Musical Settings
of American Poetry

Musical Settings
of American Poetry

A BIBLIOGRAPHY

Compiled by Michael Hovland

MUSIC REFERENCE COLLECTION, NUMBER 8

GREENWOOD PRESS

NEW YORK • WESTPORT, CONNECTICUT • LONDON

Library of Congress Cataloging-in-Publication Data

Hovland, Michael A.
   Musical settings of American poetry.

   (Music reference collection, ISSN 0736-7740 ; no. 8)
   Includes indexes.
   1. Vocal music—Bibliography. 2. American poetry—
Musical settings—Bibliography. I. Title. II. Series.
ML128.V7H67 1986   016.7843   86-402
ISBN 0-313-22938-4 (lib. bdg. : alk. paper)

Library of Congress Catalog Card Number: 86-402
ISBN: 0-313-22938-4
ISSN: 0736-7740

First published in 1986

Greenwood Press, Inc.
88 Post Road West, Westport, Connecticut 06881

Printed in the United States of America

The paper used in this book complies with the
Permanent Paper Standard issued by the National
Information Standards Organization (Z39.48-1984).

10 9 8 7 6 5 4 3 2 1

For my parents

Contents

Preface

Ever since my student days at Luther College in Decorah, Iowa I have tried in various ways to bring together my interests in literature and music. For several years I casually noted down musical settings of poems that I heard in concerts and recitals and during the many hours I listened to Minnesota Public Radio. During the bicentennial year when we were deluged with Americana of one sort or another it was radio, in fact, that first suggested to me the usefulness of a catalog of musical settings. A radio station might want to celebrate Emily Dickinson's birthday, for example, by playing a song or choral setting of one of her poems. This suggested further uses. A choral director might want to organize a program around one writer or several writers from a certain period or place, or even a point of view—such as the transcendentalists. A singer might want to base a recital on certain themes, characters, or poetic forms. A literature teacher might find a musical setting helpful in demonstrating the rhythmic and melodic richness of an E.E. Cummings poem or to bring out the more subtle metrics in a poem by Whitman or Sandburg.

It was easy to be drawn in by the idea of the project, but I had no real sense of its probable scope until I saw Gooch and Thatcher's *Musical Settings of Late Victorian and Modern British Literature* (1978), with its more than 7,700 entries. This first volume of their excellent comprehensive series at once excited and discouraged me. I was excited by the possibilities yet discouraged by the prospect of trying to locate what I assumed would be a considerable amount of music.

And there was, in fact, a considerable amount of music—more than I could deal with comprehensively. So I had to limit the scope of the project in several ways which are described below. If I were beginning the work again, I probably would include several more nineteenth century writers such as Henry Van Dyke whose poems were popular with composers. As it stands, I believe the bibliography is comprehensive enough to serve as a necessary first step to further research in the field.

Scope

Musical Settings of American Poetry: A Bibliography comprises musical settings of the writings of 99 American authors. It includes approximately 5,800 settings, 2,100 composers, and 2,400 titles of literary works. My principal aim in the book has been to link American literary texts with their published musical settings. It is intended for use by musicians and singers, choral and instrumental conductors, radio station program directors, music retailers and publishers, teachers, literary and music bibliographers, and literary and music scholars. It is not intended for use as a descriptive bibliography because I was not able to examine all of the music.

Most of the settings are of poems. Some prose settings are also included, as well as dramatic works (chiefly verse dramas), and librettos written by the authors themselves. Excluded are operatic and stage adaptations in which the authors had no direct involvement, incidental music based on literary texts or authors' lives, instrumental music which includes literary inscriptions, works in translation unaccompanied by a text in English, and unpublished music. For the purposes of this bibliography, published music includes music commercially published, music privately published, music available on commercial recordings, and music available in facsimile edition from organizations such as American Composers Alliance.

Description

Title of literary work [Any necessary descriptive information]. *Volume* (date); Variant title(s), etc.

Entry number Composer's name. "Musical title if different from literary title." *Title of larger work in which it appears* (if any). Place of publication: name of publisher(s), date of publication or copyright. Form of the musical composition: vocal specifications, accompaniment required. Subsequent publications, arrangements, variant titles, collections, etc.

Sample Entry

JAMES AGEE (1909–1955)

Description of Elysium. *Permit Me Voyage* (1934).

> 2 Barber, Samuel. "Sure on This Shining Night" in *Four Songs for Voice and Piano* op. 13 no. 3. New York: G. Schirmer, 1941. Song: low or med. and high v edns, pf. Text from stanzas 6, 7, and 8. In coll. BCS. New York: G. Schirmer, 1961. Chorus: SATB, pf. In coll. BCC.

Under each author the settings are arranged alphabetically by title of literary work or first line of text. Within each title the settings are arranged alphabetically by composer or, for anonymous settings, by musical title. A miscellaneous section arranged alphabetically by composer or musical title comes at the end of each author's entries. It includes incorrect attributions and settings for which the exact source(s) of the literary texts could not be identified.

Spelling, punctuation, and terminology do not always conform to the original musical settings and literary texts. I have corrected obvious mistakes in spelling, typography, etc.

Text Entry

The titles of individual poems appear in roman type followed by a period. Untitled poems or sections of larger works are indicated by first lines of texts in quotation marks. Titles that originally appeared in quotation marks are capitalized within those quotation marks. Titles of plays, longer poems, novels, and other individual works are italicized. All titles of literary works are ended by a period that supersedes any terminal punctuation in the title itself. Whenever the first word in the title of a literary work is an article in English, the second word determines the alphabetical listing, except when there is no title and the first line is used.

For poems, the *volume* indicates the first collected edition or first located collected edition in which the poem appears. I chose to use first collected editions for the reader's convenience in locating texts while giving some sense of chronology. Readers should always refer to descriptive author bibliographies for authoritative publication data.

Setting Entry

Entry numbers followed by a letter (e.g. 3795a) indicate interpolated entries. Composers' names are not always given exactly as they appear on the music. Pseudonyms are not identified in the main entries but are fully cross-referenced in the *Index to Composers*. Initials, when I was able to identify them, are printed out as full names; e.g., F.B. is listed in the main entry as Francis Boott. Many settings in songbooks and hymnals are compilations in which the listed composer had no direct involvement. This is clear in most cases—as in a Mozart setting of Whitman—but difficult to determine in other cases. I have identified editors and arrangers as such when that information was available and necessary.

Musical titles are omitted if they are the same as the title of the literary work except when opus numbers are included. I have changed capitalization and punctuation to follow standard conventions.

Not all multiple locations for publishers are listed. The *date* is usually the date of publication but may in some cases be the copyright date.

Vocal specifications for larger works in most cases indicate the forces required for the entire work. For vocal music, descriptions of range do not generally go beyond what is given on the music or beyond the standard library designations of high, medium, or low voice. For further descriptive information on vocal specifications, readers should consult Carman, Gaeddert, and Resch's *Art-Song in the United States, 1801–1976: An Annotated Bibliography* [CAUS], Espina's *Repertoire for the Solo Voice* [ERS], and Kagen's *Music for the Voice* [KMV].

I have not attempted to catalog all subsequent editions of musical compositions. Priority was given to variant arrangements and publishers, and especially to recent re-issues and issues in collections as an aid in locating older music.

Other Resources

Readers interested in locating further descriptive information on some settings or in locating unpublished music, manuscripts, translations, opera, and other adaptations which were excluded from this bibliography may consult the following:

Amer. Music Center   *Composer/Librettist Program Collection at the American Music Center* [AMCCL]
Catalog of the American Music Center Library [AMC-CA]

Aus. Music Centre	*Catalogue of Instrumental and Chamber Music* [AMCI]
	Catalogue of Orchestral Music [AMCO]
	Dramatic Music [AMCD]
	Electronic Music [AMCE]
	Vocal and Choral Music [AMCV]
Block, Neuls-Bates	*Women in American Music* [BlW]
G. Bordman	*American Musical Theatre* [BAM]
Boston Public Lib.	*Dictionary Catalog of the Music Collection* [BPL]
R.L. Brown	*Music, Printed and Manuscript, in the James Weldon Johnson Memorial Collection of Negro Arts and Letters* [BMJ]
M. Bruccoli	*First Printings of American Authors* [BFB]
Can. League of Comps.	*Catalogue of Orchestral Music* [CLCO]
Can. Music Centre	*Canadian Vocal Music* [CaMCV]
	Catalogue of Canadian Choral Music [CaMCCM]
	Catalogue of Chamber Music [CaMCM]
	Catalogue of Microfilms of Unpublished Canadian Music [CaMCU]
	Catalogue of Orchestral Music of the Canadian Music Centre [CaMCOM]
	List of Canadian Chamber Music [CaMCLC]
Central Opera Serv.	"Directory of American and Foreign Contemporary Operas and American Opera Premieres, 1967–1975; 1975–1980" [COSD]
M. Cole	"*Afrika singt*: Austro-German Echoes of the Harlem Renaissance" [CoAS]
J.M. Edwards	*Literature for Voices in Combination with Electronic and Tape Music* [EL]
H. Johnson	*Operas on American Subjects* [JoAS]
Lib. of Congress	*The National Union Catalog: Music and Phonorecords* [LCMP]
A. Loewenberg	*Annals of Opera 1597–1940* [LAAO]
National Opera Assn.	*The National Opera Association Catalog of Contemporary American Operas* [NOAC]
C. Northouse	*Twentieth Century Opera in England and the United States* [NTO]
New York Public Lib.	*Dictionary Catalog of the Music Collection* [NYPL]

Readers may also wish to consult articles on American authors in the forthcoming *New Grove Dictionary of Music in the United States.* Sources pertinent to individual authors only are listed at the head of each section in the main body.

Collections

Some collections are fully described in the main entries, but the majority are indicated by abbreviated forms which are fully described in the *List of Works Cited*. All of the relevant entries from the following reference works have been included: Cushing's *Children's Song Index* [CuCS], De Charms and Breed's *Songs in Collections: An Index* [BSC], and Sears' *Song Index* [SSI].

Hymns

The cataloging of hymns is problematic due to their multiple locations and variant texts, as well as to the large number of compilations, editions, and arrangements. The most extensive hymn indexes available are Katherine Diehl's *Hymns and Tunes: An Index* [DHT] and John Julian's *Dictionary of Hymnology* [JDH]. Because the primary aim of my book is to provide information on which texts have been set, I have not included all the various settings cataloged by Diehl and Julian, although at least one representative setting of each text is included. I have covered more extensively those hymnals and collections not included in DHT and JDH.

Recordings

I have not attempted to provide an extensive discography. Selected recordings are listed for unpublished music and those settings for which no published edition was discovered. Also included are recordings that may be too recent to be found in previously published discographies. Other recordings may be located through the Library & Museum of the Performing Arts *Dictionary Catalog of the Rodgers and Hammerstein Archives of Recorded Sound* [RHD], Carol Oja's *American Music Recordings* [OAM], Sibley Music Library *Catalog of Sound Recordings* [ESMC], and Dorothy Stahl's *Select Discography of Solo Song* [SDSS], as well as in bibliographies of individual authors and composers.

Acknowledgements

Samuel Johnson described lexicographers as "harmless drudges." I am not sure if that humorous description applies equally well to bibliographers, but I can vouch for the fact that much of the work is drudgery. I hope soon to forget the boxes upon boxes of note-cards and the numbers of wasted days spent skimming volumes of poetry in search of elusive texts. What I will remember are the people I have worked with, the new friends I have made, and the many kindnesses shown to me.

I owe special thanks to many faculty and staff from the University of Iowa: L.E. Folsom, William Kupersmith, Brooks Landon, Susan Lohafer (English Department); Richard Bloesch, Robert Eckert, Albert Gammon, Donald Jenni, Donald Moses (School of Music); Esther Bierbaum and Carl Orgren (School of Library and Information Science); Peter Brokaw, Diane Eglseder, Diana Harris, Christine Pruess (Weeg Computing Center); and to George Mullally, Wayne Rawley, the late Dorothy Kestel, and the staff of the University of Iowa Libraries for their many services. I would also like to thank Dianne M. Gutscher and Susan Ravdin of the Bowdoin College Library, as well as the staffs of American Music Center, Inc. Library, Ball State University Library, Boston Public Library, Johns Hopkins University Library, Newberry Library, Music Library and Rare Book Library of the University of Illinois at Urbana-Champaign, University of Northern Iowa Library, and the Music Library and Beinecke Rare Book and Manuscript Library of Yale University. Above all my appreciation goes to Elizabeth Auman and the entire staff of the Music Division, Library of Congress, without whose support I could not have completed this project.

I am grateful to the Graduate Council of the University of Northern Iowa for monetary support early in the project, and to the University of Iowa Department of English for computer funds.

Many music retailers and publishers were helpful in supplying me with recently published music: Associated Music Publishers, Inc., Belwin-Mills Publishing Corp., Boelke-Bomart Publications, Boosey & Hawkes, Inc., Boston Music Company, Alexander Broude, Inc., Broude Bros., Ltd., Composers Recordings, Inc., Galaxy Music Corp., General Music Publishing Co., Inc., Hal Leonard Publishing Corp., Margun Music, Inc., Edward B. Marks Music Corp., Oxford University Press, Inc., G. Schirmer, Inc., Seesaw Music Corp., Shawnee Press, Inc., Southern Music Company, World Library Publications, Inc., and especially American Composers Alliance, Luyben Music, Theodore Presser Company, and Merrill Jones and the staff of Wingert-Jones Music, Inc.

I am indebted to Bryan N.S. Gooch and David Thatcher (University of Victoria) whose series of catalogs on musical settings of British literature have set a high standard for all such reference works, and to Elizabeth

Wilford for her care and patience with many tasks. I am also indebted to Gregory Awbrey and Jeffrey Nelson of Compositors, Inc., and to Marilyn Brownstein, Acquisitions Editor of Greenwood Press, who was interested in the project from the beginning and who periodically encouraged me to finish.

I would also like to thank Janet Ashman, Eric Austin, Ernst Bacon, Miriam Barndt-Webb, Rae Linda Brown, Elliott Carter, Kathleen Haefliger, Richard Jackson, Richard C. Johnson, David Lasocki, Karen Lehmann, Joel Myerson, Verna Ritchie, Colleen Schultz, Edward Wagner, Ruth Watanabe, and Ruth M. Wilson. Finally, I would like to thank Nancy Jones for her help with the *Preface* and for her patient encouragement.

Iowa City, Iowa
17 February 1985

List of Works Cited

AA   *Anthology of American Song.* High voice and low voice edns. New York: G. Schirmer, 1911.

AB 1–4   *Album of Bass Songs.* 4 vols. New York: G. Schirmer, 1888–94.

AMCCA   American Music Center, New York. *Catalog of the American Music Center Library.* Ed. by Karen McNerney Famera. New York: American Music Center. Vol. 1, *Catalog of Choral and Vocal Works,* 1975. Vol. 2, *Chamber Music,* 1978.

AMCCL   American Music Center, New York. *Composer/Librettist Program Collection at The American Music Center.* New York: American Music Center, 1979.

AMCD   Australia Music Centre. *Dramatic Music.* Catalogues of Australian Compositions, vol. 5. Sydney: Australia Music Centre, 1977.

AMCE   Australia Music Centre. *Electronic Music.* Catalogues of Australian Compositions, vol. 7. Sydney: Australia Music Centre, 1977.

AMCI   Australia Music Centre. *Catalogue of Instrumental and Chamber Music.* Sydney: Australia Music Centre, 1976.

AMCO   Australia Music Centre. *Catalogue of Orchestral Music.* Catalogues of Australian Compositions, vol. 1. Sydney: Australia Music Centre, 1976.

AMCV   Australia Music Centre. *Vocal and Choral Music.* Catalogues of Australian Compositions, vol. 4. Sydney: Australia Music Centre, 1976.

ArF 1–2   Armitage, Marie Teresa, ed. *Folk Songs and Art Songs for Intermediate Grades.* 2 vols. Boston: C.C. Birchard, 1925.

ArJ   Armitage, Marie Teresa, ed. *Junior Laurel Songs: Teachers' Edition.* Boston: C.C. Birchard, 1916.

BAA   Breach, William, ed. *Art-song Argosy.* 2 vols. New York: G. Schirmer, 1937.

BacFS   Bacon, Ernst. *Fifty Songs.* Georgetown, Calif.: Dragon's Teeth Press, 1974.

BacQA   Bacon, Ernst. *Quiet Airs.* New York: Mercury Music, 1952.

BacSE   Bacon, Ernst. *Songs from Emily Dickinson.* San Francisco: Bacon, [BAL n.d., 1932].

BacSP   Bacon, Ernst. *Songs at Parting.* San Francisco: Bacon, 1930.

BacT   Bacon, Ernst. *Tributaries.* Berkeley, Calif.: The Musical Offering, 1978.

BAL   Blanck, Jacob. *Bibliography of American Literature.* 7 vols. New Haven: Yale Univ. Press, 1955–.

BAM   Bordman, Gerald Martin. *American Musical Theatre: A Chronicle.* New York: Oxford Univ. Press, 1978.

BAS 1–2   *Baritone Songs.* 2 vols. London: Boosey, 1921.

BCC   Barber, Samuel. *Complete Choral Music.* New York: G. Schirmer, 1979.

BCS   Barber, Samuel. *Collected Songs.* New York: G. Schirmer, 1955; rev. edn. 1971. High voice and low voice edns.

BD   Bispham, David, ed. *The David Bispham Treasury of Song.* Chicago and Philadelphia: John C. Winston Co., 1920.

BeBB   Beattie, John W., et al. *The Blue Book of Favorite Songs.* Chicago: Hall & McCreary, 1928.

BeBBN   Beattie, John W. *The New Blue Book of Favorite Songs, the Golden Book of Favorite Songs and the Gray Book of Favorite Songs.* Chicago: Hall & McCreary, 1941.

Ben 2–4   Bentley, Alys Eliza. *The Song Series.* Vols. 2–4. Chicago: Laidlaw Bros., 1923.

BFB   Bruccoli, Matthew, ed. *First Printings of American Authors: Contributions toward Descriptive Checklists.* 4 vols. Detroit: Gale Research Co., 1977–79.

BLC   British Library. Dept. of Printed Books. *The Catalogue of Printed Music in the British Library to 1980.* 29 vols. to date. London: K.G. Saur, 1981.

BlW   Block, Adrienne Fried, and Carol Neuls-Bates. *Women in American Music: A Bibliography of Music and Literature.* Westport, Conn.: Greenwood Press, 1979.

BMJ   Brown, Rae Linda. *Music, Printed and Manuscript, in the James Weldon Johnson Memorial Collection of Negro Arts and Letters: An Annotated Catalog.* New York: Garland Pub., 1982.

Bo   Bonsall, Elizabeth H. *Famous Hymns.* 2d edn. rev. Philadelphia: American Sunday School Union, 1927.

BoAS 2   Boott, Francis. *Album of Songs No. 2.* Boston: O. Ditson, 1897.

BoAS 3   Boott, Francis. *Album of Songs No. 3.* Boston: O. Ditson, 1902.

BoC   Botsford, Florence Hudson, ed. *Botsford Collection of Folk-Songs.* 3 vols. New York: G. Schirmer, 1930.

BoF   Boott, Francis. *Florence.* Boston: O. Ditson, 1858, c1857.

BoS   Boott, Francis. *Songs by Harte, Longfellow, Whittier, Thackeray, Coleridge.* Boston: O. Ditson, 1857–73.

BP   Burleigh, Henry Thacker. *Plantation Melodies Old and New.*
                New York: G. Schirmer, 1901.

BPL   Boston Public Library. *Dictionary Catalog of the Music Collection,*
                Boston Public Library. 20 vols. Boston: G.K. Hall, 1972. Sup-
                plement. 1st–. Boston: G.K. Hall, 1977–.

BSC   Breed, Paul F., and Desiree De Charms. *Songs in Collections:*
                An Index. Detroit: Information Service, 1966.

BSE   Bacon, Mary S., Mrs., ed. *Songs Every Child Should Know.* New
                York: Grosset and Dunlap, 1906.

BSP   Balfe, Michael William. *Seven Poems by Longfellow.* London:
                Boosey, [BLC 1855?].

BST   Baltzell, Winton James. *Something to Sing: Old and New Master-*
                pieces for the Voice. Boston: O. Ditson, 1916.

BuE   Busch, Carl. *Eight Indian Songs.* Boston: O. Ditson, 1917.

BuS   Busch, Carl. *Six Indian Songs.* Boston: O. Ditson, 1907.

BYC   Bozyan, Hagop Frank, and Sidney Lovett, eds. *The Yale Carol*
                Book. London: Humphrey Milford, Oxford Univ. Press; New
                Haven: Pub. for the Church of Christ in Yale Univ. by Yale
                Univ. Press, 1944.

CaCL   Carpenter, Edward, ed. *Chants of Labour.* London: Swan Son-
                nenschein, 1888.

CaLCO   Canadian League of Composers. *Catalogue of Orchestral Music*
                (Including Works for Small Orchestra and Band, Concertos, Vocal-
                Orchestral and Choral-Orchestral Works). Toronto: Canadian
                League of Composers, 1957.

CaMCCM   Canadian Music Centre, Toronto. *Catalogue of Canadian Cho-*
                ral Music Available for Perusal from the Library of the Canadian
                Music Centre. Toronto: Canadian Music Centre, 1966.

CaMCLC   Canadian Music Centre, Toronto. *List of Canadian Chamber Music Supplementary to the CMC 1967 Catalogue of Canadian Chamber Music.* Toronto: Canadian Music Centre, 1976.

CaMCM   Canadian Music Centre, Toronto. *Catalogue of Chamber Music Available on Loan from the Library of the Canadian Music Centre.* Toronto: Canadian Music Centre, 1967.

CaMCOM   Canadian Music Centre, Toronto. *Catalogue of Orchestral Music at the Canadian Music Centre, Including Orchestra, Band, Concertos, Operas and Vocal-Orchestra.* Toronto: Canadian Music Centre, 1963. *List of Canadian Orchestral Music Supplementary to the CMC 1963 Catalogue.* Toronto: Canadian Music Centre, 1968.

CaMCU   Canadian Music Centre, Toronto. *Catalogue of Microfilms of Unpublished Canadian Music.* Toronto: Canadian Music Centre, 1970.

CaMCV   Canadian Music Centre, Toronto. *Canadian Vocal Music, available for Perusal from the Library of the Canadian Music Centre.* Toronto: Canadian Music Centre, 1967.

CASH   *Contemporary Art Song Album for High Voice.* Cleveland Composers Guild Publications Series. New York: Galaxy Music, 1969.

CASM   *Contemporary Art Song Album for Medium Voice.* Cleveland Composers Guild Publication Series. New York: Galaxy Music, 1972.

CAST   *Contemporary Art Songs: 28 Songs by American and British Composers.* New York: G. Schirmer, 1970.

CAUS   Carman, Judith E., William K. Gaeddert, and Rita M. Resch. *Art-Song in the United States, 1801–1976: An Annotated Bibliography.* New York: National Assn. of Teachers of Singing, 1976. *First Supplement,* 1978.

CB   *Classic Baritone and Bass Songs.* Boston: Oliver Ditson, 1888.

CCS   *Cos Cob Song Volume*. New York: Cos Cob Press; reissued under the auspices of Arrow Music Press, 1935.

ChAH   Christ-Janer, Albert, Charles W. Hughes, and Carleton S. Smith. *American Hymns Old and New*. 2 vols. New York: Columbia Univ. Press, 1980.

ChN   Cheatham, Katherine S. *Nursery Garland*. New York: G. Schirmer, 1917.

CHS   Chamberlain, David B., and Karl P. Harrington, eds. *Songs of All the Colleges*. New York: Hinds & Noble, 1903.

CJS   *Cole and Johnson Song Folio, The*. New York: Jos. W. Stern, 1904.

CNA   Clark, Rogie, comp. and arr. *Negro Art Songs*. New York: E.B. Marks, 1946.

CoAS   Cole, Malcolm S. "*Afrika singt*: Austro-German Echoes of the Harlem Renaissance." *Journal of the American Musicological Society* 30 (Spring 1977), pp. 72–95.

COSD   Central Opera Service, New York. "Directory of American and Foreign Contemporary Opera Premieres, 1967–1975." *Central Opera Service Bulletin* 17(2) (1975). "Directory of American and Foreign Contemporary Opera Premieres, 1975–1980." *Central Opera Service Bulletin* 22(2) (1980).

CS 1–2   *Contralto Songs*. 2 vols. London: Boosey, n.d.

CSB 1–6   *The Clarendon Song Books*. Ed. by W.G. Whittaker, Herbert Wiseman, and John Wishart. 6 vols. New York: C. Fischer, 1929–30.

CSS 1–2   *Choice Sacred Solos*. 2 vols. Boston: O. Ditson, 1883–1917.

CU   *Columbia University Songs*. Boston: O. Ditson, 1904.

CuBH   Currier, Thomas Franklin. *A Bibliography of Oliver Wendell Holmes.* Ed. by Eleanor M. Tilton for the Bibliographic Society of America. New York: New York Univ. Press, 1953.

CuBW   Currier, Thomas Franklin. *A Bibliography of John Greenleaf Whittier.* Cambridge: Harvard Univ. Press, 1937.

CuCS   Cushing, Helen Grant. *Children's Song Index.* New York: H.W. Wilson, 1936. Reprint. St. Clair Shores, Mich.: Scholarly Press, 1977.

DagA   Damrosch, Walter J., George H. Gartlan, and Karl W. Gehrkens, eds. *New Universal School Music Series: Art Songs and Part Songs.* New York and Philadelphia: Hinds, Hayden & Eldredge, 1933–35.

DagI   Damrosch, Walter J., George H. Gartlan, and Karl W. Gehrkens, eds. *New Universal School Music Series: Introduction to Part Singing.* New York and Philadelphia: Hinds, Hayden & Eldredge, 1933–35.

DagM   Damrosch, Walter J., George H. Gartlan, and Karl W. Gehrkens, eds. *New Universal School Music Series: My First Song Book.* New York and Philadelphia: Hinds, Hayden & Eldredge, 1933–35.

DagR   Damrosch, Walter J., George H. Gartlan, and Karl W. Gehrkens, eds. *New Universal School Music Series: Rhythm Songs.* New York and Philadelphia: Hinds, Hayden & Eldredge, 1933–35.

DagU   Damrosch, Walter J., George H. Gartlan, and Karl W. Gehrkens, eds. *New Universal School Music Series: Unison Songs.* New York and Philadelphia: Hinds, Hayden & Eldredge, 1933–35.

Dar 1–6   Dann, Hollis E., ed. *Hollis Dann Music Course.* 6 vols. New York: American Book Co., 1914–17.

DarJ   Dann, Hollis E., ed. *Junior Songs.* New York: American Book Co., 1925.

DavB   Davison, Archibald T., Thomas W. Surette, and Augustus D. Zanzig, comps. *Book of Songs.* Boston: E.C. Schirmer, 1924.

DCD   Ditson, Oliver, Company. *Oliver Ditson Company's Complete Descriptive Catalogue of Vocal Music.* Boston, 1900?

DHT   Diehl, Katharine S. *Hymns and Tunes: An Index.* New York: Scarecrow Press, 1966.

DM 1-2   Duncan, Edmondstowne, ed. *The Minstrelsy of England.* 2 vols. London: Augener, 1905-10.

DNM   *Danish National Music.* Copenhagen: Wilhelm Hansen, 1939.

DNS   Dunstan, Ralph, ed. *A Second Book of Christmas Carols.* London: Reid Bros., 1923.

DSB   Davison, Archibald T., Thomas W. Surette, and Augustus D. Zanzig, comps. *A Book of Songs.* Boston: E.C. Schirmer, 1931.

DSC   Davison, Archibald T., Thomas W. Surette, and Augustus D. Zanzig, comps. *The Home and Community Song Book.* Rev. and enl. edn. Boston: E.C. Schirmer, 1903?

DSO   Dolph, Edward A. *Sound Off!* New York: Cosmopolitan Book Corp., 1929.

DTA   Downes, Olin, and Elie Siegmeister, eds. *A Treasury of American Song.* New York: Howell, Soskin, 1940.

DTAR   Downes, Olin, and Elie Siegmeister, eds. *A Treasury of American Song.* Music arr. by Elie Siegmeister. 2d edn. rev. and enl. New York: Knopf, 1943.

Ea   Earhart, Will, and Elias H. Sneath, eds. *Songs of Purpose: Advanced Music.* New York: Macmillan, 1929.

EFL   Ehret, Walter, and Ivan Trusler, eds. *Functional Lessons in Singing.* 2d edn. Englewood Cliffs, N.J.: Prentice-Hall, 1972.

EH Edmunds, John. *Hesperides: Fifty Songs.* Georgetown, Calif.: Dragon's Teeth Press, 1975.

EL Edwards, J. Michele. *Literature for Voices in Combination with Electronic and Tape Music: An Annotated Bibliography.* Ann Arbor, Mich.: Music Library Assn., 1977.

EMEP Evans, May Garrettson. *Music and Edgar Allan Poe: A Bibliographical Study.* Baltimore: Johns Hopkins Press, 1939.

ERS Espina, Noni. *Repertoire for the Solo Voice.* 2 vols. Metuchen, N.J.: Scarecrow Press, 1977

ES *Encore Songs.* Boston: O. Ditson, 1910. High voice and low voice edns.

ESMC Eastman School of Music, Rochester, N.Y. Sibley Music Library. *Catalog of Sound Recordings: The University of Rochester, Eastman School of Music, Rochester, New York.* Boston: G.K. Hall, 1977.

FAS *Fifty Art Songs from the Modern Repertoire.* New York: G. Schirmer, 1939.

FMES *Fifty Modern English Songs.* Selected by and published for the Society of English Singers. London: Boosey, 1923?

Fo 1-6 Foresman, Robert, ed. *Books of Songs: First–Sixth.* 6 vols. New York and Boston: American Book Co., 1925-32.

FoH Foresman, Robert, ed. *High Road of Song.* New York: American Book Co., 1931.

FoT 1-3 Foresman, Robert, ed. *Three Book Series.* 3 vols. New York: American Book, 1933.

FSS 1-8 *Franklin Square Song Collection.* 8 vols. New York: Harper, 1881-92.

FRM   Frey, Hugo, ed. *Robbins Mammoth Collection of American Songs.* New York: Robbins Music Corp., 1941.

FRMS   Frey, Hugo, ed. *Robbins Mammoth Collection of American Songs.* A shorter edn. New York: Robbins Music Corp., 1941.

FRMW   Frey, Hugo, ed. *Robbins Mammoth Collection of World Famous Songs.* New York: Robbins Music Corp., 1939.

GaL   Gallagher, Elizabeth L., and Carlo Peroni, comps. *Hymns and Carols for Children to Play and Sing.* New York: Elizabeth Gallagher, 1930.

GaO   Gallagher, Elizabeth L., and Carlo Peroni, comps. *100 Favorite Songs for Children to Play and Sing.* New York: Elizabeth Gallagher, 1930.

GAS 1-2   Glenn, Mabelle, and Alfred Spouse, eds. *Art Songs for School and Studio.* First Year and Second Year vols. Medium high voice and medium low voice edns. Boston: O. Ditson, 1930.

GE   *Gems of English Song.* Boston: O. Ditson, 1875.

GEB   Gallup, Donald. *T.S. Eliot: A Bibliography.* London: Faber & Faber, 1969.

GEP   Gallup, Donald. *Ezra Pound: A Bibliography.* Charlottesville, Va.; Univ. Press of Virginia, 1983.

GeS   George, Marian M., ed. *Songs in Season.* Chicago: A. Flanagan, 1916.

Gi 1-4   Giddings, Thaddeus P., et al., eds. *Music Education Series: The Home Edition.* 4 vols. Boston: Ginn, 1925, 1928.

GiA   Giddings, Thaddeus P., et al., eds. *Adventures in Music.* Boston and New York: Ginn, 1931.

GiJr   Giddings, Thaddeus P., et al., eds. *Junior Music.* Boston and New York: Ginn, 1924.

GilM Giddings, Thaddeus P., et al., eds. *Intermediate Music.* Boston and New York: Ginn, 1924.

GiTh Giddings, Thaddeus P., et al., eds. *Three-part Music.* Boston and New York: Ginn, 1925.

GiTw Giddings, Thaddeus P., et al., eds. *Two-part Music.* Boston and New York: Ginn, 1927.

GO Gilbert, Henry F.B., ed. *One Hundred Folk-songs from Many Countries.* Boston: C.C. Birchard, 1910.

Gord Gordon, Edgar B., and Irene Curtis. *Music for Youth.* Milwaukee, Wisc. and Columbus, Ohio: E.M. Hale, 1930. *Teacher's Music Book,* 1931.

GOS 1-2 *Good Old Songs We Used To Sing.* Comp. by J.C.H. 2 vols. Boston: O. Ditson, 1887-95.

HC Hutchins, Charles L., ed. *Carols Old and Carols New.* Boston: Parish Choir, 1916.

HCA Heinrich, Max, ed. *Classic Song Album.* New York: C. Fischer, 1914.

He Hesser, Ernest G., and Bessie S. Dustman, comps. *Treasure Chest of Songs.* New York: American Book Co., 1932.

HoA Hofer, Marie R., comp. *Christmas in Peasant France.* Chicago: Clayton F. Summy, 1926.

HSC *Home Songs.* Boston: O. Ditson, 1906.

HSD *Heart Songs Dear to the American People.* Boston: Chapple Pub. Co., 1909.

HSE 1-3 Hatton, John L., and Eaton Faning, eds. *The Songs of England.* 3 vols. London: Boosey, n.d.

HST   Hughes, Rupert, ed. *Songs by Thirty Americans*. Boston: O. Ditson, 1904.

INS   Ives, Charles. *Nineteen Songs*. Bryn Mawr, Pa.: Merion Music, 1935.

IOS   Ives, Charles. *114 Songs*. New York: Associated Music Publishers and Peer International; Bryn Mawr, Pa.: Theodore Presser, 1975.

ISS   Ives, Charles. *Seven Songs*. New York: Associated Music Publishers, 1957.

ITS   Ives, Charles. *Thirty-four Songs by Charles Ives*. New Music Edn. Bryn Mawr, Pa.: Merion Music, 1933.

JDH   Julian, John. *A Dictionary of Hymnology*. London: Murray, 1908. Reprint, 2 vols. New York: Dover Publications, 1957.

JO   Johnson, Helen Kendrick, ed. *Our Familiar Songs and Those Who Made Them*. New York: H. Holt, 1909.

JoAS   Johnson, Harold E. *Operas on American Subjects*. New York: Coleman-Ross, 1964.

JR   Johnson, John Rosamond. *Rolling Along in Song*. New York: Viking, 1937.

JS   Johnson, Charles W., ed. *Songs of the Nation*. Boston: Silver, Burdett, 1912.

JSE   Johnson, Clifton, ed. *Songs Every One Should Know*. New York and Cincinnati: American Book Co., 1908.

JSY   Jordan, Philip Dillon, comp. *Songs of Yesterday: A Song Anthology of American Life*. Garden City, N.Y.: Doubleday, Doran, 1941.

KCC   Kvame, Torstein O. *The Christmas Carolers' Book in Song and Story*. Chicago: Hall & McCreary, 1935.

KMV   Kagen, Sergius. *Music for the Voice.* Rev. edn. Bloomington: Indiana Univ. Press, 1968.

Kn   Knowlton, Fanny S., comp. *Nature Songs for Children.* Springfield, Mass.: Milton Bradley, 1898.

LAAO   Loewenberg, Alfred. *Annals of Opera 1597–1940.* Cambridge: W. Heffer & Sons, 1943.

LAAS   Levermore, Charles H., ed. *The Abridged Academy Song-book.* Boston: Ginn, 1903.

LAASR   Levermore, Charles H., ed. *The Abridged Academy Song-book.* Rev. edn. Boston: Ginn, 1918.

LAS   Levermore, Charles H., ed. *The American Song Book.* Boston: Ginn, 1917.

LBR   Lawrence, William M., and Orlando Blackman, eds. *Riverside Song Book.* Boston: Houghton Mifflin, 1893.

LBW   *Lutheran Book of Worship.* Minneapolis: Augsburg Publishing House, 1978.

LCMP   Library of Congress Catalogs. *The National Union Catalog: Music and Phonorecords.* [Variant publishers, 1958–.]

LNB   Laurence, Dan A. *Robert Nathan: A Bibliography.* New Haven: Yale Univ. Press, 1960.

LoPM   "Longfellow's Poems with Musical Settings." *The Musician* 13 (Jan. 1908), 52.

LWP   Lawrence, Vera Brodsky, ed. *The Wa-Wan Press: 1901–1911.* 5 vols. New York: Arno Press & The New York Times, 1970.

MaB   McConathy, Osbourne, John W. Beattie, and Russell Van Dyke, eds. *Music of Many Lands and Peoples.* New York and Boston: Silver, Burdett, 1932.

MalS   McLaughlin, James M., and William W. Gilchrist. *Song Reader*. Boston: Ginn, 1910.

MAS   Maddy, Joseph Edgar, and W.O. Miessner, eds. *All-American Song Book: A Community Song Book, for Schools, Homes, Clubs, and Community Singing*. New York: Robbins Music Corp., 1942.

MasBS   Mason, Martin, ed. *Bass Songs*. Philadelphia: O. Ditson, 1936.

MasSS   Mason, Martin, ed. *Singable Songs for Studio and Recital*. Philadelphia: O. Ditson, 1936. High voice and medium voice edns.

MCS   McCaskey, John P., ed. *Christmas in Song, Sketch, and Story*. New York: Harper, 1890.

MFS   McCaskey, John P., ed. *Favorite Songs and Hymns for School and Home*. New York: American Book Co., 1899.

MM   *Magic Melodies from the World of Song*. New York: Remick, 1943.

MoFB   Morton, Bruce. *John Gould Fletcher: A Bibliography*. Kent, Ohio: Kent State Univ. Press, 1979.

MP   *The Most Popular Songs of Patriotism*. New York: Hinds, Hayden & Eldredge, 1916.

MPC   *The Most Popular College Songs*. Rev. edn. New York: Hinds, Hayden & Eldredge, 1906.

MRAB   McLeod, J.R. *Theodore Roethke: A Bibliography*. Kent, Ohio: Kent State Univ. Press, 1973.

MSF 1-2   *Modern Song Favorites*. 2 vols. New York: G. Schirmer, 1882?

MSS   MacLean, Douglas, arr. [pseud. of Frank Campbell-Watson]. *Song Session: A Community Song Book*. New York: Remick, 1953.

Mu 1–5   *The Music Hour.* 5 vols. Ed. by Edward B. Birge, et al. New York: Silver, Burdett, 1928–30.

MuC 1–5   *The Music Hour.* Catholic Edn. 5 vols. Ed. by Gregory Huegle, Sister Alice Marie, and Joseph Schrembs. New York and Boston: Silver, Burdett, 1931.

MuENC   Music Educators National Conference. *Contemporary Music Project for Creativity in Music Education: The CMP Library.* 3 vols. Washington, D.C.: Music Educators National Conference, 1967–68.

MuO   *The Music Hour, One-book Course.* Ed. by Edward B. Birge, et al. New York and Boston: Silver, Burdett, 1932.

MuT 2   *The Music Hour: Intermediate Teacher's Book.* New York and Boston: Silver, Burdett, 1931.

MuT 3   *The Music Hour: Teacher's Guide for the Fifth Book.* New York: Silver, Burdett, 1931.

NAA   *A New Anthology of American Songs: 25 Songs by Native American Composers.* High voice and low voice edns. New York: G. Schirmer, 1942.

NAS   Nevin, Ethelbert. *Album of Songs by Ethelbert Nevin.* Boston: O. Ditson, 1899.

NGS   Newell, George, ed. *Girl Scout Song Book.* Rev. edn. New York: Girl Scouts, 1929.

NMH   Noble, Gilbert C., ed. *The Most Popular Home Songs.* New and enl. edn. New York: Hinds, Hayden & Eldredge, 1913.

NML   Noble, Gilbert C., ed. *The Most Popular Love Songs.* New York: Hinds, Hayden & Eldredge, 1906.

NMS   Noble, Gilbert C., ed. *The Most Popular Songs for Every Occasion.* New York: Hinds, Hayden & Eldredge, 1912.

NOAC   National Opera Association. *The National Opera Association Catalog of Contemporary American Operas.* Denton, Texas: National Opera Assn., 1976.

NoBS   Northcote, Sydney, ed. and arr. *Bass Songs.* New Imperial edn. New York: Boosey, 1952.

NoSS   Northcote, Sydney, ed. and arr. *Soprano Songs.* New Imperial edn. New York: Boosey, 1952.

NoTS   Northcote, Sydney, ed. *Tenor Songs.* London and New York: Boosey, 1903.

NTO   Northouse, Cameron. *Twentieth Century Opera in England and the United States.* Boston: G.K. Hall, 1976.

NVS   *New Vistas in Song.* New York: Marks Music, 1964.

NYPL   New York Public Library. Research Libraries. *Dictionary Catalog of the Music Collection.* 33 vols. Boston: G.K. Hall, 1964. *Supplement,* 1964–71.

OAM   Oja, Carol. *American Music Recordings: A Discography of 20th Century U.S. Composers.* Brooklyn, N.Y.: Institute for Studies in American Music, Conservatory of Music, Brooklyn College of the City University of New York, 1982.

OH   *The One Hundred and One Best Songs.* Rev. edn. Chicago: Cable Co., 1925.

ONAS   Oberndorfer, Marx, comp. *The New American Song Book.* Chicago: Hall & McCreary, 1933–41.

PaAS   Patterson, Willis C., comp. *Anthology of Art Songs by Black American Composers.* New York: Edward B. Marks, 1977.

Par 1–4   Parker, Horatio W., et al., eds. *The Progressive Music Series.* Books 1–4. New York: Silver, Burdett, 1920.

ParO   Parker, Horatio W., et al., eds. *The Progressive Music Series: One-book Course.* New York and Boston: Silver, Burdett, 1917.

ParT 1-3   Parker, Horatio W., et al., eds. *The Progressive Music Series: Teacher's Manual.* 3 vols. New York and Boston: Silver, Burdett, 1919.

PBC   Perry, Margaret. *A Bio-bibliography of Countee P. Cullen, 1903–1946.* Westport, Conn.: Greenwood Pub. Co., 1971.

PCS   Preuss, Theodore, comp. and ed. *Christmas in Song.* Chicago: Rubank, 1947.

PoMM   Pollin, Burton R. "More Music to Poe." *Music and Letters* 54 (Oct. 1973), pp. 391–404.

PouH   Poulsson, E. *Holiday Songs and Every Day Songs and Games.* Springfield, Mass.: Milton Bradley Co., 1901.

Pr   Pratt, Waldo S., comp. *St. Nicholas Songs.* New York: Century Co., 1885.

RFA   Rorem, Ned. *14 Songs on American Poetry.* New York: Henmar Press, 1970.

RHD   Rodgers and Hammerstein Archives of Recorded Sound. [New York Public Library. Library & Museum of the Performing Arts.] *Dictionary Catalog of the Rodgers and Hammerstein Archives of Recorded Sound.* Boston: G.K. Hall, 1981.

ScNS   Schirmer, G., publishers. *New Singing Teacher's Guide.* New York: G. Schirmer, 1922.

SDSS   Stahl, Dorothy. *A Selected Discography of Solo Song.* Detroit Studies in Music Bibliography, vol. 13. Detroit: Information Coordinators, 1968. *A Selected Discography of Solo Song: A Cumulation through 1971.* Detroit Studies in Music Bibliography, vol. 24. Detroit: Information Coordinators, 1972. *A Selected Discography of Solo Song: Supplement, 1971–1974.* Detroit Studies in Music Bibliography, vol. 34. Detroit: Information Coordinators, 1976.

SFB   Spicker, Max, comp. *Favorite Bass Songs.* New York: G. Schirmer, 1909.

SLS   *Songs We Love to Sing.* Chicago: Hall & McCreary, 1938.

SM 1–4   *Song Miscellany.* 4 vols. New York: G. Schirmer, 1902.

SmASH   Smith, Henry Augustine, ed. *The American Student Hymnal.* New York: Century Co., 1928.

SmNH   Smith, Henry Augustine, ed. *The New Hymnal for American Youth.* New York: Century Co., 1930.

SmPS   Smith, Henry Augustine, ed. *Praise and Worship: Hymns with Tunes for Christian Worship.* New York: Century Co., 1932.

SnKW   Snider, Lee, ed. *Kurt Weill in America: A Folio of 50 Songs Celebrating the 75th Anniversary of Kurt Weill's Birth.* New York: Chappell, 1975.

SRW   Spaeth, Sigmund G. *Read 'Em and Weep.* Garden City, N.Y.: Doubleday, Page, 1926.

SSI   Sears, Minnie Earl. *Song Index.* New York: H.W. Wilson, 1926. *Supplement,* 1934. Reprint. n.p.: Shoestring Press, 1966.

SSS   *The Scottish Students' Song Book.* London: Bayley and Ferguson, n.d.

St   Stanley-Brown, Katharine, comp. *The Song Book of the American Spirit.* New York: Harper & Bros., 1927.

STC   Simon, Henry William, ed. *A Treasury of Christmas Songs and Carols.* Boston: Houghton Mifflin, 1955.

TaCA   Taylor, Bernard, ed. *Contemporary American Art Songs.* Bryn Mawr, Pa.: O. Ditson, 1977.

TaCAS   Taylor, Bernard, comp. and ed. *Contemporary American Songs.*

High voice and low voice edns. Evanston, Ill.: Summy-Birchard, 1960.

TaCS   Taylor, Bernard, ed. *Contemporary Songs in English: Songs by American and English Composers for Recital, Concert, and Studio Use.* Medium high voice and medium low voice edns. New York: C Fischer, 1956.

TaSE   Taylor, Bernard, ed. *Songs in English: 19 Contemporary Settings by English and American Composers.* High voice and low voice edns. New York: C. Fischer, 1970.

TaST   Taylor, Bernard, comp. *Songs by 22 Americans.* High voice and low voice edns. New York: G. Schirmer, 1960.

TFB   *Twice 55 Community Songs for Male Voices: The Blue Book.* Boston: C.C. Birchard, 1926.

TFC 1–2   *Twice 55 Community Songs.* 2 vols. Boston: C.C. Birchard, 1919–23.

TFG   *Twice 55 Community Songs: The New Green Book.* Boston: C.C. Birchard, 1930.

TFO   *Twice 55 Part Songs for Boys: The Orange Book.* Boston: C.C. Birchard, 1927.

TFP   *Twice 55 Plus Community Songs: The New Brown Book.* Boston: C.C. Birchard, 1930.

TFR   *Twice 55 Community Songs for Treble Voices: The Rose Book.* Boston: C.C. Birchard, 1927.

ThAF   Thomas, John Charles. *John Charles Thomas Album of Favorite Songs and Arias.* New York: G. Schirmer, 1946.

TL   Tomlins, William L., ed. *Laurel Song Book.* Boston: C.C. Birchard, 1901.

TLM   Tomlins, William L., ed. *The Laurel Song Book: Morris High School Edition.* Boston: C.C. Birchard, 1913.

To   Tomlins, William L., ed. *The Laurel Music-Reader.* Boston: C.C. Birchard, 1914.

TMT   Tomlins, William L., ed. *The Laurel Music-Reader: Teacher's Edition.* Boston: C.C. Birchard, 1914.

TuJS   Turner, Michael R., ed. *Just a Song at Twilight: The Second Parlour Song Book.* London: Michael Joseph, 1975.

TuPS   Turner, Michael R., ed. *The Parlour Song Book: A Casquet of Vocal Gems.* London: Michael Joseph, 1972.

TwAS   *20th Century Art Songs.* New York: G. Schirmer, 1967.

UHC   Unitarian Universalist Hymnbook Commission. *Hymns for the Celebration of Life.* Boston: Beacon Press, 1964.

US   U.S. Naval Academy, Annapolis. Trident Society. *The Book of Navy Songs.* Garden City, N.Y.: Doubleday, Page, 1926.

USNSV   Untermeyer, Louis, Clara Mannes, and David Mannes, eds. *New Songs for New Voices.* New York: Harcourt, Brace, 1928.

VCS   Van Doren, Mark. *Carl Sandburg: With a Bibliography of Sandburg Materials in the Collections of the Library of Congress.* Washington, D.C.: Library of Congress, 1969.

WaMS   Wannamaker, John Samuel. "The Musical Settings of the Poetry of Walt Whitman: A Study of Theme, Structure, and Prosody." Ph.D. dissertation, Univ. of Minnesota, 1972.

WC   Waite, Henry R., comp. *College Songs.* New and enl. edn. Boston: O. Ditson, 1918.

WCP   *The World's Collection of Patriotic Songs and Airs of the Different Nations.* Boston: O. Ditson, 1903.

WieA   Wier, Albert E. *The American Home Music Album*. New York and Chicago: D. Appleton, 1915.

WieBT   Wier, Albert E. *The Book of a Thousand Songs*. New York: Mumil Pub. Co., 1918.

WieBW   Wier, Albert E. *Ballads the Whole World Sings*. New York: D. Appleton, 1917.

WieF   Wier, Albert E., comp. *Songs to Sing to Children*. New York: Harcourt, Brace, 1935.

WieL   Wier, Albert E., ed. *Love Songs the Whole World Sings*. New York: D. Appleton, 1916.

WieSW   Wier, Albert E. *Songs the Whole World Sings*. New York: D. Appleton, 1915.

Wig   Wiggin, Kate Douglas (Smith), Mrs., ed. *Kindergarten Chimes*. Rev. and enl. edn. Boston: O. Ditson, 1913.

WiGS   Wilson, Robert A. *Gertrude Stein: A Bibliography*. New York: Phoenix Bookshop, 1974.

WM 2   Werrenrath, Reinald, ed. *Modern Scandinavian Songs*. 2 vols. Boston: O. Ditson, 1926.

YBEM   Yost, Karl. *A Bibliography of the Works of Edna St. Vincent Millay*. New York: Harper, 1937.

List of Abbreviations

A	alto voice	edn(s)	edition
a cap	a cappella	elec tape	electronic tape
a cl	alto clarinet	Eng.	English
a sax	alto saxophone	ens	ensemble
ACA	American Composers Alliance	fl	flute
		Fr.	French
acc.	accompaniment/ accompanied	Ger.	German
		glock	glockenspiel
ad lib	ad libitum	gtr	guitar
a.k.a.	also known as	hn	horn
amplif	amplifier/amplified	hp	harp
arr.	arranger/arranged	incid	incidental
avail.	available	instr(s)	instrument/instrumental
B	bass voice		
b.	born	Ital.	Italian
b drum	bass drum	keybd	keyboard
b trb	bass trombone	M	mezzo-soprano voice
Bar	baritone voice	med.	medium
bcl	bass clarinet	MS	manuscript
bsn	bassoon	n.d.	no date
C	contralto voice	n.p.	no publisher/ no place
c	copyright	n.t.	no title
ca.	circa	narr.	narrator/narrated
c-T	counter-tenor	ob	oboe
cel	celeste	obl	obligato
cham.	chamber	opt	optional
cl	clarinet	orch	orchestra
coll.	collection	org	organ
d.	died	p.p.	privately published
Dan.	Danish	perc	percussion
db	double bass	pf	piano
div.	divisi	picc	piccolo
e-hn	english horn	proj	projector(s)
ed.	editor/edited	pt.	part

pubd.	published
qnt	quintet
qrt	quartet
(R)	rental
recit	recitation
red.	piano reduction
rev.	revised
Russ.	Russian
S	soprano voice
sax	saxophone
sc.	scene
secs	sections
sn dr	snare drum
Span	Spanish
str	string(s)
str bass	string bass(es)
Swed.	Swedish
t trb	tenor trombone
tba	tuba
timp	timpani
tpt	trumpet
trans.	translator/translated
trb	trombone
u.d.	unknown date
u.p.	unknown publisher/ unknown place
u.t.	unknown title
unacc.	unaccompanied
unpub	unpublished
v	voice
vc	violoncello
vib	vibraphone
vla	viola
vn	violin
ww	woodwind
xylo	xylophone

Musical Settings
of American Poetry

JAMES AGEE (1909–1955)

A Chorale. *Permit Me Voyage* (1934).

    1 Diamond, David. "Chorale." New York: Southern Music Publishing, 1951. Chorus: SSAATTBB, a cap.

Description of Elysium. *Permit Me Voyage* (1934).

    2 Barber, Samuel. "Sure on This Shining Night" in *Four Songs for Voice and Piano* op. 13 no. 3. New York: G. Schirmer, 1941. Song: low or med. and high v edns, pf. Text from stanzas 6, 7, and 8. In coll. BCS. New York: G. Schirmer, 1961. Chorus: SATB, pf. In coll. BCC.

"For love departed, lover, cease to mourn." *Permit Me Voyage* (1934).

    3 Pasatieri, Thomas. n.t. in *Permit Me Voyage*. Melville, N.Y.: Belwin-Mills, 1976. Chorus: SATB, S solo, orch.

"How Many Little Children Sleep." *The Collected Poems of James Agee* (1968).

    4 Pasatieri, Thomas. In *Three Poems of James Agee*. Melville, N.Y.: Belwin-Mills, 1974. Song: M, pf.

"I have been fashioned on a chain of flesh." *Permit Me Voyage* (1934).

    5 Pasatieri, Thomas. n.t. in *Permit Me Voyage*. Melville, N.Y.: Belwin-Mills, 1976. Chorus: SATB, S solo, orch.

"Is love then royal on some holy height?" *Permit Me Voyage* (1934).

    6 Pasatieri, Thomas. n.t. in *Permit Me Voyage*. Melville, N.Y.: Belwin-Mills, 1976. Chorus: SATB, S solo, orch.

"Just this: from now on, to go on foot." *The Collected Poems of James Agee* (1968).

    7 Pasatieri, Thomas. "Sonnet" in *Three Poems of James Agee*. Melville, N.Y.: Belwin-Mills, 1974. Song: v, pf.

Knoxville, Summer 1915; In *A Death in the Family* (1957).

7a Barber, Samuel. "Knoxville: Summer of 1915." New York: G. Schirmer, 1949. Song: high v, orch; pf red. by Barber. Recording: Unicorn, UNI-72016 (1978).

A Lullaby. *The Collected Poems of James Agee* (1968).

8 Cumberworth, Starling. "Sleep, Child." New York: C. Fischer, 1956. Song: med. v, pf.

9 Horvit, Michael. Boston: E.C. Schirmer, u.d. Chorus: SAB, pf.

10 Klein, Phillip G. New York: Lawson-Gould, u.d. Chorus: SATB, a cap.

11 Nelson, Paul. New York: Broude Brothers, 1959. Chorus: TTBB, a cap.

12 Pasatieri, Thomas. In *Three Poems of James Agee*. Melville, N.Y.: Belwin-Mills, 1974. Song: v, pf.

"Now stands our love on that still verge of day." *Permit Me Voyage* (1934).

13 Carpenter, John A. "Morning Fair" in *Two Songs for High Voice and Piano*. New York: G. Schirmer, 1936. Song: high v, pf.

"Our doom is in our being. We began." *Permit Me Voyage* (1934).

14 Pasatieri, Thomas. n.t. in *Permit Me Voyage*. Melville, N.Y.: Belwin-Mills, 1976. Chorus: SATB, S solo, orch.

Permit Me Voyage. *Permit Me Voyage* (1934).

15 Pasatieri, Thomas. n.t. in *Permit Me Voyage*. Melville, N.Y.: Belwin-Mills, 1976. Chorus: SATB, S solo, orch.

"So it begins. Adam is in his earth." *Permit Me Voyage* (1934).

16 Pasatieri, Thomas. n.t. in *Permit Me Voyage*. Melville, N.Y.: Belwin-Mills, 1976. Chorus: SATB, S solo, orch.

"The wide earth's orchard of your time of knowing." *Permit Me Voyage* (1934).

17 Pasatieri, Thomas. n.t. in *Permit Me Voyage*. Melville, N.Y.: Belwin-Mills, 1976. Chorus: SATB, S solo, orch.

"The years have passed, and made a perfect wheel." *The Collected Poems of James Agee* (1968).

18 Diamond, David. "Warning." Bryn Mawr, Pa.: Elkan-Vogel, 1973. Chorus: SATB, tabular bells.

"What dynasties of destinies undreamed." *Permit Me Voyage* (1934).

19 Pasatieri, Thomas. n.t. in *Permit Me Voyage*. Melville, N.Y.: Belwin-Mills, 1976. Chorus: SATB, S solo, orch.

"Why am I here? Why do you look at me." *Permit Me Voyage* (1934).

20 Pasatieri, Thomas. n.t. in *Permit Me Voyage*. Melville, N.Y.: Belwin-Mills, 1976. Chorus: SATB, S solo, orch.

Miscellaneous

21 Entry cancelled.

22 Williams, Edgar W., Jr. *Two Lyrics of James Agee*. Hillsdale, N.Y.: Boelke-Bomart, 1975. Song: S, pf.

CONRAD AIKEN (1889–1973)

April Rain. *Atlantic Monthly* 15 (May 1915), p. 599.

23 Crist, Bainbridge. New York: C. Fischer, 1915. Song: high and low v edns, pf; New York: C. Fischer, 1937. Chorus or Part Song: SATB, pf.

Discordants. 1 ["Music I heard with you was more than music"]. *Turns and Movies and Other Tales in Verse* (1916).

24 Bernstein, Leonard. "Music I Heard with You" in *Songfest*. New York: Boosey & Hawkes, 1977. Cycle: SAMTBarB, orch.

25 Cory, George. "Music I Heard with You." New York: General, 1969. Song: S or T, pf.

26 Elwell, Herbert. "Music I Heard with You." u.p.: Broadcast Music, 1946. Song: v, pf.

27 Faith, Richard. "Music I Heard with You." New York: G. Schirmer, 1971. Chorus: SATB, pf.

28 Fast, Willard S. "Bread and Music." New York: Associated Music, 1967. Chorus: TTBB, a cap.

29 Hageman, Richard. "Music I Heard with You." New York: Galaxy, 1938. Song: high and low v edns, pf or orch (R).

30 Hughes, Rupert. "Music I Heard with You" in *Three Songs of Love*. New York: G. Schirmer, 1920. Song: high and low v edns, pf or orch (R).

31 Nordoff, Paul. "Music I Heard with You." u.p.: Schott, 1938. Song: v, pf.

32 Robbins, Reginald C. "Bread and Music" in *Songs by Reginald C. Robbins*. Hollywood: Golden West Music, 1941. Song: high v, pf.

33 Spencer, James. "Bread and Music." New York: Composers Press, 1938. Song: med. to high v, pf.

34 Treharne, Bryceson. "Music I Heard" in *Songs by Bryceson Treharne*. Boston: O. Ditson, 1921. Song: high and med. v edns, pf.

35 Williams, Richard H. "Music I Heard." Glen Rock, N.J.: J. Fischer, 1964. Part Song: TBB, pf.

Priapus and the Pool. 4 ["This is the shape of the leaf, and this of the flower"]. *Priapus and the Pool and Other Poems* (1925).

36 Nordoff, Paul. "This Is the Shape of the Leaf." u.p.: Schott, 1937. Song: med. v, pf.

Senlin: A Biography. *The Charnel Rose, Senlin: A Biography, and Other Poems* (1918).

37 Crist, Bainbridge. "By a Silent Shore" in *Four Songs*. New York: G. Schirmer, 1934. Song: high v, pf or orch (R). Text is the first 12 lines from part 3 of "His Dark Origins."

38 Crist, Bainbridge. "Evening" in *Four Songs*. New York: G. Schirmer, 1934. Song: high v, pf or orch (R). Text is 8 lines from part 8 of "His Futile Preoccupations."

39 Crist, Bainbridge. "Knock on the Door" in *Four Songs*. New York: G. Schirmer, 1934. Song: high v, pf or orch (R). Text is 8 lines from part 1 of "His Futile Preoccupations." In coll. NAA.

40 Crist, Bainbridge. "Noontime" in *Four Songs*. New York: G. Schirmer, 1934. Song: high v, pf or orch (R). Text is from part 7 of "His Futile Preoccupations."

Stone Too Can Pray. *Brownstone Eclogues* (1942).

41 Persichetti, Vincent. n.t. in *Hymns and Responses* op. 68 no. 20. Philadelphia: Elkan-Vogel, 1956. Opening Response for choir and congregational use.

Variations. *The Charnel Rose, Senlin: A Biography, and Other Poems* (1918).

42 Crist, Bainbridge. "The Dark King's Daughter." Cincinnati: J. Church, 1920. Song: v, pf. Text from "Variations. 7."

43 Crist, Bainbridge. "Enchantment." Cincinnati: J. Church, 1920. Song: v, pf. Text from "Variations. 6."

White Nocturne. *Nocturne of Remembered Spring and Other Poems* (1917).

44 Crist, Bainbridge. "White Hours Like Snow." New York: C. Fischer, 1926. Song: high v, pf. Text from "White Nocturne. 7."

45 Nordoff, Paul. "White Nocturne." Philadelphia: O. Ditson, 1942. Song: med. v, pf. Text from "White Nocturne. 4."

EDWARD ALBEE (B. 1928)

Miscellaneous

46 Flanagan, William. *Bartleby.* New York: Composers Facsimile Edn, 1968. Opera in 4 scenes and prologue, based on Melville. Libretto by Albee, James Hinton, and Flanagan.

47 Flanagan, William. "The Lady of Tearful Regret." New York: Peer International, 1977. Song: Coloratura S and Bar, fl, cl, 2 vn, vla, vc, pf. Recording: Composers Recordings, CRI 163 (1963).

48 Flanagan, William. "Song for a Winter Child." New York: Peer International, 1964. Song: v, pf.

THOMAS BAILEY ALDRICH (1836–1907)

Across the Street. *Flower and Thorn* (1877).

49 Schlesinger, Sebastian B. "Mignonette" in *Six Songs*. Boston: C. Prüfer, 1884.

After the Rain. *The Ballad of Babie Bell and Other Poems* (1859).

50 Freer, Eleanor E. In *Six Songs to Nature* op. 10 no. 3. Milwaukee: W.A. Kaun, [1913?]. Song: v, pf.

Andalusian Cradle-Song. *Mercedes and Later Lyrics* (1884).

51 Schlesinger, Sebastian B. "Andalusian Song." Boston: C. Prüfer, 1883.

A Ballad. *The Ballad of Babie Bell and Other Poems* (1859).

52 Dana, Henshaw. "The Blackbird Sings in the Hazel-bush." Boston: A.P. Schmidt, 1883.

A Ballad of Nantucket. *The Ballad of Babie Bell and Other Poems* (1859).

> 53 Kennedy, Walter S.G. Worcester, Mass.: M. Steinert, 1898.
>
> 54 Marston, G.W. "Where Go You, Lovely Maggie?" Boston: O. Ditson, 1867. Ballad: v, pf.
>
> 55 Seaverns, C.L. "Where Go You, Pretty Maggie." Chicago: Root & Cady, 1868. Song?

Before the Rain. *Cloth of Gold and Other Poems* (1875).

> 56 Freer, Eleanor E. In *Six Songs of Nature* op. 10 no. 2. Milwaukee: W.A. Kaun, [1913?]. Song: v, pf.

The Betrothal. *The Ballad of Babie Bell and Other Poems* (1859).

> 57 Pommer, W.H. "I've Placed a Golden Ring." New York: G. Schirmer, 1888. Romance.
>
> 58 Reden, Karl. "The Golden Ring." Cincinnati: J.L. Peters, 1867. Song and Chorus: v, SATB, pf.

Cradle Song. *Unguarded Gates* (1895).

> 59 Atherton, Percy L. In *Four Songs* op. 20 no. 2. Boston: Boston Music, 1903. Song: med. v, pf.
>
> 60 Bauer, George F. New York: Luckhardt & Belder, 1896.
>
> 61 De Koven, Reginald. Boston: O. Ditson, 1896. Song: high, med. and low v edns, pf or orch (R). In coll. HST.
>
> 62 Grant-Schaefer, G.A. "Ere the Moon Begins to Rise." Boston: A.P. Schmidt, 1912.
>
> 63 Manney, Charles F. "Ere the Moon Begins to Rise." Boston: O. Ditson, 1906.
>
> 64 Semmann, Liborius. Milwaukee: Wm. A. Kaun, 1909.
>
> 65 Shackley, F.N. "Ere the Moon Begins to Rise." Boston: A.P. Schmidt, 1898.
>
> 66 Weidig, Adolf. "Cradle Song" op. 80 no. 1 in *Three Songs to Poems by Thomas Bailey Aldrich*. New York: G. Schirmer, 1927. Song: v, pf.

Dead. *The Ballad of Babie Bell and Other Poems* (1859).

> 67 Dana, C. Henshaw. "The One White Rose." Boston: G.D. Russell, 1876. Song: v, pf.

December, 1863. *The Poems of Thomas Bailey Aldrich* (1865).

> 68 "Only the Sea Intoning." Boston: A.P. Schmidt, 1887.

Epics and Lyrics. *Later Lyrics* (1896).

> 69 Semmann, Liborius. Milwaukee: Wm. A. Kaun, 1909.

Forever and a Day. *Poems* (1897).

> 70 Dieckmann, C.W. "Forever and a Day." u.p.: W.H. Willis, 1910.
>
> 71 Hadley, Henry K. In *Twelve Songs* op. 12 no. 1. Boston: A.P. Schmidt, 1898. Song: med. v, pf.
>
> 72 Harris, Victor. u.p.: E. Schuberth, 1898.
>
> 73 Johns, Clayton. Philadelphia: Hatch Music, 1898. Song: high and low v edns, pf.
>
> 74 Mack, Albert A. "Forever and a Day" in *Five Songs* op. 12 no. 1. New York: G. Schirmer, 1903. Song: med. v, pf. In coll. AA.
>
> 75 Townsend, Stephen. Boston: A.P. Schmidt, 1905.

Glamourie. *The Poems of Thomas Bailey Aldrich* (1865).

> 76 Dana, C. Henshaw. Boston: G.D. Russell, 1876. Song: v, pf.
>
> 77 Pommer, W.H. In *Four Songs*. St. Louis: Balmer & Weber, u.d.

"I'll Not Confer with Sorrow." *The Sisters' Tragedy, with Other Poems, Lyrical and Dramatic* (1891).

> 78 Hume, G.Y. "Joy" in coll. ArF 1.

In the Old Church Tower. *Pampinea and Other Poems* (1861).

> 79 Mignon, August. San Francisco: M. Gray, 1883.

It Was a Knight of Aragon. *The Ballad of Babie Bell and Other Poems* (1859).

> 80 Dana, C. Henshaw. Boston: A.P. Schmidt, 1878. Song: Bar or B, pf.

Kathie Morris. *Pampinea and Other Poems* (1861).

> 81 Dana, C. Henshaw. Boston: G.D. Russell, 1876. Ballad: S or T, pf.

Kriss Kringle. *Mercedes and Later Lyrics* (1884).

> 82 Mozart, W.A. Arr. to the Air: "Drink to Me Only with Thine Eyes" in coll. LBR.

Little Maud. *The Ballad of Babie Bell and Other Poems* (1859).

> 83 Reden, K. "O Where Is Our Dainty, Our Darling." u.p.,u.p. Song and chorus.
>
> 84 Webster, Joseph P. Chicago: H.M. Higgins, 1865. Song and Chorus: v and SATB, pf.

Maple Leaves. *Flower and Thorn* (1876).

85 Ives, Charles. New York: Cos Cob Press, ca. 1930. In coll. IOS, ISS.

May. *The Ballad of Babie Bell and Other Poems* (1859).

86 Mason, Daniel G. In *Two Songs*. Boston: Boston Music, 1892. Song: M or Bar, pf.

Mercedes ["Soldier's Song," act 1 sc. 2]. *Mercedes and Other Lyrics* (1884).

87 Pease, Alfred H. "Soldier's Song." New York: Wm. A. Pond, 1878. Song: v, pf.

88 Schlesinger, Sebastian B. "Reposez Vous Bons Chevaliers." Boston: C. Prüfer, 1883. Song: v, pf. Text in Eng.

The Merry Bells Shall Ring. *The Ballad of Babie Bell and Other Poems* (1859).

89 Dana, C. Henshaw. "Marguerite." Boston: G.D. Russell, 1876. Song: v, pf.

90 Hyatt, N. Irving. "Marguerite." Boston: A.P. Schmidt, 1901.

91 Marston, G.W. [Cover of music has C.W. Marston; inside it is listed as G.W.]. "Marguerite." Portland, Maine: Ira C. Stockbridge, 1871. Song: v, pf.

92 Pommer, W.H. "Marguerite." St. Louis: Balmer & Weber, 1892.

93 Reden, Karl. "Marguerite." Boston: O. Ditson, 1867. Song: v, pf.

Nameless Pain. *The Ballad of Babie Bell and Other Poems* (1859).

94 Lang, Margaret R. Boston: A.P. Schmidt, 1889. Song: v, pf.

Necromancy. *Unguarded Gates and Other Poems* (1895).

95 Weidig, Adolf. In *Three Songs to Poems by Thomas Bailey Aldrich* op. 80 no. 2. New York: G. Schirmer, 1927. Song: v, pf.

No Songs in Winter. *The Sisters' Tragedy, with Other Poems, Lyrical and Dramatic* (1891).

96 Butler, C. "In Winter" in coll. ArF 2. 2d stanza by H.W. Loomis.

Nocturne. *Flower and Thorn* (1877).

97 Barnes, A.L. New York: E. Schuberth, 1898. Song: v, pf.

98 Chadwick, George W. In *Two Songs*. Boston: A.P. Schmidt, 1886. Song: v, pf.

99 Dana, C. Henshaw. "Up to Her Chamber Window." Boston: A.P. Schmidt, 1877. Song: v, pf.

100 Foote, Arthur. "Up to Her Chamber Window" in *Six Songs* op. 43 no. 5. Boston: A.P. Schmidt, 1899. Song: high and low v edns, pf.

101 Foster, Fay. "In the Ilex Shadows." New York: Boosey, 1916. Song: high, med., and low v edns, pf.

102 Loth, L. Leslie. "Romeo's Ladder." New York: Enoch & Sons, 1926. Song: high and med. v edns.

103 Mack, Albert A. In *Three Songs* op. 14 no. 2. New York: G. Schirmer, 1904. Song: low v, pf.

104 Nevin, Ethelbert. "Nocturne" op. 20 no. 7. Boston: Boston Music, 1893. Song: high and med. v edns, pf.

105 Pommer, W.H. St. Louis: Balmer & Weber, 1892.

106 Redding, Joseph D. "Romeo's Ladder." New York: Wm. A. Pond, 1891.

107 Schlesinger, Sebastian B. "Up to Her Chamber Window." Boston: C. Prüfer, 1882. Song: v, pf.

108 Seymour, J.W. New York: G. Schirmer, 1887. Song: high and med. v edns, pf.

109 Train, A. "The Rose" in *Two Songs*. New York: G. Schirmer, 1893. Song: med. v, pf.

110 Underhill, Charles D. "Up to Her Chamber Window." Boston: O. Ditson, 1896. Song: high v, pf.

Nora McCarty. *Poems* (1863).

111 Boott, Francis. "Nora Macarty." Boston: O. Ditson, 1878. Song: v, pf.

112 Brown, O.B. "Nora Is Pretty." Boston: G.D. Russell, 1873. Song: v, pf.

113 Howson, Frank A. "Nora Is Pretty" in *Six Songs*. New York: J.N. Pattison, 1870. Song.

Palabras Cariñosas. *The Ballad of Babie Bell and Other Poems* (1859).

114 Caverly, Cecil M. "Good Night." Boston: C.W. Thompson, 1901. Song: v, pf.

115 Goldsborough, Arthur T. "Good Night." u.p.: H. Eberbach, 1891.

116 Pease, Alfred H. "Good Night." New York: Beer & Schmidt, 1866. Song: edns for S or T, and M or A, pf.

117 Thayer, Arthur W. "Good Night." Boston: A.P. Schmidt, 1886.

118 White, Maude V. "Good Night." u.p.: Chappell, 1904.

Seadrift. *Poems* (1863).

> 119 Coleridge-Taylor, Samuel. London: Novello, 1908. Rhapsody: SSAATTBB, a cap.

A Serenade. *Unguarded Gates and Other Poems* (1895).

> 120 Atkinson, Robert. "Bagatelle." Boston: O. Ditson, 1895.
>
> 121 Haesche, William E. "Imp of Dreams." New York: M. Witmark, 1912.

Sleep. *The Writings of Thomas Bailey Aldrich* (1897).

> 122 Foote, Arthur. Boston: A.P. Schmidt, 1929. Chorus: female voices, pf.

A Snowflake. *The Writings of Thomas Bailey Aldrich* (1891).

> 123 Loth, L. Leslie. New York: G. Schirmer, 1926. Song: high v, pf.

Songs. 4 ["Out from the depths of my heart"]. *Poems* (1863).

> 124 Hardee, Noble A. "Only to Die." Boston: Boston Music, 1901. Song: C or Bar, pf.

Two Songs from the Persian. 1 ["O cease, sweet music, let us rest!"] *Poems* (1863).

> 125 Pommer, W.H. "Song from the Persian." St. Louis: Balmer & Weber, 1892.
>
> 126 Sternberg, Constantin. "O, Cease! Sweet Music!" Milwaukee: Wm. Rohlfing, 1888.

Two Songs from the Persian. 2 ["Ah! sad are they who know not love"]. *Poems* (1863).

> 127 Chadwick, George W. "Song from the Persian" in *Two Songs*. Boston: A.P. Schmidt, 1886. Song: v, pf.
>
> 128 Fisher, William A. "Sad Are They Who Know Not Love." Boston: O. Ditson, 1897.
>
> 129 Foote, Arthur. "A Song from the Persian." Boston: A.P. Schmidt, 1894. Vocal Duet: SA.
>
> 130 Ford, Bertha. "Persian Love Song." New York: Brentano's Literary Emporium, 1881. Song: v, pf.
>
> 131 Paine, Lucy H. "Passion's Tears." New York: E. Schuberth, 1908. Song: v, pf.

The Unforgiven." *The Ballad of Babie Bell and Other Poems* (1859).

132 Dana, C. Henshaw. "In the Hushes of the Midnight." Boston: G.D. Russell, 1876. Song: v, pf.

Unsung. *Flower and Thorn* (1876).

133 Schlesinger, Sebastian B. "The Last Word." New York: E. Schuberth, 1886.

The Voice of the Sea. *Mercedes and Other Lyrics* (1884).

134 Ferrero, Carlo. u.p.: Alberto Himan, 1887.

135 Gilchrist, W.W. Boston: A.P. Schmidt, 1885.

136 O'Shea, John A. Miles & Thompson, 1890.

137 Schlesinger, Sebastian B. "In the Hush of the Autumn Night." Boston: C. Prüfer, 1882.

Wyndham Towers (1890).

138 Beach, Amy Cheney. "Sweetheart, Sigh No More" in *Song Album*. Boston: A.P. Schmidt, 1886.
    In *Song Album*. Boston: A.P. Schmidt, 1891.
    "Sweetheart, Sigh No More" op. 14 no. 3. Boston: A.P. Schmidt, 1901. Song: high v, pf. Rev. edn.

139 Brackett, Frank H. "Sweetheart Sigh No More" in *Two Songs*. Boston: Miles & Thompson, 1892. Song: v, pf.

140 Bullard, Frederic F. "Sweetheart, Sigh No More!" Cincinnati: J. Church, n.d. Song: low v, pf. Also pubd. for Chorus: TTBB, B solo, and Quartet: TTBB, 2d B solo.

141 Carmichael, M. "Sweetheart, Sigh No More" in *Three Songs*. New York: G. Schirmer, 1898. Song: high and med. v edns, pf.

142 Dana, Henshaw. "It Was with Doubt and Trembling." Boston: A.P. Schmidt, 1877. Song: v, pf.

143 Ferrero, Carlo. "It Was with Doubt and Trembling." New York: Alberto Himan, 1886.

144 Glover, William L. "Sweetheart, Sigh No More." Chicago: C.F. Summy, n.d.

145 Manney, Charles F. "Sweetheart, Sigh No More!" Boston: O. Ditson, 1898. Song: v, pf; Revised edn, Boston: O. Ditson, 1915. Song: high and med. v edns, pf, vn obl.

146 Young, Charles I. "Sweetheart, Sigh No More." Boston: O. Ditson: 1890. Song: T or Bar, pf.

Miscellaneous

147 Boyden, Georgie. "Carlotta." New York: Brentano's, 1883. Song.
Text: "Felipe and she at the play, Felipe and she at the ball. . . ."

148 Pease, Alfred H. "To the Queen's Health." New York: Wm. Pond,
1878. Song: B, pf. Text: "I drink I dare not say to whom. . . ."

149 Reden, K. "Down by the Summer Sea." u.p.,u.p. Song and Chorus.

150 Sainton-Dolby, Charlotte H. "Marjorie's Almanac." New York: Wm.
A. Pond, 1872. This is the earliest known printing of the text [BAL
273].

151 Schlesinger, S.B. "Bronze-Brown Eyes" in coll. Pr.

152 Warren, S.P. "Marjorie's Almanac" in coll. Pr [BAL 309].

153 Weidig, Adolf. "A Refrain" in *Three Songs by Thomas Bailey Aldrich* op.
80 no. 3. New York: G. Schirmer, 1927. Song: v, pf. Text: "High in
the tower she sings . . . passing by beneath. . . ."

MAXWELL ANDERSON (1888–1959)

Knickerbocker Holiday (1938).

154 Weill, Kurt. New York: Crawford Music, 1938. Musical comedy in
2 acts. Book and lyrics by Anderson.
> William Stickles, arr. "September Song" from *Knickerbocker
> Holiday*. New York: De Sylva, Brown & Henderson, 1949.
> Chorus: SATB, pf.
> "It Never Was You," "September Song," "There's Nowhere
> to Go but Up," "Will You Remember Me?" in coll. SnKW.
> Song: v, pf.

Lost in the Stars (1950). The Dramatization of Alan Paton's Novel, *Cry, the
Beloved Country*.

155 Weill, Kurt. *Lost in the Stars*. New York: Chappell, 1950. Musical
Tragedy.
> "Big Mole." New York: Chappell, 1949. Song: v, pf.
> "Lost in the Stars" from *Lost in the Stars*. New York: Crawford
> Music, 1946. Song: v, pf.
> William, Stickles, arr. "Lost in the Stars" from *Lost in the
> Stars*. New York: Crawford Music, 1946. Setting for TTBB,
> pf.

"Big Mole," "The Little Gray House," "Lost in the Stars," "Stay Well," "Thousands of Miles," "Trouble Man" in coll. SnKW. Song: v, pf.

St. Agnes' Morning. *You Who Have Dreams* (1925).

156 Cowell, Henry. New York: Music Press, 1947. Song: med. v, pf.

Miscellaneous

157 Herrmann, Bernard. "A Christmas Carol: A Musical Version of Charles Dickens' *A Christmas Carol.*" New York: Chappell, 1955. Libretto by Anderson.

158 Weill, Kurt. "Apple Jack," "The Catfish Song," "Come in Mornin'," "River Chanty," "This Time Next Year" in *Songs for Huckleberry Finn.* New York: Chappell, 1954. Song: v, pf. In coll. SnKW.

159 Weill, Kurt. "The Ballad of Magna Carta." New York: Chappell, 1940. Cantata: mixed chorus, soli, pf.

JOHN ASHBERY (B. 1927)

Fear of Death. *Self-Portrait in a Convex Mirror* (1975).

160 Rorem, Ned. In *The Nantucket Songs.* New York: Boosey & Hawkes, 1981. Song: v, pf.

The Grapevine. *Some Trees* (1956).

161 Rorem, Ned. In *Some Trees.* New York: Boosey & Hawkes, 1970. Song: S, M, B-Bar, pf. Recording: Composers Recordings, CRI 238 SD (1969).

Our Youth. *The Tennis Court Oath* (1962).

162 Rorem, Ned. In *Some Trees.* New York: Boosey & Hawkes, 1970. Song: S, M, B-Bar, pf. Recording: Composers Recordings, CRI 238 SD (1969).

Some Trees. *Some Trees* (1956).

163 Rorem, Ned. New York: Boosey & Hawkes, 1970. Song: S, M, B-Bar, pf. Recording: Composers Recordings, CRI 238 SD (1969).

Syringa. *Houseboat Days* (1975).

>   163a Carter, Elliott. New York: Associated Music, 1980. Setting for M, B, gtr, 10 instr.

Thoughts of a Young Girl. *The Tennis Court Oath* (1962).

>   164 Rorem, Ned. In *The Nantucket Songs.* New York: Boosey & Hawkes, 1981. Song: v, pf.

ROSEMARY BENÉT (1900–1962)

Abigail Adams. *A Book of Americans* (1933).

>   165 Kubik, Gail. New York: G. Schirmer, 1949. Chorus: SATB, pf.

Dolly Madison. *A Book of Americans* (1933).

>   166 London, Edwin. In *Portraits of Three Ladies.* New York: Henmar, 1973. Song: M, narr., instr. ens, slides, opt male dancer.

Jesse James. *A Book of Americans* (1933).

>   167 Shaw, Arnold. In *Sing a Song of Americans.* New York: Musette, 1941. Song: v, pf.

Nancy Hanks. *A Book of Americans* (1933).

>   168 Davis, Katherine K. New York: Galaxy, 1941. Song: S, pf; New York: Galaxy, 1945. Chorus: SSA, pf; New York: Galaxy, 1946. Chorus: SATB, pf.
>
>   169 Kubik, Gail. New York: G. Schirmer, 1949. Chorus: SSAATTBB, A and Bar soli, pf.
>
>   170 London, Edwin. In *Portraits of Three Ladies.* New York: Henmar, 1973. Song: M, narr., instr. ens, slides, opt male dancer.
>
>   171 Shaw, Arnold. In *Sing a Song of Americans.* New York: Musette, 1941. Song: v, pf.
>
>   172 Siegmeister, Elie. In *American Legends: Six Songs for Voice and Piano.* New York: E.B. Marks, 1947. Song: v, pf.

Pocahontas. *A Book of Americans* (1933).

>   173 London, Edwin. In *Portraits of Three Ladies.* New York: Henmar, 1973. Song: M, narr., instr. ens, slides, opt male dancer.

STEPHEN VINCENT BENÉT (1898–1943)

Abraham Lincoln. *A Book of Americans* (1933).

> 174 George, Earl. In *Four American Portraits*. New York: Southern Music Publishing, 1955. Chorus: SATB.

> 175 Shaw, Arnold. In *Sing a Song of Americans*. New York: Musette, 1941. Song: v, pf.

Apology. *A Book of Americans* (1933).

> 176 Shaw, Arnold. In *Sing a Song of Americans*. New York: Musette, 1941. Song: v, pf.

The Ballad of William Sycamore. *Ballad of William Sycamore* (1923).

> 177 Moore, Douglas S. New York: King's Crown Music, 1974. Opera (1 act): B, fl, trb, pf.

> 178 Stevens, Halsey. New York: Highgate Press, 1961. Chorus: SATB, orch.

A Book of Americans (1933). *See also* for individual titles under Stephen V. Benét and Rosemary Benét.

> 179 Snyder, Leo. *A Book of Americans*. New York: Leeds Music, 1962. Juvenile Opera or Cantata.

Captain Kidd. *A Book of Americans* (1933).

> 180 Shaw, Arnold. In *Sing a Song of Americans*. New York: Musette, 1941. Song: v, pf.

Chemical Analysis. *Tiger Joy* (1925).

> 181 Thompson, Randall. In *Rosemary*. Boston: E.C. Schirmer, 1930. Chorus: SSAA, a cap.

Christopher Columbus. *A Book of Americans* (1933).

> 182 Kubik, Gail. New York: Ricordi, 1960. Chorus: SATB, pf. Additional spoken lines by the composer.

Cotton Mather. *A Book of Americans* (1933).

> 183 Bone, Gene and Howard Fenton. New York: C. Fischer, 1949.

> 184 Trubitt, Allen. New York: G. Schirmer, 1979. Setting for SATB, Bar solo, gtr.

Daniel Boone. *A Book of Americans* (1933).

> 185 George, Earl. In *Four American Portraits*. New York: Southern Music Publishing, 1955. Chorus: SATB.

Daniel Drew. *A Book of Americans* (1933).

> 186 Kubik, Gail. New York: Arrow Music, 1940. Setting for SATB qrt or chorus, vc and db; acc. arr. for pf.

The Devil and Daniel Webster (1938, 1939).

> 187 Moore, Douglas S. New York: Boosey & Hawkes, 1943. Opera (1 act); selections from the opera pubd separately: "I've Got a Man" (Bar solo), "Now May there Be a Blessing" (S solo or female chorus).

For All Blasphemers. *Ballads and Poems 1915–1930* (1931).

> 188 Simons, Netty. MS, u.d., avail. ACA. Chorus: TTBB, a cap.

George Washington. *A Book of Americans* (1933).

> 189 Kubik, Gail. New York: G. Ricordi, 1960. Chorus: mixed voices, divisi, pf. Add. prose by the composer.

Hernando De Soto. *A Book of Americans* (1933).

> 190 Shaw, Arnold. In *Sing a Song of Americans*. New York: Musette, 1941. Song: v, pf.

In a Glass of Water before Retiring. *Tiger Joy* (1925).

> 191 Bergsma, William. New York: C. Fischer, 1947. Chorus: SATB, S solo, pf.

John Brown's Body (1928).

> 192 Bingham, Seth D. In *Wilderness Stone*. New York: H.W. Gray, 1937. Folk Cantata: SATB chorus, soli, narr., orch.
>
> 193 Cowell, Henry. "American Muse," "Swift Runner," and "Immensity of Wheel" in *American Muse*. New York: Music Press, 1943. Part Songs: SA, pf.
>
> 194 Delaney, Robert. "John Brown's Song." Boston: E.C. Schirmer, 1932. Choral Poem: mixed voices, pf or orch (R). Text from the sec. "John Brown's Speech" (Book One).

John James Audubon. *A Book of Americans* (1933).

> 195 Raphling, Sam. New York: Edition Musicus, 1952. Song: v, pf.

John Quincy Adams. *A Book of Americans* (1933).

196 George, Earl. In *Four American Portraits*. New York: Southern Music Publishing, 1955. Chorus: SATB.

197 Shaw, Arnold. In *Sing a Song of Americans*. New York: Musette, 1941. Song: v, pf.

Johnny Appleseed. *A Book of Americans* (1933).

198 Alexander, Josef. In *Three American Episodes*. New York: H.W. Gray, 1947. Chorus: SATB, pf.

199 Siegmeister, Elie. New York: Maxwell Weaner, 1941. Chorus: SATB, pf.
    New York: Maxwell Weaner, 1941. Song: v, pf.
    In *American Legends: Six Songs for Voice and Piano*. New York: Edward B. Marks, 1947. Song: v, pf.
    New York: Mercury, 1949. Song: v, pf.
    In coll. DTA, DTAR.
    Siegmeister lists Rosemary Benét as the author of the text.

The Last Speech. *Radio's Best Plays* (1947).

200 Cooper, Lou. "The Last Speech" in *Radio's Best Plays,* ed. by Joseph Liss. New York, 1947. Cantata, with words by Benét, Cecil Carmer, and Franklin D. Roosevelt.

Miles Standish. *A Book of Americans* (1933).

201 Kubik, Gail. New York: Southern Music Publishing, 1950. Chorus: SSAATTBB, pf.

Negro Spirituals. *A Book of Americans* (1933).

202 Alexander, Josef. In *Three American Episodes*. New York: H.W. Gray, 1947. Chorus: SATB, pf.

A Nonsense Song. *Tiger Joy* (1925).

203 Thompson, Randall. In *Rosemary*. Boston: E.C. Schirmer, 1930. Chorus: SSA, a cap.

Oliver De Lancey. *A Book of Americans* (1933).

204 Kubik, Gail. In *Choral Profiles*. New York: G. Schirmer, 1949. Chorus: TTBB, T and B soli, pf; also arr. for chorus: SSAATTBB, pf (1949).

205 Shaw, Arnold. In *Sing a Song of Americans*. New York: Musette, 1941. Song: v, pf.

P.T. Barnum. *A Book of Americans* (1933).

206 Kubik, Gail. New York: G. Ricordi, 1960. Chorus: SSAATTBB, SATB soli, narr., pf. Add. prose by the composer.

207 Shaw, Arnold. In *Sing a Song of Americans*. New York: Musette, 1941. Song: v, pf.

Peregrine White and Virginia Dare. *A Book of Americans* (1933).

208 Kubik, Gail. New York: Southern Music Publishing, 1950. Chorus: SSA, a cap.

209 Shaw, Arnold. In *Sing a Song of Americans*. New York: Musette, 1941. Song: v, pf.

Peter Stuyvesant. *A Book of Americans* (1933).

210 Shaw, Arnold. In *Sing a Song of Americans*. New York: Musette, 1941. Song: v, pf.

Prayer. *Prayer. A Child Is Born* (1944).

211 Moore, Douglas S. "Prayer for the United Nations." New York: H.W. Gray, 1943. Chorus: SATB, A and Bar soli, pf or orch.

A Sad Song. *Tiger Joy* (1925).

212 Thompson, Randall. In *Rosemary*. Boston: E.C. Schirmer, 1930. Chorus: SSA, a cap.

Southern Ships and Settlers. *A Book of Americans* (1933).

213 Kubik, Gail. New York: Southern Music Publishing, 1950. Chorus: SSAATTBB, a cap.

Theodore Roosevelt. *A Book of Americans* (1933).

214 Kubik, Gail. New York: Southern Music Publishing, 1950. Chorus: SSAATTBB, pf.

215 Shaw, Arnold. In *Sing a Song of Americans*. New York: Musette, 1941. Song: v, pf.

Thomas Jefferson. *A Book of Americans* (1933).

216 George, Earl. In *Four American Portraits*. New York: Southern Music Publishing, 1955. Chorus: SATB.

217 Shaw, Arnold. In *Sing a Song of Americans*. New York: Musette, 1941. Song: v, pf.

To Rosemary, on the Methods by Which She Might Become an Angel. *Tiger Joy* (1925).

218 Thompson, Randall. In *Rosemary.* Boston: E.C. Schirmer, 1930. Chorus: SSAA, pf.

Western Star (1945).

219 Dello Joio, Norman. "Song of Affirmation." New York: C. Fischer, 1953. Symphonic Cantata: SATB chorus, S solo, narr., full orch. Text adapted.

220 Goldstein, David. "Prelude to 'Western Star.'" New York: G. Schirmer, 1978. Chorus: SATB, a cap. Text from the "Prelude."

221 Lockwood, Normand. "Americans" and "Lend Me Your Music" in *Prelude to "Western Star."* New York: Boosey & Hawkes, 1961. Arr. by Erich Kunzel for TTBB chorus, pf; orig. for M, pf.

Western Wagons. *A Book of Americans* (1933).

222 Alexander, Josef. In *Three American Episodes.* New York: H.W. Gray, 1947. Chorus: SATB, pf.

223 Shaw, Arnold. In *Sing a Song of Americans.* New York: Musette, 1941. Song: v, pf.

Wilbur Wright and Orville Wright. *A Book of Americans* (1933).

224 Shaw, Arnold. In *Sing a Song of Americans.* New York: Musette, 1941. Song: v, pf.

Winged Man. *Ballads and Poems 1915–1930* (1931).

225 Bassett, Leslie. n.t. in *Moon Canticles.* New York: C.F. Peters, 1971. Chorus: SATB, narr., a cap, vc obl.

Woodrow Wilson. *A Book of Americans* (1933).

226 Kubik, Gail. New York: Southern Music Publishing, 1950. Chorus: SSATTBB, pf.

227 Shaw, Arnold. In *Sing a Song of Americans.* New York: Musette, 1941. Song: v, pf.

Miscellaneous

227a Moore, Douglas S. 'Perhaps to Dream.' New York: C. Fischer, 1938. Chorus: SSA, a cap.

WILLIAM ROSE BENÉT (1886–1950)

The Fawn in the Snow. *Man Possessed* (1927).

> 228 Couper, Mildred. In coll. UNSNV. Song: v, pf.
>
> 229 Smith, Dorothy B. In coll. UNSNV. Song: v, pf.

Jesse James: American Myth. *Man Possessed* (1927).

> 230 George, Earl. "A Ballad of Jesse James." New York: Southern Music
> Publishing, 1957. Chorus: SATB, a cap.
>
> 231 Hiller, Lejaren A. Setting for vocal qrt, pf. Recording: Orion, ORS
> 78287 (1978).

Judgment. *Golden Fleece* (1935).

> 232 Ames, William T. New York: Music Press, 1947. Song: med. v, pf.

Ritual. *Merchants from Cathay* (1913).

> 233 Babin, Victor. London: Augener, 1950. Song: v, pf.

Song Heard in Sleep. *The Stairway of Surprise* (1947).

> 234 Read, Gardner. "Song Heard in Sleep" op. 88a. New York: Lawson-
> Gould, 1958. Chorus: 4-pt. mixed voices, pf.

WENDELL BERRY (B. 1934)

The Arrival. *The Country of Marriage* (1973).

> 235 Jenni, Donald. In *Songs from the "Country of Marriage."* MS, 1982, avail.
> ACA. Cycle: med. v, pf.

Her First Calf. *The Country of Marriage* (1973).

> 236 Jenni, Donald. In *Songs from the "Country of Marriage."* MS, 1982, avail.
> ACA. Cycle: med. v, pf.

A Song Sparrow Singing in the Fall. *The Country of Marriage* (1973).

> 237 Jenni, Donald. In *Songs from the "Country of Marriage."* MS, 1982, avail.
> ACA. Cycle: med. v, pf.

The Wild Geese. *The Country of Marriage* (1973).

> 238 Jenni, Donald. In *Songs from the "Country of Marriage."* MS, 1982, avail. ACA. Cycle: med. v, pf.

Zero. *The Country of Marriage* (1973).

> 239 Jenni, Donald. In *Songs from the "Country of Marriage."* MS, 1982, avail. ACA. Cycle: med. v, pf.

ELIZABETH BISHOP (1911–1979)

MacMahon, Candace W. *Elizabeth Bishop: A Bibliography, 1927–1979.* Charlottesville, Va.: University Press of Virginia, 1980, p. 168.

Anaphora. *North & South* (1946).

> 240 Carter, Elliott. In *A Mirror on Which to Dwell.* New York: Associated Music, 1977. Song: S, cham orch.

Argument. *Poems: North & South—A Cold Spring* (1955).

> 241 Carter, Elliott. In *A Mirror on Which to Dwell.* New York: Associated Music, 1977. Song: S, cham orch.

Conversation [No. 1 of "Four Poems"]. *Poems: North & South—A Cold Spring* (1955).

> 242 Rorem, Ned. New York: Boosey & Hawkes, 1969. Song: med. v, pf.

Insomnia. *Poems: North & South—A Cold Spring* (1955).

> 243 Carter, Elliott. In *A Mirror on Which to Dwell.* New York: Associated Music, 1977. Song: S, cham orch.

O Breath [No. 4 of "Four Poems"]. *Poems: North & South—A Cold Spring* (1955).

> 244 Carter, Elliott. In *A Mirror on Which to Dwell.* New York: Associated Music, 1977. Song: S, cham orch.

Sandpiper. *Questions of Travel* (1965).

> 245 Carter, Elliott. In *A Mirror on Which to Dwell.* New York: Associated Music, 1977. Song: S, cham orch.

View of the Capitol from the Library of Congress. *Poems: North & South—A Cold Spring* (1955).

246 Carter, Elliott. In *A Mirror on Which to Dwell.* New York: Associated Music, 1977. Song: S, cham orch.

Visits to St. Elizabeth's. *Questions of Travel* (1965).

247 Rorem, Ned. New York: Composers Editions, 1959; New York: Boosey & Hawkes, 1964. Song: med. v, pf.

LOUISE BOGAN (1897–1970)

To Be Sung on the Water. *Collected Poems 1923–1953* (1954).

248 Barber, Samuel. "To Be Sung on the Water" op. 42 no. 2. New York: G. Schirmer, 1969. Chorus: SATB.

ANNE BRADSTREET (1612?–1672)

To My Dear and Loving Husband. *Works of Anne Bradstreet* (1967).

248a Bacon, Ernst. "To a Loving Husband" in coll. BacFS. Song: v, pf.

249 Bassett, Leslie. In *Five Love Songs.* Bryn Mawr, Pa.: Merion Music, 1977. Song: S, pf.

250 Bernstein, Leonard. In *Songfest.* New York: Boosey & Hawkes, 1977. Cycle: SAMTBarB, orch.

251 Rorem, Ned. In *Women's Voices.* New York: Boosey & Hawkes, 1979. Cycle: S, pf.

"What God is like to him I serve." *Works of Anne Bradstreet* (1967).

252 Sims, Ezra. MS, u.d, avail. ACA. Chorus: SATB, a cap.

Miscellaneous

253 Avshalomov, Jacob. In *City upon a Hill.* MS, u.d., avail. ACA. Cantata: SATB chorus, speaker, orch.

254 Boyd, Jack. *Three Contemplations of Anne Bradstreet.* Cincinnati: World Library Publications, u.d. Chorus: SATB.

255 Gideon, Miriam. In *Spirit above the Dust.* MS, u.d., avail. ACA. Cycle: med. v, fl, ob, bsn, hn, str qrt.

256 Pinkham, Daniel. "The Happy Flood" in *O Beautiful! My Country.* Boston: Ione Press, 1976. Chorus: SSAATTBB, opt pf.

WILLIAM CULLEN BRYANT (1794–1878)

Abraham Lincoln; The Death of Lincoln. *Poems* (1871) [BAL 1694].

257 Ringwald, Roy. n.t. in *The Song of America.* East Stroudsburg, Pa.: Shawnee, 1951. Cantata: SATB chorus, narr., pf 4 hands. Recording: Decca, DAU 816.

The Centennial Hymn. *The Poetical Works of William Cullen Bryant* (1883).

258 Ringwald, Roy. n.t. in *Heritage.* Delaware Water Gap, Pa.: Shawnee, 1975. National Hymn for the Bicentennial: SATB, pf or org. Verse "D" from "Centennial Hymn" by Bryant, "Through calm and storm the years have led our country on from stage to stage. . . ." Choral voicings avail. are SATB, SSA, SAB, SA, STBB. Band acc. avail. (R). Also avail. is a transparency with the melody and words to permit audience participation.

Earth. *Poems* (1836).

259 Bassett, Leslie. In *Of Wind and Earth.* New York: C.F. Peters, 1978. Chorus: SATB, pf.

The Gladness of Nature. *Poems* (1832).

260 Demarest, Clifford. New York: J. Fischer, 1937. Part Song: SSA, pf.

261 Merriam, R.H. Chatham, N.J.: Joseph Dunham, 1934. Chorus: SATB, pf.

262 Molloy, J.L. "An Arbor Day Song" in coll. FSS 8.

"How Amiable Are Thy Tabernacles." *Hymns* (1864).

263 Pond, Sylvanus B. "O Thou Whose Own Vast Temples Stand" in coll. ChAH. Hymn.

The Hunter's Serenade. *Poems* (1832).

264 "The Hunter's Serenade." Arr. from a German Air. In coll. LBR.

265 Ives, E., Jr. Philadelphia: Kretschmar & Nunns, [BAL n.d., ca. 1834–1836].

Hymn of the City. *Poems* (1832).

266 Warren, Elinor R. New York: C. Fischer, 1970 (R), Chorus: SATB, pf or orch.

The Indian Girl's Lament. *Poems* (1832).

267 Mendelssohn, Felix, arr. from. In coll. LBR.

March. *Poems* (1832).

268 Hanson, H. In coll. Mu 5, MuC 5, MuT 3.

The New Moon. *Poems* (1832).

269 Ives, E., Jr. New York: Firth & Hall, 1837.

A Northern Legend [From the German of Uhland]. *The White-Footed Deer and Other Poems* (1844).

270 Schnecker, P.A. New York: G. Schirmer, 1895.

Not Yet. *Thirty Poems* (1864).

271 "Not Yet" in *Songs for War Time: German Airs with English Words, for the Army, the Family, and the School.* Boston: Gould & Lincoln, 1863.

"Oh, Fairest of the Rural Maids." *Poems* (1832).

272 McNaughton, J.H. Buffalo: Penn & Remington, 1865. Song.

273 Pollen, J. Shelton. "Maid of the Sylvan Wild." Boston: Chas. W. Homeyer, 1903.

"Other Sheep I Have, Which Are Not of This Fold." *The Poetical Works of William Cullen Bryant* (1883).

274 Buck, Percy C. "Look from Your Sphere of Endless Day" in coll. LBW. Hymn.

Our Country's Call. *Thirty Poems* (1864).

275 "Our Country's Call." Arr. to the Air: Der Tannenbaum. In coll. LBR.

The Planting of the Apple Tree. *Thirty Poems* (1864).

276 Roeske, C.C. In coll. PouH.

Robert of Lincoln. *Poems* (1854).

   277 Conrade, M.S. In coll. GeS.

   278 Osgood, J. Boston: G.P. Reed, 1856.

The Saw-Mill. *The Poetical Works of William Cullen Bryant* (1883).

   279 Saroni, Herman A. New York: Wm. Hall, 1848. Song: v, pf.

The Serenade [From the Spanish]. *The Fountain and Other Poems* (1842).

   280 Gilberté, Hallett. "Spanish Serenade." Boston: C.W. Thompson, 1900.

   281 Moore, Mary C. "May with Life and Music" op. 28 no. 1. New York: M. Witmark, 1912. Song: v, pf.

   282 Singer, Florence M. "If Slumber Sweet." Boston: O. Ditson, 1893.

   283 Thompson, Alexander S. Boston: O. Ditson, 1887. Song: v, pf.

The Siesta [From the Spanish]. *Poems* (1832).

   284 Sargent, S.A. In *Three Songs*. Boston: O. Ditson, 1885. Song: v, pf.

   285 Werrenrath, Reinald. New York: G. Schirmer, 1913. Chorus: TTBB, a cap.

Song of Marion's Men. *Poems* (1832).

   285a Durst, Sidney C. Cincinnati: J. Church, 1902. Quartet: male voices, pf.

A Song of Pitcairn's Island. *Poems* (1832).

   286 Ives, E., Jr. "Come Take Our Boy and We Will Go." Philadelphia: Bacon, Weygandt, 1833. Song: v, pf; "A Song of Pitcairn's Island 'Come Take Our Boy and We Will Go.'" Philadelphia: Geo. Willig, n.d. [BAL ca. 1833]. Song: v, pf.

Song of the Greek Amazon. *Poems* (1832).

   287 Ives, E., Jr. Philadelphia: Kretschmar & Nunns, n.d. [BAL ca. 1833–1834]. Song: v, pf; "The Greek Amazon: I Buckle to My Slender Side." New York: J.F. Nunns, n.d. Song: v, pf.

The Star of Bethlehem. *The Poetical Works of William Cullen Bryant* (1883).

   288 Cutler, H.S. "As Shadows Cast by Cloud and Sun" in coll. LAASR; "All Saints" in coll. LAAS.

   289 Oliver, Henry K. "As Shadows Cast by Cloud and Sun" in coll. ChAH.

The Stream of Life. *Poems* (1847).

    290 Hair, Frank N. Worcester, Mass.: C.L. Gorham, 1886.

A Summer Ramble. *The White Footed Deer and Other Poems* (1844).

    291 Bright, Houston. "August Noon." Delaware Water Gap, Pa.: Shawnee, 1963. Chorus: SATB, a cap. Text adapted.

    292 Brook, Harry. "The Quiet August Noon." London: J. Curwen, 1936. 2-pt. song for equal voices, pf.

    293 Pasmore, Henry B. "Come Thou in Whose Soft Eyes I See." San Francisco: J.D. Pasmore, 1880. Song: v, pf.

Thanatopsis. *Poems* (1821).

    293a Heiss, John. "from 'Thanatopsis' " in *Songs of Nature.* n.p.: Boosey & Hawkes, 1978. Song Cycle: M, fl, cl, vn, vc, pf. Recording: Nonesuch H 71351.

    294 Mosenthal, Joseph. New York: G. Schirmer, 1891. Chorus: TTBB, pf.

"The Lord Giveth Wisdom." *The Poetical Works of William Cullen Bryant* (1883).

    295 Zundel, John. "Mighty One, Before Whose Face" in coll. ChAH. 3 stanzas.

"The May Sun Sheds an Amber Light." *Poems* (1854).

    296 Dempster, William R. Boston: O. Ditson, 1852. Song: v, pf.

    297 Doerinckel, Fred. R. New York: E. Schuberth, 1877. Song: v, pf. Text in Eng. and Ger.

"Thou Hast Put All Things Under His Feet." *The Poetical Works of William Cullen Bryant* (1883).

    298 Davis, Katherine K. "His Kingdom Is Begun." u.p.: The New Music Co., 1977.

To a Cloud. *Poems* (1832).

    299 Burleigh, Cecil. "To a Cloud" op. 49 no. 2. Cincinnati: J. Church, 1919. Song: v, pf.

To a Waterfowl. *Poems* (1821).

    300 Crist, Bainbridge. New York: C. Fischer, 1947. Chorus: SSA, pf.

To the Fringed Gentian. *Poems* (1832).

301 Kern, C.A. In coll. Mu 5, MuC 5.

302 Lang, Margaret R. In coll. TL. Setting for SATB, pf.

The West Wind. *Poems* (1832).

303 Parker, J.C.D. "The West Wind" in *7 Part Songs*. Boston: Ditson, 1875. Setting for SATB, pf.

304 Woodman, R.H. In coll. Par 4.

The Yellow Violet. *Poems* (1821).

304a Heiss, John. In *Songs of Nature*. n.p.: Boosey & Hawkes, 1978. Setting for M, fl, cl, vn, vc, pf. Recording: Nonesuch H 71351.

Miscellaneous

305 Busch, Carl. "America." Newark, N.J.: Festival Pub. co., 1916. Cantata: chorus, 2 soli, orch.

306 Emerson, L.O. "We Are Coming, Father Abra'am." Boston: O. Ditson, 1862. The poem is not by Bryant, although it is frequently attributed to him. The author was James Sloan Gibbons [BAL 1673].

307 Linley, G. "Fading of the Flowers." Cited in DCD. Duet.

308 Pasmore, Henry B. "In the Wood" in *Song Album*. Boston: O. Ditson, 1890. Song: M or Bar, pf. Words in Eng. and Ger., trans. by Paul Torek.

[HAROLD] WITTER BYNNER (1881–1968)

After a Rain at Mokanshan. *Against the Cold* (1940).

309 Graham, Robert. New York: Associated Music, 1958. Song: med. v, pf.

"Any other time would have done." *New Poems* (1960).

310 Rorem, Ned. "Any Other Time" in *Santa Fe Songs*. New York: Boosey & Hawkes, 1980. Cycle: med. v, vn, vla, vc, pf.

Autumn Bird. *Take Away the Darkness* (1947).

311 Graham, Robert. Philadelphia: Elkan-Vogel, 1961. Chorus: SSA, pf.

The Boatmen. *The Beloved Stranger* (1919).

312 Babin, Victor. In *Beloved Stranger*. London: Augener, 1950. Song: low v, pf.

A Boy. *A Canticle of Pan and Other Poems* (1920).

313 Mason, Daniel G. In *Russians* op. 18 no. 4. New York: G. Schirmer, 1920. Song: Bar, pf or orch (R).

Cherry-Blossoms. *The Beloved Stranger* (1919).

314 Babin, Victor. In *Beloved Stranger*. London: Augener, 1950. Song: low v, pf.

Clover. *An Ode to Harvard and Other Poems* (1907).

315 Watts, Wintter. Cincinnati: J. Church, 1906. Song: high and low v edns, pf.

"Coming down the stairs." *New Poems* (1960).

316 Rorem, Ned. In *Santa Fe Songs*. New York: Boosey & Hawkes, 1980. Cycle: med. v, vn, vla, vc, pf.

A Concertina-Player. *A Canticle of Pan and Other Poems* (1920).

317 Mason, Daniel G. In *Russians* op. 18 no. 2. New York: G. Schirmer, 1920. Song: Bar, pf or orch (R).

The Crown. *The Beloved Stranger* (1919).

318 Babin, Victor. In *Beloved Stranger*. London: Augener, 1950. Song: low v, pf.

Dream. *The Beloved Stranger* (1919).

319 Babin, Victor. In *Beloved Stranger*. London: Augener, 1950. Song: low v, pf.

A Drunkard. *A Canticle of Pan and Other Poems* (1920).

320 Mason, Daniel G. In *Russians* op. 18 no. 1. New York: G. Schirmer, 1920. Song: Bar, pf or orch (R).

Dusk. *The Beloved Stranger* (1919).

321 Babin, Victor. In *Beloved Stranger*. London: Augener, 1950. Song: low v, pf.

El Musico. *Selected Poems* (1977, 1978).

> 322 Rorem, Ned. In *Santa Fe Songs*. New York: Boosey & Hawkes, 1980. Cycle: med. v, vn, vla, vc, pf.

The Gold-Thread Robe [Co-translator, Kiang Kang-Hu]. *Freeman* (January 4, 1922).

> 323 Mennin, Peter. New York: C. Fischer, 1948. Chorus: SATB, a cap.

"He never knew what was the matter." *New Poems* (1960).

> 324 Rorem, Ned. "He Never Knew" in *Santa Fe Songs*. New York: Boosey & Hawkes, 1980. Cycle: med. v, vn, vla, vc, pf.

Lament. *The Beloved Stranger* (1919).

> 325 Babin, Victor. In *Beloved Stranger*. London: Augener, 1950. Song: low v, pf.

Lightning. *The Beloved Stranger* (1919).

> 326 Babin, Victor. In *Beloved Stranger*. London: Augener, 1950. Song: low v, pf.

Moving Leaves. *Indian Earth* (1929).

> 327 Rorem, Ned. In *Santa Fe Songs*. New York: Boosey & Hawkes, 1980. Cycle: med. v, vn, vla, vc, pf.

Opus 101. *Spectra* (1916).

> 328 Rorem, Ned. In *Santa Fe Songs*. New York: Boosey & Hawkes, 1980. Cycle: med. v, vn, vla, vc, pf.

A Prophet. *A Canticle of Pan and Other Poems* (1920).

> 329 Mason, Daniel G. In *Russians* op. 18 no. 5. New York: G. Schirmer, 1920. Song: Bar, pf.

A Revolutionary. *A Canticle of Pan and Other Poems* (1920).

> 330 Mason, Daniel G. In *Russians* op. 18 no. 3. New York: G. Schirmer, 1920. Song: Bar, pf.

Santa Fe. *Selected Poems* (1977, 1978).

> 331 Rorem, Ned. In *Santa Fe Songs*. New York: Boosey & Hawkes, 1980. Cycle: med. v, vn, vla, vc, pf.

Singing. *The Beloved Stranger* (1919).

332 Babin, Victor. In *Beloved Stranger*. London: Augener, 1950. Song: low v, pf.

Snickerty Nick & the Giant (1935).

333 Ridgway, Charles A. Los Angeles: Sutton House, 1935. By Julia Ellsworth (Shaw) Ford. Rhymes by Bynner. Music by Ridgway. Illustrations by Arthur Rackham.

A Song of the Palace. *The Jade Mountain* (1929).

334 Mennin, Peter. New York: C. Fischer, 1948. Chorus: SATB. Trans. from a poem by Kiang Kang-Hu.

The Sowers. *Against the Cold* (1940).

335 Rorem, Ned. In *Santa Fe Songs*. New York: Boosey & Hawkes, 1980. Cycle: med. v, vn, vla, vc, pf.

"Summer, O Summer, fill thy shadowy trees." *Against the Cold* (1940).

336 Rorem, Ned. "Sonnet" in *Santa Fe Songs*. New York: Boosey & Hawkes, 1980. Cycle: med. v, vn, vla, vc, pf.

A Tent Song. *Book of Lyrics* (1955).

337 Owen, Richard. "Till We Watch the Last Low Star." New York: General, 1962. Song: high v, pf.

To a Phoebe-Bird. *Bellman* 17 (Aug. 1, 1914), p. 148.

338 Bricken, Carl. In coll. UNSNV. Song: v, pf.

Tree-Toads. *The Beloved Stranger* (1919).

339 Babin, Victor. In *Beloved Stranger*. London: Augener, 1950. Song: low v, pf.

The Two Windows. *Take Away the Darkness* (1947).

340 Graham, Robert. Philadelphia: Elkan-Vogel, 1962. Chorus: SSA, pf.

Voices. *A Canticle of Pan and Other Poems* (1920).

341 Duke, John. New York: Boosey & Hawkes, 1949. Song: high v, pf.
342 Hageman, Richard. New York: Galaxy, 1943. Song: med. v, pf.

The Wall. *The Beloved Stranger* (1919).

343 Babin, Victor. In *Beloved Stranger*. London: Augener, 1950. Song: low v, pf.

Water-Hyacinths. *Indian Earth* (1929).

> 344 Rorem, Ned. In *Santa Fe Songs*. New York: Boosey & Hawkes, 1980. Cycle: med. v, vn, vla, vc, pf. Setting of both secs. of the poem.

The Wave. *The Beloved Stranger* (1919).

> 345 Babin, Victor. In *Beloved Stranger*. London: Augener, 1950. Song: low v, pf.

The Wintry Mind. *Against the Cold* (1940).

> 346 Rorem, Ned. In *Santa Fe Songs*. New York: Boosey & Hawkes, 1980. Cycle: med. v, vn, vla, vc, pf.

"Yes I hear them." *New Poems* (1960).

> 347 Rorem, Ned. In *Santa Fe Songs*. New York: Boosey & Hawkes, 1980. Cycle: med. v, vn, vla, vc, pf.

Miscellaneous

> 348 Blair, William. "Resignation." Cincinnati: J. Church, 1917. Song: v, pf.
>
> 348a "Feast of Lanterns," "The Lily," "Longing," "A Love Song," "Yoh-Wu-Mo" in coll. BoC. Song: v, pf.

JAMES FENIMORE COOPER (1789–1951)

"My Brigantine!" [Text from chap. 15]. *The Water-Witch* (1831).

> 349 Rodwell, George H. New York: E.S. Mesier, ca. 1830.
>
> 350 Saar, Louis V. In coll. TL.

[HAROLD] HART CRANE (1899–1932)

Enrich My Resignation. *The Collected Poems of Hart Crane* (1933).

> 350a Harbison, John. In *The Flower-Fed Buffaloes*. New York: Associated

Music, u.d. Cycle: 6-pt. chorus, Bar solo, 7 instrs. Recording: None-such, H-71366 (1979).

Voyages. *White Buildings* (1926).

351 Blumenfeld, Harold. Recording: Composers Recordings, CRI SD 387 (1978).

351a Carter, Elliott. South Hadley, Mass.: Valley Music Press, 1945; New York: Associated Music, 1973. Song: high v, pf.

Miscellaneous

352 Fussell, Charles. *Poems for Chamber Orchestra and Voices, after Hart Crane* in coll. MuENC. Setting for cham orch and SSAATTBB soli.

353 Entry cancelled.

354 Ordansky, Jerold A. *Four Poems by Hart Crane.* MS, 1978, avail. ACA. Song: high v, pf.

STEPHEN CRANE (1871–1900)

"A spirit sped." *The Black Riders and Other Lines* (1895).

355 Kay, Ulysses. "A Spirit" in *Stephen Crane Set.* New York: Duchess Music, 1972. Chorus: SATB, 13 players.

"Black riders came from the sea." *The Black Riders and Other Lines* (1895).

356 Kay, Ulysses. "Black Riders" in *Stephen Crane Set.* New York: Duchess Music, 1972. Chorus: SATB, 13 players.

"Do not weep, maiden, for war is kind." *War Is Kind* (1899).

357 Carter, John. "War Is Kind." Macomb: R. Dean, 1976. Chorus: SATB, Bar solo, pf.

358 Hennagin, Michael. "War Is Kind" in *The Unknown.* New York: Walton Music, 1968, 1972. Setting for SATB chorus, pf, fl, 6 perc, 2 slide proj, elec tape, (slides [R]).

359 Kay, Ulysses. "War Is Kind" in *Stephen Crane Set.* New York: Duchess Music, 1972. Chorus: SATB, 13 players.

360 Waters, James. "War Is Kind" in coll. CASM. Song: v, pf.

"Each small gleam was a voice." *War Is Kind* (1899).

361 Barrett-Thomas, N. "Each Small Gleam" in *Songs of Singing*. Boston: Artists' Forum, 1970. Cycle: A, pf.

"I have heard the sunset song of the birches." *War Is Kind* (1899).

362 Barrett-Thomas, N. "I Have Heard the Sunset Song" in *Songs of Singing*. Boston: Artists' Forum, 1970. Cycle: A, pf.

"I saw a man pursuing the horizon." *The Black Riders and Other Lines* (1895).

363 Owen, Richard. u.p.: General, 1966. Song: high v, pf.

364 Spino, Pasquale J. "I Saw a Man" in *Five Poetic Songs*. u.p.: J. Boonin, u.d. Chorus: SATB, a cap.

365 Zonn, Paul. "I Saw a Man Pursuing" in *3 Folk Songs of Stephen Crane*. MS, 1967, avail. ACA. Song: C, unacc.

"I stood upon a high place." *The Black Riders and Other Lines* (1895).

366 Boyd, Jack. "Comrade! Brother!" New York: G. Schirmer, 1968. Chorus: SATB, a cap.

"I was in the darkness." *The Black Riders and Other Lines* (1895).

367 Schuyler, William. "Darkness" in *A Song Cycle*. St. Louis: Thiebes-Stierlin Music, 1900. Song: v, pf. Music not seen; text presumably from this poem.

"In Heaven,/ Some little blades of grass." *The Black Riders and Other Lines* (1895).

368 Bauer, Marion. "A Parable." New York: G. Schirmer, 1922. Song: v, pf.

"In the desert." *The Black Riders and Other Lines* (1895).

369 Boyd, Jack. Ft. Lauderdale: Music 70, 1982. Chorus: SATB, a cap.

"Mystic shadow, bending near me." *The Black Riders and Other Lines* (1895).

370 Kay, Ulysses. "Mystic Shadow" in *Stephen Crane Set*. New York: Duchess Music, 1972. Chorus: SATB, 13 players.

"On a horizon the peaks assembled." *The Black Riders and Other Lines* (1895).

371 Schuyler, William. "The March of the Mountains" in *A Song Cycle*. St. Louis: Thiebes-Stierlin Music, 1900. Song: v, pf.

"Once, I knew a fine song." *The Black Riders and Other Lines* (1895).

> 372 Barrett-Thomas, N. In *Songs of Singing*. Boston: Artists' Forum, 1970. Cycle: A, pf.

"Places among the stars." *The Black Riders and Other Lines* (1895).

> 373 Farley, Roland. New York: New Music Press, 1933. Song: high or med. v, pf.

A Prologue. *Roycroft Quarterly* (May 1896), p. 38; In *The University of Virginia Edition of the Works of Stephen Crane* [Vol. 8] (1973).

> 374 Boyd, Jack. "Prologue for an Unwritten Play." New York: Warner Bros., 1972. Chorus: SATB, cl, chimes, pf.

"The livid lightnings flashed in the clouds." *The Black Riders and Other Lines* (1895).

> 375 Barrett-Thomas, N. "The Vivid Lightnings Flashed" in *Songs of Singing*. Boston: Artists' Forum, 1970. Cycle: A, pf.

"There came whispering in the winds." *The Black Riders and Other Lines* (1895).

> 376 Schuyler, William. "Good Bye" in *A Song Cycle*. St. Louis: Thiebes-Stierlin Music, 1900. Song: v, pf. Music not seen; text presumably from this poem.

"There was a man with tongue of wood." *War Is Kind* (1899).

> 377 Barrett-Thomas, N. "Tongue of Wood" in *Songs of Singing*. Boston: Artists' Forum, 1970. Cycle: A, pf.

> 378 Boyd, Jack. "A Tongue of Wood." New York: G. Schirmer, 1968. Chorus: SATB, S solo, a cap.

> 379 Zonn, Paul. "There Was a Man with Tongue" in *3 Folk Songs on Stephen Crane*. MS, 1967, avail. ACA. Song: C, a cap.

"There were many who went in huddled procession." *The Black Riders and Other Lines* (1895).

> 380 Owen, Richard. u.p.: General, 1966. Song: med. v, pf.

"The wayfarer." *War Is Kind* (1899).

> 381 Zonn, Paul. In *3 Folk Songs of Stephen Crane*. MS, 1967, avail. ACA. Song: C, unacc.

Miscellaneous

382 Roosevelt, J. Willard. n.t. in *Our Dead Brothers Bid Us Think of Life*. MS, 1976, avail. ACA. Stage work: S and male narr., woman dancer, pf, cham orch.

383 Schuyler, William. "Consecration," "Longing" in *A Song Cycle*. St. Louis: Thiebes-Stierlin Music, 1900. Song: v, pf.

ADELAIDE CRAPSEY (1878–1914)

Cradle-Song. *Verse* (1915).

384 Lockwood, Normand. u.p.: Shawnee, 1953. Chorus: SATB, a cap.

Dirge. *Verse* (1915).

385 Binkerd, Gordon. "Never the Nightingale" in *Three Songs for Mezzo-Soprano*. New York: Boosey & Hawkes, 1971. Song: M, pf.

386 Enders, Harvey. New York: G. Schirmer, 1927. Song: med. v, pf.

387 Huerter, Charles. "Never the Nightingale." New York: H. Flammer, 1919. Song: v, pf.

388 Kerr, Harrison. In *Six Songs for Voice and Piano to Poems by Adelaide Crapsey*. u.p.: E.B. Marks, 1952. Song: med. or high v, pf.

389 Weisgall, Hugo. In *Four Songs* op. 1 no. 4. u.p.: Axelrod Publications, 1940. Song: S, pf.

Fate Defied. *Verse* (1915).

390 Antheil, George. In *Five Songs*. New York: Cos Cob Press, 1934. Song: high v, pf.

391 Kerr, Harrison. "Fate" in *Six Songs for Voice and Piano to Poems by Adelaide Crapsey*. u.p.: E.B. Marks, 1952. Song: med. or high v, pf.

Laurel in the Berkshires. *Verse* (1915).

392 Clarke, Henry L. In *Four Songs for a Young Lady*. MS, 1961, avail. ACA. Song: high v, pf.

The Lonely Death. *Verse* (1915).

393 Robbins, Reginald C. Paris: M. Senart, 1937. Song: high v, pf.

Night Winds. *Verse* (1915).

> 394 Kerr, Harrison. "The Old Old Winds" in *Six Songs for Voice and Piano to Poems by Adelaide Crapsey.* u.p.: E.B. Marks, 1952. Song: med. or high v, pf.

November Night. *Verse* (1915).

> 395 Antheil, George. In *Five Songs.* New York: Cos Cob Press, 1934. Song: high v, pf.

> 396 Fetler, Paul. New York: Lawson-Gould, 1957. Chorus: SATB, a cap.

> 397 Jones, Marjorie. In *Four Short Solos.* u.p.: Gentry Publications, 1971. Song: med. v, pf.

> 398 Spratlan, Lewis. In *Images.* Northampton, Mass.: New Valley Music, 1977. Cycle: S, pf.

> 399 Strilko, Anthony. In *Three Cinquains.* New York: Rongwen Music, 1955. Chorus: AATB, a cap.

Oh, Lady, Let the Sad Tears Fall. *Verse* (1915).

> 400 Lockwood, Normand. u.p.: Music Press, 1947. Song: med. v, pf.

> 401 Weisgall, Hugo. In *Four Songs* op. 1 no. 3. u.p.: Axelrod Publications, 1940. Song: med. or high v, pf.

Old Love. *Verse* (1915).

> 402 Kerr, Harrison. In *Six Songs for Voice and Piano to Poems by Adelaide Crapsey.* u.p.: E.B. Marks, 1952. Song: med. or high v, pf.

> 403 Sacco, John. "More Dim than Waning Moon." Boston: Boston Music, 1943. Song: high and med. or low v edns, pf.

> 404 Weisgall, Hugo. In *Four Songs* op. 1 no. 1. u.p.: Axelrod Publications, 1940. Song: med. or high v, pf.

On Seeing Weather-Beaten Trees. *Verse* (1915).

> 405 Jones, Marjorie. In *Four Short Solos.* u.p.: Gentry Publications, 1971. Song: med. v, pf.

Rapunzel. *Verse* (1915).

> 406 Duke, John. New York: Music Press, 1947. Song: med. v, pf.

> 407 Sacco, John. In *Three Songs.* Boston: Boston Music, 1941. Song: high v, pf.

Rose-Mary of the Angels. *Verse* (1915).

408 Cox, Ralph. "Little Sister Rose-Marie." Boston: A.P. Schmidt, 1918.

409 Jones, Marjorie. "Little Sister Rose-Marie" in *Four Short Solos.* u.p.: Gentry Publications, 1971. Song: med. v, pf.

Song. *Verse* (1915).

410 Kerr, Harrison. "Triolet" in *Six Songs for Voice and Piano to Poems by Adelaide Crapsey.* u.p.: E.B. Marks, 1952. Song: v, pf.

411 Sacco, John. "Where the Lilac Blows" in *Three Songs.* Boston: Boston Music, 1941. Song: high v, pf.

412 Weisgall, Hugo. In *Four Songs* op. 1 no. 2. u.p.: Axelrod Publications, 1940. Song: med. or high v, pf.

Susanna and the Elders. *Verse* (1915).

413 Antheil, George. In *Five Songs.* New York: Cos Cob Press, 1934. Song: high v, pf.

Triad. *Verse* (1915).

414 Antheil, George. In *Five Songs.* New York: Cos Cob Press, 1934. Song: high v, pf.

415 Jones, Marjorie. In *Four Short Solos.* u.p.: Gentry Publications, 1971. Song: med. v, pf.

416 Strilko, Anthony. In *Three Cinquains.* New York: Rongwen Music, 1955. Chorus: AATB, a cap.

Vendor's Song. *Verse* (1915).

417 McKay, George F. Chicago: Gamble-Hinged, 1936. Chorus: SSA, pf.

The Warning. *Verse* (1915).

418 Antheil, George. In *Five Songs.* New York: Cos Cob Press, 1934. Song: high v, pf.

419 Kerr, Harrison. "A White Moth Flew" in *Six Songs for Voice and Piano to Poems by Adelaide Crapsey.* u.p.: E.B. Marks, 1952. Song: med. or high v, pf.

420 Spratlan, Lewis. "Moth" in *Images.* Northampton, Mass.: New Valley Music, 1977. Cycle: S, pf.

421 Strilko, Anthony. In *Three Cinquains.* New York: Rongwen Music, 1955. Chorus: SATB, S solo, a cap.

422 Jenni, Donald. "Snow Toward Evening and Cinquain." MS, u.d., avail. ACA. Song: high v, pf.

ROBERT CREELEY (B. 1926)

The Eye. *For Love: Poems 1950–1960* (1962).

423 Adler, Samuel. In *Begin My Muse*. New York: Oxford Univ. Press, 1969. Chorus: TTBB, 6 perc.

COUNTEE CULLEN (1903–1946)

Perry, Margaret. *A Bio-Bibliography of Countee P. Cullen*. Westport, Conn.: Greenwood, 1971, pp. 90–94.

A Brown Girl Dead. *Color* (1925).

424 Bonds, Margaret. "To a Brown Girl, Dead." Boston: R.D. Row, 1956. Song: high and low v edns, pf.

425 Whithorne, Emerson. n.t. in *Saturday's Child: An Episode in Color* op. 42. Boston: C.C. Birchard, 1926. Cycle: M, T, pf or cham orch.

Christus Natus Est. *On These I Stand* (1947).

426 Marsh, Charles. Flushing, N.Y.: D.L. Schroeder, 1945. Song for mixed voices.

The Dance of Love. *Color* (1925).

427 Whithorne, Emerson. n.t. in *Saturday's Child: An Episode in Color* op. 42. Boston: C.C. Birchard, 1926. Cycle: M, T, pf or cham orch.

Dear Friends and Gentle Hearts. *On These I Stand* (1947).

428 Lawrence, William. New York: Chappell, 1943. Song: v, pf.

For a Poet. *Color* (1925).

429 Cohen, Cecil. "Epitaph for a Poet." New York: E.B. Marks, 1942. In coll. CNA. Song: v, pf.

430 Moore, Dorothy R. In *From the Dark Tower*. New York: Composers Facsimile Edn, 1970. Cycle: M, pf, vc.

431 Schickele, Peter. "Epitaph for a Poet" in *Baptism: A Journey through Our Time*. Song. Recording: Vanguard, VSD 79275 (1968).

For Joseph Conrad. *Color* (1925).

432 Schuman, William. "Epitaph for Joseph Conrad" in *Four Canonic Choruses*. New York: G. Schirmer, 1942. Chorus: SSTB, a cap.

For Paul Lawrence Dunbar. *Color* (1925).

433 DiDomenica, Robert. In *Black Poems*. Newton Centre, Mass.: Margun Music, [1976?]. Setting for Bar, pf, tape (R).

From the Dark Tower. *Copper Sun* (1927).

434 Moore, Dorothy R. In *From the Dark Tower*. New York: Composers Facsimile Edn, 1970. Cycle: M, pf, vc; New York: Composers Facsimile Edn, 1972. Setting for M, orch.

Gods. *Color* (1925).

435 Whithorne, Emerson. n.t. in *Saturday's Child: An Episode in Color* op. 42. Boston: C.C. Birchard, 1926. Cycle: M, T, pf or cham orch.

Hunger (To Emerson Whithorne). *Copper Sun* (1927).

436 Whithorne, Emerson. "Hunger" in *The Grim Troubadour* op. 45. New York: C. Fischer, 1927. Song: med. v, str qrt or pf.

If You Should Go. *Color* (1925).

437 Still, William G. In *Songs of Separation*. New York: Leeds, 1949. Song: v, pf.

Lament. *Copper Sun* (1927).

438 Walker, George. In coll. PaAS. Song: v, pf.

439 Whithorne, Emerson. In *The Grim Troubadour* op. 45. New York: C. Fischer, 1927. Song: med. v, str qrt or pf.

The Love Tree. *Copper Sun* (1927).

440 Whithorne, Emerson. In *The Grim Troubadour* op. 45. New York: C. Fischer, 1927. Song: med. v, str qrt or pf.

The Medea of Euripides. *The Medea and Some Poems* (1935).

441 Thomson, Virgil. "O Gentle Heart," "Love, Like a Leaf," "Immortal Zeus Controls the Fate of Man," "O, Happy Were Our Fathers," "Weep for the Little Lambs," "Go Down, O Sun," "Behold, O Earth" in *Seven Choruses from the Medea of Euripides*. New York: Weaner-Levant, 1942. Chorus: SSAA, a cap, perc ad lib.

On Going. *Color* (1925).

442 Bone, Gene and Howard Fenton. "Tryst." New York: C. Fischer, 1950. Song: high or med. v, pf.

Requiescam. *Color* (1925).

443 Whithorne, Emerson. n.t. in *Saturday's Child: An Episode in Color* op. 42. Boston: C.C. Birchard, 1926. Cycle: M, T, pf or cham orch.

Saturday's Child. *Color* (1925).

444 Whithorne, Emerson. n.t. in *Saturday's Child: An Episode in Color* op. 42. Boston: C.C. Birchard, 1926. Cycle: M, T, pf or cham orch.

She of the Dancing Feet Sings. *Color* (1925).

445 Whithorne, Emerson. n.t. in *Saturday's Child: An Episode in Color* op. 42. Boston: C.C. Birchard, 1926. Cycle: M, T, pf or cham orch.

A Song of Praise. *Color* (1925).

446 Whithorne, Emerson. n.t. in *Saturday's Child: An Episode in Color* op. 42. Boston: C.C. Birchard, 1926. Cycle: M, T, pf or cham orch.

To One Who Said Me Nay. *Color* (1925).

447 Whithorne, Emerson. n.t. in *Saturday's Child: An Episode in Color* op. 42. Boston: C.C. Birchard, 1926. Cycle: M, T, pf or cham orch.

Wisdom Cometh with the Years. *Color* (1925).

448 Adler, Samuel. New York: Southern Music Publishing, 1968. Chorus: SATB, cham orch (R).

Youth Sings a Song of Rosebuds. *Copper Sun* (1927).

449 Moore, Dorothy R. In *Sonnets on Love, Rosebuds, and Death*. New York: Composers Facsimile Edn, 1976. Cycle: S, pf, vn.

Miscellaneous

450 Samuels, W. "Clinton My Clinton." *The Magpie* 21 (January 1922), p. 14. Arr. by L.F. West.

E[DWARD] E[STLIN] CUMMINGS (1894–1962)

Firmage, George J. *E.E. Cummings: A Bibliography.* Middletown, Conn.: Wesleyan Univ. Press, 1960, pp. 89–92.

"a great." *73 Poems* (1963).

451 Ballou, Esther W. In *5-4-3.* MS, 1966, avail. ACA. Song: S, vla, hp.

"a politician is an arse upon." *1 X 1* (1944).

452 Persichetti, Vincent. "A Politician" in *Glad and Very* op. 129 no. 5. Philadelphia: Elkan-Vogel, 1976. Chorus: SA or TB or SATB, pf.

"a pretty a day." *50 Poems* (1940).

452a Rathaus, Karol. Bryn Mawr, Pa.: T. Presser, 1959. Chorus: SATB, a cap.

"a wind has blown the rain away and blown." *Tulips and Chimneys* (1923).

453 Garwood, Margaret. "A Wind Has Blown the Rain Away" in *Lovesongs: 6 Songs to Poems of E.E. Cummings.* East Greenville, Pa.: composer, 1963. Song: S, pf.

454 Imbrie, Andrew W. "A Wind Has Blown the Rain Away." u.p.: Malcolm Music, 1970. Chorus: SAB, pf.

455 King, Jeffrey. "A Wind Has Blown the Rain Away." u.p.: Boosey & Hawkes, u.d. Chorus: SATB, pf.

456 Ung, Chinary. n.t. in *Tall Wind.* New York: C.F. Peters, 1975. Song: fl, ob, gtr, vc.

"air." *50 Poems* (1940).

457 Feldman, Morton. In *4 Songs to E.E. Cummings.* New York: C.F. Peters, 1962. Song: v, vc, pf.

"All in green went my love riding." *Tulips and Chimneys* (1923).

458 Diamond, David. New York: Southern Music Publishing, 1950. Chorus: SSA, a cap.

459 Keyes, Nelson. In coll. MuENC. Chorus: SATB, a cap.

460 Schickele, Peter. In *Baptism: A Journey through Our Time*. Song. Recording: Vanguard, VSD 79275 (1968).

"all nearness pauses, while a star can grow." *95 Poems* (1958).

461 Wright, Maurice. n.t. in *Loneliness*. MS, 1978, avail. ACA. Chorus: SSA, tpt, vc, pf.

"all which isn't singing is mere talking." *73 Poems* (1963).

462 Ballou, Esther W. In *5-4-3*. MS, 1966, avail. ACA. Song: S, vla, hp.

"anyone lived in a pretty how town." *50 Poems* (1940).

463 Alexander, Josef. New York: Lawson-Gould, u.d. Chorus: SATB, a cap.

464 Hamm, Charles. Northampton, Mass.: Valley Music, 1956. Song: high v, pf.

465 Keats, Donald. New York: Boosey & Hawkes, 1968. Chorus: SSATBB, a cap.

466 Martino, Donald. In *Portraits*. Boston: Ione Press, 1970. Chorus: SATB, pf 4 hands, opt perc. Acc. originally for orch.

467 Orr, Buxton. In *Many Kinds of Yes*. London: B.V.F. Anglo-Continental, 1973. Duet: S and C, pf.

"Beautiful." *95 Poems* (1958).

468 Fennelly, Brian. In *Songs with Improvisations*. MS, 1970, avail. ACA. Song: med. v, cl, pf.

"because it's." *73 Poems* (1963).

469 Fortner, Jack. In *S pr ING*. Paris: Société des editions Jobert, 1967. Song: female v, vc, bsn, vla, alto sax, db, hp, vib, pf.

470 Harper, Edward. n.t. in *Seven Poems by E.E. Cummings*. New York: Oxford Univ. Press, n.d., avail. on Rental. Song: S, orch.

471 Harrex, Patrick. In *Sonata*. London: Ars Viva, 1969. Song: female v, fl, perc.

472 Siegmeister, Elie. "Because It's Spring" in *Five Cummings Songs*. u.p.: Alfred Music Publishing, 1978. Song: M, pf.

"between green/ mountains." *XLI Poems* (1925).

473 Kaplan, Elliot. n.t. in *Six Etudes for Voice and Piano*. New York: Galaxy, 1965. Song: v, pf.

"birds(/here,inven." *No Thanks* (1935).

474 Boulez, Pierre. "Cummings ist der Dichter." London: Universal Edition, 1976. Chorus: 4 S, 4 A, 4 T, 4 B, cham orch. Recording: Telefunken, 6.48066–1 (EK) (1974).

475 Peyton, Malcolm. n.t. in *Choruses from E.E. Cummings*. Hillsdale, N.Y.: Mobart Music, 1979. Double Chorus: SSAATTBB, a cap.

"!blac." *50 Poems* (1940).

476 Feldman, Morton. In *4 Songs to E.E. Cummings*. New York: C.F. Peters, 1962. Song: v, vc, pf.

"Buffalo Bill's." *Tulips and Chimneys* (1923).

477 Yannatos, James. In *Three Settings of E.E. Cummings*. New York: Associated Music, 1972. Chorus: TTBB, a cap.

" 'but why should.' " *95 Poems* (1958).

478 Wright, Maurice. n.t. in *Loneliness*. MS, 1978, avail. ACA. Chorus: SSA, vc, tpt, pf.

"buy me an ounce and i'll sell you a pound." *50 Poems* (1940).

479 Blank, Allan. MS, u.d., avail. ACA. Song: high v, pf.

"crazy jay blue)." *95 Poems* (1958).

480 Fennelly, Brian. In *Songs with Improvisations*. MS, 1970, avail. ACA. Song: med. v, cl, pf.

481 Roosevelt, J. Willard. n.t. in *Four Songs*. MS, 1975, avail. ACA. Song: S, vla.

"cruelly, love." *XLI Poems* (1925).

482 Garwood, Margaret. In *Lovesongs: 6 Songs to Poems of E.E. Cummings*. East Greenville, Pa.: composer, 1963. Song: S, pf.

"curtains part)." *is 5* (1926).

483 Beckwith, John. In *Four Songs to Poems by E.E. Cummings*. Waterloo, Ont.: Waterloo Music, 1975. Song: v, pf.

"dim." *95 Poems* (1958).

484 Schickele, Peter. "Dim/l(a" in *Three Choruses from E.E. Cummings*. u.p.: Tetra Music, 1967. Chorus: SATB, a cap.

"Doll's boy's asleep." *Tulips and Chimneys* (1923).

485 Bergsma, William. In *Six Songs to Poems by E.E. Cummings*. New York: C. Fischer, 1947. Song: high v, pf.

486 Nordoff, Paul. In *Eight Songs to Poems by E.E. Cummings*. u.p.: Independent Music Publishers, 1948. Song: v, pf.

"dominic has." *95 Poems* (1958).

487 Persichetti, Vincent. "Dominic Has a Doll" in *Four Cummings Choruses* op. 98. Philadelphia: Elkan-Vogel, 1966. Chorus: SATB, SA, or TB; pf.

488 Schickele, Peter. "Dominic Has a Doll" in *Three Choruses from E.E. Cummings*. u.p.: Tetra Music, 1967. Chorus: SATB, a cap.

"enter no(silence is the blood whose flesh." *73 Poems* (1963).

489 Harper, Edward. n.t. in *Seven Poems by E.E. Cummings*. New York: Oxford Univ. Press, n.d. (Rental only), setting for S, orch.

"first robin the." *95 Poems* (1958).

490 Fortner, Jack. In *S pr ING*. Paris: Société des editions Jobert, 1967. Song: female v, vc, bsn, vla, fl, alto sax, db, hp, vib, pf.

"from spiralling ecstatically this." *95 Poems* (1958).

491 Wright, Maurice. n.t. in *Loneliness*. MS, 1978, avail. ACA. Chorus: SSA, vc, tpt, pf.

"hist whist." *Tulips and Chimneys* (1923).

492 Bergsma, William. "Hist Whist Little Ghost Things" in *Six Songs to Poems by E.E. Cummings*. New York: C. Fischer, 1947. Song: high v, pf.

493 Cage, John. In *Five Songs for Contralto*. New York: Henmar Press, 1960. Song: C, pf.

494 De Jong, Conrad. New York: G. Schirmer, 1971. Song: med. v, fl, vla, perc.

495 Duke, John. New York: Southern Music Publishing, 1957. Song: med. v, pf.

495a Engel, Lehman. n.t. in *Chansons Innocentes*. New York: Arrow Music, 1939. Chorus: SSA, pf obl.

496 Jones, Robert W. Delaware Water Gap, Pa.: Shawnee, 1970. Setting for SATB speech choir, perc, opt orch (R).

497 Kaplan, Elliot. n.t. in *Six Etudes for Voice and Piano.* New York: Galaxy, 1965. Song: v, pf.

498 Martirano, Salvatore. n.t. in *Chansons Innocentes.* London: Schott, 1967; New York: Associated Music Publishing. Song: high v, pf. Recording: Composers Recordings, CRI SD 324 (1974).

499 Myers, Robert. n.t. in *Chansons Innocentes.* In coll. MuENC. Chorus: SA, perc.

500 Persichetti, Vincent. "Hist Whist" op. 46 no. 2. New York: C. Fischer, 1952. Chorus: SA, a cap.

501 Pollock, Robert E. "Theater Piece." Hillsdale, N.Y.: Mobart Music, 1977. Chamber Chorus: SSA, prepared pf.

"!hope." *73 Poems* (1963).

502 Ballou, Esther W. In *5-4-3.* MS, 1966, avail. ACA. Song: S, vla, hp.

"i am so glad and very." *50 Poems* (1940).

503 Persichetti, Vincent. In *Glad and Very* op. 129 no. 2. Philadaplhia: Elkan-Vogel, 1976. Chorus: SATB or SA or TB; pf.

"i carry your heart with me(i carry it in." *95 Poems* (1958).

504 Duke, John. "I Carry Your Heart." New York: G. Schirmer, 1962. Song: S, pf.

505 Harper, Edward. n.t. in *Seven Poems by E.E. Cummings.* New York: Oxford Univ. Press, n.d., avail. on Rental. Song: S, orch.

506 Mathew, David. "I Carry Your Heart." u.p.: Piedmont Music, 1974. Chorus: SATB, a cap.

"i love you much(most beautiful darling.)" *95 Poems* (1958).

507 Malipiero, Riccardo. In *In Time of Daffodils.* Milan: Edizoni Suvini Zerboni, 1964. Cycle: S, Bar, 7 instruments. Words in English.

"i shall imagine life." *95 Poems* (1958).

508 Diamond, David. New York: Southern Music Publishing, 1968. Song: med. v, pf.

"i thank You God for most this amazing." *XAIPE* (1950).

509 Avshalomov, Jacob. "I Thank You, God" in *Praises from the Corners of the Earth.* New York: Duchess Music, 1971. Chorus: SATB, org, perc.

509a Dickinson, Peter. "I Thank You God" in *An E.E. Cummings Song Cycle.* u.p.: Novello, 1965, rev. 1970. Song Cycle: M, pf.

510 McKay, David. "I Thank You, God." Melville, N.Y.: J. Fischer, u.d. Chorus: SAB, org.

511 Moe, Daniel. "Which Is Yes." Chapel Hill, N.C.: Hinshaw Music, 1979. Chorus: SATB, a cap.

512 Peyton, Malcolm. n.t. in *Choruses from E.E. Cummings.* Hillsdale, N.Y.: Mobart Music, 1979. Double Chorus: SSAATTBB, a cap.

513 Pfautsch, Lloyd. "I Thank You, God." New York: Lawson-Gould, u.d. Chorus: SATB, a cap.

514 Tipton, Clyde. "I Thank You, God." u.p.: Belwin-Mills, 1975. Chorus: SSAA, fl, handbells, org.

"if i have made,my lady,intricate." *is 5* (1926).

515 Helm, Everett. "For My Lady" in *Two Love Songs.* New York: Music Press, 1947. Song: med. v, pf.

"if night's mostness(and whom did merely day." *No Thanks* (1935).

516 Peyton, Malcolm. n.t. in *Choruses from E.E. Cummings.* Hillsdale, N.Y.: Mobart Music, 1979. Double Chorus: SSAATTBB, a cap.

"if the." *XAIPE* (1950).

517 Persichetti, Vincent. "If the Green" in *Spring Cantata.* Philadelphia: Elkan-Vogel, 1964. Chorus: SSA, pf.

"If you can't eat you got to." *50 Poems* (1940).

518 Bernstein, Leonard. In *Songfest.* New York: Boosey & Hawkes, 1977. Cycle: SAMTBarB, orch; New York: Amberson Enterprises, 1981. Setting for T solo, men's voices, pf, with opt str bass and perc.

519 Diamond, David. "If You Can't" in *Three Songs.* New York: Leeds, 1950. Song: high v, pf.

"in" [Poem no. 62]. *XAIPE* (1950).

520 Argento, Dominick. "In Spring Comes" in *Songs about Spring.* New York: Boosey & Hawkes, 1980. Cycle: S, pf or cham orch (R).

"in Just." *Tulips and Chimneys* (1923).

521 Argento, Dominick. "In Just Spring" in *Songs about Spring.* New York: Boosey & Hawkes, 1980. Cycle: S, pf or cham orch (R).

522 Blank, Allan. MS, u.d., avail. ACA. Song: high v, pf.

523 Cage, John. In *Five Songs for Contralto*. New York: Henmar Press, 1960. Song: C, pf.

524 Duke, John. "Just-Spring." New York: C. Fischer, 1954. Song: high v, pf. In coll. TaSE.

524a Engel, Lehman. n.t. in *Chansons Innocentes*. New York: Arrow Music, 1939. Chorus: SSA, pf obl.

525 Fortner, Jack. In *S pr ING*. Paris: Société des editions Jobert, 1967. Song: female v, vc, bsn, vla, fl, alto sax, db, hp, vib, pf.

526 Harrex, Patrick. In *Sonata*. London: Ars Viva, 1969. Song: female v, fl, perc.

527 Martirano, Salvatore. n.t. in *Chansons Innocentes*. London: Schott, 1967; New York: Associated Music Publishers. Song: high v, pf. Recording: Composers Recordings, CRI SD 324 (1974).

528 Myers, Robert. n.t. in *Chansons Innocentes*. In coll. MuENC. Chorus: SA, perc.

529 Persichetti, Vincent. In *Spring Cantata*. Philadelphia: Elkan-Vogel, 1964. Chorus: SSA, pf.

530 Tubb, Monte. "In Just-Spring." New York: Lawson-Gould, 1966. Setting for mixed chorus.

531 Weigl, Vally. "In Just Spring." MS, u.d., avail. ACA. Chorus: SATB, soli, a cap.

532 Yannatos, James. In *Three Settings of E.E. Cummings*. New York: Associated Music Publishers, 1972. Chorus: SSATB, a cap.

"in spite of everything." *is* 5 (1926).

533 Copland, Aaron. "Song" in coll. CCS; "Poet's Song." New York: Boosey & Hawkes, 1967. Song: high v, pf.

534 Kaplan, Elliot. n.t. in *Six Etudes for Voice and Piano*. New York: Galaxy, 1965. Song: v, pf.

535 Siegmeister, Elie. In *Five Cummings Songs*. u.p.: Alfred Music, 1978. Song: M, pf.

"in the rain." *XLI Poems* (1925).

536 Rorem, Ned. In *Poems of Love and the Rain*. New York: Boosey & Hawkes, 1965. Cycle: M, pf. Numbers 1 and 7 are contrasting settings of this poem.

"in time of daffodils(who know." *95 Poems* (1958).

537 Malipiero, Riccardo. In *In Time of Daffodils*. Milan: Edizoni Suvini Zerboni, 1964. Cycle: S, Bar, 7 instruments. Words in Eng.

"it is so long since my heart has been with yours." *is* 5 (1926).

538 Helm, Everett. "It Is So Long" in *Two Love Songs*. New York: Music Press, 1947. Song: med. v, pf.

"it may not always be so; and i say." *Tulips and Chimneys* (1923).

539 Bergsma, William. "It May Not Always Be So" in *Six Songs to Poems by E.E. Cummings*. New York: C. Fischer, 1947. Song: T, pf.

540 Garwood, Margaret. "It May Not Always Be So" in *Lovesongs: 6 Songs to Poems of E.E. Cummings*. East Greenville, Pa.: composer, 1963. Song: S, pf.

"jake hates/ all the girls(the." *XAIPE* (1950).

541 Persichetti, Vincent. "Jake Hates All the Girls" in *Glad and Very* op. 129 no. 4. Philadaplhia: Elkan-Vogel, 1976. Chorus: SATB or SA or TB; pf.

"Jimmie's got a goil/ goil/ goil,/ Jimmie." *is* 5 (1926).

542 Bergsma, William. "Jimmie's Got a Goil" in *Six Songs to Poems by E.E. Cummings*. New York: C. Fischer, 1947. Song: high v, pf.

543 Blitzstein, Marc. "Jimmie's Got a Goil" in coll. CCS. Song: med. v, pf.

544 Persichetti, Vincent. "Jimmie's Got a Goil." New York: G. Schirmer, 1949. Chorus: SB, SA, or TB, pf 4 hands.

"l(a." *95 Poems* (1958).

545 Schickele, Peter. "Dim/l(a" in *Three Choruses from E.E. Cummings*. u.p.: Tetra Music, 1967. Chorus: SATB, a cap.

546 Wright, Maurice. n.t. in *Loneliness*. MS, 1978, avail. ACA. Chorus: SSA, tpt, vc, pf.

"lady will you come with me into." *W [ViVa]* (1931).

547 Gruen, John. Recording: Desto 7411/412.

"(listen.)" *73 Poems* (1963).

548 Harper, Edward. n.t. in *Seven Poems by E.E. Cummings*. New York: Oxford Univ. Press, n.d., avail. on Rental. Song: S, orch.

"little man." *No Thanks* (1935).

549 Persichetti, Vincent. In *Glad and Very* op. 129 no. 1. Philadelphia: Elkan-Vogel, 1976. Chorus: SATB, SA, or TB; pf.

"Little tree." *XLI Poems* (1925).

550 Cage, John. "Little Christmas Tree" in *5 Songs for Contralto*. New York: Henmar Press, 1960. Song: C, pf.

551 Diamond, David. "Christmas Tree." Philadelphia: Elkan-Vogel, 1972. Song: med. v, pf.

552 Nordoff, Paul. In *Eight Songs to Poems by E.E. Cummings*. u.p.: Independent Music Publishers, 1948. Song: v, pf; New York: American Music Edn, 1960. Song: v, pf.

"love is more thicker than forget." *50 Poems* (1940).

553 Diamond, David. "Love Is More." New York: Southern Music Publishing, 1954. Song: med. v, pf.

553a Dickinson, Peter. "Love Is More Thicker" in *An E.E. Cummings Song Cycle*. u.p.: Novello, 1965, rev. 1970. Song Cycle: M, pf.

554 George, Earl. "A Definition." New York: Lawson-Gould, 1956. Chorus: SSAA, a cap.

555 Orr, Buxton. In *Many Kinds of Yes*. London: B.V.F. Anglo-Continental, 1973. Song: C, pf.

556 Phillips, Burrill. "Love" in *Declaratives*. Philadelphia: Elkan-Vogel, 1945. Chorus: SSAA, pf or cham orch.

557 Wiener, Ivan. New York: Rongwen Music, 1971. Chorus: SATB, a cap.

"love is the every only god." *50 Poems* (1940).

557a Dickinson, Peter. In *An E.E. Cummings Song Cycle*. u.p.: Novello, 1965, rev. 1970. Song Cycle: M, pf.

"love our so right." *XAIPE* (1950).

558 Peyton, Malcolm. n.t. in *Choruses from E.E. Cummings*. Hillsdale, N.Y.: Mobart Music, 1979. Double Chorus: SSAATTBB, a cap.

"maggy and milly and molly and may." *95 Poems* (1958).

559 Fuller, Jeanne W. New York: Associated Music Publishers, u.d. Chorus: SA, a cap.

560 Orr, Buxton. In *Many Kinds of Yes*. London: B.V.F. Anglo-Continental, 1973. Duet: S and C, pf.

561 Persichetti, Vincent. In *Four Cummings Choruses*. Philadelphia: Elkan-Vogel, 1966. Chorus: SATB or SA or TB; pf.

562 Schickele, Peter. In *Three Choruses from E.E. Cummings*. u.p.: Tetra Music, 1967. Chorus: SATB, a cap.

"may i be gay." *73 Poems* (1963).

> 563 Ballou, Esther W. In *5-4-3*. MS, 1966, avail. ACA. Song: S, vla, hp.
>
> 564 Harper, Edward. n.t. in *Seven Poems by E.E. Cummings.* New York: Oxford Univ. Press, n.d., avail. on Rental. Song: S, orch.

"may my heart always be open to little." *Collected Poems* (1938).

> 565 De Gastyne, Serge. "May My Heart." Philadelphia: Elkan-Vogel, 1958. Song: med. v, pf.

"maybe god." *XAIPE* (1950).

> 566 Persichetti, Vincent. In *Glad and Very* op. 129 no. 3. Philadelphia: Elkan-Vogel, 1976. Chorus: SATB or SA or TB; pf.

"moan." *50 Poems* (1940).

> 567 Feldman, Morton. In *4 Songs to E.E. Cummings.* New York: C.F. Peters, 1962. Song: v, vc, pf.

"my father moved through dooms of love." *50 Poems* (1940).

> 568 Prendergast, Roy M. "My Father Moved through Dooms." New York: C. Fischer, 1977. Chorus: SSAA, reader, vib, chimes, timp, vc, cel, pf.

"my sweet old etcetera." *is 5* (1926).

> 569 Starer, Robert. New York: Leeds, 1967. Song: Bar, pf.
>
> 570 Weisgall, Hugo. In *Soldier Songs for Baritone.* u.p.: Merrymount Music, 1953. Cycle: Bar, pf.

"my uncle." *is 5* (1926).

> 571 Diamond, David. "Four Uncles" in *7 Songs by David Diamond.* Philadelphia: Elkan-Vogel, 1946. Song: high v, pf.
>
> 572 Persichetti, Vincent. "Uncles" in *Four Cummings Choruses.* Philadelphia: Elkan-Vogel, u.d. Chorus: SATB or SA or TB, pf.

"n//OthI." *73 Poems* (1963).

> 573 Harper, Edward. n.t. in *Seven Poems by E.E. Cummings.* New York: Oxford Univ. Press, n.d. (Rental only). Setting for S, orch.

" 'next to of course god america i." *is 5* (1926).

> 574 Brooks, Richard J. "Next to, of Course, God." MS, u.d., avail. ACA. Setting for SATB, pf, brass, perc.

"no time ago." *XAIPE* (1950).

> 574a Dickinson, Peter. In *An E.E. Cummings Song Cycle.* u.p.: Novello, 1965, rev. 1970. Song Cycle: M, pf.

"Nobody wears a yellow." *is 5* (1926).

> 575 Beckwith, John. "Nobody Wears a Yellow Flower in His Button Hole" in *Four Songs to Poems by E.E. Cummings.* Waterloo, Ont.: Waterloo, Music , 1975. Song: v, pf.

"nouns to nouns." *50 Poems* (1940).

> 576 Persichetti, Vincent. In *Four Cummings Choruses.* Philadelphia: Elkan-Vogel, u.d. Chorus: SATB or SA or TB, pf.

"now all the fingers of this tree(darling)have." *XAIPE* (1950).

> 577 Garwood, Margaret. "Now All the Fingers of This Tree" in *Love-songs: 6 Songs to Poems of E.E. Cummings.* East Greenville, Pa.: composer, 1963. Song: S, pf.

"Now i lay(with everywhere around)." *73 Poems* (1963).

> 578 Fortner, Jack. In *S pr ING.* Paris: Société des editions Jobert, 1967. Song: female v, vc, bsn, fl, alto sax, db, hp, vib, pf.

> 579 Kolb, Barbara. "Now I Lay" in *Songs Before an Adieu.* New York: Boosey & Hawkes, 1979. Cycle: S, fl, gtr.

"now(more near ourselves than we)." *95 Poems* (1958).

> 580 Fuller, Jeanne W. New York: Associated Music Publishers, u.d. Chorus: SATB, pf.

> 581 Gruen, John. Recording: Desto 7411/412.

"now that,more nearest even than your fate." *73 Poems* (1963).

> 582 Blank, Allan. "Poem." Song: S, cl, vc, hp. Recording: Composers Recordings, CRI SD 250 (1970).

"n(o)w/ the." *W [ViVa]* (1931).

> 583 Berio, Luciano. n.t. in *Circles.* London: Universal Edition, 1961. Song: high female v, hp, 2 perc. Recording: Time 58003.

"o by the by." *1 X 1* (1944).

> 584 Blitzstein, Marc. In *From Marion's Book.* New York: Chappell, 1962. Cycle: med. v, pf.

585 Dougherty, Celius. In *Songs by E.E. Cummings.* New York: G. Schirmer, 1946. Song: med. v, pf.

"O sweet spontaneous." *Tulips and Chimneys* (1923).

586 Morrill, Dexter. "O Sweet Spontaneous Earth." In coll. MuENC. Chorus: SATB, pf.

"O the sun comes up-up-up in the opening." *73 Poems* (1963).

587 Ballou, Esther W. MS, u.d., avail. ACA. Chorus: SSA, a cap; New York: Composers Facsimile Edn, 1966.

"off a pane)the." *95 Poems* (1958).

588 Fennelly, Brian. In *Songs with Improvisations.* MS, 1970, avail. ACA. Song: med. v, cl, pf.

"open your heart." *1 X 1* (1944).

589 Blitzstein, Marc. In *From Marion's Book.* New York: Chappell, 1962. Cycle: med. v, pf.

"pity this busy monster,manunkind." *1 X 1* (1944).

590 Caviani, Ronald. u.p.: Foster, u.d. Chorus: SSAATTBB, narr., tape.

591 Fennelly, Brian. In *Songs with Improvisations.* MS, 1970, avail. ACA. Song: med. v, cl, pf.

"purer than purest pure." *XAIPE* (1950).

592 Persichetti, Vincent. "Star" in *Hyms and Responses* op. 68 no. 5. Philadelphia: Elkan-Vogel, 1956. Hymn for choir and congregational use. In coll. ChAH.

"rain or hail." *1 X 1* (1944).

593 Nordoff, Paul. "Sam" in *Eight Songs to Poems by E.E. Cummings.* u.p.: Independent Music Publishers, 1948. Song: v, pf; New York: American Music Edn, 1960. Song: v, pf.

594 Persichetti, Vincent. "Sam Was a Man." New York: G. Schirmer, 1948. Chorus: SATB or SA or TB; pf.

"raise the shade." *& [AND]* (1925).

595 Siegmeister, Elie. In *Five Cummings Songs.* u.p.: Alfred Music, 1978. Song: M, pf.

"riverly is a flower." *& [AND]* (1925).

596 Berio, Luciano. n.t. in *Circles*. London: Universal Edition, 1961. Song: high female v, hp, 2 perc. Recording: Time 58003.

"silence." *95 Poems* (1958).

597 Malipiero, Riccardo. In *In Time of Daffodils*. Milan: Edizoni Suvini Zerboni, 1964. Cycle: S, Bar, 7 instruments. Words in Eng.

"silent unday by silently not night." *No Thanks* (1935).

598 Blitzstein, Marc. In *From Marion's Book*. New York: Chappell, 1962. Cycle: med. v, pf.

"(sitting in a tree)." *Poems* (1940).

599 Feldman, Morton. In *Four Songs to E.E. Cummings*. New York: C.F. Peters, 1962. Song: v, vc, pf.

600 Nordoff, Paul. In *Eight Songs to Poems by E.E. Cummings*. u.p.: Independent Music Publsihers, 1948. Song: v, pf.

601 Orr, Buxton. In *Many Kinds of Yes*. London: B.V.F. Anglo-Continental, 1973. Song: S, pf.

"somewhere i have never travelled,gladly beyond." *W [ViVa]* (1931).

602 Binkerd, Gordon. "Somewhere I Have Never Travelled." New York: ACA, 1955. New York: Boosey & Hawkes, 1969. Song: high v, pf.

603 Blank, Allan. "Somewhere I Have Never Travelled." MS, u.d., avail. ACA. Song: M, pf.

604 Randall, James K. "Improvisation on a Poem by E.E. Cummings." New York: American Society of Univ. Composers, 1961. Song: S or C, a cl, a sax, tpt, gtr, pf.

"Spring is like a perhaps hand." *& [AND]* (1925).

605 Argento, Dominick. In *Songs about Spring*. New York: Boosey & Hawkes, 1980. Cycle: S, pf or cham orch (R).

606 Gruen, John. Recording: Desto 7411/412.

607 Persichetti, Vincent. In *Spring Cantata* op. 94. Philadelphia: Elkan-Vogel, 1964. Chorus: SSA, pf.

"spring!may." *95 Poems* (1958).

608 Roosevelt, J. Willard. n.t. in *Four Songs*. MS, 1975, avail. ACA. Song: S, vla.

"stand with your lover on the ending earth." *95 Poems* (1958).

609 Wright, Maurice. n.t. in *Loneliness.* MS, 1978, avail. ACA. Chorus: SSA, tpt, vc, pf.

"stinging." *Tulips and Chimneys* (1923).

610 Berio, Luciano. n.t. in *Circles.* London: Universal Edition, 1961. Song: high female v, hp, 2 perc. Recording: Time 58003.

611 Silsbee, Ann L. "Diffraction." MS, 1975, avail. ACA. Chorus: SATB, S solo, fl, pf, 2 perc.

612 Spratlan, Lewis. u.t. in *Images.* Northampton, Mass.: New Valley Music, 1977. Cycle: S, pf.

613 Ung, Chinary. n.t. in *Tall Wind.* New York: C.F. Peters, 1975. Song: S, fl, ob, gtr, vc.

" 'sweet spring is your." *1 X 1* (1944).

614 Beckwith, John. "Sweet Spring Is Your Time Is My Time Is Our Time" in *Four Songs to Poems by E.E. Cummings.* Waterloo, Ont.: Waterloo Music, 1975. Song: v, pf.

615 Binkerd, Gordon. "And Viva Sweet Love." New York: Boosey & Hawkes, 1970. Chorus: TBB, pf 4 hands.

616 De Gastyne, Serge. "Sweet Spring." Philadelphia: Elkan-Vogel, u.d. Song: med. v, pf.

617 Dougherty, Celius. "Sweet Spring Is Your Time." New York: G. Schirmer, u.d. Setting for vocal duet.

618 Nordoff, Paul. "Sweet Spring" in *Eight Songs to Poems by E.E. Cummings.* u.p.: Independent Music Publishers, 1948. Song: v, pf.

619 Orr, Buxton. "Sweet Spring Is Your" in *Many Kinds of Yes.* London: B.V.F. Anglo-Continental, 1973. Duet: S and C, pf.

"the first of all my dreams was of." *73 Poems* (1963).

620 Siegmeister, Elie. "The First of all My Dreams" in *Four Cummings Songs.* u.p.: Alfred Music, 1978. Song: M, pf.

"the glory is fallen out of." *Tulips and Chimneys* (1923).

621 Beckwith, John. "The Glory Is Fallen out of the Sky" in *Four Songs to Poems by E.E. Cummings.* Waterloo, Ont.: Waterloo Music, 1975. Song: v, pf.

622 Diamond, David. "The Glory Is Fallen out of the Sky." New York: Southern Music Publishing, 1950. Chorus: SSA, a cap.

"the great advantage of being alive." *XAIPE* (1950).

623 Peyton, Malcolm. n.t. in *Choruses from E.E. Cummings.* Hillsdale, N.Y.: Mobart Music, 1979. Double Chorus: SSAATTBB, a cap.

"the rose." *Tulips and Chimneys* (1923).

624 Yannatos, James. In *Three Settings of E.E. Cummings.* New York: Associated Music, 1972. Chorus: SSAA, a cap.

"the/ sky/ was." *XLI Poems* (1925).

625 Fennelly, Brian. In *Songs with Improvisations.* MS, 1970, avail. ACA. Song: med. v, cl, pf.

626 Kaplan, Elliot. n.t. in *Six Etudes for Voice and Piano.* New York: Galaxy, 1965. Song: v, pf.

"these children singing in stone a." *50 Poems* (1940).

626a Nordoff, Paul. "These Children Singing in Stone." New York: American Music Edn, 1960. Song: v, pf.

"this is the garden: colours come and go." *XLI Poems* (1925).

627 Diamond, David. "This Is the Garden." New York: C. Fischer, 1940. Chorus: SATB, a cap.

628 Glass, Philip. "This Is the Garden." In coll. MuENC. Chorus: SATB, a cap.

629 Persichetti, Vincent. "This Is the Garden" op. 46 no. 1. New York: C. Fischer, 1952. Chorus: SSA, a cap.

630 Zupko, Ramon. "This Is the Garden" in coll. MuENC.. Chorus: SATB, winds, str, perc.

"t,h;r:u;s,h;e:s." *73 Poems* (1963).

631 Harper, Edward. n.t. in *Seven Poems by E.E. Cummings.* New York: Oxford Univ. Press, n.d., avail. on Rental. Song: S, orch.

"Thy fingers make early flowers of." *Tulips and Chimneys* (1923).

632 Bergsma, William. "Thy Fingers Make Early Flowers" in *Six Songs to Poems by E.E. Cummings.* New York: C. Fischer, 1947. Song: high v, pf.

633 Dougherty, Celius. "Thy Fingers Make Early Flowers" in *Songs by E.E. Cummings.* New York: G. Schirmer, 1946. Song: high v, pf.

"Tumbling-hair/ picker of buttercups/ violets." *Tulips and Chimneys* (1923).

634 Cage, John. "Another Comes" in *5 Songs for Contralto.* New York: Henmar Press, 1960. Song: C, pf.

634a Engel, Lehman. n.t. in *Chansons Innocentes*. New York: Arrow Music, 1939. Chorus: SSA, pf obl.

635 Kaplan, Elliot. n.t. in *Six Etudes for Voice and Piano*. New York: Galaxy, 1965. Song: v, pf.

636 Martirano, Salvatore. n.t. in *Chansons Innocentes*. London: Schott, 1967. Song: high v, pf. Recording: Composers Recordings, CRI SD 324 (1974).

637 Mennin, Peter. "Tumbling-Hair." New York: C. Fischer, 1949. Chorus: SSA, pf.

638 Myers, Robert. n.t. in *Chansons Innocentes*. In coll. MuENC. Chorus: SA, perc.

639 Nordoff, Paul. "Tumbling-Hair" in *Eight Songs to Poems by E.E. Cummings*. u.p.: Independent Music Publishers, 1948. Song: v, pf; New York: American Music Edn, 1960. Song: v, pf.

"un." *Collected Poems* [Section entitled, "New Poems"] (1938).

640 Kaplan, Elliot. n.t. in *Six Etudes for Voice and Piano*. New York: Galaxy, 1965. Song: v, pf.

"un(bee)mo." *95 Poems* (1958).

641 Fennelly, Brian. In *Songs with Improvisations*. MS, 1970, avail. ACA. Song: med. v, cl, pf.

"until and i heard." *1 X 1* (1944).

642 Blitzstein, Marc. In *From Marion's Book*. New York: Chappell, 1962. Cycle: med. v, pf.

643 Dougherty, Celius. In *Songs by E.E. Cummings*. New York: G. Schirmer, 1946. Song: med. v, pf.

644 Nordoff, Paul. In *Eight Songs to Poems by E.E. Cummings*. u.p.: Independent Music Publishers, 1948. Song: v, pf.

"up into the silence the green." *50 Poems* (1940).

644a Dickinson, Peter. "Up into the Silence" in *An E.E. Cummings Song Cycle*. u.p.: Novello, 1965, rev. 1970. Song Cycle: M, pf.

645 Nordoff, Paul. "Up into the Silence" in *Eight Songs to Poems by E.E. Cummings*. u.p.: Independent Music Publishers, 1948. Song: v, pf.

646 Siegmeister, Elie. "Up into the Silence" in *Five Cummings Songs*. u.p.: Alfred Music, 1978. Song: M, pf.

"what a proud dreamhorse pulling(smoothloomingly)through." *No Thanks* (1935).

647 Garwood, Margaret. "What a Proud Dreamhorse" in *Lovesongs: 6 Songs to Poems of E.E. Cummings*. East Greenville, Pa.: composer, 1963. Song: S, pf.

"what if a much of a which of a wind." *1 X 1* (1944).

648 Ballou, Esther W. MS, u.d., avail. ACA. Chorus: SBB, ww qnt; New York: Composers Facsimile Edn, 1959.

649 Blitzstein, Marc. In *From Marion's Book*. New York: Chappell, 1962. Cycle: med. v, pf.

649a Downey, John W. "What If?" Bryn Mawr: T. Presser, u.d. Chorus: voices, brass ens, perc. Recording: Orion, ORS 77267 (1977).

650 Wernick, Richard. In coll. MuENC. Chorus: SATB, prepared pf 4 hands.

"when any mortal (even the most odd)." *95 Poems* (1958).

651 Clarke, Henry L. "When Any Mortal." MS, 1965, avail. ACA. Song: med. v, pf.

"when faces called flowers float out of the ground." *XAIPE* (1950).

652 Argento, Dominick. In *Songs about Spring*. New York: Boosey & Hawkes, 1980. Cycle: S, pf or cham orch (R).

653 Duke, John. "The Mountains Are Dancing." New York: C. Fischer, 1956. Song: high v, pf.

"when god lets my body be." *Tulips and Chimneys* (1923).

654 Bergsma, William. In *Six Songs to Poems by E.E. Cummings*. New York: C. Fischer, 1947. Song: high v, pf.

"when life is quite through with." *XLI Poems* (1925).

655 Blitzstein, Marc. In *From Marion's Book*. New York: Chappell, 1962. Cycle: med. v, pf.

"wherelings whenlings." *50 Poems* (1940).

656 Cage, John. "Forever and Sunsmell." New York: Henmar Press, 1960. Song: low v, perc duo. Words freely adapted.

"who(is?are)who." *95 Poems* (1958).

657 Malipiero, Riccardo. In *In Time of Daffodils*. Milan: Edizoni Suvini Zerboni, 1964. Cycle: S, Bar, 7 instruments. Words in Eng.

"who is this." *73 Poems* (1963).

658 Ballou, Esther W. In *5-4-3*. MS, 1966, avail. ACA. Song: S, vla, hp.

"who knows if the moon's." *&* *[AND]* (1925).

659 Argento, Dominick. "Who Knows if the Moon's a Balloon" in *Songs about Spring*. New York: Boosey & Hawkes, 1980. Cycle: S, pf or cham orch (R).

660 Garwood, Margaret. "Who Knows if the Moons a Balloon" in *Lovesongs: 6 Songs to Poems of E.E. Cummings*. East Greenville, Pa.: composer, 1963. Song: S, pf.

661 Harrex, Patrick. In *Sonata*. London: Ars Viva, 1969. Song: female v, fl, perc.

"why" [No. 21]. *73 Poems* (1963).

662 Malipiero, Riccardo. n.t. in *In Time of Daffodils*. Milan: S. Zerboni, 1965. Cycle: S, Bar, fl, e-hn, bcl, perc, gtr, vla, db.

"why did you go." *XLI Poems* (1925).

663 Cage, John. "Little Four Paws" in *5 Songs for Contralto*. New York: Henmar Press, 1960. Song: C, pf.

664 Dougherty, Celius. "Little Fourpaws" in *Songs by E.E. Cummings*. New York: G. Schirmer, 1946. Song: med. v, pf.

"yes is a pleasant country." *1 X 1* (1944).

665 Blitzstein, Marc. In *From Marion's Book*. New York: Chappell, 1962. Cycle: med. v, pf.

"you shall above all things be glad and young." *Collected Poems* [Section entitled, "New Poems"] (1938).

666 Pfautsch, Lloyd. "Learn How to Sing." New York: C. Fischer, 1971. Setting for mixed voices, opt unison chorus, narr., solo tpt, perc, pf, or band or orch (R).

"youful." *50 Poems* (1940).

667 Koch, Frederick. n.t. in *Sound Particles*. New York: General, 1973. Setting for speaker, pf, perc.

Miscellaneous

668 Boone, Charles. "Trois Motets." Paris: Musique Contemporaine, 1971. Chorus: SATB.

669 Cage, John. "Experiences II." New York: C.F. Peters, u.d. Song: med. v, pf.

670 Entry cancelled.

671 Entry cancelled.

672 Fennelly, Brian. u.t. in *Songs with Improvisations*. MS, 1970, avail. ACA. Song: med. v, cl, pf.

673 Hoffman, Allen. "Mass for . . . the Passing of All Shining Things." New York: C.F. Peters, u.d. Setting for SATB, T or Bar solo.

673a Kresky, Jeffrey. *Chansons Innocentes: Three Songs for Soprano and Piano on Texts by E.E. Cummings*. New York: Composers Facsimile Edn, 1969. Song: high v, pf.

674 Lerdahl, Fred. "Wake." Hillsdale, N.Y.: Boelke-Bomart, 1968. Setting for S, str trio, hp, perc.

675 Mellnäs, Arne. "Dream." u.p.: Wilhelm Hansen Edition, u.d. Chorus: SATB, a cap.

676 Reck, David. "Night Sounds (and Dream)." Davis, Calif.: Composer/Performer Edn, u.d. Song: S, perc, db.

677 Tarlow, Karen Anne. "Chansons Innocentes." New York: Seesaw, u.d. Setting for women's chorus, amplif harpsichord and amplif vc.

JAMES DICKEY (B. 1923)

Apollo. *The Eye-Beaters, Blood, Victory, Madness, Buckhead, and Mercy* (1970).

678 Perera, Ronald. "So Long," "The Moon Comes," "You Lean Back," "You Hang Mysteriously" in *Apollo Circling*. Boston: E.C. Schirmer, 1977. Cycle: high v, pf.

Sleeping out at Easter. *Into the Stone and Other Poems* (1960).

679 Karlén, Robert. "All Dark Is Now No More." u.p.: Schmitt, u.d. Setting for SATB, tape.

EMILY DICKINSON (1830–1886)

Buckingham, Willis J. *Emily Dickinson: An Annotated Bibliography*. Bloomington, Ind.: Indiana Univ. Press, 1970.

"A Drop fell on the Apple Tree" [J. 794]. *Poems of Emily Dickinson* (1890).

> 680 Bacon, Ernst. In *From Emily's Diary*. New York: G. Schirmer, 1947. Cantata: SSAA chorus, S solo, pf or orch.

> 681 Dickinson, Clarence. "Summer Shower" in *Six Songs*. Chicago: Samuel Merwin, 1897. Song: v, pf.

> 682 Farwell, Arthur. "Summer Shower" in *Three Dickinson Poems* op. 73 no. 1. New York: G. Schirmer, 1928. Song: med. or high v, pf.

> 683 Kent, Richard. In *Spring Songs*. Cincinnati: World Library, 1971. Chorus: SSA, a cap or TTBB, a cap.

"A Light exists in Spring" [J. 812]. *Poems by Emily Dickinson* (1896).

> 684 Kent, Richard. In *Spring Songs*. Cincinnati: World Library, 1971. Chorus: SSA, a cap or TTBB, a cap.

"A Shady friend—for Torrid days" [J. 278]. *Poems by Emily Dickinson* (1891).

> 685 Baksa, Robert. In *Seven Songs to Poems of Emily Dickinson* op. 38 no. 5. u.p.: Composers Library Editions, 1977. Cycle: v, pf.

"A solemn thing—it was—I said" [J. 271]. *Poems by Emily Dickinson* (1896).

> 686 Mollicone, Henry. "A Solemn Thing It Was" in *Five Poems of Love*. Boston: E.C. Schirmer, 1966. Chorus: SSAA, pf or hp.

"A Sparrow took a Slice of Twig" [J. 1211]. *Bolts of Melody* (1945).

> 687 Green, Ray. "Sparrow" in *Three Choral Songs*. New York: American Music Edition, 1954, Chorus: SSA, a cap.

"A Spider sewed at Night" [J. 1138]. *Poems by Emily Dickinson* (1891).

> 688 Bacon, Ernst. "A Spider" in *Nature*. Boston: E.C. Schirmer, 1971. Chorus: SA, pf; "A Spider" in coll. BacFS. Song: high v, pf.

> 688a Grantham, Donald. In *Seven Choral Settings of Poems by Emily Dickinson*. Boston: E.C. Schirmer, 1983. Chorus: SATB, a cap. Recording: Composers Recordings, CRI SD 488.

"A train went through a burial gate," [J. 1761]. *Poems of Emily Dickinson* (1890).

689 Dickinson, Clarence. In *Six Songs*. Chicago: Samuel Merwin, 1897. Song: v, pf.

"Alter! When the Hills do" [J. 729]. *Poems of Emily Dickinson* (1890).

690 Bacon, Ernst. "O Friend." New York: Associated Music Publishers, 1946. Song: med. v, pf.

691 Persichetti, Vincent. "When the Hills Do" in *Emily Dickinson Songs* op. 77 no. 3. Philadelphia: Elkan-Vogel, 1958. Song: v, pf.

"Ample make this Bed" [J. 829]. *Poems by Emily Dickinson* (1891).

692 Horvit, Michael. In *Three Songs of Elegy*. Boston: E.C. Schirmer, 1970. Song: S, pf.

693 Kay, Ulysses. In *Emily Dickinson Set*. u.p.: Duchess Music, 1964. Chorus: SSA, pf.

"An awful Tempest mashed the air" [J. 198]. *Poems by Emily Dickinson* (1891).

694 Duke, John. In *Six Poems by Emily Dickinson*. New York: Southern Music Publishing, 1978. Song: S, pf.

"And this of all my Hopes" [J. 913]. *Further Poems of Emily Dickinson* (1929).

695 Bacon, Ernst. In *Five Poems by Emily Dickinson*. New York: G. Schirmer, 1944. Song: high v, pf.

"Answer July" [J. 386]. *Unpublished Poems of Emily Dickinson* (1935).

696 Berger, Jean. In *Three Poems by Emily Dickinson*. New York: Broude Bros., 1973. Chorus: SATB, pf.

697 Schwartz, Paul. In *Three Choruses on Poems by Emily Dickinson*. New York: Rongwen Music, 1981. Chorus: SATB, pf.

"Apparently with no surprise" [J. 1624]. *Poems of Emily Dickinson* (1890).

698 Dinerstein, Norman. In *Four Settings for Soprano and String Quartet*. New York: Boosey & Hawkes, 1972. Song: S, str qrt.

699 Lindenfeld, Harris. n.t. in *Three Dickinson Songs*. MS, u.d., avail. ACA. Song: S, e flat cl, pf.

"As if some little Artic flower" [J. 180]. *Poems of Emily Dickinson* (1890).

700 Bacon, Ernst. In *Nature*. Boston: E.C. Schirmer, 1971. Chorus: SA, pf.

"As if the Sea should part" [J. 695]. *Further Poems of Emily Dickinson* (1929).

701 Bacon, Ernst. In *Songs from Emily Dickinson*. San Francisco: Priv. pubd. by Bacon, 1932. Song: v, pf; "The Sea" in *Nature*. Boston: E.C. Schirmer, 1971. Chorus: SSAA, pf; "Eternity" in coll. BacFS, BacT. Song: high v, pf.

702 Riegger, Wallingford. "Eternity" op. 32a. New York: H. Flammer, 1945. Chorus: SSA, fl, 2 hn, db.

"As imperceptibly as Grief" [J. 1540]. *Poems by Emily Dickinson* (1891).

703 Bacon, Ernst. "Summer's Lapse" in coll. BacFS. Song: S, pf.

704 Kent, Richard. In *Autumn Songs*. New York: Lawson-Gould, u.d. Setting for female chorus.

705 Thygerson, Robert. Richmond, Ind.: Richmond Music, 1980. Chorus: SSA, pf.

"At last, to be identified!" [J. 174]. *Poems of Emily Dickinson* (1890).

706 Farwell, Arthur. "Resurgam" in *Two Poems by Emily Dickinson* op. 66 no 2. New York: G. Schirmer, 1926. Song: med. or high v, pf.

"At least—to pray—is left—is left" [J. 502]. *Poems by Emily Dickinson* (1891).

707 Laderman, Ezra. n.t. in *Magic Prison*. New York: Oxford Univ. Press, 1970. Melodrama: 2 narr., pf and orch (R). Texts selected by MacLeish.

"Beauty—be not caused—It Is" [J. 516]. *Further Poems of Emily Dickinson* (1929).

708 Clarke, Henry L. n.t. in *Emily Dickinson Canons*. MS, 1965, avail. ACA. Song: med. v, vn or vla.

709 Dougherty, Celius. "Beauty Is Not Caused." New York: Associated Music, 1948. Song: med. v, pf.

710 Perle, George. In *Thirteen Dickinson Songs*. Song: v, pf. Recording: Composers Recordings, CRI SD 403.

"Because I could not stop for Death" [J. 712]. *Poems of Emily Dickinson* (1890).

711 Copland, Aaron. "The Chariot" in *Twelve Poems by Emily Dickinson*. New York: Boosey & Hawkes, 1951. Cycle: M, pf.

712 Kagen, Sergius. New York: Leeds Music, 1951. Song: med. v, pf.

"Bee! I'm expecting you!" [J. 1035]. *Bolts of Melody* (1945).

713 Duke, John. In *Six Poems by Emily Dickinson*. New York: Southern Music Publishing, 1978. Song: S, pf.

"Belshazzar had a Letter" [J. 1459]. *Poems of Emily Dickinson* (1890).

714 Berger, Jean. In *Three Poems by Emily Dickinson*. New York: Broude Bros., 1973. Chorus: SATB, pf.

"Come slowly—Eden!" [J. 211]. *Bolts of Melody* (1945).

715 Bacon, Ernst. "Eden" in *Quiet Airs*. New York: Mercury, 1952. Song: high v, pf; In coll. BacFS, BacT.

716 Springer, Philip. Boston: Boston Music, 1966. Song: M or S, pf.

"Dear March—Come in" [J. 1320]. *Poems by Emily Dickinson* (1896).

717 Copland, Aaron. In *Twelve Poems of Emily Dickinson*. New York: Boosey & Hawkes, 1951. Cycle: M, pf.

"Departed—to the Judgment" [J. 524]. *Poems of Emily Dickinson* (1890).

718 Dickinson, Peter. n.t. in *Winter Afternoons*. Sevenoaks, Kent: Novello, 1974. Cantata: AATTBB soli, db.

"Did the Harebell loose her girdle" [J. 213]. *Poems by Emily Dickinson* (1891).

719 Mollicone, Henry. In *Five Poems of Love*. Boston: E.C. Schirmer, 1966. Chorus: SSAA, pf or hp.

"Each Life Converges to some Centre" [J. 680]. *Poems by Emily Dickinson* (1891).

720 Pinkham, Daniel. In *An Emily Dickinson Mosaic*. New York: C.F. Peters, 1963. Chorus: SSAA, pf or cham orch.

"Elysium is as far as to" [J. 1760]. *Poems of Emily Dickinson* (1890).

721 Kay, Ulysses. "Elysium Is As Far" in *Emily Dickinson Set*. u.p.: Duchess Music, 1964. Chorus: SSA, pf.

722 Weiss, Adolf. "Elysium" in *Seven Songs for Soprano and String Quartet*. New York: Composers Facsimile Edn, 1952. Cycle: S, str qrt.

"Exhiliration is the Breeze" [J. 1118]. *The Single Hound* (1914).

723 Pinkham, Daniel. In *An Emily Dickinson Mosaic*. New York: C.F. Peters, 1963. Chorus: SSAA, pf or cham orch.

"Experiment to me" [J. 1073]. *Poems by Emily Dickinson* (1891).

724 Luening, Otto. In *Songs to Poems of Emily Dickinson*. New York: Galaxy, 1961. Cycle: med. v, pf.

"Far from Love the Heavenly Father" [J. 1021]. *Poems by Emily Dickinson* (1896).

> 725 Pasatieri, Thomas. "Far from Love." Melville, N.Y.: Belwin-Mills, 1976. Song: S, cl, vn, vc, pf.

"Few, yet enough" [J. 1596]. *Poems by Emily Dickinson* (1896).

> 726 Luening, Otto. In *Songs to Poems of Emily Dickinson*. New York: Galaxy, 1961. Cycle: med. v, pf.

"For each extatic instant" [J. 125]. *Poems by Emily Dickinson* (1891).

> 726a Grantham, Donald. In *Seven Choral Settings of Poems by Emily Dickinson*. Boston: E.C. Schirmer, 1983. Chorus: SATB, a cap. Recording: Composers Recordings, CRI SD 488.

"From Blank to Blank" [J. 761]. *Further Poems of Emily Dickinson* (1929).

> 727 Bacon, Ernst. In coll. BacSE. Song: v, pf: "A Threadless Way" in coll. BacFS. Song: high or med. v, pf.

> 728 Kagen, Sergius. In *The Mob Within the Heart*. New York: Mercury, 1956. Song: v, cl or cham orch.

"Going to Heaven!" [J. 79]. *Poems by Emily Dickinson* (1891).

> 729 Copland, Aaron. In *Twelve Poems of Emily Dickinson*. New York: Boosey & Hawkes, 1951. Cycle: M, pf.

"Going to Him! Happy Letter!" [J. 494]. *Poems by Emily Dickinson* (1891).

> 730 Pasatieri, Thomas. "Going to Him! Happy Letter! Tell Him" in *Far from Love*. Melville, N.Y.: Belwin-Mills, 1976. Cycle: S, cl, vn, vc, pf.

"Good Morning—Midnight" [J. 425]. *Further Poems of Emily Dickinson* (1929).

> 731 Duke, John. In *Six Poems by Emily Dickinson*. New York: Southern Music Publishing, 1978. Song: S, pf.

"Have you got a Brook in your little heart," [J. 136]. *Poems of Emily Dickinson* (1890).

> 732 Boyle, George F. "The Silent Brook." New York: Galaxy, 1937. Song: v, pf.

> 733 Dickinson, Clarence. In *Six Songs*. Chicago: Samuel Merwin, 1897. Song: v, pf.

> 734 Duke, John. In *Four Poems by Emily Dickinson*. Song: S, pf. Recording: Cambridge, CRS 2776 (1979).

735 Mollicone, Henry. "Have You Got a Brook" in *Five Poems of Love.* Boston: E.C. Schirmer, 1966. Chorus: SSAA, pf or hp.

736 Parker, Etta. Boston: Miles & Thompson, 1896.

"Heart, not so heavy as mine" [J. 83]. *Poems by Emily Dickinson* (1891).

737 Carter, Elliott. New York: Arrow Music Press, 1939. Chorus: SATB, a cap.

"Heart! We will forget him!" [J. 47]. *Poems by Emily Dickinson* (1896).

738 Copland, Aaron. In *Twelve Poems of Emily Dickinson.* New York: Boosey & Hawkes, 1951. Cycle: M, pf.

739 Duke, John. In *Six Poems by Emily Dickinson.* New York: Southern Music Publishing, 1978. Song: S, pf.

740 Escher, Rudolf. In *Songs of Love and Eternity.* Amsterdam: Donemus, 1956. Chorus: 7–10 mixed voices.

741 Smith, Russell. In *Three Songs from Emily Dickinson.* New York: F. Colombo, u.d. Chorus: SSA, a cap.

742 Steiner, Gitta. n.t. in *Five Poems for Mixed Chorus.* New York: Seesaw, 1971. Chorus: SATB, a cap.

" 'Hope' is the thing with feathers" [J. 254]. *Poems by Emily Dickinson* (1891).

743 Berkowitz, Leonard. "Hope" in *Four Songs on Poems of Emily Dickinson.* New York: Associated Music, 1968. Chorus: SATB, a cap.

744 Binkerd, Gordon. New York: Boosey & Hawkes, u.d. Chorus: SSAA, a cap.

745 Luening, Otto. In *Songs to Poems of Emily Dickinson.* New York: Galaxy, 1961. Cycle: med. v, pf.

746 Starer, Robert. New York: Music Corporation of America, 1977. Chorus: SATB, a cap.

747 Sydeman, William. "Hope is a thing with feathers" in *Three Songs after Emily Dickinson.* Boston: Ione Press, 1970. Song: S or T, vc.

"How happy is the little Stone" [J. 1510]. *Poems by Emily Dickinson* (1891).

748 Bacon, Ernst. "The Little Stone" in *Quiet Airs.* New York: Mercury, 1952. Song: med. v, pf.

749 Brown, Allyson. n.t. in *Songs from Emily.* Delaware Water Gap, Pa.: Shawnee, 1975. Chorus: SA, pf.

749a Heiss, John. "from 'If I Shouldn't Be Alive' and 'How Happy Is the Little Stone' " in *Songs of Nature.* n.p.: Boosey & Hawkes, 1978. Cycle: M, fl, cl, vn, vc, pf. Recording: Nonesuch H71351.

"How still the Bells in Steeples stand" [J. 1008]. *Poems by Emily Dickinson* (1896).

750 Bacon, Ernst. "How Still the Bells" in coll. BacSE. Song: v, pf.

"I died for Beauty—but was scarce" [J. 449]. *Poems of Emily Dickinson* (1890).

751 Baksa, Robert. "I Died for Beauty" in *Seven Songs to Poems of Emily Dickinson* op. 38 no. 4. u.p.: Composers Library, 1977. Cycle: v, pf.

752 Clarke, Henry L. "I Died for Beauty." MS, 1963, avail. ACA. Song: med. v, pf.

753 Dinerstein, Norman. "I Died for Beauty" in *Four Settings for Soprano and String Quartet.* New York: Boosey & Hawkes, 1972. Song: S, str qrt.

754 Lindenfeld, Harris. n.t. in *3 Dickinson Songs.* MS, u.d., avail. ACA. Song: S, e flat cl, pf.

"I dreaded that first Robin, so" [J. 348]. *Poems by Emily Dickinson* (1891).

755 Laderman, Ezra. n.t. in *Magic Prison.* New York: Oxford Univ. Press, 1970. Melodrama: 2 narr., pf and orch (R). Texts selected by MacLeish.

"I dwell in Possibility" [J. 657]. *Further Poems of Emily Dickinson* (1929).

756 Bacon, Ernst. In *From Emily's Diary.* New York: G. Schirmer, 1947. Chorus: S solo, pf (complete work, SSAA, S and A soli, pf).

"I envy Seas, whereon He rides" [J. 498]. *Poems by Emily Dickinson* (1896).

757 Mollicone, Henry. "I Envy Seas" in *Five Poems of Love.* Boston: E.C. Schirmer, 1966. Chorus: SSAA, pf or hp.

"I felt a Cleaving in my Mind" [J. 937]. *Poems by Emily Dickinson* (1896).

758 Horvit, Michael. "I Felt a Cleavage in My Mind" in *Three Songs of Elegy.* Boston: E.C. Schirmer, 1970. Song: S, pf.

759 Kagen, Sergius. "I Felt a Cleavage in My Mind" in *The Mob within the Heart.* New York: Mercury, 1956. Song: v, cl or cham orch.

760 Luening, Otto. "I Felt a Cleavage" in *Songs to Poems of Emily Dickinson.* New York: Galaxy, 1961. Cycle: med. v, pf.

"I felt a Funeral, in my Brain," [J. 280]. *Poems by Emily Dickinson* (1896).

761 Copland, Aaron. In *Twelve Poems of Emily Dickinson.* New York: Boosey & Hawkes, 1951. Cycle: M, pf.

762 Horvit, Michael. In *Three Songs of Elegy.* Boston: E.C. Schirmer, 1970. Song: S, pf.

"I have no Life but this" [J. 1398]. *Poems by Emily Dickinson* (1891).

> 763 Pasatieri, Thomas. In *Far from Love*. Melville, N.Y.: Belwin-Mills, 1976. Cycle: S, cl, vn, vc, pf.

> 764 Steiner, Gitta. In *4 Choruses of Emily Dickinson*. New York: Seesaw, u.d. Chorus: SATB, a cap.

"I heard a Fly buzz—when I died" [J. 465]. *Poems by Emily Dickinson* (1896).

> 765 Dinerstein, Norman. "Dying" in *Four Settings for Soprano and String Quartet*. New York: Boosey & Hawkes, 1972. Song: S, str qrt.

> 766 Sydeman, William. In *Three Songs after Emily Dickinson*. Boston: Ione Press, 1970. Song: S or T, vc.

"I held a Jewel in my fingers" [J. 245]. *Poems by Emily Dickinson* (1891).

> 767 Mollicone, Henry. "I Held a Jewel" in *Five Poems of Love*. Boston: E.C. Schirmer, 1966. Chorus: SSAA, pf or hp.

"I know a place where Summer strives" [J. 337]. *Poems by Emily Dickinson* (1891).

> 768 Perera, Ronald. "I Know a Place" in *Five Summer Songs*. Boston: E.C. Schirmer, 1976. Song: S or M, pf.

"I know some lonely Houses off the Road" [J. 289]. *Poems of Emily Dickinson* (1890).

> 769 Perle, George. In *Thirteen Dickinson Songs*. Song: v, pf. Recording: Composers Recordings, CRI SD 403.

"I like to see it lap the Miles" [J. 585]. *Poems by Emily Dickinson* (1891).

> 770 Perle, George. In *Thirteen Dickinson Songs*. Song: v, pf. Recording: Composers Recordings, CRI SD 403.

> 771 Rogers, W.K. In *Three Songs from Emily Dickinson*. u.p.: BMI Canada, 1948. Chorus: SATB, a cap.

> 772 Weiss, Adolf. "The Railway Train" in *Seven Songs for Soprano and String Quartet*. New York: Composers Facsimile Edn, 1952. Cycle: S, str qrt.

"I live with Him—I see His face" [J. 463]. *Poems by Emily Dickinson* (1896).

> 773 Laderman, Ezra. n.t. in *Magic Prison*. New York: Oxford Univ. Press, 1970. Melodrama: 2 narr., pf and orch (R). Texts selected by MacLeish.

> 774 Pasatieri, Thomas. In *Far from Love*. Melville, N.Y.: Belwin-Mills, 1976. Cycle: S, cl, vn, vc, pf.

775 Steiner, Gitta. n.t. in *Five Poems for Mixed Chorus.* New York: Seesaw, 1971. Chorus: SATB, a cap.

"I many times thought Peace had come" [J. 739]. *Poems by Emily Dickinson* (1891).

776 Gold, Ernest. "Peace" in *Songs of Love and Parting.* New York: G. Schirmer, 1963. Cycle: high v, pf or orch (R).

777 Pasatieri, Thomas. "Reflection." Melville, N.Y.: Belwin-Mills, 1977. Song: v, pf.

"I never felt at Home—Below" [J. 413]. *Further Poems of Emily Dickinson* (1929).

778 Dougherty, Celius. "New England Pastoral" in *Three Songs.* New York: Boosey & Hawkes, 1949. Song: med. v, pf.

"I never saw a Moor" [J. 1052]. *Poems of Emily Dickinson* (1890).

779 Berkowitz, Leonard. In *Four Songs on Poems of Emily Dickinson.* New York: Associated Music, 1968. Chorus: SATB, a cap.

780 Freed, Isadore. "Chartless." New York: Fischer, 1946. Song: med.-high or med.-low v, pf. In coll. TaCS.

781 Leavitt, H.S. "Chartless" in coll. Gi 3, GiTh.

782 Muczynski, Robert. New York: G. Schirmer, u.d. Chorus: SATB, a cap.

783 Sacco, John. "Revelation" in *Three Songs.* Boston: Boston Music, 1941. Song: high v, pf.

784 Weiss, Adolf. "Chartless" in *Seven Songs for Soprano and String Quartet.* New York: Composers Facsimile Edn, 1952. Cycle: S, str qrt.

"I reason, Earth is short" [J. 301]. *Poems of Emily Dickinson* (1890).

785 Laderman, Ezra. n.t. in *Magic Prison.* New York: Oxford Univ. Press, 1970. Melodrama: 2 narr., pf and orch (R). Texts selected by MacLeish.

"I reckon—when I count at all" [J. 569]. *Further Poems of Emily Dickinson* (1929).

786 Weiss, Adolf. "Poets" in *Seven Songs for Soprano and String Quartet.* New York: Composers Facsimile Edn, 1952. Cycle: S, str qrt.

"I robbed the Woods" [J. 41]. *Poems by Emily Dickinson* (1891).

787 Baksa, Robert. "Who Robbed the Woods" in *More Songs to Poems of*

Emily Dickinson op. 40. u.p.: Composers Library Edns, 1978. Song: M, pf.

"I shall know why—when Time is over" [J. 193]. *Poems of Emily Dickinson* (1890).

788 Farwell, Arthur. "I Shall Know Why" in *Two Poems by Emily Dickinson* op. 66 no. 1. New York: G. Schirmer, 1926. Song: med. v, pf.

"I taste a liquor never brewed" [J. 214]. *Poems of Emily Dickinson* (1890).

789 Dickinson, Clarence. In *Six Songs.* Chicago: Samuel Merwin, 1897. Song: v, pf.

790 Duke, John. In *Four Poems by Emily Dickinson.* Song: S, pf. Recording: Cambridge, CRS 2776 (1979).

791 Escher, Rudolf. In *Songs of Love and Eternity.* Amsterdam: Donemus, 1956. Chorus: 7–10 mixed voices.

792 Gettel, William. New York: C. Fischer, u.d. Chorus: SATB, a cap.

793 Sydeman, William. n.t. in *Three Songs after Emily Dickinson.* Boston: Ione Press, 1970. Song: S or T, vc.

794 Ward, Robert. "Intoxication" in *Sacred Songs for Pantheists.* n.p.: Highgate Press, 1966. Song: S, or orch (R). Recording: Composers Recordings, CRI 206 (1966).

795 Weiss, Adolf. "I Taste a Liquor" in *Seven Songs for Soprano and String Quartet.* New York: Composers Facsimile Edn, 1952. Cycle: S, str qrt.

"I took my Power in my Hand" [J. 540]. *Poems by Emily Dickinson* (1891).

796 Baksa, Robert. In *Seven Songs to Poems of Emily Dickinson* op. 38 no. 3. u.p.: Composers Library, 1977. Cycle: v, pf.

"I went to Heaven" [J. 374]. *Poems by Emily Dickinson* (1891).

797 Walker, George. u.p.: General, 1971. Song: S or M, pf.

"If I can stop one Heart from breaking" [J. 919]. *Poems of Emily Dickinson* (1890).

798 Bartlett, Floy L. "I Shall Not Live in Vain." Boston: A.P. Schmidt, 1915. Song: high and med. v edns, pf.

799 Hageman, Richard. "Charity." New York: G. Schirmer, 1921. Song: high and low v edns, pf.

800 Kennedy, John B. In *Sails, Robins, and Butterflies.* New York: Boosey & Hawkes, 1966. Chorus: 2-pt. treble voices, a cap.

801 Luening, Otto. In *Songs to Poems of Emily Dickinson.* New York: Galaxy, 1961. Cycle: med. v, pf.

802 Lutkin, Peter C. In coll. SmNH. Hymn. Optional stanza by Earl Marlatt; In coll. ChAH. Hymn.

803 MacDermid, James G. In *Songs.* Chicago: MacDermid, 1908.

804 Patterson, Janie A. "Not In Vain: Song." Philadelphia: Presser, 1944.

805 Persichetti, Vincent. "Robin" in *Hymns and Responses* op. 68 no. 3. Philadelphia: Elkan-Vogel, 1956. Hymn for choir and congregational use.

806 Speaks, Oley. "Charity." New York: G. Schirmer, 1911.

807 Towner, E. "Not In Vain" in coll. Gi 4, GiJr.

"If I shouldn't be alive" [J. 182]. *Poems of Emily Dickinson* (1890).

807a Heiss, John. "from 'If I Shouldn't Be Alive' and 'How Happy Is the Little Stone' " in *Songs of Nature.* n.p.: Boosey & Hawkes, 1978. Cycle: M, fl, cl, vn, vc, pf. Recording: Nonesuch H 71351.

"If I'm lost—now" [J. 256]. *Bolts of Melody* (1945).

808 Perle, George. In *Thirteen Dickinson Songs.* Song: v, pf. Recording: Composers Recordings, CRI SD 403.

"If you were coming in the Fall" [J. 511]. *Poems of Emily Dickinson* (1890).

809 Laderman, Ezra. n.t. in *Magic Prison.* New York: Oxford Univ. Press, 1970. Melodrama: 2 narr., pf and orch (R). Texts selected by MacLeish.

"I'll tell you how the Sun rose" [J. 318]. *Poems of Emily Dickinson* (1890).

810 Brown, Allyson. n.t. in *Songs from Emily.* Delaware Water Gap, Pa.: Shawnee, 1975. Chorus: SA, pf.

811 Kettering, Eunice L. "The Sun." New York: C. Fischer, 1955. Chorus: SSA, a cap.

812 Knowlton, F.S. "A Day" in coll. Kn.

813 McAfee, Don. Philadelphia: Elkan-Vogel, u.d. Chorus: SATB, a cap.

814 Raymond-Ward, Adeline. "A Day." Boston: Homeyer, 1913.

"I'm Nobody! Who are you?" [J. 288]. *Poems by Emily Dickinson* (1891).

815 Bacon, Ernst. "I'm Nobody" in coll. BacSE, BacFS. Song: S, pf.

816 Baksa, Robert. "I'm Nobody" in *Seven Songs to Poems of Emily Dickinson* op. 38 no. 7. u.p.: Composers Library, 1977. Cycle: v, pf.

817 Berkowitz, Leonard. "I'm Nobody" in *Four Songs on Poems of Emily Dickinson.* New York: Associated Music, 1968. Chorus: SATB, a cap.

817a Davis, Sharon. "I'm Nobody" in *Three Moods of Emily Dickinson*. Los Angeles: Western International Music, 1981. Song: S, pf trio.

818 Kagen, Sergius. "I'm Nobody." New York: Weintraub, 1950. Song: S, pf.

819 Kennedy, John B. New York: Boosey & Hawkes, 1966. Chorus: SATB, a cap.

820 Laderman, Ezra. n.t. in *Magic Prison*. New York: Oxford Univ. Press, 1970. Melodrama: 2 narr., pf and orch (R). Texts selected by MacLeish.

821 Persichetti, Vincent. "I'm Nobody" in *Emily Dickinson Songs* op. 77 no. 2. Philadelphia: Elkan-Vogel, 1958. Song: high v, pf.

822 Riley, Dennis. "On Life" in *Three Little Commentaries*. In coll. MuENC. Chorus: SAB, str ens.

823 Starer, Robert. "I'm Nobody." New York: MCA Music, 1968. Chorus: SSA, a cap.

824 Steiner, Gitta. "I'm Nobody" in *4 Choruses of Emily Dickinson*. New York: Seesaw, u.d. Chorus: SATB, a cap.

"I'm 'wife'—I've finished that" [J. 199]. *Poems of Emily Dickinson* (1890).

825 Laderman, Ezra. n.t. in *Magic Prison*. New York: Oxford Univ. Press, 1970. Melodrama: 2 narr., pf and orch (R). Texts selected by MacLeish.

"It sifts from Leaden Sieves" [J. 311]. *Poems by Emily Dickinson* (1891).

826 Bacon, Ernst. "Snowfall" in coll. BacFS; "Alabaster Wool" in coll. BacT. Song: v, pf.

"It was not Saint—it was too large" [J. 1092]. *Further Poems of Emily Dickinson* (1929).

827 Clarke, Henry L. n.t. in *Emily Dickinson Canons*. MS, 1965, avail. ACA. Song: med. v, pf.

"It's all I have to bring today" [J. 26]. *Poems by Emily Dickinson* (1896).

828 Bacon, Ernst. "It's All I Have to Bring" in *Five Poems by Emily Dickinson*. New York: G. Schirmer, 1944. Song: high v, pf; "This and My Heart" in coll. BacT.

829 Kennedy, John B. Melville, N.Y.: Belwin-Mills, 1973. Chorus: SSA, a cap.

"It's Coming—the postponeless Creature" [J. 390]. *Further Poems of Emily Dickinson* (1929).

830 Bacon, Ernst. In coll. BacSE; "The Postponeless Creature" in coll. BacT. Song: v, pf; In *From Emily's Diary*. New York: G. Schirmer, u.d. Chorus: SSAA, S and A soli, pf.

"It's such a little thing to weep" [J. 189]. *Poems by Emily Dickinson* (1896).

831 Bacon, Ernst. "Weeping and Sighing" in coll. BacFS. Song: v, pf.

"I've heard an Organ talk, sometimes" [J. 183]. *Unpublished Poems of Emily Dickinson* (1935).

832 Copland, Aaron. In *Twelve Poems by Emily Dickinson*. New York: Boosey & Hawkes, 1951. Cycle: M, pf.

"Let down the Bars, Oh Death" [J. 1065]. *Poems by Emily Dickinson* (1891).

833 Bacon, Ernst. "Let Down the Bars" in coll. BacSE. Song: v, pf.

834 Barber, Samuel. "Let Down the Bars, O Death" op. 8 no. 2. u.p.: C. Schirmer, u.d. Chorus: SATB, a cap.

835 Duke, John. In *Six Songs by Emily Dickinson*. New York: Southern Music Publishing, 1978. Song: S, pf.

836 Pasatieri, Thomas. In *Far from Love*. Melville, N.Y.: Belwin-Mills, 1976. Cycle: S, cl, vn, vc, pf.

837 Weigl, Vally. MS, u.d., avail. ACA. Chorus: TTBB, pf.

"Lightly stepped a yellow star" [J. 1672]. *The Single Hound* (1914).

838 Rogers, W.K. In *Three Songs from Emily Dickinson*. u.p.: BMI Canada, 1948. Chorus: SATB, a cap.

"Love's stricken, 'why' " [J. 1368]. *Letters of Emily Dickinson* (1894).

839 Rorem, Ned. In *Poems of Love and the Rain*. New York: Boosey & Hawkes, 1965. Cycle: M, pf. Numbers 4 and 14 are contrasting settings of this poem.

"Mine—by the Right of the White Election!" [J. 528]. *Poems of Emily Dickinson* (1890).

840 Farwell, Arthur. "Mine" in *Three Dickinson Poems* op. 73 no. 2. New York: G. Schirmer, 1928. Song: high v, pf.

"Mine Enemy is growing old" [J. 1509]. *Poems by Emily Dickinson* (1891).

841 Kagen, Sergius. In *The Mob Within the Heart*. New York: Mercury, 1956. Song: v, cl or cham orch.

"Much Madness is divinest Sense" [J. 435]. *Poems of Emily Dickinson* (1890).

842 Baksa, Robert. In *Seven Songs to Poems of Emily Dickinson* op. 38 no. 1. u.p. Composers Library, 1977. Cycle: v, pf.

843 Kagen, Sergius. In *The Mob within the Heart.* New York: Mercury, 1956. Song: v, cl or cham orch.

844 Lindenfeld, Harris. n.t. in *3 Dickinson Songs.* MS, u.d., avail. ACA. Song: S, e flat cl, pf.

"Musicians wrestle everywhere" [J. 157]. *Poems by Emily Dickinson* (1891).

845 Carter, Elliott. New York: Music Press, 1948. Madrigal: SSATB, a cap or str orch.

846 Mennin, Peter. In *Reflections of Emily.* New York: G. Schirmer, 1979. Chorus: SSA, hp, pf, perc.

"My Cocoon tightens—Colors teaze" [J. 1099]. *Poems of Emily Dickinson* (1890).

847 Pasatieri, Thomas. In *Far from Love.* Melville, N.Y.: Belwin-Mills, 1976. Cycle: S, cl, vn, vc, pf.

"My life closed twice before its close" [J. 1732]. *Poems by Emily Dickinson* (1896).

848 Gold, Ernest. "Parting" in *Songs of Love and Parting.* New York: G. Schirmer, 1963. Cycle: high v, pf or orch (R).

849 Laderman, Ezra. n.t. in *Magic Prison.* New York: Oxford Univ. Press, 1970 Melodrama: 2 narr., pf and orch (R). Texts selected by MacLeish.

"My River runs to thee" [J. 162]. *Poems of Emily Dickinson* (1890).

850 Bacon, Ernst. In coll. BacSE. Song: v, pf; In *From Emily's Diary.* New York: G. Schirmer, 1947. Cantata: SSAA, pf or orch.

851 Steiner, Gitta. n.t. in *Five Poems for Mixed Chorus.* New York: Seesaw, 1971. Chorus: SATB, a cap.

"My Soul—accused me—And I quailed" [J. 753]. *Further Poems of Emily Dickinson* (1929).

852 Clarke, Henry L. n.t. in *Emily Dickinson Canons.* MS, 1965, avail. ACA. Song: med. v, vla or vn.

"Nature—the Gentlest Mother is," [J. 790]. *Poems by Emily Dickinson* (1891).

853 Bacon, Ernst. "The Gentlest Mother" in *Nature.* Boston: E.C. Schirmer, 1971. Chorus: SSA, S and A soli, pf.

854 Copland, Aaron. In *Twelve Poems by Emily Dickinson*. New York: Boosey & Hawkes, 1951. Cycle: M, pf.

"New feet within my garden go" [J. 99]. *Poems of Emily Dickinson* (1890).

855 Duke, John. In *Four Poems by Emily Dickinson*. Song: S, pf. Recording: Cambridge, CRS 2776 (1979).

856 Kent, Richard. In *Spring Songs*. Cincinnati: World Library, 1971. Chorus: SSA, a cap or TTBB, a cap.

857 Perera, Ronald. In *Five Summer Songs*. Boston: E.C. Schirmer, 1976. Song: S or M, pf.

"No matter—now—Sweet" [J. 704]. *Bolts of Melody* (1945).

858 Baksa, Robert. In *More Songs to Poems of Emily Dickinson* op. 40. u.p.: Composers Library Editions, 1978. Song: M, pf.

"Nobody knows this little Rose" [J. 35]. *Bolts of Melody* (1945).

859 Duke, John. In *Six Songs by Emily Dickinson*. New York: Southern Music Publishing, 1978. Song: S, pf.

860 Roy, William. "This Little Rose." New York: G. Schirmer, 1947. Song: low, med., and high v edns, pf. In coll. TaST; New York: G. Schirmer, 1950. Also arr. for SSA chorus, pf and SATB chorus, pf.

"Not what We did, shall be the test" [J. 823]. *Further Poems of Emily Dickinson* (1929).

861 Bacon, Ernst. In *From Emily's Diary*. New York: G. Schirmer, 1947. Chorus: SSAA, S and soli, pf.

"Of all the Souls that stand create" [J. 664]. *Poems by Emily Dickinson* (1891).

862 Shearer, C.M. "Of All the Souls." San Antonio: Southern Music, 1982. Chorus: SATB, a cap.

"Of God we ask one favor" [J. 1601]. *Letters of Emily Dickinson* (1894).

863 Laderman, Ezra. n.t. in *Magic Prison*. New York: Oxford Univ. Press, 1970. Melodrama: 2 narr., pf and orch (R). Texts selected by MacLeish.

"On this wondrous sea" [J. 4]. *Poems by Emily Dickinson* (1896).

864 Bacon, Ernst. "In the Silent West" in coll. BacFS. Song: v, pf; "On this Wondrous Sea." Song: v, pf. Recording: Cambridge, CRS-1707.

865 Weigl, Vally. "From Time and Eternity." MS, u.d., avail. ACA.

Chorus: SSA, a cap. Arr. for SATB chorus (1953) and SMATB chorus, a cap (1955).

"One dignity delays for all" [J. 98]. *Poems of Emily Dickinson* (1890).

866 Dickinson, Peter. n.t. in *Winter Afternoons*. Sevenoaks, Kent: Novello, 1974. Cantata: AATTBB soli, db.

"One need not be a Chamber—to be Haunted" [J. 670]. *Poems by Emily Dickinson* (1891).

866a Grantham, Donald. In *Seven Choral Settings of Poems by Emily Dickinson*. Boston: E.C. Schirmer, 1983. Chorus: SATB, a cap. Recording: Composers Recordings, CRI SD 488.

"Our share of night to bear" [J. 113]. *Poems of Emily Dickinson* (1890).

867 Bacon, Ernst. In *From Emily's Diary*. New York: G. Schirmer, 1947. Cantata: SSAA, pf or cham orch.

868 Luening, Otto. In *Songs to Poems of Emily Dickinson*. New York: Galaxy, 1961. Cycle: med. v, pf.

869 Steiner, Gitta. In *4 Choruses of Emily Dickinson*. New York: Seesaw, u.d. Chorus: SATB, a cap.

"Pain—has an Element of Blank" [J. 650]. *Poems of Emily Dickinson* (1890).

870 Kagen, Sergius. In *The Mob Within the Heart*. New York: Mercury, 1956. Song: v, cl or cham orch.

871 Starer, Robert. In *On the Nature of Things*. New York: Music Corp. of America, 1969. Chorus: SATB, a cap.

"Perhaps you'd like to buy a flower," [J. 134]. *Poems of Emily Dickinson* (1890).

872 Perle, George. In *Thirteen Dickinson Songs*. Song: v, pf. Recording: Composers Recordings, CRI SD 403.

873 Steiner, Gitta. n.t. in *Five Poems for Mixed Chorus*. New York: Seesaw, 1971. Chorus: SATB, a cap.

"Pigmy seraphs—gone astray" [J. 138]. *Poems by Emily Dickinson* (1891).

874 Bacon, Ernst. "Velvet People." New York: C. Fischer, 1948. Song: med. v, pf.

"Pink—small—and punctual" [J. 1332]. *Poems of Emily Dickinson* (1890).

875 Bacon, Ernst. "With the First Arbutus" in *Nature*. Boston: E.C. Schirmer, 1971. Chorus: SSA, pf. In coll. BacT.

"Poor little Heart!" [J. 192]. *Poems by Emily Dickinson* (1896).

876 Bacon, Ernst. In *Five Poems by Emily Dickinson*. New York: G. Schirmer, 1944. Song: high v, pf.

877 Baksa, Robert. In *More Songs to Poems of Emily Dickinson* op. 40. u.p.: Composers Library Editions, 1978. Song: M, pf.

878 Dickinson, Clarence. In *Six Songs*. Chicago: Samuel Merwin, 1897. Song: v, pf.

"Put up my lute!" [J. 261]. *Unpublished Poems of Emily Dickinson* (1935).

879 Samuel, Gerhard. u.p.: Belwin-Mills, u.d. Setting for S, 30 db, perc. Recording: Composers Recordings, CRI SD 422.

"Read—Sweet—how others—strove" [J. 260]. *Poems of Emily Dickinson* (1890).

880 Harris, Roy. In coll. ChAH.

881 Mennin, Peter. In *Reflections of Emily*. New York: G. Schirmer, 1979. Chorus: SSA, hp, pf, perc.

"Remorse—is Memory—awake" [J. 744]. *Poems by Emily Dickinson* (1891).

882 Kagen, Sergius. In *The Mob Within the Heart*. New York: Mercury, 1956. Song: v, cl or cham orch.

"Safe in their Alabaster Chambers" [J. 216]. *Poems of Emily Dickinson* (1890).

883 Murray, Bain. New York: Galaxy, 1968. Chorus: SATB, e-hn and vc or org. Recording: Composers Recordings, CRI SD 182 (1964).

884 Pinkham, Daniel. n.t. in *Safe in their Alabaster Chambers*. Boston: Ione Press, 1974. Song: med. v, electronic tape.

"Savior! I've no one else to tell" [J. 217]. *Further Poems of Emily Dickinson* (1929).

885 Bacon, Ernst. "Savior" in coll. BacSE; "The Imperial Heart" in coll. BacQA, BacFS. Song: v, pf.

885a Grantham, Donald. "Father, I Bring Thee Not Myself" in *Seven Choral Settings of Poems by Emily Dickinson*. Boston: E.C. Schirmer, 1983. Chorus: SATB, a cap. Recording: Composers Recordings, CRI SD 488. "Father—I bring thee—not Myself" is the first line of the packet copy of this poem.

"She bore it till the simple veins" [J. 144]. *Unpublished Poems of Emily Dickinson* (1935).

886 Perle, George. In *Thirteen Dickinson Songs*. Song: v, pf. Recording: Composers Recordings, CRI SD 403.

"She died—this was the way she died" [J. 150]. *Poems by Emily Dickinson* (1891).

887 Ward, Robert. "Vanished." New York: Peer International, 1951. Song: high v, pf.

"She went as quiet as the Dew" [J. 149]. *Poems of Emily Dickinson* (1890).

888 Bacon, Ernst. In coll. BacSE; "She Went" in coll. BacFS. Song: S, pf.

"Sleep is supposed to be" [J. 13]. *Poems of Emily Dickinson* (1890).

889 Copland, Aaron. In *Twelve Poems of Emily Dickinson*. New York: Boosey and Hawkes, 1951. Cycle: M, pf.

"So bashful when I spied her!" [J. 91]. *Poems of Emily Dickinson* (1890).

890 Bacon, Ernst. "So Bashful" in *Five Poems by Emily Dickinson*. New York: G. Schirmer, 1944. Song: high v, pf.

891 Weld, Arthur. "Bashfulness" in *Seven Songs*. New York: T.B. Harms, u.d. Song: v, pf.

"So well that I can live without" [J. 456]. *Further Poems of Emily Dickinson* (1929).

892 Bacon, Ernst. "As Well As Jesus" in coll. BacFS. Song: v, pf.

"Soul, Wilt thou toss again?" [J. 139]. *Poems of Emily Dickinson* (1890).

893 Luening, Otto. In *Songs to Poems of Emily Dickinson*. New York: Galaxy, 1961. Cycle: med. v, pf.

"South Winds jostle them" [J. 86]. *Poems by Emily Dickinson* (1891).

894 Perera, Ronald. In *Five Summer Songs*. Boston: E.C. Schirmer, 1976. Song: S or M, pf.

"Split the Lark—and you'll find the Music" [J. 861]. *Poems by Emily Dickinson* (1896).

895 Schwartz, Paul. "Split the Lark" in *Three Choruses on Poems by Emily Dickinson*. New York: Rongwen Music, 1981. Chorus: SATB, pf.

"Spring comes on the World" [J. 1042]. *Bolts of Melody* (1945).

896 Smith, Russell. In *Three Songs from Emily Dickinson*. New York: F. Colombo, u.d. Chorus: SSA, a cap.

"Spring is the Period" [J. 844]. *Bolts of Melody* (1945).

897 Roy, William. "Spring." New York: G. Schirmer, 1948. Song: v, pf.

"Success is counted sweetest" [J. 67]. *Poems of Emily Dickinson* (1890).

  898 Leichtling, Alan. In *3 Songs by Emily Dickinson* op. 47 no. 3. New York: Seesaw, 1969. Song: Bar, vc.

"Summer for thee, grant I may be" [J. 31]. *Poems by Emily Dickinson* (1896).

  899 Steiner, Gitta. "Summer for Thee" in *4 Choruses of Emily Dickinson*. New York: Seesaw, u.d. Chorus: SATB, a cap.

"Surgeons must be very careful" [J. 108]. *Poems by Emily Dickinson* (1891).

  900 Brown, Allyson. n.t. in *Songs from Emily*. Delaware Water Gap, Pa.: Shawnee, 1975. Chorus: SA, pf.

"Sweet is the swamp with its secrets," [J. 1740]. *Poems by Emily Dickinson* (1896).

  901 Bacon, Ernst. "The Swamp" in coll. BacFS. Song: v, pf.

"Talk not to me of Summer Trees" [J. 1634]. *Bolts of Melody* (1945).

  902 Kaderavek, Milan. "Talk Not to Me." Cincinnati: Westwood Press, 1967. Chorus: SATB, a cap.

"That I did always love" [J. 549]. *Poems of Emily Dickinson* (1890).

  903 Mennin, Peter. In *Reflections of Emily*. New York: G. Schirmer, 1979. Chorus: SSA, hp, pf, perc.

  904 Pasatieri, Thomas. In *Far from Love*. Melville, N.Y.: Belwin-Mills, 1976. Cycle: S, cl, vn, vc, pf.

"The Bat is dun, with wrinkled Wings" [J. 1575]. *Poems by Emily Dickinson* (1896).

  905 Bacon, Ernst. "The Bat" in coll. BacFS, BacT. Song: S, pf.

"The Bobolink is gone—the Rowdy of the Meadow" [J. 1591] *Bolts of Melody* (1945).

  906 Green, Ray. "Bobolink" in *Three Choral Songs*. New York: American Music Edition, 1954. Chorus: SSA, a cap.

"The Brain—is wider than the Sky" [J. 632]. *Poems by Emily Dickinson* (1896).

  907 Pinkham, Daniel. In *An Emily Dickinson Mosaic*. New York: C.F. Peters, 1963. Chorus: SSAA, pf or cham orch.

"The Bustle in a House" [J. 1078]. *Poems of Emily Dickinson* (1890).

> 908 Dinerstein, Norman. In *Four Settings for Soprano and Strinq Quartet*. New York: Boosey & Hawkes, 1972. Song: S, str qrt.

"The butterfly obtains" [J. 1685]. *The Single Hound* (1914).

> 909 Schwartz, Paul. "The Butterfly" in *Three Choruses on Poems by Emily Dickinson*. New York: Rongwen Music, 1981. Chorus: SATB, pf.

"The Crickets sang" [J. 1104]. *Poems by Emily Dickinson* (1896).

> 910 Bacon, Ernst. In *Nature*. Boston: E.C. Schirmer, 1971. Chorus: SSA, pf.

"The Daisy follows soft the Sun" [J. 106]. *Poems of Emily Dickinson* (1890).

> 911 Bacon, Ernst. In *From Emily's Diary*. New York: G. Schirmer, 1947. Chorus: SSAA, S and A soli, pf.

"The Grass so little has to do" [J. 333]. *Poems of Emily Dickinson* (1890).

> 912 Bacon, Ernst. In coll. BacSE; "The Grass." New York: Associated Music, 1944. Song: med. v, pf.
>
> 913 Bergh, Arthur. "The Grass." New York: Robbins Music, 1954. Chorus: SA, pf.
>
> 914 Persichetti, Vincent. "The Grass" in *Emily Dickinson Songs* op. 77 no. 4. Philadelphia: Elkan-Vogel, 1958. Song: med. v, pf.
>
> 915 "The Grass." Arr. from a Swiss Air in coll. DSB, DavB.

"The hallowing of Pain" [J. 772]. *Bolts of Melody* (1945).

> 916 Leichtling, Alan. In *3 Songs by Emily Dickinson* op. 47 no. 2. New York: Seesaw, 1969. Song: Bar, vc.

"The Heart asks Pleasure—first" [J. 536]. *Poems of Emily Dickinson* (1890).

> 917 Bacon, Ernst. In coll. BacSE. Song: v, pf; "The Heart" in coll. BacQA.
>
> 918 Perle, George. In *Thirteen Dickinson Songs*. Song: v, pf. Recording: Composers Recordings, CRI SD 403.
>
> 919 Rogers, W.K. In *Three Songs from Emily Dickinson*. u.p.: BMI Canada, 1948. Chorus: SATB, a cap.

"The Heart is the Capital of the Mind" [J. 1354]. *Further Poems of Emily Dickinson* (1929).

> 920 Pinkham, Daniel. In *An Emily Dickinson Mosaic*. New York: C.F. Peters, 1963. Chorus: SSAA, pf or cham orch.

"The Loneliness One dare not sound" [J. 777]. *Bolts of Melody* (1945).

921 Perle, George. In *Thirteen Dickinson Songs*. Song: v, pf. Recording: Composers Recordings, CRI SD 403.

"The Mind Lives on the Heart" [J. 1355]. *Bolts of Melody* (1945).

922 Pinkham, Daniel. In *An Emily Dickinson Mosaic*. New York: C.F. Peters, 1963. Chorus: SSAA, pf or cham orch.

"The Moon was but a Chin of Gold" [J. 737]. *Poems by Emily Dickinson* (1896).

923 Binkerd, Gordon. "Her Silver Will" in *Four Songs for High Soprano*. New York: Boosey & Hawkes, 1976.

"The morns are meeker than they were" [J. 12]. *Poems of Emily Dickinson* (1890).

924 Baksa, Robert. In *More Songs to Poems of Emily Dickinson* op. 40. u.p.: Composers Library Editions, 1978. Song: M, pf.

925 Brown, Allyson. n.t. in *Songs from Emily*. Delaware Water Gap, Pa.: Shawnee, 1975. Chorus: SA, pf.

926 Clarke, Henry L. "Autumn." MS, 1979, avail. ACA. Song: med. v, pf.

927 Kent, Richard. In *Autumn Songs*. New York: Lawson-Gould, u.d. Chorus: SSA, a cap.

928 Marzo, E. "Autumn" in coll. Gi 2, Gi 3.

"The Mountain sat upon the Plain" [J. 975]. *Poems of Emily Dickinson* (1890).

929 Bacon, Ernst. "The Mountain" in *Nature*. Boston: E.C. Schirmer, 1971. Chorus: SSA, pf.

"The Mountains—grow unnoticed" [J. 757]. *Further Poems of Emily Dickinson* (1929).

930 Adler, Samuel. In *In Nature's Ebb and Flow*. New York: Southern Music Publishing, 1968. Chorus: SSAA, pf.

931 Clarke, Henry L. n.t. in *Emily Dickinson Canons*. MS, 1965, avail. ACA. Song: med. v, vla or vn.

"The Murmur of a Bee" [J. 155]. *Poems of Emily Dickinson* (1890).

932 Weiss, Adolf. "Mysteries" in *Seven Songs for Soprano and String Quartet*. New York: Composers Facsimile Edn, 1952. Cycle: S, str qrt.

"The One who could repeat the Summer day" [J. 307]. *Poems by Emily Dickinson* (1891).

933 Perera, Ronald. In *Five Summer Songs*. Boston: E.C. Schirmer, 1976. Song: S or M, pf.

"The right to perish might be tho't" [J. 1692]. *The Single Hound* (1914).

934 Kagen, Sergius. "The Right to Perish" in *The Mob Within the Heart*. New York: Mercury, 1956. Song: v, cl or cham orch.

"The Rose did caper on her cheek" [J. 208]. *Poems by Emily Dickinson* (1891).

935 Dickinson, Clarence. "The Lovers" in *Six Songs*. Chicago: Samuel Merwin, 1897. Song: v, pf.

936 Duke, John. In *Four Poems by Emily Dickinson*. Song: S, pf. Recording: Cambridge, CRS 2776 (1979).

"The Show is not the Show" [J. 1206]. *Poems by Emily Dickinson* (1891).

937 Luening, Otto. In *Songs to Poems of Emily Dickinson*. New York: Galaxy, 1961. Cycle: med. v, pf.

"The Sky is low—the Clouds are mean" [J. 1075]. *Poems of Emily Dickinson* (1890).

938 Iannaccone, Anthony. Boston: E.C. Schirmer, 1979. Chorus: mixed voices, a cap.

939 Kent, Richard. In *Autumn Songs*. New York: Lawson-Gould, u.d. Chorus: SSA, a cap.

"The Soul selects her own Society" [J. 303]. *Poems of Emily Dickinson* (1890).

940 Baksa, Robert. In *Seven Songs to Poems of Emily Dickinson* op. 38 no. 6. u.p.: Composers Library, 1977. Cycle: v, pf.

"The Spider as an Artist" [J. 1275]. *Poems by Emily Dickinson* (1896).

940a Grantham, Donald. In *Seven Choral Settings of Poems by Emily Dickinson*. Boston: E.C. Schirmer, 1983. Chorus: SATB, a cap. Recording: Composers Recordings, CRI SD 488.

"The Sun kept setting—setting—still" [J. 692]. *Poems of Emily Dickinson* (1890).

941 Bacon, Ernst. "No Dew upon the Grass" in *Six Songs*. New Music (Jan. 1942). Song: low v, pf.

"The Sun went down—no Man looked on" [J. 1079]. *Further Poems of Emily Dickinson* (1929).

942 Bacon, Ernst. "The Sun Went Down" in coll. BacSE; "Sunset" in coll. BacFS, BacT. Song: S or M, pf.

"The Wind—tapped like a tired Man" [J. 436]. *Poems by Emily Dickinson* (1891).

> 943 Escher, Rudolf. In *Songs of Love and Eternity*. Amsterdam: Donemus, 1956. Setting for 7–10 mixed voices.

> 944 Perle, George. In *Thirteen Dickinson Songs*. Song: v, pf. Recording: Composers Recordings, CRI SD 403.

"The Wind took up the Northern Things" [J. 1134]. *Bolts of Melody* (1945).

> 945 Berkowitz, Leonard. "The Wind" in *Four Songs on Poems of Emily Dickinson*. New York: Associated Music, 1968. Chorus: SATB, a cap.

"The World—feels Dusty" [J. 715]. *Further Poems of Emily Dickinson* (1929).

> 946 Copland, Aaron. In *Twelve Poems of Emily Dickinson*. New York: Boosey & Hawkes, 1951. Song: M, pf.

"There came a Day at Summer's full" [J. 322]. *Poems of Emily Dickinson* (1890).

> 947 Bacon, Ernst. "There Came a Day" in *Nature*. Boston: E.C. Schirmer, 1971. Chorus: SA, pf.

> 948 Laderman, Ezra. n.t. in *Magic Prison*. New York: Oxford Univ. Press, 1970. Melodrama: 2 narr., pf and orch (R). Texts selected by MacLeish.

"There came a Wind like a Bugle" [J. 1593]. *Poems by Emily Dickinson* (1891).

> 949 Bacon, Ernst. "A Wind Like a Bugle" in *Nature*. Boston: E.C. Schirmer, 1971. Chorus: SSAA, pf.

> 950 Bliss, Milton. Evanston, Ill.: Summy-Birchard, u.d. Chorus: SSA, a cap.

> 951 Copland, Aaron. In *Twelve Poems of Emily Dickinson*. New York: Boosey & Hawkes, 1951. Cycle: M, pf.

> 952 Pasatieri, Thomas. In *Far from Love*. Melville, N.Y.: Belwin-Mills, 1976. Cycle: S, cl, vn, vc, pf.

> 953 Perle, George. In *Thirteen Dickinson Songs*. Song: v, pf. Recording: Composers Recordings, CRI SD 403.

"There is a solitude of space" [J. 1695]. *The Single Hound* (1914).

> 954 Bacon, Ernst. "Solitude" in coll. BacFS. Song: C, pf.

> 955 Pierce, Brent. "Solitude of Space." u.p.: Walton, u.d. Setting for SATB, pf.

"There is no Silence in the Earth—so silent" [J. 1004]. *Bolts of Melody* (1945).

956 Leichtling, Alan. "There Is No Silence" in *3 Songs by Emily Dickinson* op. 47 no. 1. New York: Seesaw, 1969. Song: Bar, vc.

"There's a certain Slant of light," [J. 258]. *Poems of Emily Dickinson* (1890).

957 Bacon, Ernst. "Winter Afternoons" in *Nature*. Boston: E.C. Schirmer, 1971. Chorus: SA, pf.

958 Baksa, Robert. In *More Songs to Poems of Emily Dickinson* op. 40. u.p.: Composers Library Editions, 1978. Song: M, pf.

958a Davis, Sharon. In *Three Moods of Emily Dickinson*. Los Angeles: Western International Music, 1981. Song: S, pf trio.

959 Dickinson, Peter. n.t. in *Winter Afternoons*. Sevenoaks, Kent: Novello, 1974. Cantata: AATTBB soli, db.

960 Pinkham, Daniel. n.t. in *Safe in Their Alabaster Chambers*. Boston: Ione Press, 1974. Song: med. v, electronic tape.

"These are the days when Birds come back" [J. 130]. *Poems of Emily Dickinson* (1890).

961 Escher, Rudolf. In *Songs of Love and Eternity*. Amsterdam: Donemus, 1956. Setting for 7–10 mixed voices.

962 Ferris, William. "Indian Summer." New York: Oxford Univ. Press, 1979. Chorus: SATB, pf.

963 Kay, Ulysses. "Indian Summer" in *Emily Dickinson Set*. n.p.: Duchess Music, 1964. Chorus: SSA, pf.

964 McKay, George F. "Indian Summer." New York: G. Schirmer, 1967. Chorus: SSA, pf.

965 Pasatieri, Thomas. "These Are the Days." New York: Belwin-Mills, 1977. Song: high v, pf.

966 Perle, George. In *Thirteen Dickinson Songs*. Song: v, pf. Recording: Composers Recordings, CRI SD 403.

967 Pinkham, Daniel. n.t. in *Safe in Their Alabaster Chambers*. Boston: Ione Press, 1974. Song: med. v, electronic tape.

"These—saw Visions" [J. 758]. *Unpublished Poems of Emily Dickinson* (1935).

968 Farwell, Arthur. "These Saw Vision." New York: Galaxy, 1944. Song: low v, pf.

"This is my letter to the World" [J. 441]. *Poems of Emily Dickinson* (1890).

968a Grantham, Donald. In *Seven Choral Settings of Poems by Emily Dickinson*. Boston: E.C. Schirmer, 1983. Chorus: SATB, a cap. Recording: Composers Recordings, CRI SD 488.

969 Levy, Frank. New York: Seesaw, u.d. Chorus: SATB, a cap.

970 Mennin, Peter. In *Reflections of Emily*. New York: G. Schirmer, 1979. Chorus: SSA, hp, pf, perc.

"This—is the land—the Sunset washes" [J. 266]. *Poems of Emily Dickinson* (1890).

971 Bacon, Ernst. "The Banks of the Yellow Sea" in *Six Songs*. *New Music* (Jan. 1942). Song: A or Bar, pf. In coll. BacT; "Sunset" in coll. BacFS.

972 Farwell, Arthur. "The Sea of Sunset" in *Three Dickinson Poems* op. 26. New York: G. Schirmer, 1928. Song: med. v, pf; In *The Art of Music*. Vol. 14. New York, 1916. Ed. by Daniel G. Mason.

"This quiet Dust was Gentlemen and Ladies" [J. 813]. *The Single Hound* (1914).

973 Weiss, Adolf. "A Cemetery" in *Seven Songs for Soprano and String Quartet*. New York: Composers Facsimile Edn, 1952. Cycle: S, str qrt.

"This was in the White of the Year" [J. 995]. *Complete Poems of Emily Dickinson* (1924).

974 Pasatieri, Thomas. In *Far from Love*. Melville, N.Y.: Belwin-Mills, 1976. Cycle: S, cl, vn, vc, pf.

"'Tis so much joy! 'Tis so much joy!" [J. 172]. *Poems of Emily Dickinson* (1890).

975 Mennin, Peter. "Tis So Much Joy" in *Reflections of Emily*. New York: G. Schirmer, 1979. Chorus: SSA, hp, pf, perc.

"To be alive—is Power" [J. 677]. *The Single Hound* (1914).

976 Pinkham, Daniel. "To Be Alive" in *An Emily Dickinson Mosaic*. New York: C.F. Peters, 1963. Chorus: SSAA, pf or cham orch.

"To fight aloud, is very brave" [J. 126]. *Poems of Emily Dickinson* (1890).

977 Laderman, Ezra. n.t. in *Magic Prison*. New York: Oxford Univ. Press, 1970. Melodrama: 2 narr., pf and orch (R). Texts selected by MacLeish.

"To hear an Oriole sing" [J. 526]. *Poems by Emily Dickinson* (1891).

978 Kunz, Alfred. Waterloo, Ont.: Waterloo Music, 1965. Chorus: SSA, a cap.

"To know just how He suffered—would be dear" [J. 622]. *Poems of Emily Dickinson* (1890).

979 Pasatieri, Thomas. In *Far from Love*. Melville, N.Y.: Belwin-Mills, 1976. Cycle: S, cl, vn, vc, pf.

"To make a prairie it takes a clover and one bee," [J. 1755]. *Poems by Emily Dickinson* (1896).

980 Bacon, Ernst. "To Make a Prairie" in *Five Poems by Emily Dickinson*. New York: G. Schirmer, 1944. Song: high v, pf; "If Bees Are Few" in coll. BacT.

981 Berger, Jean. "To Make a Prairie" in *Three Poems by Emily Dickinson*. New York: Rongwen Music, 1973. Chorus: SATB, pf.

982 Escher, Rudolf. "To Make a Prairie it Takes a Clover" in *Songs of Love and Eternity*. Amsterdam: Donemus, 1956. Setting for 7–10 mixed voices.

983 Perera, Ronald. "To Make a Prairie" in *Five Summer Songs*. Boston: E.C. Schirmer, 1976. Song: S or M, pf.

"To venerate the simple days" [J. 57]. *Poems by Emily Dickinson* (1896).

984 Bacon, Ernst. "Simple Days" in coll. BacT. Song: v, pf.

"Two Butterflies went out at Noon" [J. 533]. *Poems by Emily Dickinson* (1891).

985 Baksa, Robert. In *More Songs to Poems of Emily Dickinson* op. 40. u.p.: Composers Library Editions, 1978. Song: M, pf.

986 Green, Ray. "Butterflies" in *Three Choral Songs*. New York: American Music Edition, 1954. Chorus: SSA, a cap.

987 Kennedy, John B. In *Sails, Robins, and Butterflies*. New York: Boosey & Hawkes, 1966. Chorus: 2-pt. treble voices, a cap.

"Under the Light, yet under," [J. 949]. *Bolts of Melody* (1945).

988 Perle, George. In *Thirteen Dickinson Songs*. Song: v, pf. Recording: Composers Recordings, CRI SD 403.

" 'Unto Me?' I do not know you" [J. 964]. *Further Poems of Emily Dickinson* (1929).

989 Bacon, Ernst. "Unto Me?" in *From Emily's Diary*. New York: G. Schirmer, 1947. Chorus: SSAA, S and A soli, pf.

"Upon Concluded Lives" [J. 735]. *Bolts of Melody* (1945).

990 Green, Ray. "Concluded Lives." New York: American Music Edition, 1962. Song: med. v, pf.

"Water, is taught by thirst" [J. 135]. *Poems by Emily Dickinson* (1896).

991 Bacon, Ernst. "Water" in coll. BacT. Song: v, pf.

"We Cover Thee—Sweet Face" [J. 482]. *Poems by Emily Dickinson* (1896).

992 Bacon, Ernst. "Farewell" in coll. BacFS. Song: M, pf.

"We never know we go when we are going" [J. 1523]. *Poems by Emily Dickinson* (1896).

993 Bacon, Ernst. "We Never Know" in coll. BacFS. Song: M, pf.

"We pray—to Heaven" [J. 489]. *Further Poems of Emily Dickinson* (1929).

994 Bacon, Ernst. "Unto Me?" in *From Emily's Diary*. New York: G. Schirmer, 1947. Cantata: SSAA, pf or cham orch. Second stanza.

"We talked as Girls do" [J. 586]. *Further Poems of Emily Dickinson* (1929).

995 Smith, Russell. In *Three Songs from Emily Dickinson*. New York: F. Colombo, u.d. Chorus: SSA, a cap.

"What if I say I shall not wait!" [J. 277]. *Poems by Emily Dickinson* (1891).

996 Perle, George. In *Thirteen Dickinson Songs*. Song: v, pf. Recording: Composers Recordings, CRI SD 403.

"What Inn is this" [J. 115]. *Poems by Emily Dickinson* (1891).

997 Baksa, Robert. In *Seven Songs to Poems of Emily Dickinson* op. 38 no. 2. u.p.: Composers Library, 1977. Cycle: v, pf.

998 Rorem, Ned. In *Women's Voices*. New York: Boosey & Hawkes, 1979. Cycle: S, pf.

"What Soft—Cherubic Creatures" [J. 401]. *Poems by Emily Dickinson* (1896).

999 Bacon, Ernst. In *From Emily's Dairy*. New York: G. Schirmer, 1947. Chorus: SSAA, S and A soli, pf.

"When I hoped I feared" [J. 1181]. *Poems by Emily Dickinson* (1891).

1000 Luening, Otto. In *Songs to Poems of Emily Dickinson*. New York: Galaxy, 1961. Cycle: med. v, pf.

"When Night is almost done" [J. 347]. *Poems of Emily Dickinson* (1890).

1001 Baksa, Robert. In *More Songs to Poems of Emily Dickinson* op. 40. u.p.: Composers Library Edns., 1978. Song: M, pf.

"When Roses cease to bloom, Sir" [J. 32]. *Poems by Emily Dickinson* (1896).

1002 Bacon, Ernst. "When Roses Cease to Bloom" in *From Emily's Diary*. New York: G. Schirmer, 1947. Chorus: SSAA, S and A soli, pf.

"When they come back—if Blossoms do" [J. 1080]. *Further Poems of Emily Dickinson* (1929).

1003 Copland, Aaron. "When They Come Back" in *Twelve Poems of Emily Dickinson*. New York: Boosey & Hawkes, 1951. Cycle: v, pf.

"Whether my bark went down at sea" [J. 52]. *Poems of Emily Dickinson* (1890).

1004 Kennedy, John B. In *Sails, Robin, and Butterflies*. New York: Boosey & Hawkes, 1966. Chorus: 2-pt. treble voices, a cap.

"Why—do they shut Me out of Heaven?" [J. 248]. *Further Poems of Emily Dickinson* (1929).

1005 Copland, Aaron. In *Twelve Poems of Emily Dickinson*. New York: Boosey & Hawkes, 1951. Cycle: v, pf.

1006 Heilner, Irwin. "Poem." MS, n.d. [comp. 1930, rev. 1972], avail. ACA. Song: med. v, pf.

"Wild Nights—Wild Nights!" [J. 249]. *Poems by Emily Dickinson* (1891).

1007 Bacon, Ernst. "Wild Nights" in coll. BacSE. Song: v, pf.

1007a Davis, Sharon. "Wild Nights" in *Three Moods of Emily Dickinson*. Los Angeles: Western International Music, 1981. Song: S, pf trio.

1008 Escher, Rudolf. "Wild Nights" in *Songs of Love and Eternity*. Amsterdam: Donemus, 1956. Chorus: 7–10 mixed voices.

1009 Golub, Peter. "Wild Nights" in *3 Songs*. MS, 1977, avail. ACA. Song: S, fl, hp.

"Will there really be a 'Morning'?" [J. 101]. *Poems by Emily Dickinson* (1891).

1010 Bacon, Ernst. "Is There Such a Thing As Day?" New York: Associated Music, 1944. Song: med. v, pf.

1011 Persichetti, Vincent. "Out of the Morning" in *Emily Dickinson Songs* op. 77. Philadelphia: Elkan-Vogel, 1958. Song: v, pf.

1012 Willeby, Charles. "Little Pilgrim (A Child's Fancy)." Cincinnati: J. Church, 1907. Song: high and low v edns, pf.

"Without a smile—Without a Throe" [J. 1330]. *Bolts of Melody* (1945).

1012a Grantham, Donald. In *Seven Choral Settings of Poems by Emily Dickinson*. Boston: E.C. Schirmer, 1983. Chorus: SATB, a cap. Recording: Composers Recordings, CRI SD 488.

"You left me—Sire—two Legacies" [J. 644]. *Poems of Emily Dickinson* (1890).

> 1013 Pasatieri, Thomas. "You Left Me, Sweet, Two Legacies" in *Far from Love*. Melville, N.Y.: Belwin-Mills, 1976. Cycle: S, cl, vn, vc, pf.

Miscellaneous

> 1014 Bottje, Will G. "Wayward Pilgrim: A Musical Biography of Emily Dickinson." MS, 1963, avail. ACA. Setting for S, cham chorus, cham orch.

> 1014a Butterworth, Neil. *Letter to the World*. London: Chiltern Music, 1983. Song: Bar, pf.

> 1015 Davis, Sharon. *Three Moods of Emily Dickinson*. Los Angeles: Avant Music, 1977. Song: S, pf, vn, vc.

> 1016 Fine, Vivian. In *The Women in the Garden*. Shaftsbury, Vt.: Catamount Facsimile Edn, 1977. Setting for solo SSMAT, fl, cl, bsn, timp, perc.

> 1017 Hammond, Harold E. "A Book, a Rose, a Prairie." Chicago: C.F. Summy, 1920. Song: v, pf.

> 1018 Kagen, Sergius. "My God, What Is a Heart" in *The Mob Within the Heart*. New York: Mercury, 1956. Song: v, cl or cham orch.

> 1019 Silverman, Faye-Ellen. *In Shadow*. New York: Seesaw, 1973. Song: S, cl, gtr.

> 1020 Weigl, Vally. *Songs of Remembrance*. New York: Composers Facsimile Edn, 1953. Song: M, str qrt; New York: Composers Facsimile Edn, 1957. Song: M, fl, pf, opt cl or vn.

HILDA DOOLITTLE [H.D.] (1886–1961)

Charioteer. *Collected Poems of H.D.* (1925).

> 1021 Robbins, Reginald C. "Charioteer: Epilog." Hollywood: Golden West Music, 1941. Song: high v, pf.

Fire, Flood, and Olive Tree. *Selected Poems* (1957).

> 1022 Nierenberg, Roger. Delaware Water Gap, Pa.: Shawnee, 1975. Chorus: SATB, pf, woodblocks, tom toms, b drum. Text from sec. 4: "Thou hast been slain."

Lethe. *Collected Poems of H.D.* (1925).

  1023 Robbins, Reginald C. Hollywood: Golden West Music, 1941. Song: high v, pf.

Oread. *Collected Poems of H.D.* (1925).

  1024 Fetler, Paul. New York: Associated Music, 1957. Chorus: SATB, a cap.

  1025 Haussermann, John. In *Five Singing Miniatures* op. 12 no. 3. New York: Composers Press, u.d. Song: v, pf.

The Pool. *Collected Poems of H.D.* (1925).

  1026 Becker, John J. MS, 1933, avail. ACA. Chorus: SSA, pf.

Miscellaneous

  1027 Johnston, Jack. "Hymn" in coll. MuENC. Chorus: SATB, org.

PAUL LAURENCE DUNBAR (1872–1906)

Angelina. *Lyrics of the Hearthside* (1899).

  1028 Peycke, Frieda. Chicago: T.S. Denison, 1928.

An Ante-Bellum Sermon. *Majors and Minors* (1895).

  1029 Burleigh, Harry T. In *Plantation Melodies Old and New*. New York: G. Schirmer, 1901. Song: v, pf. Arr. from the tune, "Joshua Fit de Battle ob Jerico." In coll. SM 4.

At Candle-Lightin' Time. *Lyrics of the Hearthside* (1899).

  1030 Coleridge-Taylor, Samuel. "Candle-Lightin' Time." Cincinnati: J. Church, 1911. Song: high and low v edns, pf.

At Sunset Time. *Lyrics of Sunshine and Shadow* (1905).

  1031 Lora, Antonio. MS, u.d., avail. ACA. Song: M, str qrt.

Ballad. *Majors and Minors* (1895).

  1032 Coleridge-Taylor, Samuel. In *African Romances* op. 17 no. 5. London: Augener, 1897. Song: high v, pf.

Beyond the Years. *Majors and Minors* (1895).

    1033 Wendt, Theophil. In *Six Songs*. London: Boosey, 1901. Song: v, pf.

The Boogah Man. *Lyrics of Love and Laughter* (1903).

    1034 Lea, Mary Jordan. Franklin, Ohio: Eldridge Entertainment House, 1910.

Compensation. *Lyrics of Sunshine and Shadow* (1905).

    1035 DiDomenica, Robert. In *Black Poems*. Newton Centre, Mass.: Margun Music, [1976?]. Setting for Bar, pf, tape (R).

    1036 Lloyd, Charles Jr. In coll. PaAS. Song: v, pf.

A Corn-Song. *Majors and Minors* (1895).

    1037 Coleridge-Taylor, Samuel. New York: Boosey, 1897. Song: v, pf, str and hp (R).

Dawn. *Majors and Minors* (1895).

    1038 Coleridge-Taylor, Samuel. In *African Romances* op. 17 no. 4. London: Augener, 1897. Song: high v, pf.

    1039 Hall, Frederick D. In coll. CNA. Song: v, pf.

    1040 Leoni, Franco. "The Birth of Morn." New York: Chappell, 1902.

Day. *Lyrics of Sunshine and Shadow* (1905).

    1041 Cowell, Henry. In *Day, Evening, Night, Morning*. New York: Peer Intl., 1950. Chorus: TTBBB, falsetto or boys' voices ad lib, a cap.

A Death Song. *Lyrics of the Hearthside* (1899).

    1042 Swanson, Howard. New York: Leeds, 1951. Song: med. v, pf. Words both in dialect and in written edited Eng.

Dreamin' Town. *Lyrics of Sunshine and Shadow* (1905).

    1043 Cadman, Charles W. "Come away to Dreaming Town." Chicago: C.F. Summy, 1905. Song: v, pf.

    1044 Hall, Frederick D. "Mandy Lou." Chicago: Homer A. Rodeheaver, 1926. Song: v, pf. In coll. CNA.

    1045 Hier, Ethel G. Cincinnati: Willis Music, 1919. Song: v, pf.

    1046 Riker, Franklin W. "Dreamin' Town or Mandy Lou." New York: T.B. Harms, 1904.

Encouragement. *Lyrics of Love and Laughter* (1903).

> 1047 Sawyer, Henry S. "Speak up, Ike, an' 'Spress Yo'se'f." Chicago: T.S. Denison, u.d.

Evening. *The Complete Poems of Paul Laurence Dunbar* (1913).

> 1048 Cowell, Henry. In *Day, Evening, Night, Morning*. New York: Peer Intl., 1950. Chorus: TTBBB, falsetto or boys' voices ad lib, a cap.

Good-Night. *Majors and Minors* (1895).

> 1049 Boyd, Wynn L. "Slumber Song" in *American Art Songs*. New York: The Golden Eagle Music Publ., 1964. Song: v, pf.
>
> 1050 Smith, N. Clark. In *Two Songs*. Chicago: N.C. Smith, 1923. Song: v, pf and vc obl.

How Shall I Woo Thee. *Majors and Minors* (1895).

> 1051 Coleridge-Taylor, Samuel. In *African Romances* op. 17 no. 7. London: Augener, 1897. Song: high v, pf; single song edn in D, 1898, edn in F, 1902.

A Hymn ["Lead gently, Lord, and slow"]. *Lyrics of the Hearthside* (1899).

> 1052 Boyd, Wynn L. "Lead Gently, Lord" in *American Art Songs*. New York: Golden Eagle Music, 1964. Song: v, pf.

Hymn ["O li'l' lamb out in de col' "]. *Lyrics of the Hearthside* (1899).

> 1053 Haufrecht, Herbert. "O Li'l Lamb." New York: Edwin H. Morris, 1951. Chorus: SATB, a cap; MS, u.d., avail. ACA. Song: med. v, pf.

In May. *Lyrics of Love and Laughter* (1903).

> 1054 Barnett, Alice. Boston: O. Ditson, 1925. Song: high and med. v edns, pf.

Invitation to Love. *Majors and Minors* (1895).

> 1055 English, Granville. New York: Chappell, 1923. Song: v, pf; "Come to My Heart." London: Chappell, 1923.
>
> 1056 Wendt, Theophil. In *Six Songs*. London: Boosey, 1901. Song: v, pf.

Itching Heels. *Lyrics of Love and Laughter* (1903).

> 1057 Koerner, C. In *Spoken Songs*. Cited in ScNS.

Life. *Lyrics of Lowly Life* (1896).

1058 Haufrecht, Herbert. MS, u.d., avail. ACA. Settings for SATB chorus, a cap, and for high or low v, pf.

1059 Salter, Mary T. In *Five Songs*. New York: G. Schirmer, 1916. Song: low v, pf.

Li'l' Gal. *Lyrics of Love and Laughter* (1903).

1060 Johnson, J. Rosamond. New York: Joseph W. Stern, 1902. Song: v, pf; high and low v edns, pf (1917); In coll. CNA, JR.

"Love is the light of the world, my dear." *Lyrics of Love and Laughter* (1903).

1061 Bergh, Arthur. "Love Is the Light of the World" op. 28 no. 2. Cincinnati: J. Church, 1926. Song: med. v, pf.

Love's Apotheosis. *Lyrics of the Hearthside* (1899).

1062 Boyd, Wynn L. "Love's Exaltation" in *American Art Songs*. New York: Golden Eagle Music, 1964. Song: v, pf.

Love's Phases. *Lyrics of the Hearthside* (1899).

1063 Boyd, Wynn L. In *American Art Songs*. New York: Golden Eagle Music, 1964. Song: v, pf.

Lullaby. *Lyrics of the Hearthside* (1899).

1064 Gilchrist, W.W. "Southern Lullaby." Philadelphia: T. Presser, 1897.

A Madrigal. *Majors and Minors* (1895).

1065 Kay, Ulysses. In *Two Dunbar Lyrics*. New York: Duchess Music, 1966. Chorus: SATB, a cap.

The Master-Player. *Lyrics of Lowly Life* (1896).

1066 Coerne, Louis A. "The Master-Player" op. 167 no. 4. Boston: O. Ditson, 1925. Chorus: SATB, pf.

Morning. *Lyrics of Sunshine and Shadow* (1905).

1067 Cowell, Henry. In *Day, Evening, Night, Morning*. New York: Peer Intl., 1950. Chorus: TTBBB, falsetto or boys' voices ad lib, a cap.

A Negro Love Song. *Majors and Minors* (1895).

1068 Dawson, William L. "Jump Back, Honey, Jump Back." Kansas City, Mo.: Wunderlichs Piano, 1923. Song: v, pf.

1069 Gilroth, James. "Seen My Lady Home Las' Night." Boston: De-Bross Pub., u.d.

Night. *Lyrics of Sunshine and Shadow* (1905).

> 1070 Cowell, Henry. In *Day, Evening, Night, Morning*. New York: Peer Intl., 1950. Chorus: TTBBB, falsetto or boys' voices ad lib, a cap.

On the Road. *Lyrics of the Hearthside* (1899).

> 1071 Andrews, M. New York: G. Schirmer, 1913. Song: med. or low v, pf.

Over the Hills. *Lyrics of the Hearthside* (1899).

> 1072 Bauer, Marion. Boston: A.P. Schmidt, 1912. Song: high and med. v edns, pf.

> 1073 Coleridge-Taylor, Samuel. In *African Romances* op. 17 no. 6. London: Augener, 1897. Song: high v, pf; single song edn in B, 1902.

> 1074 Hadley, Henry K. "My Star" op. 9 no. 5. Boston: A.P. Schmidt, 1897. Song: v, pf.

Parted ["De breeze is blowin' cross de bay"]. *Lyrics of the Hearthside* (1899).

> 1075 Cook, Will M. "My Lady" in *Two Negro Ballads*. New York: G. Schirmer, 1914. Song: v, pf.

> 1076 Foster, F. "Sol' Down de Stream" in *Two Songs*. New York: G. Schirmer, 1912. Song: med. and low v edns, pf.

Parted ["She wrapped her soul in a lace of lies"]. *Lyrics of Sunshine and Shadow* (1905).

> 1077 Still, William G. In *Songs of Separation*. New York: Leeds, 1949. Song: v, pf.

A Plea. *Lyrics of Love and Laughter* (1903).

> 1078 Carpenter, John A. "Treat Me Nice." u.p.: Frank K. Root, 1905. Song: 2 v edns; In *Three Songs*. New York: G. Schirmer, 1918. Song: med. v, pf. In coll. BAA.

A Prayer. *Majors and Minors* (1895).

> 1079 Coleridge-Taylor, Samuel. In *African Romances* op. 17 no. 2. London: Augener, 1897. Song: high v, pf.

> 1080 Dett, Robert N. "O Lord, the Hard-Won Miles." New York: G. Schirmer, 1934. Song: high and low v edns, pf.

Response. *Lyrics of Love and Laughter* (1903).

> 1081 Walker, George. u.p.: General, 1971. Song: v, pf.

Riding to Town. *Majors and Minors* (1895).

>1082 Haufrecht, Herbert. MS, u.d., avail. ACA. Chorus: SATB, Bar solo, a cap.

>1083 Kerr, Thomas H., Jr. In coll. PaAS. Song: v, pf.

The Rising of the Storm. *Lyrics of Lowly Life* (1896).

>1084 Smith, David S. Cincinnati: J. Church, 1902. Song: low v, pf.

A Sailor's Song. *Lyrics of the Hearthside* (1899).

>1085 Margetson, Edward. In coll. CNA. Song: v, pf.

Song ["My heart to thy heart"]. *Majors and Minors* (1895).

>1086 Bull, Harry G. "An African Love Song." Keeseville, N.Y.: Ulysses Press, 1954. Song: v, pf.

>1087 Coleridge-Taylor, Samuel. "An African Love Song" in *African Romances* op. 17 no. 1. London: Augener, 1897. Song: high v, pf.

>1088 Nevin, Ethelbert. "An African Love Song." Cincinnati: J. Church, 1901. Song: v, pf.

A Song ["On a summer's day as I sat by a stream"]. *Lyrics of Sunshine and Shadow* (1905).

>1089 Boyd, Wynn L. In *American Art Songs*. New York: Golden Eagle Music, 1964. Song: v, pf.

A Song ["Thou art the soul of a summer's day"]. *Lyrics of Sunshine and Shadow* (1905).

>1090 Ball, Ernest R. "Who Knows?" New York: M. Witmark, 1908. Song: v, pf.

Spring Fever. *Lyrics of Love and Laughter* (1903).

>1091 Koerner, C. In *Spoken Songs*. Cited in ScNS.

A Starry Night. *Majors and Minors* (1895).

>1092 Coleridge-Taylor, Samuel. In *African Romances* op. 17 no. 3. London: Augener, 1897. Song: high v, pf.

>1093 Kay, Ulysses. In *Two Dunbar Lyrics*. New York: Duchess Music, 1966. Chorus: SATB, a cap.

The Sum. *Lyrics of the Hearthside* (1899).

>1094 Carrington, John. "A Little Dreaming by the Way." New York: M. Witmark, 1899.

Two Songs ["Bird of my lady's bower"]. *Lyrics of Lowly Life* (1896).

1095 Smith, David S. "Bird of My Lady's Bower." Cincinnati: J. Church, 1902. Song: high v, pf.

The Valse. *Lyrics of Love and Laughter* (1903).

1096 Koerner, C. In *Spoken Songs*. Cited in ScNS.

When All Is Done. *Lyrics of the Hearthside* (1899).

1097 Boyd, Wynn L. In *American Art Songs*. New York: Golden Eagle Music, 1964. Song: v, pf.

Why Fades a Dream? *Majors and Minors* (1895).

1098 Boyd, Wynn L. In *American Art Songs*. New York: Golden Eagle Music, 1964. Song: v, pf.

1099 Busch, Marie F. Boston: Boston Music, 1954. Song: med.-high v, pf.

Winter's Approach. *Lyrics of Sunshine and Shadow* (1905).

1100 Still, William G. New York: G. Schirmer, 1928. Song: high v, pf.

Miscellaneous

1100a Berger, Jean. "A Crust of Bread" in *Of Life*. New York: C. Fischer, 1975. Choral Cycle: SATB, v solo, instr.

1101 Coleridge-Taylor, Samuel. *Dream Lovers* op. 25. London: Boosey, 1898. Operatic romance.

1101a Cook, Will Marion. *Clorindy, or the Origin of the Cakewalk*. New York: Witmark, 1898.

1102 Cook, Will M. "Down de Lover's Lane." New York: G. Schirmer, 1900. Song: high v, pf.

1103 Cook, Will M. "Good Evenin'." Music Supplement of the *New York American and Journal* (Sunday March 22, 1903).

1104 Cook, Will M. *In Dahomey*. London: Keith, Prowse, 1902. A negro musical comedy with lyrics by Dunbar and others; "On Emancipation Day." New York, Chicago: Harry von Tilzer Music, 1902.

1105 Cook, William M. *Jes Lak White Fo'ks*. New York: Will M. Cook, 1900. A one act Negro Operetta by Cook with additional lyrics by Dunbar; "Evah Dahkey Is a King," as sung by Williams & Walker in Dunbar & Cook's operetta, *In Dahomey*. Music Supplement of Hearst's *Chicago American* (Sunday Oct. 26, 1902). Text in collaboration with E.P. Moran. "Although the title-page states that this song is in *In Dahomey* it does not appear in the 1903 libretto of that musical comedy. The song had prior publication in *Jes Lak White Fo'ks*" [BAL 4941].

1106 Entry cancelled.

1107 Cook, Will M. "Returned." Chicago: Harry von Tilzer Music, u.d. Song: v, pf.

1107a Cook, Will Marion. *Uncle Eph's Christmas.* New York: Will M. Cook and Paul L. Dunbar, 1900. A one act Negro musical sketch.

1108 Hammon, Grace A. "Dusky Sleep-Song." Philadelphia: Presser, 1922.

1109 Jacobs-Bond, Carrie. u.t. in *Love and Sorrow.* Chicago: Bond Shop, 1908. Cycle: Bar, pf.

1110 "Returned." Music Supplement of the *New York American and Journal* (Sunday Sept. 21, 1902). A Negro Ballad as sung by Miss Abbie Mitchell at Mrs. Cornelius Venderbilt's Newport Theater Party [BAL 4940].

1111 "The Tuskegee Song" in *Selected Songs Sung by Students of Tuskegee Normal and Industrial Institute.* Tuskegee, Ala., 1904. It was issued ca. 1905 in sheet music form; originally sung to the tune of "Fair Harvard" until 1907–08 when music was written especially for it by N. Clarke Smith [BAL 4953].

1112 Wendt, Theophil. "A Dream." London: E. Ascherberg, 1904. Song: v, pf. Text: "If life were but a dream of love. . . ."

1113 Wendt, Theophil. "Love's Forgetfulness" in *Six Songs.* London: Boosey, 1901. Song: v, pf.

ROBERT DUNCAN (B. 1919)

Often I Am Permitted to Return to a Meadow. *The Opening of the Field* (1960).

1114 Mellers, Wilfrid. In *The Happy Meadow.* London: Novello, 1964. Cantata: speaker, children's voices, recorder consort, glock, xylo, perc.

T[HOMAS] S[TEARNS] ELIOT (1888–1965)

Gallup, Donald. *T.S. Eliot: A Bibliography.* London: Faber & Faber, 1969 [GEB].

Gooch, Bryan N.S. and Thatcher, David S. *Musical Settings of Late Victorian and Modern British Literature: A Catalogue.* New York: Garland, 1976.

Ash-Wednesday (1930).

> 1115 Crawford, John C. New York: Oxford Univ. Press, 1971 (R). Oratorio: SATB chorus, S and Bar soli, narr.

Burnt Norton. *Collected Poems 1909–1935* (1936).

> 1116 Whear, Paul W. Cleveland: Ludwig Music, u.d. (R). Setting for speaker, fl, ob, 2 cl, 2 hn, vn, db, timp, perc.

Bustopher Jones: The Cat about Town. *Old Possum's Book of Practical Cats* (1939).

> 1117 Rawsthorne, Alan. In *Practical Cats.* London: Oxford Univ. Press, n.d. (R). Setting for speaker, orch. Recording: Angel 30002; New version (unpub.) performed London, May 1971.

Cape Ann. *Two Poems* (1935); Landscapes. 5. *Collected Poems 1909–1935* (1936).

> 1118 Archer, Violet. In *Landscapes.* Waterloo: Waterloo Music, 1973. Chorus: SATB, a cap.

> 1119 Holloway, Robin. "Voices of Birds" in *Five Madrigals.* London: Oxford Univ. Press, 1976. Chorus: SATB, a cap.

> 1120 Paynter, John. In *Landscapes.* London: Oxford Univ. Press, 1972. Choral Suite: SATB, div., a cap, opt ob.

> 1121 Smith, Gregg. In *Landscapes.* New York: G. Schirmer, 1962. Chorus: SATB, a cap.

> 1122 Thomas, Alan. In *Five Landscapes.* Bryn Mawr, Pa.: T. Presser, 1957. Cycle: high v, pf.

> 1123 Young, Douglas. In *Landscapes and Absences.* London: Faber, u.d. (R). Cycle: T, e-hn, with interludes for e-hn and str trio.

East Coker (1940).

> 1124 Whettam, Graham. "The Wounded Surgeon Plies the Steel" op. 41 no. 1. London: Boosey & Hawkes, 1960. Anthem: SATB, a cap. Not issued until 1962 because of an error in the 1960 printing.

Eyes That I Saw Last in Tears. *Collected Poems 1909–1935* (1936).

    1125 Christou, Jani. In *Symphony No. 1*. Rome: DeSantis, [GEB 1953?]. Song in the middle section of the symphony; In *Six Songs for Mezzo-soprano & Orchestra*. Wiesbaden: Impero, [GEB 1959?]. Text in Ger. and Eng.

    1126 Holloway, Robin. In *Five Madrigals*. London: Oxford Univ. Press, 1976. Chorus: AATTBB, a cap.

    1127 McCabe, John. In *Five Elegies*. London: Oxford Univ. Press, u.d. (R). Setting for v, fl, ob, cl, bsn, hn, perc, 2 vn, vla, vc, db.

La Figlia che Piange. *Prufrock and Other Observations* (1917).

    1128 Cone, Edward T. New York: E.B. Marks, u.d. (R). Song: T, cham ens.

    1129 Reif, Paul. New York: General Music, 1957. Song: Bar, pf.

Five-Finger Exercises. *Collected Poems 1909–1935* (1936).

    1130 Reif, Paul. New York: Leslie Productions, 1957. Cycle: Bar, pf. Setting of all five secs.

Four Quartets (1943). *See also* "Burnt Norton," *East Coker,* and *Little Gidding*.

    1131 Pollin, Claire. *Infinito*. New York: Seesaw Music, 1973. Requiem: SATB chorus, S solo, narr., a sax. All quotations from *Four Quartets*.

    1132 Tavener, John. *Sections from T.S. Eliot's "Four Quartets."* Composed 1963–1964. Song: v, pf. Tape: BIRS M 1687 W.

Growltiger's Last Stand. *Old Possum's Book of Practical Cats* (1939).

    1133 Searle, Humphrey. In *Two Practical Cats*. London: Oxford Univ. Press, 1956. Setting for speaker, fl (doubling picc), gtr, vc.

Gus: The Theatre Cat. *Old Possum's Book of Practical Cats* (1939).

    1134 Rawsthorne, Alan. In *Practical Cats*. London: Oxford Univ. Press, n.d. (R). Setting for speaker, orch. Recording: Angel 30002; New version (unpub.) performed London, May 1971.

The Hollow Men. *Poems 1909–1925* (1925).

    1135 ApIvor, Denis. London: Oxford Univ. Press, 1951. Setting for TTBB chorus, Bar solo, orch.

    1136 Baaren, Kees van. Amsterdam: Donemus, 1949. Cantata: chorus, S and Bar soli, small orch.

    1137 Keats, Donald. New York: Boosey & Hawkes, 1976. Chorus: mixed voices, pf.

Journey of the Magi (1927).

    1138 Britten, Benjamin. "Canticle IV: Journey of the Magi" op. 86. London: Faber, 1972. Trio: c-T, T, Bar, pf.

Lines for an Old Man. *Collected Poems 1909–1935* (1936).

    1139 Diamond, David. "For an Old Man." New York: Southern Music Publishing, 1951. Song: v, pf.

Little Gidding (1942).

    1140 Bliss, Arthur. *Shield of Faith*. London: Novello, 1975. Cantata: SATB chorus, S and Bar soli, org. Includes extracts from *Little Gidding*.

    1141 Harvey, Jonathan. London: Novello, 1975. Anthem: SATB, org. Setting of lines beginning, "The dove descending breaks the air. . . ."

    1142 Lourié, Arthur. "The Dove" in *The Third Hour* 4 (1949), pp. 51–58. Song: v, pf.

    1143 Stravinsky, Igor. "Anthem (The Dove Descending Breaks the Air)." London: Boosey & Hawkes, 1962. Chorus: SATB, a cap.

Macavity: The Mystery Cat. *Old Possum's Book of Practical Cats* (1939).

    1144 Searle, Humphrey. In *Two Practical Cats*. London: Oxford Univ. Press, 1956. Setting for speaker, fl (doubling picc), gtr, vc.

Mélange Adultère de Tout. *Poems* (1919).

    1145 Christou, Jani. In *Six Songs for Mezzo-soprano & Orchestra*. Wiesbaden: Impero, [GEB 1959?]. Song: M, orch. Text in Eng. and Ger.

Murder in the Cathedral (1935).

    1146 Buck, Percy. "Dead upon the Tree, My Saviour" in *Hymn Book*. Oxford: Clarendon, 1936. Hymn: v, org. Tune: "Judicum." Setting of lines beginning, "Dead upon the tree my saviour. . . ."

    1147 Fortner, Wolfgang. "Aria." Mainz: B. Schott's, 1951. Aria: M or A, fl, vla, cham orch.

The Naming of Cats. *Old Possum's Book of Practical Cats* (1939).

    1148 Keats, Donald. New York: Boosey & Hawkes, 1962. Setting for SATB, pf.

    1149 Rawsthorne, Alan. In *Practical Cats*. London: Oxford Univ. Press, n.d. (R). Setting for speaker, orch. Recording: Angel 30002; New version (unpub.) performed London, May 1971.

New Hampshire. *Words for Music* (1935); Landscapes. 1. *Collected Poems 1909–1935* (1936).

> 1150 Archer, Violet. In *Landscapes*. Waterloo: Waterloo Music, 1973. Chorus: SATB, a cap.

> 1151 Burt, George. New York: Continuo, 1967. Chorus: double chorus of female voices, a cap.

> 1152 Christou, Jani. In *Six Songs for Mezzo-soprano & Orchestra*. Wiesbaden: Impero, [GEB 1959?]. Song: M, orch. Text in Eng. and Ger.

> 1153 Holloway, Robin. "Children's Voices" in *Five Madrigals*. London: Oxford Univ. Press, 1976. Chorus: SSAA, a cap.

> 1154 Paynter, John. In *Landscapes*. London: Oxford Univ. Press, 1972. Choral Suite: SATB, div., a cap, opt ob.

> 1155 Smith, Gregg. In *Landscapes*. New York: G. Schirmer, 1962. Chorus: SATB, a cap.

> 1156 Thomas, Alan. In *Five Landscapes*. Bryn Mawr, Pa.: T. Presser, 1957. Cycle: high v, pf.

> 1157 Young, Douglas. In *Landscapes and Absences*. London: Faber, u.d. (R). Cycle: T, e-hn, with interludes for e-hn and str trio.

Old Deuteronomy. *Old Possum's Book of Practical Cats* (1939).

> 1158 Rawsthorne, Alan. In *Practical Cats*. London: Oxford Univ. Press, n.d. (R). Setting for speaker, orch. Recording: Angel 30002; New version (unpub.) performed London, May 1971.

The Old Gumbie Cat. *Old Possum's Book of Practical Cats* (1939).

> 1159 Rawsthorne, Alan. In *Practical Cats*. London: Oxford Univ. Press, n.d. (R). Setting for speaker, orch. Recording: Angel 30002; New version (unpub.) performed London, May 1971.

Old Possum's Book of Practical Cats (1939). *See also* under individual titles.

> 1160 Webber, Andrew L. *Cats*. Musical. Lyrics by T.S. Eliot and Trevor Nunn. Recording: Geffen 2GHS 2031, 2017.

Preludes. *Collected Poems 1909–1935* (1936).

> 1161 Rautavaara, Einojuhani. *Two Preludes*. Helsinki: Ylioppilaskunnan Laulajat, 1967. Setting for TTBB div, a cap. Setting of lines beginning, "The winter evening settles down . . .," and "The morning comes to consciousness. . . ."

> 1162 Swanson, Howard. *Four Preludes*. New York: Weintraub, 1952. Song: high v, pf.

Rannoch, by Glencoe [Landscapes. 4]. *Collected Poems 1909–1935* (1936).

1163 Paynter, John. In *Landscapes*. London: Oxford Univ. Press, 1972. Choral Suite: SATB, div., a cap, opt ob.

1164 Smith, Gregg. In *Landscapes*. New York: G. Schirmer, 1962. Chorus: SATB, a cap.

1165 Thomas, Alan. In *Five Landscapes*. Bryn Mawr, Pa.: T. Presser, 1957. Cycle: high v, pf.

1166 Young, Douglas. In *Landscapes and Absences*. London: Faber, u.d. (R). Cycle: T, e-hn, with interludes for e-hn and str trio.

The Rock (1934).

1167 Frith, Michael. "The River Flows, the Seasons Turn." London: Oxford Univ. Press, 1976. Anthem: SATB chorus, S solo, org.

1168 Hanson, Howard. n.t. in *New Land, New Covenant*. New York: C. Fischer, 1976. Chorus: SATB, opt children's chorus, S and Bar soli, narr., org and small orch. Text compliled by Howard C. Kee.

1169 Leighton, Kenneth. u.t. in *The Light Invisible*. London: Novello, 1958. Sinfonia Sacra: SATB chorus, T solo, orch. Setting of lines beginning, "The eagle soars in the summit. . . ."

1170 Shaw, Martin. "The Builders: Song from 'The Rock.' " London: J.B. Cramer, 1934. Chorus: unison voices, pf or orch (R). Also arr. as a part song.

1171 Shaw, Martin. "The Greater Light." London: J. Curwen, 1966. Anthem: double chorus, T solo, org.

1172 Wills, Arthur. "The Light Invisible." London: J. Weinberger, 1976. Chorus: double chorus, perc, harp, org.

The Song of the Jellicles. *Old Possum's Book of Practical Cats* (1939).

1173 Howell, Dorothy. London: Edward Arnold, 1953. Part Song: 2-pt. voices, pf.

1174 Price, Beryl. In *A Cycle of Cats*. London: Oxford Univ. Press, 1972. Chorus: SSA, pf.

1175 Rawsthorne, Alan. In *Practical Cats*. London: Oxford Univ. Press, n.d. (R). Setting for speaker, orch. Recording: Angel 30002; New version (unpub.) performed London, May 1971.

Sweeney Agonistes (1932).

1176 Dankworth, John. London: Faber, u.d. (R). Melodrama: 2 female voices (med. to low), 5 male voices (med. to high), jazz band of cls, tpt, ob, pf, drums.

Usk. *Two Poems* (1935); Landscapes. 3. *Collected Poems 1909–1935* (1936).

 1177 Paynter, John. In *Landscapes*. London: Oxford Univ. Press, 1972. Choral Suite: SATB, div., a cap, opt ob.

 1178 Smith, Gregg. In *Landscapes*. New York: G. Schirmer, 1962. Chorus: SATB, a cap.

 1179 Thomas, Alan. In *Five Landscapes*. Bryn Mawr, Pa.: T. Presser, 1957. Cycle: high v, pf.

 1180 Young, Douglas. In *Landscapes and Absences*. London: Faber, u.d. (R). Cycle: T, e-hn, with interludes for e-hn and str trio.

Virginia. *Words for Music* (1935); Landscapes. 2. *Collected Poems 1909–1935* (1936).

 1181 Christou, Jani. In *Six Songs for Mezzo-soprano & Orchestra*. Wiesbaden: Impero, [GEB 1959?]. Song: M, orch. Text in Eng. and Ger.

 1182 Holloway, Robin. "Red River" in *Five Madrigals*. London: Oxford Univ. Press, 1976. Chorus: SATB, a cap.

 1183 Paynter, John. In *Landscapes*. London: Oxford Univ. Press, 1972. Choral Suite: SATB, div., a cap, opt ob.

 1184 Rathaus, Karol. In *Three Songs*. Bryn Mawr, Pa.: T. Presser, 1959. Song: SATB, a cap.

 1185 Smith, Gregg. In *Landscapes*. New York: G. Schirmer, 1962. Chorus: SATB, a cap.

 1186 Thomas, Alan. In *Five Landscapes*. Bryn Mawr, Pa.: T. Presser, 1957. Cycle: high v, pf.

 1187 Young, Douglas. In *Landscapes and Absences*. London: Faber, u.d. (R). Cycle: T, e-hn, with interludes for e-hn and str trio.

The Waste Land (1922).

 1188 Christou, Jani. "Death by Water" in *Six Songs for Mezzo-soprano & Orchestra*. Wiesbaden: Impero, [GEB 1959?]. Song: M, orch. Text in Eng. and Ger. Setting of sec. 4 of the poem.

 1189 MacInnis, Donald. "From 'The Waste Land' [Part 4, 'Death by Water']." Hollywood: Cameo Music, 1956. Chorus: 2-pt. men's voices.

The wind sprang up at four o'clock. *Collected Poems 1909–1935* (1936).

 1190 Christou, Jani. In *Six Songs for Mezzo-soprano & Orchestra*. Wiesbaden: Impero, [GEB 1959?]. Song: M, orch. Text in Eng. and Ger.

Miscellaneous

1191 Berio, Luciano. *Laborinthus II.* Recording: RCA LSC 3267. Includes words by Eliot.

1192 Joyce, Mary A. *The Passion, Death, and Resurrection of Jesus Christ.* St. Louis: Washington Univ. Press, 1970. Passion: SATB chorus, orch. Includes words by Eliot.

RALPH WALDO EMERSON (1803–1882)

Myerson, Joel. *Ralph Waldo Emerson: A Descriptive Bibliography.* Pittsburgh: Univ. of Pittsburgh Press, 1982.

The Apology. *Poems* (1847).

1193 Schuyler, Georgina. " 'Song' from the Poems of Ralph Waldo Emerson." London: p.p., 1875. Song: v, pf; New York: G. Schirmer, 1882. Song: v, pf; In *Album of Songs by Georgina Schuyler.* New York: G. Schirmer, 1894. Song: med. v, pf.

Bacchus. *Poems* (1847).

1194 McKay, George F. "Bacchanal" in *The Seer.* New York: J. Fischer, 1946. Choral Rhapsody: SSAATTBB, pf.

Brahma. *May-Day and Other Pieces* (1867).

1195 Nevin, Gordon B. New York: G. Schirmer, 1933. Chorus: TTBB, pf.

Concord Hymn. *Selected Poems* (1876).

1196 Beethoven, Ludwig van, arr. from. In coll. LBR, He.

1197 Birge, Edward B. Song: v, pf. In coll. TMT, To.

1198 Jarrett, Jack. In *Choral Rhapsody on American Poems.* New York: C. Fischer, 1970. Chorus: SATB, pf; band or orch (R).

1199 Kent, Richard. New York: Lawson-Gould, 1973. Chorus: SATB, 2 tpt.

1200 Mailman, Martin. "Concord Hymn" op. 20. New York: Mills, 1968. Chorus: SATB, ob (or fl or cl), hp (or pf or gtr).

1201 Ringwald, Roy. In *The Song of America.* East Stroudsburg, Pa.: Shawnee, 1951. Chorus: SATB chorus, narr., pf 4 hands. Recording: Decca, DAU 816; East Stroudsburg, Pa.: Shawnee, 1953. Chorus: men's voices, pf 4 hands.

1202 Ward, Robert. New York: Merrymount, 1949. Chorus: SSATTBB, a cap.

1203 Wood, Kevin. Ft. Lauderdale, Fla.: Plymouth Music, 1981. Chorus: SSAATTBBB(B), a cap.

Days. *May-Day and Other Pieces* (1867).

1204 Bassett, Leslie. n.t. in *Time and Beyond.* New York: C.F. Peters, 1980. Song: Bar, cl, vc, pf.

1205 Gaul, Harvey B. "Daughters of Time." New York: G. Schirmer, 1929. Part Song for male voices, Bar solo, pf 4 hands.

"Dearest, where thy shadow falls." *May-Day and Other Pieces* (1867).

1206 Curtis, Natalie. "Dearest, Where Thy Shadow Falls" op. 1 no. 1. New York: G. Schirmer, 1898. Song: high v, pf.

Each and All. *Poems* (1847).

1207 McKay, George F. "Unto Each and Unto All" in *The Seer.* New York: J. Fischer, 1946. Choral Rhapsody: SSAATTBB, pf.

Fable. *Poems* (1847).

1208 Berger, Jean. "The Mountain and the Squirrel." New York: G. Schirmer, 1958. Chorus: SATB, a cap.

1209 Bucci, Mark. "The Squirrel" in *The Wondrous Kingdom.* n.p.: Duchess Music, 1962. Chorus: SATB, a cap.

1210 Gyring, Elizabeth. MS, u.d., avail. ACA. Song: S, pf.

Fame. *Poems* (1884).

1211 Stoker, Richard. "Aspects 1 in 3." New York: C.F. Peters, 1972. Song: med. v, pf. This piece is 3 contrasting settings of the same poem.

Father in Heaven We Thank Thee. *Grade Teacher* 50 (Nov. 1932), p. 196. Text most certainly not by Emerson.

1212 Ambrose, P. "We Thank Thee" in coll. Mu 3, MuT 2.

1213 George, M.M. "We Thank Thee" in coll. GeS.

1214 Graham, R.Z. "We Thank Thee" in coll. ArF 2.

1215 Jewitt, Jessie Mae. "Father We Thank Thee." New York: M. Witmark, 1914. Song: high and med. v edns, pf. Also pubd for duet: S or T and C or Bar edn; M or T and C or Bar edn.

1216 Sharman, Cecil. "A Spring Prayer." London: Edward Arnold, 1937. Song: unison voices, pf.

Give All to Love. *Poems* (1847).

1217 Rorem, Ned. New York: Boosey & Hawkes, 1981. Chorus: 2-pt. mixed voices, pf.

Good-bye. *Poems* (1847).

1218 Toch, Ernest. "Good-bye, Proud World." Los Angeles: Affiliated Musicians, u.d. Chorus: mixed voices.

Hamatreya [Sec. entitled "Earth-Song"]. *Poems* (1847).

1219 Clarke, Henry L. "Earth Song" in *Four Elements*. MS, 1962, avail. ACA. Song: S, vc.

1220 Erickson, Frank. "Earth-Song." New York: G. Schirmer, 1969.

The Humble-Bee. *Poems* (1847).

1221 "The Humble-Bee" in coll. LBR. Arr. to a German Air.

1222 Neidlinger, W.H. In coll. TL. Chorus: SATB, a cap.

Hymn ["There is in all the sons of men"]. *Poems* (1904).

1223 Smith, Gregg. "Spirit" in *Four Concord Chorales*. New York: G. Schirmer, 1967. Chorus: SATB, org or pf 4 hands. Text by Alicia Smith based on poem by Emerson.

Hymn, Sung at the Second Church, at the Ordination of Rev. Chandler Robbins. *Selected Poems* (1876).

1224 Mason, Lowell. n.t. in coll. ChAH.

Music. *Poems* (1904).

1225 Atherton, Percy Lee. "Let Me Go Where'er I Will" in *Four Songs* op. 15 no. 2. London: Breitkopf & Härtel, 1901. Song: v, pf. Text abridged.

1226 Harold, Thomas. n.p.,n.p., 1912. Song: S and C, pf.

1227 Kay, Ulysses. In *Triumvirate*. New York: Peer, 1954. Chorus: TTBB, a cap.

1228 Kücken, F.W. "The Poet" in coll. LBR. Song: v, pf.

1229 Marshall-Loepke, G. "Sky Born Music" in coll. ArJ.

Nature [Essay]. *The Complete Works of Ralph Waldo Emerson* (1903–1904).

1230 Averre, Dick. "As a Plant upon the Earth." Winona, Minn.: Hal Leonard, 1981. Chorus: SATB, pf. Text from vol. 1 sec. 7, p. 64. Setting of lines beginning: "As a plant upon the earth so a man rests upon the bosom of God. . . ."

1231 Averre, Dick. "If the Stars Should Appear." Winona, Minn.: Hal Leonard, 1981. Chorus: SATB, pf. Text from vol. 1 sec. 1, p. 7. Setting of lines beginning: "If the stars should appear one night in a thousand. . . ."

Ode Inscribed to W.H. Channing. *Poems* (1847).

1232 McKay, George F. "The Scourge" in *The Seer*. New York: J. Fischer, 1946. Choral Rhapsody: SSAATTBB, pf.

Ode Sung in the Town Hall, Concord, July 4, 1857. *May-Day and Other Pieces* (1867).

1233 Bacon, Ernst. "Ode." New York: Mercury, 1951. Chorus: SATB, pf.

On Man & God (1961).

1234 Averre, Dick. "Yes, I Am Willing." Winona, Minn.: Hal Leonard, 1981. Chorus: SA, pf. Setting of lines on page 27 beginning: "Nature wishes that woman should attract man. . . ."

The Snow-Storm. *Poems* (1847).

1235 Husted, Benjamin. "Snow Storm." Cincinnati: World Library, u.d. Chorus: SATB.

1236 Sacco, P. Peter. In *Collected Songs. Vol. 2* op. 136 no. 5. Daly City, Calif.: Ostara Press, 1975. Song: med.-high v, pf; str orch (R).
New York: Lawson-Gould, u.d. Chorus: TTBB, pf; SATB, pf.

Sunrise. *Poems* (1884).

1237 Burleigh, Cecil. "Sunrise" op. 49 no. 4. Cincinnati: J. Church, 1920. Song: high and low v edns, pf.

"Teach me your mood, O patient stars!" *Poems* (1884).

1238 Bassett, Leslie. "Teach Me Your Mood, O Patient Stars" in *Five Love Songs*. Bryn Mawr, Pa.: Merion Music, 1977. Song: S, pf.

Terminus. *May-Day and Other Pieces* (1867).

1239 Ivey, Jean E. New York: C. Fischer, 1972. Song: M, tape. Recording: Folkways, FTS 33439.

Thine eyes still shined. *Poems* (1847).

1240 Kreutzer, Konradin. In coll. LBR. Song: v, pf.

1241 Parry, Hubert. "Thine Eyes Still Shined for Me" in *English Lyrics,* Set 4. London: Novello, Ewer, 1896. Song: v, pf.

1242 Schneider, Edwin. New York: G. Ricordi, 1918. Song: v, pf.

To Ellen, at the South. *Poems* (1847).

1243 Schuyler, Georgina. New York: G. Schirmer, 1882; In *Album of Songs by Georgina Schuyler.* New York: G. Schirmer, 1894. Song: med. v, pf.

Voluntaries [Sec. 3 beginning, "In an age of fops and toys"]. *May-Day and Other Pieces* (1867).

1244 Ives, Charles. "Duty." New York: Mercury, 1933. Song: med. v, pf. In coll. IOS, ITS.

1245 Mendelssohn-Bartholdy, Felix. "Duty" in coll. Mu 3, MuC 3.

Waldeinsamkeit. *May-Day and Other Pieces* (1867).

1246 Mendelssohn, Felix, arr. from. In coll. LBR. Chorus: SATB.

Water. *Poems* (1884).

1247 Bacon, Ernst. New York: Galaxy, 1959. Chorus: SA, pf or org.

Woodnotes. I. *Poems* (1847).

1248 Müller, Wenzel. "Woodnotes" in coll. LBR. Setting for SATB.

Woodnotes. II [Text beginning, "Hearken! Hearken!/ If thou wouldst know the mystic song . . ."]. *Poems* (1847).

1249 McKay, George F. "Mystic Song" in *The Seer.* New York: J. Fischer, 1946. Choral Rhapsody: SSAATTBB, pf.

The World-Soul. *Poems* (1847).

1250 Tracy, G.L. "Thanks to the Morning Light" in coll. ArJ.

Miscellaneous

1251 Felciano, Richard. "Cosmic Festival" in *Two Public Pieces*. Boston: E.C. Schirmer, u.d. Setting for unison voices, electronic tape, opt slides, film, or dancers.

1252 Gartlan, G.H. "A Nation's Builders" in coll. DagA.

1253 Hadley, Henry K. "How Silent, How Spacious" op. 39 no. 1. Boston: A.P. Schmidt, 1904, 1931. Chorus: SSAA, pf.

1254 Korte, Karl. "Marriage" in *Aspects of Love*. Boston: E.C. Schirmer, 1971. Chorus: SA, TB, or SATB, pf.

1255 Smith, Gregg. "Nature" in *Four Concord Chorales*. New York: G. Schirmer, 1967. Chorus: SATB, org or pf 4 hands. Text by Alicia Smith based on poems by Emerson.

1255a "We Sing of Golden Mornings" in coll. UHC. Text loosely based on "The World-Soul."

LAWRENCE FERLINGHETTI (B. 1919)

"Away above a harborful." *Pictures of the Gone World* (1955).

1256 Farr, Ian. In *Pictures*. u.p.: J. Albert & Son (R), 1971. Cycle: S, pf, fl.

Big Fat Hairy Vision of Evil. *Starting from San Francisco* (1967).

1257 Jergenson, Dale. "The Vision." New York: G. Schirmer, 1971. Chorus: full chorus, 7 soli, a cap.

1258 Siegmeister, Elie. In *A Cycle of Cities*. New York: C. Fischer, 1975. Chorus: SATB, S and T soli, pf or orch (R).

"Don't let that horse/ eat that violin." *A Coney Island of the Mind* (1958).

1259 Blank, Allan. New York: Okra Music, 1975. Song: M, bsn. Recording: Composers Recordings, CRI SD 370 (1977).

1260 Yavelow, Christopher. "The Horse with Violin in Mouth." MS, 1975, avail. ACA. Chorus: SSAA, pf or str orch.

"Dove sta amore." *A Coney Island of the Mind* (1958).

1261 Perera, Ronald. Boston: E.C. Schirmer, 1973. Song: S, quadraphonic tape, 2 channel.

"for all I know maybe she was happier." *Pictures of the Gone World* (1955).

> 1262 Farr, Ian. In *Pictures.* u.p.: J. Albert & Son (R), 1971. Cycle: S, pf, fl.

"Fortune/ has its cookies to give out." *Pictures of the Gone World* (1955).

> 1263 Siegmeister, Elie. "Fortune Has Its Cookies" in *A Cycle of Cities.* New York: C. Fischer, 1975. Chorus: SATB, S and T soli, pf or orch (R).

"Terrible a horse at night." *Pictures of the Gone World* (1955).

> 1264 Farr, Ian. In *Pictures.* u.p.: J. Albert & Son (R), 1971. Cycle: S, pf, fl.

"The pennycandy store beyond the El." *A Coney Island of the Mind* (1958).

> 1265 Blank, Allan. New York: Okra Music, 1975. Song: M, bsn. Recording: Composers Recordings, CRI SD 370 (1977).

> 1266 Bernstein, Leonard. In *Songfest.* New York: Boosey & Hawkes, 1977. Cycle: SAMTBarB, orch.

JOHN GOULD FLETCHER (1886–1950)

Morton, Bruce. *John Gould Fletcher: A Bibliography.* Kent, Ohio: Kent State Univ. Press, 1979, pp. 112–113 [MoFB].

Blue Symphony. *Goblins and Pagodas* (1916).

> 1267 Bauer, Marion. "Through the Upland Meadows" in *Four Poems* op. 16 no. 1. New York: G. Schirmer, 1924. Song: high v, pf. Text from sec. 2.

> 1268 Elwell, Herbert. *Blue Symphony: Five Songs for Voice and String Quartet.* Fairport, N.Y.: Rochester Music Publishers, 1962. Song: v, str qrt. Texts taken from the 5 secs. of the symphony.

Golden Symphony. *Goblins and Pagodas* (1916).

> 1269 Bauer, Marion. "In the Bosom of the Desert" in *Four Poems* op. 16 no. 4. New York: G. Schirmer, 1924. Song: high v, pf. Text taken from sec. 3 of the symphony.

Lincoln. *Selected Poems* (1938).

1270 Elwell, Herbert. "Lincoln: Requiem Aeternum." New York: Broadcast Music, 1946. Chorus: SATB, Bar solo, pf or orch.

Midsummer Dreams (Symphony in White and Blue). *Goblins and Pagodas* (1916).

1271 Bauer, Marion. "Midsummer Dreams" in *Four Poems* op. 16 no. 3. New York: G. Schirmer, 1924. Song: high v, pf.

Violet Symphony. *Goblins and Pagodas* (1916).

1272 Bauer, Marion. "I Love the Night" in *Four Poems* op. 16 no. 2. New York: G. Schirmer, 1924. Song: high v, pf.

The Yardstick. *Goblins and Pagodas* (1916).

1273 Clarke, Henry L. In *Four Songs for Young Lady*. MS, 1961, avail. ACA. Song: high v, pf.

Miscellaneous

1274 Powell, Laurence. "Arkansas Centennial Office Ode." Boston: Birchard, 1936. Setting in 4-pt. harmony.

1275 Powell, Laurence. "The Weak and Rambling One." Boston: Birchard, 1936. "Words collected by Fletcher, song arranged by Powell. This song was taken down by dictation from the singing of Mrs. Dusenberry of Mena, Arkansas, in 1934" [MoFB].

PHILIP FRENEAU (1752–1832)

America Independent. *The Poems of Philip Freneau* (1902–1907).

1276 Pinkham, Daniel. "Take Warning, Tyrants" in *O Beautiful! My Country*. Boston: Ione Press, 1976. Chorus: SSAATTBB, pf opt.

The Battle of Stonington. *The Poems of Philip Freneau* (1902–1907).

1277 "The Battle of Stonington" In coll. DSO.

Mars and Hymen. *The Poems of Philip Freneau* (1902–1907).

1278 Tepper, Albert. "Song of Thyrsis." Oceanside, N.J.: Boosey & Hawkes, 1979. Chorus: SATB, pf.

Ode. *The Poems of Philip Freneau* (1902–1907).

   1279 Jacobi, Frederick. "Ode to Freedom" in *Three Songs*. New York: Boosey & Hawkes, 1949. Song: med.-high v, pf. Text: "God save the rights of man. . . ."

On the Sleep of Plants. *The Poems of Philip Freneau* (1902–1907).

   1280 Jacobi, Frederick. In *Three Songs*. New York: Boosey & Hawkes, 1955. Song: med.-high v, pf.

Reflections. *The Poems of Philip Freneau* (1902–1907).

   1281 Haufrecht, Herbert. "Speak, for You Must." New York: Peer International, 1952. Chorus: TTBB, a cap. Text: "Left to himself wherever man is found. . . ."

To a Caty-Did. *The Poems of Philip Freneau* (1902–1907).

   1282 Braine, R. "To a Katy-did" in coll. DagI.

The Wild Honey Suckle. *The Poems of Philip Freneau* (1902–1907).

   1283 Jacobi, Frederick. "Elegy" in *Three Songs*. New York: Boosey & Hawkes, 1949. Song: med.-high v, pf.

Miscellaneous

   1284 Avshalomov, Jacob. In *City upon a Hill*. MS, u.d., avail. ACA. Cantata: SATB chorus, speaker, orch.
   1285 Verrall, John. "Colonial Heritage." MS, u.d., avail. ACA. Song: high or low v, pf.

ROBERT FROST (1874–1963)

Acquainted with the Night. *West-Running Brook* (1928).

   1286 Duke, John. New York: Southern Music Publishing, 1964. Song: med. v, pf.
   1287 Freed, Arnold. New York: Boosey & Hawkes, 1965. Song: v, pf.

Birches. *Mountain Interval* (1916).

1288 Reif, Paul. New York: Boosey & Hawkes, 1966. Song: high v, pf.

1289 Spratlan, Lewis. "Prologue" in *Images*. Northampton, Mass.: New Valley Music, 1977. Cycle: S, pf.

Choose Something Like a Star. *Come In* (1943); Take Something Like a Star. *Complete Poems of Robert Frost* (1949).

1290 Thompson, Randall. "Choose Something Like a Star" in *Frostiana*. Boston: E.C. Schirmer, 1959. Chorus: SATB, pf; Boston: E.C. Schirmer, 1971. Chorus: SSAA, pf.

Come In. *A Further Range* (1936).

1291 Thompson, Randall. In *Frostiana*. Boston: E.C. Schirmer, 1959. Chorus: SAA, pf.

Departmental. *A Further Range* (1936).

1292 Berkowitz, Leonard. "Chamber Music." New York: Associated Music, 1968. Chorus: SSA, S solo, vn and vla, or pf.

A Dream Pang. *A Boy's Will* (1913).

1293 Ames, William T. New York: Associated Music, 1946. Song: med. v, pf.

Dust of Snow. *New Hampshire* (1923).

1294 Ames, William T. New York: Seesaw, 1945. Song: high v, pf.

1295 Carter, Elliott. New York: Associated Music, 1947. Song: med. v, pf; In *Three Poems of Robert Frost*. New York: Associated Music, 1975.

Fire and Ice. *New Hampshire* (1923).

1296 Ames, William T. New York: Associated Music, 1944. Song: med. v, pf.

1297 Cowell, Henry. Boston: Boston Music, 1944. Chorus: TTBB, military band, orch, or pf.

1298 Moritz, Edvard. Bryn Mawr, Pa.: Presser, 1939. Song: high v, pf.

1299 Taylor, Clifford. In *Five Songs on English Texts* op. 4 no. 5. New York: Associated Music, 1954. Song: high v, pf.

The Gift Outright. *A Witness Tree* (1942).

1300 Thompson, Randall. In *A Concord Cantata*. Boston: E.C. Schirmer, 1975. Cantata: SATB chorus, pf or orch.

A Girl's Garden. *Mountain Interval* (1916).

1301 Thompson, Randall. In *Frostiana*. Boston: E.C. Schirmer, 1959. Chorus: SAA, pf.

The Hill Wife [Pt. 5, "The Impulse"]. *Mountain Interval* (1916).

1302 Owen, Richard. "The Impulse." New York: General, 1966. Song: med. v, pf.

The Last Word of a Bluebird. *Mountain Interval* (1916).

1303 Duke, John. New York: G. Schirmer, 1959. Song: med. v, pf.

The Line-Gang. *Mountain Interval* (1916).

1304 Carter, Elliott. In *Three Poems of Robert Frost*. New York: Associated Music, 1975. Song: med. v, pf.

A Minor Bird. *West-Running Brook* (1928).

1305 Ames, William T. New York: Associated Music, u.d. Song: med. v, pf.

1306 Behrend, Jeanne. In *Songs*. Philadelphia: J. Behrend, 1943. Song: v, pf.

1307 Dougherty, Celius. In coll. TwAS. Song: M, pf.

Nothing Gold Can Stay. *New Hampshire* (1923).

1308 Ames, William T. New York: Associated Music, 1944. Song: med. v, pf.

1309 Bentz, Cecil. In *Two Short Poems by Robert Frost*. New York: Lawson-Gould, u.d. Chorus: mixed voices, pf.

1310 Spino, Pasquale. Turnersville, N.J.: Standard Music Publishing, 1971. Chorus: SATB, a cap.

Now Close the Windows. *A Boy's Will* (1913).

1311 Murray, Bain. In coll. CASM. Song: med. v, pf.

"Out, Out." *Mountain Interval* (1928).

1312 Phelps, Lewis A. New York: Galaxy, u.d. Song: med. v, cl, pf.

The Pasture. *North of Boston* (1914).

1313 Cowell, Henry. In coll. NVS. Song: high v, pf.

1314 Gordon, Philip. New York: Lawson-Gould, 1958. Chorus: SATB, a cap.

1315 Murray, Bain. In coll. TaCAS. Song: high and low v edns, pf.

1316 Naginski, Charles. In *Four Songs.* New York: G. Schirmer, 1940. Song: med. v, pf. In coll. TaST.

1317 Thompson, Randall. In *Frostiana.* Boston: E.C. Schirmer, 1959. Chorus: TBB, pf.

A Patch of Old Snow. *Mountain Interval* (1916).

1318 Ames, William T. New York: Associated Music, u.d. Song: med. v, pf.

1319 Spino, Pasquale. Turnersville, N.J.: Standard Music Publishing, 1971. Chorus: SATB, a cap.

A Prayer in Spring. *A Boy's Will* (1913).

1320 Canning, Thomas. "O, Give Us Pleasure in the Flowers Today" in coll. ChAH. Hymn.

1321 McKay, George F. New York: J. Fischer, 1950. Chorus: SSAATTBB, S solo, a cap.

1321a Taylor, Cyril V. "Oh, Give Us Pleasure in the Flowers Today" in coll. UHC.

The Road Not Taken. *Mountain Interval* (1916).

1322 Elwell, Herbert. New York: G. Schirmer, 1942. Song: med. or high v, pf.

1323 Thompson, Randall. In *Frostiana.* Boston: E.C. Schirmer, 1959. Chorus: SATB, pf.

The Rose Family. *West-Running Brook* (1928).

1324 Carter, Elliott. New York: Associated Music, 1947. Song: med. v, pf; In *Three Poems of Robert Frost.* New York: Associated, 1975.

The Sound of the Trees. *Mountain Interval* (1916).

1325 Elwell, Herbert. New York: Broadcast Music, 1946. Song: v, pf.

Spring Pools. *West-Running Brook* (1928).

1326 Ames, William T. New York: Associated Music, 1946. Song: high v, pf.

Stopping by Woods on a Snowy Evening. *New Hampshire* (1923).

1327 Diers, Ann M. New York: Galaxy, 1953. Song: med. v, pf.

1328 Duke, John. Song: S, pf. Recording: Cambridge, CRS 2776 (1979).

1329 Glazer, Frank. New York: Broadcast Music, 1946. Song: v, pf.

1330 Gruenberg, Louis. In *Four Songs* op. 24 no. 3. Vienna: Universal Edition, 1927. Song: med. v, pf.

1331 Hoskins, William. MS, u.d., avail. ACA. Song: M, pf.

1332 La Montaine, John. New York: Galaxy, 1963. Song: Bar or M, pf.

1333 Mortensen, Otto. In *Four Songs*. Copenhagen: W. Hansen, 1945. Song: v, pf.

1334 Sargent, Paul. New York: G. Schirmer, 1950. Song: med. v, pf. In coll. CAST.

1335 Schmutz, Albert. New York: Lawson-Gould, u.d. Chorus: SATB, a cap.

1336 Thompson, Randall. In *Frostiana*. Boston: E.C. Schirmer, 1959. Chorus: TBB, pf.

The Telephone. *Mountain Interval.* (1916).

1337 Birch, Robert F. "Voices" op. 34 no. 3. New York: J. Patelson, 1959. Duet: Bar and M, pf.

1338 Thompson, Randall. In *Frostiana*. Boston: E.C. Schirmer, 1959. Chorus: SAATTBB, pf.

To the Thawing Wind. *A Boy's Will* (1913).

1339 Duke, John. New York: Southern Music Publishing, 1964. Song: v, pf.

Tree at My Window. *West-Running Brook* (1928).

1340 Jackson, Francis. London: Oxford, 1951. Song.

Waspish. *A Further Range* (1936).

1341 Bentz, Cecil. In *Two Short Poems by Robert Frost.* New York: Lawson-Gould, u.d. Chorus: mixed voices, pf.

ALLEN GINSBERG (B. 1926)

Howl. *Howl and Other Poems* (1959).

1342 White, Michael. "I'm with You in Rockland." In coll. MuENC. Chorus: SATB, a cap.

Sunflower Sutra. *Howl and Other Poems* (1959).

1343 Felciano, Richard. "To Allen Ginsberg," "To Patrick Sweeney" in *Two Hymns to Howl By.* Boston: E.C. Schirmer, 1972. Setting for chorus of equal voices.

PAUL GOODMAN (1911–1972)

Absalom. *The Lordly Hudson* (1962).

1344 Rorem, Ned. New York: Boosey & Hawkes, 1972. Song: med. v, pf.

"Creator of the worlds, O joy" [Little Prayers. 24]. *The Lordly Hudson* (1962).

1345 Rorem, Ned. "Creator of the Worlds" in *Little Prayers.* New York: Boosey & Hawkes, 1976. Chorus: SATB, S and Bar soli, orch.

"Creator spirit, please let your." *Hawkweed* (1967).

1346 Rorem, Ned. "Creator Spirit, Please" in *Little Prayers.* New York: Boosey & Hawkes, 1976. Chorus: SATB, S and Bar soli, orch; "Creator Spirit, Please" in *Three Prayers.* New York: Boosey & Hawkes, 1973. Chorus: SATB.

"Creator Spirit, who dost lightly hover" [Little Prayers. 1]. *The Lordly Hudson* (1962).

1347 Rorem, Ned. In *Three Prayers.* New York: Boosey & Hawkes, 1973. Chorus: SATB; "Creator Spirit Who Dost" in *Little Prayers.* New York: Boosey & Hawkes, 1976. Chorus: SATB, S and Bar soli, orch.

"Father, guide, and lead me stray." *Empire City* (1959).

1348 Rorem, Ned. "Father, Guide and Lead Me" in *Three Prayers.* New York: Boosey & Hawkes, 1973. Chorus: SATB; "Father, Guide and Lead Me" in *Little Prayers.* New York: Boosey & Hawkes, 1976. Chorus: SATB, S and Bar soli, orch.

Four Senseless Little Prayers of Convalescence. *Homespun of Oatmeal Gray* (1969, 1970).

1349 Rorem, Ned. "On all, the wicked and . . ." in *Little Prayers.* New York: Boosey & Hawkes, 1976. Chorus: SATB, S and Bar soli, orch. Setting of the first 8 lines of the text.

"God bless this small home that." *Hawkweed* (1967).

> 1350 Rorem, Ned. "God Bless My Small Home" in *Little Prayers*. New York: Boosey & Hawkes, 1976. Chorus: SATB, S and Bar soli, orch.

"God, I prayed, to me restore." *Hawkweed* (1967).

> 1351 Rorem, Ned. In *Little Prayers*. New York: Boosey & Hawkes, 1976. Chorus: SATB, S and Bar soli, orch.

"How like a wildflower untended" [p. 422]. *Collected Poems* (1973).

> 1352 Rorem, Ned. "For Susan" in *Three Poems of Paul Goodman*. New York: Boosey & Hawkes, 1968. Song: v, pf.

"I thought I woke: the Midnight sun." *The Lordly Hudson* (1962).

> 1353 Rorem, Ned. "The Midnight Sun" in *Four Songs*. Boston: E.C. Schirmer, 1968. Song: med.-high v, pf.

"I waited in the parlor, Lord." *Hawkweed* (1967).

> 1354 Rorem, Ned. "I Waited in the Parlor" in *Little Prayers*. New York: Boosey & Hawkes, 1976. Chorus: SATB, S and Bar soli, orch.

Long Lines ["I opened with my key, to my astonished joy"]. *Hawkweed* (1967).

> 1355 Rorem, Ned. In *Little Prayers*. New York: Boosey & Hawkes, 1976. Chorus: SATB, S and Bar soli, orch.

The Lordly Hudson. *The Lordly Hudson* (1962).

> 1356 Rorem, Ned. New York: Music Press, 1947. Song: med. v, pf. In coll. TaCA.

"My world, my only! as I see" [Little Prayers. 30]. *The Lordly Hudson* (1962).

> 1357 Powell, Mel. n.t. in *Two Prayer Settings*. New York: G. Schirmer, 1964. Song: T, ob, vn, vla, vc.

1943. *The Lordly Hudson* (1962).

> 1358 Rorem, Ned. "What Sparks and Wiry Cries" in *Three Poems of Paul Goodman*. New York: Boosey & Hawkes, 1968. Song: v, pf.

"O God of fire and the secret mus—" [Little Prayers. 12]. *The Lordly Hudson* (1962).

> 1359 Rorem, Ned. "O God of Fire and the Secret" in *Little Prayers*. New York: Boosey & Hawkes, 1976. Chorus: SATB, S and Bar soli, orch.

"Of the millions, I know, who have gone to the grave" [Sentences. 14]. *The Lordly Hudson* (1962).

>1360 Rorem, Ned. u.t. in *The Poets' Requiem*. New York: Boosey & Hawkes, 1976. Chorus: SATB, S solo, pf or orch. Texts compiled by Goodman.

Out of the Tulip Tree. *The Lordly Hudson* (1962).

>1361 Rorem, Ned. "The Tulip Tree" in *Four Songs*. Boston: E.C. Schirmer, 1968. Song: med.-high v, pf.

"Rest well thy weary head and heart" [Little Prayers. 27]. *The Lordly Hudson* (1962).

>1362 Rorem, Ned. "Rest Well" in *Little Prayers*. New York: Boosey & Hawkes, 1976. Chorus: S and Bar soli, orch. There are three separate settings of this text.

Sally's Smile. *The Lordly Hudson* (1962).

>1363 Rorem, Ned. New York: Henmar Press, 1957. Song: high v, pf. In coll. RFA.

"Such beauty as hurts to behold." *The Lordly Hudson* (1962).

>1364 Rorem, Ned. New York: Henmar Press, 1961. Song: v, pf. In coll. RFA.

Three Little Prayers to Saint Harmony. *Homespun of Oatmeal Gray* (1969, 1970).

>1365 Rorem, Ned. "A Prayer to Saint Harmony" in *Little Prayers*. New York: Boosey & Hawkes, 1976. Chorus: SATB, S and Bar soli, orch.

To Dawn (Manner of Sappho). *The Lordly Hudson* (1962).

>1366 Rorem, Ned. "Dawn" in *Sun*. New York: Boosey & Hawkes, 1969. Cycle: Song: high v, pf or orch (R).

"We see that novices of art" [Little Prayers. 5]. *The Lordly Hudson* (1962).

>1367 Rorem, Ned. "Novices of Art Understate" in *Little Prayers*. New York: Boosey & Hawkes, 1976. Chorus: SATB, S and Bar soli, orch.

Miscellaneous

>1368 Rorem, Ned. "A Sermon on Miracles." New York: Boosey & Hawkes, 1970. Chorus: unison voices, solo v, strings or keyboard.

1369 Rorem, Ned. "Rain in Spring." New York: Boosey & Hawkes, 1956. Song: med. v, pf. Text: "There fell a beautiful clear rain. . . ."

1370 Rorem, Ned. "Clouds" in *Three Poems of Paul Goodman*. New York: Boosey & Hawkes, 1968. Song: v, pf. Text: "So effortlessly we are not given. . . ."

[FRANCIS] BRET[T] HARTE (1836–1902)

Cadet Gray [Sec. 13 of canto 2]. *West Point Tic Tacs* (1878).

1371 Griswold, Gertrude. "Not Yet." London: Boosey, 1904. Song: v, pf.

1372 Millard, Harrison. "Not Yet!" in *West Point Tic Tacs* [pp. 24–25]. Song: v, pf.

Chiquita. *Poems* (1871).

1373 Boott, Francis. Boston: Ditson, 1871. Song: v, pf. In coll. BoS.

Effie [Tit. "Jessie" in *St. Nicholas Magazine*]. *Stories and Poems* (1914).

1374 Allen, N.H. "Jessie" in coll. Pr, p. 139.

1375 Damrosch, Leopold. "Jessie" in coll. Pr, p. 1.

Fate. *Poems* (1871).

1376 Philp, Elizabeth. London: Mills, [BPL 186–?]. Song: v, pf.

1377 Wiles, Cora Y. Cincinnati: Willis Music, 1915. Song: med. v, pf.

A Greyport Legend. *East and West* (1871).

1378 Hascall, W.F. Boston: A.P. Schmidt, 1884. Song: v, pf.

Guild's Signal. *Poetical Works of Bret Harte* (1882).

1379 Henriette. "The Engineer." London: Cunningham, Boosey, [BPL 187–?]. Song: v, pf.

In the Tunnel. *Poems* (1871).

1380 Boott, Francis. "Flynn of Virginia." Boston: O. Ditson, 1870. Song: v, pf. In coll. BoS.

Jim. *Poems* (1871).

1381 Boott, Francis. Boston: O. Ditson, 1871. Song: v, pf. In coll. BoS.

The Mission Bells of Monterey. *Poetical Works of Bret Harte* (1896).

1382 Gounod, Charles. New York: Novello, Ewer, 1887.

Penelope. *Poems* (1871).

1383 "Penelope" in the "Ballon Post" for April 13, 1871. Boston: O. Ditson, 1871. Music topography by Giles and Gould.

Plain Language from Truthful James. *Poems* (1871).

1384 Boott, F. "The Heathen Chinee." Boston: O. Ditson, 1870. Song: v, pf. In coll. BoS. [BAL 7248d.]

1385 Keller, M. "The Heathen Chinee." Boston: J.F. Laughlin, 1871. [BAL 7248h.]

1386 Towner, Charles. "The Heathen Chinee." Chicago: Root & Cady, 1870. Song and Chorus: v, SATB, pf. [BAL 7248c.]

The Reveille. *Lost Galleon* (1867).

1387 Elgar, Edward. London: Novello, 1908. Part Song: TTBB, a cap; London: Novello, 1926. Arr. for SATB, a cap.

1388 Foote, Arthur. Boston: Silver, Burdett, 1920. Setting for 4-pt. mixed voices.

1389 Montell, John B. New York: E. Schuberth, 1918. Song: v, pf.

1390 Read, Gardner. New York: Seesaw Music, u.d. Chorus: SATB, 2 bsn, 4 hn, 4 tpt, 4 trb, tba, timp, perc, org.

The Society upon the Stanislaus. *Poems* (1871).

1391 Boott, Francis. "Upon the Stanislow." Boston: O. Ditson, 1871. Song and Chorus.

Twenty Years. *Poems* (1871).

1392 Boott, Francis. Boston: O. Ditson, 1871. Song: v, pf. In coll. BoS.

Under the Guns. *Stories and Poems* (1914).

1393 Addison, D.C. Cincinnati: J. Church, 1880.

1394 Felt, D.F. New York: Joseph P. Felt, 1881. Song: v, pf.

1395 Hascall, W.F. Boston: A.P. Schmidt, 1884. Song: B, pf.

What the Bullet Sang. *Poetical Works of Bret Harte* (1882).

1396 Henry, Harold. "What the Bullet Sang" op. 13. New York: C. Fischer, 1921. Song: high v, pf.

What the Chimney Sang. *Echoes of the Foot-Hills* (1875).

1397 Griswold, Gertrude. New York: G. Schirmer, 1890. Song: high and med. v edns, pf. [BAL 7515.]

1398 Hopkins, E.G. In coll. LBR.

1399 Remick, E.T. Detroit: E.T. Remick, 1893. Song: v, pf.

Miscellaneous

1400 "The Jolly Switzer." Arr. from a Swiss Air. In coll. TFO, TFR; In coll. ArF 1. Second stanza by K. Lloyd.

1401 Leach, S.W. "Row, Boys, Row!" San Francisco: Salvator Rosa, 1869. The Boat song, as sung in Formosa, at the California Theater, by Mr. Lawrence Barrett, Mr. Leach & chorus. Words by Frank Bret Harte. [BAL 7245.]

1402 Miller, Lillian. "Manuela of La Torre." New York: G. Schirmer, 1904. Song: M or Bar, pf. Text: "Know I not thou mayst be carved upon this olive tree. . . ."

1403 Tucker, Stephen. "That Heathen Chinee and Other Poems Mostly Humorous." London: John C. Hotten, n.d. [BAL 1871].

NATHANIEL HAWTHORNE (1804–1864)

The Ocean. *The Mariner's Library or Voyager's Companion* (1833).

1404 White, Edward L. "The Ocean." Philadelphia: Geo. Willig, 1836. Words from the *Boston Spectator*. Hawthorne's name does not appear on the music [BAL 7579].

ROBERT HILLYER (1895–1961)

George Arents Research Library. Manuscripts Dept. *Robert Silliman Hillyer: A Register of His Papers in the Syracuse University Library.* Syracuse, N.Y.: Syracuse Univ. Library, 1964.

The Assassination. *Pattern of a Day* (1940).

1405 Dello Joio, Norman. New York: C. Fischer, 1949. Song: low v, pf. Text adapted by the composer.

Christmas Eve. *Collected Poems* (1961).

1406 Pinkham, Daniel. Boston: E.C. Schirmer, 1956. Chorus: SATB, a cap.

Early in the Morning. *The Suburb by the Sea* (1952).

1407 Duke, John. "Morning in Paris." New York: C. Fischer, 1956. Song: high v, pf.

1408 Rorem, Ned. New York: Henmar Press, 1958. Song: v, pf. In coll. RFA.

Folk Song: Elegy. *Poems for Music* (1949).

1409 Pinkham, Daniel. "Elegy." Boston: E.C. Schirmer, 1964. Chorus: SATB, a cap. Recording: Composers Recordings, CRI 102; Boston: E.C. Schirmer, 1964. Song: med. v, pf.

Folk Song: The Stars Came. *Poems for Music* (1949).

1410 Ferguson, Edwin E. New York: Associated Music, u.d. Chorus: SSA, pf.

Hickory Hill. *Poems for Music* (1949).

1411 Sargent, Paul. New York: C. Fischer, 1955. Song: med. v, pf.

Madrigal ["Piping Anne and Husky Paul"]. *Poems for Music* (1949).

1412 Pinkham, Daniel. "Piping Ann and Husky Paul." Boston: E.C. Schirmer, 1964. Madrigal: SATB, a cap. Recording: Composers Recordings, CRI 102.

1413 Schwartz, Paul. New York: Broude Bros., 1972. Chorus: SATB, a cap.

Moo! *Collected Poems* (1961).

1414 Kalmanoff, Martin. New York: Broude Bros., 1960. Chorus: SATB, T solo, pf.

Out of Lucretius. *Poems for Music* (1949).

1415 Mollicone, Henry. MS, 1967, avail. ACA. Chorus: SSA, str qrt.

Overheard. *Collected Poems* (1961).

1416 Clarke, Henry L. MS, 1955, avail. ACA. Song: high and low v edns, pf or org.

Serenade. *Collected Poems* (1961).

1417 Robbins, Reginald C. "Lute-Music." Hollywood: Golden West Music, 1941. Song: high v, pf.

1418 Schwartz, Paul. New York: Rongwen Music, 1959. Chorus: SSA, pf.

XXth Century. *The Gates of the Compass* (1930).

1419 Duke, John. In *Two Songs.* u.p.: Valley Music Press, 1948. Song: v, pf.

1420 Kalmanoff, Martin. "Twentieth Century." In coll. TaCAS. Song: high and low v edns, pf.

1421 Leich, Roland. u.p.: Shawnee, 1963. Chorus: SATB, a cap.

1422 Sargent, Paul. New York: Sprague-Colman, 1940. Song: high and low v edns, pf.

Visitants. *Pattern of a Day* (1940).

1423 Dello Joio, Norman. "Visitants at Night" in *Evocations.* New York: E.B. Marks, 1970. Chorus: SATB, pf or orch (R).

Miscellaneous

1424 Adler, Samuel. "Pastoral" in *Contrasts.* u.p.: Mills Music, u.d. Chorus: SATB, a cap.

1425 Baldwin, R.L. "At Anchor" in coll. Gi 2, GiTw. Text beginning, "Quiet now at her mooring. . . ."

1426 Baldwin, R.L. "Morning Song" in coll. Gi 3, GiTh. Text: "Darkness has rolled from the valley lawn. . . ."

1427 Brown, W.E. "The Bold Traveler" in coll. Gi 2, GiTw.

1428 Clokey, Joseph W. "For He Is Risen" op. 54. Boston: C.C. Birchard, 1926. Cantata: mixed chorus, soli, antiphonal chorus of treble voices, pf.
"O Make Our Hearts to Blossom." Boston: C.C. Birchard, 1953. Anthem: SSAATTBB, a cap.

1429 Earhart, W. "At Dawn" in coll. Gi 2, GiTw. Text: "Oh, now I can follow. . . ."

1430 Earhart, W. "Northeaster" in coll. Gi 3, GiTh. Text beginning, "High up the yellow sand. . . ."

1431 Crane-Leavitt. "Days of Brocade" in coll. Gi 3, GiTh.

1432 Hewitt, E. "The Dauntless" in coll. Gi 3, GiTh.

1433 Horsford, A.C. "Outward Bound" in coll. Gi 2, GiTw. Text beginning, "High tide and dawn of day. . . ."

1434 Hosmer, E.S. "Hands and Heart" in coll. Gi 2, GiTw.

1435 Hosmer, E.S. "Pastorale" in coll. Gi 2, GiTw. Text: "Shepherds, leave your hills and brooks. . . ."

1436 Leavitt, H.S. "The Question" in coll. Gi 2, GiTw. Text: "Oh, days should be a playtime. . . ."

1437 "Magic" arr. to a Bohemian Air. In coll. Gi 3, GiTh. Text: "Where have you found the rose. . . ."

1438 Manney, C.F. "On the Shore" in coll. Gi 3, GiTh.

1439 Manney, C.F. "Secrets" in coll. Gi 2, GiTw. Text: "Would you hear the lonely word. . . ."

1440 Mozart, Wolfgang A. "At Close of Day" in coll. Gi 3, GiTh. Text: "Now the wind that turns the mill. . . ."

1441 Pinkham, Daniel. "Evergreen." Boston: Ione Press, 1974. Christmas carol: unison voices, opt tape, and one or more of the following: org, pf, harpsichord, 2 gtrs, hp. Text: "How fine the sweetness from the bow. . . ."

1442 Pinkham, Daniel. "The King and the Shepherds." Boston: Ione Press, 1978. Chorus: SATB, a cap.

1443 Pinkham, Daniel. *The Song of Jephthah's Daughter.* New York: C.F. Peters, 1966. Cantata: SSA chorus, S and Bar soli, pf.

1444 Scott, B.M. "Remembering" in coll. Gi 3, GiTh. Text: "Happy, we still can hold. . . ."

1445 Scott, B.M. "The Sun Turns North" in coll. Gi 3, GiTh. Text: "Oh hearken, oh hearken the south wind is chanting. . . ."

1446 Spencer, R. McC. "The Naiad" in coll. Gi 2, GiTw. Text beginning, "Over the foaming spray. . . ."

1447 Towner, E. "Outdoors and In" in coll. Gi 2, GiTw.

1448 Weidig, A. "The Whippoorwill" in coll. Gi 3, GiTh. Text: "The ghostly hermit thrush is still. . . ."

OLIVER WENDELL HOLMES (1809–1894)

Currier, Thomas Franklin. *A Bibliography of Oliver Wendell Holmes.* Ed. by E.M. Tilton. New York: New York Univ. Press, 1953 [CuBH].

Army Hymn [CuBH pp. 93–97; BAL 8805, 8822]. *Songs in Many Keys* (1862).

> 1449 Dresel, Otto. Boston: G.D. Russell, 1863. Song: v, chorus ad lib, pf 2 or 4 hands.

> 1450 Lwolff, A.T. von. In coll. JSE.

> 1451 Oliver, H.K. In coll. LAASR

> 1452 Peabody, George. Boston: O. Ditson, n.d. [CuBH ca. 1886]. Music with introductory march for military band.

A Ballad of the Boston Tea-Party. *Songs of Many Seasons* (1875).

> 1453 Ringwald, Roy. n.t. in *The Song of America.* u.p.: Shawnee, 1951. Cantata: SATB chorus, narr., pf 4 hands or orch (R). Recording: Decca, DAU 816.

The Ballad of the Oysterman. *Poems* (1836).

> 1454 Bailey, Eben H. "The Young Oysterman." Boston: Miles & Thompson, 1894.

> 1455 Grant-Schaefer, G.A. Boston: A.P. Schmidt, 1929. Cantata: SAB, pf.

> 1456 Hatton, John L. Boston: O. Ditson, 1849. Song: v, pf.

> 1457 Shaw, Mr. "The Tall Young Oysterman." Philadelphia: George Willig, 1842.

> 1458 Stevenson, R. "Love and Oysters." New York: Firth & Hall, [BAL n.d., not after 1831]. Parody on Hero and Leander, written and arranged to the celebrated "Air partant pour la syrie" [BAL 8720].

> 1459 "The Young Oysterman." Arr. from the Air: Son of a Gambolier. In coll. SRW.

The Chambered Nautilus. *The Autocrat of the Breakfast-Table* (1858).

> 1460 Andrews, Mark. "Build Thee More Stately Mansions." New York: G. Schirmer, 1920. Anthem: Mixed qrt, Bar solo, org.
> > New York: G. Schirmer, 1924. Song: high and low v edns, pf.
> > Charles Dews, arr. New York: G. Schirmer, 1933. Setting for unison treble voices, opt A, org.
> > Kenneth Downing, arr. New York: G. Schirmer, 1946. Chorus: SSA, org.

1461 Beach, H.H.A., Mrs. "The Chambered Nautilus" op. 66. Boston: A.P. Schmidt, 1907. Cantata: SSAA chorus, A and C soli, pf and org ad lib.

1462 Farwell, Arthur. "Build Thee More Stately Mansions." Boston: C.C. Birchard, 1901, 1929. Chorus: SATB, pf. Setting for SATB in coll. TL.

1463 Fearis, John S. Chicago: J.S. Fearis, 1921. Cantata: SATB chorus, med. v solo, pf.

1464 Gartlan, George H. u.p.: George Gartlan, 1910.

1465 La Munyon, George. Westerly, R.I.: Geo. La Munyon, 1906. Song: low v, pf.

1466 Miles, Russell H. New York: H.W. Gray, 1944. Cantata: SATB, A and S soli, pf or pf and org (R).

1467 Mueller, Carl F. "Build Thee More Stately Mansions." New York: H. Flammer, 1936. Chorus: SATB, a cap.

1468 Taylor, Deems. "The Chambered Nautilus" op. 7. Boston: O. Ditson, 1914. Cantata: SATB, pf, org and orch.

1469 Young, Gordon. "Build Thee More Stately Mansions" in *Voices in Praise*. u.p.: T. Presser, u.d. Chorus: SATB.

The Comet. *Poems* (1836).

1470 Lang, M.R. In coll. Par 3, ParT 3.

Departed Days. *Poems* [London] (1846).

1471 Fearis, J.S. Chicago: J.S. Fearis, 1908. Song: low v, pf.

An Evening Thought. *Poems* (1836).

1472 Van Antwerp, Yates. Philadelphia: Lee & Walker, [BAL has 1872 and CuBH has 1878 for the same plate number].

Fantasia. *The Poet at the Breakfast-Table* (1872).

1473 Cowen, Frederic H. In *Six Songs*. London: J. Williams, u.d. Song: v, pf.

1474 German, Edward. "Beauteous Morn." London: Novello, 1912. Part Song: SCC; H.A. Chambers, arr. London: Novello, 1933. Part Song: 2 female voices, pf.

1475 Protheroe, Daniel. "Diamond Dew." Chicago: H.T. FitzSimmons, 1925. Chorus: SS or SA, pf.

1476 Rodgers, Sara K. "Kiss My Eyelids." u.p.: Schmidt, 1890. [CuBH, p. 506.]

The Flower of Liberty. *Songs in Many Keys* (1862).

> 1477 Brown, O.B. Boston: Russell & Patee, 1862. Song and Chorus.
>
> 1478 Keens, H.P. "What Flower Is this?" New York: Wm. A. Pond, 1877. Ballad: T, chorus.
>
> 1479 Neidlinger, W.H. Boston: C.C. Birchard, 1904. Setting for SATB in coll. To.
>
> 1480 Treharne, Bryceson. Boston: Boston Music, 1942. Chorus: SAB, pf.
>
> 1481 Wilhelm, Carl. Arr. from the Air: "Die Wacht am Rhein." Setting for SATB in coll. LBR. In coll. He.

Freedom, Our Queen [CuBH p. 524]. *Songs in Many Keys* (1862).

> 1482 Burton, Frederick R. New York: Luckhardt & Belder, 1901.
>
> 1483 Herman, R.L. Boston: A.P. Schmidt, 1918. Setting for S or T, A or Bar. Also pubd for mixed voices, men's voices, and women's trio.
>
> 1484 Howard, Francis E. In *The Knickerbocker Series of School Songs. Book III.* Ed. by F.E. Howard. New York: Novello, Ewer, 1898.
>
> 1485 Page, N.C. In coll. ArJ.
>
> 1486 Paine, John K. New York: Novello, Ewer, 1902. Part Song.
>
> 1487 Parker, Horatio. "Freedom, Our Queen" op. 66 no. 4. New York, Boston, Chicago: Silver, Burdett, 1911. Setting for SSAB or SATB.
>
> 1488 Severns, W.F. In coll. Ea.

From a Bachelor's Private Journal. *Poems* (1836).

> 1489 Hoby, Charles. "Sweet Mary" in *Four Songs.* New York: G. Schirmer, n.d. [BAL 1880–1892].

God Save the Flag! *Songs of Many Seasons* (1875).

> 1490 Louis, L. "Our Flag." Boston: Henry Tolman, 1865.

Hail, Columbia! [CuBH pp. 312–314]. *Before the Curfew, and Other Poems* (1888).

> 1491 Hopkinson, Francis. "The New 'Hail Columbia' " in coll. LAASR. Tune: "The President's March."
>
> 1492 Phile, P. In coll. FSS 5, LAASR, MFS.

The Height of the Ridiculous. *Poems* (1836).

> 1493 Hart, Charles H. Cincinnati: J. Church, 1909. Song: Bar.
>
> 1494 Homer, Sidney. "The Height of the Ridiculous" op. 37 no. 5. New York: G. Schirmer, 1920. Song: high and low v edns, pf.

1495 Williams, C. Lee. London: Novello, 1906. Part Song: TTBB, pf ad lib.

The Hudson. *Songs in Many Keys* (1862).

1496 Lloyd, Thos. Spencer. "Recollections." Washington, Boston: Nathan Richardson, 1855. Song.

Hymn for the Class-Meeting. *Songs of Many Seasons* (1875).

1497 Heward, Leslie. "Choral Song for a Reunion." London: Novello, 1932. Sacred Song: unison voices, org or pf.

1498 Hews, George. n.t. in coll. SmPS. Hymn.

A Hymn of Peace [BAL 8869]. *Songs of Many Seasons* (1875).

1499 Keller, Matthias. Boston: O. Ditson, 1869. Quartet. Adapted to Keller's "American Hymn."
Humphrey Mitchell, arr. "Angel of Peace." Boston: C.C. Birchard, 1915. Setting for SATB. Also pubd for treble voices.
"Angel of Peace" in coll. ArJ, ChAH, FSS 4, GOS 2, LAAS, LAASR, LBR, WCP.

Hymn of Trust. *The Professor at the Breakfast-Table* (1860).

1500 Adams, Carrie B. "Thou Art Near." Dayton, Ohio: Lorenz, 1924. Duet: M and T.

1501 Allen, Nathan H. "O Love Divine" in *Two Sacred Duets*. Boston: H.B. Stevens, 1897; London: S. Lucas, Weber, Pitt & Hatzfeld, 1897. Song: S and T, pf.

1502 Allitsen, Frances. "Hymn of Trust." New York: Boosey, 1903. Song: v, org or harmonium ad lib.

1503 Baker, Henry. n.t. in coll. SmPS. Hymn. In coll. Bo.

1504 Beach, H.H.A., Mrs. "Hymn of Trust" in *Song Album*. Boston: Boston Music, 1891. Song: v, pf; "Hymn of Trust" op. 13. Boston: A.P. Schmidt, 1901. Song: v, pf, vn ad lib.

1505 Hammond, William G. "O Love Divine." Boston: O. Ditson, 1921. Sacred song.

1506 Harvey, Maitland. "O Love Divine." New York: Birdwell Press, 1937. Hymn-Anthem: mixed voices.

1507 Haydn, F.J., arr. from. "O Love Divine" in coll. CSS 1.

1508 Holden, Albert J. "Thou Art Near." New York: Wm. A. Pond, 1883. Song: S and C edns.

1509 MacFarlane, Will C. "O Love Divine." New York: G. Schirmer, 1902. Sacred Duet: SA.

1510 Marshall, Leonard. "Though Long the Weary Way We Tread." Boston: O. Ditson, 1885.

1511 Marston, G.W. "O Love Divine." Boston: A.P. Schmidt, 1900. Song: S or T, pf.

1512 Nevin, George B. "O Love Divine!" Cincinnati: J. Church, 1896. Sacred Song: C.

1513 Oliver, Henry K. "O Love Divine, That Stooped to Share" in coll. ChAH. Hymn.

1514 Plumpton, A. "Thou Art Near." Cincinnati: J. Church, 1875.

1515 Protheroe, Daniel. "O Love Divine." Chicago: H.T. FitzSimmons, 1926. Chorus: mixed voices, org ad lib.

1516 Vance, J.P. "O Love Divine." New York: C.H. Ditson, 1888. Song.

Hymn, Written for the Great Central Fair in Philadelphia, 1864 [CuBH p. 120]. *The Complete Poetical Works of Holmes* (Cambridge Edition) (1895).

1517 Grüber, Franz. Arr. from "Holy Night." Issued as a broadside, June 1864.

Hymn, Written for the Twenty-Fifth Anniversary of the Reorganization of the Boston Young Men's Christian Union. *The Complete Poetical Works of Holmes* [Cambridge Edition] (1895).

1518 Lewis, Leo R. "Our Father! While Our Hearts Unlearn" in coll. ChAH.

An Impromptu, at the Walcker Dinner upon the Completion of the Great Organ for Boston Music Hall in 1863. *The Complete Poetical Works of Holmes* [Cambridge Edition] (1895).

1519 Penfield, S.N. "I Asked Three Little Maidens" in *Five Songs*. Boston: O. Ditson, 1895. Song: T or M, pf.

International Ode: Our Father's Land. *Songs in Many Keys* (1862) [This Ode was sung in unison by twelve hundred children of the public schools to the Air of "God Save the Queen" at the visit of the Prince of Wales to Boston, October 18, 1860.]

1520 Engel, Carl. "God Rest Our Glorious Land." Boston: C.C. Birchard, 1932. Setting for SATB and unison chorus, pf; Boston: C.C. Birchard, 1940. Chorus: SATB and unison chorus, pf or orch (R). 3d verse by David Stevens.

An Invocation [Trans. from the Arabic]. *The Poetical Works of Oliver Wendell Holmes* [Cambridge Edition] (1975).

> 1521 Allen, Nathan H. "Invocation" in *Two Sacred Duets*. Boston: H.B. Stevens, 1897; London: S. Lucas, Weber, Pitt & Hatzfeld, 1897. Song: C and T, org.

The Last Leaf. *Poems* (1836).

> 1522 Clokey, Joseph W. Boston: C.C. Birchard, 1938. Chorus: SATB, a cap.
>
> 1523 Darley, Francis J.S. Philadelphia: A. Fiot, 1850.
>
> 1524 Griswold, D.D. "The Last of the Knickerbockers (or the Last Leaf)." New York: G.B. Demarest, 1855.
>
> 1525 Homer, Sidney. In *Four Songs* op. 14 no. 1. New York: G. Schirmer, 1903. Song: high and low v edns, pf.
>
> 1526 Rinker, Alton. In *American Poets' Suite*. Delaware Water Gap, Pa.: Shawnee, 1968. Chorus: SATB, pf. Arr. by Hawley Ades.

The Last Reader. *Poems* (1836).

> 1527 Ives, Charles. In *New Music* 7 (1933). Song: v, pf. In coll. IOS.

Lexington. *Poems* [Second Issue] (1849).

> 1528 Heath, L. "Battle of Lexington." Boston: O. Ditson, 1858.

L'Inconnue. *Poems* (1836).

> 1529 Hoby, Charles. In *Four Songs*. New York: G. Schirmer, n.d. [BAL 1880-1892].

Lines by a Clerk. *Poems* (1836).

> 1530 Goodrich, A.J. "The Song of a Clerk." New York: C.H. Ditson, 1836.

The Mother's Secret. *The Professor at the Breakfast-Table* (1860).

> 1531 Leshure, John. "The Choral Host." c1926 by Leshure, assigned to A.P. Schmidt, 1927. Chorus: mixed voices.

Never or Now [BAL 8820]. *Songs of Many Seasons* (1875).

> 1532 Culver, Richard. "Now or Never!" Boston: O. Ditson, n.d. [ca. 1862-1863].
>
> 1533 Webster, J.P. "Fill up the Ranks Boys." Chicago: H.M. Higgins, 1862. Song: v, pf.

No Time Like the Old Time. *Before the Curfew, and Other Poems* (1888).

    1534 Bishop, T. Brigham. "The Dear Old Times." San Francisco: Bancroft, Knight, 1879.

    1535 Ford, John. "There Is No Time Like the Old Time." Philadelphia: F.A. North, 1877. Song.

    1536 Gilbert, J.L. Boston: White, Smith, 1878. Song: v, pf.

    1537 Gretchen, A.M. San Francisco: C.M.P. Company, 1879. Song and Chorus. Arr. by Gretchen, from "Joseph in Egypt," 1865.

    1538 Hennings, R.E. "There Is No Time Like the Old Time." Cincinnati: J. Church, 1867. Song and Chorus.

    1539 Hutchinson, Asa B. "There's No Time Like the Old Time." Boston: O. Ditson, 1866. Song and Chorus: voices, pf.

    1540 Leslie, Ernest. Boston: G.D. Russell, 1865. Duet.

    1541 Roe, J.J. "There's No Time Like the Old Time." Toledo, Ohio: W.W. Whitney, 1882. Song and Chorus.

    1542 S.D.S. New York: Beer & Schirmer, 1866. Song.

    1543 Wilson, R. Bruce. New York: Harding's Music Office, n.d. [BAL ca. 1900].

Ode for a Social Meeting. *The Autocrat of the Breakfast-Table* (1858).

    1544 Schlesinger, Sebastian B. "Maidens Who Laughed Thro' the Vines." New York: C.H. Ditson, 1885.

Ode for Washington's Birthday. *Songs in Many Keys* (1862).

    1545 Beethoven, Ludwig van. Boston: O. Ditson, n.d. [BPL 188–?]. Part Song: voices, pf. Music from the Ninth (Choral) Symphony op. 125. N. Clifford Page, arr. Boston: O. Ditson, 1931. Chorus: SATB.
        In coll. LBR.

    1546 Heise, P. In coll. Ea.

    1547 Rossini, Gioacchino. In coll. He.

Old Ironsides. *Poems* [as a part of the Phi Beta Kappa poem "Poetry"]. (1836).

    1548 Klein, Bruno O. Boston: C.C. Birchard, 1914, 1942. Chorus: SATB, pf. In coll. TFC 2, TFG, TMT.

    1549 Lardner, William. In coll. MP, FRM, FRMS.

    1550 "Old Ironsides" in coll. LBR.

    1551 "Old Ironsides" in coll. US.

1552 Royce, Edward. Boston: A.P. Schmidt, 1921. Song: med. v, pf.

1553 Scott, Charles P. Boston: A.P. Schmidt, 1925. Chorus: TTBB, a cap? Boston: A.P. Schmidt, 1925. Chorus: SATB, a cap?

1554 Wilder, Burt G. Boston: O. Ditson, 1912. Song: Bar or B, pf; N. Clifford Page, arr. Boston: O. Ditson, 1916. Part Song for mixed or school voices.

Our Yankee Girls. *Poems* (1836).

1555 Comer, Thomas. "God Bless Our Yankee Girls." Boston: O. Ditson, 1854. Song: v, pf.

1556 King, Charles M. "Our Yankee Girls!" New York: Firth & Hall, 1836.

1557 Kotzschmar, Hermann. "Our Yankee Girls" op. 8. Portland: J.S. Paine, 1852.

The Parting Word. *Poems* [London] (1846).

1558 Hoby, Charles. In *Four Songs.* New York: G. Schirmer, n.d. Song: v, pf.

Questions and Answers. *Poems* [Stereotyped Edition] (1849).

1559 "Questions and Answers" In coll. LAASR.

1560 "The Visions of Morning." In coll. FSS 1.

Song, Written for the Dinner Given to Charles Dickens by the Young Men of Boston, February 1, 1842. *Poems* [London] (1846).

1561 Maeder, James C. "The Stars Their Early Vigils Keep." Boston: W.H. Oakes, 1842. Sung to the Scotch Air "Gramachree" by Dr. Holmes [BAL 8735].

1562 White, E.L. "The Stars Their Early Vigils Keep." Boston: Henry Prentiss, 1842. Adapted to the Scotch Air "Gramachree," with symphonies and accompaniments by White.

Spring Has Come. *The Autocrat of the Breakfast-Table* (1858).

1563 Birge, E.B. In coll. Par 4.

Stanzas. *Poems* (1836).

1564 Cameron, Cecil. "Little Azure Rings." New York: G. Schirmer, 1918. Song: med. v, pf.

1565 Franke-Harling, W. "Meditation" op. 14. Boston: Boston Music, 1912. Song: high and med. v edns, pf.

Star-Spangled Banner [CuBH pp. 519–23; BAL 8806]. *The Poetical Works of Oliver Wendell Holmes* [Cambridge Edition] (1975).

> 1566 Bruen, C., arr. Cleveland: S. Brainard's, 1861. Song and chorus, with additional fifth verse by Holmes.

> 1567 Smith, Edward J. Glenmont, N.Y.: E.J. Smith, 1942. Setting for mixed, women's, men's, adult, or childern's voices in unison, or any combination of these. Also pubd for solo voice.

> 1568 Smith, John S. Boston: O. Ditson, 1861. Song and Chorus: voices, pf. Additional fifth verse by Holmes.

> 1569 "The Star-Spangled Banner." Boston, New York, Chicago: White-Smith Music, 1889. Song & Chorus: voices, pf. Additional verse by Holmes.

Sun and Shadow. *The Autocrat of the Breakfast-Table* (1858).

> 1570 Roney, H.B. "Sun and Shadow (Licht und Schatten)." Detroit: C.J. Whitney, 1871. Setting for qrt, or wrt and chorus. Text in Eng. and Ger.

A Sun-Day Hymn. *The Professor at the Breakfast-Table* (1860).

> 1571 Beazley, William E. "Lord of All Being." Boston: C.W. Thompson, 1911. Sacred Song: v, pf.

> 1572 Elvey, George J. n.t. in coll. SmPS. Hymn.

> 1573 Hatton, John L. "Lord of All Being" in coll. DSC.

> 1574 Linley, Francis. "Lord of All Being" in coll. LBR.

> 1575 Moore, Mary C. "Sun of Our Life" op. 87 no. 3. Los Angeles: W.A. Quincke, 1927. Sacred Song: M or Bar.

> 1576 Oliver, Henry Kemble. "Lord of All Being, Throned Afar." In coll. ChAH.

> 1577 Ritter, G.P. "Lord of All Being." Boston: A.P. Schmidt, 1891.

> 1578 Shepherd, Thomas G. "Lord of All Being." New York: William Maxwell, 1902.

> 1579 Taylor, Virgil C. "Lord of All Being, Throned afar." In coll. BeBBN, LBR, ONAS, SLS.

The Sweet Little Man. *Songs in Many Keys* (1862).

> 1580 "The Sweet Little Man." Arranged to the Air "Bonnie Dundee" in coll. LBR.

To an Insect. *Poems* (1836).

1581 Busch, Carl. "To a Katydid." Philadelphia: T. Presser, 1929. Cantata: children's voices, pf.

1582 "The Katydid." Arr. from a German Air in coll. LBR.

1583 Ritter, G.P. "Katydid." Boston: A.P. Schmidt, 1896. Setting for women's voices.

To Canaan [BAL 8825]. *Songs of Many Seasons* (1875).

1584 Kelly, Eben A. Providence, R.I.: Clapp & Cory, 1862. Song.

1585 Leslie, Ernest. Boston: Russell & Pattee, 1862. Song.

1586 Oliver, Henry K. "To Canaan, or 'Where Are You Going Soldiers?' " Boston: O. Ditson, n.d. Setting for 3 voices.

1587 Thayer, W.E. Boston: O. Ditson, n.d. Song & Chorus.

To the Reverend S.F. Smith, D.D. *The Poetical Works of Oliver Wendell Holmes* [Cambridge Edition] (1975).

1588 Sibley, Luthera A. "One Breath of Song." Boston: Sibley, 1922. Song.

The Toadstool. *Poems* (1836).

1589 Lester, W. In coll. Mu 5, MuC 5, MuT 3.

1590 Wilson, H. Chilver. London: J.B. Cramer, 1898. Song.

Too Young for Love. *Over the Teacups* (1891).

1591 Barraja, Enrico. "Too Young for Love" op. 41 no. 1. New York: C. Fischer, 1917. Song: high and med. v edns, pf.

1592 Kunkel, Charles. Saint Louis: Kunkel Bros., 1890. Song. Text in Ger. and Eng.

1593 Rogers, Clara K. "Too Young for Love" op. 30 no. 2. Boston: A.P. Schmidt, 1893. Song.

1594 Rotoli, Augusto. In *Two Love Songs*. Boston: Boston Music, 1890. Song: high, med., and low v edns, pf.

Under the Violets. *The Professor at the Breakfast-Table* (1860).

1595 Hoby, Charles. In *Four Songs*. New York: G. Schirmer, n.d. Song: v, pf.

Union and Liberty. *Songs in Many Keys* (1862).

1596 Boott, Francis. Boston: O. Ditson, 1894. Chorus: SATB, pf. In coll. BoAS 3.

1597 Brown, O.B. Boston: Russell & Patee, 1862. Song and Chorus.

1598 Coombs, C. Whitney. "Flag of Freedom." New York: H. Flammer, 1917. Song: v, pf; New York: H. Flammer, 1917. Patriotic Song: SATB chorus, pf.

1599 Day, Edgar J. Published for the benefit of the New York Ladies Educational Union, 1862.

1600 Degenhard, Charles G. Toledo: Louis Doebele, 1863.

1601 Kennedy, Walter S.G. Boston: M. Steinert, c1898 by Charles A. Williams. Setting for chorus and S solo.

1602 Kimball, C.E. "Flag of the Heroes." Boston: O. Ditson, 1861.

1603 Parker, Horatio. "Union and Liberty" op. 60. New York: G. Schirmer, 1905. Chorus: SATB, pf.

1604 Perkins, H.S. "Up with the Banner." Chicago: H.M. Higgins, 1863. Song and Chorus.

1605 "Union and Liberty." Philadelphia: Lee & Walker, 1862. Song: v, pf. Melody by John Seltzer, arr. for pf by Edmund Mattoon.

Welcome to the Nations. *The Poetical Works of Holmes* [Household Edition] (1877).

1606 Keller, Matthias. Boston: O. Ditson, 1876. Setting for mixed voices to the music of Keller's "American Hymn."

Miscellaneous

1607 u.t. in *Songs for War Time: German Airs with English Words, for the Army, the Family, and the School.* Boston: Gould and Lincoln, 1863.

RICHARD HOVEY (1864–1900)

"And if he should come again" [Text from act 1 sc. 1]. *The Birth of Galahad* (1898).

1608 Kernochan, Marshall R. "Song of Ylen." New York: Galaxy, 1911. Song: v, pf.

At the Crossroads. *Last Songs from Vagabondia* (1900). Poems by Hovey and Bliss Carman.

1609 Malotte, Albert H. New York: G. Schirmer, 1941. Song: med. v, pf.

Child's Song. *Last Songs from Vagabondia* (1900). Poems by Hovey and Bliss Carman.

1610 Kernochan, Marshall. "A Child's Song." New York: Galaxy, 1914, rev. ed., 1933. Song: high v, pf.

Comrades. *Songs from Vagabondia* (1894). Poems by Hovey and Bliss Carman.

1611 Dunhill, Thomas F. "Comrades" op. 19. London: Ascherberg, Hopwood & Crew, 1912. Song: Bar, pf.

Hanover Winter-Song. *Along the Trail* (1898).

1612 Bullard, Frederic F. "Winter Song." u.p.: Ditson, 1914. Song: T, Bar, B v edns, pf.

Hunting-Song: From "King Arthur." *More Songs from Vagabondia* (1896).

1613 Nordheimer, Albert. "Hunting Song 'Tarantara.'" Toronto, Hamilton, Montreal, London: Nordheimer Piano and Music, 1908. "Although the text is credited to Bliss Carman, the author was Richard Hovey" [BAL 9396].

The Kavanagh. *Songs from Vagabondia* (1894).

1614 Bullard, Frederic F. Boston: O. Ditson, 1901. Song: med. and low v edns, pf; Boston: O. Ditson, 1901. Duet: T and Bar. Also pubd for TBarB trio.

Love in the Winds. *Along the Trail* (1898).

1615 Hageman, Richard. New York: Galaxy, 1941. Song: high v, pf.

The Open Door. *Last Songs from Vagabondia* (1900). Poems by Hovey and Bliss Carman.

1616 Bullard, Frederic F. "Love Me, Love Me Not." Boston: O. Ditson, 1905. Song: high and med. v edns, pf.

The Sea Gypsy. *More Songs from Vagabondia* (1896).

1617 Clough-Leighter, Henry. "Sea Gypsy" op. 65 no. 1. Boston: Boston Music, 1919. Song: Bar, pf.

1618 O'Hara, Geoffrey. New York: Chappell-Harms, 1933. Chorus or Quartet: TTBB, pf.

A Stein Song. *More Songs from Vagabondia* (1896); Spring. *Along the Trail* (1898) and *Dartmouth Lyrics* (1924).

1619 Bullard, Frederic F. "A Stein Song." Boston: O. Ditson, 1896. Song: T, pf; Boston: O. Ditson, 1898. Song: T or Bar edn, and B edn, pf; in coll. CU, MasBS, WC.

1620 Bullard, Frederic F. "When Good Fellows Get Together." Boston: O. Ditson, 1919. Chorus: male voices, pf. Text by Hovey and Bliss Carman.

A Toast. *Songs from Vagabondia* (1894); "Here's a Health to Thee, Roberts." *Dartmouth Lyrics* (1924).

1621 Bullard, Frederic F. Boston: Boston Music, 1897. Song: Bar and B edns, pf.

You Remind me, Sweeting [Text from act 3 sc. 1]. *The Marriage of Guenevere* (1898); "You Remind Me, Sweeting." *Dartmouth Lyrics* (1924).

1622 Bullard, Frederic F. Cincinnati: J. Church, 1900. Song: high and low v edns, pf; also pubd for T and Bar duet, and part song for male voices with T or S solo, a cap.

Miscellaneous

1623 Dello Joio, Norman. "Promise of Spring" in *Evocations*. New York: E.B. Marks, 1970. Chorus: SATB, orch (R). Text: "Hear hear hear o hear the first stirring. . . ."

1624 Ivey, Jean E. "I Dreamed of Sappho" in *Three Songs of Night*. New York: C. Fischer, 1973. Song: S, alto fl, cl, vla, vc, pf, tape. Text: "I dreamed of Sappho on a summer night. . . ."

1625 MacDowell, Edward. "Summer Wind." Boston: A.P. Schmidt, 1902. Setting for women's voices. [BAL 9394.]

WILLIAM DEAN HOWELLS (1837–1920)

The Battle in the Clouds. *Poems* (1873).

1626 Keller, Matthias. Jefferson, Ohio: J.A. Howells, 1864

By the Sea. *Poems* (1873).

1627 Boott, Francis. "The Song of the Sea." New York: C.H. Ditson, 1872. Song: v, pf.

Don't Wake the Children.

> 1628 Bowers, Clarence W. Jefferson, Ohio: J.A. Howells, 1895.

The First Cricket. *Poems* (1873).

> 1629 Boott, Francis. Boston: O. Ditson, 1876. Song: v, pf.

For One Who Killed. *Poems* (1873).

> 1630 Daniels, Mabel W. "Glory and Endless Years" op. 27 no. 1. Boston: A.P. Schmidt, 1921, 1923. Chorus: TTBB, pf.

Gone. *Poems* (1873).

> 1631 MacDowell, Edward. "Folk Song" in *Eight Songs* op. 47 no. 3. Leipzig: Breitkopf & Härtel, 1893, 1906, 1907. Song: v, pf.

Pleasure-Pain. *Poems* (1873).

> 1632 Kjerulf, Halfdan. In coll. LBR.
>
> 1633 MacDowell, Edward. "The Sea" in *Eight Songs* op. 47 no. 7. Leipzig: Breitkopf & Härtel, 1893, 1906, 1907. Song: med. v, pf.

A Sea-Change or Love's Stowaway (1888).

> 1634 Henschel, Isidor Georg. "A Sea Change." Boston: A.P. Schmidt, 1884. Comic opera in 2 acts and an epilogue, pf acc.

Through the Meadows. *Poems* (1873).

> 1635 MacDowell, Edward. "Through the Meadow" in *Eight Songs* op. 47 no. 8. Leipzig: Breitkopf & Härtel, 1893, 1906, 1907. Song: Bar or T, pf.

Miscellaneous

> 1636 Daniels, M. "The Poet's Friends" in coll. Gi 3, Gilm. Text: "The robin sings in the elm. . . ."
>
> 1637 Scollard, W.F. "The Whispering Stream" in coll. ArF 2. Text beginning, "All the long August afternoon. . . ."

[JAMES] LANGSTON HUGHES (1902–1967)

After Many Springs. *The Weary Blues* (1926).

   1638 Raphling, Sam. In *Shadows in the Sun: Eleven Poems by Langston Hughes*. Hastings-on-Hudson, N.Y.: General, 1971. Cycle: v, pf.

Alabama Earth. *The Dream Keeper and Other Poems* (1932).

   1639 Stilson, Harold W. San Pedro, Calif.: H.W. Stilson, 1956.

As I Grew Older. *The Weary Blues* (1926).

   1640 Raphael, Günter. In *My Dark Hands*. Cologne: H. Gerig, 1965. Song: Bar, pf, ob, perc. Text in Eng. and Ger.

Beggar Boy. *The Weary Blues* (1926).

   1641 Piket, Frederick. In *Sea Charm*. New York: Associated Music, 1948. Chorus: SATB, a cap.

   1642 Raphling, Sam. In *Shadows in the Sun: 11 Poems by Langston Hughes*. Hastings-on-Hudson, N.Y.: General, 1971. Cycle: v, pf.

A Black Pierrot. *The Weary Blues* (1926).

   1643 Still, William G. In *Songs of Separation*. New York: Leeds Music, 1949. Song: v, pf.

Blues at Dawn. *Montage of a Dream Deferred* (1951).

   1644 Feather, Leonard. "Blues Fantasy (I Don't Dare Start Thinking in the Morning)." New York: Model Music, 1960.

Blues Fantasy. *The Weary Blues* (1926).

   1645 Carpenter, John A. "The Cryin' Blues" in *Four Negro Songs*. New York: G. Schirmer, 1927. Song: med. v, pf.

Border Line. *Fields of Wonder* (1947).

   1646 Hovey, Serge. In *I, Too, Sing America*. Elkins Park: Music Publications, 1950. Song: v, pf.

   1647 Owens, Robert. "Border Line" op. 24. Munich: Orlando-Musikverlag, 1970. Cycle: v, pf.

Bound No'th Blues. *Fine Clothes to the Jew* (1927).

   1648 Koval, Marian. "Road, Road, Road" in *Oh, What Singers*. Moscow:

Editions de l'Art de l'URSS, 1939. Song: v, pf. Text in Eng. and Russ.

The Breath of a Rose. *13 Against the Odds,* by Edwin Embree (1947), p. 118.

1648a Still, William G. New York: G. Schirmer, 1928. Song: high and med. v edns, pf. In coll. NAA.

Carolina Cabin. *Fields of Wonder* (1947).

1649 Berger, Jean. In *Four Songs.* New York: Broude Bros., 1951. Song: v, pf.

Danse Africaine. *The Weary Blues* (1926).

1650 Muse, Clarence and Connie Bemis. "African Dance." New York: Exclusive Publications, 1939. Song: v, pf.

1651 Work, John W. New York: Ethyl Smith Music, 1951. Chorus: SATB, S solo, pf, perc; New York: Ethyl Smith Music, 1955. Chorus: TTBB, T solo, pf, perc.

Death of an Old Seaman. *The Weary Blues* (1926).

1652 Cohen, Cecil. In coll. PaAS. Song: v, pf.

1653 Piket, Frederick. In *Sea Charm.* New York: Associated Music, 1948. Chorus: SATB, a cap.

Democracy. *One-Way Ticket* (1949).

1654 Heilner, Irwin. MS, 1966, avail. ACA. Song: med. v, gtr.

Desert. *Fields of Wonder* (1947).

1655 Raphael, Günter. In *My Dark Hands.* Cologne: H. Gerig, 1965. Song: Bar, pf, ob, perc. Text in Eng. and Ger.

Desire. *Fields of Wonder* (1947).

1656 Owens, Robert. In *Desire.* Munich: Orlando-Musikverlag, n.d. Cycle: T, pf.

The Dove. *The Panther and the Lash* (1967).

1657 Siegmeister, Elie. In *The Face of War.* New York: C. Fischer, u.d. Recording: Composers Recordings, CRI SD 416 (1979).

Dream. *Fields of Wonder* (1947).

1658 Owens, Robert. In *Desire.* Munich: Orlando-Musikverlag, n.d. Cycle: T, pf.

Dream Deferred. *The Panther and the Lash* (1967).

1659 Brazinski, Frank W. In *Names in Uphill Letters*. In coll. MuENC. Song: Bar or T, unacc.

The Dream Keeper. *The Weary Blues* (1926).

1659a De Jong, Conrad. In *Four Choruses after Langston Hughes*. New York: G. Schirmer, 1966. Chorus: SSA, a cap.

1660 Hovey, Serge. In *I, Too, Sing America*. Elkins Park: Music Publications, 1950. Song: v, pf.

1661 Raphling, Sam. In *Shadows in the Sun: 11 Poems by Langston Hughes*. Hastings-on-Hudson, N.Y.: General, 1971. Cycle: v, pf.

Dream Variation. *The Weary Blues* (1926).

1662 Bonds, Margaret. In *Three Dream Portraits*. New York: G. Ricordi, 1959. Song: high and med. v edns, pf.

Dreams. *The Dream Keeper and Other Poems* (1932).

1662a De Jong, Conrad. In *Four Choruses after Langston Hughes*. New York: G. Schirmer, 1966. Chorus: SSA, a cap.

Dressed Up. *Fine Clothes to the Jew* (1927).

1663 Keyes, Nelson. In coll. MuENC. Chorus: SSA, pf.

Drum. *Selected Poems of Langston Hughes* (1959).

1664 Adler, Samuel. In *Contrasts*. New York: Mills Music, u.d. Chorus: SATB, a cap.

1665 Fetler, Paul. New York: Associated Music, 1957. Chorus: SATB, a cap.

1666 Kagen, Sergius. New York: Mercury, 1954. Song: med. v, pf.

1667 Raphael, Günter. In *My Dark Hands*. Cologne: H. Gerig, 1965. Song: Bar, pf, ob, perc. Text in Eng. and Ger.

1668 Reutter, Hermann. "Trommel" in *Meine dunklen Hände*. Mainz: B. Schott's Söhne, 1958. Song: Bar, pf. Text in Ger. and Eng.

Evenin' Air Blues. *Shakespeare in Harlem* (1942).

1669 Goodloe, Lucille E. Toledo: Langston Hughes & Lucille Goodloe, 1951.

Faithful One. *Fields of Wonder* (1947).

1670 Owens, Robert. In coll. PaAS. Song: med. v, pf.

Feet o' Jesus. *Fine Clothes to the Jew* (1927).

1671 Harper, Toy. "At the Feet of Jesus." New York: C. Fischer, 1947. Song: med. v, pf. Arr. by Hall Johnson.

Genius Child. *Fields of Wonder* (1947).

1672 Owens, Robert. In coll. PaAS. Song: med. v, pf.

God to Hungry Child. *Good Morning Revolution* (1973).

1673 Rzewski, Frederic. "Lullaby: God to a Hungry Child" in *Three Songs*. Setting for Bar, vib, cl. Recording: Folkways, FTS 33903.

Gypsy Man. *Fine Clothes to the Jew* (1927).

1674 Enders, Harvey. New York: Galaxy, 1933. Chorus: SSAA, cl.

Harlem Night Club. *The Weary Blues* (1926).

1675 Carpenter, John A. "Jazz-Boys" in *Four Negro Songs*. New York: G. Schirmer, 1927. Song: med. v, pf. Recording: Desto 7411/412.

Heart. *Fields of Wonder* (1947).

1676 Berger, Jean. In *Four Songs*. New York: Broude Bros., 1951. Song: v, pf.

Homesick Blues. *Fine Clothes to the Jew* (1927).

1677 Donato, Anthony. New York: Mercury, u.d. Chorus: TTBB, a cap.

1678 Koval, Marian. In *Oh, What Singers*. Moscow: Editions de l'Art de l'Urss, 1939. Song: v, pf. Text in Russ. and Eng.

1679 Wolfe, Jacques. "Sad Song in de Air." New York: M.G. Mayer, 1934. Song: v, pf.

I, Too [Epilogue]. *The Weary Blues* (1926).

1680 Bernstein, Leonard. "I, Too, Sing America" in *Songfest*. New York: Boosey & Hawkes, 1977. Cycle: SAMTBarB, orch.

1681 Bonds, Margaret. In *Three Dream Portraits*. New York: G. Ricordi, 1959. Song: high and med. v edns, pf.

1682 Hovey, Serge. "I, Too, Sing America" in *I, Too, Sing America*. Elkins Park: Music Publications, 1950. Song: v, pf.

1683 Mortensen, Otto. In *Four Songs*. Copenhagen: W. Hansen, 1945. Song.

In Time of Silver Rain. *Fields of Wonder* (1947).

> 1684 Berger, Jean. In *Four Songs.* New York: Broude Bros., 1951. Song: v, pf.

> 1685 Owens, Robert. "In Time of Silver Rain" op. 11. Munich: Orlando-Muiskverlag, n.d.

> 1686 Swanson, Howard. New York: Weintraub Music, 1950. Song: high v, pf.

Irish Wake. *The Dream Keeper and Other Poems* (1932).

> 1687 Piket, Frederick. In *Sea Charm.* New York: Associated Music, 1948. Chorus: SATB, a cap.

Joy. *The Weary Blues* (1926).

> 1688 Swanson, Howard. New York: Leeds Music, 1950. Song: med. or low, and high v edns, pf. Recording: American Recording Society, ARS-10 (1953); Music Library Recordings, ML-SP 1–2.

Juliet. *Fields of Wonder* (1947).

> 1689 Owens, Robert. In *Desire.* Munich: Orlando-Musikverlag, n.d. Cycle: T, pf.

Last Call. *New Poems by American Poets,* ed. by Rolfe Humphries (1957).

> 1690a Brazinski, Frank W. In *Names in Uphill Letters* in coll. MuENC. Song: T or Bar, unacc.

Laughers. *Fine Clothes to the Jew* (1927).

> 1690 Koval, Marian. "My People" in *Oh, What Singers.* Moscow: Editions de l'Art de l'URSS, 1939. Song: v, pf. Text in Eng. and Russ.

Life Is Fine. *One-Way Ticket* (1949).

> 1691 Siegmeister, Elie. In *A Cycle of Cities.* New York: C. Fischer, 1975. Chorus: SATB, S and T soli, pf or orch (R).

Lincoln Monument: Washington. *The Dream Keeper and Other Poems* (1932).

> 1692 Raphling, Sam. "Lincoln Monument." New York: Mercury Music, 1932. Song: v, pf; New York: Beekman Music, 1958.

Little Song. *Fields of Wonder* (1947).

> 1693 Berger, Jean. "Lonely People" in *Four Songs.* New York: Broude Bros., 1951. Song: v, pf; New York: Broude Bros., 1970. Chorus: SATB div, a cap, or instr acc. ad lib.

Long Trip. *The Weary Blues* (1926).

    1694 Piket, Frederick. In *Sea Charm*. New York: Associated Music, 1948. Chorus: SATB, a cap.

Madam and the Census Man. *One-Way Ticket* (1949).

    1695 Siegmeister, Elie. In *Madam to You*. New York: Henmar Press, 1975. Cycle: high v, pf.

Madam and the Fortune Teller. *One-Way Ticket* (1949).

    1696 Siegmeister, Elie. In *Madam to You*. New York: Henmar Press, 1975. Cycle: high v, pf.

Madam and the Minister. *One-Way Ticket* (1949).

    1697 Siegmeister, Elie. In *Madam to You*. New York: Henmar Press, 1975. Cycle: high v, pf.

Madam and the Number Writer. *One-Way Ticket* (1949).

    1698 Siegmeister, Elie. "Madam and the Number Runner" in *Madam to You*. New York: Henmar Press, 1975. Cycle: high v, pf.

Madam and the Rent Man. *One-Way Ticket* (1949).

    1699 Siegmeister, Elie. In *Madam to You*. New York: Henmar Press, 1975. Cycle: high v, pf.

Madam and the Wrong Visitor. *One-Way Ticket* (1949).

    1700 Siegmeister, Elie. In *Madam to You*. New York: Henmar Press, 1975. Cycle: high v, pf.

Mama and Daughter. *One-Way Ticket* (1949).

    1701 Siegmeister, Elie. In *Madam to You*. New York: Henmar Press, 1975. Cycle: high v, pf.

Man. *Fields of Wonder* (1947).

    1702 Owens, Robert. In *Desire*. Munich: Orlando-Musikverlag, n.d. Cycle: T, pf.

March Moon. *The Weary Blues* (1926).

    1703 Smith, Hale. In *Beyond the Rim of Day*. New York: E.B. Marks, 1970. Cycle: high v, pf.

Mexican Market Woman. *The Weary Blues* (1926).

1704 Piket, Frederick. In *Sea Charm*. New York: Associated Music, 1948. Chorus: SATB, a cap.

1705 Raphling, Sam. In *Shadows in the Sun: Eleven Poems by Langston Hughes*. Hastings-on-Hudson, N.Y.: General, 1971. Cycle: v, pf.

Militant. *The Panther and the Lash* (1967).

1706 Koval, Marian. "Pride" in *Oh, What Singers*. Moscow: Editions de l'Art de l'URSS, 1939. Song: v, pf. Text in Eng. and Russ.

Minstrel Man. *The Dream Keeper and Other Poems* (1932).

1707 Bonds, Margaret. In *Three Dream Portraits*. New York: G. Ricordi, 1959. Song: high and med. v edns, pf.

1708 Raphael, Günter. In *My Dark Hands*. Cologne: H, Gerig, 1965. Song: Bar, pf, ob, perc. Text in Eng. and Ger.

1709 Reutter, Hermann. "Bänkelsänger" in *Meine dunklen Hände*. Mainz: B. Schott's Söhne, 1958. Song: Bar, pf. Text in Ger. and Eng.

Misery. *Fine Clothes to the Jew* (1927).

1710 Carpenter, John A. "That Soothin' Song" in *Four Negro Songs*. New York: G. Schirmer, 1927. Song: med. v, pf.

Moan. *Fine Clothes to the Jew* (1927).

1711 Harris, Edward. New York: J. Fischer, 1934. Song: v, pf.

Mother to Son. *The Weary Blues* (1926).

1712 Johnson, Hall. New York: C. Fischer, 1970. Song: med.-high v, pf.

1713 Thomas, Frances. "No Crystal Stair." Berkeley, Calif.: Musi-Craft Productions, 1957. Song: v, pf.

The Negro Speaks of Rivers. *The Weary Blues* (1926).

1714 Berger, Jean. "I've Known Rivers." Boston: R.D. Row, 1953. Chorus: male voices, a cap.

1715 Bonds, Margaret. New York: Handy Bros., 1942. Song: v, pf; New York: Handy Bros., 1942. Chorus: SATB, pf.

1716 Swanson, Howard. New York: Leeds, 1949. Song: low v, pf. In coll. PaAS. Recording: Music Library Recordings, ML-SP 1-2; American Recording society, ARS-10 (1953).

1717 Work, John W. "I've Known Rivers." New York: Galaxy, 1955. Chorus: SSAATTBB, a cap.

Night and Morn. *Dream Keeper* (1932).

1718 Keyes, Nelson. In coll. MuENC. Chorus: SSA, M solo, pf.

Night: Four Songs. *Fields of Wonder* (1947).

1719 Hovey, Serge. In *I, Too, Sing America.* Elkins Park: Music Publications, 1950. Song: v, pf.

Night Song. *Fields of Wonder* (1947).

1720 Swanson, Howard. New York: Weintraub, 1950. Song: v, pf. Recording: American Recording Society, ARS-10 (1953).

Official Notice. *The Panther and the Lash* (1967).

1721 Siegmeister, Elie. In *The Face of War.* New York: C. Fischer, u.d. Recording: Composers Recordings, CRI SD 416 (1979).

On a Christmas Night. *The Crisis* 65(10) (1958), p. 616

1721a Huntley, Jobe. New York: Circle Blue Print Co., 1954.

On a Pallet of Straw. *The Crisis* 65(10) (1958), p. 614.

1721b Meyerowitz, Jan. New York: Rongwen Music, 1954. Carol: SSAA chorus, S solo, pf.

Parisian Beggar Woman. *The Dream Keeper and Other Poems* (1932).

1722 Piket, Frederick. In *Sea Charm.* New York: Associated Music, 1948. Chorus: SATB, a cap.

Peace. *The Panther and the Lash* (1967).

1723 Siegmeister, Elie. In *The Face of War.* New York: C. Fischer, u.d. Recording: Composers Recordings, CRI SD 416 (1979).

Pierrot. *The Weary Blues* (1926).

1724 Swanson, Howard. New York: Weintraub, 1950. Song: low v, pf.

Po' Boy Blues. *Fine Clothes to the Jew* (1927).

1725 Koval, Marian. "Po' Boys' Blues" in *Oh, What Singers.* Moscow: Editions de l'art de l'URSS, 1939. Song: v, pf. Text in Eng. and Russ.

Poem (To F.S.). *The Weary Blues* (1926).

1726 Green, Ray. "I Loved My Friend" in *American Artsong Anthology.* Vol. 1. New York: Galaxy, 1982.

1727 Raphling, Sam. In *Shadows in the Sun: Eleven Poems by Langston Hughes.* Hastings-on-Hudson, N.Y.: General, 1971. Cycle: v, pf.

Poème d'Automne. *The Weary Blues* (1926).

1728 Smith, Hale. In *In Memoriam—Beryl Rubenstein.* New York: Galaxy, u.d. Chorus: SATB, cham orch? Recording: Composers Recordings, CRI 182 SD (1964).

Prayer. *Fields of Wonder* (1947).

1729 Kagen, Sergius. New York: Leeds, 1951. Song: med. v, pf.

Quiet Girl. *The Dream Keeper and Other Poems* (1932).

1729a De Jong, Conrad. In *Four Choruses after Langston Hughes.* New York: G. Schirmer, 1966. Chorus: SSA, a cap.

Red Sun Blues. *The Langston Hughes Reader* (1958).

1730 Hague, Albert. New York: Reis Publications, 1957.

Sailor. *The Dream Keeper and Other Poems* (1932).

1731 Piket, Frederick. In *Sea Charm.* New York: Associated Music, 1948. Chorus: SATB, a cap.

Sea Calm. *The Weary Blues* (1926).

1732 Piket, Frederick. In *Sea Charm.* New York: Associated Music, 1948. Chorus: SATB, a cap.

Sea Charm. *The Weary Blues* (1926).

1733 Green, Ray. In *New Music* 7(3) (1934). Chorus: TTBB.

1734 Harris, Edward C. New York: Boosey & Hawkes, 1950. Song: 2 v edns, pf.

1735 Piket, Frederick. In *Sea Charm.* New York: Associated Music, 1948. Chorus: SATB, a cap.

Seascape. *The Weary Blues* (1926).

1736 Piket, Frederick. In *Sea Charm.* New York: Associated Music, 1948. Chorus: SATB, a cap.

Share-Croppers. *Shakespeare in Harlem* (1942).

1737 Rubel, Joseph. New York: Transcontinental Music, 1939. Song: v, pf.

Sick Room. *The Weary Blues* (1926).

1738 Raphling, Sam. In *Shadows in the Sun: Eleven Poems by Langston Hughes.* Hastings-on-Hudson, N.Y.: General, 1971. Cycle: v, pf.

Silhouette. *One-Way Ticket* (1949).

1739 Hovey, Serge. In *I, Too, Sing America.* Elkins Park: Music Publications, u.d. Song: v, pf.

Simply Heavenly. *The Langston Hughes Reader* (1958).

1740 Martin, David. *Simply Heavenly.* Book and Lyrics by Hughes; music and orch. by Martin. Recording: Columbia, OL 5240 (1957).
> "Deep in Love with You." New York: Bourne, 1958. Song: v, pf.
> "Did You Ever Hear the Blues?" New York: Bourne, 1956. Song: v, pf.
> "Gatekeeper of My Castle." New York: Bourne, 1957. Song: v, pf.
> "Good Old Girl." New York: Bourne, 1957. Song: v, pf.
> "I'm Gonna Be John Henry." New York: Bourne, 1957. Song: v, pf.
> "I Want Somebody to Come Home to." New York: Bourne, 1958. Song: v, pf.
> "Let's Ball Awhile." New York: Bourne, 1957.
> "Look for the Morning Star." New York: Bourne, 1957. Song: v, pf.
> "Simply Heavenly." New York: Bourne, 1956. Song: v, pf.
> "A Sweet Worriation." New York: Bourne, 1958. Song: v, pf.
> "When I'm in a Quiet Mood." New York: Bourne, 1957. Song: v, pf.

Snail. *Fields of Wonder* (1947).

1741 Raphael, Günter. In *My Dark Hands.* Cologne: H. Gerig, 1965. Song: Bar, pf, ob, perc. Text in Eng. and Ger.

Soledad (A Cuban Portrait). *The Weary Blues* (1926).

1742 Raphling, Sam. In *Shadows in the Sun: Eleven Poems by Langston Hughes.* Hastings-on-Hudson, N.Y.: General, 1971. Cycle: v, pf.

Song ["Lovely, dark, and lonely one"]. *The Dream Keeper and Other Poems* (1932).

1743 Burleigh, Harry T. "Lovely, Dark, and Lonely One." New York: G. Ricordi, 1935. Song: v, pf.

Song for a Banjo Dance. *The Weary Blues* (1926).

1744 Carpenter, John A. "Shake Your Brown Feet, Honey" in *Four Negro Songs*. New York: G. Schirmer, 1927. Song: med. v, pf.

Song for a Dark Girl. *Fine Clothes to the Jew* (1927).

1745 Moore, Dorothy R. In *Sonnets on Love, Rosebuds, and Death.* New York: Composers Facsimile Edn, 1976. Cycle: S, pf, vn.

1746 Reutter, Hermann. "Lied für eine dunlkles Mädchen" in *Meine dunklen Hände.* Mainz: B. Schott's Söhne, 1958. Song: Bar, pf. Text in Ger. and Eng.

1747 Revueltas, Silvestre. "Canto de una muchacha negra." New York: E.B. Marks, 1948. Song: v, pf. Text in Eng. and Span.

Songs to the Dark Virgin. *The Weary Blues* (1926).

1748 Price, Florence B. New York: G. Schirmer, 1941. Song: med. or high v, pf. In coll. PaAS.

Spirituals. *Fields of Wonder* (1947).

1749 Brazinski, Frank W. In *Names in Uphill Letters.* n coll. MuENC. Song: Bar or T, unacc.

Stars. *Fields of Wonder* (1947).

1750 Brazinski, Frank W. In *Names in Uphill Letters* in coll. MuENC. Song: Bar or T, unacc.

1751 Hovey, Serge. In *I, Too, Sing America.* Elkins Park: Music Publications, 1950. Song: v, pf.

Stony Lonesome. *Selected Poems of Langston Hughes* (1959).

1752 Brazinski, Frank W. In *Names in Uphill Letters* in coll. MuENC. Song: Bar or T, unacc.

Street Scene (1948).

1752a Weill, Kurt. *Street Scene.* New York: Chappell, 1948. An American opera based on Elmer Rice's play. Book by Rice. Lyrics by Hughes. Pf score edn by William Tarrasch. Recording: Columbia, ML 4139 (1947).

   "A Boy Like You." New York: Chappell, 1947. Song: v, pf.
   "Lonely House." New York: Chappell, 1946. Song: v, pf.
   "Moon-Faced, Starry-Eyed." New York: Chappell, 1947. Song: v, pf.

"We'll Go Away Together." New York: Chappell, 1947. Song: v, pf.

"What Good Would the Moon Be." New York: Chappell, 1946. Song: v, pf.

"A Boy Like You," "Lonely House," "Moon-Faced, Starry-Eyed," "We'll Go Away Together," "What Good Would the Moon Be?" in coll. SnKW. Song: v, pf.

Suicide's Note. *The Weary Blues* (1926).

1753 Hibbs, Cleo A. Los Angeles: Saunders Publications, 1933. Song: v, pf.

1754 Raphling, Sam. In *Shadows in the Sun: Eleven Poems by Langston Hughes*. Hastings-on-Hudson, N.Y.: General, 1971. Cycle: v, pf.

Tambourines. *Selected Poems of Langston Hughes* (1959).

1755 Brazinski, Frank W. In *Names in Uphill Letters* in coll. MuENC. Song: Bar or T, unacc.

Tambourines to Glory (1958).

1755a Huntley, Jobe. *Tambourines to Glory*. New York: Chappell, n.d. Book and Lyrics by Hughes. Recording: Folkways Records, FG 3538 (1958).

"As I Go." New York: Kraft Music, 1952. Chorus: mixed voices.

Frances K. Reckling, arr. "God's Got a Way." New York: Chappell, n.d. Song: v, pf.

"Home to God." New York: Chappell, n.d. Song: v, pf.

"I'm Gonna Testify." New York: Chappell, n.d. Song: v, pf.

"Let the Church Say Amen." New York: Chappell, n.d. Song: v, pf.

"Lord Above." New York: Chappell, n.d. Song: v, pf.

"Moon Outside My Window." New York: Chappell, 1964. Song: v, pf.

"Upon This Rock." New York: Chappell, n.d. Song: v, pf.

"When I Touch His Garment." New York: Chappell, n.d. Song: v, pf.

To a Little Lover-Lass Dead. *The Weary Blues* (1926).

1756 Smith, Hale. In *Beyond the Rim of Day*. New York: E.B. Marks, 1970. Cycle: high v, pf.

To the Dark Mercedes of El Palacio de Amor. *The Weary Blues* (1926).

1757 Raphling, Sam. In *Shadows in the Sun: Eleven Poems by Langston Hughes.* Hastings-on-Hudson, N.Y.: General, 1971. Cycle: v, pf.

Troubled Woman. *The Weary Blues* (1926).

1758 Raphling, Sam. In *Shadows in the Sun: Eleven Poems by Langston Hughes.* Hastings-on-Hudson, N.Y.: General, 1971. Cycle: v, pf.

1759 Smith, Hale. In *Beyond the Rim of Day.* New York: E.B. Marks, 1970. Cycle: high v, pf.

Two Kids. *Cuba Libre* (1968).

1759a Smith, Hale. "Two Kids." u.p.: E.B. Marks, 1973. Chorus: SATB, a cap. Text from "Cuba Libre" by Nicolás Guillén, trans. by Hughes and Frederic Carruthers.

War. *The Panther and the Lash* (1967).

1760 Siegmeister, Elie. In *The Face of War.* New York: C. Fischer, u.d. Recording: Composers Recordings, CRI SD 416 (1979).

Water-Front Streets. *The Weary Blues* (1926).

1761 Piket, Frederick. In *Sea Charm.* New York: Associated Music, 1948. Chorus: SATB, a cap.

The Weary Blues. *The Weary Blues* (1926).

1762 Moore, Dorothy R. In coll. PaAS. Song: med. or high v, pf.

When Sue Wears Red. *The Weary Blues* (1926).

1763 Reutter, Hermann. "Wenn Susanna Jones trägt Rot" in *Meine dunklen Hände.* Mainz: B. Schott's, 1958. Song: Bar, pf. Text in Ger. and Eng.

Without Benefit of Declaration. *The Panther and the Lash* (1967).

1764 Siegmeister, Elie. "Listen Here, Joe" in *The Face of War.* New York: C. Fischer, u.d. Recording: Composers Recordings, CRI SD 416 (1979).

Winter Sweetness. *The Dream Keeper and Other Poems* (1932).

1764a De Jong, Conrad. In *Four Choruses after Langston Hughes.* New York: G. Schirmer, 1966. Chorus: SSA, a cap.

Young Bride. *The Weary Blues* (1926).

1765 Raphling, Sam. In *Shadows in the Sun: Eleven Poems by Langston Hughes.* Hastings-on-Hudson, N.Y.: General, 1971. Cycle: v, pf.

Miscellaneous

1766 Adomián, Lan. *Play de Blues.* New York: G. Schirmer, 1979. Choral Cycle: mixed voices, pf.

1767 Amram, David. "Let Us Remember." New York: C.F. Peters, u.d. Cantata: SATB chorus, SATB soli, orch (R). Recording: Sound Recording, LUR 400.

1768 Bonds, Margaret. *The Ballad of the Brown King.* New York: Sam Fox Publishing, 1961. Christmas Cantata: SATB chorus, STBar soli, pf; "Mary Had a Little Baby." New York: Sam Fox Publishing, 1962. Song: v, pf; chorus: SSA, pf (1963).

1769 Bonds, Margaret. "When the Dove Enters In." New York: Sam Fox Publishing, u.d. Song: v, pf.

1770 Entry cancelled.

1771 Feather, Leonard. "Regardless." New York: Model Music, 1960.

1772 Feather, Leonard. "(Lovely Night) Without You." New York: Model Music, 1960.

1773 Hague, Albert. "I Kiss Your Lips." u.p.: Chappell, 1952. Song: v, pf.

1774 Handy, William C. "Golden Brown Blues." New York: W.C. Handy, 1926. Song: v, pf or ukelele.

1775 Handy, William C., and Clarence M. Jones. "Go and Get the Enemy Blues." New York: Handy Bros., 1942. Song: v, pf.

1776 Harper, Emerson. "I'm Marching Down Freedom Road." New York: Musette, 1942. Song: v, pf.
    "Freedom Road." New York: Musette, 1942. Song: v, pf.
    Cornel Tanassy, arr. New York: Musette, 1942. Band score.

1777 Harper, Emerson. "That Eagle." New York: Musette, 1942. Song: v, pf.

1778 Harper, Toy and Langston Hughes. "Grab It and Hold It!" New York: Independent Music Publishers, n.d.

1779 Harper, Toy and La Villa Tullos. "This Is My Land." New York: Musette, 1945.

1780 Heilner, Irwin. "Mammy Sings." MS, u.d., avail. ACA. Song: med. v, pf.

1781 Heyward, Sammy. "Checkin' on the Freedom Train." New York: Handy Bros., 1947. Song: v, pf.

1782 Hughes, Langston. "Freedom Land." New York: Ralph Satz Publications, 1964. Song: v, pf. Words and music by Hughes, as featured in the Hughes Song Play, *Jerico-Jim Crow.*

1783 Entry cancelled.

1784 Entry cancelled.

1785 Huntley, Jobe. "Jesus Is His Name." New York: J. Huntley, 1953. Setting for solo v with chorus acc.

1786 Huntley, Jobe. "Oh Lord, I Want to Be Ready." New York: J. Huntley, 1959. Chorus: mixed voices.

1787 Entry cancelled.

1788 Entry cancelled.

1789 Entry cancelled.

1790 Johnson, Hall. "On the Dusty Road." New York: C. Fischer, 1947. Song: med. v, pf. Work song based on a theme by Toy Harper.

1791 Martin, David. "Don't Put That Washing Out." New York: Independent Music Publishers, n.d.

1792 Meyerowitz, Jan. "How Godly Is the House of God." New York: Rongwen Music, 1959. Chorus: SATB, org or brass ens (org and timp ad lib).

1793 Meyerowitz, Jan. "The Glory Round His Head." New York: Broude Bros., 1953. Cantata of the Resurrection: chorus, soli, orch.
> "My Body and My Blood." New York: Broude Bros., u.d. Chorus: SATB, keybd.
> "Thy Will Be Done." New York: Broude Bros., 1978. Chorus: SATB, keybd.

1794 Entry cancelled.

1795 Moore, Dorothy. "Dream Variation" in *From the Dark Tower*. New York: Composers Facsimile Edn, 1970. Cycle: M, pf, vc; New York: Composers Facsimile Edn, 1972. Setting for M, orch.

1796 Muse, Clarence. "Louisiana." New York: Chappell, 1937. Song: v, pf.

1797 Nordoff, Paul. "Heaven, Heaven, Heaven Is the Place" in coll. ChAH. Hymn.

1798 Schuman, William. "The Lord Has a Child." Bryn Mawr, Pa.: Merion Music, 1957. Song: high and med. v edns, pf; also arr. for chorus: SSA, pf; chorus: SATB, pf or org; In coll. ChAH.

1799 Segure, Roger. "Love Is Like Whiskey." New York: Exclusive Publications, 1938. Song: v, pf.

1800 Segure, Roger. "Night-Time." San Francisco: Sherman Clay, 1936. Song: v, pf.

1801 Siegmeister, Elie. "Chalk Marks on the Sidewalk," "Childhood Memories" in *Two Songs of the City*. u.p.: Alfred Music Publishing, 1978. Song: M or Bar, pf.

1802 Siegmeister, Elie. "A New Wind A-Blowin'." New York: Musette, 1942. Song: v, pf; also arr. for SATB, pf. In coll. DTAR. Text: "There's a brand new wind a-blowin'. . . ."

1803 Entry cancelled.

1804 Smith, Lawrence. "The Spring That Did Not Become Summer." n.p.: Eagle Music, 1951. Song: v, pf.

1805 Smith, Lawrence. "You Took the Sunshine." New York: Cardinal Music, 1952. Song: v, pf.

1806 Entry cancelled.

1807 Tullos, La Villa. "You Know How It Is These Days." New York: Independent Music Publishers, n.d.

1808 Entry cancelled.

1809 Willett, Chappie. " 'Let My People Go' Now!" New York: Text Music, 1944. Chorus: SATB, pf.

WASHINGTON IRVING (1783–1859)

Miscellaneous

1810 Northrup, Theodore H. "A Legende Strange." New York: G. Schirmer, 1891. Song: high and med. v edns, pf.

1811 Perry, George. "The Moorish Drum." New York: Hewitt & Jaques, [1837–1841].

ROBINSON JEFFERS (1887–1962)

Ante Mortem. *Apology for Bad Dreams* (1930).

1812 Huston, Scott. In *Ante Mortem and Post Mortem.* New York: General, u.d. Song: Bar, pf.

Granite and Cypress. *Roan Stallion, Tamar and Other Poems* (1925).

1813 Ames, William. MS, u.d., avail. ACA. Chorus: SATB, orch, timp, perc, hp.

Joy. *Roan Stallion, Tamar and Other Poems* (1925).

1814 Mechem, Kirke. In *The Children of David* op. 37 no. 2. New York: Boosey & Hawkes, 1974. Chorus: SATB, M solo, org.

Medea (1946).

1815 Krenek, Ernst. "Medea." 1951. Dramatic monologue: S, orch. Text after Euripides.

Post Mortem. *Roan Stallion, Tamar and Other Poems* (1935).

1816 Huston, Scott. In *Ante Mortem and Post Mortem*. New York: General, u.d. Song: Bar, pf.

Rearmament. *Solstice and Other Poems* (1935).

1817 Smith, Leland. In *Three Pacifist Songs*. MS, n.d., avail. ACA. Song: med. v, pf.

Shine, Perishing Republic. *Roan Stallion, Tamar and Other Poems* (1925).

1818 Lockwood, Normand. MS, u.d., avail. ACA. Chorus: SATB, org, 3 tpt, tbn, 2 vla, timp, 2 perc.

JAMES WELDON JOHNSON (1871–1938)

The Awakening. *Fifty Years & Other Poems* (1917).

1819 Johnson, J. Rosamond. New York: G. Ricordi, 1913. Song: 2 v edns, pf.

The Creation. *God's Trombones* (1927).

1820 Fortner, Wolfgang. Mainz: B. Schott's, 1957. Song: med. v, orch. Text in Eng. and Ger.

1821 Gruenberg, Louis. "The Creation, a Negro Sermon for Voice and Eight Instruments" op. 23. New York: Universal-Edition, 1926. Song: v, fl, cl, bsn (or vc), hn, vla, pf, timp, perc. Text in Eng. and Ger., trans. by R. St. Hoffman.

1822 Ringwald, Roy. In *God's Trombones*. Delaware Water Gap, Pa.: Shawnee, 1955. Dramatic Sequence: SATB chorus, 2 speakers, soli, small orch.

1823 Scott, Thomas J. Bryn Mawr, Pa.: T. Presser, 1950. Chorus: SATB, narr., a cap.

An Explanation. *Fifty Years & Other Poems* (1917).

 1824 Cook, Will M. New York: G. Schirmer, 1914. Song: v, pf.

The Ghost of Deacon Brown. *Fifty Years & Other Poems* (1917).

 1825 Johnson, J. Rosamond. New York: J.W. Stern, 1906. Song: v, pf.

The Glory of the Day Was in Her Face. *Fifty Years & Other Poems* (1917).

 1826 Burleigh, Harry T. In *Passionale.* New York: G. Ricordi, 1915. Song: high and low v edns, pf.

Go Down Death—A Funeral Sermon. *God's Trombones* (1927).

 1827 Ringwald, Roy. "Go Down Death" in *God's Trombones.* Delaware Water Gap, Pa.: Shawnee, 1955. Dramatic Sequence: SATB chorus, 2 speakers, soli, small orch.

God's Trombones (1927). *See also* under individual titles.

 1828 Myers, Gordon. "God's Trombones: A Prayer and 7 Negro Folk Sermons by James Weldon Johnson." New York: Eastlane Music, 1967, c1961–1962. Setting for mixed chorus, soli, solo trbs, five brass or orch; Trenton, N.J.: Eastlane Music, 1972.

Her Eyes Twin Pools. *Fifty Years & Other Poems* (1917).

 1829 Burleigh, Harry T. In *Passionale.* New York: G. Ricordi, 1915. Song: high and low v edns, pf.

The Judgment Day. *God's Trombones* (1927).

 1830 Ringwald, Roy. In *God's Trombones.* Delaware Water Gap, Pa.: Shawnee, 1955. Dramatic Sequence: SATB chorus, 2 speakers, soli, small orch.

Lift Every Voice and Sing. *Saint Peter Relates an Incident* (1935).

 1831 Johnson, J. Rosamond. New York: E.B. Marks, 1912. Song: v, pf.
  New York: E.B. Marks, 1921. Song: v, pf.
  New York: E.B. Marks, 1921. Chorus: SATB, pf.
  "Lift Ev'ry Voice and Sing." New York: E.B. Marks, 1923. Orchestration by Jas. Harrington.
  New York: E.B. Marks, 1928. Setting for male qrt.
  New York: E.B. Marks, 1932. Chorus: SABar.
  New York: E.B. Marks, 1932. Quartet: TTBB.
  New York: E.B. Marks, 1932. Song: v, pf.
  New York: E.B. Marks, 1932. Quartet: 4-pt. mixed voices.

New York: E.B. Marks, 1940. Song: v, pf.

New York: E.B. Marks, 1940. Song: v, orch.

"Lift Ev'ry Voice and Sing." New York: E.B. Marks, 1940. Song: v, pf.

New York: E.B. Marks, 1943. Chorus: SSA.

Robert Cray, arr. New York: E.B. Marks, 1947. Song: v, band.

John Coates, Jr., arr. "Lift Ev'ry Voice and Sing." Delaware Water Gap, Pa: Shawnee, 1973. Chorus: SATB, pf. Music and text arranged and adapted.

In coll. LBW. Hymn.

Listen, Lord—A Prayer. *God's Trombones* (1927).

1832 Ringwald, Roy. "Opening: A Prayer," "Closing: A Prayer" in *God's Trombones*. Delaware Water Gap, Pa.: Shawnee, 1955. Dramatic Sequence: SATB chorus, 2 speakers, soli, small orch.

Ma Lady's Lips Am Like de Honey. *Fifty Years & Other Poems* (1917).

1833 Cook, Will M. New York: G. Schirmer, 1915. Song: med. v, pf; New York: G. Schirmer, 1915. Chorus: SATB, a cap.

Morning, Noon, and Night. *Fifty Years & Other Poems* (1917).

1834 Johnson, J. Rosamond. In *Two Love Songs*. New York: G. Schirmer, 1916. Song: high v, pf.

Nobody's Lookin' but de Owl an' de Moon. *Fifty Years & Other Poems* (1917).

1835 Johnson, J. Rosamond. New York: J.W. Stern, 1901. Song: v, pf. Words by Bob Cole and J.W. Johnson.

O Southland. *Fifty Years & Other Poems* (1917).

1836 Burleigh, Harry T. New York: G. Ricordi, 1914. Chorus: TTBB, pf; New York: G. Ricordi, 1919. Chorus: SATB, pf.

1837 Johnson, J. Rosamond. "O, Southland." New York: G. Schirmer, 1919. Chorus: SATB, S solo, pf.

The Prodigal Son. *God's Trombones* (1927).

1838 Elmore, Robert H. "The Prodigal Son (A Sermon in Swing.)" New York: H.W. Gray, 1940. Chorus: men's voices, pf or orch (R).

Sence You Went Away. *Fifty Years & Other Poems* (1917).

1839 Johnson, J. Rosamond. New York: J.W. Stern, 1900. Song: v, pf.

Words by Bob Cole and J.W. Johnson; New York: G. Ricordi, 1913. Song: 3 v edns, pf. In coll. CJS.

1840 Mortensen, Otto. In *Four Songs*. Copenhagen: W. Hansen, 1945. Song: v, pf.

The Young Warrior. *Fifty Years & Other Poems* (1917).

1841 Burleigh, Harry T. "The Young Warrior (Il giovane guerriero)." New York: G. Ricordi, 1915. Song: v, pf. Ital. text by Edoardo Petro.

You's Sweet to Yo' Mammy Jes' the Same. *Fifty Years & Other Poems* (1917).

1842 Johnson, J. Rosamond. New York: J.H. Remick, 1911. Song: v, pf.

Miscellaneous

1843 Burleigh, Harry T. "Elysium." New York: G. Ricordi, 1914. Song: high v, pf.

1844 Burleigh, Harry T. "Your Eyes So Deep" in *Passionale*. New York: G. Ricordi, 1915. Song: T, pf.

1845 Burleigh, Harry T. "Your Lips Are Wine" in *Passionale*. New York: G. Ricordi, 1915. Song: T, pf.

1846 Cole, Bob. "Como le Gusta (How Do You Like Me)." New York: J.W. Stern, 1904. Song: v, pf.

1847 Cole, Bob. "Don't Wake Him up Let Him Dream." New York: J.W. Stern, 1904. Song: v, pf.

1848 Cole, Bob. "Everybody Wants to See the Baby." New York: J.W. Stern, 1903. Song: v, pf. In coll. CJS.

1849 Cole, Bob. "Gimme de Leavin's." New York: J.W. Stern, 1904. Song: v, pf.

1850 Cole, Bob. "I Don't Want to Be No Actor Man No Mo'." New York: J.W. Stern, 1901. Song: v, pf. Words by J. Rosamond and J.W. Johnson.

1851 Cole, Bob. "The Katy-did, the Cricket and the Frog." New York: J.W. Stern, 1903. Song: v, pf; New York: E.B. Marks, 1932.

1852 Cole, Bob. "Lindy." New York: J.W. Stern, 1903. Song: v, pf. Music by Cole and J. Rosamond Johnson.

1853 Cole, Bob. "Louisiana Lize." New York: J.W. Stern, 1899. Song: v, pf. Words by J. Rosamond and J.W. Johnson. In coll. CJS.

1854 Cole, Bob. "The Maiden with the Dreamy Eyes." New York: J.W. Stern, 1901. Song: v, pf. New York: E.B. Marks, 1920.

1855 Cole, Bob. "Man, Man, Man." New York: J.W. Stern, 1904. Song: v, pf.

1856 Cole, Bob. "Mexico." New York: J.W. Stern, 1904. Song: v, pf. Words by Cole and J.W. Johnson. New York: E.B. Marks, 1921.

1857 Cole, Bob. "My Angemima Green." New York: J.W. Stern, 1902? Song: v, pf. In coll. CJS.

1858 Cole, Bob. "My Lulu Sam (A Japanese Love Song)." New York: J.W. Stern, 1905. Song: v, pf.

1859 Cole, Bob. "A Prepossessing Little Maid." New York: J.W. Stern, 1904. Song: v, pf.

1860 Cole, Bob. "Sambo and Dinah." New York: J.W. Stern, 1904. Song: v, pf. Words by Cole and J.W. Johnson.

1861 Cole, Bob. "Save It for Me." New York: J.S. Stern, 1903. Song: v, pf.

1862 Cole, Bob. "There Is Something about You That I Love, Love, Love." New York: J.W. Stern, 1904. Song: v, pf. Arr. by J. Rosamond Johnson.

1863 Cole, Bob. "When the Band Plays Ragtime." New York: J.W. Stern, 1902. Song: v, pf. In coll. CJS.

1864 Cole, Bob. "Zel Zel." New York: J.W. Stern, 1905. Song: v, pf.

1865 [Cook,] Will M. "If the Sands of the Seas Were Pearls." New York: J.H. Remick, 1914. Song: v, pf.

1866 Europe, James R. "What It Takes to Make Me Love You You've Got It." New York: J.W. Stern, 1914. Song: v, pf.

1867 Granados y Campiña, Enrique. "The Goddess in the Garden (Mañanica Era)." New York: G. Schirmer, 1916. Song: high or med. v. English version by Johnson.

1868 Granados y Campiña, Enrique. "Goyescas." New York: G. Schirmer, 1915. Opera in three tableaux. The book by Fernando Periquet, Eng. version by Johnson. Text in Span. and Eng; New York: G. Schirmer, 1944.

1869 Johnson, J. Rosamond. "Ain't dat Scan'lous." New York: J.W. Stern, 1901. Song: v, pf. Words by Bob Cole and J.W. Johnson; New York: E.B. Marks, 1932. In coll. CJS.

1870 Johnson, J. Rosamond. "The Animal's Convention." New York: J.W. Stern, 1902. Song: v, pf. In coll. CJS.

1871 Johnson, J. Rosamond. "Can You Forget." New York: T.B. Harms & Francis, Day & Hunter, 1910.

1872 Johnson, J. Rosamond. "Come Out, Dinah, on the Green." New York: H.H. Taylor, 1901. Song: v, pf. Words by Bob Cole and J.W. Johnson.

1873 Johnson, J. Rosamond. "Congo Love Song." New York: J.W. Stern, 1903. Song: v, pf; New York: E.B. Marks, 1921. Song: v, pf.
  Claude G. Garreau, arr. In *Time to Harmonize* [vol. 1 p. 56]. New York: E.B. Marks, 1948. Setting for TTBB.
  Eva Jessye, arr. New York: E.B. Marks, 1956. Chorus: TTBB, pf.

1874 Johnson, J. Rosamond. "The Creole Belle." New York: J.W. Stern, 1910. Song: v, pf.

1875 Johnson, J. Rosamond. "Cupid's Ramble." New York: J.W. Stern, 1901. Song: v, pf. Words by Bob Cole and J.W. Johnson.

1876 Johnson, J. Rosamond. "De Bo'd of Education." New York: J.W. Stern, 1906. Song: v, pf.

1877 Johnson, J. Rosamond. "De Little Pickaninny's Gone to Sleep." Boston: O. Ditson, 1910. Part Song: mixed voices, opt pf; Boston: O. Ditson, 1910. Setting for men's qrt or chorus, pf.

1878 Johnson, J. Rosamond. "Dem Lovin' Words Sound Mighty Good to Me." New York: J.W. Stern, 1905. Song: v, pf.

1879 Johnson, J. Rosamond. "Dis Ain't No Time for an Argument." New York: J.W. Stern, 1906. Song: v, pf.

1880 Johnson, J. Rosamond. "Don't Butt In." New York: J.W. Stern, 1901. Song: v, pf. Words by Bob Cole and J.W. Johnson. In coll. CJS.

1881 Johnson, J. Rosamond. "Down in Mulberry Bend." New York: J.W. Stern, 1904. Song: v, pf.

1882 Johnson, J. Rosamond. "Echoes of the Day." New York: J.W. Stern, 1903. Song: v, pf; "Echoes of the Day (Daylight Is Fading)." New York: E.B. Marks, 1930. Song: v, pf.

1883 Johnson, J. Rosamond. "Every Woman's Eyes." New York: J.W. Stern, 1912. Song: v, pf.

1884 Johnson, J. Rosamond. "Excuse Me Mister Moon." New York: J.W. Stern, 1912. Song: v, pf.

1885 Johnson, J. Rosamond. "Fishing." New York: J.W. Stern, 1904. Song: v, pf; New York: E.B. Marks, 1921; New York: E.B. Marks, 1932.

1886 Johnson, J. Rosamond. "Floating Down the Nile." New York: J.W. Stern, 1906. Song: v, pf.

1887 Johnson, J. Rosamond. "Hello Ma Lulu." New York: J.W. Stern, 1905. Song: v, pf.

1888 Johnson, J. Rosamond. "I Aint Gwine ter Work No Mo'." New York: J.W. Stern, 1900. Song: v, pf. Words by Bob Cole and J.W. Johnson.

1889 Johnson, J. Rosamond. "If You'll Be My Eve I'll Build an Eden for You." New York: J.W. Stern, 1912. Song: v, pf.

1890 Johnson, J. Rosamond. "I'll Keep a Warm Spot in My Heart for You." New York: J.W. Stern, 1906. Song: v, pf; Claude Garreau, arr. In *Time to Harmonize* [vol. 2 p. 56]. New York: E.B. Marks, 1948. Setting for TTBB.

1891 Johnson, J. Rosamond. "I've Got Troubles of My Own." New York: J.W. Stern, 1900. Song: v, pf. Words by Bob Cole and J.W. Johnson.

1892 Johnson, J. Rosamond. "Lovely Daughter of Allah." New York: J.W. Stern, 1912. Song: v, pf.

1893 Johnson, J. Rosamond. "Ma Mississippi Belle." New York: J.W. Stern, 1900. Song: v, pf. Words by Bob Cole and J.W. Johnson. In coll. CJS.

1894 Johnson, J. Rosamond. "Magdaline My Southern Queen." New York: J.W. Stern, 1900. Song: v, pf. Words by Bob Cole and J.W. Johnson; "Madalene My Southern Queen" in coll. CJS.

1895 Johnson, J. Rosamond. "The Maid of Timbuctoo." New York: J.W. Stern, 1903. Song: v, pf.

1896 Johnson, J. Rosamond. "My Castle on the Nile." New York: J.W. Stern, 1901. Words by Bob Cole and J.W. Johnson. In coll. CJS; New York: E.B. Marks, 1921; New York: E.B. Marks, 1932.

1897 Johnson, J. Rosamond. "My Creole Belle." New York: Hurtig & Seamon, 1900. Song: v, pf.

1898 Johnson, J. Rosamond. "My Heart's Desiah Is Miss Moriah." New York: J.W. Stern, 1901. Song: v, pf. Words by Bob Cole and J.W. Johnson. In coll. CJS.

1899 Johnson, J. Rosamond. "No Use Askin' 'Cause You Know Why." New York: J.W. Stern, 1901. Song: v, pf. In coll. CJS.

1900 Johnson, J. Rosamond. "Oh! Didn't He Ramble." New York: J.W. Stern, 1902. Song: v, pf. Words by Bob Cole and J.W. Johnson; New York: E.B. Marks, 1912.

1901 Johnson, J. Rosamond. "Oh, You Sweet Boy." New York: J.W. Stern, 1913. Song: v, pf.

1902 Johnson, J. Rosamond. "The Old Flag Never Touched the Ground." New York: J.W. Stern, 1901. Song: v, pf. Words by Bob Cole and J.W. Johnson. In coll. CJS.

1903 Johnson, J. Rosamond. "On Lalawana's Shore." New York: J.W. Stern, 1904. Song: v, pf.

1904 Johnson, J. Rosamond. "The Pussy and the Bow-wow." New York: J.W. Stern, 1904. Song: v, pf.

1905 Johnson, J. Rosamond. "Roll Them Cotton Bales." New York: J.W. Stern, 1914. Song: v, pf; New York: E.B. Marks, 1920.

1906 Johnson, J. Rosamond. "Run, Brudder Possum, Run." New York: Roger's Bros., Music Publishing, 1900. Song: v, pf.

1907 Johnson, J. Rosamond. "The Soldier Is the Idol of the Nation." New York: J.W. Stern, 1903. Song: v, pf.

1908 Johnson, J. Rosamond. "The Spirit of the Banjo!" New York: J.W. Stern, 1903. Song: v, pf. Words by Bob Cole and J.W. Johnson.

1909 Johnson, J. Rosamond. "Sweet Saloma." New York: J.W. Stern, 1901. Song: v, pf. Words by Bob Cole and J.W. Johnson. In coll. CJS.

1910 Johnson, J. Rosamond. "Tell Me, Dusky Maiden." New York: H.H. Taylor, 1908. Song: v, pf. Words by Bob Cole and J.W. Johnson.

1911 Johnson, J. Rosamond. "There's a Very Pretty Moon To-night." New York: J.W. Stern, 1903. Song: v, pf.

1912 Johnson, J. Rosamond. "Three Questions." New York: H. Flammer, 1917. Song: high and low v edns, pf.

1913 Johnson, J. Rosamond. "Treat Me Like a Baby Doll." New York: J.W. Stern, 1914. Song: v, pf.

1914 Johnson, J. Rosamond. "Two Eyes." New York: J.W. Stern, 1903. Song: v, pf.

1915 Johnson, J. Rosamond. "Under the Bamboo Tree." New York: J.W. Stern, 1902. Song: v, pf. New York: E.B. Marks, 1932.

1916 Johnson, J. Rosamond. "When de Jack O' Lantern Starts to Walk About." New York: J.W. Stern, 1901. Song: v, pf. Words by Bob Cole and J.W. Johnson. In coll. CJS.

1917 Johnson, J. Rosamond. "Why Don't the Band Play." New York: J.W. Stern, 1900. Song: v, pf. Words by Bob Cole and J.W. Johnson. In coll. CJS.

1918 Johnson, J. Rosamond. "You Go Your Way and I'll Go Mine." New York: J.W. Stern, 1915. Song: v, pf.

1919 Moore, Dorothy R. "O Black and Unknown Bards" in *From the Dark Tower*. New York: Composers Facsimile Edn, 1970. Cycle: M, pf, vc; New York: Composers Facsimile Edn, 1972. Setting for M, orch.

1920 Williams, Egbert A. "When It's All Goin' Out and Nothin' Comin' In." New York: J.W. Stern, 1902. Song: v, pf. Words and Music by Williams and Walker; words revised by J.W. Johnson.

KENNETH KOCH (B. 1925)

The Artist. *Thank You and Other Poems* (1962).

1921 Reif, Paul. New York: Seesaw, 1970. Setting for C or Bar, narr., fl, bcl, bsn, hn, tpt, vn, perc. Includes speaking parts for instrumentalists. Can be performed in dramatization or concert form. Music not seen; text presumably from this poem.

Bertha. *Bertha & Other Plays* (1966).

1922 Rorem, Ned. New York: Boosey & Hawkes, 1973. One act opera.

The Circus. *Thank You and Other Poems* (1962).

1923 Reif, Paul. *The Circus: A Cycle of Nine Songs.* New York: Seesaw, 1970. Cycle: S, pf. Setting of secs. 3, 4, 6, 7, 8, 9, 10, 11, 12.

Collected Poems. *Thank You and Other Poems* (1962).

1924 Thomson, Virgil. New York: Southern Music Publishing, 1978. Duet: S and Bar, pf. The Bar line sings the "titles," and the soprano line follows with the one line text.

Down at the Docks. *Thank You and Other Poems* (1962).

1925 Rorem, Ned. In *Hearing: A Cycle of Poems by Kenneth Koch.* New York: Boosey & Hawkes, 1969. Cycle: med.-low v, pf.

1926 Thomson, Virgil. In *Mostly About Love.* New York: G. Schirmer, 1964. Song: v, pf.

In Love with You. *Thank You and Other Poems* (1962).

1927 Rorem, Ned. In *Hearing: A Cycle of Poems by Kenneth Koch.* New York: Boosey & Hawkes, 1969. Cycle: med.-low v, pf.

Poem. *Thank You and Other Poems* (1962).

1928 Rorem, Ned. In *Hearing: A Cycle of Poems by Kenneth Koch.* New York: Boosey & Hawkes, 1969. Cycle: med.-low v, pf.

Spring. *Thank You and Other Poems* (1962).

1929 Rorem, Ned. In *Hearing: A Cycle of Poems by Kenneth Koch.* New York: Boosey & Hawkes, 1969. Cycle: med.-low v, pf.

1930 Thomson, Virgil. "Let's Take a Walk" in *Mostly About Love.* New York: G. Schirmer, 1964. Song: v, pf.

To You. *Thank You and Other Poems* (1962).

    1931 Thomson, Virgil. "Love Song" in *Mostly About Love*. New York: G. Schirmer, 1964. Song: v, pf.

ALFRED KREYMBORG (1883–1966)

Ballad of All Women. *The Selected Poems, 1912–1944, of Alfred Kreymborg* (1945).

    1932 Heller, Hans Ewald. "Ode to Our Women." New York: E.B. Marks, 1944. Cantata: SSAATTBB, pf.

Ballad of Decoration Days. *Ten American Ballads* (1942).

    1933 Padwa, Vladimir. "This Is the Day." New York: E.B. Marks, 1943. Song: med. v, pf.

    1934 Wagner, Joseph. "Ballad of Memorial Days" in *American Ballad Set*. New York: Southern Music Publishing, 1967. Chorus: SATB, a cap.

Ballad of the Common Man. *Ten American Ballads* (1942).

    1935 Wagner, Joseph. In *American Ballad Set*. New York: Southern Music Publishing, 1967. Chorus: SATB, a cap.

Ballad of the Lincoln Penny. *Ten American Ballads* (1942).

    1936 Siegmeister, Elie. "The Lincoln Penny." New York: E.B. Marks, 1943. Song: v, pf; "The Lincoln Penny" in *American Legends: Six Songs for Voice and Piano*. New York: E.B. Marks, 1947. Song: med. v, pf.

    1937 Wagner, Joseph. In *American Ballad Set*. New York: Southern Music Publishing, 1967. Chorus: SATB, a cap.

Ballad of Valley Forge. *Ten American Ballads* (1942).

    1938 North, Alexander. New York: E.B. Marks, 1942. Song: low v, pf.

Down in the Clover. *Ten American Ballads* (1942).

    1939 North, Alexander. "Child in the Clover." New York; E.B. Marks, 1943. Song: v, pf.

Old Manuscript. *Mushrooms* (1916).

1940 McKay, Francis H. New York: C. Fischer, 1966. Chorus: SATB, pf.

Privelege and Privation. *One Act Play Magazine* 1 (June 1937), pp. 141–152.

1941 Becker, John. "Privelege and Privation" [Stagework no. 5c]. New York: C.F. Peters, u.d. A playful affair with music.

Song Sparrow [Eight Movements. 8]. *Scarlet and Mellow* (1926).

1942 Hier, Ethel G. "The Song Sparrow." New York: Composers Facsimile Edn, 1955. Song: v, pf.

There's a Nation. *Ten American Ballads* (1942).

1943 North, Alexander. New York: E.B. Marks, 1942. Song: med. v, pf.

Miscellaneous

1944 Hageman, Richard. "Scherzetto." New York: Galaxy, 1952. Song: med. v, pf.

1945 Read, Gardner. "Lullaby for a Dark Hour" op. 68 no. 1. New York: Boosey & Hawkes, 1950. Song: v, pf. Text: "O hearts that are heavy with earth. . . ."

1946 Siegmeister, Elie. "Funnybone Alley, a Musical Cartoon for American Children." New York: Leeds Music, 1945. Story and lyrics by Kreymborg. A note on the music says, "Except for a number of lyrics the present work is totally different in plot and character from an earlier version published by the Macauley Company."

1947 Wagner, Joseph. "Ballad of Brotherhood." Philadelphia: Elkan-Vogel, 1949. Chorus: SATB, orch or orch without chorus. Text: "Leaves of grass, none of you shall ever pass. . . ."

SIDNEY LANIER (1842–1881)

Baby Charley. *Poems of Sidney Lanier* (1884).

1948 "Baby Charley." Arr. from an "Old College Air" in coll. LBR.

1949 Camp, John Spencer. In *Five Songs* op. 15 no. 5. Cincinnati: J. Church, 1903. Song: v, pf.

A Ballad of Trees and the Master. *Poems of Sidney Lanier* (1884).

1950 Adams, Carrie B. "Into the Woods My Master Went." Dayton, Ohio: Lorenz, 1931. Song: med. and low v edns, pf.

1951 Briel, Marie. "Into the Woods My Master Went." Chicago: H.T. Fitzsimmons, 1934. Setting for 4-pt. mixed voices, a cap.

1952 Chadwick, George W. Boston: O. Ditson, 1899. Song: high, med., and low v edns, pf.
   N. Clifford Page, arr. Boston: O. Ditson, 1899. Song: v, orch.
   Boston: O. Ditson, 1929. Chorus: 4-pt. mixed voices, pf or org.

1953 Dupont-Hansen, George. Chicago: C.F. Summy, 1950.

1954 Dyckman, H.W. Cincinnati: J. Church, 1924. Song: v, pf, vc obl.

1955 Fearis, John S. "The Trees." Chicago: J.S. Fearis & Bro., 1927. Cantata: mixed voices, pf.

1956 Goldman, Maurice. New York: M. Witmark, 1949. Chorus: SATB, S and T soli.

1957 Griswold, Ruth R. Chicago: Clayton F. Summy, 1921. Song: med. v, pf or org.

1958 Hamilton, Janie A. Cincinnati: Willis Music, 1917. Song: v, pf.

1959 Helyer, Marjorie. Vancouver: Western Music, 1954. 3-pt. song.

1960 James, Philip. "A Ballad of Trees and the Master" op. 22 no. 2. Boston: O. Ditson, 1920. Song: high or med. v, pf; "A Ballad of Trees and the Master" op. 22 no. 1. Boston: O. Ditson, u.d. Chorus: SATB.

1961 Lekberg, Sven. New York: Galaxy, 1950. Song: high v, pf.

1962 Lippa, Kate O. "Trees and the Master." Pittsburgh: Volkwein Bros., 1934. Song: v, pf.

1963 Lorenz, Ellen J. "The Trees and the Master." Dayton, Ohio: Lorenz, 1959. Anthem: SATB, pf or org. Based on a hymn tune by Peter C. Lutkin.

1964 Lutkin, Peter C. n.t. in coll. ChAH, SmASH, SmPS. Hymn.

1965 McCaskey, J.P. "The Trees and the Master" in coll. LAAS. Harmonized and adapted by John Hyatt Brewer; In coll. FSS 6, LAASR, MFS.

1966 McCollin, Frances. "Into the Woods My Master Went." New York: J. Fischer, 1940. Song: high or med. v, pf.

1967 McCray, Walter C. Rockford, Ill.: Ogren & Uhe, 1933. Song: v, pf.

1968 Matthews, H. Alexander. New York: G. Schirmer, 1921. Anthem: SATB, a cap.

1969 Mills, Charles. MS, u.d., avail. ACA. Setting for SATB a cap.

1970 Nevin, George B. "Into the Woods My Master Went." Boston: O. Ditson, 1926. Anthem: SATB, pf or org; Boston: O. Ditson, 1928. Song: high and low v edns, pf. Also pubd for men's voices.

1971 Noble, T. Tertius. "Into the Woods My Master Went." Boston: A.P. Schmidt, c1922 by Banks & Son, assigned to Schmidt, 1926. Setting for SATB, org.

1972 Patterson, Janie A. "A Ballad of Trees and the Master." u.p.,u.p.

1973 Protheroe, Daniel. "The Trees and the Master." New York: G. Schirmer, 1908. Part Song: SATB, a cap; Boston: Boston Music, 1927. Sacred Song: high and low v edns, pf.

1974 Protheroe, Daniel, arr. Melody by David E. Roberts. "Into the Woods My Master Went." Cleveland: Women's Welsh Club of America, 1921. Setting for SATB.

1975 Ross, Orvis. Chicago: C.F. Summy, 1952. Setting for SATB.

1976 Sheldon, Robert. u.p.: Motif Publications, 1959. Song: med. or low v, pf.

1977 Shelley, Harry R. "Into the Woods My Master Went." New York: G. Schirmer, 1940. Song: high and low v edns, pf or org.

1978 Shepherd, Arthur. Boston: C.C. Birchard, 1935. Chorus: SAATTBB, a cap.

1979 Snow, Francis W. "Into the Woods My Master Went." Boston: C.W. Homeyer, 1935. Chorus: TTBB, a cap.

1980 Entry cancelled.

1981 Urban, Francis. Baltimore: Otto Sutro, 1886. Song: v, pf.

1982 Vaughan Williams, Ralph. "Into the Woods My Master Went" in *Songs of Praise.* Ed. by Percy Dearmer, Martin Shaw, and Vaughan Williams. London and New York: Oxford University Press, 1931. Hymn: SATB.

1983 Williams, David H. "Into the Woods My Master Went." Glenrock, N.J.: J. Fischer, u.d. Anthem for mixed voices.

1984 Wilson, Harry R. New York: Boosey & Hawkes, 1955. Setting for SATB.

The Centennial Meditation of Columbia [BAL 11248].

1985 Buck, Dudley. New York: G. Schirmer, 1876. A Cantata for the Inaugural.

1985a Hadley, H. "America" in coll. ArJ.

Evening Song. *Poems of Sidney Lanier* (1884).

1986 Buck, Dudley. "Sunset" in *Five Songs* op. 76 no. 4. New York: G. Schirmer, 1877. Song: C or Bar, pf.

1987 Bumstead, Gladys P. "Look off, Dear Love." Boston: O. Ditson, 1926. Song: high and med. v edns, vn obl.

1988 Camp, John S. In *Five Songs* op. 15 no. 3. Cincinnati: J. Church, 1903. Song: v, pf.

1989 Colan, Rosslyn L. "The Good Night Kiss." Edinburg: Paterson & Sons, 1910. Song: v, pf.

1990 De Koven, Reginald. "A Love Song." u.p.: u.p., 1896.

1991 De Packh, Maurice B. New York: Harms, 1927. Song: v, pf.

1992 Fallberg, Carl. Chicago: Clayton F. Summy, 1917. Song: v, pf.

1993 Freer, Eleanor E. "Evening Song" op. 20 no. 3. Berlin: R. Kaun, 1907. Song: v, pf.

1994 Griffes, Charles T. New York: G. Schirmer, 1941. Song: high v, pf.

1995 Hadley, Henry K. In *Three Songs* op. 53 no. 3. New York: G. Schirmer, 1915. Song: high and med. v edns, pf.

1996 James, Philip. "Evening Song" in *A Sea Symphony* [Movement 2]. u.p.: Mills Music (R). Setting for B-Bar, pf or orch.

1997 Menges, Edward E. New York: C. Fischer, 1937. Song: high and low v, edns, pf.

1998 Rodgers, James H. "Look off, Dear Love." u.p.: u.p., 1899.

1999 Root, Grace W. "A Sunset Song." Chicago: C.F. Summy, 1891.

2000 Russell, Alexander. "Sunset." Cincinnati: J. Church, 1910. Song: high and low v edns, pf.

In the Foam. *Poems of Sidney Lanier* (1884).

2001 Camp, John S. In *Five Songs* op. 15 no. 4. Cincinnati: J. Church, 1903. Song: v, pf.

Little Ella. *The Centennial Edition of Sidney Lanier* (1945).

2002 Lanier, Sidney. Montgomery, Ala.: R.W. Offut, 1868. Ballad.

Marsh Hymns. *Poems of Sidney Lanier* (1884).

2002a Pettis, Ashley. "Marsh Hymn." New York: C. Fischer, 1925. Song: v, pf.

The Marshes of Glynn. *The Centennial Edition of Sidney Lanier* (1945).

2003 Blair, William. "When the Tide Comes In." Cincinnati: J. Church, 1915. Song: v, pf.

"May the Maiden." *Poems of Sidney Lanier* (1884).

2004 Barnby, J. In coll. LBR.

2005 Carmichael, Mary. "A May Song." Boston: O. Ditson, [18--?]. Song: M or T, pf. In coll. WBT, WBW.

2006 Carpenter, John A. Boston: O. Ditson, 1912. Song: high and low v edns, pf. In coll. MasSS.

2007 De Koven, Reginald. "May, the Maiden" op. 130 no. 4. New York: G. Schirmer, 1897. Song: M or Bar, pf.

2008 Hill, K. "Marie" in *3 Songs*. Riga: P. Neldner, n.d. Song: v, pf.

Psalm of the West. *Poems* (1877).

2009 Saminsky, Lazare. In *From the American Poets* op. 46 no. 3. New York: Beekman Music, 1956. Chorus: SATB, pf (perc and org ad lib,) or orch (R).

The Raven Days. *Poems of Sidney Lanier* (1884).

2010 Barnett, David. Weston, Conn.: Ledgebrook Associates, 1977. Song: A, pf.

Rose-Morals. *Poems* (1877).

2010a Sawyer, Harriet Priscilla. "Rose Morals." Boston: C.W. Thompson, 1903. Song: v, pf.

2011 Ware, Harriet. "Rose Moral no. 1." New York: T.B. Harms, 1901. Song: v, pf. Setting of "White Rose," verse 1, and "Red Rose," verse 3.

2012 Ware, Harriet. "Rose Moral no. 2." New York: T.B. Harms, 1901. Song: v, pf. Setting of "Red Rose" verses 1 and 2.

A Song of the Future. *Poems of Sidney Lanier* (1884).

2013 Camp, John S. In *Five Songs* op. 15 no. 1. Cincinnati: J. Church, 1903. Song: v, pf.

2014 James, Philip. New York: H.W. Gray, 1923. Double Chorus: SAATBB and SATBB, a cap.

2015 Ware, Harriet. New York: T.B. Harms, 1901. Song: v, pf.

The Symphony. *Poems* (1877).

2016 Harold, Thomas. "Dear Eyes," "Love Song." u.p.: Harold, 1912. Song: S and C, pf.

Thou and I. *Poems of Sidney Lanier* (1891).

2017 Alling, Willis H. New York: Wm. Maxwell, 1902. Song: 2 v edns, pf.

2018 Camp, John S. In *Five Songs* op. 15 no. 2. Cincinnati: J. Church, 1903. Song: v, pf.

2019 Palmer, Clara B. New York: u.p., 1902.

2020 Rihm, Alexander. In *Three Songs.* New York: G. Schirmer, 1918. Song: high v, pf.

Miscellaneous

2021 Clark, Frederic H. "The Red Rose" op. 10. Chicago: C.F. Summy, 1900.

2022 Gow, George C. "Love-Song" in *Five Songs* op. 2 no. 2. Boston: Boston Music, 1888. Song: v, pf.

2023 Entry cancelled.

2024 Entry cancelled.

2025 Entry cancelled.

DENISE LEVERTOV (B. 1923)

Hymn to Eros. *The Sorrow Dance* (1967).

2026 Weigl, Vally. In *Songs Newly Seen in the Dusk.* MS, u.d., avail. ACA. Song: M, vc.

In Praise of Krishna: Songs from the Bengali [Trans. by Edward C. Dimock, Jr. and Denise Levertov] (1967).

2027 Rochberg, George. "Songs in Praise of Krishna." Bryn Mawr: T. Presser, 1977. Recording: Composers Recordings, CRI SD 360 (1976).

Living. *The Sorrow Dance* (1966).

2028 Weigl, Vally. "The Fire in Leaf and Grass" in *Songs Newly Seen in the Dusk.* MS, u.d., avail. ACA. Song: M, vc.

A Man. *The Sorrow Dance* (1967).

2029 Weigl, Vally. "Living a Life" in *Songs Newly Seen in the Dusk.* MS, u.d., avail. ACA. Song: M, vc.

What Were They Like? *The Sorrow Dance* (1967).

2030 Heilner, Irwin. MS, u.d., avail. ACA. Song: med. v, gtr.

Who Is at My Window. *O Taste and See* (1964).

2031 Weigl, Vally. MS, 1969, avail. ACA. Song: med. v, pf.

VACHEL LINDSAY (1879–1931)

Abraham Lincoln Walks at Midnight. *The Congo and Other Poems* (1914).

2032 Bradley, Ruth O. Philadelphia: Composers Press, 1959. Cantata: mixed chorus, pf.

2033 Harris, Roy. New York: Associated Music, 1955, 1962. Song: M, vn, vc, pf.

2034 Siegmeister, Elie. u.p.: Arrow Music, 1939. Chorus: SATB, pf or orch (R).

2035 White, John. In *Three Madrigals*. New York: G. Schirmer, 1972. Chorus: SATB, pf or orch (R).

The Amaranth. *Collected Poems by Vachel Lindsay* (1925).

2036 Harbison, John. In *The Flower-Fed Buffaloes*. New York: Associated Music, u.d. Choral Cycle: 6-pt. chorus, Bar solo, 7 instrs. Recording: Nonesuch, H-71366 (1979).

The Booker Washington Trilogy [Pt. 1, "Simon Legree—A Negro Sermon"]. *The Chinese Nightingale and Other Poems* (1917).

2037 Moore, Douglas S. "Simon Legree." New York: C. Fischer, u.d. Chorus: TTBB, Bar solo, pf.

The Congo. *The Congo and Other Poems* (1914).

2038 Bergh, Arthur. "The Congo" op. 25. Boston: O. Ditson, 1918. Song: Bar, pf; Maynard Klein, arr. Philadelphia: O. Ditson, 1941. Choral Fantasy: SSATB, instr.

2039 Cheslock, Louis. New York: Independent Music Publishers, 1942? Chorus: SATB, orch.

2040 Paviour, Paul. "The Congo Jive." New York: Boosey & Hawkes, 1974. Setting for school chorus, pf, perc.

2041 Wolfe, Jacques. New York: C. Fischer, 1948. Song: med.·low v, pf.

Daniel. *The Golden Whales of California* (1920).

2042 Chappell, Herbert. "The Daniel Jazz" op. 103. London: Novello, 1963. Cantata: unison voices, pf.

2043 Enders, Harvey. St. Louis: Shattinger Piano and Music, 1925. Song: v, pf; arr. for male chorus, pf.

2044 Gruenberg, Louis. "The Daniel Jazz" op. 21. Vienna: Universal Edition, 1925. Song: v, cl, c tpt, 2 vn, vla, vc, pf, perc. Words in Eng. and Ger., trans. by R.S. Hoffman.

A Dirge for a Righteous Kitten. *The Congo and Other Poems* (1914).

2045 Gruenberg, Louis. In *Animals and Insects* op. 22 no. 4. Vienna: Universal Edition, 1925. Song: med. v, pf.

2046 Kettering, Eunice L. Chicago: C.F. Summy, 1949. Chorus: SSA, S solo, pf red.

Drying Their Wings. *The Congo and Other Poems* (1914).

2047 Kettering, Eunice L. Chicago: C.F. Summy, 1950. Chorus: SSA, a cap.

The Eagle That Is Forgotten. *General William Booth Enters into Heaven and Other Poems* (1913).

2048 Bottje, Will G. "To an Eagle Forgotten." MS, 1962, avail. ACA. Chorus: SATB, 7 brass, pf, perc.

Euclid. *The Congo and Other Poems* (1914).

2049 Tepper, Albert. New York: Edwin H. Morris, 1951. Chorus: SSA, pf.

An Explanation of the Grasshopper. *The Congo and Other Poems* (1914).

2050 Gruenberg, Louis. In *Animals and Insects* op. 22 no. 2. Vienna: Universal Edition, 1925. Song: med. v, pf.

Factory Windows Are Always Broken. *The Congo and Other Poems* (1914).

2051 Kettering, Eunice L. Cincinnati: Willis Music, 1950. Chorus: SATB, a cap.

The Flower-Fed Buffaloes. *Selected Poems of Vachel Lindsay* (1963).

2052 Harbison, John. In *The Flower-Fed Buffaloes*. New York: Associated Music, u.d. Choral Cycle: 6-pt. chorus, Bar solo, 7 instrs. Recording: Nonesuch, H-71366 (1979).

Foreign Missions in Battle Array. *General William Booth Enters into Heaven and Other Poems* (1913).

2052a Smart, Henry. "An Endless Line of Splendor" in *Christian Worship: A Hymnal.* Philadelphia: Judson Press, 1941.

General William Booth Enters into Heaven. *General William Enters into Heaven and Other Poems* (1913).

2053 Homer, Sidney. New York: G. Schirmer, 1926. Song: med. or low v, pf.

2054 Ives, Charles E. In coll. INS. Song: med. v, pf. Recording: Composers Recordings, CRI SD 390; John J. Becker, arr. Merion Music, 1964. Setting for solo v or chorus, small orch.

2055 James, Philip. New York: M. Witmark, 1933. Chorus: TTBB, tpt, trb, perc, 2 pf or pf and org; also pubd for chorus, a cap.

Ghosts in Love. *General William Enters into Heaven and Other Poems* (1913).

2056 Swanson, Howard. New York: Weintraub, 1950. Song: med. v, pf.

How Samson Bore away the Gates of Gaza. *The Chinese Nightingale* (1917).

2057 MacMahon, Desmond. "Samson at the Gates of Gaza" in *Three Pictures in Sepia.* London: Wm. Paxton, 1950. Chorus: SSA, solo v, pf.

2058 Maconchy, Elizabeth. "Samson and the Gates of Gaza." London: Chappell, 1967. Chorus: SATB, 1 or 2 pf or orch (R).

I Went Down into the Desert. *The Congo and Other Poems* (1914).

2059 Gruenberg, Louis. In *Four Songs* op. 24 no. 1. Vienna: Universal Edition, 1927. Song: med. v, pf.

In Praise of Johnny Appleseed. *Collected Poems of Vachel Lindsay* (1923).

2060 Jarrett, Jack. In *Choral Symphony on American Poems.* New York: C. Fischer, 1970. Chorus: SATB, pf, band or orch (R).

2061 Kubik, Gail. New York: F. Colombo, 1962. Cantata: SATB chorus, B/Bar solo, 2 pf (R) or orch (R).

The Leaden-Eyed. *The Congo and Other Poems* (1914).

2062 McKay, George F. "Pieta" in *Two Modern Madrigals.* New York: Lawson-Gould, 1967. Chorus: SATB, a cap.

2062a Wise, Michael. "Let Not Young Souls Be Smothered Out" in coll. UHC.

The Lion. *The Congo and Other Poems* (1914).

>   2063 Gruenberg, Louis. In *Animals and Insects* op. 22 no. 1. Vienna: Universal Edition, 1925. Song: med. v, pf.

The Little Turtle. *The Golden Whales of California* (1920).

>   2064 Carpenter, J.A. In coll. Mu 5, MuC 5, MuO, MuT 3.

>   2065 Enders, Harvey. New York: G. Schirmer, 1926. Song: high or med. v, pf.

>   2065a Sherman, Helen. New York: The Composers Press, u.d. Song: v, pf.

>   2066 Weigl, Vally. In *7 Songs*. MS, 1962, avail. ACA. Song: med. v, pf.

The Moon's the North Wind's Cooky. *The Congo and Other Poems* (1914).

>   2067 Kettering, Eunice L. Chicago: C.F. Summy, 1949. Chorus: SSA, a cap.

The Mouse That Knawed the Oak Tree Down. *The Congo and Other Poems* (1914).

>   2068 Dello Joio, Norman. "A Fable." New York: C. Fischer, 1947. Chorus: SATB, T solo, pf.

>   2069 Gruenberg, Louis. In *Animals and Insects* op. 22 no. 6. Vienna: Universal Edition, 1925. Song: med. v, pf.

The Mysterious Cat. *The Congo and Other Poems* (1914).

>   2070 Gruenberg, Louis. In *Animals and Insects* op. 22 no. 5. Vienna: Universal Edition, 1925. Song: med. v, pf.

>   2071 Kettering, Eunice L. Cincinnati: Willis Music, 1950. Chorus: SATB, a cap.

>   2072 Moore, Douglas S. Evanston: Summy-Birchard, 1960. Chorus: SSA, a cap.

The Spider and the Ghost of the Fly. *The Congo and Other Poems* (1914).

>   2073 Gruenberg, Louis. In *Animals and Insects* op. 22 no. 3. Vienna: Universal Edition, 1925. Song: med. v, pf.

The Statue of Old Andrew Jackson. *The Golden Whales of California* (1920).

>   2074 Jarrett, Jack. In *Choral Symphony on American Poems*. New York: C. Fischer, 1970. Chorus: SATB, pf, band or orch (R).

The Sun Says His Prayers. *The Congo and Other Poems* (1914).

2075 Kettering, Eunice L. Chicago: C.F. Summy, 1949. Chorus: SSA, a cap.

Two Old Crows. *The Chinese Nightingale and Other Poems* (1920).

2076 Dello Joio, Norman. "Of Crows and Clusters." New York: E.B. Marks, 1972. Chorus: SATB, pf. Based on the poem.

2077 Enders, Harvey. "Two Old Crows (An Exercise in Stuttering for Male Voices)." New York: Galaxy, 1932. Chorus: TTBB, a cap.

2078 Gruenberg, Louis. In *Animals and Insects* op. 22 no. 7. Vienna: Universal Edition, 1925. Song: med. v, pf.

2079 Kettering, Eunice L. Chicago: C.F. Summy, 1950. Chorus: SSAA, pf red.

Miscellaneous

2080 Hageman, Richard. "To a Golden-Haired Girl." New York: C. Fischer, 1938. Song: v, pf. Text: "You are a sunrise. . . ."

2081 McKay, George F. "To a Golden-Haired Girl." Chicago: Gamble-Hinged Music, 1936. Chorus: SATB, a cap.

HENRY WADSWORTH LONGFELLOW (1807–1882)

Aftermath. *Aftermath* (1873).

2082 Boott, Francis. Boston: O. Ditson, 1873. Song: v, pf.

2083 Maree, C. Josie. Boston: O. Ditson, 1874.

2084 Paine, Francis M. "Aftermath" op. 1 no. 4. Hyde Park, Mass.: F.L. Hodgdon, n.d. Song: v, pf (fl or vn obl).

Afternoon in February. *Poems* (1845).

2085 Aguilar, Emanuel. London: Duncan Davison, n.d. Song: v, pf.

2086 Blunt, Arthur C. "The Day Is Ending." London: Duncan Davison, n.d. Song: v, pf.

2087 Cottam, Arthur. London: Rudall, Rose, Carte, n.d. Song: v, pf.

2088 Haakman, J. Jacques. "Afternoon in February" op. 5 no. 1. London: C. Woolhouse, n.d. Song: v, pf.

2089 Hullah, John. In coll. LBR.

2090 Noble, T. Tertius. "Winter." New York: G. Schirmer, 1917. Song: high and low v edns, pf.

2091 Zabel, Rudolph. "Day Is Ending." Milwaukee: H.N. Hempsted, 1875.

"Ah, Love!" [act 3 sc. 1]. *The Spanish Student* (1843).

2092 Hawtree, F. "Ah, Love." London: Ashdown & Parry, 1868. Ballad: v, pf.

"All are sleeping, weary heart!" [act 2 sc. 4]. *The Spanish Student* (1843).

2093 Coleridge-Taylor, Samuel. "All Are Sleeping, Weary Heart." London: J. Curwen, 1910. Part Song: TTBB, pf.

2094 Johnson, W. Noel. "All Are Sleeping, Weary Heart" in *Four Songs.* London: C. Woolhouse, n.d. Song: v, pf.

2095 Pasmore, Henry B. "All are Sleeping." New York: G. Schirmer, 1881. Song: high v, pf, vn; In *Song Album.* Boston: O. Ditson, 1890. Song: v, pf.

Allah [Trans. from the poem of Siegfried August Mahlmann]. *Kéramos and Other Poems* (1878).

2096 Chadwick, George W. Boston: A.P. Schmidt, 1887. Song: high and med. v edns, pf.

2097 Clark, Victor I. Springfield Gardens, L.I.: Emalvic, 1932. Song: v, pf; New York: Mid-Town Music, 1932.

2098 Foulds, John. London: W. Paxton, 1925. Song.

2099 Gibson, Alexander S. Cincinnati: J. Church, 1906. Song: v, pf.

2100 Jordan, Jules. Boston: A.P. Schmidt, 1890. Song: high, med., and low v edns, pf; "The Bedouin's Prayer." Boston: A.P. Schmidt, 1890. Song: high, med., and low v edns, pf.

2101 Kramer, A. Walter. "Allah" op. 29 no. 2. Boston: O. Ditson, 1912. Song: high, med., and low v edns, pf.

2102 Protheroe, Daniel. Milwaukee: Joseph Flanner, 1896. Song: C or Bar, pf; Chicago: H.T. FitzSimmons, 1928. Chorus: TTBB, pf.

2103 Schaaf, E.O. In *German and English Poems in Song* vol. 2 op. 3. u.p.: E.O. Schaaf, 1902.

2104 Steere, William C. In *Four Songs* op. 15 no. 1. Cincinnati: J. Church, 1910. Song: v, pf.

2105 Wald, Max R. Boston: Boston Music, 1906. Song: 2 v edns, pf.

2106 Weil, Hermann. Boston: O. Ditson, 1917. Song: high and med. v edns, pf.

The Angel and the Child [Trans from the poem, "L'Ange et l'enfant: elégie à une mère," of Jean Reboul]. *Three Books of Song* (1872).

2107 Gabriel, Virginia. Boston: O. Ditson, [BAL n.d., not before 1870].

Annie of Tharaw [Trans. from the poem, "Anke von Tharau," of Simon Dach]. *The Poets and Poetry of Europe* (1845).

2108 Balfe, Michael W. London: Boosey, n.d., [BPL 187-?]. Ballad: v, pf. In coll. BSP.

The Arrow and the Song. *The Belfry of Bruges and Other Poems* (1846).

2109 Balfe, Michael W. Boston: O. Ditson, [BAL n.d., 1858-1876]. Song: med. v, pf. In coll. CS 1, DM 1, HSE 1, Jo.

2110 Beach, H.H.A., Mrs. In coll. DagI.

2111 Beecroft, G.A.B. "The Arrow & the Song." London: Weekes, n.d. Song: v, pf.

2112 Blair, William. Cincinnati: J. Church, 1915. Song: v, pf.

2113 Blockley, John. London: John Blockley, n.d. Song: v, pf.

2114 Bonvin, Ludwig. "Pfeil und Lied (The Arrow and the Song)" in *Zwei Lieder* op. 40. no 1. Leipzig: Breitkopf & Härtel, 1898. Song: M or Bar, pf. Words in Eng. and Ger.

2115 Chenoweth, Wilbur. New York: M. Witmark, 1936. Song: v, pf.

2116 Coerne, Louis A. In *Ten Songs* op. 28 no. 3. Boston: Everett E. Truette, 1894. Song: v, pf.

2117 Colburn, S.C. New York: G. Schirmer, 1910. Song: high or med. v, pf.

2118 Davis, Miss. London: Metzler, [BPL 188-?]. Song: v, pf.

2119 Elliot, C.S. Boston: G.D. Russell, 1880.

2120 Erlanger, Frédéric d'. London: Schott, 1934. Chorus: SSAATTBB, a cap.

2121 Falk, L. "The Arrow and the Song" op. 22. Privately pubd by Falk, 1869. Song: v, pf.

2122 Foote, A. In coll. Par 4.

2123 Gounod, Charles. Philadelphia: W.F. Shaw, 1884. London: Metzler, n.d. Song: high, med., and low v edns, pf.

2124 Hawley, C.B. New York: Wm. A. Pond, 1883. Song: v, pf.

2125 Hay, Walter. Boston: O. Ditson, n.d. Part Song: SATB,

2126 Henschel, Georg. "I Shot an Arrow into the Air." New York: G. Schirmer, 1880. Song: high and low v edns, pf.

2127 Hime, Edward L. London: Duff & Stewart, n.d. Song: v, pf.

2128 Mulligan, Wm. Ed. New York: E. Schuberth, 1887.

2129 Newell, J.E. In *Twelve Two Part Songs for the Use of Schools and Classes*. London: E. Donajowski, n.d. Part Song: 2 voices, pf.

2130 Ord, George. Dunham: George Ord, n.d. Song: v, pf.

2131 Pinsuti, Ciro. Philadelphia: W.F. Shaw, n.d. [BAL not before 1870]. Song: v, pf; George L. Tracy, arr. [Boston?]: C.C. Birchard, 1916. Chorus: SATB, pf.

2132 Thomas, F. In coll. ArJ.

2133 Van Curt, W.E. Philadelphia: F.A. North, 1887. Song: v, pf.

2134 Watson, Michael. London: Metzler, n.d. Part Song: 2 treble voices.

The Arsenal at Springfield. *Poems* (1845).

2135 Høffding, Finn. "Fantasia Sinfonica" op. 54. Copenhagen: Samfundet til udgivelse af dansk musik, 1958. Cantata: SATB chorus, SABar soli, org and orch. Words in Eng.

2136 Jones, J. Owen. London: Rowland's, 1929. Chorus: TTBB, pf or orch.

2137 Speer, Charlton, T. " 'The Arsenal' or 'War and Peace.' " London: Weekes, [BPL 1884?]. Cantata: chorus, SATBarB soli, pf or orch.

2138 Warden, David A. "The Voice of Christ." Philadelphia: Lee & Walker, 1862.

Auf Wiedersehen, in Memory of J.T.F. *In The Harbor: Ultima Thule—Part II*. (1882).

2139 Temple, Hope. "Auf Wiederseh'n." New York: Boosey, 1893.

Autumn Within. *In the Harbor: Ultima Thule—Part II* (1882).

2140 Colburn, S.C. New York: G. Schirmer, Jr., 1907; Boston: Boston Music, 1907. Song: med. v, pf.

2141 Deis, Carl. "The Waning" in *Two Plaints*. New York: G. Schirmer, 1920. Song: low v, pf.

The Ballad of Carmilhan. *Three Books of Song* (1872).

2142 Arnott, Archibald D. "The Ballad of Carmilhan" op. 10. London: Novello, Ewer, 1894. Setting for chorus, Bar solo, orch.

The Beleaguered City. *Voices of the Night* (1839).

2143 Fisher, Bernard W. London: R. Cocks, n.d. Song: v, pf.

The Belfry of Bruges. *The Belfry of Bruges, and Other Poems* (1846).

2144 Weiss, Willoughby H. London: Weekes, 1896. Song: v, pf.

The Bells of San Blas. *In the Harbor: Ultima Thule—Part II* (1882).

2145 Boott, Francis. Boston: O. Ditson, 1882. Setting for qrt of equal v, pf.

Beware! [Trans. from the poem, "Hüt Du Dich!"]. *Voices of the Night* (1839).

2146 A.H.N.B. "She Is Fooling Thee." Cited in DCD.

2147 Allen, G.B. London: Duff & Stewart, n.d. Song: v, pf.

2148 Balfe, Michael W. "Trust Her Not." New York: Firth, Pond, [BAL n.d., not before 1856]. Duet: MM, pf. In coll. BSP.

2149 Blockley, John. London: John Blockley, n.d. Song: v, pf. Also pubd for duet.

2150 Brown, O.B. Boston: O. Ditson, n.d., c1880 by J.M. Russell. Quartet: TTBB, a cap.

2151 C.S.T. "I Know a Maiden Fair." New York: Firth and Hall, 1842: Song: v, pf.

2152 Dance, Caroline A. London: Robt. W. Ollivier, n.d. Song: v, pf.

2153 Dendy, A.H. London: Letchford, n.d. Song: v, pf.

2154 Dow, Howard M. Boston: O. Ditson, 1876.

2155 Elliot, C.S. Boston: G.D. Russell, 1880. Song: v, pf.

2156 Fickenscher, Arthur. "I Know a Maiden Fair to See." New York: G. Schirmer, 1912. Chorus: SSAA, pf.

2157 Gilbert, B.F. Boston: O. Ditson, 1876. Song: S, pf.

2158 Glover, Stephen R. London: Brewer, n.d. Song: v, pf.

2159 Gounod, Charles. New York: Wm. A. Pond, [BAL n.d., not before 1863].

2160 Hatton, John L. New York: G. Schirmer, 1890. Part Song: TTBB and SATB edns, pf; New York: G. Schirmer, 1890. Chorus: SATB, a cap. In coll. BD.

2161 Herbert, Arthur. London: C. Woolhouse, n.d. Song: v, pf.

2162 Heuberer, Charles F. Boston: H. Prentiss, 1845.

2163 James, Philip. "I Know a Maiden Faire to See" op. 3 no. 2. New York: H.W. Gray, u.d. Chorus: SATB.

2164 Jordan, Jules. "I Know a Maiden." Boston: O. Ditson, 1888. Quartet: TTBB, pf.

2165 Kolar, Victor. "Beware" op. 18 no. 2. New York: C. Fischer, 1912. Song: med. v, pf.

2166 Kullak, Franz. "Beware! Beware!" London: Sheard, [BPL 186–?]. Song: v, pf.

2167 Lancelott, F. London: Davidson, n.d. Song: v, opt 3-pt. refrain, pf.

2168 Landor, Margaret. "Warning" in *Six Songs*. Minneapolis: Lloyd Publishing, 1903. Song: v, pf.

2169 Lent, Ernest. Washington, D.C.: Columbia Music Pub., 1908. Song: high v, pf.

2170 Merz, Karl. New York: C.M. Tremaine, 1866.

2171 Moulton, Charles. "Beware! Take Care." New York: Beer & Schirmer, 1865. Song: high and med. v edns, pf; "Beware" (Prends garde à toi). London: J. Williams, n.d. Song: v, pf. Text in Eng. and Fr., trans. by Victor Wilder.

2172 Newell, J.E. London: Osborn & Tuckwood, n.d. Part Song: SATB, a cap.

2173 Pasmore, Henry B. Boston: O. Ditson, 1907. Part Song: SSAA, pf.

2174 Perring, James Ernest. New York: Wm. A. Pond, 1864. Song: high v, pf; London: Cramer, n.d. Song: v, pf. The title page mistakenly has J.G. Perring.

2175 R., F.W. "I Know a Maiden Fair to See." Richmond, Va.: George Dunn, 1863. Song: v, pf.

2176 Redhead, Alfred. "I Know a Maiden." London: S. Lucas, Weber, Pitt & Hatzfeld, [ca. 1883]. Madrigal: SATB, pf.

2177 Rossini, Gioacchino. Boston: O. Ditson, n.d., c1891 J.M. Russell. Part Song: 3 women's voices, a cap.

2178 Schaide, M. Boston: O. Ditson, 1851.

2179 Sudds, W.F. "Trust Her Not." Boston: Thompson & Odell, 1882.

2180 Terry, R.R., arr. by Maurice Jacobson. Setting for male chorus, a cap.

2181 Thayer, Arthur W. Boston: A.P. Schmidt, 1886. Song: v, pf.

2182 Thayer, W. Eugene. In *Three Songs*. Boston: G.D. Russell, 1865. Song: v, pf.

2183 Thomson, Sydney. Boston: O. Ditson, 1901. Part Song: TTBB, a cap.

2184 "Trust Her Not." London: Boosey, n.d. Duet: 2 M, pf.

2185 Van Vactor, David. In *New Music* 17 (1944). Song: v, pf.

2186 Whittlesey, Orramel. "Take Care." New York: Gould & Berry, 1852. Song: v, pf.

The Black Knight [Trans. from the poem, "Der schwarze Ritter," of Johann Ludwig Uhland]. *Hyperion* (1839).

2187 Elgar, Edward. "The Black Knight" op. 25. London: Novello, Ewer, 1893. Cantata: SATB chorus, orch.

Blessed Are the Dead [Trans. from the poem, "Selig sind, die in dem Herrn Sterben," of Simon Dach].

2188 Lyon, James. "Blessed Are the Dead (Selig sind die Toten)" op. 28. London: Breitkopf & Härtel, n.d. Chorus: SSAATTBB, pf or orch (R). Text in Eng. and Ger.

Blind Bartimeus. *Ballads and Other Poems* (1842).

2189 Austin, Walter. London: Boosey, n.d. Song: v, pf.

2190 Bell, Doyne C. London: R. Mills, n.d. Song: v, pf.

The Blind Girl of Castèl Cuillè [Trans. from the poem of Jacques Jasmin]. *The Seaside and the Fireside* (1849).

2191 Coleridge-Taylor, Samuel. "The Blind Girl of Castèl-Cuillè" op. 43. London: Novello, 1901. Cantata: SATB chorus, S and Bar soli, orch.

2192 Corder, Frederick. London: J. Williams, 1893. Cantata: SSA chorus, S and C soli, pf.

2193 Morton, Marguerite W, arr. New York: Edgar S. Werner, 1892. Illustrated tableaux with musical acc.

The Boy and the Brook. *The Poetical Works* [BAL n.d., not before May 1872].

2194 Hatton, John L. London: Ransford, n.d. [BPL 187–?]. Song: v, pf.

2195 Kellie, Lawrence. London: Robert Cocks, 1893.

The Bridge. *Poems* (1845).

2196 Armitage, R.K. London: E. Ashdown, n.d. Song: v, pf.

2197 Barnett, John. London: Lamborn Cock, Hutchings, n.d. Song: v, pf.

2198 Blockley, John. London: Addison & Hollier, n.d. Song: v, pf; New York: Benjamin W. Hitchcock, 1869.

2199 Bucalossi, P. "The Midnight Hour." Boston: O. Ditson, [BAL n.d., not before 1881].

2200 Carew, Lady. New York: J.L. Peters, n.d. [BAL ca. 1870]. Song: v, pf; St. Louis: Kunkel Bros., 1883. Song: low v, pf. Text in Eng. and Ger. Also pubd for women's chorus and mixed chorus (arr. by P.A. Schnecker). In coll. GE.

2201 Cottell, Lansdowne. London: London Conservatoire of Music, n.d. Song: v, pf.

2202 Dolores. London: C. Jefferys, n.d. Song: v, pf.

2203 Landon, Agnes. Boston: O. Ditson, [BAL n.d., not before 1854]. Song: v, pf.

2204 Lindsay, M., Miss. [Mrs. M. Bliss]. Philadelphia: Lee & Walker, [BAL 1856?]. Song: med. v, pf. In coll. FSS 3, HSC, LBR, NMH, WBT.

2205 Romer, Frank. London: Lamborn Cock, Hutchings, n.d. Song: v, pf.

2206 Smallwood, Samuel. Philadelphia: F.A. North, [BAL n.d., not before 1872].

2207 Stevens, M.L. London: Weekes, n.d. Song: v, pf.

2208 Walker, J.H. London: Addison & Hollier, n.d. Song: v, pf.

The Brook [Trans. from the poem, "A un arroyuelo"]. *Voices of the Night* (1839).

2209 Volpé, A.D. In *Three Songs*. New York: G. Schirmer, 1906. Song: high v, pf.

The Brook and the Wave. *Aftermath* (1873).

2210 Boott, Francis. "The Brooklet." Boston: O. Ditson, 1874. Duet: M and T or Bar, pf.

2211 C.E.N.C. "The Brook and the Wave." n.p., n.d. Song: v, pf.

2212 Cadman, Charles W. "The Brooklet Came from the Mountain." New York: G. Schirmer, u.d. Song: low v, pf. 1944?

2213 Lautz, Henry J. "The Brook and the Wave (Das Bächlein und die Walle)." New York: A.P. Schmidt, 1902. Text in Ger. and Eng.

2214 Molloy, James L. Boston: O. Ditson, [BAL n.d., not before 1858, not after 1876]. Song: v, pf.

2215 Parr, Amy Ursula. London: Hopwood & Crew, n.d. Song: v, pf.

2216 Pontet, Henry. London: John Blockley, n.d. Song: v, pf.

2217 Scott, Charles P. Boston: A.P. Schmidt, 1897.

The Builders. *Poems: Lyrical and Dramatic* (1848).

2218 Blockley, John. London: Duff & Hodgson, n.d. Song: v, pf.

The Building of the Ship. *The Seaside and the Fireside* (1849).

2219 Barnett, John F. London: Patey & Willis, [ca. 1880]. Cantata: SATB chorus, soli, pf.

2220 Beethoven, Ludwig van, arr. from. "The Ship of State" in coll. Gi 4, GiJr.

2221 Cole, Rossetter G. "Sail On, O Ship of State" in coll. To. Setting for SA, B ad lib.

2222 Cowles, Eugene. "The Ship of State." Boston: O. Ditson, 1908. Song: B, pf.

2223 Kratz, Lee G. "Sail On, Sail On." Boston: O. Ditson, 1895. Part Song: TTBB, a cap.

2224 Lahee, Henry. London: Tonic Solfa Agency, 1869. Cantata: chorus, soli, pf and harmonium. Also pubd for 3-pt. women's chorus ("Sail Forth out into the Sea") and mixed chorus, S obl ("Sail On, Nor Fear").

2225 Maddison, A. "Sail On, O Ship of State." London: Augener, n.d. Song: v, pf.

2226 Ringwald, Roy. n.t. in *The Song of America.* East Stroudsburg, Pa.: Shawnee, 1951. Setting for SATB chorus, narr., pf 4 hands. Recording: Decca, DAU 816.

2227 Scott, Charles P. "Sail On! O Ship of State." Boston: A.P. Schmidt, 1936. Chorus: 3-pt. mixed voices, pf.

2228 "The Ship of State." Arr. from a German Air. In coll. LBR.

2229 "The Ship of State" in coll. FSS 8, LAASR, WBT.

2230 Stewart, N. Coe. "The Ship of State." New York: The New Singing Society, 1917. Chorus: mixed voices.

2231 Weyse, C.E., adapted from. "The Ship of State" in coll. Ea.

2232 Wilson, Ira B. Chicago: J.S. Fearis, 1924. Cantata: SABar, [pf or orch?].

Carillon. *Poems* (1845).

2233 Gordon, J. Hart. Liverpool: Music Publishing Cooperative Society, 1894. Duet: 2 voices in canon, pf.

The Castle by the Sea [Trans. from the poem, "Das Schloss am Meere," of Johann Ludwig Uhland]. *Hyperion* (1839).

2234 Brandeis, Frederick. New York: Wm. A. Pond, 1864.

2235 Romer, Frank. London: Lamborn, Cock, Hutching, [BPL 186-?]. Romance: v, pf.

Catawba Wine. *The Courtship of Miles Standish, and Other Poems* (1858).

2236 Adams, Charles R. "Wine Song." Boston: O. Ditson, 1879. Song: v, pf.

2237 Clough-Leighter, H. "Catawba Wine" op. 1 no. 2. Washington, D.C.: Henry White, 1902. Song: v, pf.

2238 Dempster, William R. Boston: O. Ditson, 1858. Song: v, pf.

Changed. *Aftermath* (1873).

2239 Boott, Francis. Boston: O. Ditson, 1873. Song: v, pf. In coll. BoS.

2240 Paine, Francis M. "Changed" op. 1 no. 3. Hyde Park, Mass.: F.L. Hodgdon, n.d. Song: M or T, pf (fl or vn obl).

Charles Sumner. *The Masque of Pandora and Other Poems* (1875).

2241 Heilner, Irwin. "Garlands and Flowers." MS, 1945, avail. ACA. Song: high v, pf.

2242 Rinck, Christian H. "Alike Are Life and Death" in coll. LBR. Setting for SATB.

The Child Asleep [Trans. from the poem, "Verslets à mon premier né," of Clotilde de Surville]. *Voices of the Night* (1839).

2243 Schaaf, E.O. In *German and English Poems in Song* vol. 2 op. 3. u.p.: E.O. Schaaf, 1902.

2244 Volpé, A.D. "The Child Asleep (Das schlafende Kind)." Boston: O. Ditson, 1905. Song: med. v, pf. Text in Eng. and Ger., trans. by Melanie Guttman.

Children. *The Courtship of Miles Standish, and Other Poems* (1858).

2245 Anderton, Thomas. "Come to Me O Ye Children." London: Patey & Willis, n.d. Song: v, pf.

2246 Baker, George. [BAL Galt, Canada, 1878].

2247 Bainton, Edgar L. "To the Children." London: J.B. Cramer, 1923. Song: v, pf.

2248 Batten, Robert. "Living Poems." London: Boosey, 1905. Song: v, pf, org ad lib.

2249 Cecil, Arthur. London: Chappell, n.d. Song: v, pf.

2250 Chase, Charles Coes. "Come to Me, O Ye Children." Boston: O. Ditson, 1900. Chorus: SATB, pf ad lib.

2251 Dempster, William R. Boston: O. Ditson, 1859.

2252 Driver, J.M. "Longfellow's Work Song." Boston: O. Ditson, 1886.

2253 Hatton, John L. London: J. Williams, n.d. Song: v, pf.

2254 Kingston, Matthew. "Come to Me, O Ye Children." London: B. Williams, n.d. Song: v, pf.

2255 Linley, George. London: F. Brooks, n.d. Song: v, pf.

2256 Macirone, C.A. "Come to Me Oh Ye Children." London: Robt. W. Ollivier, n.d. Song: v, pf.

2257 Maker, F.C. London: Patey & Willis, n.d. Song: v, pf.

2258 Martinez, Isidora. "Living Poems." Chicago: Clayton F. Summy, 1912. Song: v, pf.

2259 Matthews, Charles. "Come to Me, O Ye Children." London: Hutchings & Romer, n.d. Song: v, pf.

2260 Maynard, Walter. London: Chappell, [BPL 186–?]. Song: v, pf.

2261 Mountfort, J. London: J. Blockley, n.d. Song: v, pf.

2262 Newell, J.E. "The Eastern Window." London: W. Morley, n.d. Song: v, pf.

2263 Romer, Frank. London: A.W. Hammond, n.d. Song: v, pf.

2264 Selle, Louis. "Come to Me O Ye Children." New York: H. Waters, 1862. Song: v, pf.

2265 Sullivan, Arthur. "Living Poems." Philadelphia: W.H. Boner, [BAL n.d., after 1864]. Song: v, pf.

2266 Watkis, Helena. "Children's Voices." London: Weekes, n.d. Song: v, pf.

2267 Whyte, Dorothy J. "Living Poems." London: Keith, Prowse, 1922. Song: v, pf.

The Children's Hour. *Tales of a Wayside Inn* (1863).

2268 Allen, George B. London: E. Nichol, n.d. Song: v, pf.

2269 Blockley, John. London: John Blockley, n.d. Song: v, pf.

2270 Cottam, Arthur. London: Addison & Lucas, n.d. Song: v, pf.

2271 Gaul, Arthur R. Boston: O. Ditson, n.d. Part Song: SATB, pf.

2272 Ives, Charles. In coll. IOS, ITS. Song: v, pf.

2273 Kay, Ulysses. In *Triumvirate*. New York: Peer International, 1954. Chorus: TTBB, a cap.

2274 Maeder, J. Gaspar. New York: Firth, Pond, 1860.

2275 Mirana. London: Metzler, n.d. Song: v, pf.

2276 Williams, Langton. London: W. Williams, n.d. Song: v, pf.

Christmas Bells. *Household Poems* (1865).

2277 Barnes, A. Fairbairn. "I Heard the Bells on Christmas Day." London: Stainer & Bell, 1934. Carol: SATB, org.

2278 Bentley, W.H. In *Six Songs* op. 2 no. 5. London: London Music Publishing, n.d. Song: v, pf.

2279 Bergh, Arthur. "I Heard the Bells on Christmas Day." Boston: C.C. Birchard, 1950. Carol: SATB, acc?

2280 Bishop, H., attr. to. "I Heard the Bells on Christmas Day." Tune: "Illsey." In coll. STC.

2281 Brewer, A.H. "I Heard the Bells on Christmas Day" in coll. HC.

2282 Bullard, F.F. In coll. Bo.

2283 Calkin, John Baptiste. "I Heard the Bells on Christmas Day." Waltham (tune). In coll. BB, BeBBN, KCC, MAS, PCS, SLS.

2284 Dunstan, R. "I Heard the Bells on Christmas Day" in coll. DNS.

2285 Earhart, W. In coll. Gi 2, GiA, GiTw.

2286 Fontein-Tuinhout, F.R. "Three Christmas-Bells" in *Three Serious Songs* op. 11. Middleburg: A.A. Noske, 1906. Song: A or B-Bar, pf.

2287 Hatton, John L. "The Bells." Boston: O. Ditson, [BAL n.d., after 1869]. In coll. HSE 3; "Christmas Bells." London: Boosey, n.d. Song: v, pf.

2288 Hesser, E. In coll. DagM, DagR, DagU.

2289 J.T. n.t. In coll. ChAH. Hymn.

2290 Lane, Charles F. "Bells on Christmas." New York: Tullar-Meredith, 1936. Cantata: mixed voices, pf. Text adapted by Edith Sanford Tillotson.

2291 Liddle, S. London: Chappell, 1907. Song: v, pf.

2292 Matthews, J. Sebastian. New York: H.W. Gray, 1916. Carol-Anthem: SATB, a cap.

2293 O'Hara, Geoffrey. "Good-will to Men." New York: Chappell-Harms, 1932. Song: med. and low v edns, pf; New York: Chappell-Harms, 1932. Anthem or Chorus: SATB, pf.

2294 Ramsey, B. Mansell. "I Heard the Bells on Christmas Day." London: J. Curwen, n.d. Chorus: 2 equal treble voices.

2295 Sawyer, H.P. St. Louis: Balmer & Weber, 1881. Song: v, pf.

A Christmas Carol ["I hear along our street"]. *The Seaside and the Fireside* (1849).

2296 Chester, Lilly Lawrence. n.p., n.d. Song: v, pf.

2297 Clare, Professor. "Christmas Carol." London: Holdernesse, n.d. Song and Chorus: v, SATB, pf.

2298 Lane, Carl A. London: Augener, n.d. Song: v, pf.

2298a Noël Bourguignon" in coll. HoA.

2298b "Nuns in Frigid Cells." Carol. In coll. STC.

2299 Speranza, L. London: Lamborn, Cock, Addison, n.d. Song: v, pf.

2300 Wilson, Mackenzie, Mrs. London: R. Cocks, n.d. Song: v, pf.

2301 Wilson, William. London: Addison, Hollier & Lucas, n.d. Song: v, pf.

Chrysoar. *The Seaside and the Fireside* (1849).

2302 Busch, Carl. "Song of a Star." Boston: O. Ditson, 1904. Part Song: TTBB, a cap.

2303 Indy, Vincent d'. "The Evening Star" in coll. Par 4.

2304 Nevin, Arthur F. New York: G. Schirmer, 1907. Chorus: SATB, pf.

Coplas de Manrique. *Voices of the Night* (1839).

2305 Berger, Francesco. "The Way of the World" in *Two-Part Songs*. London: Patey & Willis, n.d. Part Song: boys' or girls' voices, pf.

2306 Romer, Frank. "Our Lives Are Rivers." London: Wickins, n.d. Song: v, pf.

The Courtship of Miles Standish. *The Courtship of Miles Standish and Other Poems* (1858).

2307 Wilson, Ira B. Dayton: Lorenz Music, 1929. Cantata for 2-pt. voices, pf. Text adapted by Edith Sanford Tillotson.

The Cumberland. *Tales of a Wayside Inn* (1863).

2308 Boott, Francis. Boston: O. Ditson, 1863. Song with chorus ad lib, pf. In coll. BoS.

2309 Marshall, Charles. London: Boosey, [BPL 188–?]. Song: v, pf.

Curfew. *Poems* (1845).

2310 Anderton, Thomas. London: Cassell, Peter, and Alpin, n.d. Part Song: SATB, pf.

2311 Bentley, W.H. In *Six Songs* op. 2 no. 6. London: London Music Publishing, n.d. Song: v, pf.

2312 Berger, Francesco. In *Two-Part Songs*. London: Patey & Willis, n.d. Part Song: boys' or girls' voices, pf.

2313 Beta. In *Gems of Longfellow*. London: R.W. Ollivier, n.d.

2314 Blockley, John. Baltimore: Miller & Beacham, [BAL n.d., not before 1854]. Pubd. as a song and a duet.

2315 Chadwick, George W. "The Curfew." Boston: A.P. Schmidt, 1914. Song: high and med. v edns, pf.

2316 "Curfew" in coll. LBR.

2317 Dinelli, Giuseppe. London: Marriott & Williams, n.d. Song: v, pf.

2318 Distin, Theodore. "No Sound in the Hall." London: Ransford, n.d. Song: v, pf.

2319 Finck, E.J. Boston: O. Ditson, [BAL n.d., not before 1867].

2320 Gaul, Harvey B. Chicago: C.F. Summy, 1934. Chorus: mixed v, pf.

2321 Gilchrist, W.W. "The Curfew" in coll. To. Setting for SSA, a cap?

2322 Glover, Stephen R. "The Curfew Bell." Chicago: National Music, [BAL n.d., after 1880]. Duet.

2323 Gow, George C. "Curfew" in *Five Songs* op. 2 no. 4. Boston: G. Schirmer, Jr., 1888. Song: v, pf; In *A Group of Songs*. Boston, 1896.

2324 Gower, Allis. "The Curfew Bell." London: Metzler, [BPL 188-?]. Song: v, pf.

2325 Guglielmo, P.D. "The Curfew Bell." London: Guglielmo's Music Depot, n.d. Song: v, pf.

2326 Hatton, John L. Boston: White Smith & Perry, 1869. Song: C or Bar, pf.

2327 Marchant, A.W. London: Osborn & Tuckwood, n.d. Part Song: 2 ladies' voices, pf.

2328 Newell, J.E. "The Curfew Bell" in *Twelve Two Part Songs for the Use of Schools and Classes*. London: E. Donajowski, n.d. Part Song: 2 voices, pf.

2329 Perabeau, H. "Curfew Bell." Boston: O. Ditson, [BAL n.d., 1844–1857].

2330 Read, J.F.H. London: Lamborn Cock, n.d. Song: C or Bar, pf.

2331 Seward, Theo. F. "The Curfew." Rochester, N.Y., 1862.

2332 Silas, E. "The Curfew." London: Cramer, Beale & Chappell, [BPL 186-?]. Song: Bar or C, pf.

2333 Smart, Henry. London: Novello, Ewer, n.d. Setting for SATB, pf. No. 142 of *Novello's Part-Song Book* (Second Series).

2334 Waley, S.W. London: Jullien, n.d. Song: Bar or B, pf.

The Day Is Done. *Poems* (1845).

2335 Allen, George B. London: Cramer, Beale, n.d. Song: v, pf.

2336 Andrews, R. London: Metzler, n.d. Song: v, pf.

2337 Balfe, Michael W. Philadelphia: Lee & Walker, [BAL n.d., not before 1856]. Song: low v, pf. In coll. BSP, GE.

2338 Beta. In *Gems of Longfellow*. London: Robt. W. Ollivier, n.d. Song: v, pf.

2339 Blockley, John J., the Younger. London: Cramer, Beale, n.d. Song: v, pf.

2340 Carter, O.L. "The Day Is Done" op. 53. Boston: O. Ditson, 1896. Quartet: ladies' voices, unacc.

2341 Castelnuovo-Tedesco, Mario. In *Two Longfellow Songs* op. 149. New York: Mills, 1962. Chorus: SATB, pf.

2342 Davis, L.S. San Francisco: Bancroft, Knight, 1875. Song: v, pf.

2343 E.W. London: R. Cocks, n.d. Song: v, pf.

2344 Gaul, Alfred R. London: Novello, Ewer, [BPL 188-?]. Descriptive choral song for unaccompanied singing.

2345 Kinney, John J. New York: Wm. A. Pond, 1878.

2346 Löhr, Hermann. London: Chappell, 1908. Duet: voices, pf, org ad lib.

2347 Loud, Annie F. Boston: O. Ditson, 1882. Song: v, pf.

2348 Neidlinger, W.H. "Resting." Brooklyn: F.H. Chandler, 1879. Song: v, pf.

2349 Reinhardt, Carl. London: Sheard, [BPL 186-?]. Song: v, pf.

2350 Schäffer, Wilhelm. New York: M. Witmark, 1932. Reading, pf.

2351 Sellé, W.C. London: A. Hammond, n.d. Song: v, pf.

2352 Smart, Henry. London: Ashdown & Parry, [BPL 187-?]. Song: v, pf.

2353 Williams, Eliza. London: Addison & Lucas, n.d. Song: v, pf.

2354 Wood, Arthur L. In *The Musical Record* 21, pp. 41-43. c1877 by F.W. Helmick. Song: v, pf.

A Day of Sunshine. *The Courtship of Miles Standish and Other Poems* (1858).

2355 Beethoven, Ludwig van. In coll. Mu 5, MuC 5, MuO, MuT 3.

2356 Butler, Eugene. "Paean of Joy." Chapel Hill: Hinshaw Music, 1977. Chorus: SATB, pf.

2357 Luttman, Willie L. London: Reid Bros., n.d. Song: v, pf.

2358 Entry cancelled.

Daybreak. *The Courtship of Miles Standish, and Other Poems* (1858).

2359 Balfe, Michael W. Boston: O. Ditson, [BAL n.d., 1858-1876]. Song: med. v, pf.

2360 Barbour, Florence N. "Awake! It Is the Day." Boston: A.P. Schmidt, 1910. Song: high and med. v edns, pf.

2361 Berger, Francesco. In *Two-Part Songs*. London: Patey & Willis, n.d. Part Song: boys' or girls' voices, pf.

2362 Blockley, John. London: Addison, Hollier & Lucas, n.d. Song: v, pf.

2363 Branscombe, Gena. "A Wind from the Sea." Boston: A.P. Schmidt, 1924. Setting for SSA, pf.

2364 Braunschiedl, Johannes. "A Wind Came up out of the Sea." New York: C.H. Ditson, 1883.

2364a Broadhead, G.F. New York: Associated Music Publishers, u.d. Chorus: SSA.

2365 Burleigh, Cecil. "Awake, It Is the Day" op. 47 no. 1. Boston: O. Ditson, 1920. Song: high and med. v edns, pf.

2366 Camp, John S. Philadelphia: T. Presser, 1918. Part Song: SATB, pf.

2367 Clippingdale, J. London: Forsyth Bros., n.d. Song: v, pf.

2368 Dubois, T. In coll. ArF 1.

2369 Faning, Eaton. Cincinnati: W.H. Willis, 1904. Setting for mixed chorus, pf; Bryceson Treharne, arr. Cincinnati: W.H. Willis, 1933. School Song, pf.

2370 Fisher, William A. Boston: O. Ditson, 1901. Chorus: male voices.

2371 Gaul, Alfred R. London: Patey & Willis, 1883. Part Song: SATB, pf; New York: G. Schirmer, 1891. Part Song: SATB, a cap.

2372 Georgette. "A Wind Came up out of the Sea." London: J. Bath, n.d. Song: v, pf.

2373 Gerard, V.C. London: Lyric Music Publishing, n.d. Duet: voices, pf.

2374 Gould, Monk. London: Novello, n.d. Song: med. and low v edns, pf.

2375 Homer, Sidney. "Daybreak" op. 11 no. 1 in *Four Songs*. New York: G. Schirmer, 1903. Song: high and low v, edns, pf.

2376 Lindsay, M., Miss. Boston: O. Ditson, [BAL n.d., 1858–1876]. Song: v, pf.

2377 Macfarren, Walter. London: Stanley Lucas, Weber, n.d. Part Song: SATB, pf.

2378 Mallard, Clarisse. London: C. Woolhouse, 1900. Song: v, pf or orch.

2379 Mallinson, Albert. Leipzig: Wilhelm Hansen, 1898. Song: v, pf. Words in Eng. and Ger.

2380 Malmene, Waldemar. New York: R.A. Saalfield, 1873. Descriptive Song: v, pf.

2381 Mamlock, Ursula. MS, u.d., avail. ACA. Song: S or M, pf.

2382 Marston, G.W. New York: G. Schirmer, 1877. Song: med. v, pf.

2383 Nevin, Arthur F. New York: G. Schirmer, 1907. Chorus: SATB, pf.

2384 Newell, J.E. In *Twelve Two Part Songs for the Use of Schools and Classes*. London: E. Donajowski, n.d. Part Song: voices, pf.

2385 Parker, J.C.D. "Day-break." Boston: O. Ditson, 1875. Chorus: SATB; In *7 Part Songs*. Boston: O. Ditson, 1875. Part Song: SATB, pf.

2386 Pennell, H. Chalmondeley. "A Wind Came up out of the Sea." London: Addison, Hollier & Lucas, n.d. Song: v, pf.

2387 Perkins, W.O. Boston: O. Ditson, 1895. Part Song: female trio, pf.

2388 Peuret, O. Boston: A.P. Schmidt, 1884. 4-pt. song for female voices, a cap.

2389 Romer, Frank. London: Lamborn Cock, Hutchings, [BPL 186–?]. Song: v, pf.

2390 Sacco, P. Peter. In *Collected Songs* vol. 1, op. 135 no. 1. Daly City, Calif.: Ostara Press, 1971. Song: med.-high v, pf (str orch [R]); Los Angeles: Western International Music, u.d. Chorus: SATB, pf.

2391 Smith, David Stanley. "Daybreak" op. 33 no. 2. *Songs of Dawn*. New York: G. Schirmer, 1917. Chorus: SATB, a cap.

Daylight and Moonlight. *The Courtship of Miles Standish, and Other Poems* (1858).

2392 Berger, Francesco. In *Two-Part Songs*. London: Patey & Willis, n.d. Part Song: boys' or girls' voices, pf.

2393 Pope, H. Campbell. "Daylight & Moonlight." London: Weekes, n.d. Song: v, pf.

The Dead. *Voices of the Night* (1839).

2394 Coleridge-Taylor, Samuel. "How They So Softly Rest" op. 35 no. 2. London: Augener, 1898. 3-pt. song for female voices, pf.

2395 Hodges, Faustina H. "The Holy Dead." New York: Firth, Pond, [BAL n.d., 1848–1853]. Trio: 3 treble voices, pf.

2396 Van Antwerp, Yates. In *Two Poems*. Philadelphia: Lee & Walker, 1872. Song: v, pf.

Decoration Day. *In the Harbor: Ultima Thule—Part II* (1882).

2396a Geyer, Johann Aegidius. In coll. LBR. Setting for SATB, a cap.

Delia. *Kéramos and Other Poems* (1878).

2397 Bischoff, J.W. "Sweet Remembrance." Cincinnati: J. Church, 1890.

2398 Busch, Carl. "Remembrance." Boston: O. Ditson, 1900. Song: med. and low v edns, pf.

2399 Christie, Kenneth. n.p.: O. Ditson, 1950. Song: med. v, pf.

2400 Coerne, Louis A. In *Ten Songs* op. 28 no. 1. Boston: Everett E. Truette, 1894. Song: v, pf.

2401 Cowen, Frederic H. "Thy Remembrance" in *Album of Twelve Songs.* New York: G. Schirmer, [BAL n.d., after 1879]. Song: med. v, pf; Boston: O. Ditson, n.d. Song: high v, pf.

2402 Hamilton, W.K. In *Three Songs.* Biarritz, France: Hamilton, n.d. Song: v, pf.

2403 Heymann, Jacob. In *Three Songs.* New York: E. Schuberth, 1932. Song: med. v, pf.

2404 Ives, Arthur. London: Grahame & Black, 1910. Song: med. and low v edns, pf.

2405 Waldrop, Uda. "Thy Remembrance." Cincinnati: J. Church, n.d. Song: high and med. v edns, pf.

Drinking Song. *The Belfry of Bruges, and Other Poems* (1846).

2406 Harvey, S. "The Head of Old Silenus." London: F. Pitman, n.d. Duet: T and B, pf.

Endymion. *Ballads and Other Poems* (1842).

2407 Berger, Francesco. In *Two-Part Songs.* London: Patey & Willis, n.d. Part Song: boys' or girls' voices, pf.

2408 Claypole, Arthur C. "Love's Life." London: A. Rotherham, 1913. Song: v, pf.

2409 Lehmann, Liza. Cincinnati: J. Church, 1899. Song: S, A, M edns, pf. Cincinnati: J. Church, 1917. Chorus: SSAA, pf.

2410 Levey, W.C. "The Rising Moon Has Hid the Stars." London: Doremi, n.d. Duet: S or T, and C or B, pf.

2411 Turpin, Edmund H. London: Weekes, n.d. Song: v, pf.

2412 Verrinder, C.G. "Endymion" op. 11. London: J.B. Cramer, n.d. Song: v, pf.

Evangeline: A Tale of Acadie (1847).

2413 Andrews, Mark. "Fair Was She to Behold." New York: H.W. Gray, 1912. Song: v, pf.

2414 Bedford, Herbert. "Evangeline Passes." London: Goodwin, Tabb, 1922. Song: v, unacc.

2415 Blockley, John. Boston: O. Ditson, [BAL n.d., after 1854]. Song, v, pf. Poem adapted by Charlotte Young; "Gabriel and Evangeline." London: J. Blockley, u.d. Duet; "Gabriel's Lament for Evangeline." London: J. Blockley, u.d. Song.

2416 Cain, Noble. Chicago: Raymond H. Hoffman, 1929. Cantata: S and A, pf.

2417 Forster, Cuthbert. n.p.: Yorks, Banks, 1936. Chorus: male voices, a cap.

2418 Gabriel, Mary Ann Virginia. "Sad Heart, O Take Thy Rest." Boston: O. Ditson, [BAL n.d., after 1857]. Cantata.

2419 Entry cancelled.

2420 Ringwald, Roy. n.t. in *The Song of America*. East Stroudsburg, Pa.: Shawnee, 1951. Setting for SATB chorus, narr., pf 4 hands. Recording: Decca, DAU 816.

2421 Spross, Charles G. Cincinnati: J. Church, 1930. Cantata: female voices, Bar solo, pf. Text adapted by Frederick H. Martens.

Excelsior. *Ballads and Other Poems* (1842).

2422 Balfe, Michael W. Boston: O. Ditson, n.d. [BAL not before 1858]. London: Boosey, n.d. Duet: S and C edn, T and Bar edn. George B. Nevin, arr. Setting for men's chorus. In coll. TuPS. Duet: TB, pf.

2423 Berger, Francesco. Boston: O. Ditson, [BAL n.d., not before 1877]. Trio: SCBar, pf.

2424 Birch, W.H. Boston: O. Ditson, n.d. Part Song: SATB, a cap; London: J. Curwen, 1881. Part Song: male voices.

2425 Bird, Joseph. "Issued without place or date. A copy in CH inscribed by Longfellow, Sept. 1847" [BAL vol. 5 p. 622].

2426 Blockley, John. London: Blockley, n.d. Song: v, pf; Also pubd for duet: ST, SC, or SB; Boston: O. Ditson, n.d. Duet: TBar, pf.

2427 Catty, Corbett S. London: C. Jefferys, n.d. Song: v, pf.

2428 Clarke, Frederic W. In *Album of Songs*. London: Novello, Ewer, n.d. Song: v, pf.

2429 "Excelsior." Boston: O. Ditson, 1884.

2430 Glover, Stephen R. Boston: O. Ditson, [BAL n.d., 1844-1857].

2431 Goldbeck, Robert. [BAL n.p., 1885].

2432 Hatton, John L. London: Addison & Hollier, [BPL 186-?]. Song: v, pf.

2433 Heins, Nicholas. London: Howard, n.d. Song: v, pf.

2434 Hutchinson Family, The. New York: Firth & Hall, 1843; New York: J.L. Hewitt, 1843. Part Song: SATB, pf. In coll. JSY.

2435 Lindsay, M., Miss. Boston: O. Ditson, [BAL n.d. 1844-1857]. Song: v, pf. Also pubd for duet; Mrs. G. Worthington Bliss. London: R. Cocks, u.d.

2436 Lyon, Robert H. London: W. Williams, n.d. Song: v, pf.

2437 Normann, Jules. London: Sheard, [BPL 186-?]. Song: v, pf.

2438 Peabody, George. Boston: O. Ditson, 1884.

2439 Perkins, Charles C. [Cover destroyed.] Song: v, pf. Text in Eng. and Fr., trans. by Ch. Monselet.

2440 Pinsuti, Ciro E. London: Addison & Hollier, n.d. Song: v, pf.

2441 Russell, George. London: Leader & Cock, n.d. Song: v, pf.

2442 Schnecker, P.A. Boston: O. Ditson, 1910. Ballad: SATB school chorus, pf, org and cathedral chimes ad lib.

2443 Spaulding, H.G., arr. "Upidee" (A College Song and Chorus as Sung by the Students of Harvard College). Boston: O. Ditson, 1859.

2444 Thouless, A.H. In *Album of Ten Songs*. London: Stanley Lucas, Weber, n.d. Song: v, pf.

2445 Tilleard, J. London: Davidson, n.d. Song: v, pf.

2446 "Upidee." Arr. from a College Air. In coll. DSC, FSS 1, HSD, JS, JSE, LAASR, MPC, NMH, SSS, WA, WBT, WC, WSW.

2447 "Upidee." Arr. from a College Air. In coll. JSE, LAASR. Variation on Longfellow's words beginning, "The shades of night were a-comin' down swift."

Eyes So Tristful, Eyes So Tristful [Trans. from the poem, "Ojos Tristes, Ojos Tristes," of Diego de Saldaña]. *Aftermath* (1873).

2448 Cowen, Frederic H. "Eyes So Wistful" in *Longfellow's Songs*. Boston: O. Ditson, 1892. Song: med. v, pf; "Eyes so Tristful" in *Nine Songs*. London: Metzler, 1892. Song: high and med. v edns, pf.

The Fiftieth Birthday of Agassiz. *The Courtship of Miles Standish, and Other Poems* (1858).

2449 Hatton, John L. "It Was Fifty Years Ago." London: Boosey, n.d. [BPL 187-?]. In coll. HSE 3.

Flowers. *Voices of the Night* (1839).

2450 Romer, Frank. London: Lamborn Cock, Hutchings, n.d. Song: v, pf.

Footsteps of Angels. *Voices of the Night* (1839).

2451 Baer, Frank. New York: Wm. Hall, [BAL n.d., not before 1848].

2452 Blockley, John. London: Addison, Hollier & Lucas, n.d. Song: v, pf.

2453 Davis, Miss. London: Ashdown & Parry, n.d. Song: v, pf.

2454 Dempster, William R. Boston: O. Ditson, 1848. Song: v, pf.

2455 "Evening Song." Chicago: Chicago Music, 1881.

2456 "Footsteps of Angels." London: Music-Publishing Co., n.d. Song: v, pf. Text adapted to a melody by Weber.

2457 "Footsteps of Angels." London: J. Williams, n.d. Song: v, pf. Text adapted to the last song of Carl Maria von Weber.

2458 Gaul, Alfred R. London: Novello, Ewer, n.d. [BPL 188–?]. Descriptive choral song for unacc. singing.

2459 Harding, Emma. New York: Horace Waters, 1856. Recitative and Air: v, pf.

2460 Harding, Joseph R.W. "Footsteps of Angels: A Vison." London: Metzler, [BPL 186–?]. Song: v, pf.

2461 Hime, Edward L. London: Duff & Stewart, n.d. Song: v, pf.

2462 Linley, George. London: Brewer, n.d. Song: v, pf.

2463 Normann, Jules, arr. London: Musical Bouquet Office, n.d. Song: v, pf. Text adapted to the last song of Carl Maria von Weber.

2464 Perkins, Frank. "The Evening Reverie, or Footsteps of Angels." London: J. Shepherd, n.d. Song: v, pf.

2465 Romer, Frank. New York: Wm. Hall, n.d. [BPL 185–?]. Song: v, pf.

2466 Schulz, E. London: Cramer, Beale, n.d. Song: v, pf; London: Musical Bouquet, 1856. Adapted to the last song of Carl Maria von Weber.

Four by the Clock. *In the Harbor: Ultima Thule—Part II* (1882).

2467 Mallinson, Albert. London: Reynolds, 1901. Song: v, pf. "Four by the Clock (Um Vier Uhr Morgens)" in *Song Album No. 3*. London: Frederick Harris, 1906. Song: low v, pf. Text in Eng. and Ger.

Fox-Song. *Hyperion* (1839).

2468 "The Fox." A celebrated student song, translated from the German. Troy, N.Y.: E.P. Jones, 1859. Song and Chorus.

From My Arm-Chair. *Ultima Thule* (1880).

2469 Jephson, T.L. "My Arm-Chair." Boston: O. Ditson, 1880.

2470 Mallinson, Albert. In *Song Album No. 3*. London: Fredrick Harris, 1901. Song: low v.

Gaspar Becerra. *The Seaside and the Fireside* (1850).

2471 Bennett, Wentworth. "The Sculptor." London: Novello, Ewer, 1887. Song: v, vc obl.

2472 Bradshaw, W.F. London: Novello, Ewer, 1882. Cantata.

2473 Tuddenham, Horatio. London: English College of Music, n.d. Song: v, pf.

A Gleam of Sunshine. *Poems* (1845).

2474 Balfe, Michael W. "This Is the Place, Stand Still My Steed." London: Boosey, n.d. Song: v, pf. In coll. BSP.

2475 Blockley, John. "This Is the Place, Stand Still My Steed." London: Cramer, Beale, n.d. Song: v, pf.

2476 Campbell-Tipton, Louis. London: C. Sheard, n.d. Song: high v, pf; Boston and New York: Whyte-Smith, 1893. Song: high and med. v edns, pf. Text adapted.

2477 Romer, Frank. "The Past and Present." London: Leader & Cock, [BPL 187-?]. Romance: v, pf.

2478 Romer, Frank. "Still I Thought of Thee." London: Hutchings & Romer, n.d. Song: v, pf. [A different setting.]

2479 Sotheby, E.M. "Memories." n.p.: Sotheby, n.d. Song: v, pf.

The Golden Legend (1851). *See also* "My Redeemer and my Lord," "The night is calm and cloudless," "O gladsome light."

2480 Buck, Dudley. "Scenes from Longfellow's 'The Golden Legend.'" Cincinnati: John Church, 1880, 1908. Symphonic Cantata: mixed chorus, STBarB soli, orch.

2481 Carew, Lester. "The Monk Felix." London: Weekes, 1895. Recitation, pf.

2482 Carter, George. London: London Music Publishing and General Agency, n.d. Cantata: SATB chorus, soli, orch.

2483 Dawson, A. "Come Back! Come Back Ye Friendships Long Departed." London: Augener, n.d.

2484 Hodson, Henry E. London: Novello, Ewer, 1881. Dramatic Cantata: SATB chorus, soli, pf or orch (R).

2485 Liszt, Franz. "Die Glocken des Strassburger Münster." Leipzig: J. Schuberth, 1875. Setting for mixed voices. Text in Ger. and Eng. Based on the prologue, "The Spire of Strassburg Cathedral," of the *Golden Legend* with a prelude incorporating ideas from Longfellow's poem, "Excelsior." *See* the article, "Liszt and Longfellow," in the *Musical Quarterly* (Jan. 1955).

"The Bells of Strassburg." New York: G. Schirmer, ca. 1889. Chorus: mixed voices, pf.

2486 Romer, Frank. "The Angels Song." London: Hutchings & Romer, n.d. Song: v, pf.

2487 Romer, Frank. "Hail to Thee Jesus of Nazareth!" London: Hutch-ings & Romer, n.d. Sacred Carol: v, chorus ad lib, pf.

2488 Sullivan, Arthur. London: Novello, Ewer, 1887. Cantata: chorus, soli, and orch. Poem adapted by Joseph Bennett

The Golden Mile-Stone. *The Courtship of Miles Standish, and Other Poems* (1858).

2489 Romer, Frank. London: Lamborn, Cock, Hutchings, n.d. Song: v, pf.

"Good night! Good night, beloved!" [act 2 sc. 10]. *The Spanish Student* (1843).

2490 Abt, Franz. Cited in LoPM for male chorus, Bar solo.

2491 Balfe, Michael W. New York: Firth, Pond; Cleveland: S. Brainard's, [Both BAL n.d., not before 1856]. Song: v, pf. In coll. BSP, DM 1, HSE 3, TS.

2492 Barnard, J.G. "Good Night, Beloved." New York: Wm. A. Pond, 1870.

2493 Blockley, John. "Good Night." London: Cramer, Beale, n.d. Song: v, pf. Also pubd as a duet.

2494 Busch, Carl. "Good Night, Beloved." Boston: O. Ditson, 1903. Song: high v, pf.

2495 Chase, Charles A. "Good Night! Beloved." Boston: O. Ditson, 1897. Song: v, pf.

2496 Chase, C. Coes. Cited in LoPM for Song: high v, pf.

2497 Cirillo, Vincenzo. "Good Night, Beloved." Portland, Maine: Ira C. Stockbridge, 1874. Ballad: v, pf.

2498 Coombs, C.W. "Serenade" op. 3 in *Two Songs*. Stuttgart: G.A. Zumsteeg, 1883. Song: v, pf. Words in Eng. and Ger; "Good Night, Beloved" op. 3. New York: G. Schirmer, 1886. Song: v, pf. Text in Eng. and Ger.

2499 Dalton, Sydney. New York: C. Fischer, 1918. Song: high and low v edns, pf.

2500 Denza, Luigi. "Good-night!" New York: T.B. Harms, [BAL n.d., ca. 1883-1884]. Song: high and med. v edns, pf. Words in Eng. and Ital.

2501 Dolores. "Good Night, Beloved." New York: Wm. J. Hall, [BAL n.d., not before 1848]. Song: v, pf.

2502 Dormand, Frederic. "Good Night Beloved" in *Three Love Songs*. London: Novello, n.d. Song: v, pf.

2503 E.A.B. "Good Night" in *Two Songs*. London: Addison & Hollier, n.d. Song: v, pf.

2504 Forrester, J. Cliffe. "Serenade." London: C. Woolhouse, n.d. Song: v, pf.

2505 Gilder, Frank. "To Be Near Thee." Boston: O. Ditson, 1879. Song: v, pf.

2506 Glover, Stephen. "Good Night, Beloved." Philadelphia: Lee & Walker, [BAL n.d., not before 1856].

2507 Graham, W.H.J. "Good Night, Beloved." New York: Wm. A. Pond, 1864.

2508 Jerome, H. "Serenade." London: Novello, n.d. Song: v, pf.

2509 Johnson, W. Noel. In *Four Songs.* London: C. Woolhouse, n.d. Song: v, pf.

2510 Jones, J. Tomlins. "The Serenade from Longfellow's *Spanish Student.*" London: Addison, Hollier & Lucas, n.d. Song: v, pf.

2511 Kimball, E.S. "Good Night, Beloved." Washington, D.C.: John F. Ellis, 1885.

2512 Laciar, S.L. Philadelphia: T. Presser, 1916. Part Song: TTBB, a cap.

2513 Löhr, F.N. "Good-Night, Beloved." Boston: O. Ditson, n.d. Trio: SSA, pf.

2514 Moir, Frank L. Boston: O. Ditson, [BAL n.d., not before 1858]. Song: B, pf. In coll. CB.

2515 Monk, E.G. "Good Night, Beloved!" *The Musical Times* no. 196, n.d. Part Song: TTBB, a cap.

2516 Neidlinger, W.H. "The Weary Hours." New York: Wm. Maxwell, 1904. Song: v, pf; In *Six Songs.* New York: Wm. Maxwell, 1907. Song: v, pf.

2517 Nevin, Ethelbert. New York: G. Schirmer, 1888. Song: high and med. v edns, pf; New York: G. Schirmer, 1911. Chorus: SSA, pf. In coll. MSF 1, SM 2.

2518 Newell, J.E. "Good Night." London: Osborn & Tuckwood, n.d. Part Song: SATB, a cap.

2519 Perabeau, H. "Serenade." Boston: O. Ditson, [BAL n.d., not before 1853].

2520 Philp, Elizabeth. "Good Night, Beloved." Boston: O. O. Ditson, [BAL n.d., not before 1855]. Song: v, pf.

2521 Pinsuti, Ciro. New York: G. Schirmer, 1887. Chorus: SATB, pf.
    u.p.: J. Curwen, 1909. Chorus: TTBB a cap.
    Cited in LoPM are 2 arr. by J.C.M. for men's chorus and mixed chorus.
    In coll. TFG, TFC 2 (arr. unknown).
    H. Elliott Button, arr. In coll. TuPS. Chorus: ATTB, a cap.

Henry Leslie, ed. London: Novello, Ewer, u.d. Chorus: SATB.

2522 Protheroe, Daniel. "Good Night, Beloved" op. 23 no. 3. Scranton, Pa.: Lyric Music, 1894. Song: T, pf; In *Six Lyrics* op. 59 no. 3. Milwaukee: Nau & Schmidt, 1901. Song: T, pf; Chicago: H.T. FitzSimmons, 1933. Chorus: SATB, pf.

2523 Reed, William. Boston: O. Ditson, 1897. Quartet: TTBB, a cap.

2524 Reinhardt, Carl. "Good Night, Beloved, Good Night." London: Sheard, [BPL 186–?]. Song: v, pf.

2525 Schehlmann, L. Cited in the Poet Subject Card Catalog at the Music Division of the Library of Congress.

2526 Silsby, Mae. "Good Night, Beloved." Bangor, Maine: George S. Silsby, [BAL n.d., not before 1880].

2527 Sired, W.G. "Good-Night Beloved." n.p.: H.B. Stevens, 1896. Part Song: TTBB, a cap.

2528 Spence, William R. Boston: O. Ditson, 1897. Quartet: TTBB, a cap.

2529 Sullivan, Thomas D. "Good Night, Beloved." New York: John J. Daly, 1859.

2530 Terschak, A. "Good Night, Beloved." Cincinnati: J. Church, 1880.

The Good Part. *Poems on Slavery* (1842).

2531 Coleridge-Taylor, Samuel. "She Dwells by Great Kenhawa's Side" in *Three Choral Ballads* op. 54 no. 2. London: Breitkopf & Härtel, 1904. Chorus: SATB, pf or orch.
> "She Dwells by Great Kenhawa's Side" op. 54a no. 2. London: Breitkopf & Härtel, 1905. Chorus: female voices, pf.
> Leipzig: Breitkopf & Härtel, 1932. Chorus: 3-pt. women's voices.

The Hanging of the Crane (1875).

2532 Dunne, John. London: C. Jefferys, n.d. Cantata: SATB chorus, soli, pf.

The Happiest Land. *Voices of the Night* (1839).

2533 Balfe, Michael W. London: Boosey, [BAL n.d., 1856?]. Song: v, pf.

2534 Cramer, Oliver. London: Ashdown & Parry, n.d. Song: v, pf.

2535 Heuberer, Charles F. Boston: H. Prentiss, 1845. Ballad: v, pf.

2536 Jude, W.H. Boston: O. Ditson, 1896. Song: B, pf; "The Landlord's Daughter." London: Wickins, n.d. Song: B, pf.

2537 Montgomery, W.H. London: R. Cocks, n.d. Song: v, pf.

2538 Perring, J. Ernest. New York: Wm. A. Pond, 1870. Song: v, pf.

2539 Rogers, Frederick F. London: Duncan Davison, n.d. Song: v, pf.

2540 Watson, Michael. London: Agate, n.d. Song: v, pf.

Haroun Al Raschid. *Kéramos and Other Poems* (1878).

2541 Heymann, Jacob. In *Three Songs*. New York: E. Schuberth, 1932. Song: med. v, pf.

The Harvest Moon. *The Masque of Pandora and Other Poems* (1875).

2542 Freer, Eleanor E. In *Six Songs to Nature* op. 10 no. 4. Milwaukee: W.A. Kaun, [BlW 1913?]. Song: v, pf.

The Hemlock Tree. *Poems* (1845).

2543 Baldwin, Raymond H. In *Two Songs*. Los Angeles: R.W. Heffelfinger, 1912. Song: M, pf.

2544 Baumer, Annette. "Oh Maiden Fair." London: Duff & Hodgson, n.d. Song: v, pf.

2545 Hatton, John L. London: Novello, Ewer, n.d. Part Song: ATTB, pf.

2546 "The Hemlock Tree." Set to German Air: "Der Tannenbaum." In coll. GO. Words adapted.

2547 Whaples, B.A. New York: Blelock, 1864.

Hymn of the Moravian Nuns at Bethlehem. *Voices of the Night* (1839).

2547a Birch, William H. "Hymn of the Moravian Nuns at the Consecration of the Banner of Pulaski" in *The Choral Handbook*. No. 826. [BLC 1885.] Part Song.

2548 Blockley, John. "The Consecration of Pulaski's Banner and Hymn of the Moravian Nuns of Bethlehem." n.p.: Blockley, n.d. Song or duet.

2549 Coward, James. "Take Thy Banner." London: Lamborn Cock, n.d. Part Song: TT(A)TB, pf; also pubd for ATTBB, pf.

2550 Lindsay, M., Miss. "Hymn of the Moravian Nuns of Bethlehem at the Consecration of Pulaski's Banner." London: Cocks, [BPL 184-?].

New York: Wm. A. Pond, [BAL n.d., 1863–1877]. Song: v, pf.

London: R. Cocks, n.d. Duet: SC, pf.

Mrs. J. Worthington Bliss. London: R. Cocks, n.d. Song: v, pf.

2551 Morris, Haydn. n.p.: Tork, Banks, 1932. 8-pt. song, a cap.

Hymn to the Night. *Voices of the Night* (1839).

2552 Burleigh, Cecil. "I Heard the Trailing Garments of the Night" op. 32 no. 4. Boston: C. Ditson, 1917. Song: high and low v edns, pf.

2553 Campbell-Tipton, Louis. New York: H.W. Gray, 1910. Song: v, pf.

2554 Donovan, Richard. New York: J. Fischer, 1947. Chorus: SSA, a cap.

2555 Farebrother, Bernard. London: Novello, Ewer, n.d. Song: v, pf, vc ad lib.

2556 Genet, Marianne. New York: Galaxy, 1934. Chorus: SATB, pf; New York: Galaxy, 1936. Chorus: 2-pt. female voices, pf.

2557 Glover, Stephen R. New York: Firth, Pond, [BAL n.d., 1856–1862]; London: R. Cocks, n.d. Duet.

2558 Lane, Richard. "A Hymn to the Night." New York: Mills Music, 1962. Chorus: SATB, a cap.

2559 MacFarlane, William C. New York: G. Schirmer, 1933. Chorus: 4-pt. male voices, T solo, a cap.

2560 Orr, A. Barrington. Dublin: Bussell, n.d. Song: v, pf.

2561 Pratt, Silas G. "O Holy Night." Cincinnati: J. Church, 1883.

2562 Romer, Frank. "Beloved Night." London: Lamborn Cock, Hutchings, n.d. Song: v, pf.

2563 Steele, Clarence T. "I Heard the Trailing Garments of the Night." New York: Hamilton S. Gordon, 1892.

2564 Stevens, Henry. "I Heard the Trailing Garments of the Night." London: C. Jefferys, n.d. Song: v, pf.

2565 Ward, Robert. In *Fifth Symphony: Canticles of America.* New York: Highgate Press, 1979. Choral Symphony: mixed chorus, S and Bar soli, opt narr., orch.

2566 Wood, Joseph. MS, 1957, avail. ACA. Chorus: TTBB, a cap.

"If thou art sleeping, maiden," [act 3 sc. 6]. *The Spanish Student* (1843). [Trans. from the Portuguese of Gil Vicente].

2567 Baumann, Alfred R. "Awake." London: Novello, Ewer, 1896. Song: v, pf.

2568 Birch, Robert F. "If Thou Art Sleeping Maiden" op. 14 no. 5. New York: J. Patelson, 1953.

2569 Caracciolo, Luigi. "A Muleteer Song." Boston: O. Ditson, [BAL n.d., not before 1877]. Milan: Edizoni Ricordi, n.d. Song: v, pf. Text in Eng. and Ital., trans. by A. Zanardini.

2570 Cirillo, Vincenzo. "Morning Song." Boston: G.D. Russell, 1876. Song: v, pf.

2571 Goodall, Cecil. "If Thou Art Sleeping." London: Weekes, n.d. Song: v, pf.

2572 Gordon, Philip. Philadelphia: Elkan-Vogel, 1954. Chorus: SATB, a cap.

2573 Gounod, Charles. "If Thou Art Sleeping Maiden, Awake." London: Weeks, [NYPL 1872 or 1873]. Song: B or Bar.

2574 Grahame, Murray. London: J.E. Dallas, n.d. Song: v, pf.

2575 Johnson, W. Noel. In *Four Songs*. London: C. Woolhouse, n.d. Song: v, pf.

2576 Parker, Louis N. London: Lamborn Cock, n.d. Serenade: 2 voices, pf.

The Image of God ["La Imágen de Dios" by Francisco de Aldana]. *Voices of the Night* (1839).

2577 Wood, Charles. "O Lord That Seest from yon Starry Height." London: H.F.W. Deane, 1919. Anthem: SATB, org.

It Is Not Always May. *Ballads and Other Poems* (1842).

2577a Barnett, John F. In *The Musical Times*. No. 447. London, [?BLC 1844]. Part Song.

2578 Bell, Doyne C. London: R. Mills, n.d. Song: v, pf.

2579 Bentley, W.H. In *Six Songs* op. 2 no. 4. London: London Music Publishing, n.d. Song: v, pf.

2580 Clarke, Hamilton. London: Augener, n.d. Duet: S and C, pf.

2581 Coward, James. "The Sun Is Bright." London: S. Lucas, Weber, [NYPL 187–?]. Setting for chorus, pf or org.

2582 Cowen, Frederic H. London: Metzler, 1892. Song: high and med. v edns, pf; In *Longfellow's Songs*. Boston: O. Ditson, 1892. Song: high v, pf; In *Nine Songs*. London: Metzler, 1892. Song: high and med. v edns, pf.

2583 Gounod, Charles. London: Chappell, [NYPL 186–?]; Philadelphia: Lee & Walker, [BAL n.d., not before 1872]. Song: med. v, pf. In coll. HCA.

2584 Harris, Cuthbert. "Spring" op. 4 no. 4. School Song: equal voices in unison, pf.

2585 Hatton, John. L. London: Williams, [BPL 186–?]. Song: v, pf.

2586 Macfarren, Walter. "All Things Rejoice." London: E. Ashdown, 1893. Song: v, pf.

2587 Marchant, A.W. London: Osborn & Tuckwood, n.d. School Song: 2 equal voices, pf.

2588 Martinez, Isidora. Boston: A.P. Schmidt, 1902. Song: high and low v, edns, pf.

2589 Pinsuti, Ciro. Boston: O. Ditson, [BAL n.d., not before 1877]; London: Ashdown & Parry, n.d. Duet, pf.

2590 Reiff, Anthony. New York: Wm. A. Pond, 1887.

2591 St. John, Robert, Mrs. "Gwendoline." London: Augener, n.d. Song: v, pf.

2592 Schlesinger, H. London: London Conservatoire of Music, n.d. Song: v, pf.

2593 "Spring and Youth," arr. to a Polish dance Air. In coll. ArF 2.

2594 Stoddard, L.E., Miss. Cleveland: S. Brainard, 1866.

2595 Thamsen, Nicolai P. London: Forsyth Bros., n.d. Song: v, pf.

2596 Thomson, Sydney. New York: Wm. Maxwell, 1911. Song: v, pf; New York: Wm. Maxwell, 1911. Part Song: 2 equal voices, pf.

2596a Weber, Carl Maria von. "The Sun Is Bright" in coll. LAASR.

2597 Wickham, J.J. Birmingham: Harrison & Harrison, n.d. Song: v, pf.

The Jewish Cemetery at Newport. *The Courtship of Miles Standish, and Other Poems* (1858).

2598 Heilner, Irwin. MS, u.d., avail. ACA. Chorus: SATB, pf.

Kéramos. *Kéramos and Other Poems* (1878).

2599 Farwell, Arthur. "Kéramos: The Potter's Wheel" op. 28. New York: Remick Music, 1952. Chorus: SATB, S and T soli, pf.

2600 Gaul, Alfred R. "The Potter." London: Novello, Ewer, n.d. Part Song: SATB, pf.

2601 Mallard, Clarisse. London: C. Woolhouse, n.d. Song: v, pf.

King Christian. *Voices of the Night* (1839).

2602 Robert, D.L. "Kong Kristian." In coll. DNM. Words in Dan. and Eng.

King Robert of Sicily. *Tales of a Wayside Inn* (1863).

2603 Cole, Rossetter G. "King Robert of Sicily" op. 22. New York: G. Schirmer, 1906. Recitation, pf, or pf and org, or orch.

2604 Hattersley, Frederick K. "Robert of Sicily." London: Novello, Ewer, 1894. Cantata: chorus, soli, orch.

2605 Wootton, John J. New York: Edgar S. Werner, 1888. Recitation.

King Witlaf's Drinking-Horn. *The Seaside and the Fireside* (1849).

2606 Allon, Erskine. "King Witlaf." Cambridge: Stoakely, [BPL 188–?]. Song: v, pf. Pubd. also as "The Monks of Croyland."

2607 Gow, George C. "King Witlaf's Drinking Horn" op. 2 no. 5. Boston: G. Schirmer, Jr., 1888. Song: Bar and B edns, pf.

2608 Hatton, John L. London: Novello, n.d. Chorus: ATTB, pf.

2609 Ostlere, May. "The Monks of Croyland." London: J.B. Cramer, [BPL 187–?]. Song: v, pf. Pubd. also as "King Witlaf."

2610 Weiss, Willoughby H. London: J. Williams, n.d. Song: v, pf.

The Leap of Roushan Beg. *Kéramos and Other Poems* (1878).

2611 Dear, James R. "The Leap of Kurroglou." London: Chappell, 1907. Ballad: SATB chorus, Bar solo, orch.

2612 Parker, Horatio W. "The Leap of Roushan Beg" op. 75. New York: G. Schirmer, 1913. Ballad: TTBB chorus, T solo, orch.

The Legend Beautiful. *Tales of a Wayside Inn* (1863).

2613 Hawley, Stanley. London: R. Cocks, 1896. Recitation: v, pf.

2614 Lyon, James. "The Legend Beautiful" op. 48. London: Stainer & Bell, 1937. Chorus: mixed voices, Bar solo, pf or orch.

The Legend of the Crossbill [Trans. from the poem, "Der Kreuzschnabel, No. 3," of Julius Mosen]. *Poems* (1845).

2615 Jones, Edwin A. n.p., n.d. Song: S, pf.

2616 Hopper, Arthur. Brighton: J. & W. Chester, [NYPL 191–?]. Song: v, pf.

2617 Lemmens, Le Chevalier. Boston: G.D. Russell, 1874. Song: v, pf or org.

L'Envoi ["Ye voices, that arose"]. *Voices of the Night* (1839).

2618 Burleigh, Cecil. "Ye Voices That Arose" op. 32 no. 3. Boston: O. Ditson, 1917. Song: high and low v edns, pf.

The Light of Stars. *Voices of the Night* (1839).

2619 Anderson, Charlotte A. London: Chappell, n.d. Song: v, pf.

2620 Cowen, Frederic H. In *Longfellow's Songs*. Boston: O. Ditson, 1892. Song: low v, pf; In *Nine Songs*. London: Metzler, 1892. Song: high and med. v edns, pf.

2621 Horn, John. Cincinnati: J. Church, 1887.

2622 "The Light of Stars." Set to an Air adapted from a Swedish Folk-Song in coll. Ea.

2623 Sellé, W.C. London: A.W. Hammond, n.d. Song: v, pf.

The Lighthouse. *The Seaside and the Fireside* (1849).

2624 Burleigh, Cecil. "The Lighthouse" op. 32 no. 5. Boston: O. Ditson, 1917. Song: high and low v edns, pf.

2625 Gest, Elizabeth. Chicago: C.F. Summy, 1922. Recitation, pf.

2626 Nelson, Herbert H. London: J. Williams, 1906. Song: B or Bar, pf.

"Loud sang the Spanish cavalier" [act 3 sc. 5]. *The Spanish Student* (1843).

2627 Coleridge-Taylor, Samuel. London: J. Curwen, 1910. Part Song: TTBB, pf red.

Mad River. *In the Harbor: Ultima Thule—Part II* (1882).

2628 Brabson, M.M. Privately pubd. by the composer, 1897. Song: v, pf.

Maiden and Weathercock. *Ultima Thule* (1880).

2629 Austin, Walter. "Maiden and the Weathercock." New York: Wm. A. Pond, [BAL n.d., 1880–1896]. Song: v, pf.

2630 Lehmann, Liza. "The Weathercock." London: Boosey, 1913. Song: high and med. v edns, pf.

2631 Noyes, Charles F. Boston: O. Ditson, 1897. Part Song: men's and women's voices, pf.

2632 Pasmore, Henry B. "The Maiden and the Weathercock" in *Eight Songs*. Privately pubd. by the composer, 1931. Song: v, pf.

Maidenhood. *Ballads and Other Poems* (1842).

2633 Bartlett, Homer N. New York: Wm. A. Pond, 1881.

2634 "Bear a Lily in Thy Hand" in coll. FSS 7, LAASR.

2635 Beta. London: Robt. W. Ollivier, n.d. Song: v, pf.

2636 Blockley, John. London: Addison, n.d. Song: v, pf.

2637 Kelly, John C. "Maiden with the Meek Brown Eyes." Song: med. v, pf. Cited in LoPM.

2638 Marshall, Charles. London: J. Williams, 1905. Part Song: 2 treble voices, pf.

2639 Pitcher, R.J. London: Bach, 1910. Song: v, pf.

"Many a year is in its grave" [Chap. 6]. *Hyperion* (1839).

> 2640 Romer, Frank. "The Ferry." London: Lamborn Cock, Hutchings, n.d. Song: v, pf; London: Leader & Cock, n.d. Song: v, pf.

The Masque of Pandora. *The Masque of Pandora and Other Poems* (1875).

> 2641 Busch, Carl. "Gently Swaying." Boston: O. Ditson, 1903. Song: high v, pf. Words from pt. 6, sec. titled, "Chorus of Birds," beginning, "Gently swaying to and fro."
>
> 2642 Cale, Rosalie Balmer Smith. St. Louis, privately pubd. by the composer, 1922. A classical musical play, pageant, dramatic cantata, or legend with reader and soloists for women only or men assisting; 2 pf and hp acc.
>
> 2643 Cellier, Alfred. Arr. for the stage by Bolton Rowe. Cambridge: The Riverside Press, 1881. "Produced for the first time at the Boston Theater by the Blanche Roosevelt English Opera Company. 10th January 1881" [BAL 12225].
>
> 2644 Choveaux, Nicholas. "Birds in the Nest." London: Chappell, 1828. Song: v, pf. Words from pt. 6, sec. titled, "Chorus of Birds," beginning, "Gently swaying to and fro."
>
> 2645 Freer, Eleanor E. "The Masque of Pandora" op. 36. Milwaukee: Wm. A. Kaun, 1929. Opera in 1 act, 2 scenes. Words adapted by Freer.
>
> 2646 Gilbert, Henry Franklin B. "Zephyrus." Newton Center, Mass.: Wa-Wan Press, 1903. Song: high v, pf. Words from pt. 8 of the poem.

The Meeting. *Aftermath* (1873).

> 2647 Hatton, John L. [BAL n.p.,n.d., ca. 1876–1878].

Michael Angelo [Words from sec. titled, "Dedication"] (1882).

> 2648 Diamond, David. "Dedication" in *To Music*. New York: Southern Music Publishing, 1969. Choral Symphony: SATB, T and B-Bar soli, orch.

My Lost Youth. *The Courtship of Miles Standish, and Other Poems* (1858).

> 2649 Clarke, Henry L. "Deering's Woods." MS, 1969, avail. ACA. Chorus: SATB, pf.
>
> 2650 Lane, Rhoda. "Looking Backward." London: Forsyth Bros., n.d. Song: v, pf.
>
> 2651 Nicrine. "A Boys Will Is the Winds Will." London: Simpson, n.d. Song: v, pf.

2652 Robbins, Reginald C. Paris: M. Senart, 1922. Song: B or Bar, pf.

2653 Romer, Frank. London: Lamborn Cock, Hutchings, n.d. Song: v, pf.

"My Redeemer and my Lord" [Sec. 2]. *The Golden Legend* (1851).

2654 Buck, Dudley. "My Redeemer and My Lord." Cincinnati: J. Church, 1900. Song: high and low v edns; Charles Gilbert Spross, arr. Cincinnati: J. Church, 1928. Anthem: SATB, pf.

2655 Gallatin, Albert R. "My Redeemer and My Lord." New York: Luckhardt & Belder, 1903.

2656 Lott, Edwin M. "Elsie's Prayer." London: Wickins, [BPL 187–?]. Sacred Song: v, pf.

Nature. *The Masque of Pandora and Other Poems* (1875).

2657 Castelnuovo-Tedesco, Mario. In *Two Longfellow Songs* op. 149. New York: Mills, 1962. Chorus: SATB, a cap.

2658 Horrocks, Amy Elise. "As a Fond Mother" in *Twelve Songs*. London: J. Williams, [NYPL ca. 1890]. Song: v, pf, vn obl.

The Nature of Love. *The Poets and Poetry of Europe* (1845).

2659 Fontaine, Leon J. London: Leonard, n.d. Song: v, pf.

"The night is calm and cloudless" [Sec. 5]. *The Golden Legend* (1851).

2660 Boott, Francis. "Kyrie Eleison." Boston: O. Ditson, 1857; "The Night Is Calm and Cloudless." Boston: O. Ditson, 1857. Song: v, pf; In *Boott's Album of Songs No. 2*. Boston: O. Ditson, 1897.

2661 Borrow, W. "The Music of the Sea." London: Metzler, n.d. Song: v, pf.

2662 Coward, J. Munro. "Christe Eleison." London: Metzler, n.d. Song: high, med., and low v edns, pf.

2663 Done, Emily. "Elsie's Song to the Sea." London: Stanley, Lucas, Weber, n.d. Song: v, pf.

2664 Dyson, George. "The Night Is Calm and Cloudless" in *Four Songs for Sailors*. London: Novello, 1949. Chorus: SCTB, pf or str orch (R), opt 2 timp, 2 tpt in C, 3 trb.

2665 Harvey, R.F. "Christie Eleison." London: Osborn & Tuckwood, [BPL 187–?]. Song: v, pf.

2666 Hatton, John L. "The Night Is Calm and Cloudless." Philadelphia: Lee & Walker, n.d. Song: v, pf.

2667 Loveland, Benj. W. "The Music of the Sea." New York: C.H. Ditson, 1887.

2667a Mosenthal, Joseph. "The Music of the Sea." New York: G. Schirmer, 1883. Chorus: TTBB, a cap; In *Three Songs for Male Voices*. New York: G. Schirmer, 1883.

2668 Nelson, J.W. "The Night Is Calm and Cloudless." London: Weippert, n.d. Duet: voices, pf.

The Norman Baron. *Poems* (1845).

2669 Anderton, Thomas. London: Novello, Ewer, 1884. Cantata: SATB chorus, pf.

2670 Baxter, Frederick N. London: Novello, Ewer, 1898. Choral Ballad: chorus, S solo, orch.

2671 Francis, G.T. "The Norman Baron" op. 25. London: Murdoch, Murdoch, 1925. Ballad: chorus, orch.

"O gladsome light" [Sec. 2]. *The Golden Legend* (1851).

2672 C.K.S. "O Gladsome Light." London: Augener, n.d. Part Song: SATB, pf or org.

2673 Mahnke, Allan. "Oh, Gladsome Light" in coll. LBW. Hymn.

The Occultation of Orion. *Poems* (1845).

2674 Gyring, Elizabeth. "The Reign of Violence Is Over." MS, u.d., avail. ACA. Cantata: SATB, pf and str orch.

2675 Hill, Clarence S. "Orion." London: Novello, n.d. Song: v, pf.

The Old Bridge at Florence. *The Masque of Pandora and Other Poems* (1875).

2676 Mallinson, Albert. London: J.B. Cramer, 1922. Song: v, pf.

The Old Clock on the Stairs. *The Belfry of Bruges* (1846).

2677 Allitsen, Francis. "Old Clock on the Stairs." London: Boosey, 1896. Song: v, pf.

2678 Bliss, J. Worthington, Mrs. London: R. Cocks, n.d. Song: v, pf.

2679 Blockley, John. London: Cramer, Beale, n.d. Song: v, pf. Also pubd for duet.

2680 Boott, Francis. Boston: O. Ditson, 1886. Song: v, pf.

2681 Bricher, T. Boston: O. Ditson, 1846. Boston: C. Bradlee, 1846. Song: v, pf.

2682 Callcott, J.G. London: J.B. Cramer, n.d. Part Song: SATB, pf ad lib.

2683 Carew, Lady. London: R. Mills, n.d. Song: v, pf.

2684 Dolores. "Old Clock on the Stairs." Boston: O. Ditson, [BAL n.d., not before 1854].

2685 Hatton, John L. London: Addison, Hollier & Lucas, [BPL 184–?]. Song: v, pf.

2686 Hime, Edward L. London: Duff & Stewart, n.d. Song: v, pf.

2687 Hutchinson, John W. Boston: O. Ditson, 1891. Song: med. v, pf.

2688 Landon, Agnes. London: Chappell, n.d. Song: v, pf.

2689 Marshall, L. "The Old Timepiece on the Stairs." Boston: O. Ditson, [BAL n.d., after 1857].

2690 Marston, G.W. "Old Clock on the Stairs." Boston: A.P. Schmidt, 1881. Song: v, pf.

2691 Montgomery, W.H. London: D'Almaine, n.d. Song: v, pf.

2692 Pease, Frederic H. Detroit: C.J. Whitney, 1876. Cantata: qrt and chorus of mixed voices; Boston: C.W. Thompson, 1908. Cantata: soli, chorus, orch.

2693 Stöpel, R. London: Sheard, [BPL 186–?]. Song: v, pf.

2694 Trannack, Marie. "The Old Clock." London: Magazine of Music Office (Magazine of Music Supplement, Aug. 1891). Song: v, pf.

2695 Watson, Michael. "The Old Timepiece." London: Patey & Willis, n.d. Song: v, pf.

The Open Window. *The Seaside and the Fireside* (1849).

2696 Andrews, R. London: Weekes, n.d. Song: v, pf.

2697 Bennett, James. "The Old House by the Lindens Stood." London: Leader & Cock, n.d. Song: v, pf.

2698 Blockley, John. "The Old House by the Lindens." London: J. Blockley, n.d. Song: v, pf.

2699 Davis, Miss. London: Lamborn Cock, Addison, n.d. Song: v, pf.

2700 Dolores. London: E. Donajowski, n.d. Song: v, pf.

2701 Fontein-Tuinhout, F.R. In *Three Serious Songs.* op. 10 no. 1. Middleburg: A.A. Noske, 1906. Song: A or B-Bar, pf.

2702 Frost, Charles J. London: Lyric Music Publishing, n.d. Duet: S and C, pf.

2703 Gatty, Alfred S. Philadelphia: Ditson, [BPL 187–?]. Song: v, pf. In coll. LBR.

2704 Glover, Howard. "The Old House by the Lindens." London: D. Davison, n.d. Song: v, pf.

2705 Hime, Edward L. London: Duff & Stewart, n.d. Song: v, pf.

2706 Liebling, Georg. "The Open Window (Wie flüchtig rinnt die stunde)" op. 36. London: Novello, 1899. Song: v, pf. Text in Eng. and Ger., trans. by E. Geibel.

2707 Martin, G.W. London: Addison & Hollier, n.d. Song: v, pf.

2708 Miller, Charles M. London: A. White, n.d. Song: v, pf.

2709 Minima. "The Old House by the Lindens." London: Cramer, Beale, n.d. Song: v, pf.

2710 Mitchell, W.H. "The Old House by the Lindens." London: Alphonse Bertini, Seymour, n.d. Song: v, pf.

2711 Redan. "Old House by the Lindens." London: Weekes, n.d. Song: v, pf.

2712 Rosewig, A.H. "The Old House by the Lindens. The Faces of the Children They Were No Longer There." Philadelphia: Lee & Walker, 1880. [Song?]. Inserted are two letters from Longfellow to Rosewig, the first giving him permission to set the poem, and the second thanking him for a copy of the song [BPL].

2713 Weiss, Willoughby H. "The Old House by the Lindens." London: J. Williams, n.d. Song: v, pf.

Paul Revere's Ride. *Tales of a Wayside Inn* (1863).

2714 Buck, Dudley. New York: G. Schirmer, 1898. Cantata: male voices, T and Bar soli, orch.

2715 Busch, Carl. Boston: O. Ditson, 1905. Cantata: SATB chorus, Bar solo, orch.

2716 Cain, Noble. London: Boosey & Hawkes, 1939. Setting for 2 pt. intermediate or junior high voices, med. v solo, pf or orch.

2717 Gantvoort, Arnold J. Cincinnati: J. Church, 1921. Cantata for mixed voices.

2718 Mason, Derrick. London: Keith, Prowse, 1968. Part Song for voices, pf, perc (R).

2719 Ringwald, Roy. n.t. in *The Song of America*. Delaware Water Gap, Pa.: Shawnee, 1951. Chorus: SATB, pf 4 hands. Recorded Decca, DAU 816; "Paul Revere's Ride." East Stroudsburg, Pa.: Shawnee, 1953. Chorus: TTBB, pf 4 hands.

2720 Schehl, J. Alfred. "The Midnight Ride of Paul Revere" op. 27. Cincinnati: Willis Music, 1936. Chorus: SATB, pf. Words adapted by Walter J. Brunsman.

2721 Vernon, Mary Strawn. Chicago: Raymond A. Hoffman, 1930. Cantata: S and A, pf. Music by Vernon and Nora Loraine Olin. Also pubd for SABar, pf.

The Phantom Ship. *The Courtship of Miles Standish, and Other Poems* (1858).

2722 Tirbutt, J. Charles B. London: J. Williams, n.d. Choral Ballad: SATB, orch.

The Poet's Calendar. *In the Harbor: Ultima Thule—Part II* (1882).

2723 Cadman, Charles W. "I Martius Am." New York: G. Schirmer, 1910. Recitative and Air from the cycle, *The Morning of the Year.*

2724 Olds, W.B. "January." In coll. NMS.

Praise of Little Women [Trans. from the poem of Juan Ruiz de Hita]. *The Poets and Poetry of Europe* (1845).

2725 Gordon, Philip. New York: Sam Fox, 1955. Chorus: TTBB, pf.

Prelude. *Voices of the Night* (1839).

2726 Balfe, Michael W. "The Green Trees Whispered Low and Mild." Boston: O. Ditson, [BAL n.d., not before 1858]. Song: v, pf. In coll. BSP, CS 1, HSE 3.

2727 Blockley, John. "The Green Trees Whispered Low & Mild." Boston: O. Ditson, [BAL n.d., not before 1858].

2728 Knight, Joseph P. "The Green Trees Whispered Low and Mild." London: F. Moutrie, n.d. Song: v, pf.

2729 Reinhardt, Carl. "The Green Trees Whispered Low and Mild." London: Musical Bouquet Office, [BPL 185–?]. Song: v, pf.

A Psalm of Life. *Voices of the Night* (1839).

2730 Barker, George. London: Woodward, [BPL 186–?]. Song: v, pf.

2731 Beecher, Charles. n.t. in coll. ChAH.

2732 Bellamy, Louisa. London: A. Hays, n.d. Song: v, pf.

2733 Berger, Francesco. In *Two-Part Songs.* London: Patey & Willis, n.d. Part Song: boys' or girls' voices, pf.

2734 Beuthin, J.C. "Psalm of Life." London: J. Shepherd, n.d. Setting for 3-pt. song, pf.

2735 Bliss, J. Worthington, Mrs. London: R. Cocks, n.d. Song: v, pf.

2736 Blockley, John. Boston: O. Ditson, [BAL n.d., not before 1858]. Song: v, pf. Also pubd for duet.

2736a Clemens, Theodor L. In *J.B. Cramer's Select Library of Part Songs.* No. 38. London: J.B. Cramer, [BLC 1880?]. Part Song: 2T, 2B.

2737 Clifford, Alan. London: H.E. Angless, n.d. Song: v, pf.

2738 Coote, Charles, Jr. "All Things Are Not What They Seem." London: Chappell, n.d. Song: v, pf.

2739 Cowen, Frederic H. London: Boosey, 1895. Song: v, pf.

2740 Dugmore, F.S. In *Voices of the Night.* London: Stanley Lucas, Weber, n.d. Song: M or Bar, pf or org.

2741 Emerson, L.O. "Tell Me Not in Mournful Numbers." Arr. from a melody by Franz Schubert. Boston: O. Ditson, 1854. Song: v, pf.

2742 Glover, Steven. "Psalm of Life." London: C. Jefferys, n.d. Song: v, pf.

2743 Guglielmo, P.D. "Life." London: Guglielmo's Music Depot, Duncan Davison, n.d. Song: v, pf.

2744 Hewitt, G.W. Philadelphia: Lee & Walker, 1869. Song: v, pf.

2745 Hime, Edward L. London: Duff & Stewart, n.d. Song: v, pf.

2746 Hodges, Faustina H. New York: G. Schirmer, 1884. Song: high and low v edns, pf.

2747 Kinross, James. London: Novello, Ewer, in *The Musical Times* (Sept. 1, 1882). Part Song: SATB, pf.

2748 Lane, Arthur. London: Reid Bros., n.d. Song: v, pf.

2749 Leroux, Paul. "A Quotation" in coll. ArF 1.

2750 Miller, C.C. Cleveland: S. Brainard's, [BAL n.d., not before 1866]. Song: v, pf.

2751 Montgomery, W.H. London: D'Almaine, n.d. Song: v, pf.

2752 Peale, Dudley. Chicago: H.T. FitzSimmons, 1932. Chorus: SATB, pf or org.

2753 Peel, F., Air adapted from. In coll. Ea.

2754 Proch, Heinrich. London: Davidson, n.d. Song: v, pf.

2755 Purday, Charles H. "Tell Me Not in Mournful Numbers." London: C.H. Purday, n.d. Song: v, pf.

2756 Römele, J.M. Louisville, Ky.: Henry Knöfel, 1882.

2757 Romer, Frank. London: Lamborn Cock, Hutchings, n.d. Song: v, pf.

2758 Smart, Henry. In coll. LBR.

2759 Spencer, Henry C. "Fourths" in *Songs Illustrating the Intervals*. London: Augener, n.d. Song: v, pf.

2760 Stocker, M.A. London: H. May, n.d. Song: v, pf.

2761 Tepé, Frank A. "Life Is Not an Empty Dream." Baltimore: Henry McCaffrey, 1855.

2762 Tillett, Clara. "Tell Me Not in Mournful Numbers." London: C. Herzog, n.d. Song: v, pf.

2763 Titus, Amanda W. "Footprints on the Sands of Time." Philadelphia: Lee & Walker, 1873. Song: v, pf.

2764 Wakefield, Margaret, Miss. London: Cramer, Beale & Chappell, n.d. Song: v, pf.

2765 Warburton, Augustus, Mrs. London: Boosey, n.d. Song: v, pf.

2766 Ward, John C. "Lives of Great Men." London: Stanley Lucas, Weber, n.d. Song: v, pf.

2767 Ward, Robert. In *Fifth Symphony: Canticles of America.* New York: Highgate Press, 1979. Choral Symphony: mixed chorus, S and Bar soli, opt narr., orch.

2768 Westrop, E.J. London: Sheard, [BPL 185–?]. Song: v, pf.

2769 Wood, Albert H. New York: Beer & Schirmer, 1862.

The Quadroon Girl. *Poems on Slavery* (1842).

2770 Balfe, Michael W. London: Boosey, n.d. Song: v, pf.

2771 Coleridge-Taylor, Samuel. In *Five Choral Ballads* op. 54 no. 4. Leipzig: Breitkopf & Härtel, 1904. Chorus: SATB, pf or orch; In *Two Choral Ballads* op. 54 no. 4. London: Breitkopf & Härtel, 1905. Chorus: female voices, Bar solo, orch.

Rain in Summer. *Poems* (1845).

2772 Burleigh, Cecil. "Rain in Summer" op. 33 no. 7. New York: C. Fischer, 1917. Song: high v, pf.

2773 Weigl, Vally. MS, u.d., avail. ACA. Song: med. v, pf.

The Rainy Day. *Ballads and Other Poems* (1842).

2774 Ames, Henry, Mrs. Manchester: Hime, Beale, n.d. Song: v, pf.

2775 Balfe, Michael W. London: Boosey, n.d. Song: v, pf.

2776 Barnby, J. Cited in DCD.

2777 Behrend, A.H. New York: C.H. Ditson, 1878. Song: v, pf.

2778 Bergen, Alfred Hiles. "The Day Is Dark and Dreary." Chicago: H.T. FitzSimmons, 1936. Setting for male v, pf.

2779 Berger, Francesco. In *Two-Part Songs.* London: Patey & Willis, n.d. Part Song: boys' or girls' voices, pf.

2780 Bischoff, J.W. Cincinnati: J. Church, 1886.

2781 Blockley, John. "The Day Is Cold, and Dark and Dreary." Boston: O. Ditson, [BAL n.d., not before 1858]. Pubd. as a song and a duet.

2782 Blumenthal, Jacques. Cincinnati: J. Church, 1901. Song: high and low v edns, pf.

2783 Bonvin, Ludwig. "Regentag (The Rainy Day)" in *Zwei Lieder.* Leipzig: Breitkopf & Härtel, 1898. Song: M or Bar, pf. Words in Ger. and Eng.

2784 Camille. "The Day Is Dark and Dreary." Boston: G.D. Russell, 1973. Song: Bar, pf.

2785 Cheney, Amy Marcy. Boston: O. Ditson, 1883. Song: v, pf.

2785a Clemens, Matthew. In *The Choral Handbook*. No. 805. London: u.p., 1885, etc. Part Song [BLC vol. 12 p. 276].

2786 Cowen, Frederic H. New York: T.B. Harms, [BAL n.d., not before 1881].

2787 Dempster, William R. Boston: O. Ditson, 1847. Song: v, pf. In coll. GOS 1, HSD, JO, LBR.

2788 Despommier, Victor. "A Rainy Day." New York: J. Fischer, 1911. Song: high, med., and low v edns, pf.

2789 Ellerton, J.L. "The Day Is Dark & Dreary." London: C. Lonsdale, n.d. Song: v, pf.

2790 Elliott, A.E.P. London: J. Shepherd, n.d. Song: v, pf.

2791 Emerson, L.O. Cited in LoPM. Setting for mixed chorus.

2792 Goldbeck, R. "The Day Is Cold." Chicago: Root & Cady, 1870. Song: B or C, pf.

2793 Gorst, Harold. London: E. Ashdown, n.d. Song: v, pf.

2794 Grylls, Cordelia. London: B. Mocatta, n.d. Song: v, pf.

2795 Harraden, Ethel. London: Forsyth Bros., n.d. Song: v, pf.

2796 Harrison, W. Edinburgh: Paterson, n.d. Song: v, pf.

2797 Hatton, John L. New York: Beer & Schirmer, [BAL n.d., not after 1866]. Song: v, pf.

2798 Hodges, Faustina H. "The Dreary Day." New York: C. Breusing, 1860. Song: med. v, pf.

2799 Johnson, Croshaw. "Be Still Sad Heart." London: Ashdown & Parry, n.d. Song: v, pf.

2800 Lee, Myntora J. Wagoner, Okla.: Privately pubd. by Myntora Lee, n.d. Song: v, pf.

2801 Marchant, A.W. London: Osborn & Tuckwood, n.d. School Song: 2-pt. song for ladies' voices, pf.

2802 Maynard, Walter. London: Lamborn Cock, Addison, n.d. Song: v, pf.

2803 Morrow, Katharine. London: W.G. Hallifax, n.d. Song: v, pf.

2804 Pasmore, Henry B. Boston: O. Ditson, 1880. Song: v, pf.

2805 Piaggio, I. Chicago: National Music, 1890.

2806 Pratt, Silas G. "The Rainy Day" op. 20. Chicago: F.S. Chandler, 1872. Setting for SATB qrt, chorus ad lib, pf.

2807 Reinhardt, Carl. London: Musical Bouquet Office, [BPL 186-?]. Song: v, pf.

2808 Rudersdorff, Erminia. Boston: G.D. Russell, 1873. Song: v, pf; Madame Rudersdorff. "Dark and Dreary." London: Stanley Lucas, Weber, n.d. Song: v, pf.

2809 Shanley, Robert. New York: C. Fischer, 1939. Song: med. v, pf.

2810 Sullivan, Arthur. London: Novello, n.d. Part Song: SATB, pf.

2811 Swinstead, Felix. London: J.W. Cramer, 1912. Song: v, pf.

2812 Wiebé, Edward. Boston: Henry Tolman, 1867.

The Reaper and the Flowers. *Voices of the Night* (1839).

2813 Balfe, Michael W. Boston: O. Ditson, [BAL n.d., not before 1858]. Song: v, pf. In coll. BSP.

2814 Banks, Collingwood. London: R. Cocks, n.d. Song: v, pf.

2815 Blockley, John. London: J. Blockley, n.d. Song: v, pf; New York: Benjamin W. Hitchcock, 1869. Duet, pf.

2816 Clay, Frederic. London: Cramer, Wood, n.d. Song: v, pf.

2817 Cowen, Frederic H. Boston: O. Ditson, [BAL n.d., not before 1877].

2818 Emerson, L.O. In coll. LBR.

2819 Fitzgerald, James. London: Novello, Ewer, n.d. Song: v, pf.

2820 Fontein-Tuinhout, F.R. In *Three Serious Songs* op. 10 no. 2. Middleburg: A.A. Noske, 1906. Song: A or B-Bar, pf.

2821 Hempel, Carl F. London: Jewell & Letchford, n.d. Song: v, pf.

2822 Hime, Edward L. London: Duff & Stewart, n.d. Song: v, pf.

2823 Hobbs, J.W. London: R. Cocks, [BPL 186-?]. Song: v, pf.

2824 Marshall, Charles. "Heavenly Blossoms." London: W. Morley, n.d. Song: high, med., and low v edns, pf.

2825 Melville, Frank. "The Reaper & the Flowers." London: J. Guest, n.d. Song: v, pf.

2826 Mendelssohn, F. In coll. HCA.

2827 Montgomery, W.H. London: Ashdown & Parry, n.d. Song: v, pf.

2828 O'Reilly, Kathleen. London: Lamborn Cock, n.d. Song: v, pf.

2829 Pinsuti, Ciro. "There Is a Reaper." London: Leader & Cock, n.d. Setting for trio, pf.

2830 Reinhardt, Carl. London: Sheard, [BPL 185-?]. Song: v, pf.

2831 Stap, Henry. Liverpool: J. Smith, n.d. Song: v, pf.

2832 Thomas, J.R. Boston: O. Ditson, 1861.

2833 Zeta. London: Leader & Cock, n.d. Song: v, pf.

Resignation. *The Seaside and the Fireside* (1849).

2834 Blockley, John. London: J. Blockley, n.d. Song: v, pf.

2835 Claribel. London: G. Emery, [BPL 186-?]. Song: v, pf.

2836 Gould, John Edgar. Boston: O. Ditson, 1850. Song: v, opt pf.

2837 M.R.L. "Across the River." Hastings, St. Leonard's, Bournemouth: W. Slade, n.d. Song: v, pf.

2838 Mocatta, Percy G. London: Reid Bros., n.d. Song: v, pf.

2839 "Resignation." London: Jewell & Letchford, n.d. Song: v, pf.

2840 Romer, Frank. London: Hutchings & Romer, n.d. Song: v, pf.

2841 Smith, Samuel. London: Addison, Hollier & Lucas, n.d. Song: v, pf.

The Return of Spring [Trans. from the poem of Charles D'Orleans]. *The Poets and Poetry of Europe* (1845).

2842 Berger, Francesco. "A Spring Song" in *Two-Part Songs*. London: Patey & Willis, n.d. Part Song: boys' or girls' voices, pf.

2843 Foulds, John. London: W. Paxton, 1925. Song: high and low v edns, pf; "Spring Joy." London: W. Paxton, 1925. Song: high and low v edns.

Rondel ["Hence away, begone, begone," trans. from the poem of Charles D'Orleans]. *The Poets and Poetry of Europe* (1845).

2844 Manson, Willie B. "Hence Away! Begone" in *Songs of Love and Youth*. London: Boosey, 1919. Song: v, pf.

2845 Ogilvy, Frederick A. "Song Against Melancholy." London and New York: Boosey, 1932. Part Song: TTBB, a cap.

Rondel ["Love, love, what wilt thou with this heart of mine?" Trans. from the poem of Jean Froissart]. *The Poetical Works of Henry Wadsworth Longfellow* (1868).

2846 Cowen, Frederic H. "Love, What Wilt Thou with This Heart of Mine?" in *Longfellow's Songs*. Boston: O. Ditson, 1892. Song: S or T, pf; In *Nine Songs*. London: Metzler, 1892. Song: high and med. v edns, pf.

2847 Elgar, Edward. In *7 Lieder*. London: Ascherberg, Hopwood & Crew, n.d. Song: v, pf. Text in Eng. and Ger., trans. by Ed. Sachs.

2848 Gordon, Philip. New York: Skidmore Music, 1957. Chorus: SATB, a cap.

2849 Manson, Willie B. "Love! What Wilt Thou with This Heart of Mine?" in *Songs of Love and Youth*. London: Boosey, 1919. Song: v, pf.

2850 Thomson, Sydney. "Love, Love, What Wilt Thou." Boston: O. Ditson, 1901. Part Song: SATB, a cap.

The Saga of King Olaf. *Tales of a Wayside Inn* (1863).

2851 Buck, Dudley. "King Olaf's Christmas" op. 86. New York: G. Schirmer, 1881. Cantata: male chorus, Bar and T soli, reed organ, pf obl, str qnt ad lib.

2852 Buck, Dudley. "The Nun of Nidaros." New York: G. Schirmer, 1879. Setting for male chorus with T solo, pf obl, reed organ ad lib. Words from pt. 22 of the poem.

2853 Busch, Carl. "Einer Tambelskelver." Cincinnati: H.T. FitzSimmons, 1925. Cantata: male chorus, pf or orch.

2854 Busch, Carl. "King Olaf." Boston: O. Ditson, 1903. Cantata: SATB chorus, STBar soli, orch (R); "The Challenge of Thor, from 'King Olaf.' " Boston: O. Ditson, 1903. Song: v, pf. Text from pt. 1 of the poem.

2855 Edmunds, Chris M. "Thorberg's Dragon Ship." London: Bayley & Ferguson, 1923. Choral Ballad: SATB chorus, SATB soli, orch (R).

2856 Elgar, Edward. "King Olaf" op. 30. London: Novello, Ewer, 1896. Cantata: SATB chorus, STB soli, orch (R). Text alterations by H.A. Acworth.

> "As Torrents in Summer" from the cantata, "King Olaf." *The Musical Times,* Extra Supplement, no. 796 (Oct. 1, 1900). Part Song: SATB, pf.
> "The Wraith of Odin." London: Novello, 1903, 1904.
> "A Little Bird in the Air." London: Novello, 1905.
> "As Torrents in Summer." London: Novello, 1906. Quartet: 4-pt. men's voices, a cap.
> "As Torrents in Summer." London: Novello, 1927. Setting for female voices, pf. Arr. by the composer.
> "As Torrents in Summer." London: Novello, 1933. Setting for unison song, pf. Arr. by the composer.
> "As Torrents in Summer." York, Nebr.: J.A. Parks, 1933. Quartet or chorus for male voices. Arr. by J.A. Parks.
> "As Torrents in Summer." London: Novello, 1934. Chorus: TTBB. Arr. by H.A. Chambers.
> "As Torrents in Summer." New York: J. Fischer, 1934. Chorus: SSA, a cap. Arr. by William Lester.
> "As Torrents in Summer." New York: J. Fischer, 1934. Chorus: TTBB, a cap. Arr. by Frederic Joslyn.
> "As Torrents in Summer." Boston: Boston Music, 1947. Setting for 4-pt. boys' voices, TTBB, a cap. Arr. by Robert W. Gibb.

"As Torrents in Summer." Boston: McLaughlin & Reilly, 1947. Chorus: 3-pt. women's voices.

2857 Godfrey, Percy. "Legend of the North (The Saga of King Olaf)." London: Weekes, 1905. Dramatic Cantata.

2858 Protheroe, Daniel. "Drontheim (King Olaf's Christmas)." Part Song for male voices.

2859 Protheroe, Daniel. "The Nun of Nidaros" op. 63. Milwaukee: Rohlfing, 1902. Chorus: TTBB, orch. Words in Eng. and Ger., trans. by E. Buek.

2860 Romer, Frank. "Thyri the Fair." London: Lamborn Cock, Hutchings, n.d. Song: v, pf.

2861 Sveinbjörnsson, Sv. "The Challenge of Thor." London: Wood, n.d. Song: v, pf.

2862 Tinker, D. Emily. "The Thunderer." Ft. Wayne: Ten Oak Publishing, 1926. Song: Dram. T or Bar, pf.

2863 West, Alfred H. "The Challenge of Thor." London and Leipzig: Pitt & Hatzfeld; Boston: H.B. Stevens, 1891. Song: Bar or B, pf.

Sandalphon. *The Courtship of Miles Standish, and Other Poems* (1858).

2864 Loomis, Harvey W. New York: E.S. Werner, 1896. Recitation with acc.

2865 Romer, Frank. London: Lamborn Cock, Hutchings, n.d. Song: v, pf.

2866 Smart, Henry. London: Augener, n.d. Song: v, pf.

Santa Teresa's Book-Mark [Trans. from the poem, "Letrilla que llevaba por registro en su breviario," of Santa Teresa de Avila]. *The Poets and Poetry of Europe* (1871).

2867 Diamond, David. "Let Nothing Disturb Thee." New York: Associated Music, 1945. Song: med. v, pf.

2867a Takacs, Jeno. "Let Nothing Disturb Thee." Cincinnati: World Library, u.d. Chorus: SSA. Also pubd for SATB chorus.

The Sea-Diver. *Poems: Lyrical and Dramatic* (1848).

2868 Andrews, R., arr. Melody by Ricci. London: Metzler, n.d. Cavatina: v, pf.

The Sea Hath Its Pearls. *The Belfry of Bruges and Other Poems* (1846).

2869 Biermann, W. Cleveland: S. Brainard's, 1875.

2870 Bischoff, J.W. Cincinnati: J. Church, 1888. Song: v, pf.

2871 Braunschiedl, Johannes. "The Sea Hath Its Pearls." New York: C.H. Ditson, 1883.

2872 Burck, Henry. New York: C. Fischer, 1908. Song: high v, pf.

2873 Busch, Carl. Boston: O. Ditson, 1901. Song: med. v, pf.

2874 Clutsam, Fred. "The Sea Hath Its Pearls" op. 1. Melbourne: W.H. Glen, n.d. Song: S or T, pf.

2875 Cowdell, Ellen. London: Boosey, 1905. Song: high and med. v edns, pf.

2876 Cowen, Frederic H. In *Longfellow's Songs*. Boston: O. Ditson, 1892. Song: S or T, pf; In *Nine Songs*. London: Metzler, 1892. Song: high and med. v edns, pf.

2877 Davis, J.D. London: Chappell, 1910. Song: high and med. v edns, pf.

2878 Forrester, J. Cliffe. Newbury: Alphonse Cary, n.d. Song: v, pf.

2879 Frewin, T. Harrison. London: C. Woolhouse, n.d. Song: v, pf. Text in Eng. and Ger.

2880 Ganz, Rudolph. Boston: A.P. Schmidt, 1915. Song: high and med. v edns, pf.

2881 Goldbeck, Robert. New York: Pond, 1866. Song: S or T, pf.

2882 Gounod, Charles. Boston: G.D. Russell, 1872.

2883 Gulesian, M.H., Mrs. New York: G. Schirmer, 1927. Song: high v, pf.

2884 Henry, Bertram C. Boston: A.P. Schmidt, 1889. Song: v, pf.

2885 King, Oliver A. "The Sea Hath Its Pearls" in *Six Songs* op. 59. London: Novello, Ewer, 1890. Song: Bar, pf.

2886 Kolar, Victor. "The Sea Hath Its Pearls" op. 18 no. 1. New York: C. Fischer, 1912. Song: med. v, pf.

2886a Lichner, F. Cited in DCD.

2887 Macfarren, Walter. London: Enoch, n.d. Song: v, pf.

2888 Morrill, Osma C. "My Heart and the Sea and the Heaven." Washington, D.C.: John F. Ellis, 1892. Song: v, pf.

2889 Newell, J.E. London: E. Donajowski, n.d. Duet: voices, pf.

2890 O'Shea, John A. Boston: Miles & Thompson, 1890.

2891 Parker, J.C.D. In *7 Part Songs*. Boston: Ditson, 1875. Part Song: SATB, pf.

2892 Philp, Elizabeth. Boston: O. Ditson, [BAL n.d., after 1856]. Song: v, pf.

2893 Pinsuti, Ciro. Boston: O. Ditson, [BAL n.d., after 1869].
    George B. Nevin, arr. Boston: O. Ditson, 1898. Part Song:
    TTBB, a cap.
    London: Lamborn Cock, n.d. Part Song: SATB, pf ad lib.

2894 Radecki, Olga V. Boston: A.P. Schmidt, 1882.

2895 Rile, LeRoy M. New York: Hinds, Hayden & Eldredge, 1917. Song:
    v, pf.

2896 "The Sea Hath Its Pearls." Boston: Davenport Bros, 1877.

2897 Sprenger, Jules. London: Ashdown & Parry, n.d. Song: v, pf.

2898 Tours, Berthold. Boston: O. Ditson, [BAL n.d., not before 1864].
    Song: v, pf.

2899 Vincent, Charles. London: C. Vincent, n.d. Song: v, pf.

2900 Walter, Ida. London: Duncan Davison, n.d. Song: v, pf.

2901 Warren, S.P. New York: G. Schirmer, 1865. Song: v, pf.

2902 White, Maude Valérie. In *Maude Valérie White's Album of German
    Songs.* Boston: O. Ditson, 1876; "Das Meer hat seine Perlen." Lon-
    don: Stanley Lucas, Weber, n.d. Song: v, pf. Text in Eng. and Ger.

2903 Wickham, J.J. Birmingham: Harrison & Harrison, n.d. Song: v, pf.

2903a Woolf, B.E. Male quartet. Cited in DCD.

2904 Wright, Vernon O. London: J. Williams, n.d. Song: v, pf.

Seaweed. *Poems* (1845).

2905 Bright, Houston. Delaware Water Gap, Pa.: Shawnee, u.d. Chorus:
    mixed voices.

2906 Burton, F.R. "Sea-Weed" op. 14 no. 3. New York: C.H. Ditson,
    1882. Song: B, pf.

2907 Sacco, P. Peter. In *Collected Songs* vol. 2, op. 136 no. 7. Daly City,
    Calif.: Ostara Press, 1975. Song: med.-high v, pf; Los Angeles:
    Western International Music, u.d. Chorus: SATB, pf.

Silent Love. *The Poets and Poetry of Europe* (1845).

2908 Squire, W.H. "In Love's Domain." London: Boosey, 1902. Duet for
    C and Bar, pf.

The Singers. *The Seaside and the Fireside* (1849).

2909 Abt, Franz. "The Three Great Chords." London: William Czerny,
    n.d. Song: v, pf.

2910 Bell, Doyne C. London: R. Mills, n.d. Song: v, pf.

2911 Bornschein, Franz. Chicago: H.T. FitzSimmons, 1930. Cantata:
    female voices, pf.

2912 Gaul, A.R. London: Patey & Willis, 1883. Part Song; London: Novello, n.d. Part Song: SATB, a cap.

2913 Gaul, Harvey. New York: M. Witmark, 1931. Cantata: SATB chorus, S and Bar soli, pf.

2914 Harris, Cuthbert. Boston: A.P. Schmidt, 1925. Chorus: SSAA, pf.

2915 Harris, Victor, arr. "The Three Singers." Boston: O. Ditson, 1920. Part Song: SSA, pf.

2916 MacKenzie, Alexander, Sir. London: Novello, 1901. Part Song.

2917 Mitchell, Walter. London: Wood, n.d. Song: v, pf, harmonium ad lib.

2918 Osborne, G.A. "The Three Singers." London: C. Jefferys, n.d. Song: v, pf.

2919 Protheroe, Daniel. "The Minstrels." Boston: Boston Music, 1932. Chorus: TTBB, pf.

2920 Rau, Earl. n.p.: Oklahoma Music Educators Assn., 1965. Chorus: SATB, a cap.

2921 Saar, Louis V. "The Singers" op. 108a. New York: J. Fischer, 1925. Part Song: SATB.

2922 Schurig, Bruno. London: Augener, n.d. Song: v, pf.

2923 Sellew, Donald E. Cincinnati: Willis Music, 1953. Chorus: SSAATTBB, a cap.

2924 Sodero, Cesare. New York: Galaxy, 1936. Chorus: male voices, pf.

2925 Stark, Humphrey J. London: H.W. Wickins, n.d. Song: B or C, pf, harmonium obl.

2926 Tours, Berthold. "The Three Singers." Boston: O. Ditson, [BAL n.d., after 1876]. Song: high and low v edns; Victor Harris, arr. Boston: O. Ditson, 1920. Part Song: SSA, pf.

2927 Waller, Hilda. London: Novello, n.d. Cantata: SSA, pf.

2928 Work, John W. New York: Mills, 1949. Chorus: SATB, Bar solo, pf, orch.

Sir Humphrey Gilbert. *The Seaside and the Fireside* (1849).

2929 McGrath, Joseph J. "The Ballad of Sir Humphrey Gilbert." New York: H. Flammer, 1920. Chorus: SSAA, S solo.

The Skeleton in Armor. *Ballads and Other Poems* (1842).

2930 Boughton, Rutland. "The Skeleton in Armor" op. 2. London: Novello, 1909. Symphonic Poem: SATB chorus, orch.

2931 Foote, Arthur. "The Skeleton in Armor" op. 28. Boston: A.P. Schmidt, 1892. Ballad for chorus and orch.

2932 M.C.Z. "Once As I Told in Glee, or The Viking's Bride." Boston: O. Ditson, 1852. Song: v, pf.

2933 Whiting, George E. "The Tale of the Viking." New York: G. Schirmer, 1881. Dramatic Cantata: chorus, 3 soli, orch.

The Slave in the Dismal Swamp. *Poems on Slavery* (1842).

2934 Coleridge-Taylor, Samuel. "In Dark Fens of the Dismal Swamp" in *Five Choral Ballads* op. 54 no. 5. Leipzig: Breitkopf & Härtel, 1904. Chorus: SATB, pf or orch; In *Two Choral Ballads* op. 54 no. 5. London: Breitkopf & Härtel, 1905. Chorus: SATB, pf or orch.

The Slave Singing at Midnight. *Poems on Slavery* (1842).

2935 Bentley, W.H. In *Six Songs* op. 2 no. 3. London: London Music Publishing, n.d. Song: v, pf.

2936 Coleridge-Taylor, Samuel. "Loud He Sang the Psalm of David" in *Three Choral Ballads* op. 54 no. 1. London: Breitkopf & Härtel, 1904. Part Song: SATB, a cap.

2937 Glover, Stephen R. London: R. Cocks, [NYPL ca. 1860]. Vocal duet.

The Slave's Dream. *Poems on Slavery* (1842).

2938 Braunschiedl, J. New York: G. Schirmer, 1887. Song: v, pf.

2939 Coleridge-Taylor, Samuel. "Beside the Ungathered Rice He Lay" in *Three Choral Ballads* op. 54 no. 3. London: Breitkopf & Härtel, 1904. Part Song: SATB, pf or orch.

2940 Levey, Maria F. "The Vision of the Slave." London: Duff & Stewart, n.d. Song: v, pf.

2941 Matthews, Harry A. New York: G. Schirmer, 1910. Choral Ballad: SSAA, T solo, orch; New York: G. Schirmer, 1911. Choral Ballad: SATB, T solo, orch.

2942 Normann, Jules. London: Musical Bouquet Office, n.d. Song: v, pf.

2943 Renshaw, Wilmott. London: Munt Bros., n.d. Song: v, pf.

2944 Sjögren, Emil. "Slafvens dröm" op. 8. Stockholm: A. Hirsch, 1883. Song: B, pf. Words in Eng. and Swed.

2945 Weiss, Willoughby H. London: Addison, Hollier & Lucas, n.d. Song: v, pf.

Snow-Flakes. *The Courtship of Miles Standish and Other Poems* (1858).

2946 Cottam, Arthur. In *The Musical Times*. No. 278. Choral Song: SATB, pf ad lib.

2947 Jones, Edwin A. "Snowflakes." n.p.: composer, n.d. Song: v, pf.

2948 Lyon, James. "Snow Flakes" op. 85 no. 1. London: Edwin Ashdown, 1926. Part Song: SA or SS, pf.

2949 Pontet, Henry. "The Snow Flakes." London: Chappell, n.d. Song: v, pf.

2950 "The Snow" in coll. Ben 4.

2950a Trubitt, Allen. "Snowflakes." Cincinnati: World Library, u.d. Chorus: SATB. Music not seen; text presumably from this poem.

Something Left Undone. *The Courtship of Miles Standish and Other Poems* (1858).

2951 Bell, Doyne C. London: R. Mills, n.d. Song: v, pf.

Song [Trans. from the poem, "The Paradise of Love" beginning, "Hark! Hark!"]. *Outre-Mer: A Pilgrimmage Beyond the Sea* (1883).

2952 Saar, Louis V. "Hark, Hark Pretty Lark" op. 31 no. 2. New York: G. Schirmer, 1901. Song: high v, pf and vn obl.

Song ["She is a maid of artless grace"]. *Outre-Mer: A Pilgrimmage Beyond the Sea* (1883).

2953 Allen, Grace B. "The Maid of Artless Grace." London: Cramer, Beale, n.d. Song: v, pf.

2953a Blockley, John J., the Younger. "She Is a Maid of Artless Grace." London, 1863.

2954 Cairos-Burgos, Rex de. "She Is a Maid of Artless Grace." London: G. Shrimpton, 1911. Song.

Song ["Stay, stay at home, my heart, and rest"]. *Kéramos and Other Poems* (1878).

2955 Barnett, John. "Stay at Home." Boston: Carl Prüfer, [BAL n.d., ca. 1878]. Song: v, pf.

2956 Behrend, A.H. "Stay, Stay at Home." London: B. Schott's Söhne, 1896. Song: v, pf.

2957 Berger, Francesco. "Stay at Home" in *Two-Part Songs*. London: Patey & Willis, n.d. Part Song: boys' or girls' voices, pf.

2958 Brown, A. Swan, Mrs. "Stay at Home My Heart and Rest." New York: Spear & Dehnhoff, 1885. Song: v, pf.

2959 Bunning, Herbert. "Home's Best." London: Enoch, 1908. Song: med. and low v edns, pf.

2960 Camilieri, L. "To Stay at Home Is Best." Boston: O. Ditson, 1921. Part Song: SATB, a cap.

2961 Carse, A. von Ahn. "Stay, Stay at Home My Heart." London: Breitkopf & Härtel, 1907. Song: med. or low v, pf.

2962 Cate, A. ten. "To Stay at Home Is Best." In coll. LBR set for SSA chorus, a cap.

2963 Cirillo, Vincenzo. "To Stay at Home Is Best." Boston: G.D. Russell, 1878. Song: v, pf.

2964 Coerne, Louis. A. "Stay, Stay at Home My Heart" in *Ten Songs* op. 28 no. 2. Boston: Everett E. Truette, 1894. Song: med. v, pf.

2965 Cowen, Frederic H. "Stay at Home" in *Longfellow's Songs*. Boston: O. Ditson, 1892. Song: M or T, pf; In *Nine Songs*. London: Metzler, 1892. Song: high and med. v edns, pf.

2966 Cutter, E., Jr. "Song of Home." Boston: E. Cutter, Jr., 1891.

2967 Harrison, S.C. "Oh, Stay at Home My Heart." Philadelphia: T. Presser, 1914, c1909 William Maxwell Music. Song: v, pf.

2968 Kelly, John C. "Stay, Stay at Home" in *Album of Six Songs*. Boston: O. Ditson, 1896. Song: v, pf.

2969 Liddle, S. "Home Song." London: Boosey, 1896. Song: v, pf.

2970 Mednikoff, Nicolai. "To Stay at Home Is Best." New York: C. Fischer, 1925. Song: high v, pf.

2971 Phelps, Edward H. "To Stay at Home Is Best." New York: G. Schirmer, 1878. Song: v, pf.

2972 Pratt, Silas G. "Stay at Home My Heart and Rest." Cincinnati: J. Church, 1878. Song: high and med. v edns, pf.

2973 Price, James. "Stay at Home." London: London Music Publishing, n.d. Song: high and med. v edns, pf.

2974 Redfield, Edith S. "Stay at Home." Boston: C.W. Thompson, 1910. Song: v, pf.

2975 Schuler, C.C. "Stay at Home." Privately pubd by C.C. Schuler, 1883. Song: v, pf.

2976 Tours, Berthold. "To Stay at Home Is Best." New York: G. Schirmer, n.d. Part Song or Chorus: SSA, pf.

2977 Wadsworth, W. "Stay at Home." Newburgh, N.Y.: Estey Organ, 1879.

2978 Waldrop, Uda. "Stay Home My Heart." Cincinnati: J. Church, 1909. Song: high and med. v edns, pf.

2979 Walthew, R.H. "Home-Keeping Hearts." London: Boosey, 1912. Song: v, pf.

Song ["Where, from the eye of day"]. *The Early Poems of Henry Wadsworth Longfellow* (1878).

2980 Campbell, John E. "The Silent River." London: Weekes, n.d. Song: v, pf.

The Song of Hiawatha (1855).

2981 Bliss, James A. "Hiawatha's Song," "Adjidaumo," "The Rainbow," "Pau Puk Keewis Dances" in *Hiawatha Songs* op. 10. Minneapolis: J.A. Bliss, 1921. Song: v, pf.

2982 Blockley, John. "The Song of Hiawatha (I Am Happy I Am Happy)." London, 1857. Song.

2983 Braine, R. "Hiawatha's Fire-Fly Song" in coll. DagI, DagR, DagU.

2984 "Building the Canoe," arr. to an Omaha Indian Air. In coll. ArF 1.

2985 Burleigh, Cecil. "Westward" op. 62. New York: G. Schirmer, 1928. Song: med. or low v, pf.

2986 Burton, Frederick R. "Hiawatha." Boston: O. Ditson, 1898. Dramatic Cantata: SATB chorus, SATB soli, orch (R); "E-wa-yea, My Little Owlet." New York: W. Maxwell, 1903. Cradle song for C, vn, pf; "When I Think of My Beloved." New York: W. Maxwell, 1903. Setting for C.

2986a Burton, Frederick R. "Hiawatha's Death Song" in *Songs of the Ojibways*. New York: W. Maxwell, 1902. Indian and Eng. words; trans. from the Indian musical play "Hiawatha" and harmonized by Burton.

2986b Burton, Frederick R. "My Bark Canoe" in *Songs of the Ojibways*. New York: Luckhardt & Belder, 1902. Done into Eng. and harmonized for the Indian musical play "Hiawatha" by Burton.

2987 Busch, Carl. "Chibiabos" in *Six Indian Songs*. Boston: O. Ditson, 1907; In *Eight Indian Songs*. Boston: O. Ditson, 1917. Song: med. v, pf. Words in Eng. and Ger., trans. by Hermann Simon.

2988 Busch, Carl. "Death of Chibiabos" in coll. BuE, BuS. Song: med. v, pf. Words in Eng. and Ger., trans. by Hermann Simon.

2989 Busch, Carl. "Farewell Minnehaha" in coll. BuE. Song: high and med. v edns, pf. Words in Eng. and Ger., trans. by Hermann Simon.

2990 Busch, Carl. "The Four Winds." New York: H.W. Gray, 1907. Cantata: SATB chorus, S and T soli, orch. Words in Eng. and Ger., from pt. 2 of the poem.

2991 Busch, Carl. "Gitche Manito the Mighty" in coll. BuE, BuS. Song: med. v, pf. Words in Eng. and Ger., trans. by Hermann Simon.

2992 Busch, Carl. "Give Me Your Bark, O Birch-Tree" in *Three Songs*. New York: G. Schirmer, 1913. Song: high or med. v, pf. Words in Eng. and Ger., trans. by Hermann Simon.

2993 Busch, Carl. "Greeting of Hiawatha" in coll. BuE, BuS. Song: med. v, pf. Words in Eng. and Ger., trans. by Hermann Simon.

2994 Busch, Carl. "Hiawatha's Friends" in coll. BuE. Song: high and low v edns, pf. Words in Eng. and Ger., trans. by Hermann Simon.

2995 Busch, Carl. "Onaway! Awake, Beloved!" in coll. BuE, BuS. Song: med. v, pf. Words in Eng. and Ger., trans. by Hermann Simon.

2996 Busch, Carl. "Pau-Puk-Keewis' Beggar's Dance" in *Three Songs*. New York: G. Schirmer, 1913. Song: high or med. v, pf. Words in Eng. and Ger., trans. by Hermann Simon.

2997 Busch, Carl. "Take Your Bow, O Hiawatha" in *Three Songs*. New York: G. Schirmer, 1913. Song: high or med. v, pf. Words in Eng. and Ger., trans. by Hermann Simon.

2998 Busch, Carl. "When the Noiseless Night Descended." In coll. BuE, BuS. Song: med. v, pf. Words in Eng. and Ger., trans. by Hermann Simon.

2999 Coleridge-Taylor, Samuel. "The Death of Minnehaha" in *Scenes from the Song of Hiawatha* op. 30 no. 2. London: Novello, 1899. Cantata: chorus, S and Bar soli, orch.

3000 Coleridge-Taylor, Samuel. "Hiawatha's Departure" in *Scenes from the Song of Hiawatha* op. 30 no. 4. London: Novello, 1901. Cantata: chorus, STB soli, orch.

3001 Coleridge-Taylor, Samuel. "Hiawatha's Vision" in *Scenes from the Song of Hiawatha* op. 30. London: Novello, 1901. Song: Bar, orch.

3002 Coleridge-Taylor, Samuel. "Hiawatha's Wedding-Feast" in *Scenes from the Song of Hiawatha* op. 30 no. 1. London: Novello, 1900. Cantata: chorus, T solo, orch; "Onaway, Awake, Beloved!" London: Novello, 1898. Aria: T; London: Novello, 1918. Aria: Bar.

3003 Coleridge-Taylor, Samuel. "My Algonquin." Philadelphia: T. Presser, 1909. Song: v, pf.

3004 Coleridge-Taylor, Samuel. "Spring Had Come" in *Scenes from the Song of Hiawatha* op. 30. London: Novello, 1901. Song: S, orch. Text in Eng. and Ger.

3005 Converse, Charles C. "The Death of Minnehaha." Boston: O. Ditson, [BAL n.d., ca. 1855]. Song: v, pf. In coll. LBR.

3006 Converse, Charles C. "My Algonquin." Boston: O. Ditson, 1856. Song: v, pf.

3007 Converse, Charles. C. "Onaway!" Boston: O. Ditson, 1856.

3008 Converse, Frederick S. "The Peace Pipe." Boston: C.C. Birchard, 1915. Cantata: SATB, Bar solo, orch.

3009 Cowen, Frederic H. "Onaway, Awake Beloved!" London: Metzler, 1892. Song: low v, pf; In *Longfellow's Songs*. Boston: O. Ditson, 1892. Song: T, pf.

3010 Donald, H.A. "Hiawatha Dramatized." London: J. Curwen, 1927. Poem arr. in tableau, recitation and dance and set to music for female v, pf or orch.

3011 Foote, Arthur. "The Farewell of Hiawatha" op. 11. Boston: A.P. Schmidt, 1886. Chorus: male voices, Bar solo, orch.

3012 Gow, George C. "Indian Love-Song" in *Five Songs* op. 2 no. 3. Boston: Boston Music, 1888. Song: v, pf.

3013 Grant-Schaefer, G.A. "Hiawatha's Childhood." Boston: A.P. Schmidt, 1929. Cantata.

3014 Harling, W. Franke. "The Death of Minnehaha." Boston: Boston Music, 1917. Indian Pastorale: male chorus, STB soli, pf, fl, hp, cel, timp.

3015 "Hiawatha's Brothers," arr. to an Omaha Indian Air. In coll. ArF 1.

3016 "Hiawatha's Brothers," arr. to a Finnish Folk Air. In coll. MuC 4, Mu 4.

3017 Holbrook, Florence. "The Hiawatha Primer." Boston: Houghton, Mifflin, 1898. Illustrated plates and music.

3018 Lutz, W. Meyer. "The Indian Melody." London: J. Williams, n.d. Song: v, pf.

3019 O'Neill, Norman. "Dramatized Scenes from 'Hiawatha.'" London: K. Paul, Trench, Trubner, 1916. Scenes by Valérie Wyngate, music by O'Neill.

3020 Pelzer, Anne W. "Hiawatha's Farewell." London: Cramer, Beale, n.d. Song: v, pf.

3021 Prior, Clement E. "Hiawatha's Lamentation." London: Novello, 1905. Part Song: SATB.

3022 Ringwald, Roy. n.t. ["By the Shores of Gitche Gumee"] in *The Song of America.* Delaware Water Gap, Pa.: Shawnee, 1951. Chorus: SATB, pf 4 hands.

3023 Schulthes, Wilhelm. "When I Think of My Beloved." London: S. Brewer, n.d. Song: v, pf.

3024 Selle, L. "Serenade from Hiawatha." Boston: O. Ditson, [BAL n.d., not before 1858].

3025 Squire, Hope. "Listen! 'Tis My Voice You Hear," "Though You Were at a Distance" in *Two Red-Indian Love Songs.* London: Elkin, 1912. Song: v, pf.

3026 Stoepel, Robert. "Beggar Dance," "Canoe Building Song," "Chibiabo's Love Song," "Cradle Song," "Death of Minnehaha," "The Great Spirit's Allocution," "The Harvest," "Hiawatha's Birth,"

"Hiawatha's Wooing," "Magic Corn-Field Dance," "The Ravens," "Spring and Summer," "War Song," "(Winter) Ghosts, Famine and Fever" in *Hiawatha*. New York: Wm. Hall, 1863. Indian Symphony: chorus, soli, orch.

3027 "Wah-Wah-Tay-See," arr. to an American Indian Air. In coll. Fo 4, FoH.

3028 Wathall, A.G. "Wah-Wah-Tay-See" in coll. Par 1, ParT 1.

3029 Whiteley, Bessie M. "Hiawatha's Childhood." Boston: C.C. Birchard, 1914. Operetta in 1 act for unchanged voices.

3030 Wilson, Ira B. "Childhood of Hiawatha." Dayton: Lorenz Publishing, 1924. Cantata: SAB; Dayton: Lorenz Publishing, 1926. Cantata: SSA, pf.

3031 Wilson, Ira B. "The Friends of Hiawatha." Dayton: Lorenz Publishing, 1933. Cantata: SA, pf or orch.

3032 Wolfe, Jacques. "Onaway." Philadelphia: O. Ditson, 1945. Song: v, pf.

Song of the Silent Land [Trans. from the poem of Johann Gaudenz von Salis-Seewis]. *Hyperion* (1839).

3033 Bainton, Edgar L. "Into the Silent Land." London: J. Curwen, 1919. Part Song: mixed voices, a cap.

3034 Blockley, John. "The Silent Land." London: Cramer, Beale, n.d. Song: v, pf. Also pubd as a duet.

3035 Faning, Eaton. London: Novello, 1896. Setting for voices with ad lib acc: vn, vc, hp, org.

3036 Foote, Arthur. "Into the Silent Land" in *Music Sung by the Alumni at the Two Hundred and Fiftieth Anniversary of the Foundation of Harvard University November Seventh 1886.*
    Boston: A.P. Schmidt, 1886, pp. 33–37.
    Boston: A.P. Schmidt, 1889. Setting for 4-pt. women's voices, a cap.
    Boston: A.P. Schmidt, 1897. Setting for 4-pt. mixed voices, a cap.

3037 Gaul, A.R. "The Silent Land" op. 21 no. 1. London: Novello, Ewer, n.d. Part Song: SATB, a cap.

3038 Jenkins, Cyril. London: J. Curwen, 1920. Hymn symphonic for chorus, orch.

3039 Lott, Edwin M. "Into the Silent Land." London: Ashdown & Parry, n.d. Song: v, pf.

3040 Matthews, Harry A. London: Weekes, 1903. Cantata: SATB chorus, T and S soli, orch (R).

3041 Pease, Frederic H. Detroit: C.J. Whitney, 1882.

3042 Rendall, Edward D. "Into the Silent Land" in *Five Duets for Soprano and Baritone or Tenor.* London: Landy, n.d. Duet: SB or ST, pf.

3043 Romer, Frank. "The Silent Land." London: Leader & Cock, n.d. Song: v, pf.

3044 Strachauer, Hermann. Boston: O. Ditson, 1860. Cantata.

3045 Wood, Henry J. "The Silent Land" op. 16 no. 1. London: Weekes, n.d. Song: v, pf.

The Sound of the Sea. *The Masque of Pandora and Other Poems* (1875).

3046 Coerne, Louis A. In *Ten Songs* op. 28 no. 4. Boston: Everett E. Truette, 1894. Song: v, pf.

3046a Heiss, John. In *Songs of Nature.* n.p.: Boosey & Hawkes, 1978. Song Cycle: M, fl, cl, vn, vc, pf. Recording: Nonesuch H 71351.

The Spanish Student (1843). *See also* "Ah, Love!" "All are sleeping, weary heart!" "Good night! Good night, beloved!" "If thou art sleeping, maiden," "Loud sang the Spanish cavalier," "Stars of the summer night!"

3047 Edwards, Julian. "Victorian." London: Hutchings & Romer, [NYPL 187–?]; London: J. Williams, [NYPL 197–?]. Opera in 4 acts founded on *The Spanish Student.* Text adapted by J.F. Reynolds-Anderson.

3048 Freer, Eleanor Everest. "Preciosa; or, The Spanish Student" op. 37. Milwaukee: Wm. A. Kaun, 1928. Opera in 1 act 3 sc. Words adapted by Freer.

Spring [Trans. from the poem of Charles D'Orleans]. *Voices of the Night* (1839).

3049 Berger, Francesco. "Gentle Spring" in *Two-Part Songs.* London: Patey & Willis, n.d. Part Song: boys' or girls' voices, pf.

3050 Farebrother, Bernard. "Gentle Spring." London: Metzler, n.d. Cavatina: v, pf.

3051 Holbrooke, Joseph C. "In Sunshine Clad" op. 15 no. 1.

3052 Lahee, Henry. London: R. Mills, n.d. Duet: SC, pf.

3053 Marchant, A.W. "Gentle Spring." London: Osborn & Tuckwood, n.d. Part Song: 2 ladies' voices, pf.

3054 R.R. "Spring." London: Weekes, n.d. Song: v, pf; London: Leonard, 1907. Song: v, pf.

3055 Romer, Frank. "Springtime." London: Lamborn Cock, Hutchings, n.d. Song: v, pf.

"Stars of the summer night!" [act 1 sc. 3]. *The Spanish Student* (1843).

3056 Alberti, Solon. "My Lady Sleeps." New York: Michael Keane, 1937. Song: 2 v edns, pf.

3057 Amberg, J. "Serenade." Boston: Boston Music, 1913. Song: med. v, pf.

3058 Atherton, Percy Lee. In *Four Songs* op. 20 no. 3. Boston: Boston Music, 1903. Song: med. v, pf.

3059 Auld, John. London: Bayley & Ferguson, 1936. Song: v, pf.

3060 Baker, B.F. Boston: G.P. Reed, 1844; Chicago: Root & Cady, 1865. Setting for TTBB, pf.

3061 Baksa, Robert. "Serenade: Stars of the Summer Night" op. 39. u.p.: Composers Library Edns, 1977. Setting for SATB, pf.

3062 Balfe, Michael W. London: Boosey, u.d. Song: v, pf. In coll. DM 2.

3063 Barbour, Florence N. Boston: A.P. Schmidt, 1910. Song: high and med. v edns, pf.

3064 Barnes, Leonard. "Preciosa." London: W. Morley, n.d. Song: v, pf.

3065 Bartholomew, Mounsey, Mrs. London: J. Williams, n.d. Song: v, pf.

3066 Bennett, George J. London: Stanley Lucas, Weber, Pitt & Hatzfeld, 1893. Song: v, pf.

3067 Blockley, John. London: Chappell, n.d. Duet: voices, pf. Also pubd as a song.

3068 Boott, Francis. Boston: O. Ditson, 1857. Song: v, pf. In coll. BoAS 2, BoF.

3068a Brydson, John Callis. London: Francis, Day & Hunter, 1949. Part Song: SA; In *Francis & Day's Unison and Part Songs*. No. 101. [BLC vol. 9 p. 59.]

3069 Calcott, Emily B. London: Metzler, n.d. Song: v, pf.

3070 Cole, Sidney R. London: J. Roberts, 1909. Song: v, pf.

3071 Compton, C.H. Boston: O. Ditson, [BAL n.d., not after 1857]. Song: v, pf.

3072 Cowen, Frederic H. "My Lady Sleeps" in *Longfellow's Songs*. Boston: O. Ditson, 1892. Song: T, pf; In *Nine Songs*. London: Metzler, 1892. Song: high and med. v edns, pf.

3073 Cutler, Ellen G. Buffalo: Blodgett & Bradford, [BAL, n.d., ca. 1858].

3074 Dicks, Ernest A. "She Sleeps, My Lady Sleeps." London: Reynolds, 1904. Song: v, pf.

3075 Dunhill, Thomas F. "The Summer Night." Pubd. in the Extra Musical Supplement of *The Musical Times* vol. 78 no. 1134 (Aug. 1937). Setting for SSA trio, pf.

3076 E.A.B. In *Two Songs*. London: Addison & Hollier, n.d. Song: v, pf.

3077 Elgar, Edward. "Spanish Serenade (Stars of the Summer Night)" op. 23. *The Musical Times,* Extra Musical Supplement no. 644 (April 1, 1904). Chorus: SATB, pf or orch (R); "Stars of the Summer Night" op. 23. London: Novello, 1912. Chorus: SS, 2 vn, pf.

3078 Erskine, Kennedy, Miss. "My Lady Sleeps." London: A.W. Hammond, n.d. Song: v, pf.

3079 Foerster, Ad. M. Philadelphia: W.F. Shaw, 1879.

3080 Gaul, Harvey B. Boston: O. Ditson, 1905. Part Song: SATB, pf.

3081 Glover, Stephen R. New York: Firth, Pond, [BAL n.d., not before 1856]. Duet: voices, pf. Boston: O. Ditson, u.d. Duet: female or male voices, pf.

3082 Grant, Bartle. Canterbury: Tench J. White, n.d. Song: v, pf.

3083 Harvey, Richard F. London: J. Shepherd, n.d. Song: v, pf.

3084 Hatton, John L. "The Student's Serenade." London: Addison & Hollier, [BPL 186–?]. Song: v, pf.

3085 Hawley, C.B. "Dreams of the Summer Night." Cincinnati: J. Church, 1908. Song: high and low v edns, pf.

3086 Heuser, Carl. New York: C. Heuser, 1873.

3087 Hiles, Henry. "A Serenade" in *Six Songs*. London: Forsyth Bros, [NYPL ca. 1890].

3088 Hime, Edward L. "My Lady Sleeps." London: Duff & Hodgson, n.d. Part Song: SATB, a cap.

3089 Huntley, Fred H. Boston: Boston Music, 1933. Chorus: male voices, a cap.

3090 Inglis, Walter W. London: W.G. Hallifax, n.d. Song: v, pf.

3091 Johns, D.G. "My Lady Sleeps." Boston: O. Ditson, 1883.

3092 Kearton, Harper. London: Evans, n.d. Duet: high and low v edns, pf.

3093 Kleber, H. Philadelphia: Lee & Walker, 1846. Song: v, pf; Philadelphia: Lee & Walker, 1847. Song: v, gtr; arr. by A. Schmitz.

3094 Kratz, Lee G. Boston: O. Ditson, 1895. Quartet: TTBB, a cap.

3095 Lassen, Eduard. London: Osborn & Tuckwood, n.d. Song: med. and low v edns, pf.

3096 Lindsay, Miss. London: R. Cocks, n.d. Song: v, pf.

3097 McGarity, Hugh. Delaware Water Gap, Pa.: Shawnee, 1952. Chorus: SATB, pf.

3098 Marchant, A.W. London: Osborn & Tuckwood, u.d. Part Song: 2-pt. ladies' voices, pf.

3099 Marston, G.W. "My Lady Sleeps." Boston: G.D. Russell, 1977. Song: high v, pf.

3100 Masson, Eliz. London: C. Lonsdale, n.d. Duet: voices, pf.

3101 Matthews, Harry A. "A Serenade." New York: G. Schirmer, 1906. Chorus: SSA, pf.

3102 Merz, Charles J. Boston: O. Ditson, 1857.

3103 Mitchell, Ernest E. "My Lady Sleeps." London: Novello, Ewer, n.d. Part Song: SATB, pf.

3104 Nevin, Ethelbert. Boston: O. Ditson, 1887. Song: high and low v edns, pf. In coll. NAS.

3105 Oswald, Madame. London: Novello, Ewer, n.d. Song: v, pf.

3106 Palmer, E. Davidson. London: E. Ashdown, n.d. Song: v, pf, vn ad lib.

3107 Pasmore, Henry B. San Francisco: A. Waldteufel, 1886. Song: v, pf; In *Song Album*. Boston: O. Ditson, 1890. Song: T, pf.

3108 Pease, Alfred H. New York: Beer & Schirmer, 1865. Song: med. v, pf. In coll. JO.

3109 Perkins, Charles C. [Cover destroyed.] Song: v, pf. Text in Eng. and Fr., trans. by Ch. Monselet.

3110 Perkins, W.O. Boston: O. Ditson, 1896. Quartet: SSAA, a cap.

3111 Radford, Henrietta M. "My Lady, Sleeps." London: Patey & Willis, n.d. Song: v, pf.

3112 Rivarde, P.A. "Mandolina." New York: Beer & Schirmer, 1867. Song: med. v, pf.

3113 Sandford, Lucy A. New York: Wm. Hall, 1849. Duet; New York: Wm. Hall, 1849. Song: v, pf.

3114 "Serenade." In coll. CHS, CU, HSC, MP, MPC, NMH, NML, WC.

3115 "Serenade." Boston: Nathan Richardson, 1856.

3116 Shepperd, Frank N. New York: Wm. A. Pond, 1888.

3117 Smart, Henry. Boston: O. Ditson, n.d; New York: G. Schirmer, 1895. Quartet or chorus: SATB, pf. Ed. and revised by H.W. Nicholl.

3118 Spawnforth, J. n.p.,n.d. Song: v, pf.

3119 "Stars of the Summer Night" in coll. LAASR.

3120 Sudds, W.F. Boston: O. Ditson, 1883. Chorus: SATB, pf.

3121 Tosti, F. Paolo. "Dreams of the Summer Night." London: Chappell, [BPL 188–?]; Cited in ScNS, Song: high, med., and low v edns.

3122 Tours, Berthold. Philadelphia: William H. Boner, [BAL n.d., not before 1872]. Song: v, pf.

3123 Travers, Mary. London: E. Ashdown, n.d. Song: v, pf.

3124 Van Gelder, Martinus. "Spanish Serenade." Philadelphia: Philadelphia Music Academy, 1882.

3125 Walker, Ernest. London: Willcocks, 1903. Song: v, pf.

3126 Walthew, Richard N. London: Boosey, 1905. Song: high and med. v edns, pf.

3127 Webster, E.L., Mrs. "My Lady Sleeps." Boston: By the author and E.H. Wade, 1849.

3128 Weil, Oscar. San Francisco: M. Gray, 1874. Song: v, pf.

3129 Wellings, Milton. [BAL n.p., n.d., ca. 1880]. Philadelphia: W.F. Shaw, n.d. Duet: voices, pf.

3130 Werther, Rudolph. n.p.: J. Albert, 1958. Song: v, pf.

3131 West, John E. London: Novello, Ewer, 1893. Trio: SSA, pf.

3132 White, Charles A. New York: C. Fischer, 1915. Male chorale.

3133 White, Otis R. "A Summer Night Serenade." Chicago: National Music, 1892.

3134 Williams, W. "My Lady Sleeps" op. 2. Boston: O. Ditson, 1890. Part Song: TTBB, a cap.

3135 Willis, H.B. "My Lady Sleeps." Cited in LoPM for women's chorus.

3136 Withington, O.W. Boston: Geo. P. Reed, 1843. Song: v, pf.

3137 Wolf-Ferrari, E. In coll. Par 4.

3138 Woodbury, Isaac B. In coll. BeBBN, FRM, FRMS, FRMW, HSD, JS, JSE, LAASR, LBR, MAS, MSS, NGS, OH, ONAS, SLS, TFB, TFC 1, TFO, TFP, TFR, WieBT, WieL. Song: v, pf; In coll. ArF 2, ArJ, Fo 5–6, FoH, FoT 3, GaO, Gi 3, GiA, Gilm, Mab, Mals, Mu 5, MuC 5, MuO, ParO, St.

3139 Y., F. G. "She Sleeps! My Lady Sleeps!" New York: n.p., n.d.

3140 Yale Glee Club, as sung by. New York: Wm. A. Pond, 1866.

3141 Zanetti, E. London: Gustav Scheurmann, n.d. Song: v, pf.

The Statue over the Cathedral Door [Trans. from the poem, "Das Steinbild am Dome," of Julius Mosen]. *Poems* (1845).

3142 Brackett, Frank H. "Over the Cathedral Door." Boston: O. Ditson, 1882. Song: C or Bar, pf.

3143 Hamlin, Charles S. Boston: O. Ditson, 1884.

Sundown. *In the Harbor: Ultima Thule—Part II* (1882).

3144 Busch, Carl. "The Summer Sun Is Sinking Low." Boston: O. Ditson, 1905. Song: high v, vn obl.

3145 Cowen, Frederic H. Boston: O. Ditson, 1892. Song: med. v, pf; In *Longfellow's Songs*. Boston: O. Ditson, 1892. Song: M or T, pf; In *Nine Songs*. London: Metzler, 1892. Song: high and med. v edns, pf.

Suspiria. *The Seaside and the Fireside* (1849).

3146 Annie. London: R. Cocks, n.d. Song: v, pf.

3147 Blakeway, Amy. London: Moutrie, n.d. Song: v, pf.

3148 Shee, R. Jenery. Mainz: B. Schott's Söhne, n.d. Song: M or C, vn or vc ad lib.

3149 Sjögren, E. In coll. WM 2. Words in Eng. and Swed.

3150 Van Antwerp, Yates. In *Two Poems*. Philadelphia: Lee & Walker, 1872. Song: v, pf.

The Theologian's Tale: Elizabeth. *Tales of a Wayside Inn* (1863).

3151 Bedford, Herbert. "Ships That Pass in the Night." London: Ascherberg, Hopwood & Crew, 1922. Song: v, unacc.

3151a Brydson, John C. "Ships That Pass in the Night." London: J. Williams, 1958. Part Song: SATB, a cap.

3152 Burnes-Loughman, Mai. "Ships That Pass in the Night." New York: Hinds, Hayden & Eldredge, n.d. Song: 2 v edns, pf.

3153 Foote, Arthur. "Ships That Pass in the Night." Boston: A.P. Schmidt, 1921. Song: med. v, pf.

3154 Harraden, Ethel. "Ships That Pass in the Night." London: Forsyth; New York: E. Schuberth, 1894. Song: med. and low v edns, pf.

3155 Huhn, Bruno. "Ships That Pass in the Night." Boston: O. Ditson, 1918. Duet: high and med. v edns, pf.

3156 Parkyn, William. "Ships That Pass in the Night." u.p.: York, Banks, 1935. Part Song: SATB, a cap.

3157 Stephenson, T. Wilkinson. "Ships That Pass in the Night." London: Boosey, 1914. Song: med. and low v edns, pf.

There Was a Little Girl. [BAL 12252].

3158 Hiller, John S. "Song of Ye Nurserie." Cincinnati: J. Church, 1895.

3159 Needham, Alicia A. "A Naughty Little Girl." London: Schott, 1904.

Song: v, pf. Text: "There was a little girl and she had a little curl. . . ."

Three Friends of Mine [Pt. 5 beginning, "The doors are all wide open; at the gate"]. *The Masque of Pandora and Other Poems* (1875).

3160 Boott, Francis. "Three Friends of Mine." Boston: O. Ditson, 1882. Song: v, pf.

The Tide Rises, the Tide Falls. *Ultima Thule* (1880).

3161 Francis, G.T. "The Tide Rises" in *Two Songs of the Sea.* London: Murdoch, Murdoch, 1925. Song: v, pf.

3162 Heilner, Irwin. "The Tide Rises" in coll. CCS; "The Traveler." New York: Associated Music, 1945. Song: med. v, pf.

3163 Meininger, J.C. St. Louis: Balmer & Weber, 1886.

3164 Shearer, C.M. San Antonio: Southern Music, 1978. Chorus: SATB, a cap.

3165 Stewart, Kensey D. New York: Lawson-Gould, 1968. Chorus: SATB, a cap.

To-morrow [Trans. from the poem, "Mañana" of Lope de Vega"]. *Voices of the Night* (1839).

3166 Margetson, Edward. "Lord, What Am I." New York: H.W. Gray, 1936. Chorus: mixed voices, S and T soli, a cap.

To the River Charles. *Ballads and Other Poems* (1842).

3167 Beethoven, Ludwig van. Arr. by W. West. "Silent River." London: T.E. Purday, n.d. Song: v, pf.

3168 Davis, Thomas F. "The River." London: J. Williams, n.d. Song: v, pf.

3169 Romer, Frank. "Silent River." London: Leader & Cock, n.d. Song: v, pf.

Twilight. *The Seaside and the Fireside* (1849).

3170 Beach, H.H.A., Mrs. "In the Twilight" op. 85. Boston: A.P. Schmidt, 1922. Song: v, pf.

3171 Bentley, W.H. In *Six Songs* op. 2 no. 1. London: London Music Publishing, n.d. Song: v, pf.

3172 Berrow, Isaac. London: G. Emery, n.d. Song: v, pf.

3173 Blakeway, Amy. London: Moutrie, n.d. Song: v, pf.

3174 Clark, Chas. J. "Twilight by the Sea." London: Harris, n.d. Song: v, pf.

3175 Ella, R.J. London: Gustav Scheurmann, n.d. Song: v, pf.

3176 Hatton, John L. "Twilight by the Sea." London: Addison & Hollier, n.d. Song: v, pf.

3177 Marchant, A.W. London: Osborn & Tuckwood, n.d. Part Song: 2-pt. ladies' voices, pf.

3178 Morgan, Geo. W. Pubd. "free with the New York Family Story Paper, no. 257" [BAL 1878].

3179 Newell, J.E. In *Twelve Two Part Songs for the Use of Schools and Classes.* London: E. Donajowski, n.d. Part Song: 2-pt. voices, pf.

3180 Robinson, Joseph, Mrs. Dublin: Bussell, n.d. Song: v, pf.

3181 Smith, S.A. London: R. Cocks, n.d. Ballad: v, pf.

3182 Weiss, Willoughby H. "The Fisherman's Cottage." Boston: E.H. Wade, [BAL n.d., 1845–1860]. Song: v, pf.

The Two Angels. *The Courtship of Miles Standish, and Other Poems* (1858).

3183 Pinsuti, Ciro. London: J. Scrutton, n.d. Song: v, pf.

3184 Romer, Frank. London: A. Hammond, n.d. Song: v, pf.

The Two Locks of Hair. *Ballads, and Other Poems* (1842).

3185 Balfe, Michael W. London: Boosey, n.d. Song: v, pf.

3186 Blockley, John. London: J. Blockley, n.d. Song: v, pf.

3187 Bucalossi. "Love Dreams." London: Lamborn Cock, n.d. Song: v, pf.

3188 Carew, Lady. London: R. Mills, n.d. Song: v, pf.

3189 Chatterton, J. Balsir, Jr. London: Chappell, n.d. Ballad: v, pf.

3190 Houfe, Alfred E. London: Novello, 1906. Song: med. v, pf.

3191 Romer, Frank. "Two Locks of Hair." London: Lamborn Cock, Hutchings, n.d. Song: v, pf.

3192 Stewart, H.E. Worthing: Palmer, n.d. Song: v, pf.

3193 Wallworth, T.A. "The Brown and the Blond." London: A. Hammond, n.d. Song: v, pf.

The Venetian Gondolier. *The Early Poems of Henry Wadsworth Longfellow* (1878).

3194 Anderson, W.R. London: Stainer & Bell, 1932. Chorus: TTBB, pf.

Venice. *The Masque of Pandora and Other Poems* (1875).

3195 Walton, Frederic E. London: W. Morley, n.d. Song: med. and low v edns, pf.

Victor Galbraith. *The Courtship of Miles Standish, and Other Poems* (1858).

3196 Bevis, T.A. London: Vincent Music, n.d. Song: Bar or B, pf (trb or cornet).

The Village Blacksmith. *Ballads, and Other Poems* (1842).

3197 Anderton, Thomas. "The Village Blacksmith (Der Dorfschmied)." London: Williams, 1898. Cantata. Ger. words by Willy Kastner.

3198 Balfe, Michael W. London: Boosey, [BPL 186-?]. Song: v, pf.

3199 Berwald, William H. New York: J. Church, 1917. Setting for mixed voices, pf.

3200 Blockley, John J., the Younger. London, 1857. Song: v, pf.

3201 Buck, Dudley. Boston: A.P. Schmidt, 1893. Song: Bar or B, pf.

3202 Daykin, Herbert. London: Howard, n.d. Song: v, pf.

3203 Gaines, Samuel R. Boston: C.C. Birchard, 1925. Cantata: mixed voices, S and Bar soli, pf or orch.

3204 Haesche, William E. "The Village Blacksmith" op. 34. New York: M. Witmark, 1911. Cantata: male chorus, T solo, pf or orch. Ger. words by Alice Mattullath.

3205 Handel, G.F., arr. from. London: J. Blockley, n.d. Song: v, pf. Music arr. from Handel's "The Harmonius Blacksmith."

3206 Hatton, John L. In *Novello's Part-Song Book* [Second Series, vol. 6, pp. 60–66]. London: [BPL, 1870?]. Part Song: SATB; In *Novello's Part-Song Book* [Second Series, vol. 7, pp. 100–106]. Part Song: ATBB.

3207 Entry cancelled.

3208 Heuberer, Charles F. Boston: A. & J.P. Ordway, 1848. Ballad: v, pf.

3209 Jephson, T.L. Milwaukee: H.N. Hempsted, [BAL n.d., ca. 1870]. Bar Recitative & Song, pf.

3210 Kountz, Richard. New York: H.W. Gray, 1924. Cantata: SSA chorus, pf or orch.

3211 Neidlinger, W.H. Philadelphia: T. Presser, 1918. Chorus: SATB, pf or org.

3212 Nevin, George B. Boston: O. Ditson, 1893. Song: Bar or B, pf.

3213 Noyes, Charles F. Boston: O. Ditson, 1898. Chorus: mixed v, pf, org, anvil; N. Clifford Page, arr. Boston: O. Ditson, 1908. Chorus: female voices, Bar solo, pf, org, anvil.

3214 Peabody, George. Boston: O. Ditson, 1890. Song: Bar or B, pf.

3215 Reinhardt, Carl. London: Sheard, [BPL 186-?]. Song: v, pf.

3216 Rhys-Herbert, W. New York: J. Fischer, u.d. Song: v, pf.

3217 Wagner, Carl, arr. London: J.F. Pettit, n.d. Song: v, pf.

3218 Warden, David A. Philadelphia: Lee & Walker, [BAL 1867; i.e., ca. 1872]. Song: v, pf.

3219 Weiss, Willoughby H. Boston: O. Ditson, 1851; London: Cramer, Beale and Chappell, 1858. Song: med. v, pf; New York: Century Music, 1909. Rev. and ed. edn; In coll. BAS 1, DM 1, HSE 1, TuJS [edns unknown].

Walter von der Vogelweid. *Poems* (1845).

3220 Hatton, John L. "Vogelweid the Minnesinger." London: Lamborn Cock, Addison, n.d. Ballad: v, pf; In *Album of Twelve Songs*. London: J. Williams, [188– or 189–]. Song: v, pf.

3221 Rathbone, George. "Vogelweid, the Minnesinger." London: Novello, 1902. Setting for children's voices.

3222 Weiss, Willoughby H. "The Minnesinger." London: Willis, 1896. Song: v, pf.

Wanderer's Night-Songs [Trans. from the poem of Johann Wolfgang von Goethe, pt. 2 beginning, "O'er all the hill-tops"]. *The Poets and Poetry of Europe* (1871).

3223 Chaloff, Julius. "Wanderer's Night Song." New York: C. Fischer, 1919. Song: high and low v edns, pf.

3224 Coleridge-Taylor, Avril Gwendolyn. "O'er All the Hill-Tops." London: Augener, 1957. 2-pt. song, pf.

3225 Fearnley, John. "Wanderer's Night-Song." London: Novello, Ewer, n.d. Song: high and med. v edns, pf. Text in Eng. and Ger.

3226 Kaufer, Joseph. "Thou That from the Heavens Art" in *The Man with the Hoe and Other Songs*. Waukegan, Ill.: Lyric-Art, 1951. Song: high and med. v edns, pf.

3227 Reed, William. "Wanderer's Night Song I," "Wanderer's Night Song II." New York: G. Schirmer, 1902. Part Song or Chorus: SATB, a cap.

The Warden of the Cinque Ports. *The Courtship of Miles Standish, and Other Poems* (1858).

3228 Lyon, James. "The Warden of the Cinque Ports" op. 26. London: Breitkopf & Härtel, 1901. Choral Ballad: TTBB, orch.

The Wave [Trans. from the poem "Die Welle" of Christoph August Tiedge]. *Voices of the Night* (1839).

3229 Guerini, Rosa. In *Six Songs* op. 9 no. 2. London: J.B. Cramer, n.d. Song: v, pf.

3230 Munster, Countess of, The. Brighton: Bridge, n.d. Song: v, pf.

3231 Schaaf, E.O. In *German and English Poems in Song* vol. 2 op. 3. u.p.: E.O. Schaaf, 1902.

The Wayside Inn. *Tales of a Wayside Inn* (1863).

3232 Bollig, Anna Burt. "By the Firelight." Boston: C.W. Thompson, 1910. Song: v, pf.

Weariness. *Tales of a Wayside Inn* (1863).

3233 Addison, Robert B. London: Alphonse Bertini.

3234 Bolton, Lawrence. New York: G. Schirmer, 1934. Song: high, med., and low v edns, pf.

3235 Dempster, William R. "O Little Feet." New York: S. T. Gordon, 1866. Song: v, pf.

3236 Pontet, Henry. London: S.J. Brewer. n.d. Song: v, pf.

3237 Rodison, Robert B. London: Alphonse Bertini, Seymour, n.d. Song: v, pf.

Whither? [Trans. from the poem "Wohin?" of Wilhelm Müller]. *Voices of the Night* (1839).

3238 Bentley, W.H. In *Six Songs* op. 2 no. 2. London: London Music Publishing, n.d. Song: v, pf.

3239 Blockley, John. London: J. Blockley, n.d. Song: v, pf.

3240 Cox, A.H. London: Cramer, n.d. Song: v, pf.

3241 Hargitt, Charles J. London: Chappell, n.d. Song: v, pf.

3242 Harrington, Karl P. Boston: O. Ditson, 1883.

3243 Hatton, John L. London: Addison & Hollier, n.d. Song: v, pf.

3244 Howard, H.R. London: R. Cocks, n.d. Song: v, pf.

3245 Schaaf, E.O. In *German and English Poems in Song* vol. 2 op. 3. u.p.: E.O. Schaaf, 1902.

3246 Smith, Arthur O. "The Brooklet." London: Metzler, n.d. Song: v, pf.

3247 Wintle, Ogle. In *Six Songs*. London: Lamborn Cock, n.d. Song: v, pf.

The Windmill. *Ultima Thule* (1880).

3248 Lyon, James. "The Windmill" op. 85 no. 6. London: Edwin Ashdown, 1926. Part Song: SS or SA, pf.

3249 Nelson, Herbert H. London: Chappell, 1897. Song: med. and low
v edns, pf.

3250 Ogilvy, Frederick A. London: J. Curwen, 1933. Part Song: SCTB,
a cap.

3251 Rathbone, George. London: Novello, 1936. Setting for unison song
(school song), pf.

3252 Tuckerman, Gustavius. Boston: A.P. Schmidt, 1885. Song: low v,
pf.

Woods in Winter. *Voices of the Night* (1839).

3253 Bates, Fred D. "Winter." Boston: Louis H. Ross, 1885.

3254 Marchant, A.W. "A Song of Winter" in *Songs of Nature* op. 93 no.
5. London: Enoch, 1906. 2-pt. Song, pf.

3255 Sharpe, Herbert F. "Winter" in *8 Two Part Songs for Girls or Boys
Voices*. London: Patey & Willis, n.d. Duet: voices, pf.

The Wreck of the Hesperus. *Ballads, and Other Poems* (1842).

3256 Anderton, Thomas. Boston: C. Prüfer, 1882. Cantata: chorus, soli,
pf; Hollis Dann, arr. Cincinnati: Willis Music, 1906.

3257 Blockley, John J., the Younger. London: Duff & Hodgson, n.d.
Song: v, pf.

3258 Burr, Willard, Jr. "The Wreck of the Hesperus" op. 22. Boston: O.
Ditson, 1889. Dramatic Ballad: edns for S or T, A or Bar, pf.

3259 Dunkley, Ferdinand L. London: Novello, Ewer, 1893. Ballad: chorus, orch.

3260 Fisher, Arthur E. "The Wreck of the Hesperus" op. 61. Boston: O.
Ditson, [BAL n.d., after 1867]; London: J. Curwen, 1896. Cantata:
female voices.

3261 Foote, Arthur. "The Wreck of the Hesperus" op. 17. Boston: A.P.
Schmidt, 1888. Setting for mixed chorus, STB soli, pf or orch.

3262 Hatton, John L. London: Cramer, Wood and Lamborn Cock, n.d.
Descriptive Ballad: v, pf. In coll. BAS 1, HSE 1, TuJS.

3263 Hullah, J. Philadelphia: Lee & Walker, [BAL n.d., not before 1872].

3264 Hyde, James. King Williams Town, South Africa: J. Hyde, n.d.
Cantata: SATB, pf.

3265 Lewis, C.H. London: Mathias & Strickland, n.d. Cantata: SSA
chorus, pf.

3266 MacCunn, Hamish. London: Novello, 1905. Chorus: SATB, orch.

3267 Mills, Charles H. Boston: C.C. Birchard, 1917. Cantata: SATB
chorus, pf.

3268 Parker, Louis Napolean. "The Wreck of the Hesperus" op. 1. London: Cock, [BPL 1878?]. Ballad: 3 female voices, pf.

3269 Read, John Francis Holcombe. "The Hesperus." London: Novello, 1896. Cantata: chorus, SBarB soli, orch.

3270 Romer, Frank. "The Frozen Wreck." London: Leader & Cock, [BPL 186-?]. Song: v, pf.

3271 Wareing, Herbert W. London: Novello, 1895. Setting for chorus, STB soli, orch.

3272 Weiss, Willoughby H. London: Cramer, Beale, [BPL 197-?]. Song: v, pf.

3273 Wilson, R.H. London: Breitkopf & Härtel, n.d. Choral Ballad: SATB, pf.

3274 Wilson, W. London: Davidson, n.d. Song: v, pf.

Miscellaneous

3275 Aiken, Walter H. "Indian Lullaby." In coll. Dar 3, BeBBN. Words beginning, "rock-a-bye my little owlet in thy mossy swaying nest."

3276 "America: Fugitive Stanza." Attrib to H. Carey. In coll. BSE. Words beginning, "Lord, let war's tempests cease."

3277 Andrews, John C. "He Said He Came to Find Me, Do You Really Think He Did?" Boston: W.H. Oakes, 1849. Words beginning, "I waited till the twilight/ And yet he did not come/ I strayed along the brookside and slowly wandered home. . . ." BAL (vol. 5 p. 633) doubts the text is by Longfellow.

3278 Blockley, John J. "Speak Gently." London, 1857. Ballad; London, 1858. Duet.

3279 Cain, Noble. "Nocturne." New York: H. Flammer, 1936. Chorus: treble voices, pf. Also pubd for SATB chorus.

3280 Carroll, B. Hobson. "King Alfred and Othere" in *The Royal Illuminated Book of Legends,* ed. and illus. by Marcus Ward. Edinburgh: Nimmo, [BPL 187-?]. Song: v, pf.

3281 Cirillo, Vincenzo. "The Murmuring Wind." Boston: A.P. Schmidt, 1877. Song: v, pf. Words from the Spanish. ["Wind so gently gently blowing/ thou to her must give repose"] BAL (vol. 5 p. 635) says text not in the works of Longfellow.

3282 Cowen, Frederic H. "Snow Flakes." Boston: O. Ditson, [BAL n.d., 1891?]; In *Album of Twelve Songs.* New York: G. Schirmer, [BAL n.d., after 1879]. BAL (vol. 5 p. 637) notes that the text is actually by Mary Mapes Dodge.

3283 Dunn, James P. "Watch and Wait." New York: J. Fischer, 1934. Chorus: SATB, a cap.

3284 Ely, Thomas. "The Spanish Jew's Tale." London: Breitkopf & Härtel, 1905. Dramatic Cantata: chorus, orch. Text from *Tales of a Wayside Inn*.

3285 Hammond, William G. "The Dawn." Cincinnati: J. Church, 1909. Chorus: male voices, org or pf.

3286 Hatton, John L. "I Loved Her." London: Novello, Ewer, n.d. Part Song: ATTB, pf. Text: "I loved her and her azure eyes haunted me from sweet sunrise. . . ."

3287 Heuberer, Charles F., and H. Perabeau. *Euphonia: A Collection of Glees and Part Songs . . . for the Use of Musical Conventions, Teacher's Institutes, and Singing Clubs*. Boston: J.P. Jewett and B.B. Mussey; Cleveland: Jewett, Proctor & Washington, 1854. "Contains 15 pieces credited to Longfellow . . . the remaining 3 pieces "Forget Not Me" "Mary, Arise" and "Boat Song" have not been located in Longfellow's Works" [BAL, vol. 5 p. 598].

3288 Leaf, W.B. "If Thou Art Worn and Hard Beset." n.p.: composer, n.d. Song: v, pf.

3289 Lindsay, Miss C. "Too Late, Too Late." New York: S. T. Gordon, [BAL n.d., 1860–1870]. BAL (vol. 5 p. 634) notes that the text is actually by Tennyson.

3290 Linley. "Bright Star." London: Cramer, Beale, n.d. Song: v, pf. Setting of lines beginning: "Bright star! whose soft, familiar ray. . . ."

3291 Longley, C.P. "Gathering Flowers in Heaven." New York: Wm. A. Pond, 1878. Text: "Long ago I loved her! Well the angels know,/ How my soul grew rich and strong, many years ago. . . ." BAL (vol. 5 p. 635) says text not found in the works of Longfellow.

3292 Mantz, Edwin Shelly, Mrs. "The Evening Sun Is Sinking." London: Hutchings & Romer, n.d. Song: v, pf. Text probably from the poem, "Sundown."

3293 Entry cancelled.

3294 Entry cancelled.

3295 Packer, F.A. "Break." London: London Publishing, n.d. Song: v, pf. A note on the music's folder at the Bowdoin College Library indicates that the text is by Tennyson as quoted by Longfellow.

3296 Ravnkilde, N. "Slumber Song." St. Louis: Balmer & Weber, 1870. BAL (vol. 5 p. 635) notes that the text is actually by Tennyson.

3297 Schlesinger, S. "I Would Tell Her I Love Her." Philadelphia: Kretschmar & Nunns, 1834 [No author listed]; Memphis, Tenn.: F. Katzenbach, 1864. BAL (vol. 5 p. 635) notes that the text is almost surely not by Longfellow.

3298 Train, Adelaide. Snow Flakes." Leipzig: Breitkopf & Härtel, 1895. Song: v, pf. Text: "Whene'er a snowflake leaves the sky. . . ."

3299 Trinder, Walter. "The Fountain." London: J. Williams, 1935. Song: v, pf.

3300 Vaughan Williams, Ralph. "'Tis Winter Now, the Fallen Snow." London: Oxford University Press, 1925. Setting for unison voices, pf.

3301 Walcott, Charles M. "Hiawatha: Or, Ardent Spirits and Laughing Water." New York: Samuel French, 1856. A musical extravaganza in two acts. Burlesque of Longfellow.

3302 Warren, Elinor R. "To My Native Land." Boston: E.C. Schirmer, u.d. Chorus: SATB.

3303 Entry cancelled.

3304 White, Mary L. "The Golden Sunset." London: J. Williams, 1900. Song: v, pf. Words by Samuel Longfellow.

3305 Yates, George. "Bless the Little Children." London: William Reeves, n.d. Song: v, pf. Text: "God bless the little children. . . ."

AMY LOWELL (1874–1925)

Autumn. *Pictures of the Floating World* (1919).

3306 Case, James. New York: Lawson-Gould, u.d. Chorus: SSA, a cap.

A Burnt Offering. *Pictures of the Floating World* (1919).

3307 Steinert, Alexander. In *Four Lacquer Prints*. Paris: Editions Maurice Senart, 1932. Song: med. v, pf.

A Decade. *Pictures of the Floating World* (1919).

3308 Engel, Carl. In *Three Poems by Amy Lowell*. New York: G. Schirmer, 1922. Song: med. v, pf.

Falling Snow. *Pictures of the Floating World* (1919).

3309 Fox, J. Bertram. New York: J. Fischer, 1926. Song: low v, pf.

A Lady. *Sword Blades and Poppy Seed* (1914).

3310 Dougherty, Celius. "Portrait of a Lady." Boston: R.D. Row, 1953. Song: high and low v edns, pf.

Little Ivory Figures Pulled with String. *Pictures of the Floating World* (1919).

3311 Gideon, Miriam. MS, n.d., avail. ACA. Song: med.-low v, gtr.

Madonna of the Evening Flowers. *Pictures of the Floating World* (1919).

3312 Dougherty, Celius. New York: Boosey & Hawkes, 1949. Song: med. v, pf.

Merchandise. *Pictures of the Floating World* (1919).

3313 Taylor, Clifford. In *Five Songs on English Texts* op. 4. New York: Associated Music, 1954. Song: S or T, pf.

Music. *Sword Blades and Poppy Seed* (1914).

3314 Dougherty, Celius. Boston: R.D. Row, 1953. Song: med. v, pf.

Night Clouds. *What's O'Clock* (1925).

3315 Robbins, Reginald C. Hollywood: Golden West Music, 1941. Song: high v, pf.

Opal. *Pictures of the Floating World* (1919).

3316 Engel, Carl. In *Three Poems by Amy Lowell.* New York: G. Schirmer, 1922. Song: med. v, pf.

Patterns. *Men, Women, and Ghosts* (1916).

3317 Bottje, Will G. MS, 1963, avail. ACA. Song: A, pf.

3318 Owen, Richard. Hastings-on-Hudson, N.Y.: General, 1973. Song: S or M, pf.

3319 Polifrone, Jon. "Patterns" op. 27. Chicago: Society for the American Composer, 1964? Song: S, orch.

Petals. *A Dome of Many-Coloured Glass* (1912).

3320 Case, James. New York: Associated Music, u.d. Chorus: SSA, a cap.

Primavera. *What's O'Clock* (1925).

3321 Dougherty, Celius. New York: G. Schirmer, 1948. Song: S, pf. In coll. TaST.

Reflections. *Pictures of the Floating World* (1919).

3322 Zeckwer, Camille W. In *Two Poems by Amy Lowell* op. 43 no. 2. New York: G. Schirmer, 1924. Song: med. v, pf.

Sea Shell. *A Dome of Many-Coloured Glass* (1912).

3323 Engel, Carl. In *Two Lyrics by Amy Lowell*. New York: G. Schirmer, 1911. Song: med. v, pf. In coll. ChN, FRM, ThAF.

3324 White, Felix. Boston: O. Ditson, 1926. Song: med. and low v edns, pf.

1777 [Sec. 2, "The City of Falling Leaves"]. *Men, Women, and Ghosts* (1916).

3325 Hughes, Rupert. "Falling Leaves" in *Free Verse Songs*. New York: G. Schirmer, 1922. Song: med. or low v, pf.

A Shower. *Pictures of the Floating World* (1919).

3326 Zeckwer, Camille W. In *Two Poems by Amy Lowell* op. 43 no. 1. New York: G. Schirmer, 1924. Song: med. v, pf.

Solitaire. *Pictures of the Floating World* (1919).

3327 Holt, Patricia B. In *Three Songs of Contemplation*. Scarborough, Ont.: Berandol Music, 1970. Song: v, pf.

A Sprig of Rosemary. *Pictures of the Floating World* (1919).

3328 Engel, Carl. In *Three Poems by Amy Lowell*. New York: G. Schirmer, 1922. Song: med. v, pf.

3329 Koemmenich, Louis. New York: J. Fischer, 1919. Song: high and low v edns, pf.

Storm by the Seashore. *Pictures of the Floating World* (1919).

3330 Steinert, Alexander. In *Four Lacquer Prints*. Philadelphia: Elkan-Vogel, 1932; Paris: M. Senart, 1932. Song: med. v, pf.

The Taxi. *Sword Blades and Poppy Seed* (1914).

3331 Dougherty, Celius. New York: C. Fischer, 1961. Song: med. v, pf. In coll. TaSE.

3332 Hadley, Henry K. "When I Go Away from You" op. 68 no. 1. New York: C. Fischer, 1920. Song: high and low v edns, pf, vn and vc obl.

Temple Ceremony [From the Japanese of Sojo Henjo]. *Pictures of the Floating World* (1919).

3333 Steinert, Alexander. In *Four Lacquer Prints*. Philadelphia: Elkan-Vogel, 1932; Paris: M. Senart, 1932. Song: med. v, pf.

The Trout. *A Dome of Many-Coloured Glass* (1912).

> 3334 Engel, Carl. In *Two Lyrics by Amy Lowell.* New York: G. Schirmer, 1911. Song: high v, pf.

Twenty-Four Hokku on a Modern Theme [Secs. 1, 13, 22]. *What's O'Clock* (1925).

> 3335 Howe, Mary. n.t. in *Three Hokku (From the Japanese).* New York: Galaxy, 1959. Song: high v, pf; In *English Songs,* Part III. New York: Galaxy, 1959. Song: v, pf.

Vicarious. *Pictures of the Floating World* (1919).

> 3336 Steinert, Alexander. In *Four Lacquer Prints.* Philadelphia: Elkan-Vogel, 1932; Paris: M. Senart, 1932. Song: med. v, pf.

Miscellaneous

> 3337 Hubert, Jean. "Weeping Pierrot and Laughing Pierrot (Pierrot qui pleure et Pierrot qui rit)." Boston: Boston Music, 1899. A comedy with music in one act. Setting for S or M, T, T or Bar, pf or orch (R). French text by Edmond Rostand; Eng. version by Lowell.
>
> 3338 Singer, Jeanne. "Fulfilled" in *A Cycle of Love.* West Babylon, N.Y.: H. Branch, 1976. Cycle: S, pf.

JAMES RUSSELL LOWELL (1819–1891)

Agro-Dolce ["One kiss from all others prevents me"]. *Heartsease and Rue* (1888).

> 3339 Phelan, Elsie G. In *In April.* Boston: C.W. Thompson, 1907. Song: v, pf.

Aladdin. *Under the Willows and Other Poems* (1868).

> 3340 Bellini, V. In coll. LAASR, MFS.
>
> 3341 "Castles in Spain" in coll. FSS 6.
>
> 3342 Coombs, C.W. "Aladdin's Lamp." New York: G. Schirmer, 1890. Song: med. v, pf.
>
> 3343 Scott-Paine, Matilda. Detroit: C.J. Whitney, 1881. Song: T and Bar edns, pf.

Auf Wiedersehen. *Under the Willows and Other Poems* (1868).

3344 Bendix, Max. Cincinnati: J. Church, 1903. Song: high and low v edns, pf.

3345 Klein, Bern. Cecil. Philadelphia: F.A. North, 1874.

3346 Macfarlane, M.R. "Auf Wiederseh'n." New York: Wm. A. Pond, 1884. Song: M, pf.

3347 Mallinson, Albert. London: Reynolds, 1901. Song: v, pf.

3348 Pratt, Silas G. "She Said Auf Wiedersehen!" New York: G. Schirmer, 1882. Song: high and med. v edns, pf.

3349 Schlesinger, Sebastian B. Boston: C. Prüfer, 1883. Ballad: v, pf.

The Birch-Tree. *Poems* [Second Series] (1848).

3350 Burleigh, Cecil. "The Birch-Tree" op. 49 no. 3. Cincinnati: J. Church, 1919. Song: v, pf.

A Christmas Carol. *Heartsease and Rue* (1888).

3351 Donizetti, G. "Peace on Earth." In coll. FSS 5, LAAS, LAASR, MCS, MFS.

3352 Young, Philip M. "Today the Prince of Peace Is Born." Nashville: Broadman Press, 1964. Christmas Cantata: mixed chorus, med. v solo, pf.

The Falcon. *Poems* [Second Series] (1848).

3353 Silcher, Friedrich. In coll. LBR.

The Fatherland. *Poems* (1844).

3354 Bellman, C.G. In coll. LBR. Song: v, pf.

3355 Petersilea, Franz. Where Is the True Man's Fatherland?" Boston: C. Bradlee, 1845.

3356 Reichardt, F. "Thy Land" in coll. LAASR.

The First Snow-Fall. *Under the Willows and Other Poems* (1868).

3357 Sacco, P. Peter. In *Collected Songs* vol. 3, op. 137 no. 5. Daly City, Calif.: Ostara Press, 1975. Song: med.-high v, pf.

The Fountain. *Poems* (1844).

3358 Clarke, Leland. "Into the Sunshine." Boston: A.P. Schmidt, 1916. Song: high and med. v edns, pf.

3359 "The Fountain." Arr. to a German Air. In coll. JSE, LBR.

3360 Hadley, Henry K. In coll. TL.

3361 Hammond, William G. "Song of the Fountain." Cincinnati: J. Church, 1908. Song: high and low v edns, pf.

3362 Kaun, H. In coll. Par 3, ParT 3.

3363 Leroux, Paul. In coll. ArF 2.

3364 Southard, Lucien H. Boston: Nathan Richardson, 1854. Song: v, pf.

3365 Warren, S.P. Cited in ScNS.

3366 Watts, Harold E. London: Bosworth, 1936. Setting for unison song, pf.

The Heritage. *Poems* (1844).

3367 "The Heritage." Arr. from a German Air. In coll. LBR.

Jonathan to John [Words included in "Mason and Slidell: A Yankee Idyll," no. 2 from the Second Series.] *The Biglow Papers* (1862).

3368 Boott, Francis. Boston: Henry Tolman, 1862.

Longing. *Poems* [Second Series] (1848).

3369 Cole, Rossetter G. In coll. TL.

The Lost Child. *A Year's Life* (1841).

3370 Shepherd, Arthur. In *Five Songs* op. 7 no. 4. Newton Center, Mass.: Wa-Wan Press, 1909. Song: high and med. v edns, pf.

Memoriae Positum. *Under the Willows and Other Poems* (1868).

3371 Boott, Francis. "Ah! When the Fight Is Won." Boston: O. Ditson, 1892. Recitative and Air for T or S, pf. In coll. BoAS 2.

Midnight. *Poems* (1844).

3372 Warren, Elinor R. "At Midnight." New York: H.W. Gray, 1936. Part Song: mixed voices, a cap.

Ode Recited at the Harvard Commemoration. *Under the Willows and Other Poems* (1868).

3373 Chadwick, George W. "Commemoration Ode." Boston: O. Ditson, 1928. Setting for SATB, pf or orch (R).

3374 Pinkham, Daniel. "The Promised Land" in *O Beautiful! My Country*. Boston: Ione Press, 1976. Chorus: SSAATTBB, pf opt.

A Parable ["Worn and footsore was the Prophet"]. *Poems* (1844).

3375 Smith, Carrie A. "The Prophet." Boston: White-Smith, 1877. Song: v, pf.

A Prayer. *Poems* (1844).

3376 Gernert, John. Philadelphia: Keyser, 1890. Song: v, pf.

The Present Crisis. *Poems* [Second Series] (1848).

3377 Beck, John N. "The Challenge." Columbus, Ohio: Beckenhorst Press, 1976. Setting for SSAATTBB, audience, pf or org, opt 3 tpt.

3378 Bergt, A., adapted from an Air of. "Once to Every Man and Nation" in coll. Ea.

3379 Beveridge, Thomas. "Epilog" in *Once*. Delaware Water Gap, Pa.: Shawnee, 1970. Cantata: SATB chorus, org, opt brass, perc and db.

3380 Hoppin, Stuart B. "Once to Every Man and Nation." Boston: C.C. Birchard, 1941. Setting for SATB, tpt obl (acc. orig. for orch); "Once to Every Man and Nation." Arr. to a Welsh hymn melody. In coll. SmASH, SmPS. Hymn.

3381 York, David S. "Once to Every Man and Nation." Bryn Mawr, Pa.: Presser, u.d. Chorus: SATB or TTBB, org or band (R) or str orch (R).

The Secret. *Heartsease and Rue* (1888).

3382 Herbert, Victor. Privately pubd by Herbert, 1897. Song: high v, pf.

Serenade. *A Year's Life* (1841).

3383 Boott, Francis. "From the Close Shut Window." Boston: O. Ditson, 1857. Setting for song and chorus ad lib, pf. In coll. BoF, BoS.

3384 Boweryem, George. "Alone! Alone!" New York: Wm. A. Pond, 1864. Song: med. v, pf.

3385 Marston, George W. "From the Close Shut Window." New York: G. Schirmer, 1877. Song: B or C, pf.

3386 Philp, Elizabeth. "Alone." London: R. Mills, [BAL n.d., ca. 1855]; "Serenade" in *6 Songs*. Boston: O. Ditson, [BAL n.d., ca. 1855].

She Came and Went. *Poems* [Vol. 2] (1849).

3387 "She Came and Went." Arr. from a German Air. In coll. LBR.

The Shepherd of King Admetus. *Poems* (1844).

3388 Towner, Earl. Boston: C.C. Birchard, 1930. Pastoral Cantata: female voices, S and Bar soli, pf or orch.

The Singing Leaves. *Under the Willows and Other Poems* (1868).

> 3389 McCollin, Frances. Boston: O. Ditson, 1918. Cantata: SSA chorus, STBar soli.

> 3390 Mayhew, Grace. Boston: H.B. Stevens, 1897.

> 3391 Rathbone, George. London: Novello, 1912. Setting for children's voices, pf.

The Sirens. *A Year's Life* (1841).

> 3392 Gilchrist, W.W. "The Syrens." New York: G. Schirmer, 1904.

Song ["Lift up the curtains of thine eyes"]. *A Year's Life* (1841).

> 3393 Browne, J. Lewis. "A Fount of Music." Toronto: Whaley, Royce, 1896. Song: v, pf.

> 3394 Shepherd, Arthur. "Lift up the Curtains of Thine Eyes" in *Five Songs* op. 7 no. 1. Newton Center, Mass.: Wa-Wan Press, 1909. Song: high v, pf.

Song ["O moonlight deep and tender"]. *Poems* (1844).

> 3395 Aiken, George E., Mrs. "O Moonlight Deep and Tender." New York: E. Schuberth, 1883. Song: v, pf.

> 3396 Busch, Carl. "O Moonlight Deep and Tender." Boston: O. Ditson, 1902. Part Song: mixed voices.

> 3397 Clarke, Leland. "Moonlight Deep and Tender." Boston: A.P. Schmidt, 1921. Song: high and med. v edns, pf.

> 3398 Dunkley, Ferdinand. "O Moonlight Deep and Tender." Boston: O. Ditson, 1897. Song: high and low v edns, pf.

> 3399 Philp, Elizabeth. "O Moonlight Deep and Tender" in *Six Songs*. London: Cramer, 1855. Song: v, pf.

> 3400 S.D.S. "Betrothal." Philadelphia: Chas. W.A. Trumpler, 1865.

> 3401 Shepherd, Arthur. "Nocturne" in *Five Songs* op. 7 no. 2. Newton Center, Mass.: Wa-Wan Press, 1909. Song: high v, pf.

> 3402 Southard, L.H. "O Moonlight Deep and Tender." Boston: Nathan Richardson, 1855. Song: v, pf.

> 3403 Warren, S.P. "O Moonlight Deep and Tender" in *Two Songs*. Boston: G.D. Russell, 1868. Song: v, pf.

Song ["There is a light in thy blue eyes"]. *Poems* (1844).

> 3404 Shepherd, Arthur. "There Is a Light in Thy Blue Eyes" in *Five Songs* op. 7 no. 3. Newton Center, Mass.: Wa-Wan Press, 1909. Song: high v, pf.

Song ["Violet! sweet violet!"] *Poems* (1844).

3405 Burleigh, Cecil. "Violet! Sweet Violet!" op. 49 no. 4. Cincinnati: J. Church, 1920. Song: high and low v edns, pf.

3406 Class, F. Morris. "The Violet" in *Six Songs*. New York: G. Schirmer, 1907. Song: high v, pf.

Song ["What reck I of the stars . . ."]. *A Year's Life* (1841).

3407 Shepherd, Arthur. "Rhapsody" in *Five Songs* op. 7 no. 5. Newton Center, Mass.: Wa-Wan Press, 1909. Song: high v, pf.

Stanzas: Sung at the Anti-Slavery Picnic in Dedham [Later titled, "Stanzas on Freedom"]. *Poems* (1844).

3408 Bacon, Ernst. "Freedom" in *Five Hymns*. Boston: C.C. Birchard, 1952. Chorus: SATB, pf or org.

3409 Bellini, Vincenzo. In coll. CaCL. Lowell's poem set to the "War Chant of the Druids" from Bellini's opera *Norma*.

3410 Lang, Margaret R. "True Freedom." In coll. TL.

3411 Ringwald, Roy. n.t. in *The Song of America*. East Stroudsburg, Pa.: Shawnee, 1951. Cantata: SATB chorus, narr., pf 4 hands or orch (R). Recording: Decca, DAU 816.

3412 Silcher, Friedrich. "True Freedom" in coll. LBR.

3413 "Stanzas on Freedom," arr. to a Welsh Air. In coll. Ea.

Sun-Worship. *Heartsease and Rue* (1888).

3414 McKenzie, Kenneth. In *A Group of Songs*. Boston: B.F. Wood, 1895. Song: v, pf.

To the Future. *Poems* [Second Series] (1848).

3415 Burleigh, Cecil. In *Two Songs after Lowell* op. 45 no. 2. New York: G. Schirmer, 1920. Song: high v, pf.

To the Past. *Poems* [Second Series] (1848).

3416 Burleigh, Cecil. In *Two Songs after Lowell* op. 45 no. 1. New York: G. Schirmer, 1920. Song: high v, pf.

The Vision of Sir Launfal (1848).

3417 Bornschein, Franz C. New York: J. Fischer, 1927. Cantata: mixed voices, T and Bar soli, boys' choir ad lib.

3418 Cadman, Charles W. New York: G. Schirmer, 1910. Cantata: male chorus, T and Bar soli, pf and org.

3419 McCollin, Frances. "June." Boston: A.P. Schmidt, 1922. Cantata: SSAA, pf. Setting of lines beginning, "And what is so rare as a day in June?" from the "Prelude to Part First."

3420 Schnecker, P.A. "June." In coll. TL. *See* note under McCollin above.

3421 Sowerby, Leo. Boston: C.C. Birchard, 1928. Cantata: mixed voices, CTBar soli, children's chorus, pf or orch.

The Voyage to Vinland. *Under the Willows and Other Poems* (1868).

3422 Clarke, Henry L. "The New Land." MS, 1957, avail. ACA. Cantata: SATB chorus, C and T soli, pf or org. Words taken from pt. 3, "Gudrida's Prophecy."

With a Pressed Flower. *Poems* [Vol. 1] (1849).

3423 Hadley, Henry K. In *Twelve Songs* op. 12 no. 11. Boston: A.P. Schmidt, 1898. Song: med. v, pf.

"Zekle crep' up, quite unbeknown." *The Biglow Papers* [First Series] (1848).

3424 Hutchinson, J.J. "Zeekel and Huldy." Boston: G.P. Reed, 1850. Song: v, pf.

Miscellaneous

3425 Avshalomov, Jacob. u.t. in *City upon a Hill*. MS, u.d., avail. ACA. Cantata: SATB, speaker, orch.

3426 Liebling, Estelle. "Faustiana." Song: S, pf. Based on Gounod's ballet music.

3427 Rosibelli-Donimozarti, Maestro. *Il Pesceballo*. Cambridge: Riverside Press, 1862. Comic Operetta in 1 act by Francis James Child with collaboration on the text by Lowell [BAL 13047].
　　　　"The Lone Fish-Ball" in *Student Songs,* ed. Richard Storrs Willis. New York: Firth, Pond, 1855. Chorus: SATB, pf. No author listed.

3428 Ward, Robert. "Epitaphs" in *Sweet Freedom's Song*. New York: Highgate Press, 1966. Cantata: mixed chorus, narr., S and Bar soli, orch. Text: "Here lies a soldier of the revolution. . . ."

ROBERT LOWELL (1917–1977)

Across the Yard: La Ignota. *History* (1973).

　3428a Carter, Elliott. In *In Sleep, In Thunder*. u.p.: Boosey & Hawkes, u.d.
　Song Cycle.

Careless Night. *The Dolphin* (1973).

　3428b Carter, Elliott. In *In Sleep, In Thunder*. u.p.: Boosey & Hawkes, u.d.
　Song Cycle.

Dies Irae. *History* (1973).

　3428c Carter, Elliott. In *In Sleep, In Thunder*. u.p.: Boosey & Hawkes, u.d.
　Song Cycle.

Dolphin. *The Dolphin* (1973).

　3428d Carter, Elliott. In *In Sleep, In Thunder*. u.p.: Boosey & Hawkes, u.d.
　Song Cycle.

Harriet. *For Lizzie and Harriet* (1973).

　3428e Carter, Elliott. In *In Sleep and Thunder*. u.p.: Boosey & Hawkes,
　u.d. Song Cycle.

In Genesis. *History* (1973).

　3248f Carter, Elliott. In *In Sleep, In Thunder*. u.p.: Boosey & Hawkes, u.d.
　Song Cycle.

The Lesson. *For the Union Dead* (1964).

　3429 Lister, Rodney. MS, 1977, avail. ACA. Song: M, pf, 3 cl, crotals.

Phaedra [A verse trans. by Lowell from Racine's *Phèdre*] (1971).

　3430 Britten, Benjamin. "Phaedra" op. 93. London: Faber Music, 1977.
　Dramatic Cantata: M, small orch. Recording: Decca, SXL 6847.

ARCHIBALD MACLEISH (1892–1982)

Adam's Riddle. *Songs for Eve* (1954).

> 3431 Alexander, Josef. In *Songs for Eve*. Vol. II. Hastings-on-Hudson, N.Y.: General Music, 1972. Cycle: v, pf.
>
> 3432 Laderman, Ezra. "The Riddles" in *Songs for Eve*. New York: Oxford Univ. Press, 1968. Cycle: S, pf.

The American Bell. *Let Freedom Ring*, by the editors of *American Heritage* (1962).

> 3433 Amram, David. New York: C.F. Peters, u.d. Setting for narr., orch (R).

American Letter. *New Found Land* (1930).

> 3434 Johnston, Jack. "Choral Symphony: American Letter" in coll. MuENC. Choral Symphony: SATB, pf, str qrt, band.

The Babe's Riddle. *Songs for Eve* (1954).

> 3435 Alexander, Josef. In *Songs for Eve*. Vol. II. Hastings-on-Hudson, N.Y.: General Music, 1972. Cycle: v, pf.
>
> 3436 Laderman, Ezra. "The Riddles" in *Songs for Eve*. New York: Oxford Univ. Press, 1968. Cycle: S, pf.

The End of the World. *Streets in the Moon* (1926).

> 3437 Cumming, Richard. In *We Happy Few*. New York: Boosey & Hawkes, 1969. Cycle: B-Bar, pf.
>
> 3438 Duke, John. u.p.: Valley Music, 1953. Song: v, pf.
>
> 3439 Spino, Pasquale J. In *Five Poetic Songs*. u.p.: J. Boonin, u.d. Chorus: SATB, perc.

Epistle to Be Left in the Earth. *New Found Land* (1930).

> 3440 Chavez, Carlos. New York: Tetra Music, 1976. Chorus: SATB, a cap.

Eve Answers the Burdock. *Songs for Eve* (1954).

> 3441 Alexander, Josef. In *Songs for Eve*. Vol. I. Hastings-on-Hudson, N.Y.: General Music, 1972. Cycle: v, pf.

Eve Explains to the Thrush Who Repeats Everything. *Songs for Eve* (1954).

3442 Laderman, Ezra. In *Songs for Eve*. New York: Oxford Univ. Press, 1968. Cycle: S, pf.

Eve in the Dawn. *Songs for Eve* (1954).

3443 Alexander, Josef. In *Songs for Eve*. Vol. I. Hastings-on-Hudson, N.Y.: General Music, 1972. Cycle: v, pf.

3444 Laderman, Ezra. In *Songs for Eve*. New York: Oxford Univ. Press, 1968. Cycle: S, pf.

Eve Old. *Songs for Eve* (1954).

3445 Alexander, Josef. In *Songs for Eve*. Vol. II. Hastings-on-Hudson, N.Y.: General Music, 1972. Cycle: v, pf.

Eve Quiets Her Children. *Songs for Eve* (1954).

3446 Laderman, Ezra. In *Songs for Eve*. New York: Oxford Univ. Press, 1968. Cycle: S, pf.

Eve to the Storm of Thunder. *Songs for Eve* (1954).

3447 Alexander, Josef. In *Songs for Eve*. Vol. II. Hastings-on-Hudson, N.Y.: General Music, 1972. Cycle: v, pf.

Eve's Child. *Songs for Eve* (1954).

3448 Alexander, Josef. In *Songs for Eve*. Vol. II. Hastings-on-Hudson, N.Y.: General Music, 1972. Cycle: v, pf.

Eve's Exile. *Songs for Eve* (1954).

3449 Alexander, Josef. In *Songs for Eve*. Vol. I. Hastings-on-Hudson, N.Y.: General Music, 1972. Cycle: v, pf.

3450 Laderman, Ezra. In *Songs for Eve*. New York: Oxford Univ. Press, 1968. Cycle: S, pf.

Eve's Now-I-Lay-Me. *Songs for Eve* (1954).

3451 Alexander, Josef. In *Songs for Eve*. Vol. I. Hastings-on-Hudson, N.Y.: General Music, 1972. Cycle: v, pf.

3452 Laderman, Ezra. In *Songs for Eve*. New York: Oxford Univ. Press, 1968. Cycle: S, pf.

Eve's Rebuke to Her Child. *Songs for Eve* (1954).

3453 Alexander, Josef. In *Songs for Eve*. Vol. II. Hastings-on-Hudson, N.Y.: General Music, 1972. Cycle: v, pf.

3454 Laderman, Ezra. In *Songs for Eve*. New York: Oxford Univ. Press, 1968. Cycle: S, pf.

Eve's Riddle. *Songs for Eve* (1954).

3455 Alexander, Josef. In *Songs for Eve*. Vol. II. Hastings-on-Hudson, N.Y.: General Music, 1972. Cycle: v, pf.

3456 Laderman, Ezra. "The Riddles" in *Songs for Eve*. New York: Oxford Univ. Press, 1968. Cycle: S, pf.

The Fall. *Songs for Eve* (1954).

3457 Alexander, Josef. In *Songs for Eve*. Vol. I. Hastings-on-Hudson, N.Y.: General Music, 1972. Cycle: v, pf.

The Hamlet of Archibald MacLeish (1928).

3458 Finney, Ross Lee. "Bleheris." New York: C.F. Peters, u.d. Setting for T and C soli, orch (R).

3459 Finney, Ross Lee. "Edge of Shadow." New York: Henmar, 1960. Chorus: SATB, 2 pf, cel, xylo, vib, timp, perc. Text taken from throughout the poem.

Pole Star for This Year. *Public Speech* (1936).

3460 Finney, Ross Lee. u.p.: Independent Music Publishers, 1939. Setting for chorus and T solo.

The Pot of Earth (1925).

3461 Finney, Ross Lee. "The Flowers of the Sea" in *A Cycle of Songs to Poems by Archibald MacLeish*. New York: American Music Edition, 1955. Cycle: high v, pf. Text from sec. 1 of part 3: "The flowers of the sea are brief. . . ."

3462 Finney, Ross Lee. "Go Secretly" in *A Cycle of Songs to Poems by Archibald MacLeish*. New York: American Music Edition, 1955. Cycle: high v, pf. Text from sec. 3 of part 3: "Go secretly and put me in the ground. . . ."

3463 Finney, Ross Lee. "They Seemed to Be Waiting" in *A Cycle of Songs to Poems by Archibald MacLeish*. New York: American Music Edition, 1955. Cycle: high v, pf.

Salute. *New Found Land* (1930).

3464 Finney, Ross Lee. In *A Cycle of Songs to Poems by Archibald MacLeish*. New York: American Music Edition, 1955. Cycle: high v, pf.

3465 Moore, Douglas S. "Dedication." New York: Arrow Music Press, 1938. Motet: SSATBarB, a cap.

The Serpent's Riddle. *Songs for Eve* (1954).

3466 Alexander, Josef. In *Songs for Eve*. Vol. II. Hastings-on-Hudson, N.Y.: General Music, 1972. Cycle: v, pf.

3467 Laderman, Ezra. "The Riddles" in *Songs for Eve*. New York: Oxford Univ. Press, 1968. Cycle: S, pf.

Speech to a Crowd. *Public Speech* (1936).

3468 Mechem, Kirke. "Speech to a Crowd" op. 44. Tustin, Calif.: National Music Publishers, 1975. Chorus: SATB, Bar solo, 2 pf or orch.

What Eve Said. *Songs for Eve* (1954).

3469 Alexander, Josef. In *Songs for Eve*. Vol. I. Hastings-on-Hudson, N.Y.: General Music, 1972. Cycle: v, pf.

What Eve Sang. *Songs for Eve* (1954).

3470 Alexander, Josef. In *Songs for Eve*. Vol. I. Hastings-on-Hudson, N.Y.: General Music, 1972. Cycle: v, pf.

3471 Laderman, Ezra. In *Songs for Eve*. New York: Oxford Univ. Press, 1968. Cycle: S, pf.

Words in Time. *New & Collected Poems, 1917–1976* (1976).

3472 McKay, George F. "Mystery" in *Two Modern Madrigals*. New York: Lawson-Gould, 1967. Chorus: SATB, a cap.

Words to Be Spoken. *Public Speech* (1936).

3473 Finney, Ross Lee. In *Modern Canons*. New York: Music Press, 1947. Chorus: SATB, a cap.

You, Andrew Marvell. *Poems 1924–1933* (1933).

3474 Robbins, Reginald C. "Shadow of Night" in *Songs by Reginald C. Robbins*. Paris: M. Senart, 1937. Song: Bar or B, and high v edns, pf.

The Young Dead Soldiers. *Actfive and Other Poems* (1948).

3475 Schuman, William. Bryn Mawr, Pa.: Merion Music, 1976. Lamentation: S, hn, 8 woodwinds, 9 str.

Miscellaneous

3475a Breedlove, Leonard P. "Heart's Remembering" in coll. UHC. Text from MacLeish's class poem at Yale Graduation, 1915.

3476 Chanler, Theodore W. "These, My Ophelia" in coll. CCS. Song: high v, pf.

3477 Finney, Ross Lee. "These, My Ophelia" in *A Cycle of Songs to Poems by Archibald MacLeish*. New York: American Music Edition, 1955. Cycle: high v, pf.

3478 Gideon, Miriam. u.t. in *Spirit above the Dust*. MS, u.d., avail. ACA. Cycle: med. v, fl, ob, bsn, hn, str qrt.

3479 Harris, Roy. "Freedom's Land." New York: Mills Music, 1941. Song: med. v, pf.
      New York: Mills Music, 1941. Chorus: SATB, a cap.
      New York: Mills Music, 1941. Chorus: SSA, pf.
      New York: Mills Music, 1942. Chorus: TTBB, a cap.

3480 Trubitt, Allen. "The Cat in the Wood." Chorus: TTBB, a cap. Cited in *Original Music for Men's Voices: A Selected Bibliography*. 2d Edn. Ed. by William Tortolano.

3481 Warren, Elinor R. "Merry-Go-Round." New York: H.W. Gray, 1934. Part Song: TTBarB, pf. Text: "Who will ride on the merry-go-round. . . ."

EDWIN MARKHAM (1852–1940)

Shields, Sophie K. *Edwin Markham: A Bibliography*. Staten Island, N.Y.: Wagner College, 1952–, pp. 95-101.

Ann Rutledge. *The Ladies' Home Journal* 43 (1926), p. 167; In *A Magic World* [Ed. by Margery Gordon and Marie B. King] (1930).

3482 McKay, George F. "Lovely Ann, Deathless Ann" in *Lincoln Lyrics*. Boston: C.C. Birchard, 1949. Choral Suite: SATB, pf.

The Ascension. *Lincoln & Other Poems* (1901).

3483 Allen, Robert E. New York: Galleon Press, 1978. Cantata: mixed chorus, M solo, 3 tpt, hp, org, timp.

At Little Virgil's Window. *Poems of Edwin Markham* (1950).

3484 Fenn, Jean W. "Three Green Eggs." New York: J. Fischer, 1921.

The Boy and the Book. *Christian Herald* 54 (Feb. 1931).

3485 McKay, George F. In *Lincoln Lyrics*. Boston: C.C. Birchard, 1949. Choral Suite: SATB, pf.

Brotherhood. *The Man with the Hoe and Other Poems* (1899).

3486 Jeffery, J. Albert. n.t. in coll. SmPS. Hymn.

3487 Stevens, David. n.t. in coll. SmASH. Hymn.

3487a "The Crest and Crowning of All Good" in coll. UHC.

The Desire of Nations. *The Man with the Hoe and Other Poems* (1899).

3488 Ware, Harriet. "The Artisan." New York: C. Fischer, 1929.

Earth Is Enough. *The Shoes of Happiness and Other Poems* (1916).

3488a "Earth Is Enough" in coll. UHC.

3489 Warford, Claude. New York: C. Fischer, 1916.

Fay Song. *The Man with the Hoe and Other Poems* (1899).

3490 Ware, Harriet. "Fay Song." New York: T.B. Harms, 1903. Song: v, pf.

"Follow Me." *The Man with The Hoe and Other Poems* (1899).

3491 Ware, Harriet. "The Cross." New York: G. Schirmer, 1932. Chorus: SATB, T solo, pf. Arr. by Wallingford Riegger.

His Cradle Song. *Christian Herald* 54 (Feb. 1931).

3492 McKay, George F. "Natal Song (Prologue)" in *Lincoln Lyrics*. Boston: C.C. Birchard, 1949. Choral Suite: SATB, pf.

Hymn of Peace and Goodwill.

3493 Fisher, William A. Boston: O. Ditson, 1918. Chorus: mixed voices and solo qrt, pf or org, or orch (R).

The Invisible Bride. *The Man with the Hoe and Other Poems* (1899).

3494 Wachtmeister, Alex R. "The Invisible Bride." Cincinnati: J. Church, 1925. Song: v, pf.

The Joy of the Hills. *The Man with the Hoe and Other Poems* (1899).

3495 Bergh, Arthur. Chicago: C.F. Summy, u.d.

3496 Dunham, Ervin. In *A Markham Trilogy*. Delaware Water Gap, Pa.: Shawnee Press, 1972. Chorus: SATB, cel, claviette, harpsichord.

3497 Kinder, Ralph. New York: J. Fischer, 1919.

Joy of the Morning. *The Man with the Hoe and Other Poems* (1899).

　3498 Hill, Mildred J. Chicago: C.F. Summy, 1908. Song: v, pf.

　3499 Robbins, Reginald C. Paris: M. Senart, 1934. Song: high v, pf.

　3500 Ware, Harriet. New York: G. Schirmer, 1906. Song: high v, pf.

The Last Furrow. *The Man with the Hoe and Other Poems* (1899).

　3501 Wachtmeister, Alex R. Cincinnati: J. Church, 1920. Song: low v, pf.

Lincoln Slain. *Poems of Edwin Markham* (1950).

　3502 McKay, George F. "Lamentation" in *Lincoln Lyrics*. Boston: C.C. Birchard, 1949. Choral Suite: SATB, pf.

Lincoln, the Man of the People. *Lincoln & Other Poems* (1901).

　3503 Ives, Charles E. "Lincoln, the Great Commoner." San Francisco: New Music Edition, 1932. Chorus: mixed voices, orch.
　　　　New York: Peer International, 1952. Song: v, pf.
　　　　In *New Music* 26 (1953). Chorus: mixed voices, orch.
　　　　In coll. IOS.

Lincoln Triumphant. *The Ladies' Home Journal* 43 (1926), p. 8.

　3504 McKay, George F. "In All That Pities and Forgives" in *Lincoln Lyrics*. Boston: C.C. Birchard, 1949. Choral Suite: SATB, pf.

Love's Vigil. *The Man with the Hoe and Other Poems* (1899).

　3505 Ware, Harriet. Cincinnati: J. Church, 1911. Song: high and low v edns, pf.

Man-making. *The Gates of Paradise and Other Poems* (1920).

　3505a Clark, Jeremiah, attrib. to. In coll. UHC.

The Man with the Hoe. *The Man with the Hoe and Other Poems* (1899).

　3506 Kaufer, Joseph. In *The Man with the Hoe and Other Songs*. Waukegan, Ill.: Lyric-Art, 1951. Song: high and med. v, pf.

On the Gulf of Night. *The Man with the Hoe and Other Poems* (1899).

　3507 Dunham, Ervin. In *A Markham Trilogy*. Delaware Water Gap, Pa.: Shawnee Press, 1972. Chorus: SATB, cel, claviette, harpsichord.

One Music. *The Shoes of Happiness and Other Poems* (1915).

> 3508 Hovhaness, Alan. "There Is a High Place in the Upper Air" in coll. ChAH.

The Poet. *The Man with the Hoe and Other Poems* (1899).

> 3508a "The Poet" in coll. UHC.

Poet-Lore. *Lincoln, and Other Poems* (1901).

> 3508b "The Poet" in coll. UHC.

A Prayer. *The Man with the Hoe and Other Poems* (1899).

> 3509 Hammond, W.G. "Teach Me, Father, How to Go" in coll. Mab.
>
> 3510 Ware, Harriet. Cincinnati: J. Church, 1920. Song: high and low v edns, pf.

Revelation. *The Shoes of Happiness and Other Poems* (1915).

> 3511 Dunham, Arthur. "The Pilgrimage." Chicago: C.F. Summy, 1913. Song: v, pf.

Shepherd Boy and Nereid. *The Man with the Hoe and Other Poems* (1899).

> 3512 Ware, Harriet. "The Forgotten Land." Cincinnati: J. Church, 1908. Song: v, pf.

Sing a While Longer. *Gates of Paradise and Other Poems* (1920).

> 3513 O'Hara, Geoffrey. New York: C. Fischer, 1936. Chorus: SSA, pf; New York: C. Fischer, 1941. Song: high and low v edns, pf; also pubd for SATB and TTBB chorus.

The Song Unheard. *New Poems: Eighty Songs at Eighty* (1932).

> 3514 Campbell, Mary. "The Wish." New York: Galaxy, 1952. Song: v, pf.

The Valley. *The Man with the Hoe and Other Poems* (1899).

> 3515 Dunham, Ervin. In *A Markham Trilogy*. Delaware Water Gap, Pa.: Shawnee Press, 1972. Chorus: SATB, cel, claviette, harpsichord.
>
> 3516 Swanson, Howard. New York: Leeds, 1951. Song: 2 v edns, pf.
>
> 3517 Wachtmeister, Alex R. Cincinnati: J. Church, 1919. Song: high and low v edns, pf; strings, hp and fl (R).

Wind and Lyre. *The Shoes of Happiness and Other Poems* (1915).

3518 Ware, Harriet. "Wind and Lyre." Cincinnati: J. Church, 1910. Song: high and low v edns, pf.

Your Tears. *Gates of Paradise and Other Poems* (1920).

3519 Fox, Oscar. "Bring Me Your Tears." Boston: C.C. Birchard, u.d.

3520 Wise, Jessie M. "Bring Me Your Tears." Boston: Boston Music, 1932. Song: high and low v edns, pf.

Miscellaneous

3520a "Agnes," "Cherry Blossoms," "The Cossack," "Far in the Forest," "Finnish Hymn," "Flowing Water," "Fond Regrets," "Louis Kossuth," "Moan to the Moon," "One Moment," "The Perfect Rose," "Polish National Anthem," "The Spool," "There Is a Reaper" in coll. BoC. Song: v, pf.

3521 Birch, Robert F. "Summer Reverie" op. 23 no. 4. New York: Joseph Patelon Music, 1957. Song: high v, pf. Text: "There in the hills of summer let me lie. . . ."

3522 McKay, George F. "The Railsplitter," "The Spelling School," "Jubilation" in *Lincoln Lyrics*. Boston: C.C. Birchard, 1949. Choral Suite: SSAATTBB, pf or orch.

3523 Vidal, P. "The Manger Song of Mary" in coll. DagA, DagI.

3524 Wainwright, J. "Lincoln" in coll. He. Text adapted.

3525 Ware, Harriet. "April." Cincinnati: J. Church, 1911. Song: v, pf. Setting of lines beginning: "April when the blossoms start. . . ."

EDGAR LEE MASTERS (1868–1950)

Andy the Night-watch. *Spoon River Anthology* (1916).

3526 Negri, Gino. In *Antologia di Spoon River*. Milan: S. Zerboni, 1948. Cantata: SATB chorus, SMCTBarB soli, orch. Text in Eng.

Anne Rutledge. *Spoon River Anthology* (1916).

3527 Raphling, Sam. In *Spoon River Anthology*. New York: Edition Musicus, 1952. Song: med. v, pf.

3528 Trubitt, Allen. Macomb, Ill.: Roger Dean, 1975. Chorus: SATB, a cap.

3529 Williams, Vincent T. St. Louis: Schattinger, 1954. Song: med. v, pf.

Francis Turner. *Spoon River Anthology* (1916).

> 3530 Negri, Gino. In *Antologia di Spoon River*. Milan: S. Zerboni, 1948. Cantata: SATB chorus, SMCTBarB soli, orch. Text in Eng.

The Hill. *Spoon River Anthology* (1916).

> 3531 Negri, Gino. "For the Hill" in *Antologia di Spoon River*. Milan: S. Zerboni, 1948. Cantata: SATB chorus, SMCTBarB soli, orch. Text in Eng.

Jonathan Houghton. *Spoon River Anthology* (1916).

> 3532 Negri, Gino. In *Antologia di Spoon River*. Milan: S. Zerboni, 1948. Cantata: SATB chorus, SMCTBarB soli, orch. Text in Eng.

Lois Spears. *Spoon River Anthology* (1916).

> 3533 Negri, Gino. In *Antologia di Spoon River*. Milan: S. Zerboni, 1948. Cantata: SATB chorus, SMCTBarB soli, orch. Text in Eng.

Lucinda Matlock. *Spoon River Anthology* (1916).

> 3534 Negri, Gino. In *Antologia di Spoon River*. Milan: S. Zerboni, 1948. Cantata: SATB chorus, SMCTBarB soli, orch. Text in Eng.
>
> 3535 Raphling, Sam. In *Spoon River Anthology*. New York: Edition Musicus, 1952. Song: med. v, pf.

Mabel Osborne. *Spoon River Anthology* (1916).

> 3536 Negri, Gino. In *Antologia di Spoon River*. Milan: S. Zerboni, 1948. Cantata: SATB chorus, SMCTBarB soli, orch. Text in Eng.

Minerva Jones. *Spoon River Anthology* (1916).

> 3537 Negri, Gino. In *Antologia di Spoon River*. Milan: S. Zerboni, 1948. Cantata: SATB chorus, SMCTBarB soli, orch. Text in Eng.

Penniwit, the Artist. *Spoon River Anthology* (1916).

> 3538 Raphling, Sam. In *Spoon River Anthology*. New York: Edition Musicus, 1952. Song: v, pf.

Petit the Poet. *Spoon River Anthology* (1916).

> 3539 Negri, Gino. In *Antologia di Spoon River*. Milan: S. Zerboni, 1948. Cantata: SATB chorus, SMCTBarB soli, orch. Text in Eng.

William and Emily. *Spoon River Anthology* (1916).

 3540 Negri, Gino. In *Antologia di Spoon River*. Milan: S. Zerboni, 1948. Cantata: SATB chorus, SMCTBarB soli, orch. Text in Eng.

Miscellaneous

 3541 Aidman, Charles and Hirshborn, Naomi. "Spoon River Anthology." Songs. Recording: Columbia OL 6010 (1963); OS 2410 (1 1963).

HERMAN MELVILLE (1819–1891)

Freibert, L.M. "A Checklist of Musical Compositions Inspired by Herman Melville's Works." *Extracts* 23 (1975), pp. 3–5.

Billy in the Darbies. *Billy Budd and Other Prose Pieces* (1924).

 3542 Diamond, David. In *7 Songs by David Diamond*. Philadelphia: Elkan-Vogel, 1946. Song: high v, pf.

 3543 Evett, Robert. MS, 1959, avail. ACA. Song: Bar, cl, str qrt.

 3544 Flanagan, William. New York: Peer International, 1954. Chorus: SATB, pf.

C——'s Lament. *Timoleon* (1891).

 3545 Flanagan, William. "Lament" in *Time's Long Ago: A Cycle of Songs to Poems of Herman Melville*. New York: Peer International, 1978. Song: S, pf. Recording: Desto, DC 6468 (1969).

Departed the Pride, and the Glory of Mardi [Vol. 2 chap. 38]. *Mardi* (1849).

 3546 Helps, Robert. n.t. in *Two Songs*. MS, 1950, avail. ACA. Song: S, pf.

Her Bower Is Not of the Vine [Vol. 2 chap. 50]. *Mardi* (1849).

 3547 Helps, Robert. n.t. in *Two Songs*. MS, 1950, avail. ACA. Song: S, pf.

Journal up the Straits (1935).

 3548 Reynolds, Roger. "Blind Men." New York: C.F. Peters, 1967. Chorus: SATB, 3 tpt, 2 trb, b trb, tba, perc, pf. Based on a collection of fragments from *Journal up the Straits* with subsidiary words and phrases added. Recording: Composers Recordings, CRI SD 241.

The Marchioness of Brinvilliers. *Timoleon* (1891).

3549 Diamond, David. "A Portrait" in *Songs by David Diamond.* Philadelphia: Elkan-Vogel, 1947. Song: med. v, pf.

The Martyr: Indicative of the Passion of the People on the 15th Day of April, 1865. *Battle-Pieces and Aspects of the War* (1866).

3550 Diamond, David. "The Martyr." New York: Southern Music Publishing, 1951. Chorus: TTBB, a cap.

3551 Floyd, Carlisle. New York: Belwin-Mills, 1973. Chorus: SATB, 2 tpt, pf, perc.

Merry Ditty of the Sad Man. *Collected Poems of Herman Melville* (1947).

3552 Diamond, David. "Let Us All Take to Singing." New York: Southern Music Publishing, 1951. Chorus: TTBB, a cap.

Moby-Dick (1851).

3553 Bacon, Ernst. "Jonah." New York: Peer International, 1956. Chorus: SATB, pf or org. Text taken from chap. 9, "The Sermon." It is often excerpted under the title, "Jonah's Song."

3554 Bialosky, Marshall. "There Is a Wisdom That Is Woe." Bryn Mawr, Pa.: T. Presser, 1953. Chorus: SATB, a cap. Music not seen; text presumably is from chap. 96.

3555 Duffield, Brainerd. Adapted by Brainerd Duffield. Music score composed and directed by Victor Young. Recording: Decca, DL 9071 (1960).

3556 Hall, Jeffrey. n.t. in *Two Settings from Ahab.* Hillsdale, N.Y.: Mobart Music, 1978. Song: low v, pf. Text taken from paragraph 3 of chap. 135, "The Chase. Third Day," beginning, "What a lovely day again; were it a new made world. . . ."

3557 Hall, Jeffrey. n.t. in *Two Settings from Ahab.* Hillsdale, N.Y.: Mobart Music, 1978. Song: low v, pf. Text taken from the fifth paragraph from the end of chap. 114, "The Gilder," beginning, "Oh, grassy glades! oh ever vernal endless landscapes. . . ."

3558 Kastle, Leonard. n.t. in *Three Whale Songs from "Moby Dick."* New York: F. Colombo, 1963. Chorus: SATB, a cap. Text taken from chap. 9, "The Sermon." It is often excerpted under the title, "Jonah's Song."

3559 Kastle, Leonard. n.t. in *Three Whale Songs from "Moby Dick."* New York: F. Colombo, 1963. Chorus: SATB, a cap. Setting of lines beginning, "Thar she blows, thar she blows, where away. . . ."

3560 Kastle, Leonard. n.t. in *Three Whale Songs from "Moby Dick."* New York: F. Colombo, 1963. Chorus: SATB, a cap. Text taken from chap. 40, "Forecastle.-Midnight," the song of the 1st Nantucket sailor beginning, "Our captain stood upon the deck. . . ."

3560a Mailman, Martin. "The Whalemen's Chorale from 'Moby Dick.'" New York: Mills Music, u.d. Setting for band with opt SATB chorus.

3561 McCabe, John. "Aspects of Whiteness." Sevenoaks, Kent: Novello, 1972. Cantata: SSAATTBB, pf. Text adapted by McCabe.

3562 Reynolds, Roger. "Masks." New York: C.F. Peters, u.d. Chorus: 8 pt mixed voices, orch (R). Music not seen; text possibly from the well-known passage in chap. 36, "The Quarter-Deck," beginning with the lines, "All visible objects, man, are but as pasteboard masks. . . ."

Monody. *Timoleon* (1891).

3563 Diamond, David. In *5 Songs by David Diamond*. Philadelphia: Elkan-Vogel, 1947. Song: med. v, pf.

3564 Flanagan, William. In *Time's Long Ago: A Cycle of Songs to Poems of Herman Melville*. New York: Peer International, 1978. Song: S, pf. Recording: Desto, DC 6468 (1969).

The Night-March. *Timoleon* (1891).

3565 Flanagan, William. In *Time's Long Ago: A Cycle of Songs to Poems of Herman Melville*. New York: Peer International, 1978. Song: S, pf. Recording: Desto, DC 6468 (1969).

3566 Kay, Ulysses. In *Triumvirate*. New York: Peer International, 1954. Chorus: TTBB, a cap. Music not seen; text presumably from this poem.

On the Grave of a Young Cavalry Officer Killed in the Valley of Virginia. *Battle-Pieces and Aspects of the War* (1866).

3567 Diamond, David. "Epitaph." New York: Associated, 1946. Song: med. v, pf.

On the Slain Collegians. *Battle-Pieces and Aspects of the War* (1866).

3568 Evett, Robert. "Youth Is the Time When Hearts Are Large" in *The Mask of Cain*. New York: Peer International, 1953. Chorus: mixed voices.

Pisa's Leaning Tower. *Timoleon* (1891).

3569 Flanagan, William. In *Time's Long Ago: A Cycle of Songs to Poems of Herman Melville*. New York: Peer International, 1978. Song: S, pf. Recording: Desto, DC 6468 (1969).

The Portent. *Battle-Pieces and Aspects of the War* (1866).

3570 Evett, Robert. "Portent" in *The Mask of Cain*. New York: Peer International, 1953. Chorus: mixed voices.

Shiloh: A Requiem. *Battle-Pieces and Aspects of the War* (1866).

3571 Evett, Robert. "Shiloh" in *The Mask of Cain*. New York: Peer International, 1953. Chorus: mixed voices.

3572 Weisgall, Hugo. In *Soldier Songs for Baritone*. n.p.: Merrymount Music, 1953. Cycle: Bar, orch.

Time's Long Ago! *Collected Poems of Herman Melville* (1947).

3573 Flanagan, William. In *Time's Long Ago: A Cycle of Songs to Poems of Herman Melville*. New York: Peer International, 1978. Song: S, pf. Recording: Desto, DC 6468 (1969).

Under the Ground. *Collected Poems of Herman Melville* (1947).

3574 Flanagan, William. In *Time's Long Ago: A Cycle of Songs to Poems of Herman Melville*. New York: Peer International, 1978. Song: S, pf. Recording: Desto, DC 6468 (1969).

3575 Entry cancelled.

EDNA ST. VINCENT MILLAY (1892–1950)

Yost, Karl. *A Bibliography of the Works of Edna St. Vincent Millay*. New York: Harper, 1937 [YBEM].

Afternoon on a Hill. *Renascence and Other Poems* (1917).

3576 Becker, Grace. Berkeley: J.R. Walker, 1934. Song: v, pf.

3577 Besly, Maurice. In *Charivaria*. London: Boosey, 1933. Song: v, pf.

3578 Briccetti, Thomas. In *Millaydy's Madrigals* in coll. MuENC. Chorus: SAB, pf.

3579 Farwell, Arthur. New York: Galaxy, 1945. Song: v, pf. In coll. UNSNV, WieF.

3580 Morrill, Dexter. In coll. MuENC. Chorus: SSA, a cap.

"And you as well must die, beloved dust." *Second April* (1921).

3581 Poùhe, Joseph F. In *The Amorous Line*. Toronto: E.C. Kerby, 1971. Song: med. v, pf.

Aria Da Capo (1921).

3582 Baksa, Robert. Opera: Coloratura S, 2 T, Bar, B-Bar, orch.

Ashes of Life. *Renascence and Other Poems* (1917).

3583 Alette, Carl. In *Three Secular Songs*. Hattiesburg, Miss.: Tritone Press, 1963. Song: med. v, pf.

Autumn Chant. *The Harp-Weaver and Other Poems* (1923).

3584 Pisk, Paul A. Los Angeles: Delkas Music, 1946. Chorus: SSA, a cap.

Baccalaureate Hymn (1917); *Collected Poems* (1956).

3585 Millay, Edna St. Vincent. "Baccalaureate Hymn." Tune: "St. Vincent." Words and music by Millay. [YBEM pp. 76–79.]

The Ballad of the Harpweaver. *The Harp-Weaver and Other Poems* (1923).

3586 Warren, Elinor R. "The Harp Weaver." New York: H.W. Gray, 1932. Choral Ballad: 3-pt. women's voices, Bar solo, pf, 2 hp.

Being Young and Green. *The Buck in the Snow* (1928).

3587 Bliss, Arthur. In *Seven American Poems*. London: Boosey, 1942. Song: low v, pf.

The Cameo. *The Buck in the Snow* (1928).

3588 Kelly, Robert. In *Song Cycle*. MS, 1964, avail. ACA. Cycle: S, pf.

"Clearly my ruined garden as it stood." *Fatal Interview* (1931).

3589 Warren, Elinor R. n.t. in *Sonnets*. New York: C. Fischer, 1974. Song: S, str qrt or str orch.

The Death of Autumn. *Second April* (1921).

3590 Kerr, Harrison. In *Three Songs*. New York: Conatus, 1975. Song: S, pf.

Departure. *The Harp-Weaver and Other Poems* (1923).

3591 Kelly, Robert. In *Song Cycle*. MS, 1964, avail. ACA. Song: S, pf.

Ebb. *Second April* (1921).

> 3592 Kerr, Harrison. In *Three Songs*. New York: Conatus, 1975. Song: S, pf.

Elaine. *Second April* (1921).

> 3593 Herreshoff, Constance M. New York: J. Fischer, 1931.

Feast. *The Harp-Weaver and Other Poems* (1923).

> 3594 Bliss, Arthur. In *Seven American Poems*. London: Boosey, 1942. Song: low v, pf.

First Fig. *A Few Figs from Thistles* (1920).

> 3595 Besly, Maurice. "My Candle Burns at Both Ends" in *Charivaria*. London: Boosey, 1933. Song: v, pf.
> 3596 Buchanan, Annabel M. "My Candle." New York: G. Ricordi, 1928. Music not seen; text presumably from this poem.

"For you there is no song . . ." ["To Elinor Wylie. 2"]. *Huntsman, What Quarry?* (1939).

> 3597 Adams, Leslie. In coll. PaAS. Song: v, pf.

From a Very Little Sphinx. *Poems Selected for Young People* (1929).

> 3598 Fink, Michael. In *From a Very Little Sphinx*. Boston: E.C. Schirmer, 1969. Chorus: SSAA, S solo, str qrt or str orch (R). Setting of sections 1, 2, 4, 5, and 7.
> 3599 Smith, Kenneth. "Horse Shoe." In coll. UNSNV. Song: v, pf. In coll. WieF.
> 3600 Wagenaar, Bernard. In *From a Very Little Sphinx*. New York: G. Schirmer, 1926. Song: S or M, pf. Setting of all sections.

God's World. *Renascence and Other Poems* (1917).

> 3601 Adler, Samuel. In *In Nature's Ebb and Flow*. New York: Southern Music Publishing, 1968. Chorus: SSAA, pf.
> 3602 Alette, Carl. Hattiesburg, Miss.: Tritone Press, 1963. Song: S, pf.
> 3603 Colville, Thomas. New York: Galaxy, 1976. Chorus: SSATB, a cap.
> 3604 Harmati, Sandor. New York: Galaxy, 1934. Song: v, pf.
> 3605 Schuman, William. New York: Marks Music, 1933. Song: high v, pf.
> 3606 Wolfe, Jacques. New York: G. Schirmer, 1932. Song: high and low or med. v edns, pf.

"Gone in good sooth you are: not even in dream." *Fatal Interview* (1931).

> 3607 Gideon, Miriam. n.t. in *Sonnets from "Fatal Interview."* MS, 1961, avail. ACA. Song: v, pf; "Gone in Good Sooth You Are" in *American Artsong Anthology.* Vol. 1. New York: Galaxy, 1982.

Humoresque. *The Harp-Weaver and Other Poems* (1923).

> 3608 Bliss, Arthur. In *Two American Poems.* New York: Boosey & Hawkes, 1980. Song: v, pf.

> 3609 Poùhe, Joseph F. In *The Amorous Line.* Toronto: E.C. Kerby, 1971. Song: med. v, pf.

"I said, seeing how the winter gale increased." *Fatal Interview* (1931).

> 3610 Kohs, Ellis B. "Farewell" in *Fatal Interview.* MS, n.d., avail. ACA. Cycle: low v, pf.

"I shall go back again to the black shore." *The Harp-Weaver and Other Poems* (1923).

> 3611 Briccetti, Thomas. "Sonnet" in *Millaydy's Madrigals* in coll. MuENC. Chorus: SSATB, pf.

"I too beneath your moon, almighty sex." *Hunstman, What Quarry?* (1939).

> 3612 Poùhe, Joseph F. In *The Amorous Line.* Toronto: E.C. Kerby, 1971. Song: med. v, pf.

"If I should learn, in some quite casual way." *Renascence and Other Poems* (1917).

> 3613 Cohen, Michael. "If I Should Learn." u.p.: Bourne, u.d. Chorus: SATB, pf.

Journey. *Second April* (1921).

> 3614 Christie, Kenneth. Bryn Mawr, Pa.: Presser, 1950. Song: v, pf.

The King's Henchman (1926).

> 3615 Taylor, Deems. *The King's Henchman* op. 19. New York: J. Fischer, 1926. Lyric Drama in 3 acts. *See* YBEM pp. 110–117 for the publishing history.
> "Hearest Thou the Wind?" New York: J. Fischer, 1926. Chorus: mixed voices, Bar solo, pf.

Lament. *Second April* (1921).

3616 Ricketts, Lucy W. In *Elegiac Songs*. New York: Composers Press, 1945. Song: v, pf.

Memorial to D.C. *Second April* (1921).

3617 Bacon, Ernst. "Epitaph" in *Four Songs for Soprano*. New York: Music Press, 1946. Song: S, pf.

3618 Besly, Maurice. "Epitaph" in *Charivaria*. London: Boosey, 1933. Song: v, pf.

3619 Burtt, Ben. "A Prayer to Persephone." New York: Galaxy, 1936. Chorus: SSAA, pf; New York: Galaxy, 1936. Song: v, pf.

3620 Ricketts, Lucy W. "Chorus," "Prayer to Persephone" in *Elegiac Songs*. New York: Composers Press, 1945. Song: v, pf.

3621 Entry cancelled.

3622 Schuman, William. "Epitaph" in *Four Canonic Choruses*. New York: G. Schirmer, 1942. Chorus: SSTB, a cap.

"Moon, that against the lintel of the west." *Fatal Interview* (1931).

3623 Gideon, Miriam. n.t. in *Sonnets from "Fatal Interview."* MS, 1961, avail. ACA. Song: v, pf.

"Night is my sister, and how deep in love." *Fatal Interview* (1931).

3624 Gideon, Miriam. n.t. in *Sonnets from "Fatal Interview."* MS, 1961, avail. ACA. Song: v, pf.

3625 Warren, Elinor R. n.t. in *Sonnets*. New York: C. Fischer, 1974. Song: S, str qrt or str orch.

"Now by this moon, before this moon shall wane." *Fatal Interview* (1931).

3626 Kohs, Ellis B. "Absence" in *Fatal Interview*. MS, u.d., avail. ACA. Cycle: low v, pf.

3627 Poùhe, Joseph F. In *The Amorous Line*. Toronto: E.C. Kerby, 1971. Song: med. v, pf.

"Oh, sleep forever in the Latmian Cave." *Fatal Interview* (1931).

3628 Themmen, Ivana M. In *Shelter This Candle from the Wind*. Song: S, orch. Recording: Louisville Orchestra, LS 767 (1979).

"Oh, think not I am faithful to a vow!" *A Few Figs from Thistles* (1920).

3629 Poùhe, Joseph F. In *The Amorous Line*. Toronto: E.C. Kerby, 1971. Song: med. v, pf.

On Hearing a Symphony of Beethoven. *The Buck in the Snow* (1928).

> 3630 Pfautsch, Lloyd. New York: Lawson-Gould, 1966. Chorus: SSA, S solo, a cap.

> 3631 Themmen, Ivana M. In *Shelter This Candle from the Wind.* Song: S, orch. Recording: Louisville Orchestra, LS 767 (1979).

The Pear Tree. *Collected Poems* (1956).

> 3632 Spino, Pasquale J. In *Five Poetic Songs.* u.p.: J. Boonin, u.d. Chorus: SATB, a cap.

"Pity me not because the light of day." *The Harp-Weaver and Other Poems* (1923).

> 3633 Kelly, Robert. "Pity Me Not" in *Song Cycle.* MS, 1964, avail. ACA. Cycle: S, pf.

"Rain comes down" [act 5 sc. 1]. *The Lamp and the Bell* (1921).

> 3634 Bliss, Arthur. New York: Boosey & Hawkes, 1940. Song: low v, pf; In *Seven American Poems.* London: Boosey, 1942.

> 3635 Fink, Michael. Boston: E.C. Schirmer, 1969. Song: S, pf.

Recuerdo. *A Few Figs from Thistles* (1920).

> 3636 Bond, Victoria. In *From an Antique Land.* New York: Seesaw, 1976. Cycle: S, pf.

> 3637 Castelnuovo-Tedesco, Mario. New York: C. Fischer, 1941. Song: high v, pf.

> 3638 House, Margueritte. Coral Gables: Univ. of Miami, 1971. Chorus: SATB, pf.

> 3639 Lessard, John. New York: Joshua Corp., 1964. Song: med. v, pf.

Renascence. *Renascence and Other Poems* (1917).

> 3640 Persichetti, Vincent. n.t. in *Hymns and Responses* op. 68 no. 19. Philadelphia: Elkan-Vogel, 1956. Opening Response for choir and congregational use. Setting of lines beginning: "The heart can push the sea and land. . . ."

> 3641 Porter, Hugh. "O God, I Cried. No Dark Disguise" in coll. ChAH. Hymn.

> 3641a White, Benjamin F. "The World Stands out on Either Side" in coll. UHC.

The Return. *Wine from These Grapes* (1934).

3642 Kelly, Robert. In *Song Cycle*. MS, 1964, avail. ACA. Cycle: S, pf.

The Return from Town. *The Harp-Weaver and Other Poems* (1923).

3643 Bliss, Arthur. In *Two American Poems*. New York: Boosey & Hawkes, 1980. Song: v, pf.

3644 Briccetti, Thomas. In *Millaydy's Madrigals* in coll. MuENC. Chorus: SATB, pf.

3644a Carroll, J. Robert. In *Songs of the Heart*. New York: G. Schirmer, 1968. Chorus: SSA.

3645 Herreshoff, Constance. New York: J. Fischer, 1928.

The Road to Avrillé. *The Buck in the Snow* (1928).

3646 Lekberg, Sven. New York: G. Schirmer, 1971. Song: high v, pf.

"Shall I be prisoner till my pulses stop." *Fatal Interview* (1931).

3647 Kohs, Ellis B. "Perfidious Prince" in *Fatal Interview*. MS, u.d., avail. ACA. Cycle: low v, pf.

Siege. *The Harp-Weaver and Other Poems* (1923).

3648 Bliss, Arthur. In *Seven American Poems*. London: Boosey, 1942. Song: low v, pf.

"Since of no creature living the last breath." *Fatal Interview* (1931).

3649 Kohs, Ellis. "Immortality" in *Fatal Interview*. MS, u.d., avail. ACA. Cycle: low v, pf.

Song. *The Buck in the Snow* (1928).

3650 Bliss, Arthur. "Gone, Gone Again Is Summer" in *Seven American Poems*. London: Boosey, 1942. Song: low v, pf.

3651 Harris, Edward. "Vanished Summer." New York: Galaxy, 1936. Song: v, pf.

Spring. *Second April* (1921).

3652 Mechem, Kirke. In *Five Centuries of Spring*. Boston: E.C. Schirmer, u.d. Madrigal Cycle: SSA, a cap.

The Spring and the Fall. *The Harp-Weaver and Other Poems* (1923).

3653 Bond, Victoria. "In the Spring and the Fall" in *From an Antique Land*. New York: Seesaw, 1976. Cycle: S, pf.

3654 Lekberg, Sven. New York: G. Schirmer, 1971. Song: S, pf.

"Sweet love, sweet thorn, when lightly to my heart." *Fatal Interview* (1931).

> 3655 Kohs, Ellis B. "Post Mortem" in *Fatal Interview*. MS, u.d., avail. ACA. Cycle: low v, pf.

Tavern. *Renascence and Other Poems* (1917).

> 3656 Vanderlip, Ruth W. "The Little Tavern." Boston: O. Ditson, 1929. Song: high and med. v edns, pf.

"The heart once broken is a heart no more." *Fatal Interview* (1931).

> 3657 Warren, Elinor R. n.t. in *Sonnets*. New York: C. Fischer, 1974. Song: S, str qrt or str orch.

"This beast that rends me in the sight of all." *Fatal Interview* (1931).

> 3658 Warren, Elinor R. n.t. in *Sonnets*. New York: C. Fischer, 1974. Song: S, str qrt or str orch.

Thursday. *A Few Figs from Thistles* (1920).

> 3659 Brussels, Iris. New York: American Music, 1933. Song: high and low v edns, pf.
>
> 3660 Johnson, Horace. New York: G. Schirmer, 1923.

"Time does not bring relief; you all have lied." *Renascence and Other Poems* (1917).

> 3661 Gold, Ernest. "Time Does Not Bring Relief" in *Songs of Love and Parting*. New York: G. Schirmer, 1963. Cycle: high v, pf or orch (R).

To the Maid of Orleans. *Make Bright the Arrows* (1940).

> 3662 McLain, Margaret S. "The Maid of Orleans." Boston: R.D. Row, 1942. Chorus: SATB, pf or orch (R).

To the Not Impossible Him. *A Few Figs from Thistles* (1920).

> 3663 Besly, Maurice. In *Charivaria*. London: Boosey, 1933. Song: v, pf.

To the Wife of a Sick Friend. *The Buck in the Snow* (11928).

> 3664 Themmen, Ivana M. In *Shelter This Candle from the Wind*. Song: S, orch. Recording: Louisville Orchestra, LS 767 (1979).

The Unexplorer. *A Few Figs from Thistles* (1920).

> 3665 Besly, Maurice. In *Charivaria*. London: Boosey, 1933. Song: v, pf.

"What lips my lips have kissed, and where, and why." *The Harp-Weaver and Other Poems* (1923).

> 3666 Alette, Carl. "What Lips My Lips Have Kissed" in *Three Secular Songs*. Hattiesburg, Miss.: Tritone Press, 1963. Song: med. v, pf.

> 3667 Bernstein, Leonard. "What Lips My Lips Have Kissed" in *Songfest*. New York: Boosey & Hawkes, 1977. Cycle: SAMTBarB, orch.

> 3668 Fink, Michael. "What Lips My Lips Have Kissed." Boston: E.C. Schirmer, 1963. Song: S, pf.

> 3669 Kelly, Robert. "What Lips My Lips Have Kissed" in *Song Cycle*. MS, 1964, avail. ACA. Cycle: S, pf.

> 3670 Poùhe, Joseph F. In *The Amorous Line*. Toronto: E.C. Kerby, 1971. Song: med. v, pf.

Wild Swans. *Second April* (1921).

> 3671 Duke, John. u.p.: Music Press, 1947. Song: med. v, pf.

> 3672 Fetler, Paul. New York: Associated Music, 1957. Chorus: SATB, a cap.

> 3673 Kerr, Harrison. In *Three Songs*. New York: Conatus, 1975. Song: S, pf.

> 3674 Themmen, Ivana M. In *Shelter This Candle from the Wind*. Song: S, orch. Recording: Louisville Orchestra, LS 767 (1979).

"Women have loved before as I love now." *Fatal Interview* (1931).

> 3675 Poùhe, Joseph F. In *The Amorous Line*. Toronto: E.C. Kerby, 1971. Song: med. v, pf.

Wraith. *Second April* (1921).

> 3676 Themmen, Ivana M. In *Shelter This Candle from the Wind*. Song: S, orch. Recording: Louisville Orchestra, LS 767 (1979).

Miscellaneous

> 3676a "Sowing the Rue," "Wedding Joy," "Why, Oh Mother?" in coll. BoC. Song: v, pf.

> 3677 Zaimont, Judith L. "Love's White Heat," "An Older Love," "Disdainful, Fickle Love" in *The Ages of Love*. MS, 1971, avail. ACA. Cycle: Bar, pf.

> 3678 Zaimont, Judith L. "Love's Autumn," "A Season's Song" in *Greyed Sonnets*. MS, 1975, avail. ACA. Song: S, pf. Recording: Golden Crest, ATH 5051.

3679 Zaimont, Judith L. "Soliloquy" in *Greyed Sonnets*. MS, 1975, avail. ACA. Cycle: S, pf. Recording: Golden Crest, ATH 5051; In *American Artsong Anthology*. Vol. 1. New York: Galaxy, 1982.

JOAQUIN MILLER (1837–1913)

Byron. *The Complete Poetical Works of Joaquin Miller* (1897).

3680 Miller, Juanita. "Judge Not." u.p.: Kohler & Chase, 1917. Song: v, pf; In *Seven Songs*. u.p.: Juanita Miller, 1935. Song: v, pf.

California's Christmas. *The Complete Poetical Works of Joaquin Miller* (1897).

3681 Miller, Juanita. "California" in *Seven Songs*. u.p.: Juanita Miller, 1935. Song: v, pf.

Columbus. *Songs of the Soul* (1896).

3682 Dykes, J.B. In coll. He.

3683 Hosmer, E.S. Boston: O. Ditson, 1917. Cantata: SSA, pf. Also pubd for mixed voices (1917), men's voices (1917), and as a school cantata for SAB (1929).

3684 Ringwald, Roy. n.t. in *The Song of America*. East Stroudsburg, Pa.: Shawnee, 1951. Setting for SATB chorus, narr., pf 4 hands.

3684a "They Sailed! They Sailed! Then Spake the Mate." DHT incorrectly cites a setting of this in SmNH. Correct hymnal not discovered.

Crossing the Plains. *The Complete Poetical Works of Joaquin Miller* (1897).

3685 Freed, Isadore. New York: C. Fischer, 1947. Song: med. v, pf.

"49." *The Complete Poetical Works of Joaquin Miller* (1897).

3686 Miller, Juanita. In *Seven Songs*. u.p.: Juanita Miller, 1935. Song: v, pf.

Ina [Text from sc. 2]. *The Complete Poetical Works of Joaquin Miller* (1897).

3687 Bassett, Leslie. n.t. in *Moon Canticle*. New York: C.F. Peters, 1971. Chorus: SATB, narr., a cap, vc obl.

Magnolia Blossoms. *The Complete Poetical Works of Joaquin Miller* (1897).

3688 Cadman, Charles W. "Magnolia Blooms" op. 60 no. 2. Boston,

New York, Chicago: White-Smith Music, 1916. Song: high and med. v edns, pf.

Mothers of Men. *Joaquin Miller's Poems* [Vol. 1] (1909).

3689 Miller, Juanita. In *Seven Songs.* u.p.: Juanita Miller, 1935. Song: v, pf.

My Ship Comes In. *Surf and Wave* (1883).

3689a Millard, H. "My Ship Comes In." New York: E. Schuberth, 1876; New York: Spear & Dehnhoff, 1876. Song: high v, pf.

3689b Perkins, Walton. "My Ship Comes Sailing in from Sea." Chicago: I.L.A. Brodersen, 1880. Song: v, pf. Music not seen; text presumably from this poem.

To Russia. *The Complete Poetical Works of Joaquin Miller* (1897).

3690 Homer, Sidney. "To Russia" op. 17 no. 4. New York: G. Schirmer, 1906. Song: high and low v edns, pf.

To the Jersey Lily. *Songs of Faraway Lands* (1878).

3691 Miller, Juanita. "God's Garden" in *Songs by Juanita and Joaquin Miller.* Oakland, Calif.: The Song Shop, 1914. Song: v, pf; In *Seven Songs.* u.p.: Juanita Miller, 1935. Song: v, pf.

The Voice of the Beautiful. *The Building of the City Beautiful* (1883).

3691a Miller, Juanita. "Only One To-Day" in *Songs by Juanita and Joaquin Miller.* Oakland, Calif.: The Song Shop, 1914. Song: v, pf.

Miscellaneous

3691b Catenhusen, E. "Over the Mountains." New York: Wm. A. Pond, 1883. [BAL 13792.]

3691c Dennée, Charles. "Goodnight." Boston: A.P. Schmidt, 1894. [BAL 13836.]

3691d Fortescue, Marion T. "My Darling Have You Money." New York: Wm. A. Pond, 1881. [BAL 13782.]

3692 Entry cancelled.

3693 Miller, Juanita. "Oakland" in *Songs by Juanita and Joaquin Miller.* Oakland, Calif.: The Song Shop, 1914. Song: v, pf.

3694 Miller, Juanita. "Indian," "Berkeley" in *Seven Songs.* u.p.: Juanita Miller, 1935. Song: v, pf. For a note on "Berkeley" see BAL 13875.

3695 Entry cancelled.

3696 Smith, Carrie A. "Love Me, Love." Boston: H.W. Smith, 1878. Song: v, pf.

3697 Sousa, John P. *Tally-Ho.* Musical Drama in 3 acts. Libretto by Miller, 1883; "Tally-Ho." Washington, D.C.: J.F. Ellis, 1885. Song: Bar, pf.

3698 Wiegand, John. "Love Me." New York: J. Fischer, 1885. Song: v, pf.

MARIANNE MOORE (1887–1972)

I've Been Thinking. . . . *The Complete Poems of Marianne Moore* (1967).

3699 Thomson, Virgil. "English Usage" in *Two by Marianne Moore.* New York: G. Schirmer, 1966. Song: med. v, pf.

A Jellyfish. *O to Be a Dragon* (1959).

3700 Adler, Samuel. In *A Whole Bunch of Fun.* New York: Oxford Univ. Press, 1980. Cantata for Young Voices: SATB, a cap; complete work, pf or orch (R).

O to Be a Dragon. *O to Be a Dragon* (1959).

3701 Adler, Samuel. In *A Whole Bunch of Fun.* New York: Oxford Univ. Press, 1980. Cantata for Young Voices: SATB, a cap; complete work, pf or orch (R).

To a Chameleon. *O to Be a Dragon* (1959).

3702 Adler, Samuel. In *A Whole Bunch of Fun.* New York: Oxford Univ. Press, 1980. Cantata for Young Voices: SATB, a cap; complete work, pf or orch (R).

3703 Spratlan, Lewis. "Chameleon" in *Images.* Northampton, Mass.: New Valley Music, 1977. Cycle: S, pf.

To His Royal Highness the Dauphin. *A Marianne Moore Reader* (1961).

3704 Adler, Samuel. "To His Royal Highness the Dauphin" in *A Whole Bunch of Fun.* New York: Oxford Univ. Press, 1980. Cantata for Young Voices: unison chorus, or med. v solo, or both, alternating, pf or orch (R).

To Victor Hugo of My Crow Pluto. *Tell Me, Tell Me* (1966).

3705 Thomson, Virgil. "My Crow Pluto" in *Two by Marianne Moore*. New York: G. Schirmer, 1966. Song: med. v, pf.

Miscellaneous

3706 Robbins, Reginald C. "A Talisman." Paris: M. Senart, 1937. Song: high and C v edns, pf. Text beginning, "Under a splintered mast torn. . . ."

HOWARD MOSS (B. 1922)

Clichés for Piano and Orchestra [Sec. 3]. *The Wound and the Weather* (1946).

3707 Flanagan, William. "Plants Cannot Travel" in *Two Songs*. New York: C.F. Peters, 1963. Song: high v, pf.

Horror Movie. *A Swimmer in the Air* (1957).

3708 Flanagan, William. New York: C.F. Peters, 1965. Song: high v, pf.

If You Can. *A Winter Come, a Summer Gone* (1960).

3709 Flanagan, William. New York: C.F. Peters, 1963. Song: high v, pf.

King Midas. *A Winter Come, a Summer Gone* (1960).

3710 Flanagan, William. "See How They Love Me." New York: C.F. Peters, 1965. Song: high v, pf. Text from part 7, "The Princess' Song."

3711 Rorem, Ned. *King Midas*. New York: Boosey & Hawkes, 1970. Cantata: T and/or S, pf.

3712 Rorem, Ned. "See How They Love Me." New York: Henmar Press, 1958. Song: high v, pf. In coll. RFA.

Song. *The Toy Fair* (1954).

3713 Rorem, Ned. "The Air Is the Only" in *Poems of Love and the Rain*. New York: Boosey & Hawkes, 1965. Cycle: M, pf. Secs. 3 and 15 of the cycle are contrasting settings of the text. Recording: Desto, DC 6480 (1969).

The Upside-Down Man. *Finding Them Lost* (1965).

> 3714 Flanagan, William. New York: Peer Internatonal, 1964. Song: med. v, pf.

Miscellaneous

> 3715 Luening, Otto. "Pilgrim's Hymn." Bryn Mawr, Pa.: Merion Music, 1958. Chorus: unison or 2-pt. voices, solo or duet, pf or org. Text: "Ripe grows the grain we sow, green grows the tree. . . ."

OGDEN NASH (1902–1971)

Adventures of Isabel. *The Bad Parents' Garden of Verse* (1936).

> 3716 Mortensen, Otto. In *Three Songs*. Copenhagen: W. Hansen, 1947. Song: v, pf.

Allow Me, Madam, but It Won't Help. *Good Intentions* (1942).

> 3717 Frackenpohl, Arthur. "Women Sitting Firmly on Their Coats" in *Essays on Women*. New York: C. Fischer, 1967. Chorus: TTBB, pf.

The Anniversary. *Ave Ogden! Nash in Latin* (1973).

> 3718 Duke, Vernon. In *Four Choruses*. New York: Broude Bros., 1956. Chorus: SATB, pf.

The Ant. *I'm a Stranger Here Myself* (1938).

> 3719 Berger, Jean. In *Who's Who in the Zoo*. New York: Broude Bros., 1973. Chorus: SATB, 2 fl.
> 3720 Duke, Vernon. In *Ogden Nash's Musical Zoo*. Boston: Little, Brown, 1947. Song: v, pf. Illus. by Frank Owen.

Barnyard Cogitations. *The Bad Parents' Garden of Verse* (1936).

> 3721 Porter, Quincy. In *Modern Canons*. Ed. by Herman Reichenbach. New York: Music Press, 1947. Chorus: mixed voices.

Biological Reflection. *Hard Lines* (1931).

> 3722 Frackenpohl, Arthur. "Pants and Paint" in *Essays on Women*. New York: C. Fischer, 1967. Chorus: TTBB, pf.

The Calf. *Ogden Nash's Musical Zoo* (1947).

> 3723 Duke, Vernon. In *Ogden Nash's Musical Zoo*. Boston: Little, Brown, 1947. Song: v, pf. Illus. by Frank Owen.

The Camel. *The Primrose Path* (1935).

> 3724 Berger, Jean. In *Who's Who in the Zoo*. New York: Broude Bros., 1973. Chorus: SATB, 2 fl.

> 3725 Shearer, C.M. San Antonio: Southern Music, 1981. Chorus: SAB or SATB, a cap.

The Cantaloupe. *Good Intentions* (1942).

> 3726 Hagemann, Philip. In *A Musical Menu*. Bryn Mawr: T. Presser, 1982. Choral Suite: SATB, pf.

A Caution to Everybody. *The Private Dining Room* (1953).

> 3727 Epstein, Alvin. u.p.: Agape, u.d. Setting for 2 speakers or 2 groups of speakers, human percussionists.

A Caution to Hillbilly Singers, Harpists, Harpoonists, Channel-Swimmers, and People First in Line for World Series Tickets. *The Private Dining Room* (1953).

> 3728 Bilik, Jerry H. In *Ogden Nash Suite*. New York: Samuel French, 1959. Song: Bar, band.

Celery. *Good Intentions* (1942).

> 3729 Diemer, Emma L. In *Three Poems*. New York: H. Flammer, 1965. Chorus: TTBB, a cap.

> 3730 Hagemann, Philip. In *A Musical Menu*. Bryn Mawr: T. Presser, 1982. Choral Suite: SATB, pf.

The Centipede. *I'm a Stranger Here Myself* (1938).

> 3731 Diemer, Emma L. In *Three Poems*. New York: H. Flammer, 1965. Chorus: TTBB, a cap.

> 3732 Duke, Vernon. In *Ogden Nash's Musical Zoo*. Boston: Little, Brown, 1947. Illus. by Frank Owen.

Correction: Eve Delved and Adam Span. *The Private Dining Room* (1953).

> 3733 Frackenpohl, Arthur. "The Ladies of the Garden Clubbub" in *Essays on Women*. New York: C. Fischer, 1967. Chorus: TTBB, pf.

The Cow. *Free Wheeling* (1931).

> 3734 Berger, Jean. In *Who's Who in the Zoo*. New York: Broude Bros., 1973. Chorus: SATB, 2 fl.

> 3735 Duke, Vernon. In *Ogden Nash's Musical Zoo*. Boston: Little, Brown, 1947. Song: v, pf. Illus. by Frank Owen.

A Drink with Something in It. *The Primrose Path* (1935).

> 3735a Hagemann, Philip. "The Martini" in *A Musical Menu*. Bryn Mawr: T. Presser, 1982. Choral Suite: SATB, pf.

The Duck. *The Bad Parents' Garden of Verse* (1936).

> 3736 Duke, Vernon. In *Ogden Nash's Musical Zoo*. Boston: Little, Brown, 1947. Song: v, pf. Illus. by Frank Owen.

> 3737 Hagemann, Philip. In *A Musical Menagerie*. Bryn Mawr, Pa.: T. Presser, 1969. Chorus: SATB, pf.

The Eel. *Good Intentions* (1942).

> 3738 Diemer, Emma L. "Eels" in *Three Poems*. New York: H. Flammer, 1965. Chorus: TTBB, pf.

> 3739 Hagemann, Philip. In *A Musical Menagerie*. Bryn Mawr, Pa.: T. Presser, 1969. Chorus: SATB, pf.

The Firefly. *Good Intentions* (1942).

> 3740 Duke, Vernon. In *Ogden Nash's Musical Zoo*. Boston: Little, Brown, 1947. Song: v, pf. Illus. by Frank Owen.

> 3741 Hagemann, Philip. In *A Musical Menagerie*. Bryn Mawr, Pa.: T. Presser, 1969. Chorus: SATB, pf.

The Fish. *Hard Lines* (1931).

> 3742 Shapiro, Norman. Boston: E.C. Schirmer, 1961. Song: S, pf.

The Fly ["God in His wisdom made the fly"]. *Good Intentions* (1942).

> 3743 Hagemann, Philip. In *A Musical Menagerie*. Bryn Mawr, Pa.: T. Presser, 1969. Chorus: SATB, pf.

The Fly ["I must admit"]. *Ogden Nash's Musical Zoo* (1947).

> 3744 Duke, Vernon. In *Ogden Nash's Musical Zoo*. Boston: Little, Brown, 1947. Song: v, pf. Illus. by Frank Owen.

The Frog. *Ogden Nash's Musical Zoo* (1947).

3745 Duke, Vernon. In *Ogden Nash's Musical Zoo*. Boston: Little, Brown, 1947. Song: v, pf. Illus. by Frank Owen.

Further Reflections on Parsley. *Good Intentions* (1942).

3746 Hagemann, Philip. In *A Musical Menu*. Bryn Mawr: T. Presser, 1982. Choral Suite: SATB, pf.

The Gander. *Good Intentions* (1942).

3747 Berger, Jean. In *Who's Who in the Zoo*. New York: Broude Bros., 1973. Chorus: SATB, 2 fl.

The Germ. *The Primrose Path* (1935).

3748 Duke, Vernon. In *Ogden Nash's Musical Zoo*. Boston: Little, Brown, 1947. Song: v, pf. Illus. by Frank Owen.

Glossina Mortisans or the Tsetse. *Good Intentions* (1942).

3749 Hagemann, Philip. In *A Musical Menagerie*. Bryn Mawr, Pa.: T. Presser, 1969. Chorus: SATB, pf.

Ha! Original Sin. *The Selected Verse of Ogden Nash* (1945).

3750 Duke, Vernon. "Vanity, Vanity" in *Four Choruses*. New York: Broude Bros., 1956. Chorus: SATB, a cap.

The Hippopotamus. *I'm a Stranger Here Myself* (1938).

3751 Berger, Jean. In *Who's Who in the Zoo*. New York: Broude Bros., 1973. Chorus: SATB, 2 fl.

I Will Arise and Go Now. *Versus* (1949).

3752 Adler, Samuel. "I Will Arise And Go Now" in *A Whole Bunch of Fun*. New York: Oxford Univ. Press, 1980. Cantata: SAB chorus (young voices), pf or orch (R).

3753 Bilik, Jerry H. "The Lama (I Will Arise and Go Now)" in *Ogden Nash Suite*. New York: Samuel French, 1959. Song: Bar, band.

3754 Cohn, James. "The Lama." New York: Bourne, 1957, 1972. Chorus: SATB, opt pf and instr.

The Jellyfish. *Ogden Nash's Musical Zoo* (1947).

3755 Duke, Vernon. In *Ogden Nash's Musical Zoo*. Boston: Little, Brown, 1947. Song: v, pf. Illus. by Frank Owen.

The Kitten ["The kitten's face is soft"]. *Ogden Nash's Musical Zoo* (1947).

3756 Duke, Vernon. In *Ogden Nash's Musical Zoo*. Boston: Little, Brown, 1947. Song: v, pf. Illus. by Frank Owen.

The Kitten ["The trouble with a kitten is"]. *The Face Is Familiar* (1940).

3757 Hagemann, Philip. In *A Musical Menagerie*. Bryn Mawr, Pa.: T. Presser, 1969. Chorus: SATB, pf.

Limerick One. *The Private Dining Room* (1953).

3758 Frackenpohl, Arthur. "Lady Limericks" in *Essays on Women*. New York: C. Fischer, 1967. Chorus: TTBB, pf.

Limerick Three. *The Private Dining Room* (1953).

3759 Frackenpohl, Arthur. "Lady Limericks" in *Essays on Women*. New York: C. Fischer, 1967. Chorus: TTBB, pf.

The Lion. *Versus* (1949).

3760 Hagemann, Philip. In *A Musical Menagerie*. Bryn Mawr, Pa.: T. Presser, 1969. Chorus: SATB, pf.

Love under the Republicans (or Democrats). *Hard Lines* (1931).

3761 Reif, Paul. In *. . . and be my love*. New York: General, 1962. Song: high v, pf.

The Mermaid. *Good Intentions* (1942).

3762 Hagemann, Philip. In *A Musical Menagerie*. Bryn Mawr, Pa.: T. Presser, 1969. Chorus: SATB, pf.

The Mouse. *Ogden Nash's Musical Zoo* (1947).

3763 Duke, Vernon. In *Ogden Nash's Musical Zoo*. Boston: Little, Brown, 1947. Song: v, pf. Illus. by Frank Owen.

My My [1. My Dream 2. My Conscience]. *You Can't Get There from Here* (1957).

3764 Bates, David S. "My Dream," "My Conscience" in *Nonsense Nonsense*. In coll. MuENC. Chorus: SSAA, a cap.

The Octopus. *Good Intentions* (1942).

3765 Hagemann, Philip. In *A Musical Menagerie*. Bryn Mawr, Pa.: T. Presser, 1969. Chorus: SATB, pf.

Oh Shucks, Ma'am, I Mean Excuse Me. *Versus* (1949).

3765a Frackenpohl, Arthur. "A Nice Girl with a Naughty Word" in *Essays on Women*. New York: C. Fischer, 1967. Chorus: TTBB, pf.

One Touch of Venus (1944).

   3766 Weill, Kurt. "Foolish Heart," "Speak Low," "That's Him," "The Trouble with Women," "Westwind" in *One Touch of Venus* [Selections]. New York: Chappell, 1943. Song: v, pf. Book by S.J. Perelman and Nash.

        William Stickles, arr. "The Trouble with Women." New York: Chappell, 1943. Chorus: TTBB, pf.

        "Foolish Heart," "Speak Low," "That's Him," "The Trouble with Women," "Westwind" in coll. SnKW. Song: v, pf.

The Ostrich. *You Can't Get There from Here* (1957).

   3767 Hagemann, Philip. In *A Musical Menagerie*. Bryn Mawr, Pa.: T. Presser, 1969. Chorus: SATB, pf.

The Parsnip. *Good Intentions* (1947).

   3768 Hagemann, Philip. In *A Musical Menu*. Bryn Mawr: T. Presser, 1982. Choral Suite: SATB, pf.

The Pidgeon. *Ogden Nash's Musical Zoo* (1947).

   3769 Duke, Vernon. In *Ogden Nash's Musical Zoo*. Boston: Little, Brown, 1947. Song: v, pf. Illus. by Frank Owen.

The Pig. *Happy Days* (1933).

   3770 Duke, Vernon. In *Ogden Nash's Musical Zoo*. Boston: Little, Brown, 1947. Song: v, pf. Illus. by Frank Owen.

   3771 Hagemann, Philip. In *A Musical Menu*. Bryn Mawr: T. Presser, 1982. Choral Suite: SATB, pf.

The Pizza [Table Talk. 3]. *You Can't Get There from Here* (1957).

   3772 Bates, David S. In *Nonsense Nonsense*. In coll. MuENC. Chorus: SSAA, a cap.

   3773 Hagemann, Philip. In *A Musical Menu*. Bryn Mawr: T. Presser, 1982. Choral Suite: SATB, pf.

Please Pass the Biscuit. *Good Intentions* (1942).

   3774 Duke, Vernon. "Our Dog" in *Ogden Nash's Musical Zoo*. Boston: Little, Brown, 1947. Song: v, pf. Illus. by Frank Owen.

The Private Dining Room. *The Private Dining Room* (1953).

3775 Duke, Vernon. In *Four Choruses*. New York: Broude Bros., 1956. Chorus: SATB, pf.

The Purist. *I'm a Stranger Here Myself* (1938).

3776 Cumberworth, Starling. In *Two Macabre Whims*. In coll. CASM. Song: med. v, pf.

The Python. *The Old Dog Barks Backwards* (1972).

3776a Plog, Anthony. In *Animal Ditties*. Century City, Calif.: Wimbledon Music, 1978. Setting for narr., tr, pf.

Quartet for Prosperous Love-Children. *Happy Days* (1933).

3776b Armbruster, Robert. In *Happy Days*. New York: Simon and Schuster, 1933, pp. 77–91. Song: v, pf.

Requiem. *I'm a Stranger Here Myself* (1938).

3777 Frackenpohl, Arthur. "Lady Limericks" in *Essays on Women*. New York: C. Fischer, 1967. Chorus: TTBB, pf.

The Rhinoceros. *Happy Days* (1933).

3778 Spino, Pasquale J. In *Five Poetic Songs*. u.p.: J. Boonin, u.d. Chorus: SATB, a cap.

The Rooster. *Ogden Nash's Musical Zoo* (1947).

3779 Duke, Vernon. In *Ogden Nash's Musical Zoo*. Boston: Little, Brown, 1947. Song: v, pf. Illus. by Frank Owen.

The Sea-Gull. *Family Reunion* (1950).

3780 Duke, Vernon. In *Ogden Nash's Musical Zoo*. Boston: Little, Brown, 1947. Song: v, pf. Illus. by Frank Owen.

3781 Shapiro, Norman R. In *Songs for Soprano and Piano*. Boston: E.C. Schirmer, 1961. Song: S, pf.

Seaside Serenade. *The Bad Parents' Garden of Verse* (1936).

3782 Bilik, Jerry H. In *Ogden Nash Suite*. New York: Samuel French, 1959. Song: Bar, band.

Song to Be Sung by the Father of Infant Female Children. *Happy Days* (1933).

3783 Adler, Samuel. In *Two Songs for Three Years*. New York: Boosey & Hawkes, 1974. Song: med. v, pf.

The Sparrow. *Ogden Nash's Musical Zoo* (1947).

3784 Duke, Vernon. In *Ogden Nash's Musical Zoo*. Boston: Little, Brown, 1947. Song: v, pf. Illus. by Frank Owen.

Sweet Bye and Bye (1945).

3785 Duke, Vernon. "Just Like a Man," "Low and Lazy," "An Old-Fashioned Tune," "Round About," "Sweet Bye and Bye" in *Sweet Bye and Bye*. New York: T.B. Harms, 1946. Musical Comedy. Book by S.J. Perelman and Albert Hirschfeld; lyrics by Nash.

The Sweetbread [Table Talk. 2]. *You Can't Get There from Here* (1957).

3786 Hagemann, Philip. In *A Musical Menu*. Bryn Mawr: T. Presser, 1982. Choral Suite: SATB, pf.

Taboo to Boot. *Many Long Years Ago* (1945).

3787 Duke, Vernon. In *Four Choruses*. New York: Broude Bros., 1956. Chorus: SATB, pf.

The Termite. *Good Intentions* (1942).

3788 Duke, Vernon. In *Ogden Nash's Musical Zoo*. Boston: Little, Brown, 1947. Song: v, pf. Illus. by Frank Owen.

3789 Hagemann, Philip. In *A Musical Menagerie*. Bryn Mawr, Pa.: T. Presser, 1969. Chorus: SATB, pf. Music not seen; text presumably from this poem.

3790 Shapiro, Norman. Boston: E.C. Schirmer, 1961. Song: S, pf. Music not seen; text presumably from this poem.

The Terrible People. *Happy Days* (1933).

3791 Cohn, James. u.p.: Belwin-Mills, 1972. Chorus: SATB, opt pf.

Thoughts Thought after a Bridge Party. *Versus* (1949).

3792 Bilik, Jerry H. In *Ogden Nash Suite*. New York: Samuel French, 1959. Song: Bar, band.

Thoughts Thought on an Avenue. *Good Intentions* (1942).

3793 Frackenpohl, Arthur. "The Feminine Approach to Feminine Fashions" in *Essays on Women*. New York: C. Fischer, 1967. Chorus: TTBB, pf.

To My Valentine. *Marriage Lines* (1964).

3794 Frackenpohl, Arthur. "To My Valentine" in *Essays on Women*. New York: C. Fischer, 1967. Chorus: TTBB, pf.

The Turkey. *The Bad Parents' Garden of Verse* (1936).

3795 Duke, Vernon. In *Ogden Nash's Musical Zoo*. Boston: Little, Brown, 1947. Song: v, pf. Illus. by Frank Owen.

The Turtle. *Hard Lines* (1931).

3795a Plog, Anthony. In *Animal Ditties*. Century City, Calif.: Wimbledon Music, 1978. Setting for narr., tr, pf.

Tweedledee and Tweedledoom. *The Private Dining Room* (1953).

3796 Avshalomov, Jacob. In *Whimsies*. Boston: E.C. Schirmer, 1958. Chorus: SATB, a cap.

What's the Use? *Free Wheeling* (1931).

3797 Frackenpohl, Arthur. "Pants and Paint" in *Essays on Women*. New York: C. Fischer, 1967. Chorus: TTBB, pf.

Yorkshire Pudding [Table Talk. 1]. *You Can't Get There from Here* (1957).

3798 Hagemann, Philip. In *A Musical Menu*. Bryn Mawr: T. Presser, 1982. Choral Suite: SATB, pf.

Miscellaneous

3799 Duke, Vernon. *The Littlest Revue*. Recording: Epic, LN 3275 (1956). Lyrics and music mostly by Nash and Duke.

3800 Duke, Vernon. *Two's Company*. Musical Revue. Recording: RCA Victor, WOC 1009 (19-0031-0035) (1953?). Lyrics by Nash; additional lyrics by Sammy Cahn.

3801 Entry cancelled.

3802 Entry cancelled.

3803 Manning, Dick. "A Bunch of Bananas." New York: M. Witmark, 1954.

3803a Plog, Anthony. "Hyena," "Hog" in *Animal Ditties*. Century City, Calif.: Wimbledon Music, 1978. Setting for narr., tr, pf.

3804 Saint-Saëns, Camille. "Introduction," "Royal March of the Lions," "Cocks and Hens," "Wild Jackass," "Turtles," "Elephants," "Kangaroos," "The Aquarium," "The Mules," "The Cuckoo in the Woods," "The Birds," "The Pianists," "The Fossils," "The Swan,"

"Grand Finale" in *The Carnival of the Animals*. Recording: Columbia, ML 4355; Nash first wrote the lyrics to accompany this recording.

ROBERT NATHAN (B. 1894)

Laurence, Dan A. *Robert Nathan: A Bibliography*. New Haven: Yale Univ. Press, 1960, pp. 75–76 [LNB].

"Be not afraid because the sun goes down." *A Winter Tide* (1940); "Autumn Sonnets. 7. *The Green Leaf* (1950).

3805 Hageman, Richard. "Fear Not the Night." New York: C. Fischer, 1944. Song: high v, pf.

Dunkirk. *The Darkening Meadows* (1945).

3806 Damrosch, Walter. New York: G. Schirmer, 1943. Setting for med. v and unison chorus, str orch, pf, opt timp.

Epistle. *A Winter Tide* (1940).

3807 Helm, Everett. "Christian, Be Up" in coll. ChAH.

He Hears the Sound of Distant Bells. *Youth Grows Old* (1922); "Bells in the Country." *The Green Leaf* (1950).

3808 Heller, James. "Bells in the Country" in *Three Songs for Soprano*. Los Angeles: Affiliated Musicians, 1953. Song: S, pf.

He Thinks How Beauty Forever Escapes the Lonely Heart. *Youth Grows Old* (1922); "Beauty is ever to the lonely mind" [Sonnet XVIII]. *Selected Poems* (1935); Autumn Sonnets. 26. *The Green Leaf* (1950).

3809 Birch, Robert F. "Sonnet" op. 25 no. 10. New York: J. Patelson Music, 1956. Song: high v, pf.

He Writes His Epitaph. *Youth Grows Old* (1922); Epitaph. *Selected Poems* (1935); Epitaph for a Poet. *The Green Leaf* (1950).

3810 Birch, Robert F. "Epitaph for a Poet." New York: J. Patelson Music, 1957. Song: med. v, pf.

3811 Heller, James. "Epitaph for a Poet" in *Three Songs for Soprano*. Los Angeles: Affiliated Musicians, 1953. Song: S, pf.

"Here in this spot with you my wings are furled." *Selected Poems* (1935); The Nest. *The Green Leaf* (1950).

> 3812 Duke, John. "Here in This Spot with You." New York: G. Schirmer, 1949. Song: med. v, pf.

Home over the Hill [LNB p. 75].

> 3813 James, Philip. Philadelphia: T. Presser, 1943. Song: high or low v, pf; Philadelphia: T. Presser, u.d. Chorus: SSA, pf.

"I ride the great black horses of my heart." *A Cedar Box* (1929).

> 3814 Duke, John. "I Ride the Great Black Horses." New York: G. Schirmer, 1949. Song: med. v, pf.

"Is it indeed your voice that whispers here." *A Winter Tide* (1940).

> 3815 Hageman, Richard. "Is It You?" New York: Galaxy, 1951. Song: high v, pf.

Now Blue October. *The Darkening Meadows* (1945).

> 3816 Hageman, Richard. "So Love Returns." New York: G. Ricordi, 1960. Song: v, pf.

"Of seven virtues has my true love seven." *Selected Poems* (1935); My True Love's Virtues. *The Green Leaf* (1950).

> 3817 Hageman, Richard. "A Lover's Song." New York: Galaxy, 1955. Song: high v, pf.

The Poet Returns to His Home. *Youth Grows Old* (1922); The Waves of Quiet. *The Green Leaf* (1950).

> 3818 Heller, James. "The Waves of Quiet" in *Three Songs for Soprano*. Los Angeles: Affiliated Musicians, 1953. Song: S, pf.

The Poet Speaks to His Love. *Youth Grows Old* (1922); Hush. *The Green Leaf* (1950).

> 3819 Hageman, Richard. "Hush." New York: Galaxy, 1951. Song: high v, pf.

Watch, America. *The Darkening Meadows* (1945).

> 3820 Elwell, Herbert. Boston: C.C. Birchard, 1951.
>
> 3821 Thomas, Christopher. Cincinnati: Willis, 1942.
>
> 3822 Warren, Elinor R. "Rolling Rivers, Dreaming Forests." New York: C. Fischer, 1953. Chorus: SATB, a cap.

"When in the crowd I suddenly Behold." *A Cedar Box* (1929); The Secret. *The Green Leaf* (1950).

> 3823 Heller, James. "The Secret" in *Three Songs for Baritone*. Los Angeles: Affiliated Musicians, 1953. Song: Bar, pf.

"When in the evening I lift up my eyes." *A Cedar Box* (1929).

> 3824 Heller, James. "When in the Evening" in *Three Songs for Baritone*. Los Angeles: Affiliated Musicians, 1953. Song: Bar, pf.

"Where I am going there is no despair." *Selected Poems* (1935).

> 3825 Heller, James. "Where I Am Going" in *Three Songs for Baritone*. Los Angeles: Affiliated Musicians, 1953. Song: Bar, pf.

> 3826 Mac Nutt, Walter. "Atque Vale." Toronto: BMI Canada, 1950.

Miscellaneous

> 3827 Hageman. Richard. "At Heaven's Door (Am Himmelstor)." New York: G. Schirmer, 1958. Trans. from the German text of Conrad F. Meyer.

> 3828 Hageman, Richard. "Beggar's Love (Betterliebe)." New York: G. Schirmer, 1958. Trans. from the Ger. text of Theodore Storm.

> 3829 Hageman, Richard. "He Passed By (Il Passa)." New York: Ricordi, 1960. Trans. from the Italian text of Helene Vacaresco.

> 3830 Hageman, Richard. "O Lovely World (O Welt, du bist so wunderschon)." New York: G. Schirmer, 1958. Trans. from the German text of Julius Rodenberg.

> 3831 Hageman, Richard. "The Town (Die Stadt)." New York: G. Schirmer, 1958. Trans. from the German text of Theodore Storm.

HOWARD NEMEROV (B. 1920)

An Old Picture. *The Salt Garden* (1955).

> 3832 Bialosky, Marshall. In coll. TaCAS. Song: v, pf.

Seven Macabre Songs, dedicated to Louis Calabro. *Mirrors & Windows: Poems* (1958).

3833 Calabro, Louis. "The Ground Swayed," "The Officer," "Each a Rose," "No More Than Dust," "It Is Forbidden," "The Sunlight Pierced" in *Macabre Reflections*. Philadelphia: Elkan-Vogel, 1969. Cycle: M, pf; "Each a Rose" and "It Is Forbidden" in coll. TaCA.

A Song of Degrees. *Guide to the Ruins* (1950).

3834 Bialosky, Marshall. Bryn Mawr, Pa.: T. Presser, 1956. Chorus: SSATTBB, a cap.

DOROTHY PARKER (1893–1967)

Biographies. 1. *Enough Rope* (1926).

3835 Fetler, Paul. "Now This Is the Story." New York: C. Fischer, 1967. Chorus: SSA, pf.

Bric-Brac. *Sunset Gun* (1928).

3836 Barab, Seymour. In *Songs of Perfect Propriety*. New York: Boosey & Hawkes, 1959. Cycle: med. v, pf.

Chant for Dark Hours. *Enough Rope* (1926).

3837 Barab, Seymour. In *Songs of Perfect Propriety*. New York: Boosey & Hawkes, 1959. Cycle: med. v, pf.

The Choice. *Enough Rope* (1926).

3838 Barab, Seymour. In *Songs of Perfect Propriety*. New York: Boosey & Hawkes, 1959. Cycle: med. v, pf.

Coda. *Sunset Gun* (1928).

3839 Barab, Seymour. In *Songs of Perfect Propriety*. New York: Boosey & Hawkes, 1959. Cycle: med. v, pf.

Comment. *Enough Rope* (1926).

3840 Barab, Seymour. In *Songs of Perfect Propriety, Vol. 1*. New York: Boosey & Hawkes, 1959. Cycle: med. v, pf; fl, cl, bsn, tpt, pf (R). Recording: Urania, X.113.

The False Friends. *Enough Rope* (1926).

3841 Barab, Seymour. In *Songs of Perfect Propriety*. New York: Boosey & Hawkes, 1959. Cycle: med. v, pf.

Indian Summer. *Enough Rope* (1926).

3842 Barab, Seymour. In *Songs of Perfect Propriety*. New York: Boosey & Hawkes, 1959. Cycle: med. v, pf.

Inventory. *Enough Rope* (1926).

3843 Barab, Seymour. In *Songs of Perfect Propriety, Vol. 1*. New York: Boosey & Hawkes, 1959. Cycle: med. v, pf; fl, cl, bsn, tpt, pf (R). Recording: Urania, X.113.

3843a Wirth, Carl Anton. "Four Be the Things." New York: The Composers Press, u.d. Song: v, pf.

Love Song. *Enough Rope* (1926).

3844 Barab, Seymour. In *Songs of Perfect Propriety*. New York: Boosey & Hawkes, 1959. Cycle: med. v, pf.

Lullaby. *Enough Rope* (1926).

3845 Barab, Seymour. In *Songs of Perfect Propriety, Vol. 1*. New York: Boosey & Hawkes, 1959. Cycle: med. v, pf; fl, cl, bsn, tpt, pf (R). Recording: Urania, X.113.

Men. *Enough Rope* (1926).

3846 Barab, Seymour. In *Songs of Perfect Propriety, Vol. 1*. New York: Boosey & Hawkes, 1959. Cycle: med. v, pf; fl, cl, bsn, tpt, pf (R). Recording: Urania, X.113.

Now at Liberty. *Enough Rope* (1926).

3847 Barab, Seymour. In *Songs of Perfect Propriety, Vol. 1*. New York: Boosey & Hawkes, 1959. Cycle: med. v, pf; fl, cl, bsn, tpt, pf (R). Recording: Urania, X.113.

One Perfect Rose. *Enough Rope* (1926).

3848 Barab, Seymour. In *Songs of Perfect Propriety, Vol. 1*. New York: Boosey & Hawkes, 1959. Cycle: med. v, pf; fl, cl, bsn, tpt, pf (R). Recording: Urania, X.113.

Renunciation. *Enough Rope* (1926).

3849 Barab, Seymour. In *Songs of Perfect Propriety, Vol. 1*. New York: Boosey & Hawkes, 1959. Cycle: med. v, pf; fl, cl, bsn, tpt, pf (R). Recording: Urania, X.113.

Résumé. *Enough Rope* (1926).

> 3850 Parchman, Gen. In *Cycle of Novelties*. New York: Seesaw Music, u.d. Song: S, pf.

Rondeau Redoublé. *Enough Rope* (1926).

> 3851 Clarke, Henry L. MS, 1955, avail. ACA. Song: Bar or M, cl, bsn, vc.

Social Note. *Enough Rope* (1926).

> 3852 Barab, Seymour. In *Songs of Perfect Propriety, Vol. 1*. New York: Boosey & Hawkes, 1959. Cycle: med. v, pf; fl, cl, bsn, tpt, pf (R). Recording: Urania, X.113.

Somebody's Song. *Enough Rope* (1926).

> 3853 Barab, Seymour. In *Songs of Perfect Propriety*. New York: Boosey & Hawkes, 1959. Cycle: med. v, pf.

Song of One of the Girls. *Enough Rope* (1926).

> 3854 Barab, Seymour. In *Songs of Perfect Propriety*. New York: Boosey & Hawkes, 1959. Cycle: med. v, pf.

Song of Perfect Propriety. *Enough Rope* (1926).

> 3855 Barab, Seymour. In *Songs of Perfect Propriety, Vol. 1*. New York: Boosey & Hawkes, 1959. Cycle: med. v, pf; fl, cl, bsn, tpt, pf (R). Recording: Urania, X.113.

Symptom Recital. *Enough Rope* (1926).

> 3856 Barab, Seymour. In *Songs of Perfect Propriety*. New York: Boosey & Hawkes, 1959. Cycle: med. v, pf.

They Part. *Enough Rope* (1926).

> 3857 Barab, Seymour. In *Songs of Perfect Propriety*. New York: Boosey & Hawkes, 1959. Cycle: med. v, pf.

The Trusting Heart. *Sunset Gun* (1928).

> 3858 Barab, Seymour. In *Songs of Perfect Propriety*. New York: Boosey & Hawkes, 1959. Cycle: med. v, pf.

Ultimatum. *Death and Taxes and Other Poems* (1931).

> 3859 Barab, Seymour. In *Songs of Perfect Propriety, Vol. 1*. New York:

Boosey & Hawkes, 1959. Cycle: med. v, pf; fl, cl, bsn, tpt, pf (R). Recording: Urania, X.113.

A Very Short Song. *Enough Rope* (1926).

3860 Barab, Seymour. In *Songs of Perfect Propriety, Vol. 1.* New York: Boosey & Hawkes, 1959. Cycle: med. v, pf; fl, cl, bsn, tpt, pf (R). Recording: Urania, X.113.

Wisdom. *Sunset Gun* (1928).

3861 Barab, Seymour. In *Songs of Perfect Propriety, Vol. 1.* New York: Boosey & Hawkes, 1959. Cycle: med. v, pf; fl, cl, bsn, tpt, pf (R). Recording: Urania, X.113.

Words of Comfort to Be Scratched on a Mirror. *Enough Rope* (1926).

3862 Calvin, Susan. "Words of Comfort." New York: Associated Music, u.d. Chorus: mixed voices.

Miscellaneous

3862a Bernstein, Leonard. *Candide.* New York: G. Schirmer, 1958. Comic operetta based on Voltaire's satire. Book by Hellman; lyrics by Parker and others.

3863 King, Jack. "How Am I to Know." New York: Robbins, 1929.

3864 Robbins, Reginald C. "Threat to a Fickle Lady." Hollywood: Golden West Music, 1941. Song: high v, pf. Text: "Sweet lady sleep befriend me. . . ."

KENNETH PATCHEN (1911–1972)

Morgan, Richard G. *Kenneth Patchen: An Annotated Bibliography.* Mamaroneck, N.Y.: Paul P. Appel, 1978, p. 91.

All Is Safe. . . . *Orchards, Thrones & Caravans* (1952).

3865 Ashforth, Alden. "All Is Safe" in *Aspects of Love.* Song: T, pf. Recording: Orion, ORS 79335 (1979).

3866 Keyes, Nelson. "All Is Safe." Bryn Mawr: Elkan-Vogel, 1970. Chorus: SATB, a cap.

3867 Entry cancelled.

At the New Year. *First Will & Testament* (1939).

3868 Bauer, Marion. "At the New Year" op. 42. New York: Associated
Music, 1950. Chorus: SATB, pf.

"Be Music, Night." *Cloth of the Tempest* (1943).

3869 Bialosky, Marshall. Bryn Mawr, Pa.: T. Presser, u.d. Chorus: SSA,
a cap.

3870 Diamond, David. New York: C. Fischer, 1948. Song: high v, pf.

"Do Me That Love." *Red Wine & Yellow Hair* (1949).

3871 Carlson, Mark. In *Patchen Songs*. Song: Bar, pf. Recording: Orion,
ORS 79335 (1979).

An Easy Decision. *Orchards, Thrones & Caravans* (1952).

3871a Bedford, David. London: Universal Edition, 1978. Song: S, pf.

Fall of the Evening Star. *First Will & Testament* (1939).

3872 Bedford, David. In *Music for Albion Moonlight*. London: Universal
Edition, 1966. Song: S, 6 instr.

For Miriam ["As beautiful as the hands"]. *Orchards, Thrones & Caravans* (1952).

3873 Ashforth, Alden. "As Beautiful As" in *Aspects of Love*. Song: T, pf.
Recording: Orion, ORS 79335 (1979).

3874 Carlson, Mark. "As Beautiful As" in *Patchen Songs*. Song: Bar, pf.
Recording: Orion, ORS 79335 (1979).

For Miriam ["The sea is awash with roses O they blow"]. *The Dark Kingdom*
(1942).

3875 Ashforth, Alden. "The Sea Is Awash with Roses" in *Aspects of Love*.
Song: T, pf. Recording: Orion, ORS 79335 (1979).

"Give You a Lantern." *When We Were Together* (1957).

3876 Keyes, Nelson. Philadelphia: Elkan-Vogel, 1969. Chorus: SATB, a
cap.

The Great Birds. *When We Were Together* (1957).

3877 Bedford, David. In *Two Poems for Chorus on Words by Kenneth Patchen*.
London: Universal Edition, 1967. Chorus: 6-12 S, 6 A, 6 T, 6 B.
Recording: Deutsche Grammophon 137004 (1969).

If We Are to Know Where We Live. *First Will & Testament* (1939).

    3878 Bedford, David. In *Music of Albion Moonlight*. London: Universal Edition, 1966. Song: S, 6 instr.

In Memory of Kathleen. *First Will & Testament* (1939).

    3878a Bedford, David. "A Dream of the Seven Lost Stars." London: Universal Edition, 1971. Setting for woodwind or strings and mixed voices.

    3879 Mollicone, Henry. In *Two Love Songs*. MS, 1969, avail. ACA. Song: T, vla.

It Is the Hour. *Hurrah for Anything* (1957).

    3879a Carlson, Mark. In *Patchen Songs*. Song: Bar, pf. Recording: Orion, ORS 79335 (1979).

Lament for the Makers of Songs. *Red Wine & Yellow Hair* (1949).

    3880 Bedford, David. In *Music for Albion Moonlight*. London: Universal Edition, 1966. Song: S, 6 instr.

Lonesome Boy Blues. *Orchards, Thrones & Caravans* (1952).

    3881 Smith, William O. In *Five Songs*. New York: MJQ Music, u.d. Song: med. v, vc.

The Magical Mouse. *Orchards, Thrones & Caravans* (1952).

    3882 Smith, William O. In *Five Songs*. New York: MJQ Music, u.d. Song: med. v, vc.

My Pretty Animals. *Orchards, Thrones & Caravans* (1952).

    3883 Smith, William O. In *Five Songs*. New York: MJQ Music, u.d. Song: med. v, vc.

"O Sleeping Falls the Maiden Snow." *Pictures of Life and Death* (1946).

    3883a Carlson, Mark. "O Sleeping Lay the Maiden Snow" in *Patchen Songs*. Song: Bar, pf. Recording: Orion, ORS 79335 (1979).

    3884 Hundley, Richard. "Maiden Snow." New York: General, 1961. Song: high v, pf.

"O Now the Drenched Land Wakes." *When We Were Together* (1957).

    3885 Bedford, David. In *Two Songs for Chorus on Words by Kenneth Patchen*. London: Universal Edition, 1967. Chorus: 6–12 S, 6 A, 6 T, 6 B. Recording: Deutsche Grammophon 137004 (1969).

3886 Willis, Richard. "The Drenched Land." New York: C.F. Peters, 1963. Chorus: SATB, a cap.

"O When I Take My Love Out Walking." *Red Wine & Yellow Hair* (1949).

3887 Carlson, Mark. In *Patchen Songs*. Song: Bar, pf. Recording: Orion, ORS 79335 (1979).

The Oldest Conversation. *Orchards, Thrones & Caravans* (1952).

3888 Smith, William O. In *Five Songs*. New York: MJQ Music, u.d. Song: med. v, vc.

Pastoral. *The Dark Kingdom* (1942).

3889 Mills, Charles. MS, 1958, avail. ACA. Song: med. v, pf.

So It Ends. *Pictures of Life and Death.* (1946).

3890 Bedford, David. In *Music for Albion Moonlight*. London: Universal Edition, 1966. Song: S, 6 instr.

"The Snow Is Deep on the Ground." *Cloth of the Tempest* (1943).

3891 Carlson, Mark. In *Patchen Songs*. Song: Bar, pf. Recording: Orion, ORS 79335 (1979).

"There is Nothing False in Thee." *The Dark Kingdom* (1942).

3892 Mills, Charles. MS, u.d., avail. ACA. Song: med. v, pf.

"This Summer Earth." *Red Wine & Yellow Hair* (1949).

3893 Carlson, Mark. In *Patchen Songs*. Song: Bar, pf. Recording: Orion, ORS 79335 (1979).

The Unreturning Hosts. *Orchards, Thrones & Caravans* (1952).

3894 Mills, Charles. MS, u.d., avail. ACA. Chorus: SATB, a cap.

What There Is. *Orchards, Thrones & Caravans* (1952).

3895 Smith, William O. In *Five Songs*. New York: MJQ Music, u.d. Song: med. v, vc.

Winter Poem. *Pictures of Life and Death.* (1946).

3896 Carlson, Mark. "Winter Song" in *Patchen Songs*. Song: Bar, pf. Recording: Orion, ORS 79335 (1979).

Miscellaneous

3896a Bedford, David. "Come in Here Child." London: Universal Edition, 1968. Song: S, amplif pf.

3897 Cage, John. "The City Wears a Slouch Hat." u.p.: Broadcast Music, 1942.

3898 Hensel, Richard. "The Dark Kingdom." New York: Associated Music Publishers, u.d.

3898a Hensel, Richard. "Three Songs from the Kingdom Between." Cincinnati: World Library, u.d. Chorus: SSA.

Sylvia Plath (1932–1963)

The Applicant. *Ariel* (1965).

3899 Lambro, Phillip. In *Four Songs*. Century City, Calif.: Wimbledon Music, 1974. Song: S, orch.

Daddy. *Ariel* (1965).

3900 Lambro, Phillip. In *Four Songs*. Century City, Calif.: Wimbledon Music, 1974. Song: S, orch.

The Hanging Man. *Ariel* (1965).

3901 Rorem, Ned. In *Ariel: Five Poems of Sylvia Plath*. New York: Boosey & Hawkes, 1974. Cycle: S, cl, pf.

Lady Lazarus. *Ariel* (1965).

3902 Rorem, Ned. In *Ariel: Five Poems of Sylvia Plath*. New York: Boosey & Hawkes, 1974. Cycle: S, cl, pf.

Mirror. *Crossing the Water* (1971).

3903 Lambro, Philip. In *Four Songs*. Century City, Calif.: Wimbledon Music, 1974. Song: S, orch.

3904 Vercoe, Elizabeth. In *Herstory I*. MS, u.d., avail. ACA. Cycle: S, vib, pf.

Morning Song. *Ariel* (1965).

3905 Vercoe, Elizabeth. In *Herstory I*. MS, u.d., avail. ACA. Cycle: S, vib, pf.

The Night Dances. *Ariel* (1965).

> 3906 Ahrold, Frank. "Night Dances" in *Three Poems of Sylvia Plath*. Song: M, fl, cl, bsn, vc, vib, perc. Recording: Composers Recordings, CRI SD 380 (1978).

> 3907 Lambro, Phillip. In *Four Songs*. Century City, Calif.: Wimbledon Music, 1974. Song: S, orch.

Poppies in July. *Ariel* (1965).

> 3908 Rorem, Ned. In *Ariel: Five Poems of Sylvia Plath*. New York: Boosey & Hawkes, 1974. Cycle: S, cl, pf.

Poppies in October. *Ariel* (1965).

> 3909 Rorem, Ned. In *Ariel: Five Poems of Sylvia Plath*. New York: Boosey & Hawkes, 1974. Cycle: S, cl, pf.

Sheep in Fog. *Ariel* (1965).

> 3910 Ahrold, Frank. In *Three Poems of Sylvia Plath*. Song: M, fl, cl, bsn, vc, vib, perc. Recording: Composers Recordings, CRI SD 380 (1978).

Words. *Ariel* (1965).

> 3911 Ahrold, Frank. In *Three Poems of Sylvia Plath*. Song: M, fl, cl, bsn, vc, vib, perc. Recording: Composers Recordings, CRI SD 380 (1978).

> 3912 Rorem, Ned. In *Ariel: Five Poems of Sylvia Plath*. New York: Boosey & Hawkes, 1974. Cycle: S, cl, pf.

EDGAR ALLAN POE (1809–1849)

Archibald, R.C. "Music and Edgar Allan Poe." *Notes & Queries* 179 (Sept. 7, 1940), pp. 170–171.

Cauthen, Irby B., Jr. "Music and Edgar Allan Poe." *Notes & Queries* 194 (March 5, 1949), p. 103.

Evans, May G. *Music and Edgar Allan Poe: A Bibliographical Study*. Baltimore: Johns Hopkins Press, 1939 [EMEP].

Pollin, Burton R. "More Music to Poe." *Music and Letters* 54(4) (Oct. 1973), pp. 391–404 [PoMM].

Annabel Lee. *Collected Works of Edgar Allan Poe* [Vol. 1. Poems] (1969).

3913 Balfe, Michael W. Boston: O. Ditson, [BAL n.d., not before 1858; BPL 186-?]; London: Joseph Williams, [BAL n.d., not before 1845; EMEP 1865?]. Ballad: v, pf.

3914 Bergen, Alfred H. "Annabel Lee" op. 15 no. 1. New York: J. Fischer, 1926. Song: med. v, pf.

3915 Best, R.E. London: J.H. Jewell, 1858. Ballad.

3915a Bruner, Jane W. San Francisco: A.A. Rosenberg, 1870.

3916 Bryan, Robert. Liverpool: W.A. Lewis, 1922. Song: A, pf. Words in Eng. and Welsh.

3917 Carder, Alfred. London: Ascherberg, Hopwood & Crew, n.d. Song: v, pf.

3918 Dilworth, Don. In *The Joan Baez Songbook* [pp. 174-77]. New York: Ryerson Music, 1964. Song.

3919 Doellner, Robert. "Annabel Lee" op. 15. Boston: Boston Music, 1930. Song: v, pf; Boston: Boston Music, 1958. Words adapted. Recording: Reelfort 1250.

3920 Falconnet, E.F. Boston: O. Ditson, u.d. Song: v, pf.

3920a Farebrother, Bernard. London: Joseph Williams, [EMEP 188-]. Song.

3921 Habash, John. New York: Ashwyn Music, 1963. Setting for SATB. Words adapted by Edna Lewis.

3922 Hall, E. Joslin. London: West & Co., 1914. Song: v, pf.

3923 Heap, C. Swinnerton. London: Novello, 1880. Song: v, pf.

3924 Holbrooke, Josef. "Annabel Lee" op. 41b. London: Swan & Co., 1906. Ballad: T or Bar, pf or orch.

3925 Janowsky, Herbert. u.p.: p.p., 1965. Setting for mixed voices, T solo, a cap. Harmonized by Hall Johnson.

3926 Kerr, Anita W. u.p.: Tuckahoe Music, 1961.

3927 Kroeger, Ernest R. "Annabel Lee" op. 65 no. 7. Leipzig: Breitkopf & Härtel, 1906. Song: v, pf. Words in Eng. and Ger.

3928 Lacy, Frederick St. John. "Annabel Lee" op. 2. London: London Music Publishing, 1887. Cantata: chorus, T solo, orch (R).

3929 Law, Alice. London: Elkin, 1909. Song: v, pf.

3930 Lerner, Al. u.p.: Melo-Art Music, 1957. Words adapted by Vic Corpora. Recording: Columbia 4-41106.

3931 Leslie, Henry. London: J.B. Cramer, n.d.; Boston: O. Ditson, n.d. Song: v, pf; Howard Raymond, arr. New York: Frank Tousey's Music Publishing, 1891. Song: v, pf; In coll. TuJS; In *Bayley and Ferguson's Standard Vocal Albums: Tenor Songs*, pp. 36-39 [PoMM p. 399.]

3932 Levey, William C. "Many a Year Ago." London: Chappell, 1866. Song: v, pf.

3933 Marston, George W. Boston: A.P. Schmidt, 1891. Song: T and Bar v edns, pf.

3934 McQuown, W.R. Louisville, Ky.: D.P. Faulds, 1869. Song and Chorus, pf.

3935 Meadows, W. Cited in DCD. Song.

3936 Mount, Julian. "Many and Many a Year Ago." London: Donajowski, 1878.

3937 Pares, A.M. London: Chappell, 1860. Song: v, pf.

3938 Rinker, Alton. In *American Poets' Suite*. Delaware Water Gap, Pa.: Shawnee, 1968. Chorus: SATB, pf. Arr. by Hawley Ades.

3939 Roberton, Hugh S. London: J. Curwen, 1914. Arr. for male or SATB chorus, a cap.

3940 Roberts, Lance and Carl Friend. "Annabelle Lee." u.p.: Chapultapec Music, 1964. Words adapted.

3941 Rommé, Donald R. New York: Schirmer, 1947. Chorus: TTBB, T and Bar soli, a cap.

3942 Schiffman, Byron. Paris: Psyche, 1953. Song: T, orch. Words in Eng. and Fr., trans. by Mallarmé.

3943 Shaw, Martin. London: J.B. Cramer, 1921. Song: v, pf.

3944 Somervell, Arthur. "A Kingdom by the Sea." London: Boosey, 1901. Song: v, pf.

3945 Sousa, John P. Philadelphia: Presser, 1931. Song: med. v, pf.

3946 Strong, Templeton. Geneva: Editions Henn, 1924. Song.

3947 Van der Water, Beardsley. New York: G. Schirmer, 1891. Part Song.

3948 Vogrich, Max. New York: G. Schirmer, 1890. Duet: SM, pf.

3948a Walthew, Richard. In *Twenty Modern English Songs*. London: Boosey, 1923. [PoMM p. 403.]

3948b Weiss, W.H. "It Was Many & Many a Year Ago." London: Cramer; Lamborn, Cock, Addison; Hutchings & Romer, [BAL n.d., ca. 1863–1872].

The Bells. *Collected Works of Edgar Allan Poe* [Vol. 1. Poems] (1969).

3949 Ahrold, Frank. Glen Rock, N.J.: J. Fischer, 1967. Setting for SATB.

3950 Anderton, Thomas. "The Sleighbells." London: Hutchings and Roemer, 187–?. Song: trio of treble voices, pf.

3951 Balfe, Michael W. London: Joseph Williams, [EMEP 1865?]. Song: v, pf. Setting of stanza 1.

3952 Diemer, Emma L. New York: Boosey & Hawkes, 1961. Chorus: SATB, pf 4 hands.

3953 Duggan, J.F. "The Voices of the Bells." London: Houlston-Stoneman, 1850. Song. PoMM notes, "Probably suggested by "The Bells," with many phrases and almost all concepts derived from Poe's poem."

3954 Emeléus, John. London: Alfred Lengnick, 1962. Unison song.

3955 Ezechiels, D. New York: R.A. Saalfield, 1888. Cantata. Setting of first 2 verses.

3956 Fitzwilliam, Edward F. "Hear the Sledges with the Bells" in *Four Dramatic Songs*. London: d'Almaine, u.d. Setting of stanza 1.

3957 Foote, Arthur. In coll. TL, TLM. Setting for SATB; Boston: C.C. Birchard, 1929. Chorus: SATB, pf.

3958 Fox, George. London: Chappell, 1876. Cantata: SATB, orch.

3959 Gilchrist, W.W. New York: G. Schirmer, 1913. Chorus: SSAA, pf.

3960 Habash, John. New York: Ashwyn Music, 1963. Chorus: SATB. Words adapted by Edna Lewis.

3961 Harris, Cuthbert. "Silver Sleigh Bells." Boston: A.P. Schmidt, 1922. Arr. for SSA trio or SATB.

3962 Hawley, Stanley. London: Bosworth, 1894. Recit. with pf.

3963 Holbrooke, Josef. "The Bells (Die Glocken)" op. 50a. Leipzig: Breitkopf & Härtel, 1906. Dramatic poem for chorus and grand orch. Words in Eng. and Ger., trans. by Alice Klengel.

3964 Kebalin, Fedor. u.t. in *Canticle of Seasons*. Ann Arbor: Univ. Microfilms (doct. diss. series), 1966.

3965 Kinscella, Hazel G. Boston: Boston Music, 1938. Chorus: SSA, pf.

3966 Kjerulf, H. "The Bells" in coll. Mu 5, MuC 5.

3967 Lahee, Henry. "The Bells" op. 128 no. 1. London: Ascherberg, Hopwood & Crew, 1937. Arr. for SSA, pf by Purcell J. Mansfield.

3968 Lancelott, F. London: B. Williams, 1957. Cantata.

3969 Leoni, Franco. London: Chappell, 1908. Vocal scene for Bar or C, orch.

3970 Lorenz, Ellen J. Dayton, Ohio: Lorenz Music, 1948. Chorus: SA, pf. Music adapted from Rachmaninoff's C sharp minor prelude.
    Dayton: Lorenz Publishing, 1941. Chorus: SATB, pf.
    Dayton: Lorenz Publishing, 1942. Chorus: SSA, pf.
    Dayton: Lorenz Publishing, 1943. Chorus: SAB, pf.

3971 Lucas, Clarence. "The Bells" op. 56. New York: Boosey, 1913. Madrigal: SATB, a cap.

3971a Lucas, Clarence. "Tolling Bells." London: Ascherberg, Hopwood & Crew, 1936. Arr. for SATB or TTBB, pf, from Rachmaninoff's C sharp minor *Prelude*.

3972 Montani, Nicola A. New York: H.W. Gray, 1917. Cantata: SSA chorus, S and A soli, pf or orch (R).

3973 Ochs, Phil. New York: Appleseed Music, 1967. Chorus: SATB, pf. Arr. by Herbert Haufrecht.

3974 Peloquin, C. Alexander. New York: Boosey & Hawkes, 1964. Chorus: mixed voices, 2 pf, 2 db, perc.

3975 Petersilea, Franz. Boston: G.P. Reed, [BAL n.d., 1851].

3976 Plumpton, Alfred. London: Charles Jefferys, 1867.

3977 Rachmaninoff, Sergei. "The Bells" op. 35. Moscow-Leipzig: A. Guthiel, 1920 (agent, Galaxy). Choral Symphony: chorus, STBar soli, orch. Words in Ger., trans. by Berthold Feiwel; Russian, trans. by Konstantin Balmont; and Eng., trans. by Fanny S. Copeland. Recording: Melodiya/ Angel SR 40114 (1969).

3978 Raphling, Sam. New York: Beekman, 1958. Chorus: 6-pt. mixed voices, a cap.

3979 Roberton, Hugh S. "Hear the Sledges with the Bells." London: J. Curwen, 1919. Part Song: SSA, a cap. Setting of stanza 1.
    "The Sledge Bells." London: J. Curwen, 1909. Part Song: SATB, a cap.
    "Hear the Tolling of the Bells." London: J. Curwen, 1909. Chorus: SATB, a cap. Setting of last stanza.

3980 Sampson, Godfrey. London: Novello, 1946.

3981 Siegel, Arsene. "The Iron Bells." Chicago: Pallma Music, 1945. Song: med. v, pf.

3982 Stone, David. "Winter (The Bells)" in *Five Songs for Female Voices and Piano*. London: Boosey, 1980. Setting for SSA.

3983 Sykes, Harold H. London: Elkin, u.d. 2-pt. canon for treble voices.

3984 Wald, George. New York: Galaxy Music, 1942. Chorus: SATB, a cap.

3985 White, Michael. "The Silver Bells." London: Chappell, 1961. Chorus: mixed voices, a cap.

3986 Wilkinson, Philip. London: E. Arnold, 1954. 2-pt. song.

3987 Wilson, Harry R. Dayton, Ohio: Heritage Music, 1968.

Bridal Ballad. *The Raven and Other Poems* (1845).

> 3988 Skilton, Charles S. New York: Herbert Wilber Greene, 1894. Song: S, pf.

The City in the Sea. *The Raven and Other Poems* (1845).

> 3989 Holbrooke, Josef. In *Homage to E.A. Poe*. London: J. & W. Chester, 1908. Dramatic choral symphony: chorus, 4 soli, orch.

The Conquerer Worm. *The Raven and Other Poems* (1845).

> 3990 Habash, John. New York: Orpheus Music, 1964.

A Dream. *Tamerlane and Other Poems* (1827).

> 3991 Habash, John. New York: Orpheus Music, 1964.

> 3992 Séverac, Déodat de. "Un Rêve (A Dream)." Paris: Rouart, Lerolle & Cie, 1924. Song: v, pf. Words in Eng. and Fr. (trans. by Mallarmé; Eng. text adapted from Mallarmé by Edward Agate).

> 3993 Van Höveln-Carpé. "In Visions" op. 57c. Berlin: Breitkopf & Härtel, 1922. Song: v, pf.

Dream-Land. *The Raven and Other Poems* (1845).

> 3994 Mulder, Herman. "Dreamland." Amsterdam: Donemus, 1971. Song: Bar or C, pf or orch.

> 3995 Van Höveln-Carpé. "Dream-Land" op. 57a. Berlin: Breitkopf & Härtel, 1922. Song: v, pf.

A Dream within a Dream. *Collected Works of Edgar Allan Poe* [Vol. 1. Poems] (1969).

> 3996 Cross, Henry. New York: G. Schirmer, 1936. Chorus: SSAATTBB, a cap.

> 3997 Debusman, Emil. In *Three Songs*. New York: American Music Edition, u.d.

> 3998 Loeffler, Charles M. In *Four Poems Set to Music for Voice and Piano* op. 15 no. 2. New York: G. Schirmer, 1906.

> 3999 McKay, Neil. New York: Music 70, 1976. Chorus: SATB, a cap.

> 4000 Mount, Julian. London: W. Marshall, 1878.

> 4001 Pontet, Henry. London: Ascherberg, Hopwood & Crew, u.d. Song: v, pf; New York: O. Ditson, [BAL n.d., not before 1877].

> 4002 Sonneck, Oscar G. In *Four Poems by Edgar Allan Poe* op. 16 no. 4. New York: G. Schirmer, 1917. Song: Bar, pf.

4003 Torrance, G.W. London: Novello, 1904. Setting for SATB.

4004 Van Höveln-Carpé. "Grains of the Golden Sand" op. 54a. Berlin: Breitkopf & Härtel, 1922. Song: v, pf. Setting of stanza 2.

Eldorado. *Works* (1850).

4005 Albritton, Sherodd. u.p.: A. Broude, 1953. Chorus: SA, pf.

4006 Allen, Creighton. New York: G. Schirmer, 1935. Song: low or med. v, pf.

4007 Bairstow, Edward. London: Oxford Univ. Press, 1937. Setting for TTB.

4008 Beachcroft, R.O. London: Oxford Univ. Press, 1925. Setting for unison chorus, pf.

4009 Beeson, Jack. In *American Artsong Anthology*. Vol. 1. New York: Galaxy, 1982. Song.

4010 Bruenner, Leopold. "Eldorado" op. 1 no. 5. Cincinnati: J. Church, 1915. Song: v, pf.

4011 Davies, Harvey. Boston: R.D. Row, 1941. Chorus: TTBB, pf.

4012 De Pue, Wallace E. In coll. EFL. Song: v, pf.

4013 Dorward, David. London: Galliard, 1966. Unison song.

4014 Ezerman, E.M.C. Boston: C.W. Thompson, 1904. Song.

4015 Fisher, Truman. "El Dorado." New York: G. Schirmer, 1969. Chorus: 3-pt. female voices, pf.

4016 Geldart, Ernest, Rev. London: Novello, 1884. Harmonized by C.W. Pearce.

4017 Griffis, Elliot. New York: Composers Press, 1937. Song: med. v, pf.

4018 Habash, John. New York: Orpheus Music, 1964.

4019 Haskin, Nancy A. u.p.: p.p., 1937 [PoMM p. 398].

4020 Huhn, Bruno. Boston: A.P. Schmidt, 1914. Song: high, med., and low v edns, pf.

4021 Kelley, Edgar S. "Eldorado" op. 8 no. 1. Newton Center, Mass.: Wa-Wan Press, 1901; New York: G. Schirmer, 1912. Song: v, pf. In coll. LWP, NAA.

4022 Lara, Isidore de. London: B. Nocetta, 1892. Song.

4023 Lucas, Clarence. "Eldorado" op. 45 no. 5 in *Five Songs for Medium Voice*. Cincinnati: J. Church, 1904. Song: med. v, pf.

4024 Mallinson, J. Albert. Copenhagen: Wilhelm Hansen, 1901; London: T. Harris, 1906. Song. Words in Eng. and Ger; In *Lieder, Second Series*. London: T. Harris, 1906, 1907.

4025 Marston, George W. In *Three Songs*. Cincinnati: J. Church, 1896. Song: Bar or B, pf.

4026 Nicholls, Frederick. London: Joseph Williams, 1938. Song: high and low v edns, pf.

4027 Oberndorfer, Alfred A. In *Songs* op. 1 no. 3. Chicago: C.F. Summy, 1911. Song.

4028 Parish, F. Wilson. London: Novello, 1918. Part Song: female voices, pf.

4029 Phelps, Ellsworth S. Brooklyn: J.H. Demonet, 1892. Song: B, pf.

4030 Price, Addison. In *Two Songs*. London: J.B. Cramer, 1921. Song: v, pf.

4031 Protheroe, Daniel. Cincinnati: Willis Music, 1929. Chorus: TTBB, pf.

4032 Rinker, Alton. In *American Poets' Suite*. Delaware Water Gap, Pa.: Shawnee, 1968. Chorus: SATB, pf. Arr. by Hawley Ades.

4033 Rowse, Albert. Brooklyn: F.H. Chandler, 1877. Song: v, pf.

4034 Royle, T.P. London: Enoch and Sons, 1889.

4035 Rôze, Raymond. London: Keith, Prowse, 1903. Song: v, pf.

4036 Schaaf, Edward O. Newark, N.J.: p.p., 1900. Song: Bar, pf.

4037 Shapleigh, Bertram. London: Edwin Ashdown, 1900; In *Fünf Lieder* op. 41 no. 4. Leipzig: Breitkopf & Härtel, 1901. Song: v, pf. Words in Eng. and Ger., trans. by F.H. Schneider.

4038 Skilton, Charles S. New York: Herbert Wilber Greene, 1894. Song: v, pf.

4039 Solis, B.R. u.p.: u.p., 1927.

4040 Sonneck, Oscar G. In *Four Poems by Edgar Allan Poe* op. 16 no. 3. New York: G. Schirmer, 1917. Song: Bar, pf.

4041 Sydenham, Edwin A. London: Novello, 1869. Song: v, pf.

4042 Trubitt, Allen. Bryn Mawr, Pa.: Presser, 1980. Chorus: SATB, gtr.

4042a Ursula. London: Cramer, 1872. Cited in BAL 16223.

4043 Van Höveln-Carpé. "Eldorado" op. 57b. Berlin: Breitkopf & Härtel, 1922. Song: v, pf.

4044 Walthew, Richard. London: Boosey, 1896. Song: v, pf. In coll. FMES.

Eulalie. *The Raven and Other Poems* (1845).

4045 Habash, John. New York: Orpheus Music, 1964.

4046 Schaaf, E.O. In *German and English Poems in Song*, vol. 2 op. 3. 1902.

Evening Star. *Tamerlane and Other Poems* (1827).

> 4047 Habash, John. New York: Orpheus Music, 1964.

> 4048 Royce, Edward. New York: Composers Music Corp., C. Fischer, 1922. Song: v, pf.

The Haunted Palace. *The Raven and Other Poems* (1845).

> 4049 Bälan, Joan. "Elegie II" op. 70. Paris: Edition "Pro Musica," 1939. Song: S or T, pf.

> 4050 Habash, John. New York: Orpheus Music, 1964.

> 4051 Holbrooke, Josef. In *Homage to E.A. Poe* op. 48 no. 1. London: J. & W. Chester, 1908. Dramatic choral symphony: chorus, 4 soli, orch.

Hymn ["At morn—at noon—at twilight dim"]. *Collected Works of Edgar Allan Poe* [Vol. 1. Poems] (1969).

> 4052 Carrington, John. "Prayer." New York: G. Ricordi, 1912. Song: v, pf.

> 4053 Chadbourne, Grace. "Hymn for Solo Voice: At Morn, at Noon, at Twilight Dim." Cincinnati: J. Church, 1907.

> 4054 Cowles, Walter R. New York: G. Schirmer, 1928. Part Song: TTBB, a cap.

> 4055 Eisler, Paul. "Hymn to the Virgin." New York: G. Schirmer, 1920. Song: v, pf; New York: G. Schirmer, 1920. Chorus: SATB, org.

> 4056 Gaul, Harvey. "Poe's Fordham Prayer." New York: Galaxy, 1930. Chorus: TTBB, a cap.

> 4057 Holbrooke, Josef. In *Homage to E.A. Poe* op. 48 no 2. London: J. & W. Chester, 1908. Dramatic choral symphony: chorus, 4 soli, orch.

> 4058 Shapleigh, Bertram. "Im Dämmerlicht, wenn Tag erglüht" in *Fünf Lieder* op. 41 no. 3. Leipzig: Breitkopf & Härtel, 1901. Song: v, pf. Words in Eng. and Ger., trans. by F.H. Schneider.

Imitation. *Tamerlane and Other Poems* (1827).

> 4059 Debusman, Emil. In *Three Songs*. New York: American Music Edition, u.d.

Israfel. *Poems* (1831).

> 4060 Bernstein, Leonard. In *Songfest*. New York: Boosey & Hawkes, 1977. Cycle: SAMTBArB, orch.

> 4061 Huhn, Bruno. Boston: A.P. Schmidt, 1913. Song: high, med., and low v edns, pf.

4062 Kelley, Edgar S. "Israfel" op. 8 no. 2. Newton Center Mass.: Wa-Wan Press, 1901. Song: high v, pf; also arr. for female chorus and orch. In coll. LWP.

4063 King, Oliver. New York: G. Schirmer, [EMEP 188–?]. Song: v, pf.
  In *Musical Times* (Feb. 1, 1885), p. 113.
  Boston: O. Ditson, ca. 1891. Song: high and med. v edns, pf.
  London: Boosey, 1909.
  Daniel Protheroe, arr. Chicago: Gamble-Hinged, 1917.
  George LeRoy Lindsay, arr. New York: Mills Music, 1943. Chorus: SATB.
  In coll. AB 2.

4064 Marston, George W. Boston: A.P. Schmidt, 1896.

4065 Royce, Edward. New York: Composers Music Corp., C. Fischer, 1922. Song: v, pf.

Lenore. *Collected Works of Edgar Allan Poe* [Vol. 1. Poems] (1969).

4066 Hawley, Stanley. London: Robert Cocks, 1898. Recit. with pf.

4067 Henderson. In *Two Songs for Medium Voice*. London: Composer's and Author's Press, 1901. Song: med. v, pf [PoMM p. 398].

4068 "Lenore." London: Hopwood & Crew, 1891. Presumably this poem, but could possibly be "The Raven."

4069 Skilton, Charles S. Philadelphia: Wm. H. Boner, 1895. Cantata: chorus, qrt, Bar solo, orch.

The Raven. *The Raven and Other Poems* (1845).

4070 Barker, George. St. Louis: J.L. Peters, 1862. Recititative chant for SATB.

4071 Beman, Samuel. "The Raven" in *The Nightingale* or *The Jenny Lind Songster* vol. 1 no. 103. New York: Stringer and Townsend, 1850.

4072 Bergh, Arthur. "The Raven" op. 20. Newton Center, Mass.: Wa-Wan Press, 1910; Boston: O. Ditson, 1911. Melodrama: narr. and pf or orch(R).

4073 Dubensky, Arcady. New York: G. Ricordi, 1933. Recit. with orch.

4074 Habash, John. New York: Ashwyn Music, 1963. Chorus: SATB. Words adapted by Edna Lewis.

4075 Hawley, Stanley. London: Bosworth, 1894. Recit. with pf.

4076 Heinrich, Max. Cincinnati: J. Church, 1905. Recit. with pf. Words in Eng. and Ger.

4077 Hemberger, Theodor. "Lenore" op. 35 no. 1. Cincinnati: J. Church, 1910. Song: high and low v edns, pf. Setting of stanza 5.

4078 Levey, William C. London: Duff & Stewart, n.d. Song.

4079 Rapoport, Eda. "The Raven" op. 15. New York: Maxwell Weaner, 1939. Song: S, str qrt and db or str orch.

4080 "The Raven" in coll. LBR.

4081 Scattergood, D. u.p.: p.p., 1865. 4-pt. chant [EMEP p. 71].

4082 Shapleigh, Bertram. "The Raven" op. 50. Leipzig: Breitkopf & Härtel, 1906. Cantata: chorus, orch.

4083 Southey, Phimon L. "Lenore's Answer: Spirit Song." New York: [T.B. Harms?], 1923.

4084 Sternberg, Erich-Walter. Mainz: Schott, 1953. Song: Bar, orch.

4085 Webster, Paul F. and Harry Revel. "Quoth the Raven" from the Universal Picture *Goat Catchers*. New York: Leeds, 1944. Words adapted humorously [PoMM].

Romance. *The Raven and Other Poems* (1845).

4086 Hoskins, William. "Romance, Who Loves to Nod and Sing." MS, 1964, avail. ACA. Song: M, vla, pf.

The Sleeper. *The Raven and Other Poems* (1845).

4087 Kelley, Edgar S. In *Two Moods of Nature* op. 21 no. 1. Boston: C.C. Birchard, 1904. Chorus: mixed voices, pf. In coll. To.

Song ["I saw thee on thy bridal day"]. *The Raven and Other Poems* (1845).

4088 Habash, John. "I Saw Thee on Thy Bridal Day." New York: Orpheus Music, 1964.

4089 Smith, Leo. "I Saw Thee on Thy Bridal Day" in *Four Songs*. New York: G. Schirmer, 1914. Song: v, pf.

Sonnet—Silence. *The Raven and Other Poems* (1845).

4090 Bon, Willem F. "Silence." Amsterdam: Donemus, 1978. Song: M, wind qnt, pf.

Spirits of the Dead. *Al Aaraaf, Tamerlane, and Minor Poems* (1827).

4091 Debusman, Emil. In *Three Songs*. New York: American Music Edition, u.d.

4092 Gatwood, Dwight. New York: Tetra Music, 1977. Chorus: TTBB, tape.

The Tell-Tale Heart. *Collected Works of Edgar Allan Poe* [Vol. 2. Tales and Sketches] (1978).

4093 Foulds, John. "The Tell-Tale Heart" op. 36. London: W. Paxton, 1924. Dramatic Monologue with music.

To F—— ["Beloved! amid the earnest woes"]. *The Raven and Other Poems* (1845).

4094 Bergen, Alfred H. "Beloved." Chicago: Gamble Hinged, 1911. Song: v, pf.

4095 Royce, Edward. "Solace." New York: Composers Music Corp., C. Fischer, 1922. Song: v, pf.

4096 Shapleigh, Bertram. "Mein Lebenspfal ist rauh und wüst" in *Fünf Lieder* op. 41 no. 2. Leipzig: Breitkopf & Härtel, 1901. Song: v, pf. Words in Eng. and Ger., trans. by F.H. Schneider.

To F——s. S. O——d. *The Raven and Other Poems* (1845).

4097 Henderson. "Thou Wouldst Be Loved" in *Two Songs for Medium Voice*. London: Composer's and Author's Press, 1901. Song: med. v, pf [PoMM p. 398].

4098 Sonneck, Oscar G. "Thou Wouldst Be Loved?" in *Four Poems by Edgar Allan Poe* op. 16 no. 2. New York: G. Schirmer, 1917. Song: Bar, pf.

To Helen ["Helen, thy beauty is to me"]. *The Raven and Other Poems* (1845).

4099 Behr, Herman. "Helen." New York: H. Behr, 1933. Song: high v, pf.

4100 Dunn, James P. New York: J. Fischer, 1916. Song: high and low v edns, pf.

4101 Edmunds, John. "Helen" in coll. EH. Song: Bar, pf.

4102 Forsyth, Cecil. London: Novello, 1927. Part Song: TTBB, a cap.

4103 Griffis, Elliot. In *Songs from Poe*. New York: The Composers Press, 1946. Song: med. v, pf.

4104 Habash, John. New York: Orpheus Music, 1964.

4105 Kaufer, Joseph. In *Dover Beach and Other Songs*. Waukegan, Ill.: Lyric-Art, 1951. Song.

4106 Little, Arthur R. "Helen" in coll. LWP. Song: v, pf.

4107 Loeffler, Charles M. In *Four Poems Set to Music for Voice and Piano* op. 15 no. 3. New York: G. Schirmer, 1906. Song: v, pf.

4108 Mourant, Walter. MS, u.d., avail. ACA. Song: med. v, pf.

4109 Piggott, Harry E. London: Oxford Univ. Press, 1953. 2 pt. song with pf.

4110 Shapleigh, Bertram. "Helen, Thy Beauty Is to Me," "Helen, deiner Schönheit macht" in *Fünf Lieder* op. 41 no. 1. Leipzig: Breitkopf & Härtel, 1901. Song: v, pf. Words in Eng. and Ger., trans. by F.H. Schneider.

4111 Smith, Leo. In *Four Songs.* New York: G. Schirmer, 1914. Song: v, pf.

4112 Smith, Warren S. New York: C. Fischer, 1917. Song: high, med., and low v edns, pf.

4113 Sonneck, Oscar G. In *Four Poems by Edgar Allan Poe* op. 16 no. 1. New York: G. Schirmer, 1917. Song: Bar, pf.

4114 Taylor, Cyril V. London: Oxford Univ. Press, 1930. Song: med. v, pf.

4115 Van Höveln-Carpé. "Thy Naiad Airs" op. 54b. Berlin: Breitkopf & Härtel, 1922. Song: v, pf.

To One in Paradise. *The Raven and Other Poems* (1845).

4116 Garratt, Percival. London: Phillips & Page, 1904; In *Three Songs* op. 58 no. 2. London: Murdoch, Murdoch, n.d.

4117 Marston, George W. Portland, Maine: Ira C. Stockbridge, 1976. Song.

4118 Roberts, Lee S. New York: G. Schirmer, 1920. Song: high or med. v, pf.

4119 Sullivan, Arthur. London: Novello, 1904. Song: T, pf.

To the River ———. *The Raven and Other Poems* (1845).

4120 Allen, Creighton. New York: G. Schirmer, 1928. Song: v, pf.

4121 Griffis, Elliot. New York: Composers Press, 1937. Song: med. v, pf.

4122 Shapleigh, Bertram. "An den Fluss" in *Fünf Lieder* op. 41 no. 5. Leipzig: Breitkopf & Härtel, 1901. Song: v, pf. Words in Eng. and Ger., trans. by F.H. Schneider.

To Zante. *The Raven and Other Poems* (1845).

4123 Holbrooke, Joseph. In *Homage to E.A. Poe.* London: J. & W. Chester, 1908. Dramatic choral symphony: chorus, 4 soli, orch.

Miscellaneous

4124 Allen, Creighton. "So When in Tears." New York: Merl L. Reid, 1948. Song: v, pf. Text not by Poe [PoMM p. 394].

4125 Allen, Creighton. "Like Music Heard in Dreams" in *Two Songs.* New York: G. Schirmer, 1929. Song: high or med. v, pf. Text not by Poe [EMEP p. 30].

4126 Karnovitch, G. *Four Romances Based on Verses of Poe.* Moscow: State Music Publishing House, 1924.

4127 London, Edwin. "Poebells (a Ritual Action)." New York: C.F. Peters, u.d. Setting for v, narr., perc; or theater or dramatic music with the above; or 2 voices, narr., perc.

4128 Mulder, Ernest W. "Hymn" in *Vijf geestelijke motetten.* Amsterdam: Donemus, 1944, 1945. Song: S, instrs.

KATHERINE ANNE PORTER (1890–1980)

Anniversary in a Country Cemetery. *The Collected Essays and Occasional Writings of Katherine Anne Porter* (1970).

4129 Diamond, David. In *Three Songs for Voice and Piano.* New York: Arrow Music, 1942. Song: med. v, pf.

EZRA POUND (1885–1972)

Gallup, Donald. *Ezra Pound: A Bibliography.* Charlottesville, Va.: University Press of Virginia, 1983, pp. 437–43 [GEP].

Alba ["As cool as the pale wet leaves"]. *Lustra* (1916).

4130 Dalby, Martin. In *Four Miniature Songs from Ezra Pound.* London: Alfred Lengnick, 1971. Chorus: SATB, a cap.

Aria. *Canzoni* (1911).

4131 Rummel, Walter M. In *Three Songs of Ezra Pound.* London: Augener, 1911. Song: v, pf or instrs.

Au Bal Masqué [GEP notes that the text is printed here for the first time].

4132 Rummel, Walter M. In *Three Songs of Ezra Pound.* London: Augener, 1911. Song: v, pf or instrs.

Canto XXX. *A Draft of XXX Cantos* (1930).

4133 Binkerd, Gordon. "Compleynt, Compleynt." New York: Boosey & Hawkes, 1969. Chorus: SATB, a cap.

Canto XXXIX. *Eleven New Cantos XXXI-XLI* (1934).

4134 Zender, Hans. "Canto II." Berlin: Bote & Bock, 1968. Chorus: triple mixed choir, S solo, orch.

Canto LXXXI. *The Pisan Cantos* (1948).

4135 Avshalomov, Jacob. n.t. in *Threnos*. Boston: E.C. Schirmer, 1959. Chorus: SATB, a cap.

The Classical Anthology Defined by Confucius (1954).

4136 Cobb, Donald. "Heaven Conserve Thy Course in Quietness." New York: Galaxy, 1973. Chorus: SSAA, pf or vla. Text from part 6 of Book 1., Deer Sing, from part 2 "Elegentiae, or Smaller Odes."

4137 Kasemets, Udo. "Octagonal Octet and/or Ode." Don Mills, Ont.: BMI Canada, 1968. Setting for 8 performers using any aural/ visual/ choreographic media (chance music). ["A calceolaria (time/ space) variation based on I Ching trigrams and hexagrams and (optional) words extracted from Pound's Confucian Odes"].

4138 Shifrin, Seymour. "The Odes of Shang." New York: C.F. Peters, u.d. Chorus: mixed voices, pf, perc. Recording: New World Records NW 219 (1977). Text from Book 3 of part 4, "The Odes of Shang," setting of I. "NA" II. "Kyrie Eleison/ father of all our line/ Kyrie Eleison."

4139 Wilding-White, Raymond. *Paraphernalia: A Regalia of Madrigalia from Ezra Pound*. Divertimento: SATB, ob, cl, tpt, vn, harpsichord. Text from Book 1 of part 1, "Chou and the South," setting of secs. 1, 2, 3, 4, 5, 6, 8, 11. Recording: Composers Recordings, CRI SD 182 (1964).

Coitus. *Lustra* (1916).

4140 Lerdahl, Fred. "Eros." Hillsdale, N.Y.: Mobart, 1978. Song: M, cham ens. Recording: Composers Recordings, CRI SD 378 (1978).

Commission. *Lustra* (1916).

4141 Heider, Werner. Frankfurt: H. Litolff's Verlag, 1976. Song: Bar, cham orch.

Dance Figure. *Lustra* (1916).

4142 Gerber, Steven R. In *Doria: Three Poems of Ezra Pound.* MS, u.d., avail. ACA. Song: S, pf.

Doria. *Ripostes* (1912).

4143 Ashforth, Alden. In *Aspects of Love.* Song: T, pf. Recording: Orion, ORS 78335 (1979).

4144 Gerber, Steven R. u.t. in *Doria: Three Poems of Ezra Pound.* MS, u.d., avail. ACA. Song: S, pf.

4145 Nordheim, Arne. Copenhagen: W. Hansen, 1977. Song: T, orch.

Epitaphs. *Lustra* (1916).

4146 Avshalomov, Jacob. "Fu-Yi." MS, 1956, avail. ACA. Song: med. v, pf.

4147 Binkerd, Gordon. "Epitaphs." New York: Boosey & Hawkes, 1970. Chorus: SATB, a cap.

Fan-piece, for Her Imperial Lord. *Lustra* (1916).

4148 Dalby, Martin. "Fan-Piece" in *Four Miniature Songs from Ezra Pound.* London: Alfred Lengnick, 1971. Chorus: SATB, a cap.

The Garret. *Lustra* (1916).

4149 Holbrooke, Josef. "The Garret" op. 77 no. 2. London: J. Curwen, 1922. Song: med. v, pf; ob or vla obl.

Image from D'Orleans. *Lustra* (1916).

4150 MacMahon, Desmond. "Spring on Horseback." London: J. Curwen, 1937. Song: unison voices, pf.

An Immorality. *Ripostes* (1912).

4151 Copland, Aaron. Boston: E.C. Schirmer, 1926. Chorus: SSA, S solo, pf.

4152 Hoiby, Lee. New York: G., Schirmer, 1956. Song: high v, pf. In coll. CAST.

4153 Koch, John. New York: General, 1965. Song: v, pf.

4154 Weber, Ben. In *Four Songs* op. 40. In *New Music* 27(2) (1954). Song: S or T, vc.

In a Station of the Metro. *Lustra* (1916).

4155 Dalby, Martin. "The Faces" in *Four Miniature Songs from Ezra Pound.* London: Alfred Lengnick, 1971. Chorus: SATB, a cap.

"Ione, Dead the Long Year." *Lustra* (1916).

   4156 Strickland, William. New York: Galaxy, 1961. Song: med. v, pf.

Ladies. *Lustra* (1916).

   4157 Diamond, David. "Four Ladies." New York: Southern Music Publishing, 1966. Song: high v, pf.

Lament of the Frontier Guard. *Cathay* (1915).

   4158 Bantock, Granville. London: Boosey, 1923. Chorus: TTBB, a cap.

Madrigale. *Canzoni* (1911).

   4159 Rummel, Walter M. In *Three Songs of Ezra Pound*. London: Augener, 1911. Song: v, pf or instrs.

Praise of Ysolt. *Personae* (1909).

   4159a Carroll, J. Robert. "In Vain" in *Songs of the Heart*. New York: G. Schirmer, 1968. Chorus: SSA.

The Return. *Ripostes* (1912).

   4160 Rummel, Walter M. London: Augener, 1913. Song: v, pf.

The River-Merchant's Wife: A Letter. *Cathay* (1915).

   4160a Willingham, Lawrence. "The River Merchant's Wife" op. 20. MS, 1980, avail. ACA. Setting for S and ensemble.

Salutation. *Lustra* (1916).

   4161 Holbrooke, Josef. "Salutation" op. 77 no. 1. London: J. Curwen, 1922. Song: med. v, pf; ob or vla obl.

Song ["Love thou thy dreams . . ."]. *A Lume Spento* (1908).

   4162 Golub, Peter. "Love Thou Thy Dreams" in *3 Songs*. MS, 1977, avail. ACA. Song: S, fl, hp.

Song of the Bowmen of Shu. *Cathay* (1915).

   4163 Bantock, Granville. London: Boosey, 1923. Chorus: TTBB, a cap.

South-Folk in Cold Country. *Cathay* (1915).

   4164 Bantock, Granville. London: Boosey, 1923. Chorus: TTBB, a cap.

Tame Cat. *Lustra* (1916).

4165 Holbrooke, Josef. "Tame Cat" op. 77 no. 5. London: W. Paxton, 1923. Song: med. v, pf; cl obl.

4166 Koch, John. New York: General, 1965. Song: med. v, pf.

The Tea Shop. *Lustra* (1916).

4167 Holbrooke, Josef. "The Tea-Shop Girl" op. 77 no. 4. London: W. Paxton, 1923. Song: v, pf; cl obl.

4168 Koch, John. New York: General, 1965. Song: med. v, pf.

Threnos. *A Lume Spento* (1908).

4169 Avshalomov, Jacob. n.t. in *Threnos*. Boston: E.C. Schirmer, 1959. Chorus: SATB, a cap.

Ts'ai Chi'h. *Lustra* (1916).

4170 Dalby, Martin. In *Four Miniature Songs from Ezra Pound*. London: Alfred Lengnick, 1971. Chorus: SATB, a cap.

A Virginal. *Ripostes* (1912).

4171 Gerber, Steven R. In *Doria: Three Poems of Ezra Pound*. MS, u.d., avail. ACA. Song: S, pf.

Miscellaneous

4172 Berio, Luciano. *Laborinthus II*. Score, Material and tape on rental. Recording: RCA, LSC 3267 (U.S.), SB 6848 (Eng.).

4172a Serly, Tibor. "The Monstrous Flea." New York: Leeds Music, 1952. Song: low v, pf. Poetic translation by Pound from the Hungarian [GEP E4ka].

FREDERIC PROKOSCH (B. 1908)

"Close my darling both your eyes" [No. 30, "Nocturne"]. *The Carnival* (1938).

4173 Barber, Samuel. "Nocturne" in *Four Songs for Voice and Piano* op. 13 no. 4. New York: G. Schirmer, 1941. Song: low or med. and high v edns, pf.

"Pears from the boughs hung golden" [No. 1, "Evening"]. *The Carnival* (1938).

> 4174 Duke, John. "Evening." New York: C. Fischer, 1954. Song: med. v, pf.

JOHN CROWE RANSOM (1888–1974)

Parting, without a Sequel. *Two Gentlemen in Bonds* (1927).

> 4175 Mechem, Kirke. In *Goodbye, Farewell, and Adieu* op. 33 no. 2. New York: C. Fischer, 1979. Song: med. v, pf.

KENNETH REXROTH (1905–1982)

Mother Goose. *In Defense of the Earth* (1956).

> 4176 Hoffman, Allen. "Do Not Pick My Rosemary," "A Gold & Silver Bird," "Once There Was a Nightingale," "Last Night I Saw in the Moon" in *Madrigals*. New York: C.F. Peters, u.d. Chorus: SATB, a cap.

Miscellaneous

> 4176a Johnson, Gordon. "Mist," "In the Spring," "Pearls," "White Egret," "Recalled," "A Doe," "Fondly" in *Seven Japanese Tanka*. New York: Edward B. Marks, u.d. Chorus: SATB, a cap.

> 4176b Johnson, Gordon. "The World," "Tears," "You" in *Three Japanese Songs*. New York: Edward B. Marks, u.d. Chorus: SATB, M solo, pf.

> 4177 Schickele, Peter. "Poems from the Japanese" in *Baptism: A Journey through Our Time*. Cycle. Recording: Vanguard, USD 79275 (1968).

ADRIENNE RICH (B. 1929)

Holiday. *The Diamond Cutters* (1955).

4178 Roy, Klaus G. "Holiday" op. 25. In coll. CASH. Song: high v, pf.

Night-Pieces: for a Child [1. The Crib]. *Necessities of Life* (1966).

4179 Vercoe, Elizabeth. "For a Child: 'The Crib' " in *Herstory I.* MS, u.d., avail. ACA. Cycle: S, vib, pf.

Poem ["I haven't yet seen you," trans. from the poem of Celia Dropkin]. *A Treasury of Yiddish Poetry* (1969).

4180 Weisgall, Hugo. "Poem (1st Version)" in *Translations.* Bryn Mawr: T. Presser, 1977. Song: v, pf.

Poem ["You sowed in me, not a child," trans. from the poem of Celia Dropkin]. *A Treasury of Yiddish Poetry* (1969).

4181 Weisgall, Hugo. "Poem (2d Version)" in *Translations.* Bryn Mawr: T. Presser, 1977.

Side by Side. *Necessities of Life* (1966).

4182 Vercoe, Elizabeth. In *Herstory I.* MS, u.d., avail. ACA. Cycle: S, vib, pf.

The Stranger ["Looking as I've looked before, straight down the heart"]. *Diving into the Wreck: Poems 1971–1972* (1973).

4183 Rorem, Ned. In *Women's Voices.* New York: Boosey & Hawkes, 1979. Cycle: S, pf.

Two Songs. 1 ["Sex, as they harshly call it"]. *Necessities of Life* (1966).

4184 Weisgall, Hugo. "Song" in *Translations.* Bryn Mawr: T. Presser, 1977. Song: v, pf.

EDWIN ARLINGTON ROBINSON (1869–1935)

Calvary. *The Children of the Night* (1897).

4185 Duke, John. In *Four Poems by Edwin Arlington Robinson.* New York: C. Fischer, 1948. Song: low v, pf.

Cliff Klingenhagen. *The Children of the Night* (1897).

> 4186 Hensel, Richard. In *Three Songs on Poems of Edwin Arlington Robinson*. Cincinnati: World Library Publications, u.d. Chorus: SATB, a cap.

Credo. *The Children of the Night* (1897).

> 4187 Allcock, Stephen. New York: Boosey & Hawkes, u.d. Chorus: SATB, a cap.
>
> 4188 Souther, Louise. Boston: C.W. Homeyer, 1935. Song: v, pf.

The Dark Hills. *The Three Taverns* (1920).

> 4189 Adler, Samuel. In *In Nature's Ebb and Flow*. New York: Southern Music Publishing, 1968. Chorus: SSAA, pf.
>
> 4190 Bassett, Leslie. In *Four Songs*. MS, 1957, avail. ACA. Song: high v, pf.
>
> 4191 Bissell, Keith W. Toronto: BMI Canada Ltd., 1958. Chorus: SATB, a cap.
>
> 4192 Coker, Wilson. New York: Associated Music, 1966. Chorus: SATB, pf.
>
> 4192a "Dark Hills at Evening" in coll. UHC.
>
> 4193 Pisk, Paul A. Los Angeles: Delkas Music, 1946. Chorus: SSA, a cap.
>
> 4194 Russell, John. New York: Lawson-Gould, u.d. Chorus: SATB, a cap.
>
> 4195 Souther, Louise. Boston: C.W. Homeyer, 1937. Song: v, pf.
>
> 4196 Travis, Ralph R. New York: H. Flammer, 1936. Song: v, pf.
>
> 4197 Watts, Wintter. In *Three Songs for Low Voice*. New York: G. Schirmer, 1924. Song: low v, pf.

The House on the Hill. *The Children of the Night* (1897).

> 4198 Copland, Aaron. Boston: E.C. Schirmer, 1926. Chorus: SSAA, a cap.
>
> 4199 Mirante, Thomas. New York: Associated Music, 1968. Chorus: SATB, pf.
>
> 4200 Souther, Louise. Boston: C.W. Homeyer, 1932. Song: v, pf.

James Wetherell. *Modern American Poetry* [Ed. by Louis Untermeyer] (1950).

> 4201 Hensel, Richard. "James Wetherell" in *Three Songs on Poems of Edwin Arlington Robinson*. Cincinnati: World Library Publications, u.d. Chorus: SATB, a cap.

Luke Havergal. *The Children of the Night* (1897).

4202 Duke, John. In *Four Poems by Edwin Arlington Robinson.* New York: C. Fischer, 1948. Song: med. v, pf. In coll. TaCS.

4203 Saminsky, Lazare. In *From the American Poets* op. 46 no. 2. New York: Beekman Music, 1956. Chorus: SATB, pf; perc and org ad lib.

Miniver Cheevy. *The Town Down the River* (1910).

4204 Bornschein, Franz. Boston: R.D. Row, 1947. Chorus: TTBB, pf.

4205 Duke, John. "Miniver Cheevy (A Satire in the Form of Variations)" in *Four Poems by Edwin Arlington Robinson.* New York: C. Fischer, 1948. Song: low v, pf.

4206 James, Philip. u.p.: Mills Music, u.d. (R). Melodrama: narr., pf or orch.

4207 Watts, Wintter. In *Three Songs for Low Voice.* New York: G. Schirmer, 1924. Song: low v, pf.

Reuben Bright. *The Children of the Night* (1897).

4208 Hensel, Richard. In *Three Songs on Poems of Edwin Arlington Robinson.* Cincinnati: World Library Publications, u.d. Chorus: SATB, a cap.

Richard Cory. *The Children of the Night* (1897).

4209 Duke, John. In *Four Poems by Edwin Arlington Robinson.* New York: C. Fischer, 1948. Song: low v, pf.

4210 James, Philip. u.p.: Mills Music, u.d. (R). Melodrama: narr., pf or orch.

4211 Naginski, Charles. In *Four Songs.* New York: G. Schirmer, 1940. Song: med. or low v, pf.

4212 Reif, Paul. New York: Seesaw Music, 1971. Song: v, pf.

Sisera. *Theater Arts Monthly* 16 (January 1932), pp. 31–38.

4213 Daniels, Mabel W. "The Song of Jael" op. 37. New York: J. Fischer, 1937. Cantata: SATB, S solo, pf; "Hymn of Triumph" op. 37. New York: J. Fischer, 1937. Chorus: SATB, pf.

Twilight Song. *Captain Craig* (1902).

4214 Mason, Daniel G. New York: J. Fischer, 1934. Chorus: SATB, pf.

Variations of Greek Themes. *Captain Craig* (1902).

4215 Lewin, Frank. *Variations of Greek Themes.* MS, 1975, avail. ACA. Song: M or C, fl, vla, hp, pf. Setting of secs. 1, 2, 4, 5, 6, 8, 9, 11.

4216 Wright, Norman S. "An Inscription by the Sea." Los Angeles: Delkas Music, 1945. Song: v, pf. Setting of sec. 11.

THEODORE ROETHKE (1908–1963)

McLeod, James R. *Theodore Roethke: A Bibliography.* Kent, Ohio: Kent State Univ. Press, 1973, pp. 116–21 [MRAB].

The Apparition. *The Far Field* (1964).

4217 Rorem, Ned. In *Poems of Love and the Rain.* New York: Boosey & Hawkes, 1965. Cycle: M, pf. Numbers 5 and 13 are contrasting settings of this poem.

The Cow. *Words for the Wind: The Collected Verse of Theodore Roethke* (1958).

4218 Benshoff, Kenneth. In *American Artsong Anthology.* Vol. 1. New York: Galaxy, 1982. Song.

4219 Lindenfeld, Harris. In *American Artsong Anthology.* Vol. 1. New York: Galaxy, 1982. Song.

Dolor. *The Lost Son and Other Poems* (1948).

4220 Lindenfeld, Harris. In *American Artsong Anthology.* Vol. 1. New York: Galaxy, 1982. Song.

First Meditation. *Words for the Wind: The Collected Verse of Theodore Roethke* (1958).

4221 Bolcom, William. In *Open House.* New York: E.B. Marks, 1976, 1977. Cycle: T, pf 4 hands or cham orch.

Give Way, Ye Gates. *Praise to the End!* (1951).

4222 Bolcom, William. In *Open House.* New York: E.B. Marks, 1976, 1977. Cycle: T, pf 4 hands or cham orch.

Goo-Girl. *I Am! Says the Lamb* (1961).

4223 Adler, Samuel. "Goo-Girl" from the section "More About Myrtle" in *A Whole Bunch of Fun.* New York: Oxford University Press, 1980. Cantata: unison or 2-pt. chorus of young voices, pf or orch (R).

I Knew A Woman. *Words for the Wind: The Collected Verse of Theodore Roethke* (1958).

4224 Bolcom, William. In *Open House*. New York: E.B. Marks, 1976, 1977. Cycle: T, pf 4 hands or cham orch.

Interlude. *Open House* (1941).

4225 Rorem, Ned. In *Poems of Love and the Rain*. New York: Boosey & Hawkes, 1965. Cycle: M, pf.

The Kitty-Cat Bird. *I Am! Says the Lamb* (1961).

4226 Kubik, Gail. In *Fables in Song*. New York: Music Corp. of America, 1975. Song: med. v, pf.

The Lamb. *I Am! Says the Lamb* (1961).

4227 Kubik, Gail. In *Fables in Song*. New York: Music Corp. of America, 1975. Song: med. v, pf.

Meditations of an Old Woman ["What can I tell my bones?"] *Words for the Wind* (1957).

4228 Rorem, Ned. "What Can I Tell My Bones" in *Sun*. New York: Boosey & Hawkes, 1969. Cycle: high v, pf.

Memory. *Words for the Wind: The Collected Verse of Theodore Roethke* (1958).

4229 Rorem, Ned. In coll. RFA. Song: med. v, pf.

The Monotony Song. *I Am! Says the Lamb* (1961).

4230 Kubik, Gail. New York: G. Ricordi, 1960. Chorus: TTBB, B solo, pf.

4231 Lamb, John D. New York: Lawson-Gould, u.d. Chorus: SATB, cl.

My Papa's Waltz. *The Lost Son and Other Poems* (1948).

4232 Diamond, David. New York: Southern Music Publishing, 1968. Song: Bar, pf.

4233 Rorem, Ned. In coll. RFA. Song: med. v, pf.

Myrtle. *I Am! Says the Lamb* (1961).

4234 Adler, Samuel. "Myrtle" from the section "Limericks" in *A Whole Bunch of Fun*. New York: Oxford University Press, 1980. Cantata: unison or 2-pt. chorus of young voices, pf or orch (R).

Myrtle's Cousin. *I Am! Says the Lamb* (1961).

4235 Adler, Samuel. "Myrtle's Cousin" from the section "More about

Myrtle" in *A Whole Bunch of Fun*. New York: Oxford University Press, 1980. Cantata: unison or 2-pt. chorus of young voices, pf or orch (R).

Night Crow. *The Lost Son and Other Poems* (1948).

4236 Rorem, Ned. In coll. RFA. Song: med. v, pf.

Old Song [MRAB notes that this lyric was especially written for the setting and does not appear elsewhere].

4237 Moore, Douglas S. New York: C. Fischer, 1950. Song: med. v, pf. In coll. TaCS.

Open House. *Open House* (1941).

4238 Bolcom, William. In *Open House*. New York: E.B. Marks, 1976, 1977. Cycle: T, pf 4 hands or cham orch.

Orchids. *The Lost Son and Other Poems* (1948).

4239 Rorem, Ned. In *Two Poems of Theodore Roethke*. New York: Boosey & Hawkes, 1969. Song: med. v, pf.

Prayer. *Open House* (1941).

4240 Diamond, David. New York: Southern Music Publishing, 1968. Song: med. v, pf.

The Right Thing. *The Collected Poems of Theodore Roethke* (1966).

4241 Bolcom, William. In *Open House*. New York: E.B. Marks, 1976, 1977. Cycle: T, pf 4 hands or cham orch.

Root Cellar. *The Lost Son and Other Poems* (1948).

4242 Rorem, Ned. In coll. RFA. Song: med. v, pf.

The Serpent. *Words for the Wind: The Collected Verse of Theodore Roethke* (1958).

4243 Bolcom, William. In *Open House*. New York: E.B. Marks, 1976, 1977. Cycle: T, pf 4 hands or cham orch.

4244 Imbrie, Andrew. u.p.: Malcolm Music, 1970. Chorus: SAB, pf.

4245 Kubik, Gail. In *Fables in Song*. New York: Music Corp. of America, 1975. Song: med. v, pf.

4246 Rorem, Ned. New York: Boosey & Hawkes, 1974. Song: med. v, pf.

The Sloth. *Words for the Wind: The Collected Verse of Theodore Roethke* (1958).

4247 Kubik, Gail. In *Fables in Song.* New York: Music Corp. of America, 1975. Song: med. v, pf.

Snake. *Words for the Wind: The Collected Verse of Theodore Roethke* (1958).

4248 Rorem, Ned. In coll. RFA. Song: med. v, pf.

Song ["From whence cometh song?"] *The Far Field* (1964).

4249 Rorem, Ned. "From Whence Cometh Song" in *The Nantucket Songs.* New York: Boosey & Hawkes, 1981. Song: v, pf.

The Voice. *Words for the Wind.* (1957).

4250 Baumgartner, Hope L. In *Selected Works for Unaccompanied Chorus.* New Haven: A-R Editions, 1963.

The Waking ["I strolled across"]. *The Lost Son and Other Poems* (1948).

4251 Rorem, Ned. "I Strolled Across an Open Field" in *Two Poems of Theodore Roethke.* New York: Boosey & Hawkes, 1969. Song: v, pf.

The Waking ["I wake to sleep, and take my waking slow"]. *The Waking: Poems 1933–1953* (1953).

4252 Bolcom, William. In *Open House.* New York: E.B. Marks, 1976, 1977. Cycle: T, pf 4 hands or cham orch.

4253 Rorem, Ned. In coll. RFA. Song: med. v, pf.

Wish for a Young Wife. *The Far Field* (1964).

4254 Barber, Samuel. "My Lizard" in *Despite and Still* op. 41 no. 2. New York: G. Schirmer, 1969. Cycle: high v, pf.

The Yak. *I Am! Says the Lamb* (1961).

4255 Adler, Samuel. "The Yak" from the section "Limericks" in *A Whole Bunch of Fun.* New York: Oxford University Press, 1980. Cantata: unison or 2-pt. chorus of young voices, pf or orch (R).

CARL SANDBURG (1878–1967)

Van Doren, Mark. *Carl Sandburg: With a Bibliography of Sandburg Materials in the Collections of the Library of Congress.* Washington: Library of Congress, 1969, pp. 62–71.

A.E.F. *Smoke and Steel* (1920).

> 4256 Hennagin, Michael. n.t. in *The Unknown*. u.p.: Walton Music, 1968, 1972. Chorus: SATB, 4 T and 3 Bar soli, pf, fl, 6 perc, 2 slide proj, elec tape, slides (R).

Baby Toes. *Smoke and Steel* (1920).

> 4257 Bricken, Carl. In coll. UNSNV, WieF. Song: v, pf.

Back Yard. *Chicago Poems* (1916).

> 4258 Raphling, Sam. In *Four Chicago Poems*. Hastings-on-Hudson, N.Y.: General, 1973. Chorus: SATB, a cap.

Beat, Old Heart. *Slabs of the Sunburnt West* (1922).

> 4259 Weigl, Vally. MS, u.d., avail. ACA. Chorus: SATB, pf, opt timp?

Bricklayer Love. *Cornhuskers* (1918).

> 4260 Hughes, Rupert. In *Free Verse Songs*. New York: G. Schirmer, 1922. Song: med. or low v, pf.

Broken Sky. *Good Morning, America* (1928).

> 4261 Green, Ray. In *Four Short Songs*. u.p.: American Music Edition, u.d. Song: med. v, pf.

Buffalo Bill. *Cornhuskers* (1918).

> 4262 Gertz, Irving. Hollywood, Calif.: Middleroad Music, 1960. Chorus: SSATBarB, pf.

Cahoots. *Smoke and Steel* (1920).

> 4263 Swanson, Howard. New York: Weintraub, 1951. Song: Bar or B, pf.

Calls. *Smoke and Steel* (1920).

> 4264 Golde, Walter. New York: G. Schirmer, 1944. Song: v, pf.

Changing Light Winds. *Complete Poems* (1950).

4265 Epstein, David. "Windscape" in *Five Scenes*. New York: Mercury, 1962. Chorus: SATB, a cap.

Chicago. *Chicago Poems* (1916).

4266 Klein, Maynard. New Orleans: Tulane Univ. Press, 1941. Choral Poem: mixed voices, a cap. Music not seen; text presumably from this poem.

4267 Morse, Richard W. In *Mid-West Scenes*. New York: Boosey & Hawkes, agent, 1952. Cantata: mixed voices, soli, orch. Music not seen; text presumably from this poem.

4268 Ultan, Lloyd. MS, u.d., avail. ACA. Chorus: SATB, pf. Music not seen; text presumably from this poem.

Child. *Chicago Poems* (1916). [DHT incorrectly cites a hymn setting for this poem in SmNH. Correct hymnal not discovered.]

Clark Street Bridge. *Chicago Poems* (1916).

4269 Beach, John. In *Two Songs of Labor*. New York: G. Schirmer, 1923. Song: med. v, pf.

"Come on, superstition, and get my goat" [Sec. 53]. *The People, Yes* (1936).

4270 Russ, Elmo. "Come on, Superstition." New York: C. Fischer, 1939. Song: v, pf.

Cool Tombs. *Cornhuskers* (1918).

4271 Mellers, Wilfrid H. In *Chants and Litanies of Carl Sandburg*. London: Novello, 1966. Chorus: TTBB, pf, 2 perc.

4272 Raphling, Sam. In *Poems by Carl Sandburg*. New York: Edition-Musicus, 1952. Song: med. v, pf.

Daybreak. *Wind Song* (1960).

4273 Pisk, Paul A. In *In Memoriam Carl Sandburg*. MS, 1967, avail. ACA. Chorus: SATB, a cap.

Death Snips Proud Men. *Smoke and Steel* (1920).

4274 Weigl, Vally. "Death Snips Proud Men by the Nose." MS, u.d., avail. ACA. Song: med. v, pf.

The Family of Man; an Exhibition of Creative Photography dedicated to the dignity of man, with examples from 68 countries, conceived and executed by Edward Steichen. Prologue by Carl Sandburg. New York: The Museum of Modern Art, 1955.

4275 Hennagin, Michael. "People," "Alike and Ever Alike," "Hands Here," "There Is Only One Man" in *The Family of Man*. New York: Walton Music, 1971. Setting for SATB chorus, 4 speakers, elec. tape.

Finish. *Smoke and Steel* (1920).

4276 Mellers, Wilfrid H. In *Chants and Litanies of Carl Sandburg*. London: Novello, 1966. Chorus: TTBB, pf, 2 perc.

Fins. *Slabs of the Sunburnt West* (1922).

4277 Weigl, Vally. MS, u.d., avail. ACA. Chorus: male voices, soli, str qrt.

Fog. *Chicago Poems* (1916).

4278 Epstein, David. In *Five Scenes*. New York: Mercury, 1962. Chorus: SATB, a cap.

4279 Green, Ray. In *New Music* 7 (1934). Song: S, pf.

4280 Harris, Roy. New York: C. Fischer, 1948. Song: med. v, pf. In coll. TaCS.

4281 Hovhaness, Alan S. In *Making Music Your Own*. Vol. 6. Morristown, N.J.: Silver Burdett, 1965. Vocal line with words.

4282 Irwin, Hoyt. New York: C. Fischer, 1939. Chorus: SATB, a cap.

4283 Matthews, Holon. In *Two Sandburg Songs*. New York: Mercury, 1952. Chorus: SATB, pf.

4284 Nash, W. Gifford. New York: G. Schirmer, 1945. Chorus: SSA, a cap.

4285 Raphling, Sam. In *Poems by Carl Sandburg*. New York: Edition-Musicus, 1952. Song: med. v, pf.

4286 Schwartz, Paul. New York: Rongwen Music, 1958. Chorus: SSA, pf.

4287 Somervell, T., Lady. New York: Bourne, 1957. Chorus: SATB, pf ad lib.

4288 Stone, Louise P. New York: H.W. Gray, 1940. Chorus: SSAA, a cap; New York: H.W. Gray, 1942. Chorus: SSATBarB or TTBB, a cap.

Four Preludes on Playthings of the Wind. *Smoke and Steel* (91920).

4289 Erickson, Elaine. "Lamentations" in coll. MuENC. Chorus: SATB, narr., fl, ob, cl, bcl, pf, perc.

4290 Kantor, Joseph. "Playthings of the Wind." Recording: Crystal Records, S 890 (1976). Setting of secs. 1–4.

"From the four corners of the earth" [Sec. 1]. *The People, Yes* (1936).

4291 Weigl, Vally. "From the Far Corners." MS, u.d., avail. ACA. Chorus: SATB, solo speakers, obl instruments, pf, drums.

Gone. *Chicago Poems* (1916).

4292 Hughes, Rupert. In *Five Homely Songs*. New York: G. Schirmer, 1920. Song: high or med. v, pf.

4293 Raphling, Sam. In *Poems by Carl Sandburg*. New York: Edition-Musicus, 1952. Song: med. v, pf.

4294 Wilder, Alec. "Chick Lorimer: Gone." Boston: R.D. Row, 1953. Song: med. v, pf.

The Gong of Time. *Honey and Salt* (1963).

4295 Starer, Robert. In *Two Songs from "Honey and Salt."* New York: Leeds, 1964. Chorus: SATB, pf or 2 tpt and 2 trb.

Good Morning, America. *Good Morning, America* (1928).

4296 Warren, Elinor R. "Great Memories" in *Singing Earth*. Bryn Mawr, Pa.: T. Presser, 1950. Song: high and med. v edns, pf or orch (R).

4297 Warren, Elinor R. New York: C. Fischer, 1976. Chorus: mixed voices, narr., pf or orch.

4298 Weigl, Vally. "Sea Sunsets." MS, u.d., avail. ACA. Chorus: women's voices, pf, fl (or cl or vn) obl. Music not seen; text presumably from sec. 21.

Grass. *Cornhuskers* (1918).

4299 Hart, Frederic. New York: Mercury, 1954. Song: med. v, pf.

4300 Heath, Fenno. New York: G. Schirmer, 1953. Chorus: TTBB, Bar solo, a cap.

Halsted Street Car. *Chicago Poems* (1916).

4301 Raphling, Sam. In *Four Chicago Poems*. Hastings-on-Hudson, N.Y.: General, 1973. Chorus: SATB, a cap.

Haze Gold. *Good Morning, America* (1928).

4302 Glass, Philip. Philadelphia: Elkan-Vogel, 1964. Chorus: SATB, a cap.

I Am the People, the Mob. *Chicago Poems* (1916).

4303 Weiss, Helen L. "I Am the People." New York: Mercury, 1956. Cantata: SSAATTBB, a cap.

In Tall Grass. *Cornhuskers* (1918).

> 4304 Mellers, Wilfrid H. In *Chants and Litanies of Carl Sandburg.* London: Novello, 1966. Chorus: TTBB, pf, 2 perc.
>
> 4305 Seeger, Ruth P. In *Three Songs.* San Francisco: New Music Edition, 1933. Song: C, ob, perc, pf, with or without orch ostinato.

"In the folded and quiet yesterdays" [Sec. 27]. *The People, Yes* (1936).

> 4306 Robinson, Earl. Delaware Water Gap, Pa.: Shawnee, 1964. Chorus: SATB, Bar solo, narr., and various speakers, pf or orch (R).

The Junk Man. *Chicago Poems* (1916).

> 4307 Swanson, Howard. New York: Weintraub, 1950. Song: high v, pf.
>
> 4308 Youse, Glad R. u.p.: Remick Music, 1958. Chorus: SSA, pf.

Killers. *Chicago Poems* (1916).

> 4309 Hennagin, Michael. In *The Unknown.* u.p.: Walton Music, 1968, 1972. Chorus: mixed voices, pf, fl, 6 perc, 2 slide proj, elec tape, slides (R).
>
> 4310 Weigl, Vally. MS, u.d., avail. ACA. Chorus: SATB, Bar or T solo, 4 timp, opt trp and trb. Music not seen.

Little Girl, Be Careful What You Say. *Complete Poems* (1950).

> 4311 Pfautsch, Lloyd. "Be Careful What You Say" in *Songs of Experience.* New York: Lawson-Gould, 1978. Chorus: SATB, a cap.

Lost. *Chicago Poems* (1916).

> 4312 Hughes, Rupert. In *Free Verse Songs.* New York: G. Schirmer, 1922. Song: med. or low v, pf.
>
> 4313 Matthews, Holon. In *Two Sandburg Songs.* New York: Mercury, 1952. Chorus: SATB, pf.
>
> 4314 Smith, Melville. In *Three Songs.* South Hadley, Mass.: Valley Music, 1957. Song: high v, pf.
>
> 4315 Strassburg, Robert. New York: Hargail, 1945. Chorus: SATB, a cap.
>
> 4316 Van Buskirk, Carl. East Stroudsburg, Pa.: Shawnee, 1952. Chorus: SATB, a cap.
>
> 4317 Wolfe, Jacques. New York: G. Schirmer, 1936. Song: med. v, pf.

Love Is a Deep and a Dark and a Lonely. *Honey and Salt* (1963).

> 4318 Starer, Robert. In *Two Songs from "Honey and Salt."* New York: Leeds, 1964. Chorus: SATB, 2 tpt and 2 trb, or pf.

Mag. *Chicago Poems* (1916).

  4319 Ives, Charles. New York: Weintraub, u.d. Song: Bar, pf.

  4320 Kagen, Sergius. New York: Weintraub, 1950. Song: Bar, pf.

  4321 Raphling, Sam. In *Poems by Carl Sandburg.* New York: Edition-Musicus, 1952. Song: med. v, pf.

Mamie. *Chicago Poems* (1916).

  4322 Raphling, Sam. In *Four Chicago Poems.* Hastings-on-Hudson, N.Y.: General, 1973. Chorus: SATB, a cap.

Maybe. *Good Morning, America* (1928).

  4323 Kagen, Sergius. New York: Weintraub, 1950. Song: S, pf.

  4324 Raphling, Sam. In *Poems by Carl Sandburg.* New York: Edition-Musicus, 1952. Song: v, pf.

Mill-Doors. *Chicago Poems* (1916).

  4325 Dello-Joio, Norman. New York: C. Fischer, 1948. Song: med. v, pf. In coll. TaCS.

Monotone. *Chicago Poems* (1916).

  4326 Davisson, Genevieve. New York: G. Schirmer, 1944. Song: high v, pf.

  4327 Lockwood, Normand. Chicago: N.A. Kjos, 1937. Chorus: SATB, a cap.

Night Stuff. *Smoke and Steel* (1920).

  4328 Schuman, William. In *Four Canonic Choruses.* New York: G. Schirmer, 1942. Chorus: SST, a cap.

Nightsong. *Wind Song* (1960).

  4329 Pisk, Paul A. In *In Memoriam Carl Sandburg.* MS, 1967, avail. ACA. Chorus: SATB, a cap.

Nocturn Cabbage. *Good Morning, America* (1928).

  4330 Green, Ray. In *Four Short Songs.* u.p.: American Music Edition, u.d. Song: med. v, pf.

Nocturne in a Deserted Brickyard. *Chicago Poems* (1916).

  4331 Epstein, David. In *Five Scenes.* New York: Mercury, 1962. Chorus: SATB, a cap.

Omaha. *Smoke and Steel* (1920).

> 4332 Bacon, Ernst. In *Six Songs. New Music* (Jan. 1942). Song: low v, pf. In coll. BacFS.

"On Lang Syne Plantation they had a prayer" [Sec. 55]. *The People, Yes* (1936).

> 4333 Starer, Robert. "Oh Angel" in *The People, Yes.* Melville, N.Y.: MCA Music, 1976. Chorus: SATB, pf or orch (R).

Our Prayer of Thanks. *Chicago Poems* (1916).

> 4334 Mollicone, Henry. Philadelphia: Elkan-Vogel, 1966. Chorus: SATB, pf.

Passers-By. *Chicago Poems* (1916).

> 4335 Beach, John. In *Two Songs of Labor.* New York: G. Schirmer, 1923. Song: med. v, pf.

Prairie. *Cornhuskers* (1918).

> 4336 Foss, Lukas. New York: G. Schirmer, 1944. Cantata: SATB chorus, SATB soli, pf or orch (R). Recording: TV-S 34649 (1976); "Cool Prayers." New York: G. Schirmer, 1944. Chorus: SATB, a cap with instrumental prelude and postlude.
>
> 4337 Lockwood, Normand. "Prairie." Ann Arbor: Musical Society of the Univ. of Michigan, 1953. Chorus: 8-pt. mixed voices, orch.

Prairie Waters by Night. *Cornhuskers* (1918).

> 4338 Helm, Everett B. New York: C. Fischer, 1950. Song: med. v, pf. In coll. TaCS.
>
> 4339 Wolfe, Jacques. New York: G. Schirmer, 1935. Song: med. v, pf.

Prayers of Steel. *Cornhuskers* (1918).

> 4340 Christiansen, Paul. Minneapolis: Augsburg, 1950. Chorus: SATB, a cap.
>
> 4341 Hughes, Rupert. "The Prayer of Steel" in *Free Verse Songs.* New York: G. Schirmer, 1922. Song: med. or low v, pf.
>
> 4342 Seeger, Ruth P. In *Three Songs.* San Francisco: New Music Edition, 1973. Song: C, ob, perc, pf, with or without orch ostinato. Recording: New World Records, NW 285 (1978).
>
> 4343 Spencer, James. St. Louis: Schattinger Piano, 1937. Song: v, pf.

Rat Riddles. *Good Morning, America* (1928).

4344 Seeger, Ruth P. In *Three Songs*. San Francisco: New Music Edition, 1973. Song: C, ob, perc, pf, with or without orch ostinato.

Red-Headed Restaurant Cashier. *Smoke and Steel* (1920).

4345 Rathaus, Karol. In *Three Songs* op. 70 no. 3. Bryn Mawr, Pa.: Presser, 1957. Chorus: SATB, a cap.

Ripe Corn. *Good Morning, America* (1928).

4346 Mellers, Wilfrid H. In *Chants and Litanies of Carl Sandburg*. London: Novello, 1966. Chorus: TTBB, pf, 2 perc.

Sea Slant. *Slabs of the Sunburnt West* (1922).

4347 Clarke, Henry L. In *Four Elements*. MS, 1962, avail. ACA. Song: S, vc.

Shirt. *Smoke and Steel* (1920).

4348 Lang, Edith M. "My Shirt, Song for a Sailor." Boston: Boston Music, 1946. Chorus: TTBB, pf.

Sketch. *Chicago Poems* (1916).

4349 Smith, Melville. In *Three Songs*. South Hadley, Mass.: Valley Music, 1957. Song: high v, pf.

Small Homes. *Good Morning, America* (1928).

4350 Oliver, Madra I. In *Seven Songs for Youth*. Boston: B. Humphries, 1963. Song: v, pf.

Special Starlight. *Complete Poems* (1950).

4351 Haslam, Herbert. Bryn Mawr, Pa.: Presser, 1967. Cantata: SATB chorus, treble voices, narr., and orch (R).

Spring Grass. *Good Morning, America* (1928).

4352 Glass, Philip. Philadelphia: Elkan-Vogel, 1964. Chorus: SATB, a cap.

4353 Kreutz, Richard E. New York: Boosey & Hawkes, 1976. Chorus: SATB, a cap.

4354 Mellers, Wilfrid H. "Spring Carries Surprises" in *Chants and Litanies of Carl Sandburg*. London: Novello, 1966. Chorus: TTBB, pf, 2 perc.

4355 Weigl, Vally. MS, u.d., avail. ACA. Chorus: SATB, pf.

Stars. *Wind Song* (1960).

4356 Gerschefski, Edwin. In *Six Songs* op. 39 no. 4b. MS, 1962, avail. ACA. Chorus.

Still Life. *Cornhuskers* (1918).

4357 Swanson, Howard. New York: Weintraub, 1950. Song: med. v, pf.

Summer Grass. *Good Morning, America* (1928).

4358 Glass, Philip. In coll. MuENC. Chorus: SATB, a cap.

4359 Green, Ray. In *Four Short Songs*. u.p.: American Music Edition. Song: v, pf.

4360 Mellers, Wilfrid H. In *Chants and Litanies of Carl Sandburg*. London: Novello, 1966. Chorus: TTBB, pf, 2 perc.

4361 Pisk, Paul A. In *In Memoriam Carl Sandburg*. MS, 1967, avail. ACA. Chorus: SATB, a cap.

Summer Stars. *Smoke and Steel* (1920).

4362 Warren, Elinor R. In *Singing Earth*. Bryn Mawr, Pa.: Presser, 1950. Song: high and low v edns, pf or orch (R).

Sunsets. *Good Morning, America* (1928).

4363 Lang, Edith M. "Sunsets, Song for a Sailor." Boston: Boston Music, 1950. Chorus: TTBarB, pf.

Tawny. *Smoke and Steel* (1920).

4364 Warren, Elinor R. "Tawny Days" in *Singing Earth*. Bryn Mawr, Pa.: Presser, 1950. Cycle: high, and med. or low v edns, pf or orch (R).

A Teamster's Farewell. *Chicago Poems* (1916).

4365 Smith, Melville. In *Three Songs*. South Hadley, Mass.: Valley Music, 1957. Song: high v, pf.

"The people will live on" [Sec. 107]. *The People, Yes* (1936).

4366 Starer, Robert. In *The People, Yes*. Melville, N.Y.: MCA Music, 1976. Chorus: SATB, pf or orch (R).

"The people, yes" [Sec. 29]. *The People, Yes* (1936).

4367 Starer, Robert. In *The People, Yes*. Melville, N.Y.: MCA Music, 1976. Chorus: SATB, pf or orch (R).

"The people, yes" [Sec. 58]. *The People, Yes* (1936).

4368 Weigl, Vally. "The People, Yes, out of What Is Their Change." MS, 1976, avail. ACA. Chorus: SATB, a cap.

"The sea moves always, the wind moves always" [Sec. 35]. *The People, Yes* (1936).

4369 Starer, Robert. "The Sea Moves Always" in *The People, Yes*. Melville, N.Y.: MCA Music, 1976. Chorus: SATB, pf or orch (R).

Theme in Yellow. *Chicago Poems* (1916).

4370 Epstein, David. "Fall Yellow" in *Five Scenes*. New York: Mercury, 1962. Chorus: SATB, a cap.

Timber Moon. *Good Morning, America* (1928).

4371 Raphling, Sam. In *Poems by Carl Sandburg*. New York: Edition Musicus, 1952. Song: v, pf.

Under a Telephone Pole. *Chicago Poems* (1916).

4372 Raphling, Sam. In *Four Chicago Poems*. Hastings-on-Hudson, N.Y.: General, 1973. Chorus: SATB, a cap.

Under the Harvest Moon. *Chicago Poems* (1916).

4373 Naginski, Charles. In *Four Songs*. New York: G. Schirmer, 1940. Song: high or med. v, pf.

Uplands in May. *Chicago Poems* (1916).

4374 Epstein, David. In *Five Scenes*. New York: Mercury, 1962. Chorus: SATB, a cap.

Upstream. *Slabs of the Sunburnt West* (1922).

4375 Bricken, Carl. In coll. UNSNV. Song: v, pf.

4376 Dougherty, Celius. New York: G. Schirmer, 1960. Song: med. v, pf.

4377 Ferguson, Edwin E. New York: Lawson-Gould, 1965. Chorus: TTBB, pf.

4378 Kagen, Sergius. New York: Weintraub, 1950. Song: med. v, pf.

4379 Lundquist, Wray. "The Strong Men." New York: G. Schirmer, 1958. Chorus: SATB, a cap.

4380 Malotte, Albert H. New York: G. Schirmer, 1937. Song: med. v, pf.

Washington Monument by Night. *Slabs of the Sunburnt West* (1922).

4381 Raphling, Sam. New York: Edition Musicus, 1952. Song: med. v, pf.

"Who shall speak for the people?" [Sec. 24]. *The People, Yes* (1936).

> 4382 Kurka, Robert F. New York: Boosey & Hawkes, 1957. Chorus:
> TTBB, pf. A portion of the text is from sec. 24; text from other
> unidentified secs. also.

"Why repeat? I heard you the first time" [Sec. 42]. *The People, Yes* (1936).

> 4383 Starer, Robert. In *The People, Yes*. Melville, N.Y.: MCA Music, 1976.
> Chorus: SATB, pf or orch (R).

The Wind Sings Welcome in Early Spring. *Smoke and Steel* (1920).

> 4384 Warren, Elinor R. "The Wind Sings Welcome" in *Singing Earth*.
> Bryn Mawr, Pa.: Presser, 1950. Cycle: high, and med. or low v
> edns, pf or orch (R).

Wind Song. *Smoke and Steel* (1920).

> 4385 Glass, Philip. In coll. MuENC. Chorus: SATB, a cap.

> 4386 Koch, Frederick. u.t. [2d movement] in *String Quartet*. [?Seesaw
> Music]. Setting for M, str qrt. Recording: Crystal Records, S 531
> (1976).

Winter Gold. *Good Morning, America* (1928).

> 4387 Glass, Philip. Philadelphia: Elkan-Vogel, 1964. Chorus: SATB, a
> cap.

"You can drum on immense drums" [Sec. 26]. *The People, Yes* (1936).

> 4388 Starer, Robert. "You Can Drum" in *The People, Yes*. Melville, N.Y.:
> MCA Music, 1976. Chorus: SATB, pf or orch (R).

Miscellaneous

> 4389 Gerschefski, Edwin. "Changing Shoes" in *Six Songs* op. 39 no. 1.
> MS, 1962, avail. ACA. Chorus.

> 4390 Gerschefski, Edwin. "Clocks" in *Six Songs* op. 39 no. 5. Chorus: SSA,
> pf, perc. Text: "Clocks tell time by their faces. . . ."

> 4391 Gerschefski, Edwin. "Sky" in *Six Songs* op. 39 no. 4a. MS, 1962,
> avail. ACA. Chorus. Text: "The sky is worth looking at. . . ."

> 4392 Gerschefski, Edwin. "Snow" in *Six Songs* op. 39 no. 3. MS, 1962,
> avail. ACA. Chorus. Text: "Snow is when winter comes. . . ."

> 4393 Gerschefski, Edwin. "Think about Wheels" in *Six Songs* op. 40 no.
> 2. MS, 1962, avail. ACA. Chorus: SSA, S and A soli, a cap.

4394 Raphling, Sam. In *Sayings from "The People, Yes."* New York: Beekman, 1956. Chorus: mixed voices, pf.

4395 Weigl, Vally. *Four Choral Songs on Death and Man.* MS, u.d., avail. ACA. Chorus: SATB, pf, opt timp?

ANNE SEXTON (1928–1974)

Her Kind. *To Bedlam and Part Way Back* (1960).

4396 Vercoe, Elizabeth. In *Herstory I.* MS, u.d., avail. ACA. Cycle: S, pf, vib.

Noon Walk on the Asylum Lawn. *To Bedlam and Part Way Back* (1960).

4397 Vercoe, Elizabeth. In *Herstory I.* MS, u.d., avail. ACA. Cycle: S, pf, vib.

Old. *All My Pretty Ones* (1962).

4398 Vercoe, Elizabeth. In *Herstory I.* MS, u.d., avail. ACA. Cycle: S, pf, vib.

KARL SHAPIRO (B. 1913)

Lord, I Have Seen Too Much. *V-Letter and Other Poems* (1944).

4399 Weisgall, Hugo. In *Soldier Songs for Baritone.* u.p.: Mercury, 1953. Cycle: Bar, pf.

The Tenor: Opera in One Act (1957).

4400 Weisgall, Hugo. *The Tenor.* Bryn Mawr, Pa.: Merion Music, 1957. Opera in 1 act. Libretto by Shapiro and Ernst Lert.

GARY SNYDER (B. 1930)

Above Pate Valley. *Ripraps & Cold Mountain Poems* (1969).

4401 Harbison, John. In *The Flower-Fed Buffaloes.* New York: Associated Music, u.d. Choral Cycle: 6-pt. chorus, Bar solo, 7 instrs. Recording: Nonesuch, H-71366 (1979).

EDMUND CLARENCE STEDMAN (1833–1908)

Autumn Song. *The Blameless Prince, and Other Poems* (1869).

4402 Bergh, Arthur. Chicago: C.F. Summy, 1954. Chorus: SSA, pf.

4403 Hadley, Henry K. New York: C. Fischer, 1933. Chorus: SSAA, pf.

4404 Ives, C.F. New York: Wm. A. Pond, 1876. Song: v, pf.

4405 Pease, A.H. Boston: G.D. Russell, 1874.

4405a Veazie, G.A., Jr. "Morning Song." Boston: O. Ditson, 1877.

Cavalry Song. *Favorite Poems* (1877).

4406 Parker, Horatio W. In *Six Songs.* New York: G. Schirmer, 1891. Song: v, pf.

Centuria. *Poems Now First Collected* (1897).

4407 Mosenthal, Joseph. New York: Century Association, 1897.

Country Sleighing. *The Blameless Prince, and Other Poems* (1869).

4407a Pease, Alfred H. "Sleighing." Boston: G.D. Russell, 1874.

Creole Lover's Song. *Poems Now First Collected: By Edmund Clarence Stedman* (1897).

4408 Buck, Dudley. In *Five Songs for Tenor or Soprano* op. 79. New York: G. Schirmer, 1876. Song: S or T, pf; New York: G. Schirmer, 1877. Song: A or Bar, pf.

Falstaff's Song. *Poems Now First Collected: By Edmund Clarence Stedman* (1897).

4409 Buck, Dudley. In *Cosmopolitan* (May 1892); New York: G. Schirmer, 1899.

Hymn of the West. *Independent* 56 (May 5, 1904), pp. 996–997; *Complete Poems* (1908).

4410 Paine, John K. *Independent* 56 (May 5, 1904), p. 997; St. Louis: Thiebes-Stierlin Music, 1904. Written for the 1904 St. Louis Exhibition to celebrate the Louisiana Purchase.

Nocturne. *Lyrics and Idylls, with Other Poems* (1879).

4411 Buck, Dudley. In *Five Songs for Tenor or Soprano* op. 79. New York: G. Schirmer, 1876. Song: S or T, pf.

Peter Stuyvesant's New Year's Call. *Alice of Monmouth, an Idyl of the Great War, and Other Poems* (1863).

4412 Ringwald, Roy. n.t. in *The Song of America*. u.p.: Shawnee, 1951. Chorus: SATB, narr., pf 4 hands. Text adapted by Ringwald.

Song from a Drama. *Hawthorne, and Other Poems* (1877); Summer Night's Song. *Songs and Ballads* (1884).

4413 Bassford, Wm. K. "At Twilight."

4414 Boott, Francis. "I Know Not if Moonlight or Starlight." New York: C.H. Ditson, 1883. Song: v, pf. In coll. BoAS 3.

4415 Buck, Dudley. "I Love Thee" in *Five Songs for Tenor or Soprano* op. 79 no. 3. New York: G. Schirmer, 1876. Song: S or T, pf.

4416 Christiani, A.F. "Rapture" op. 8. New York: E. Schuberth, u.d.

4417 Korbay, F. New York: G. Schirmer, u.d.

Stanzas for Music. *Poetical Works* (1873); Psyche. *Songs and Ballads* (1884).

4418 Baltzell, W.J. "Thou Art Mine" in coll. HST. Song: high v, pf.

4419 Buck, Dudley. "Thou Art Mine" in *Five Songs for Tenor or Soprano* op. 79. New York: G. Schirmer, 1876. Song: S or T, pf.

Surf. *The Blameless Prince, and Other Poems* (1869).

4419a Moody, D.B. "O Beautiful Sea." San Francisco: Sherman & Hyde, u.d.

Toujours Amour. *The Blameless Prince, and Other Poems* (1869).

4420 Bendelari, Augusto. New York: G. Schirmer, u.d.

4420a Coleridge-Taylor, S. "Tell, O Tell Me." Boston: A.P. Schmidt, 1914.

4420b Fossier, J. "Prithee Tell Me" op. 5 no. 1. Cleveland: S. Brainard's, 1875. Ballad.

4421 St. John, Georgie B. New York: Luckhardt & Belder, u.d.

The Undiscovered Country. *The Blameless Prince, and Other Poems* (1869).

4422 Buck, Dudley. "Shadow-Land" in *Five Songs for Tenor or Soprano* op. 79 no. 2. New York: G. Schirmer, 1876. Song: S or T, pf.

Voice of the Western Wind. *Poems, Lyrical and Idyllic* (1860).

4423 Hatton, John L. London: Addison, Hollier & Lucas, [BPL 185–?]. Ballad: v, pf; London: Williams, [BPL 187–?].

The Wedding-Day. *Songs and Ballads* (1884).

4424 Mendelsohn, Jaques. Boston: G.D. Russell, u.d.

What the Winds Bring. *The Blameless Prince, and Other Poems* (1869).

4425 Hadley, Henry K. New York: C. Fischer, 1933. Chorus: SSAA, pf.

Yale Ode for Commencement Day. *Poems Now First Collected* (1897).

4426 Parker, Horatio W. "Ode for Commencement Day at Yale University, 1895." New York: G. Schirmer, 1895.

Miscellaneous

4427 Burleigh, Cecil. "Whither Away, Robin" op. 50 no. 1. New York: C. Fischer, 1921. Song: high and med. v edns, pf.

4428 Entry cancelled

GERTRUDE STEIN (1874–1946)

Wilson, Robert A. *Gertrude Stein: A Bibliography*. New York: The Phoenix Bookshop, 1974, pp. 157–160 [WiGS].

A Blue Coat. *Tender Buttons* (1914).

4429 Thomas, Alan. In *Tender Buttons*. Philadelphia: Elkan-Vogel, 1965. Chorus: SSA, a cap.

A Box ["Out of kindness comes redness . . ."]. *Tender Buttons* (1914).

4430 Thomas, Alan. In *Tender Buttons*. Philadelphia: Elkan-Vogel, 1965. Chorus: SSA, a cap.

Capital Capitals. *Operas and Plays* (1932).

> 4431 Thomson, Virgil. In *New Music* 20(3) (1947); rev. version, New York: Boosey & Hawkes, 1968. Quartet: TTBarB, pf; Chorus: male voices, TTBarB soli, pf.

A Dog. *Tender Buttons* (1914).

> 4432 Thomas, Alan. In *Tender Buttons*. Philadelphia: Elkan-Vogel, 1965. Chorus: SSAA, a cap.

Film: Deux Soeurs Qui ne Sont Pas Soeurs. *Operas and Plays* (1932).

> 4433 Thomson, Virgil. "Film: Deux Soeurs Qui ne Sont Pas Soeurs." New York: Southern Music Publishing, 1981. Song: med. v, pf. Eng. trans. by Donald Sutherland.

A Fire. *Tender Buttons* (1914).

> 4434 Thomas, Alan. In *Tender Buttons*. Philadelphia: Elkan-Vogel, 1965. Chorus: SA, a cap.

Four Saints in Three Acts. *Operas and Plays* (1932).

> 4435 Thomson, Virgil. New York: Music Press, Arrow Music Press, 1948. Opera. Book: Random House, 1934.
> > "Pigeons on the Grass Alas." New York: J. Fischer, 1935. Recitation and Air for Bar, from the opera.
> > "Saint's Procession." Mercury, u.d. Chorus: mixed voices, pf.

The Gertrude Stein First Reader & Three Plays (1946).

> 4436 Sternberg, Ann. *Gretrude Stein's First Reader*. New York: Chappell, 1976. Musical Review.

"I am Rose my eyes are blue" [Text from the sec. "There"]. *The World Is Round* (1939).

> 4437 Diamond, David. "I Am Rose." Bryn Mawr, Pa.: Elkan- Vogel, 1973. Song: med. v, pf.

> 4438 Rorem, Ned. "I Am Rose." New York: Henmar Press, 1963. Song: med. v, pf. In coll. TaCS.

In a Garden. *The Gertrude Stein First Reader & Three Plays* (1946).

> 4439 Kupferman, Meyer. New York: Mercury Music, 1951. Opera in 1 act.

Letter to Freddy [The text was printed with the musical setting by Paul (Frederick) Bowles, to whom the letter was written (WiGS p. 135)].

> 4440 Bowles, Paul. In *New Music* 8(3) (1935). Song: v, pf. Also pubd by G. Schirmer, 1946.

Many Many Women. *Matisse, Picasso, and Gertrude Stein* (1933).

> 4440a Kotik, Petr. *Many Many Women.* Setting for SCTBarB, fl, cl, tb. Recording: Labor Records, LAB-6/10 (1981).

More. *Tender Buttons* (1914).

> 4441 Thomas, Alan. In *Tender Buttons.* Philadelphia: Elkan-Vogel, 1965. Chorus: SSA, a cap.

The Mother of Us All (1947).

> 4442 Thomson, Virgil. New York: Music Press, 1947. Opera.

Nothing Elegant. *Tender Buttons* (1914).

> 4443 Thomas, Alan. In *Tender Buttons.* Philadelphia: Elkan-Vogel, 1965. Chorus: SSA, a cap.

Orange In. *Tender Buttons* (1914).

> 4444 Thomas, Alan. In *Tender Buttons.* Philadelphia: Elkan-Vogel, 1965. Chorus: SSAA, a cap.

A Paper. *Tender Buttons* (1914).

> 4445 Thomas, Alan. In *Tender Buttons.* Philadelphia: Elkan-Vogel, 1965. Chorus: SA, a cap.

A Petticoat. *Tender Buttons* (1914).

> 4446 Thomas, Alan. In *Tender Buttons.* Philadelphia: Elkan-Vogel, 1965. Chorus: SSAA, a cap.

A Portrait of F.B. *Geography and Plays* (1922).

> 4447 Thomson, Virgil. "Portrait of F.B. (Frances Blood)." New York: G. Schirmer, 1971. Song: M, pf.

Preciosilla. *Composition As Explanation* (1926).

> 4448 Thomson, Virgil. New York: G. Schirmer, 1948. Song: high v, pf. In coll. TaST.

A Red Hat. *Tender Buttons* (1914).

4449 Thomas, Alan. In *Tender Buttons*. Philadelphia: Elkan-Vogel, 1965. Chorus: SSAA, a cap.

Red Roses. *Tender Buttons* (1914).

4450 Thomas, Alan. In *Tender Buttons*. Philadelphia: Elkan-Vogel, 1965. Chorus: SSA, a cap.

Scenes from the Door: The Ford. Red Faces. *Useful Knowledge* (1928).

4451 Bowles, Paul. "Red Faces," "The Ford" in *Scenes from the Door*. New York: Editions de la Vipère, 1934.

A Sound. *Tender Buttons* (1914).

4452 Thomas, Alan. In *Tender Buttons*. Philadelphia: Elkan-Vogel, 1965. Chorus: SSAA, a cap.

Storyette H.M. *Portraits and Prayers* (1934).

4453 Bernstein, Leonard. In *Songfest*. New York: Boosey & Hawkes, 1977. Cycle: SAMTBarB, orch.

Susie Asado. *Geography And Plays* (1922).

4454 Thomson, Virgil. In coll. CCS. Song: high v, pf.

They Must, Be Wedded. To Their Wife. *Operas and Plays* (1932).

4455 Berners, Lord. "A Wedding Bouquet." London: J. & W. Chester, 1938. Opera with chorus.

Things As They Are (1950).

4456 Anderson, Beth. "She Wrote." MS, 1977, avail. ACA. Song: S, 2 vn amplif.

This Is the Dress, Aider. *Tender Buttons* (1914).

4457 Thomas, Alan. "This Is This Dress, Aider" in *Tender Buttons*. Philadelphia: Elkan-Vogel, 1965. Chorus: SSA, a cap.

Three Sisters Who Are Not Sisters. *The Gertrude Stein First Reader & Three Plays* (1946).

4458 Rorem, Ned. New York: Boosey & Hawkes, 1974. Opera in 3 acts: SSMTBar.

A Time to Eat. *Tender Buttons* (1914).

4459 Thomas, Alan. In *Tender Buttons*. Philadelphia: Elkan-Vogel, 1965. Chorus: SSA, a cap.

A Valentine to Sherwood Anderson. *Useful Knowledge* (1928).

> 4460 Flanagan, William. New York: Peer International, 1951. Song: med. v, pf.

Miscellaneous

> 4461 Carmines, Al. "In Circles." Recording: Avant Garde Records, AV 108 (1968).

> 4462 Fine, Vivian. In *The Women in the Garden.* Shaftsbury, Vt.: Catamount Facsimile Edn, 1977. Setting for SSMAT soli, fl, cl, bsn, timp, perc.

> 4463 Schuller, Gunther. "Meditation." u.p.: E.B. Marks, 1964. Song: high v, pf. In coll. NVS. Text: "Why am I if I am uncertain reasons may inclose. . . ."

WALLACE STEVENS (1879–1955)

Edelstein, Jerome M. *Wallace Stevens: A Descriptive Bibliography.* Pittsburgh: Univ. of Pittsburgh Press, 1973, pp. 265–66.

Adult Epigram. *Transport to Summer* (1947).

> 4464 Dembski, Stephen. MS, u.d., avail. ACA. Song: S, gtr.

Anecdote of the Jar. *Harmonium* (1923).

> 4465 Boros, David J. Setting for cham chorus, pf, db, bcl. Recording: Composers Recordings, CRI SD 379 (1977).

Anecdote of the Prince of Peacocks. *Harmonium* (1923).

> 4466 Connolly, Justin. In *Poems of Wallace Stevens I* op. 9 no. 2. Sevenoaks, Kent: Novello, 1978. Song: fl, cl, vib, hp, cel, vla, trp. Recording: Argo, ZRG 747.

Another Weeping Woman. *Harmonium* (1923).

> 4467 Lybbert, Donald. In *From "Harmonium."* Bryn Mawr: Merion Music, 1970. Cycle: high v, pf.

Banal Sojourn. *Harmonium* (1923).

4468 Holloway, Robin. In *Banal Sojourn*. New York: Boosey & Hawkes, 1978. Cycle: S, pf.

Bouquet of Belle Scavoir. *Parts of a World* (1942).

4469 Ordansky, Jerold A. In *4 Poems by Wallace Stevens*. MS, 1979, avail. ACA. Song: med. v, pf.

Bouquet of Roses in Sunlight. *The Auroras of Autumn* (1950).

4470 Ordansky, Jerold A. In *4 Poems by Wallace Stevens*. MS, 1979, avail. ACA. Song: med. v, pf.

A Child Asleep in Its Own Life. *Opus Posthumous* (1957).

4471 Rorem, Ned. In *Last Poems of Wallace Stevens*. New York: Boosey & Hawkes, 1974. Cycle: high v, pf.

A Clear Day and No Memories. *Opus Posthumous* (1957).

4472 Rorem, Ned. In *Last Poems of Wallace Stevens*. New York: Boosey & Hawkes, 1974. Cycle: high v, pf.

Cy Est Pourtraicte, Madame Ste Ursule, et les Unze Mille Vierges. *Harmonium* (1923).

4473 Gardner, John. In *Five Partsongs to Poems by Wallace Stevens* op. 142 no. 5. New York: Oxford Univ. Press, 1982. Chorus: SATB, a cap.

The Death of a Soldier. *Harmonium* (1931).

4474 Lybbert, Donald. In *From "Harmonium."* Bryn Mawr: Merion Music, 1970. Cycle: high v, pf.

4475 Persichetti, Vincent. In *Harmonium* op. 50. Philadelphia: Elkan-Vogel, 1959. Cycle: S, pf.

Depression before Spring. *Harmonium* (1923).

4476 Gardner, John. In *Five Partsongs to Poems by Wallace Stevens* op. 142 no. 1. New York: Oxford Univ. Press, 1982. Chorus: SATB, a cap.

Domination of Black. *Harmonium* (1923).

4477 Melby, John. In *Two Stevens Songs*. Song: S, computer-synthesized tape. Recording: Composers Recordings, CRI SD 364 (1976).

4478 Persichetti, Vincent. In *Harmonium* op. 50. Philadelphia: Elkan-Vogel, 1959. Cycle: S, pf.

The Dove in Spring. *Opus Posthumous* (1957).

4479 Rorem, Ned. In *Last Poems of Wallace Stevens*. New York: Boosey & Hawkes, 1974. Cycle: high v, pf.

Earthy Anecdote. *Harmonium* (1923).

4480 Persichetti, Vincent. In *Harmonium* op. 50. Philadelphia: Elkan-Vogel, 1959. Cycle: S, pf.

The Emperor of Ice-Cream. *Harmonium* (1923).

4481 Reynolds, Roger. New York: C.F. Peters, 1963., rev. 1974. Setting for 8 voices, pf, db, perc.

Fabliau of Florida. *Harmonium* (1923).

4482 Holloway, Robin. In *Banal Sojourn*. New York: Boosey & Hawkes, 1978. Cycle: S, pf.

Final Soliloquy of the Interior Paramour. *Selected Poems by Wallace Stevens* (1953).

4482a Persichetti, Vincent. n.t. in *Hymns and Responses* op. 68 no. 26. Philadelphia: Elkan-Vogel, 1956. An evening response.

The Green Plant. *The Collected Poems of Wallace Stevens* (1954).

4483 Ordansky, Jerold A. In *4 Poems by Wallace Stevens*. MS, 1979, avail. ACA. Song: med. v, pf.

Gubbinal. *Harmonium* (1923).

4484 Holloway, Robin. In *Banal Sojourn*. New York: Boosey & Hawkes, 1978. Cycle: S, pf.

4485 Persichetti, Vincent. In *Harmonium* op. 50. Philadelphia: Elkan-Vogel, 1959. Cycle: S, pf.

In the Clear Season of Grapes. *Harmonium* (1931).

4486 Persichetti, Vincent. In *Harmonium* op. 50. Philadelphia: Elkan-Vogel, 1959. Cycle: S, pf.

Infanta Marina. *Harmonium* (1923).

4487 Persichetti, Vincent. In *Harmonium* op. 50. Philadelphia: Elkan-Vogel, 1959. Cycle: S, pf.

Life Is Motion. *Harmonium* (1923).

4488 Gardner, John. In *Five Partsongs to Poems by Wallace Stevens* op. 142 no. 4. New York: Oxford Univ. Press, 1982. Chorus: SATB, a cap.

4489 Holloway, Robin. In *Banal Sojourn*. New York: Boosey & Hawkes, 1978. Cycle: S, pf.

Lunar Paraphrase. *Harmonium* (1931).

4490 Persichetti, Vincent. In *Harmonium* op. 50. Philadelphia: Elkan-Vogel, 1959. Cycle: S, pf.

The Men That Are Falling. *The Man with the Blue Guitar and Other Poems* (1937).

4491 Melby, John. MS, 1978, avail. ACA. Song: S, pf, computer-synthesized tape.

Metaphors of a Magnifico. *Harmonium* (1923).

4492 Persichetti, Vincent. In *Harmonium* op. 50. Philadelphia: Elkan-Vogel, 1959. Cycle: S, pf.

Not Ideas about the Thing but the Thing Itself. *The Collected Poems of Wallace Stevens* (1954).

4493 Rorem, Ned. In *Last Poems of Wallace Stevens*. New York: Boosey & Hawkes, 1974. Cycle: high v, pf.

Nuances of a Theme by Williams. *Harmonium* (1923).

4494 Spratlan, Lewis. "Nuances" in *Images*. Northampton, Mass.: New Valley Music, 1977. Cycle: S, pf.

Of Hartford in a Purple Light. *Parts of a World* (1942).

4495 Harris, Donald. Bryn Mawr: T. Presser, 1979. Song: v, pf.

Of Mere Being. *Opus Posthumous* (1957).

4496 Dembski, Stephen. MS, u.d., avail. ACA. Song: S, pf.

4497 Rorem, Ned. In *Last Poems of Wallace Stevens*. New York: Boosey & Hawkes, 1974. Cycle: high v, pf.

Of the Surface of Things. *Harmonium* (1923).

4498 Persichetti, Vincent. In *Harmonium* op. 50. Philadelphia: Elkan-Vogel, 1959. Cycle: S, pf.

The Ordinary Woman. *Harmonium* (1923).

4499 Holloway, Robin. In *Banal Sojourn*. New York: Boosey & Hawkes, 1978. Cycle: S, pf.

Peter Quince at the Clavier. *Harmonium* (1923).

> 4500 Argento, Dominick. New York: Boosey & Hawkes, 1980. Sonatina: SATB chorus, pf concertante. Four untitled movements correspond to the four sections of the poem.

> 4501 Cyr, Gordon. In *Song Cycle*. Recording: Fantasy Records, no. 5008 (1959).

> 4502 Gardner, John. In *Five Partsongs to Poems by Wallace Stevens* op. 142 no. 2. New York: Oxford Univ. Press, 1982. Chorus: SATB, a cap. Setting of sec. 1 of the poem.

The Place of the Solitaires. *Harmonium* (1923).

> 4503 Persichetti, Vincent. In *Harmonium* op. 50. Philadelphia: Elkan-Vogel, 1959. Cycle: S, pf.

The Planet on the Table. *The Collected Poems of Wallace Stevens* (1954).

> 4504 Rorem, Ned. In *Last Poems of Wallace Stevens*. New York: Boosey & Hawkes, 1974. Cycle: high v, pf.

The Pleasures of Merely Circulating. *Ideas of Order* (1935).

> 4505 Cumberworth, Starling. New York: Independent Music Publishers, 1953. Song: v, pf.

The Plot against the Giant. *Harmonium* (1923).

> 4506 Westergaard, Peter. New York: J. Boonin, 1973. Cantata: SMA chorus, pf or cl, vc, hp (R).

Ploughing on Sunday. *Harmonium* (1923).

> 4507 Gardner, John. In *Five Partsongs to Poems by Wallace Stevens* op. 142 no. 3. New York: Oxford Univ. Press, 1982. Chorus: SATB, a cap.

> 4508 Holloway, Robin. In *Banal Sojourn*. New York: Boosey & Hawkes, 1978. Cycle: S, pf.

A Postcard from the Volcano. *Ideas of Order* (1936).

> 4509 Melby, John. In *Two Stevens Songs*. Song: S, computer-synthesized tape. Recording: Composers Recordings, CRI SD 364 (1976).

The Red Fern. *Transport to Summer.* (1947).

> 4510 Ordansky, Jerold A. In *4 Poems by Wallace Stevens*. MS, 1979, avail. ACA. Song: med. v, pf.

The River of Rivers in Connecticut. *The Collected Poems of Wallace Stevens* (1954).

4511 Rorem, Ned. In *Last Poems of Wallace Stevens*. New York: Boosey & Hawkes, 1974. Cycle: high v, pf.

Sea Surface Full of Clouds. *Harmonium* (1931).

4512 Holloway, Robin. New York: Boosey & Hawkes, 1978. Chorus: SSAATTBB, SAc-TT soli, orch.

Six Significant Landscapes. *Harmonium* (1923).

4513 Persichetti, Vincent. In *Harmonium* op. 50. Philadelphia: Elkan-Vogel, 1959. Cycle: S, pf.

The Snow Man. *Harmonium* (1923).

4514 Connolly, Justin. In *Poems of Wallace Stevens I* op. 9 no. 3. Sevenoaks, Kent: Novello, 1978. Song: fl, cl, vib, hp, cel, vla, trp. Recording: Argo, ZRG 747.

4515 Persichetti, Vincent. In *Harmonium* op. 50. Philadelphia: Elkan-Vogel, 1959. Cycle: S, pf.

Sonatina to Hans Christian. *Harmonium* (1931).

4516 Persichetti, Vincent. In *Harmonium* op. 50. Philadelphia: Elkan-Vogel, 1959. Cycle: S, pf.

Tattoo. *Harmonium* (1923).

4517 Connolly, Justin. In *Poems of Wallace Stevens I* op. 9 no. 1. Sevenoaks, Kent: Novello, 1978. Song: fl, cl, vib, hp, cel, vla, trp. Recording: Argo, ZRG 747.

4518 Persichetti, Vincent. In *Harmonium* op. 50. Philadelphia: Elkan-Vogel, 1959. Cycle: S, pf.

Tea at the Palaz of Hoon. *Harmonium* (1923).

4519 Persichetti, Vincent. "Tea" in *Harmonium* op. 50. Philadelphia: Elkan-Vogel, 1959. Cycle: S, pf.

Theory. *Harmonium* (1923).

4520 Persichetti, Vincent. In *Harmonium* op. 50. Philadelphia: Elkan-Vogel, 1959. Cycle: S, pf.

Thirteen Ways of Looking at a Blackbird. *Harmonium* (1923).

4521 Blacher, Boris. "Thirteen Ways of Looking at a Blackbird. Eine Amsel dreizehnmal gesehen" op. 54. Berlin: Bote & Bock, 1958. Song: high v, str orch. Text in Eng. and Ger., trans. by Kurt Hansen. Recording: Deutsche Grammophone LPM 18 759 (1962).

4522 Blank, Allan. Song: S, vn/vla, cl/bcl, fl, vc, pf. Recording: Composers Recordings, CRI SD 250 (1970).

4523 Foss, Lukas. New York: Pembroke Music, 1979. Song: S or M, fl, pf, perc.

4524 Gruen, John. In *Song Cycle* op. 20. MS, 1953. Recording: Contemporary Records, AP 121 (1958).

4525 Hartway, James J. New York: American Soc. of Univ. Composers, 1974. Song: S, fl, perc, prepared pf.

4526 Glanville-Hicks, Peggy. New York: Weintraub Music, 1951. Song: v, pf.

4527 Persichetti, Vincent. In *Harmonium* op. 50. Philadelphia: Elkan-Vogel, 1959. Cycle: S, pf.

4528 Williams, Edgar W., Jr. "The Bawds of Euphony." Boelke-Bomart, 1974. Song: S, pf.

To the Roaring Wind. *Harmonium* (1923).

4529 Lybbert, Donald. In *From "Harmonium."* Bryn Mawr: Merion Music, 1970. Cycle: high v, pf.

Valley Candle. *Harmonium* (1923).

4530 Holloway, Robin. In *Banal Sojourn.* New York: Boosey & Hawkes, 1978. Cycle: S, pf.

4531 Lybbert, Donald. In *From "Harmonium."* Bryn Mawr: Merion Music, 1970. Cycle: high v, pf.

4532 Persichetti, Vincent. In *Harmonium* op. 50. Philadelphia: Elkan-Vogel, 1959. Cycle: S, pf.

The Weeping Burgher. *Harmonium* (1923).

4533 Persichetti, Vincent. In *Harmonium* op. 50. Philadelphia: Elkan-Vogel, 1959. Cycle: S, pf.

The Wind Shifts. *Harmonium* (1923).

4534 Persichetti, Vincent. In *Harmonium* op. 50. Philadelphia: Elkan-Vogel, 1959. Cycle: S, pf.

Miscellaneous

4535 Holloway, Robin. "The Leaves Cry" op. 27. New York: Boosey & Hawkes, 1978. Song: S, pf.

4536 Entry cancelled.

GENEVIEVE TAGGARD (1894–1948)

Holiday Song. *Long View* (1942).

> 4537 Schuman, William. New York: G. Schirmer, 1942, 1946. Song: v, pf. Also pubd for SATB chorus and pf, TTBB chorus and pf, and SAB chorus and pf.

Lark. *Not Mine to Finish* (1934).

> 4538 Clarke, Henry L. MS, u.d., avail. ACA. Song: S, unacc.

> 4539 Copland, Aaron. Boston: E.C. Schirmer, 1941. Chorus: SATB, Bar solo, a cap.

Primavera. *Long View* (1942).

> 4540 Clarke, Henry L. MS, 1955, avail. ACA. Chorus: SSA, pf or str orch.

Prologue. *Long View* (1942).

> 4541 Schuman, William H. New York: G. Schirmer, 1939. Chorus: SSATB, pf or orch.

Sea Change. *For Eager Lovers* (1922).

> 4542 Benson, Warren. In *Two Sea Poems*. New York: C. Fischer, 1976. Chorus: SATB, a cap.

Song I. *Slow Music* (1946).

> 4543 Clarke, Henry L. In *Four Elements*. MS, 1962, avail. ACA. Song: S, vc.

This Is Our Time (Secular Cantata Number 1). *Long View* (1942).

> 4544 Schuman, William. "This Is Our Time." New York: Boosey & Hawkes, 1940. Cantata: SATB chorus, orch. All five sections of the poem set.

ALLEN TATE (1899–1979)

Emblems. *Poems: 1928–1931* (1932).

4545 Carter, Elliott. New York: Music Press, 1949. Chorus: TTBB, pf.

BAYARD TAYLOR (1825–1878)

Bedouin Song. *Poems of the Orient* (1854).

4546 Adams, Charles R. Boston: A.P. Schmidt, 1882. Song: B, pf.

4547 Bonney, Avonia. "From the Desert I Come to Thee." Boston: O. Ditson, 1885. Song: v, pf.

4548 Buck, Dudley. "Bedouin Love-Song" op. 87 no. 2. New York: Wm. A. Pond, 1872. Song: high and med. v edns, pf.

4549 Chadwick, George W. "Bedouin Love Song." Boston: A.P. Schmidt, 1890. Song: high and med. v edns, pf.

4550 Coombs, Charles W. "Bedouin Love Song" in *Two Songs* op. 2. Stuttgart: G.A. Zumsteeg, 1883. Song: v, pf. Text in Eng. and Ger.; Philadelphia: Presser, 1914. Song: high and low v edns, pf.

4551 Downs, M.S. "From the Desert I Come." Boston: G.D. Russell, 1868. Song: v, pf. Text in Ital. and Eng.

4552 Foote, Arthur. "Bedouin Song." Boston: A.P. Schmidt, 1892. Chorus: Setting for 4-pt. men's chorus, pf; Also pubd in a German language edn; Boston: A.P. Schmidt, 1903. Setting for 4-pt. mixed voices, pf.

4553 Gross, A. Haller. "From the Desert I Come to Thee." Boston: O. Ditson, 1888. Song: v, pf.

4554 Hawley, C.B. "Bedouin Love Song." New York: G. Schirmer, 1897. Song: Bar and B edns, pf. In coll. SFB.

4555 Marston, G.W. "Bedouin Love Song." Boston: A.P. Schmidt, 1891. Song: T and Bar edns, pf.

4556 Morse, Constance. "Bedouin Love Song." Boston: C.W. Thompson, 1905. Song: v, pf.

4557 Neidlinger, W.H. "From the Desert I Come." New York: G. Schirmer, 1893. Song: high, med., and low v edns, pf?

4558 Pease, Alfred H. New York: Pond, 1872. Song: v, pf.

4559 Pilcher, William H. "Bedouin Love Song" op. 34 no. 1. Boston: O. Ditson, 1893. Song: v, pf.

4560 Pinsuti, Ciro. "Bedouin Love Song." u.p.: J.B. Robinson, 1904. Song: v, pf.; Richard C. Dillmore, ed.; rearranged by Johann C. Schmid, 1905; In coll. AB 2, CB, DarJ, FSS 6, MM.

4561 Protheroe, Daniel. "From the Desert" op. 55 no. 4. Boston: Boston Music, 1903. Chorus: TTBB, a cap.

4562 Sternberg, Constantin I. "Song of the Arab" op. 81. Cincinnati: J. Church, 1900. Song: v, pf.

Greeting to America. *Knickerbocker* 36 (Oct. 1850), p. 379.

4563 Benedict, Julius. "Jenny Lind's Greeting to America." New York: Firth, Pond, 1850. Song: v, pf.

Improvisations ["Near in the forest"]. *Melodies of Verse* (1884).

4564 Kreipel, J. "Near in the Forest" in coll. LBR; "The Forest Glade" in coll. JSE.

The National Ode. *Harper's Weekly* no. 20 (July 22, 1876), p. 594.

4565 Damrosch, Leopold. "National Ode." New York: G. Schirmer, 1899. Setting for TTBB solo qrt and TTBB chorus.

Persian Serenade. *Independent* (Dec. 7, 1882).

4566 Aiken, George E., Mrs. "A Persian Serenade." New York: C.H. Ditson, 1887. Song: v, pf.

4567 Cole, Rossetter G. "Persian Serenade." Cleveland and Chicago: S. Brainard's Sons, 1888. Song: v, pf.

4568 Colyn, Garrett. "Persian Serenade." New York: G. Schirmer, 1885. Song: high and med. v edns, pf.

4569 Dolliver, Sewall. "A Persian Serenade." San Francisco: W.J. Burke, 1895. Song: v, pf.

4570 Hardee, Noble A. "Persian Serenade." Song: high v, pf.

4571 Marston, G.W. "Persian Serenade." Boston: A.P. Schmidt, 1891. Song: T or S, pf.

4572 Train, Adelaide. "Persian Serenade" in *Two Songs*. New York: G. Schirmer, 1893. Song: med. v, pf.

Proposal. *Melodies of Verse* (1884).

4573 Brackett, Frank H. Boston: O. Ditson, 1884, 1899. Song: high and med. v edns, pf; In coll. BST, ES; Samuel R. Gaines, arr. Boston: O. Ditson, 1899, 1926. Part Song: SATB, pf.

4574 Downs, M.S. Boston: O. Ditson, 1871. Song: v, pf.

4575 Gluck, C.W., arr. from. "The Proposal" in coll. LBR.

4576 Goerdeler, R. "Violet Loves a Mossy Bank." Boston: O. Ditson, 1867. Song: v, pf.

4577 Hastings, Frank S. New York: G. Schirmer, 1907. Song: high, med., and low v edns, pf. There is possibly another edn of this for med. v titled "Shall I Wed Thee?"

4578 Kaiser, Charles, Jr. "Shall I Wed Thee" op. 3 no. 1. Baltimore: George Willig, 1883. Song: v, pf.

4579 Liebling, Estelle, arr. "Chopin Mazurka (The Violet Loves a Sunny Bank)." New York: Galaxy, 1945. Song: high v, pf. Arr. from "Mazurka" op. 50 no. 2.

4580 Lutkin, Peter C. "Shall I Wed Thee?" Chicago: Chicago Music, 1887. Song: v, pf.

4581 Maier, A.G. In *Two Songs*. Cincinnati: J. Church, 1891. Song: v, pf.

4582 Ross, William. Cincinnati: J. Church, 1890. Song: v, pf.

4583 Spicker, Max. "Shall I Wed Thee?" op. 37. New York: G. Schirmer, 1896. Song: high and med. v edns, pf.

The Return of Spring. *Melodies of Verse* (1884).

4584 Jones, W.H. In coll. NMS.

Saturday Night at Sea. *Poems of the Orient* (1854).

4585 Leslie, Ernest. Boston: J.M. Russell, 1860. Quartet: male voices.

Scott and the Veteran. *Poems of American Patriotism,* ed. by Brander Matthews (1917).

4586 Warden, D.A. "General Scott and Corporal Johnson." Philadelphia: D.A. Warden, 1862. Song: v, pf.

Song ["Daughter of Egypt, veil thine eyes!"] *Poems of the Orient* (1854).

4587 Freer, Eleanor E. "Daughter of Egypt Veil Thine Eyes" in *Two Songs* op. 16. Berlin: R. Kaun, 1909. Song: v, pf.

Song ["I plucked for thee the wilding rose"]. *A Book of Romances, Lyrics, and Songs* (1852).

4588 Brackett, Frank H. "Rosebuds" in *Three Songs*. Boston: O. Ditson, 1896. Song: T, pf.

Storm Song. *A Book of Romances, Lyrics, and Songs* (1852).

4589 Gluck, C.W., arr. from. "The Storm Song" in coll. LBR.

The Voyagers. *Poems of Home and Travel* (1855).

4590 Foerster, Adolphe M. Ed. by Theodore M. Finney. "The Voyagers" op. 68 no. 2. Pittsburgh: Volkwein Bros., 1937. Chorus: TTBB, a cap.

4591 Silcher, F. In coll. LBR. Arr. to the Air: "Die Lorelei."

Wind and Sea. *Poems of Home and Travel* (1855).

4592 Cauffman, Frank G. In coll. TL. Setting for SATB, pf.

4593 Schulz, J.A.P. In coll. LBR. New York: G. Schirmer, 1893. Song: med. v, pf. Text: "Hark how the twilight pale...."

Miscellaneous

4594 Allen, George N. "Ocean Star; or, Lamp of My Spirit." Cleveland: S. Brainard, 1856. Song: v, pf.

4595 Allitsen, Frances. "I Know a Little Rose." New York: G. Schirmer, 1901. Song: med. v, pf. Text in Eng. and Ger.

4596 Fairfax, C.H. "Sleep, Soldiers! Still in Honored Rest" in coll. ArF 2.

4597 Fossier, J. "Art Thou True to Me." Song: v, pf. Cited in DCD.

4598 Entry cancelled.

4599 "Learn to Live, and Live to Learn." Arr. from an Eng. Air in coll. LBR.

4600 Paine, John K. "Matin Song" in *Four Songs* op. 29 no. 1. Boston: O. Ditson, 1879. Song: high v, pf. In coll. HST.

4601 Petri, J.F. "Deutsches Jubellied." Priv. pubd by Petri, 1870. Quartet: TTBB, a cap. Text in Eng. and Ger., "We've won the sword and valiant hand...."

4602 Schulz, J.A.P. "The Summers Come and Go" in coll. LBR.

4603 Weiland, F. "Autumn Dreaming" in coll. FSS 4.

4604 White, Joseph L. "My Rose." Boston: Louis H. Ross, 1884. Song: v, pf.

4605 Wilhelm, C. "Guard on the Rhine." Song and Chorus, pf.

4606 Young, Eliza M. "Song of the Morn." Chicago: C.F. Summy, 1891. Song: v, pf.

EDWARD TAYLOR (1642–1729)

The Ebb and Flow. *Poems of Edward Taylor* (1960).

    4607 Binkerd, Gordon. New York: Boosey & Hawkes, 1967, rev. edn 1972. Chorus: SATB, a cap.

Huswifery. *Poems of Edward Taylor* (1960).

    4608 Binkerd, Gordon. New York: Boosey & Hawkes, 1970. Chorus: SATB, a cap.

    4609 Winslow, Richard K. New York: C. Fischer, 1950. Chorus: SSA, pf.

The Joy of Church Fellowship Rightly Attended. *Poems of Edward Taylor* (1960).

    4610 Gibbons, Orlando, arr. from. "In Heaven Soaring Up." Tune: "Song of the Three Children." In coll. ChAH. Hymn.

Meditation Fifty-Six. *Poems of Edward Taylor* (1960).

    4611 Cowell, Henry. "Thou Art the Tree of Life." Tune: "Tree of Life." In coll. ChAH. Hymn.

Meditation One Hundred and Ten. *Poems of Edward Taylor* (1960).

    4612 Gibbons, Orlando, arr. from. "The Angels Sung a Carol." Tune: "Song 4." In coll. ChAH. Hymn.

Meditation Twelve. *Poems of Edward Taylor* (1960).

    4613 Finzi, Gerald. "My Lovely One." New York: Boosey & Hawkes, 1948. Anthem: SATB, org.

Meditation Twenty. *Poems of Edward Taylor* (1960).

    4614 Finzi, Gerald. "God Is Gone Up." New York: Boosey & Hawkes, 1952. Anthem: SATB, org.

The Preface. *Poems of Edward Taylor* (1960).

    4615 Cowell, Henry. "If He Please." New York: C.F. Peters, 1962. Chorus: mixed voices, 3 pt boys' or women's voices, orch (R). Recording: Composers Recordings, CRI 217 USD (1963).

SARA TEASDALE (1884–1933)

Advice to a Girl. *Strange Victory* (1933).

> 4616 Behrend, Jeanne. In *Six Teasdale Songs.* Philadelphia: composer, 1943. Song: v, pf.
>
> 4617 Starer, Robert. New York: Leeds, 1951. Song: med. or high v, pf.

After Parting. *Rivers to the Sea* (1915).

> 4618 Spencer, James. Boston, New York: White-Smith, 1920. Song: high and low v edns, pf.

Alone. *Flame and Shadow* (1920).

> 4619 Murray, Bain. In *Flame and Shadow.* u.p.: Ludwig Music, 1974. Cycle: S, pf.

April Song. *Rivers to the Sea* (1915).

> 4620 Harelson, Harry B. Chicago: H.T. FitzSimmons, 1933. Chorus: SSA, pf.
>
> 4621 Milligan, Harold V. "Willow in Your April Gown." Boston: A.P. Schmidt, 1926. Song: high and med. v edns, pf.

Barter. *Love Songs* (1932).

> 4622 Clarke, Henry L. "Life Has Loveliness to Sell." MS, u.d., avail. ACA. Setting for antiphonal unison chorus, pf.

Beatrice. *Helen of Troy and Other Poems* (1911).

> 4623 Milligan, Harold V. In *3 Songs.* Boston: A.P. Schmidt, 1916. Song: S or T, pf.

Central Park at Dusk. *Helen of Troy and Other Poems* (1911).

> 4624 Duke, John. New York: Boosey & Hawkes, 1949. Song: med. v, pf.

Christmas Carol. *Helen of Troy and Other Poems* (1911).

> 4625 Kay, Ulysses. New York: Peer International, 1957. Chorus: SSA, a cap.
>
> 4626 Mechem, Kirke. "Christmas Carol" op. 35 no. 1. Boston: E.C. Schirmer, 1969. Chorus: SATB, gtr.

Come. *Rivers to the Sea* (1915).

4627 Bergh, Arthur. "Come with Arms Outstretched." New York: Galaxy, 1941. Song: v, pf.

4628 Paine, Cordelia A. New York: E. Morris, 1924. Song: v, pf.

Compensation. *Flame and Shadow* (1920).

4629 Fisher, William A. "The Singer's Wish" in *Poems by Sara Teasdale* op. 18 no. 2. Boston: O. Ditson, 1921. Song: high and med. v edns, pf.

4630 Kettering, Eunice L. In coll. TaCAS. Song: high and low v edns, pf.

A Cry. *Rivers to the Sea* (1915).

4631 Watts, Wintter. "Only a Cry" in *Two Songs by Sara Teasdale*. New York: G. Schirmer, 1923. Song: med. v, pf.

Debt. *Rivers to the Sea* (1915).

4632 Behrend, Jeanne. In *Six Teasdale Songs*. Philadelphia: composer, 1943. Song: v, pf.

Deep in the Night. *Rivers to the Sea* (1915).

4633 Brussels, Iris. New York: American Music Co., 1933. Chorus: SSA, pf; New York: American Music, 1933. Song: high and low v edns, pf.

4634 Clarke, Leland. "Over the World to You." Boston: A.P. Schmidt, 1917. Song: high and med. v edns, pf.

4635 Rihm, Alexander. Boston: O. Ditson, 1919. Song: high and low v edns, pf.

Dew. *Helen of Troy and Other Poems* (1911).

4636 Starer, Robert. New York: Leeds, 1951. Song: high v, pf.

Dusk in June. *Rivers to the Sea* (1915).

4637 Beach, Amy Cheney. "Dusk in June" op. 82. New York: G. Schirmer, 1917. Chorus: SSAA, a cap.

4638 Foster, Fay. New York: Bryant Music, 1917. Song: high and low v edns, pf.

Ebb Tide. *Love Songs* (1932).

4639 Hill, Mabel W. In *Four Poems by Sara Teasdale*. New York: G. Schirmer, 1919. Song: high v, pf.

Enough. *Rivers to the Sea* (1915).

> 4640 Cooper, Esther. New York: C. Fischer, 1950. Song: v, pf. In coll. TaCS.

> 4641 Coryell, Marian. "Contentment." Milwaukee: Seneca Pierce, 1919. Song: high v, pf.

> 4642 Samuels, Homer. New York: G. Ricordi, 1922. Song: high and low v edns, pf.

Even To-day. *Strange Victory* (1933).

> 4643 Miller, Horace A. In *Two Songs*. Mt. Vernon, Iowa: Cornell College, 1935. Song: v, pf.

A Fantasy. *Helen of Troy and Other Poems* (1911).

> 4644 Milligan, Harold V. "Her Voice Is Like Clear Water" in *5 Lyrics by Sara Teasdale*. Boston: A.P. Schmidt, 1917. Song: v, pf.

Faults. *Love Songs* (1932).

> 4645 Behrend, Jeanne. In *Six Teasdale Songs*. Philadelphia: composer, 1943. Song: v, pf.

February Twilight. *Dark of the Moon* (1926).

> 4646 Duke, John. New York: G. Schirmer, 1926? Song: high v, pf.
> 4647 Williams, Frances. In coll. UNSNV, WieF.

The Flight. *Rivers to the Sea* (1915).

> 4648 Allen, Robert E. New York: Galaxy, 1950. Song: S, pf.
> 4649 Bull, Clifton B., Jr. "But What if I Heard My First Love" in *Songs of the Heart*. New York: G. Schirmer, 1915. Song: v, pf.

Four Winds. *Helen of Troy and Other Poems* (1911).

> 4650 Cohen, Cecil. New York: E.B. Marks, 1944. Song: v, pf. In coll. CNA.

From the Sea. *Rivers to the Sea* (1915).

> 4651 Duke, John. "All Beauty Calls You to Me," "Listen, I Love You," "I Am So Weak a Thing," "All Things in All the World," "O, My Love" in *Five Songs for Soprano*. Song: S, pf. Recording: Cambridge, CRS 2776 (1979).

Gifts. *Rivers to the Sea* (1915).

4652 De Lamarter, Eric. New York: H.W. Gray, 1920. Song: v, pf.

4653 Hedge, Grace. New York: American Music Edn, u.d. In collaboration with Agnes Booe.

The High Hill. *Flame and Shadow* (1920).

4653a Murray, Bain. In *Flame and Shadow*. u.p.: Ludwig Music, 1974. Cycle: S, pf.

I Shall Not Care. *Rivers to the Sea* (1915).

4654 Behrend, Jeanne. In *Six Teasdale Songs*. Philadelphia: composer, 1943. Song: v, pf.

4655 Dallam, Helen. New York: J. Fischer, 1924. Song: high v, pf.

4656 Ilgenfritz, McNair. New York: E. Schuberth, 1934. Song: med. v, pf.

4657 Mechem, Kirke. In *The Winds of May*. Boston: E.C. Schirmer, 1965. Choral Cycle: SSAA, a cap.

I Would Live in Your Love. *Helen of Troy and Other Poems* (1911).

4658 Ivey, Jean E. In *American Artsong Anthology*. Vol. 1. New York: Galaxy, 1982. Song.

4659 Murray, Bain. In *Flame and Shadow*. u.p.: Ludwig Music, 1974. Cycle: S, pf.

"If I Must Go." *Flame and Shadow* (1920).

4660 Adler, Lawrence. "If I Must Go to Heaven's End." Paris: M. Senart, 1923. Song: v, pf.

Joy. *Rivers to the Sea* (1915).

4661 Bartlett, Floy L. "Heat-Fire and Singing." Boston: A.P. Schmidt, 1931. Song: high and med. v edns, pf.

4662 Foster, Fay. "At Last." New York: C. Fischer, 1918. Song: high, med., and low v edns, pf.

4663 Kennedy, John B. In *The Look, the Kiss, and Joy*. New York: Boosey & Hawkes, 1972. Chorus: SSA, a cap.

4664 Kramer, Arthur W. "Joy" op. 44 no. 1. New York: J. Fischer, 1917. Song: high v, pf.

4665 Murray, Bain. In *Flame and Shadow*. u.p.: Ludwig Music, 1974. Cycle: S, pf.

4666 Rihm, Alexander. In *Two Songs*. New York: Huntzinger & Dilworth, 1919. Song: high and low v, pf.

4667 Roberts, George. New York: J. Fischer, 1923. Song: high and low v edns, pf.

4668 Watts, Wintter. New York: G. Schirmer, 1922. Song: med. and low v edns, pf.

A June Day. *Stars To-Night* (1930).

4669 Kagen, Sergius. New York: Weintraub, 1950. Song: high v, pf.

The Kiss ["Before you kissed me only winds of heaven"]. *Rivers to the Sea* (1915).

4670 Fryer, Herbert. In *Five Songs*. New York: G. Schirmer, 1916. Song: high or med. v, pf.

The Kiss ["I hoped that he would love me"]. *Helen of Troy and Other Poems* (1911).

4671 Barab, Seymour. In *First Person Feminine*. New York: Boosey & Hawkes, 1970. Choral Cycle: SSA, pf.

4672 Jacchia, Agide. Boston: Boston Music, 1920. Song: med. v, pf.

4673 Kennedy, John B. In *The Look, the Kiss, and Joy*. New York: Boosey & Hawkes, 1972. Chorus: SSA, a cap.

The Lamp. *Love Songs* (1932).

4674 Hill, Mabel W. In *Five Poems by Sara Teasdale*. New York: G. Schirmer, 1919. Song: v, pf.

Late October. *Dark of the Moon* (1926).

4675 Behrend, Jeanne. In *Six Teasdale Songs*. Philadelphia: composer, 1943. Song: v, pf.

Less Than the Cloud to the Wind. *Helen of Troy and Other Poems* (1911).

4676 McGill, Josephine. "Less Than the Cloud" in *Two Songs*. New York: G. Schirmer, 1927. Song: high v, pf.

4677 Milligan, Harold V. In *5 Lyrics by Sara Teasdale*. Boston: A.P. Schmidt, 1917. Song: v, pf.

Let It Be Forgotten. *Flame and Shadow* (1920).

4678 Farley, Roland. In *Two Poems by Sara Teasdale*. New York: G. Schirmer, 1926. Song: high or med. v, pf.

4679 Kagen, Sergius. New York: Weintraub, 1950. Song: v, pf.

4680 Mechem, Kirke. In *Goodbye, Farewell, and Adieu* op. 33 no. 3. New York: C. Fischer, 1979. Song: med. v, pf.

4681 Mechem, Kirke. In *The Winds of May*. Boston: E.C. Schirmer, 1965. Choral Cycle: SATB, a cap.

4682 Merrill, Marlin. New York: Oxford Univ. Press, 1972. Chorus: SSAATB or SSAA, pf.

4683 Sacco, John. New York: C. Fischer, 1941. Song: high and low v edns, pf.

4684 Watts, Wintter. In *Two Songs by Sara Teasdale*. New York: G. Schirmer, 1923. Song: high v, pf.

4685 Zaimont, Judith L. In *Greyed Sonnets*. MS, 1975, avail. ACA. Song: S, pf. Recording: Golden Crest, ATH 5051.

Like Barley Bending. *Flame and Shadow* (1920).

4686 Lewis, Leo R. u.p.: The Tufts College Press, 1933. Chorus: TTBB, pf.

4687 Tyson, Mildred L. New York: G. Schirmer, 1932. Song: high or med. v, pf.

4688 Entry cancelled.

The Look. *Rivers to the Sea* (1915).

4689 Barab, Seymour. In *First Person Feminine*. New York: Boosey & Hawkes, 1970. Choral Cycle: SSA, pf.

4690 Behrend, Jeanne. In *Six Teasdale Songs*. Philadelphia: composer, 1943. Song: v, pf.

4691 Fish, Alice R. In *Four Songs*. New York: G. Schirmer, 1918. Song: high v, pf.

4692 Flothius, Marius. In *Four Trifles for High Voice and Piano* op. 33. Amsterdam: Donemus, 1949. Song: high v, pf. Music not seen; text is presumably from this poem.

4693 Foster, Fay. "The Kiss in Colin's Eyes." New York: Wm. A. Pond, 1917. Song: med. v, pf.

4694 Fox, Fred. New York: Galaxy, u.d. Chorus: SATB.

4695 Hill, Mabel W. In *Four Poems by Sara Teasdale*. New York: G. Schirmer, 1919. Song: low v, pf.

4696 Housman, Rosalie. In *Three Songs*. Boston: Boston Music, 1918. Song: high and low v edns, pf.

4697 Jacobi, Frederick. In *Three Songs*. New York: G. Schirmer, 1915. Song: high v, pf.

4698 Kennedy, John B. In *The Look, the Kiss, and Joy*. New York: Boosey & Hawkes, 1972. Chorus: SSA, a cap.

4699 Menges, Edward E. University City, Mo.: Autographic Music, 1937. Song: med. v, pf.

4700 Murray, Bain. In *Flame and Shadow.* u.p.: Ludwig Music, 1974. Cycle: S, pf.

4701 Rybner, Dagmar de Corval. "Pastorale." Boston: O. Ditson, 1918. Song: high and med. v edns, pf.

Love-Free. *Rivers to the Sea* (1915).

4702 De Lamarter, Eric. New York: H.W. Gray, 1920. Song: v, pf.

Love Me. *Helen of Troy and Other Poems* (1911).

4703 Barab, Seymour. In *First Person Feminine.* New York: Boosey & Hawkes, 1970. Choral Cycle: SSA, pf.

4704 Clarke, Kathleen B. "Love Me, Kiss Me" in *Four Songs.* New York: G. Schirmer, 1919. Song: high v, pf.

4705 Milligan, Harold V. In *Two Songs.* New York: G. Schirmer, 1914. Song: v, pf.

4706 Watts, Wintter. Boston: O. Ditson, 1919. Song: med. and low v edns, pf.

A Maiden. *Helen of Troy and Other Poems* (1911).

4707 Foster, Fay. New York: C. Fischer, 1918. Song: high and low v edns, pf.

Moods. *Rivers to the Sea* (1915).

4708 Andrews, Mark. New York: H.W. Gray, 1926. Song: high v, pf.

4709 Busch, Carl. Boston: O. Ditson, 1921. Song: high and med. v edns, pf.

4710 De Lamarter, Eric. New York: H.W. Gray, 1920. Song: v, pf.

4711 Farley, Roland. "I Am the Still Rain" in *Two Poems by Sara Teasdale.* New York: G. Schirmer, 1926. Song: med. or low v, pf.

4712 Spencer, James. Boston and New York: White-Smith, 1920. Song: med. and low v edns, pf.

Morning Song. *Flame and Shadow* (1920).

4713 Frederickson, Dolores. New York: Orchesis Publications, 1960. Song: low v, pf.

The Old Enemy. *Dark of the Moon* (1926).

4714 Kramer, Arthur W. "At the Evening's End." New York: J. Fischer, 1931. Song: high v, pf.

On a March Day. *Dark of the Moon* (1926).

>   4715 Duke, John. New York: Boosey & Hawkes, 1949. Song: low v, pf.

On the Dunes. *Flame and Shadow* (1920).

>   4716 Hughes, Rupert. "The Sun-Swept Dunes" in *Four Meditations*. New York: G. Schirmer, 1920. Song: v, pf.

Over the Roofs. *Rivers to the Sea* (1915).

>   4717 Mechem, Kirke. In *The Winds of May*. Boston: E.C. Schirmer, 1965. Choral Cycle: SSAATTBB, a cap; also pubd for TTBB chorus, a cap.

Peace. *Rivers to the Sea* (1915).

>   4718 Beach, Bennie. In coll. TaCAS. Song: high and low v edns, pf.

>   4719 Murray, Bain. In *Flame and Shadow*. Ludwig Music, 1974. Cycle: S, pf.

>   4720 Walker, May S. London: Augener, 1936. Song: v, pf.

Pierrot. *Helen of Troy and Other Poems* (1911).

>   4721 Andrews, Mark. New York: G. Ricordi, 1919. Song: v, pf; New York: G. Ricordi, 1929. Chorus: SSA, pf.

>   4722 Barab, Seymour. In *First Person Feminine*. New York: Boosey & Hawkes, 1970. Choral Cycle: SSA, pf.

>   4723 McGill, Josephine. New York: Luckhardt & Belder, 1914. Song: S, pf.

>   4724 Milligan, Harold V. In *5 Lyrics by Sara Teasdale*. Boston: A.P. Schmidt, 1917. Song: v, pf.

>   4725 Read, Gardner. New York: Galaxy, 1943. Song.

>   4726 Rybner, D. Cited in ScNS. Song: high and low v edns, pf.

>   4727 Samuels, Homer. New York: G. Ricordi, 1922. Song: v, pf.

>   4728 Watts, Wintter. Boston: O. Ditson, 1919. Song: high and med. v edns, pf.

The Return. *Flame and Shadow* (1920).

>   4729 Hier, Ethel G. In *The Hour and the Return*. New York: Composers Press, 1949. Song: v, pf.

>   4730 Saar, Louis V. In *Three Songs* op. 101 no. 1. New York: G. Schirmer, 1924. Song: high v, pf.

The River. *Rivers to the Sea* (1915).

4731 Lee, Norman. Chicago: McKinley Music, 1936. Song: v, pf.

The Rose. *Rivers to the Sea* (1915).

4732 Rihm, Alexander. In *Three Songs*. New York: G. Schirmer, 1918. Song: v, pf.

The Rose and the Bee. *Helen of Troy and Other Poems* (1911).

4733 Milligan, Harold V. In *Three Songs*. New York: G. Schirmer, 1914. Song: v, pf.

Sand Drift. *Dark of the Moon* (1926).

4734 Klemm, Gustav. New York: Sprague-Colman, 1940. Song: v, pf.

Song ["Love me with your whole heart"]. *Rivers to the Sea* (1915).

4735 Mechem, Kirke. In *The Winds of May*. Boston: E.C. Schirmer, 1965. Choral Cycle: SATB, a cap.

Song ["You bound strong sandals on my feet"]. *Helen of Troy and Other Poems* (1911).

4736 Milligan, Harold V. "You Bound Strong Sandals on My Feet" in *5 Lyrics by Sara Teasdale*. Boston: A.P. Schmidt, 1917. Song: v, pf.

The Song for Colin. *Helen of Troy and Other Poems* (1911).

4737 Barab, Seymour. In *First Person Feminine*. New York: Boosey & Hawkes, 1970. Choral Cycle: SSA, pf.

Spray. *Flame and Shadow* (1920).

4738 Duke, John. New York: Boosey & Hawkes, 1949. Song: med.-high v, pf.

Stars ["Alone in the night"]. *Flame and Shadow* (1920).

4739 Berwald, William H. New York: J. Fischer, 1934. Chorus: SATB, a cap.

Stars ["Night is over the park, and a few brave stars"]. *Rivers to the Sea* (1915).

4740 Kramer, Arthur W. "Swans" op. 44 no. 4. New York: G. Ricordi, 1917. Song: high and low v edns, pf; "Swans" op. 44 no. 4a. New York: G. Ricordi, 1934. Chorus: SSA, pf.

4741 Rybner, Dagmar de Corval. "Swans." New York: Luckhardt & Belder, 1918. Song: v, pf. Words in Eng. and French.

There Will Be Stars. *Dark of the Moon* (1926).

> 4742 Duke, John. New York: Boosey & Hawkes, 1953. Song: med. v, pf.

> 4743 Ferguson, Edwin E. New York: Associated Music, u.d. Chorus: SATB, pf.

> 4744 Smith, David S. "There Will Be Stars" op. 52 no. 2. Cincinnati: J. Church, 1927. Song: low v, pf.

To-Night. *Love Songs* (1932).

> 4745 Barnett, A. In *Two Even-Songs*. Song: high v, pf. Cited in ScNS.

> 4746 Spencer, James. Boston, New York: White-Smith, 1920. Song: med. and low v edns, pf.

To One Away. *Rivers to the Sea* (1915); Message. *Love Songs* (1932).

> 4747 Beach, H.H.A., Mrs. "Message" op. 93. Philadelphia: T. Presser, 1922. Song: v, pf.

> 4748 Clarke, Henry. "It Was Your Voice." Boston: C.W. Thompson, 1920. Song: v, pf.

> 4749 Fisher, William A. "I Heard a Cry" op. 18 no. 1. Boston: O. Ditson, 1916. Song: v, pf; Boston: O. Ditson, 1921. Song: high. med., and low v edns, pf. In coll. GAS 2, MasSS.

> 4750 Ivey, Jean E. In *American Artsong Anthology*. Vol. 1. New York: Galaxy, 1982. Song.

> 4751 Rihm, Alexander. In *Two Songs*. New York: Huntzinger & Dilworth, 1919. Song: high and low v edns, pf.

To the Sea. *Strange Victory* (1933).

> 4752 Miller, Horace A. In *Two Songs*. Mt. Vernon, Iowa: Cornell College, 1935. Song: v, pf.

The Tune. *Dark of the Moon* (1926).

> 4753 Mechem, Kirke. In *The Winds of May*. Boston: E.C. Schirmer, 1965. Choral Cycle: SATB, a cap.

Twilight ["Dreamily, over the roofs"]. *Helen of Troy and Other Poems* (1911).

> 4754 Milligan, Harold V. In 5 *Lyrics by Sara Teasdale*. Boston: A.P. Schmidt, 1917. Song: v, pf.

> 4755 Watts, Wintter. "Wings of Night." New York: G. Schirmer, 1917. Song: high v, pf. In coll. NAA.

Twilight ["The stately tragedy of dusk"]. *Rivers to the Sea* (1915).

4756 Bacon, Ernst. In *Quiet Airs.* New York: Mercury, 1952. Song: med. v, pf; "Dusk" in coll. BacT. Song: med. v, pf.

Vignettes Overseas. *Rivers to the Sea* (1915).

4757 Barnett, Alice. "Night Song at Amalfi" in *Four Songs.* New York: G. Schirmer, 1919. Song: high v, pf.

4758 Barnett, Alice. "Song at Capri." New York: G. Schirmer, 1923. Song: v, pf; In *Three Songs of Musing.* New York: G. Schirmer, 1923. Song: v, pf.

4759 Beach, H.H.A., Mrs. "Night Song at Amalfi" in *Songs* op. 78 no. 2. New York: G. Schirmer, 1917. Song: v, pf.

4760 Duke, John. "Capri." New York: Boosey & Hawkes, 1949. Song: med.·high v, pf.

4761 Hill, Mabel W. "A Song at Capri" in *Four Poems by Sara Teasdale.* New York: G. Schirmer, 1919. Song: v, pf.

4762 Matthews, Harry A. "Night Song at Amalfi." Philadelphia: Elkan-Vogel, 1950. Song: v, pf; Philadelphia: Elkan-Vogel, 1949. Chorus: SSA, pf.

4763 Naginski, Charles. "Night Song at Amalfi" in *Four Songs.* New York: G. Schirmer, 1942. Song: med. v, pf.

4764 Watts, Wintter. *Vignettes Overseas.* Boston: O. Ditson, 1919. Cycle: high v, pf. Setting of secs. 2–10; "Isle of Beauty (Capri)" in coll. MasSS.

4765 Williams, David H. "Night Song." Glenrock, N.J.: J. Fischer, u.d. Part Song for TB.

Water Lillies. *Flame and Shadow* (1920).

4766 Roy, William. New York: G. Schirmer, 1949. Song: med. v, pf.

4767 Warren, Elinor R. "If You Have Forgotten." New York: G. Schirmer, 1940. Song: high and low v edns, pf.

Wood Song. *Love Songs* (1932).

4768 Rihm, Alexander. Boston: O. Ditson, 1919. Song: high and low v edns, pf.

Young Love [Sec. 6, beginning, "I plucked a daisy in the fields"]. *Helen of Troy and Other Poems* (1911).

4769 Barab, Seymour. "The Daisy" in *First Person Feminine.* New York: Boosey & Hawkes, 1970. Choral Cycle: SSA, pf.

Youth and the Pilgrim. *Helen of Troy and Other Poems* (1911).

4770 Murray, Bain. In *Flame and Shadow.* u.p.: Ludwig Music, 1974. Cycle: S, pf.

Miscellaneous

4771 Barab, Seymour. "The Wayfarer" in *First Person Feminine.* New York: Boosey & Hawkes, 1970. Choral Cycle: SSA, pf. Text: "Love entered in my heart one day. . . ."

4772 Coombs, C.W. "Benediction." Cited in ScNS. Song: low v, pf.

4773 Crandall, George. "Elegy." New York: G. Ricordi, 1936. Song: v, pf.

HENRY DAVID THOREAU (1817–1862)

The Breeze's Invitation. *The Writings of Henry David Thoreau.* Vol. 7 [p. 86] (1906); *Collected Poems of Henry Thoreau* (1943).

4774 Cone, Edward T. "Excursions." New York: Rongwen Music, 1955. Chorus: SSAATBB, a cap.

Haze ["Woof of the sun, ethereal gauze"]. *Poems of Nature* (1895).

4775 De Filippi, Amadeo. "Haze" in *Three Walden Pastoral Portraits.* New York: Pride Music, 1964. Chorus: SATB, a cap.

4776 Macbride, David. "Haze." MS, u.d., avail. ACA. Chorus: SATB, a cap.

"I walked by night last moon. . . ." *The Writings of Henry David Thoreau.* Vol. 8 [pp. 283–84] (1906).

4777 Huston, T. Scott. "I Walked by Night Last Moon." Cincinnati: Canyon Press, 1971. Setting for voices, hp, Orff instrs.

"Men say they know many things." *The Writings of Henry David Thoreau.* Vol. 2 [p. 46] (1906); *Collected Poems of Henry Thoreau* (1943).

4777a Heiss, John. "Men Say" in *Songs of Nature.* n.p.: Boosey & Hawkes, 1978. Setting for M, fl, cl, vn, vc, pf. Recording: Nonesuch H 71351.

Mist ["Low-anchored cloud"]. *Poems of Nature* (1895).

4778 Burleigh, Cecil. "Mist" op. 50 no. 2. New York: C. Fischer, 1921. Song: high and med. v edns, pf.

4779 De Filippi, Amadeo. "Mist" in *Three Walden Pastoral Portraits*. New York: Pride Music, 1964. Chorus: SATB, a cap.

4780 Saminsky, Lazare. "Newfoundland Air" op. 46 no. 1. Boston: C.C. Birchard, 1936. Chorus: SSAATTBB, a cap or pf or org.

Smoke ["Light-winged smoke, Icarian bird"]. *Poems of Nature* (1895); *The Writings of Henry David Thoreau*. Vol. 2 [p. 279] (1906).

4781 De Filippi, Amadeo. "Smoke" in *Three Walden Pastoral Portraits*. New York: Pride Music, 1964. Chorus: SATB, a cap.

4782 Kilpatrick, John F. "Smoke" op. 53 no. 1. Boston: Boston Music, 1949. Chorus: SATB, a cap.

Walden (1854).

4783 Berger, Jean. "A Different Drummer." Delaware Water Gap, Pa.: Shawnee, 1974. Chorus: SSATBB, any suitable pair of bass instr or keybd.

4784 Hovhaness, Alan. "The Stars" op. 126. New York: C.F. Peters, u.d. Chorus: SATB, S solo, cham orch.

4785 Kelly, Robert T. "Walden Pond" op. 52. MS, 1976, avail. ACA. Cantata: mixed voices, S solo, narr., fl, pf, perc ens.

Miscellaneous

4785a Cage, John. "Lecture on the Weather." New York: Henmar Press, 1976. Materials for an unconducted radio broadcast or theatrical performance. Includes a series of twelve texts by Thoreau.

4785b Husa, Karel. "Every Day." New York: Associated Music Publishers, 1983. Chorus: SATB, a cap.

4786 LaMontaine, John. *Wilderness Journal* op. 41. Based on texts from the essays and journals of Thoreau.

4787 McKay, George F. "Summer." Philadelphia: Elkan-Vogel, 1948. Chorus: SSA, pf. Text: "In May and June the woodland choir is in full tune. . . ."

4788 Whear, Paul W. "From Thoreau." Champaign, Ill.: Media Press, u.d. Song: med. v, vn.

LOUIS UNTERMEYER (1885–1977)

Caliban in the Coal Mines. *Challenge* (1914).

4789 Raymond, Lewis. New York: G. Schirmer, 1936. Song: med. v, pf.

Folk-Song. *Challenge* (1914).

4790 Rothwell, Walter H. New York: C. Fischer, 1925. Song: high v, pf.

"Only of thee and me the night wind sings." *First Love* (1911).

4791 Bauer, Marion. "Only of Thee and Me" in *3 Songs*. Boston: A.P. Schmidt, 1914. Song: high and med. v edns, pf.

4792 Becker, Grace. "Only of Thee and Me" in *Five Songs*. Berkeley: J. Ralph Walker, 1934. Song: v, pf.

4793 Hart, Theron W. "Only of Thee and Me." New York: G. Ricordi, 1932. Chorus: TTTTBBBB, pf.

4794 Spencer, James. "Only of Thee and Me." New York: Michael Keane, 1937. Song: med. and low v edns, pf.

4795 Wiley, Genevieve. "Only of Thee and Me." St. Louis: Schattinger Music, 1953. Song: v, pf.

Prayer. *Challenge* (1914).

4796 Baron, Maurice. New York: G. Ricordi, 1934. Song: med. v, pf.

4796a "Prayer" in coll. UHC.

Prayer for This House. *This Singing World* (1923).

4797 McKay, George F. New York: Lawson-Gould, u.d. Chorus: mixed voices, pf.

4798 Persichetti, Vincent. n.t. in *Hymns and Responses* op. 68 no. 25. Philadelphia: Elkan-Vogel, 1956. Communion response for choir and congregational use.

4798a Quaile, Robert N. In coll. UHC.

4799 Young, Gordon. "A Prayer for This House." New York: Galaxy Music, 1951. Song: v, pf.

Swimmers. *These Times* (1917).

4800 Ives, Charles. "From 'The Swimmers.' " In coll. IOS, ITS.

A Winter Lyric. *These Times* (1917).

4801 Rothwell, Walter H. New York: C. Fischer, 1925. Song: med. v, pf.

Miscellaneous

4801a Bornschein, Franz C. "The Dying Decadent." New York: J. Fischer, 1923. Part Song.

4802 Guion, David W. "Hopi Indian Cradle Song." New York: Boosey, 1917. Song: high v, pf. Text: "Shadows are falling. . . ."

4803 Kramer, A. Walter. "The Faltering Dusk" op. 45 no. 1. Boston: O. Ditson, 1919. Song: high and low v edns, pf. Text: "Back she came in the flaming dusk. . . ."

4803a Lane, Lewis. "In Silent Countryside." New York: Composers Press, u.d. Song: v, pf.

4804 Mason, Daniel G. "Russian Lullaby" in coll. UNSNV. Song: v, pf.

4805 Robinson, Berenice. "Russian Lullaby" in coll. UNSNV, WieF.

4805a "The Spinner" in coll. BoC. Song: v, pf.

4806 Warren, Elinor R. "For You with Love." New York: G. Schirmer, 1969. Song: high or med. v, pf. Text: "Love is the whisper of earth when stars pale. . . ."

MARK VAN DOREN (1894–1972)

Another Music. *A Winter Diary and Other Poems* (1935).

4807 Carter, Elliott. "The Harmony of Morning." New York: Associated Music, 1955. Chorus: SSAA, pf or cham orch.

Down Dip the Branches. *New Poems* (1948).

4808 Lane, Richard B. In *Four Songs*. Rochester, N.Y.: Eastman School of Music, 1957. Song: S and M edns, pf or orch (R). Recording: Mercury, MG 50510, SR 90150.

4809 Polifrone, Jon. In *Four Songs for Tenor*. Chicago: Society for the American Composer, 1967. Song: T, pf.

Dunce's Song. *New Poems* (1948).

4810 Lane, Richard B. In *Four Songs*. Rochester, N.Y.: Eastman School of Music, 1957. Song: S and M edns, pf or orch (R). Recording: Mercury, MG 50150, SR 90150.

Epitaphs: For Two Men. *A Winter Diary and Other Poems* (1935).

    4811 Polifrone, Jon. "Epitaph for Two Men" in *Four Songs for Tenor.* Chicago: Society for the American Composer, 1967. Song: T, pf.

He Cut One Finger. *Spring Birth and Other Poems* (1953).

    4812 Polifrone, Jon. In *Four Songs for Tenor.* Chicago: Society for the American Composer, 1967. Song: T, pf.

Let There Be Law. *New Poems* (1948).

    4813 McDonald, Harl. "Song of Free Nations." Philadelphia: u.p., 1945. Song: high v, orch.

Mountain House: December. *Spring Thunder and Other Poems* (1924).

    4814 Lane, Richard B. In *Four Songs.* Rochester, N.Y.: Eastman School of Music, 1957. Song: M and S edns, pf or orch (R). Recording: Mercury, MG 50150, SR 90150.

    4815 Polifrone, Jon. In *Four Songs for Tenor.* Chicago: Society for the American Composer, 1967. Song: T, pf.

Never Another. *Spring Birth and Other Poems* (1953).

    4816 Thomson, Virgil. "Praise Him Who Makes Us Happy" in coll ChAH.

O World. *Late Poems* (1963).

    4817 Duke, John. New York: C. Fischer, 1970. Song: med. v, pf.

One Red Rose. *New Poems* (1948).

    4818 Duke, John. New York: C. Fischer, 1970. Song: med. v, pf.

Only for Me. *Spring Birth and Other Poems* (1953).

    4819 Duke, John. New York: Boosey & Hawkes, 1955. Song: med. v, pf.

Psalm 2 ["He sings to me when I am sad"]. *That Shining Place* (1969).

    4820 Sclater, James S. "He Sings to Me" in *Three Psalms.* Delaware Water Gap, Pa.: Shawnee, 1981. Chorus: SATB, a cap.

Psalm 3 ["Praise Orion and the Great Bear"]. *That Shining Place* (1969).

    4821 Sclater, James S. "Praise!" in *Three Psalms.* Delaware Water Gap, Pa.: Shawnee, 1981. Chorus: SATB, a cap.

Psalm 4 ["Where was I when the world was made?"]. *That Shining Place* (1969).

    4822 Sclater, James S. "Where Was I?" in *Three Psalms.* Delaware Water Gap, Pa.: Shawnee, 1981. Chorus: SATB, a cap.

Spring Thunder. *Spring Thunder and Other Poems* (1924).

    4823 Duke, John. New York: C. Fischer, 1968. Song: high and low v edns, pf. In coll. TaSE.

    4823a Laufer, Beatrice. New York: Associated Music Publishers, u.d. Chorus: SATB.

Why, Lord. *A Winter Diary and Other Poems* (1935).

    4824 Donato, Anthony. In coll. ChAH.

Will He Come Back? *New Poems* (1948).

    4825 Lane, Richard B. In *Four Songs.* Rochester, N.Y.: Eastman School of Music, 1957. Song: M and S edns, pf or orch (R). Recording: Mercury, MG 50150, SR 90150.

Miscellaneous

    4826 Bassett, Leslie. In *Time and Beyond.* New York: C.F. Peters, u.d. Song: Bar and S, vc, pf, cl.

JONES VERY (1813–1880)

The Fair Morning. *Jones Very: Selected Poems* (1966).

    4827 Binkerd, Gordon. In *Four Songs.* New York: Boosey & Hawkes, 1971. Song: S, pf.

The Hand and Foot. *Jones Very: Selected Poems* (1966).

    4828 Krush, Jay P. New York: C. Fischer, 1976. Anthem: SATB, tpt, trb, chimes, org.

The Prayer. *Jones Very: Selected Poems* (1966).

    4829 Oliver, Henry K. "Wilt Thou Not Visit Me?" in coll. ChAH. 5 stanzas.

WALT WHITMAN (1819–1892)

Neilson, Kenneth P. *The World of Walt Whitman Music: A Bibliographical Study.* n.p.: n.p., 1963.

U.S. Library of Congress Reference Dept. *Walt Whitman: A Catalog Based upon the Collections of the Library of Congress.* Washington: Library of Congress, 1955, pp. 106–118.

Wannamaker, John Samuel. "The Musical Settings of the Poetry of Walt Whitman: A Study of Theme, Structure, and Prosody." Ph.D. diss., Univ. of Minnesota, 1972 [WaMS].

Aboard at a Ship's Helm. *The Collected Writings of Walt Whitman* [Vol. 6] (1965).

> 4830 Booth, Guy. In *The Ship*. Boston: Boston Music, 1936. Chorus: mixed voices, a cap.

After the Sea-Ship. *The Collected Writings of Walt Whitman* [Vol. 6] (1965).

> 4831 Vaughan Williams, Ralph. "Scherzo—The Waves" in *A Sea Symphony*. New York, London: Breitkopf & Härtel, 1909. Setting for chorus, S and Bar soli, orch.

America. *The Collected Writings of Walt Whitman* [Vol. 6] (1965).

> 4832 Harris, Roy. In *Whitman Triptych*. New York: G. Schirmer, 1940. Chorus: 6-pt. female voices, a cap.

Among the Multitude. *The Collected Writings of Walt Whitman* [Vol. 6] (1965).

> 4833 Delius, Frederick. n.t. in *Idyll*. London: Hawkes, 1933. Setting for S and Bar soli, orch.

An Army Corps on the March. *The Collected Writings of Walt Whitman* [Vol. 6] (1965).

> 4834 Bryson, Ernest. In *Drum Taps*. London: J. Curwen, 1919. Chorus: mixed voices, ad lib side-drum, org, brass, and str.

> 4835 Hanna, James. In *War*. Hattiesburg, Miss.: Tritone Press, 1962.

> 4836 Klein, John. Boston: Boston Music, 1950. Chorus: SATB, pf.

As Adam Early in the Morning. *The Collected Writings of Walt Whitman* [Vol. 6] (1965).

> 4837 Delius, Frederick. n.t. in *Idyll*. London: Hawkes, 1933. Setting for S and Bar soli, orch.

> 4838 Rorem, Ned. New York: Henmar, 1961. Song: med. v, pf. In coll. RFA.

As I Watch'd the Ploughman Ploughing. *The Collected Writings of Walt Whitman* [Vol. 6] (1965).

> 4839 Dalmas, Philip. In *Four Songs from Whitman*. London: Novello, 1901; Philadelphia: Franklin Printing, 1928. Song: v, pf.

> 4840 Neidlinger, W.H. "Life and Death" in *Two Songs*. New York: G. Schirmer, 1900. Song: Bar or M, pf.

> 4841 Stout, Alan. "The Harvest According" in *Three Whitman Songs*. MS, 1971, avail. ACA. Song: Bar, pf.

> 4842 Ward, Robert. New York: Peer Intl., 1951. Song: high v, pf.

As If a Phantom Caress'd Me. *The Collected Writings of Walt Whitman* [Vol. 6] (1965).

> 4843 Bonner, Eugene. "Phantoms" in *Three Songs* op. 8 no. 1. London: J. & W. Chester, 1923. Song: v, pf.

As the Time Draws Nigh. *The Collected Writings of Walt Whitman* [Vol. 6] (1965).

> 4844 Delius, Frederick. n.t. in *Idyll*. London: Hawkes, 1933. Setting for S and Bar soli, orch.

> 4845 Dello-Joio, Norman. "Years of the Modern." New York: E.B. Marks, 1968. Chorus: SSAATTBB, 3 tpt, 3 hn, 2 t-trb, 1 b-trb, tba, perc. Words paraphrased.

Ashes of Soldiers. *The Collected Writings of Walt Whitman* [Vol. 6] (1965).

> 4846 Delius, Frederick. n.t. in *Idyll*. London: Hawkes, 1933. Setting for S and Bar soli, orch.

Beat! Beat! Drums! *The Collected Writings of Walt Whitman* [Vol. 6] (1965).

> 4847 Bacon, Ernst. In *Ten Songs by Ernst Bacon*. San Francisco: Bacon, 1928. Song: v, pf.

> 4848 Coleridge-Taylor, Samuel. In *Six American Lyrics* op. 56 no. 6. London: Novello, 1903. Song: Bar or C, pf or orch.

> 4849 Hanson, Howard. In *Drum Taps*. Glen Rock, N.J.: J. Fischer, 1935. Chorus: SATB, full orch. Recording: Mercury, MG 50073 (1963).

> 4850 Heath, Fenno. New York: G. Schirmer, 1955. Chorus: TTBB, pf.

> 4851 Loeffler, Charles M. Boston: C.C. Birchard, 1932. Setting for unison male voices, perc, 2 pf or wind orch (R).

> 4852 Neidlinger, W.H. In *Memories of President Lincoln*. Cincinnati: J. Church, 1920. Song: Bar or T, pf.

4853 Raphling, Sam. New York: General, 1968. Song: med. v, pf.

4854 Stoessel, Albert. New York: H.W. Gray, 1922. Chorus: SATB, pf, or tpts and drums.

4855 Vaughan Williams, Ralph. n.t. in *Dona Nobis Pacem*. London: Oxford Univ. Press, 1936. Cantata: SATB chorus, S and Bar soli, orch (R) or pf and str orch.

4856 Vrionides, Christos. In *A Cycle of Whitman Poems*. New York: Composers Facsimile Edn, 1952. Song.

4857 Weill, Kurt. In *Three Walt Whitman Songs*. New York: Chappell, 1942. Song: v, pf; Song: v, orch (1977).

Beautiful Women. *The Collected Writings of Walt Whitman* [Vol. 6] (1965).

4858 Klein, John. In *Sentences from Whitman*. New York: Associated Music, 1946. Chorus: SSAA, pf opt.

Bivouac on a Mountain Side. *The Collected Writings of Walt Whitman* [Vol. 6] (1965).

4859 Bryson, Ernest. In *Drum Taps*. London: J. Curwen, 1919. Chorus: mixed voices, ad lib side-drum, org, brass, and str.

The Bravest Soldiers. *The Collected Writings of Walt Whitman* [Vol. 6] (1965).

4860 Hanna, James. In *War*. Hattiesburg, Miss.: Tritone Press, 1962. Song: low v, pf.

4861 Nelhybel, Vaclav. In *Epitaph for a Soldier*. New York: F. Colombo, 1966. Chorus: SATB, S and A soli, a cap.

A Broadway Pageant. *The Collected Writings of Walt Whitman* [Vol. 6] (1965).

4862 Whitmer, Thomas C. u.t. in *The Soul of America*. Boston: A.P. Schmidt, 1942. Setting for solo qrt, chorus, pf, or org, or orch. Augmented with an intro. for speech choir, 1948.

By Blue Ontario's Shore. *The Collected Writings of Walt Whitman* [Vol. 6] (1965).

4863 Raphling, Sam. In *I Hear America Singing*. New York: Beekman Music, 1960. Setting for chorus, med. v solo, pf or orch.

4864 Whitmer, Thomas C. In *The Soul of America*. Boston: A.P. Schmidt, 1942. Setting for mixed chorus, pf or org or orch; augmented with an intro. for speech choir, 1948.

By the Bivouac's Fitful Flame. *The Collected Writings of Walt Whitman* [Vol. 6] (1965).

4865 Bliss, Arthur. u.t. in *Morning Heroes.* London: Novello, 1930. Symphony: chorus, orator, orch.

4866 Gaul, Harvey B. New York: G. Schirmer, 1925. Chorus: male voices, T solo, pf 4 hands.

4867 Hanson, Howard. In *Songs from "Drum Taps."* Glen Rock, N.J.: J. Fischer, 1935. Chorus: SATB, Bar solo, orch. Recording: Mercury, MG 50073 (1956).

4868 Harty, Hamilton. London: Boosey, 1912. Song: v, pf.

Cavalry Crossing a Ford. *The Collected Writings of Walt Whitman* [Vol. 6] (1965).

4869 Bryson, Ernest. In *Drum Taps.* London: J. Curwen, 1919. Chorus: mixed voices, ad lib side-drum, org, brass, and str.

Chanting the Square Deific. *The Collected Writings of Walt Whitman* [Vol. 6] (1965).

4870 Luedeke, Raymond. MS, 1974, avail. ACA. Song: 2 S, pf.

A Child's Amaze. *The Collected Writings of Walt Whitman* [Vol. 6] (1965).

4871 Schonthal, Ruth. In *By the Roadside: Six Songs to Poems by Walt Whitman.* New York: Oxford Univ. Press, 1979. Song: S, pf.

A Clear Midnight. *The Collected Writings of Walt Whitman* [Vol. 6] (1965).

4872 Bacon, Ernst. In *Six Songs. New Music* (Jan. 1942). Song: A or Bar, pf.

4873 Bonner, Eugene. In *Three Songs* op. 8 no. 2. London: J. & W. Chester, 1923. Song: v, pf

4874 Dalmas, Philip. In *Four Songs from Whitman.* London: Novello, 1901. Song.

4875 Delius, Frederick. n.t. in *Idyll.* London: Hawkes, 1933. Setting for S and Bar soli, orch.

4876 Glass, Philip. Philadelphia: Elkan-Vogel, 1967. Chorus: SATB, a cap.

4877 Hanna, James. "Clear Midnight" in *Night.* Hattiesburg, Miss.: p.p., 1967. Cycle: v, vla, pf.

4878 Entry cancelled.

4879 Kunz, Alfred. Waterloo, Ont.: Waterloo Music, 1965. Chorus: SATB, a cap.

4880 Persichetti, Vincent. In *Celebrations* op. 103. Philadelphia: Elkan-Vogel, 1967. Cantata (no. 3): chorus, wind ens.

4881 Reed, Lynnel. New York: G. Schirmer, 1920. Song: med. v, pf.

4882 Spalding, Eva R. "Minuit clair" in *Trois Melodies*. Paris: M. Senart, 1923. Song: v, pf. Words in Eng. and Fr., trans. by Léon Bazalgette.

4883 Spier, Harry R. New York: J. Fischer, 1917. Song: high v, pf; also arr. for med. v, pf and SSAA chorus.

4884 Vaughan Williams, Ralph. In *Three Poems by Walt Whitman*. London: Oxford Univ. Press, 1925. Song: v, pf.

4885 Willan, Healey. New York: Oxford Univ. Press, 1930. Chorus: SATB, a cap.

4886 Williams, Alice C. "This Is Thy Hour O Soul." New York: Paragon Music, 1953. Song: v, pf.

Come up from the Fields Father. *The Collected Writings of Walt Whitman* [Vol. 6] (1965).

4887 Nelhybel, Vaclav. In *Epitaph for a Soldier*. New York: F. Colombo, 1966. Chorus: SATB, S and A soli, a cap.

4888 Rogers, Bernard. "A Letter from Pete." New York: Southern Music Publishing, 1953. Cantata: SATB chorus, S and T soli, large or small orch.

The Commonplace. *The Collected Writings of Walt Whitman* [Vol. 6] (1965).

4889 Bacon, Ernst. New York: Associated Music, 1946. Song: v, pf.

4890 Harris, Roy. "Freedom, Toleration." New York: Mills Music, 1941. Chorus: SATB, a cap.

Crossing Brooklyn Ferry. *The Collected Writings of Walt Whitman* [Vol. 6] (1965).

4891 Kaufer, Joseph. "Crossing Brooklyn Ferry: Conclusion" in *The Man with the Hoe and Other Songs*. Waukegan, Ill.: Lyric-Art, 1951. Song: high and med. v, pf.

4892 Kaufer, Joseph. "Not upon You Alone" in *Dover Beach and Other Songs*. Waukegan, Ill.: Lyric-Art, 1951. Song: high or med. v, pf. Words from sec. 6.

4893 Thomson, Virgil. New York: Boosey & Hawkes, 1960. Chorus: SSATB, pf.

The Dalliance of the Eagles. *The Collected Writings of Walt Whitman* [Vol. 6] (1965).

4894 Dello-Joio, Norman. In *Songs of Walt Whitman*. New York: E.B. Marks, 1966. Chorus: SATB, pf or orch (R).

Darest Thou Now, O Soul. *The Collected Writings of Walt Whitman* [Vol. 6] (1965).

4895 Adler, Samuel. u.t. in *Sixth String Quartet (A Whitman Serenade)*. New York: C. Fischer, 1977. Song: med. v, str qrt.

4896 Bacon, Ernst. In coll. BacSP.

4897 Bonner, Eugene. In *Whispers of Heavenly Death*. London: J. & W. Chester, 1925. Song: v, pf or orch. Words in Eng. and Fr., trans. by Léon Bazalgette.

4898 Chadwick, George W. New York: A.P. Schmidt, 1910. Quartet: TTBB, a cap.

4899 Diggle, Roland. u.p.: Abbey Music, 1948. Chorus: mixed voices, pf.

4900 Freed, Isadore. New York: H.W. Gray, 1928. Setting for SSA, M solo, pf.

4901 Glass, Philip. In coll. MuENC. Chorus: SATB, a cap.

4902 Hennagin, Michael. n.t. in *The Unknown*. New York: Walton Music, 1968. Chorus: SSA, pf, fl, perc; New York: Walton Music, u.d. Chorus: SATB, 3 Bar and 4 T soli, pf, fl, perc, elec tape, 2 slide projectors, 3 tpt, timp.

4903 Huhn, Bruno. "The Unknown." Boston: Boston Music, 1918. Setting for 3-pt. female voices, pf and org.

4904 Lockwood, Normand. MS, 1959, avail. ACA. Chorus: SSAATTBB, pf.

4905 Schuman, William. "The Unknown Region" in *Carols of Death*. n.p.: Merion Music, 1959. Chorus: SATB, a cap.

4906 Stanford, Charles V. "To the Soul" in *Songs of Faith* op. 97 no. 4. London: Boosey, 1908. Song: v, pf.

4907 Vaughan Williams, Ralph. "Darest Thou Now O Soul." London: J. Curwen, 1925. Unison song, pf.

4908 Vaughan Williams, Ralph. "Toward the Unknown Region." London: Breitkopf & Härtel, 1907. Setting for 8-pt. chorus and orch.

4909 Whitmer, Thomas C. In *Choral Rhapsody*. New York: H.W. Gray, 1928. Setting for chorus, solo qrt, pf, or orch.

4910 Williams, David McK. New York: H.W. Gray, 1926. Anthem: chorus, S solo, org or orch.

4911 Wood, Charles. u.t. in *Ten Songs for Low Voice* [WaMS has *Two Songs.*] London: Boosey, 1927. Song: low v, pf.

Delicate Cluster. *The Collected Writings of Walt Whitman* [Vol. 6] (1965).

4912 Lo Presti, Ronald. "Tribute." New York: C. Fischer, 1962. Chorus: SATB, pf, band, or orch (R). Text adapted.

Dirge for Two Veterans. *The Collected Writings of Walt Whitman* [Vol. 6] (1965).

4913 Bryson, Ernest. "Lo, the Moon Ascending" in *Drum Taps*. London: J. Curwen, 1919. Chorus: mixed voices, ad lib side-drum, org, brass, and str.

4914 Holst, Gustav. "A Dirge for Two Veterans." London: J. Curwen, 1914. Chorus: TTBB, pf or 2 tpt, 2 trb, perc.

4915 Lockwood, Normand. New York: M. Witmark, 1936. Chorus: SATB, a cap; also arr. for TTBB chorus, T solo, pf.

4916 McDonald, Harl. Philadelphia: Elkan-Vogel, 1940. Chorus: SSAA, pf.

4917 Pasatieri, Thomas. New York: Belwin-Mills, 1977. Song: Bar or M, pf.

4918 Ritter, Frederic L. "Dirge for Two Veterans" op. 13. New York: E. Schuberth, 1880. Recit. with pf.

4919 Rogers, Bernard. Bryn Mawr, Pa.: Presser, 1969. Chorus: SATB, pf or str orch (R).

4920 Vaughan Williams, Ralph. n.t. in *Dona Nobis Pacem*. London: Oxford Univ. Press, 1036. Cantata: SATB chorus, S and Bar soli, orch (R) or pf and str orch.

4921 Weill, Kurt. In *Three Walt Whitman Songs*. New York: Chappell, 1942. Song: v, pf; Song: v, orch (1977).

4922 Wood, Charles. London: Boosey, 1901. Setting for chorus, B solo, orch.

The Dismantled Ship. *The Collected Writings of Walt Whitman* [Vol. 6] (1965).

4923 Bonner, Eugene. in *Three Songs* op. 8 no. 3. London: J. & W. Chester, 1923. Song: v, pf.

4924 Gustafson, Dwight. In *Three Songs of Parting*. u.p.: Shawnee, 1967. Chorus: SATB, pf.

An Ended Day. *The Collected Writings of Walt Whitman* [Vol. 6] (1965).

4925 Segerstam, Leif. In *Three Leaves of Grass*. London: Josef Weinberger, 1967. Song: high v, pf.

Ethiopia Saluting the Colors. *The Collected Writings of Walt Whitman* [Vol. 6] (1965).

4926 Burleigh, Harry T. New York: G. Ricordi, 1915. Song: v, pf.

4927 Wood, Charles. London: Boosey, 1898. Song: low and med. v edns, pf. In coll. NoBS.

An Evening Lull. *The Collected Writings of Walt Whitman* [Vol. 6] (1965).

4928 Harris, Roy. In *Whitman Triptych*. New York: G. Schirmer, 1940. Chorus: 6-pt. female voices, a cap.

A Farm Picture. *The Collected Writings of Walt Whitman* [Vol. 6] (1965).

4929 Klein, John. In *Four Whitman Sketches*. Boston: Boston Music, 1945. Chorus: SATB, a cap.

4930 Luening, Otto. New York: Associated Music, 1944. Song: med. v, pf. Recording: New Music Recordings 1211 B.

4931 Schonthal, Ruth. In *By the Roadside: Six Songs to Poems by Walt Whitman*. New York: Oxford Univ. Press, 1979. Song: S, pf.

Fast Anchor'd Eternal O Love! *The Collected Writings of Walt Whitman* [Vol. 6] (1965).

4932 Delius, Frederick. n.t. in *Idyll*. London: Hawkes, 1933. Setting for S and Bar soli, orch.

The First Dandelion. *The Collected Writings of Walt Whitman* [Vol. 6] (1965).

4933 Neidlinger, W.H. Chicago: C.F. Summy, 1901. Song: high and low v edns, pf.

4934 Radleigh, Arthur. In *Music Everywhere*. Book 6. Ed. by Armitage, Dykema, et al. Boston: C.C. Birchard, 1943. Unison song with pf.

For You O Democracy. *The Collected Writings of Walt Whitman* [Vol. 6] (1965).

4935 Boughton, Rutland. "The Love of Comrades" op. 17 no. 4. London: J. Curwen, 1928. Song: v, pf. Words adapted.

4936 D.F. "Love of Comrades" no. 35 in coll. CaCL.

4937 Frank, Marcel G. New York: J. Fischer, 1955. Setting for mixed voices, pf.

4938 Gertz, Irving. Hollywood, Calif.: Middleroad Music, 1959 (Criterion). Setting for mixed voices, pf.

4939 Helm, Everett. u.p.: p.p., u.d. Choral excerpt cited in WaMS.

4940 Kleinsinger, George. "Ode to Democracy" in *I Hear America Singing*. New York: E.B. Marks, 1941. Cantata: SATB chorus, Bar solo, pf or orch (R).

4941 Norris, Homer. u.t. in *The Flight of the Eagle*. Boston: G. Schirmer, Jr., 1903. Setting for S, T, Bar, pf.

4942 White, Felix H. "Love of Comrades." New York: G. Schirmer, u.d. Music not seen; text presumably from this poem.

4943 Zuckmayer, Eduard. "Kameradschaft (For You, O Democracy)." Leipzig: J. Rieter-Biedermann, 1932. Setting for unison chorus or solo v and str or wind instr.

From Montauk Point. *The Collected Writings of Walt Whitman* [Vol. 6] (1965).

4944 Delius, Frederick. "I Stand As on Some Mighty Eagle's Beak" in *Songs of Farewell (Lieder des Abschieds)*. London: Winthrop Rogers, 1931. Chorus: SSAATTBB, pf or orch. Vocal score by Eric Fenby; words in Eng. and Ger., trans. by Jelka Delius. Recording: Angel, S 36285 (1966).

From Pent-Up Aching Rivers. *The Collected Writings of Walt Whitman* [Vol. 6] (1965).

4945 Delius, Frederick. n.t. in *Idyll*. London: Hawkes, 1933. Setting for S and Bar soli, orch.

Give Me the Splendid Silent Sun. *The Collected Writings of Walt Whitman* [Vol. 6] (1965).

4946 Elsmith, Leonard. "Drum Taps" in *Walt Whitman Songs*. New York: p.p., 1960. Song: med. v, pf.

4947 Gilbert, Henry F.B. New York: H.W. Gray, 1914. Song: v, pf.

4948 Harris, Roy. New York: Associated Music, 1962. Cantata: Bar, orch.

4949 Lockwood, Normand. MS, 1961, avail. ACA. Chorus: SATB, Bar solo.

4950 Spencer, Williametta. u.p.: Fostco Music Press, 1976 (agent, Mark Foster Music). Chorus: SATB, a cap.

Gliding o'er All. *The Collected Writings of Walt Whitman* [Vol. 6] (1965).

4951 Hennagin, Michael. In *By the Roadside*. u.p.: Walton Music, 1979. Chorus: SATB, a cap.

4952 Luening, Otto. In *Three Songs*. New York: G. Schirmer, 1944. Song: T or S, pf.

4953 Rorem, Ned. In *Five Poems of Walt Whitman*. New York: Boosey & Hawkes, 1970.

4954 Stearns, Peter P. In *Whitman Cycle IV*. New York: Composer's Facsimile Edn, 1959.

A Glimpse. *The Collected Writings of Walt Whitman* [Vol. 6] (1965).

4955 Delius, Frederick. n.t. in *Idyll*. London: Hawkes, 1933. Setting for S and Bar soli, orch.

Gods. *The Collected Writings of Walt Whitman* [Vol. 6] (1965).

> 4956 Hennagin, Michael. In *By the Roadside.* u.p.: Walton Music, 1979. Chorus: SATB, a cap.

> 4957 Rorem, Ned. In *Five Poems of Walt Whitman.* New York: Boosey & Hawkes, 1970. Song: v, pf.

Good-bye My Fancy! *The Collected Writings of Walt Whitman* [Vol. 6] (1965).

> 4958 Flanagan, William. New York: Peer Intl., 1959. Song: S, fl and gtr, or pf.

> 4959 Williams, David. New York: H.W. Gray, 1956. Song: med. v, pf.

Grand Is the Seen. *The Collected Writings of Walt Whitman* [Vol. 6] (1965).

> 4960 Bacon, Ernst. In coll. BacSP. Song: v, pf; "The Unseen Soul" in coll. BacT, BacFS.

> 4961 Stearns, Peter P. MS, u.d., avail. ACA. Chorus: SATB, a cap.

Halcyon Days. *The Collected Writings of Walt Whitman* [Vol. 6] (1965).

> 4962 Lockwood, Normand. In *Four Songs—A Cycle.* MS, u.d., avail. ACA. Song: S, pf, (orig. for S, vn, org).

Hast Never Come to Thee an Hour. *The Collected Writings of Walt Whitman* [Vol. 6] (1965).

> 4963 Hennagin, Michael. In *By the Roadside.* u.p.: Walton Music, 1979. Chorus: SATB, a cap.

Here the Frailest Leaves of Me. *The Collected Writings of Walt Whitman* [Vol. 6] (1965).

> 4964 Luening, Otto. New York: Associated Music, 1944. Song: med. v, pf. Recording: New Music Recordings 1121 B.

Hospital Scenes.—Incidents. *The Collected Writings of Walt Whitman* [Vol. 7] (1965).

> 4965 Rorem, Ned. "An Incident" in *War Scenes.* New York: Boosey & Hawkes, 1971. Cycle: med.-low v, pf. Recording: Desto, DC 7101.

Hush'd Be the Camps To-day. *The Collected Writings of Walt Whitman* [Vol. 6] (1965).

> 4966 Dougherty, Celius. New York: G. Schirmer, 1948. Song: v, pf.

> 4967 Loomis, Harvey W. Boston: C.C. Birchard, 1906. Chorus: SATB, pf.

4968 Ward, Robert. New York: H.W. Gray, 1943. Chorus: mixed voices, pf. Recording: Composers Recordings, CRI 165 (1963).

I Dream'd in a Dream. *The Collected Writings of Walt Whitman* [Vol. 6] (1965).

4969 Creston, Paul. "Calamus" op. 104. New York: G. Schirmer, 1974. Chorus: SSAATTBB, Bar solo, pf or brass and perc (R); also arr. for male chorus.

I Hear America Singing. *The Collected Writings of Walt Whitman* [Vol. 6] (1965).

4970 Bay, Victor. "Keep Singing." New York: Alpha Music, 1941. Song: v, pf. Uses 2 lines.

4971 Eastham, Clark. Chicago: Raymond A. Hoffman, 1940. Chorus: SSAATTBB, a cap.

4972 Gaul, Harvey B. Boston: C.C. Birchard, 1925. Cantata: male voices, S or T, pf 4 hands; also arr. for SSAA chorus, pf 4 hands (1926).

4973 Gertz, Irving. Hollywood, Calif.: Middleroad Music, 1959. Chorus: SSAATBarB, pf.

4974 Harte, Stan, Jr. Arr. by Don McAfee. u.p.: New Era Music, 1977. Setting for SA or TB and pf.

4975 Kleinsinger, George. In *I Hear America Singing*. New York: E.B. Marks, 1941. Cantata: SATB chorus, Bar solo, pf or orch. with introductory narr. speech by soloist: "Walt Whitman Am I."

4976 Lockwood, Normand. u.t. in *I Hear America Singing*. Delaware Water Gap, Pa.: Shawnee, 1954. Setting for mixed voices, pf.

4977 Pfautsch, Lloyd. n.t. in *I Hear America Singing*. Delaware Water Gap, Pa.: Shawnee, 1970. Chorus: SATB, a cap.

4978 Raphling, Sam. In *I Hear America Singing*. New York: Beekman, 1960. Setting for chorus, med. v solo, pf or orch.

4979 Reed, Robert B. New York: J. Fischer, 1942. Chorus: mixed voices, a cap.

I Heard You Solemn-Sweet Pipers of the Organ. *The Collected Writings of Walt Whitman* [Vol. 6] (1965).

4980 Piket, Frederick. "I Heard You" in *The Speaking of Silence*. New York: Associated Music, u.d. Setting for female chorus.

I Saw in Louisiana a Live-Oak Growing. *The Collected Writings of Walt Whitman* [Vol. 6] (1965).

4981 Castelnuovo-Tedesco, Mario. "Louisiana." New York: Galaxy, 1940. Song: med. v, pf; Song: low v, pf (1949).

4982 Newlin, Dika. MS, u.d., avail. ACA. Song: med. v, pf.

I Sing the Body Electric. *The Collected Writings of Walt Whitman* [Vol. 6] (1965).

4983 Persichetti, Vincent. In *Celebrations* op. 103. Philadelphia: Elkan-Vogel, 1967. Cantata (no. 3): chorus, wind ens.

I Sit and Look Out. *The Collected Writings of Walt Whitman* [Vol. 6] (1965).

4984 Dello-Joio, Norman. "I Sit and Look out upon the World" in *Songs of Walt Whitman*. New York: E.B. Marks, 1966. Chorus: SATB, pf or orch (R).

4985 Goldstein, William. u.p.: Malcolm Music, 1971. Chorus: TTBB, T and B solo, a cap; also arr. for SATB chorus, pf.

Inauguration Ball. *The Collected Writings of Walt Whitman* [Vol. 7] (1965).

4986 Rorem, Ned. "Inauguration Ball" in *War scenes*. New York: Boosey & Hawkes, 1971. Cycle: med.-low v, pf. Recording: Desto, DC 7101.

Joy, Shipmate, Joy! *The Collected Writings of Walt Whitman* [Vol. 6] (1965).

4987 Bacon, Ernst. In coll. BacSP. Song: v, pf.

4988 Delius, Frederick. In *Songs of Farewell (Lieder des Abschieds)*. London: Winthrop Rogers, 1931. Chorus: SSAATTBB, pf or orch. Vocal score by Eric Fenby; words in Eng. and Ger., trans. by Jelka Delius. Recording: Angel, S 36285 (1966).

4989 Gustafson, Dwight. In *Three Songs of Parting*. u.p.: Shawnee, 1967. Chorus: SATB, pf.

4990 Hall, Beatrice M. Paris: Senart, u.d. Song: Words in Eng. and Fr.

4991 Paviour, Paul. In *Three Part Songs*. u.p.: Ricordi, 1975. Chorus: SATB, a cap.

4992 Persichetti, Vincent. "Voyage" in *Celebrations* op. 103. Philadelphia: Elkan-Vogel, 1967. Cantata (no. 3): chorus, wind ens.

4993 Robertson, Leroy. New York: Galaxy, 1942. Song: high v, pf.

4994 Rogers, James H. In *In Memoriam*. New York: G. Schirmer, 1919. Cycle: med. v, pf.

4995 Stanford, Charles V. u.t. in *Songs of Faith by Walt Whitman* op. 97 no. 6. London: Boosey, 1908. Song: v, pf.

4996 Vaughan Williams, Ralph. In *Three Poems by Walt Whitman*. London: Oxford Univ. Press, 1925. Song: v, pf.

4997 Whitmer, Thomas C. u.t. in *Choral Rhapsody*. New York: H.W. Gray, 1928. Setting for solo qrt, chorus, pf or orch.

The Last Invocation. *The Collected Writings of Walt Whitman* [Vol. 6] (1965).

4998 Adler, Samuel. u.t. in *Sixth String Quartet (A Whitman Serenade)*. New York: C. Fischer, 1977. Song: med. v, str qrt.

4999 Bacon, Ernst. In coll. BacT, BacSP. Song: v, pf; "At the Last" in coll. BacFS.

5000 Bergh, Arthur. "The Imprisoned Soul" op. 31 no. 1. New York: Sprague-Colman, 1939. Song: high and low v edns, pf.

5001 Besly, Maurice. "At the Last" op. 21 no. 4. London: Boosey, 1922. Song: v, pf.

5002 Binkerd, Gordon. MS, 1956, avail. ACA. Chorus: SATB, a cap.

5003 Bonner, Eugene. In *Whispers of Heavenly Death*. London: J. & W. Chester, 1925. Song: v, pf or orch. Words in Eng. and Fr., trans. by Léon Bazalgette.

5004 Boyd, Jack. Winona, Minn.: Hal Leonard, 1963. Chorus: SATB, a cap.

5005 Bridge, Frank. London: Winthrop Rogers, 1919. Song: high, med., and low v edns, pf.

5006 Campbell-Tipton, Louis. "Invocation" op. 32 no. 2. New York: G. Schirmer, 1915. Song: high and low v edns, pf.

5007 Carter, John. u.p.: E.B. Marks, 1975. Chorus: SSATB, a cap.

5008 Diggle, Roland. u.p.: Abbey Music, 1946. Setting for 4-pt. men's voices.

5009 Garratt, Percival. "The Last Invocation" op. 36. London: J. Curwen, 1920. Song: v, pf.

5010 Glass, Philip. Philadelphia: Elkan-Vogel, 1967. Chorus: SATB, a cap.

5011 Henderson, Elizabeth. Philadelphia: Elkan-Vogel, 1946.

5012 Hively, Wells. New York: Composers Facsimile Edn, 1945. Hymn for mixed voices.

5013 Kastle, Leonard. New York: G. Ricordi, 1956. Chorus: SATB, pf ad lib.

5014 Luening, Otto. "At the Last." New York: Composers Facsimile Edn, 1936. Song: S, pf. Music not seen; text presumably from this poem.

5015 Powers, Ada W. New York: E. Schuberth, 1927. Song: v, pf.

5016 Rogers, James H. In *In Memoriam*. New York: G. Schirmer, 1919. Cycle: med. v, pf.

5017 Schmutz, Albert D. New York: H.W. Gray, 1939. Chorus: mixed voices, a cap.

5018 Schuman, William. In *Carols of Death.* Bryn Mawr, Pa.: Merion Music, 1959. Chorus: SATB, a cap.

5019 Spalding, Eva R. "L'invocation suprème" in *Trois Melodies.* Paris: M. Senart, 1923. Song: v, pf. Words in Eng. and Fr., trans. by Léon Bazalgette.

5020 Storey-Smith, Warren. Boston: Bruce Humphries, 1934. Song: v, pf.

5021 Whithorne, Emerson. "Invocation" op. 29 no. 1. New York: Composers Music Corp., 1921. Song: v, pf.

5022 Whitmer, Thomas C. u.t. in *Choral Rhapsody.* New York: H.W. Gray, 1928. Setting for solo qrt, chorus, pf or orch.

Lingering Last Drops. *The Collected Writings of Walt Whitman* [Vol. 6] (1965).

5023 Bacon, Ernst. In coll. BacFS, BacT. Song: high v, pf.

5024 Segerstam, Leif. In *Three Leaves of Grass.* London: Joseph Weinberger, 1967. Song: high v, pf.

Locations and Times. *The Collected Writings of Walt Whitman* [Vol. 6] (1965).

5025 Luening, Otto. u.p.: Composers Facsimile Edition, 1932; In *Twelve Songs.* New York: Galaxy, 1976? Song: v, pf.

Long, Too Long America. *The Collected Writings of Walt Whitman* [Vol. 6] (1965).

5026 Hanna, James. "Too Long, America" in *War.* Hattiesburg, Miss.: Tritone Press, 1962. Song: low v, pf. Music not seen, text presumably from this poem.

5027 Schuman, William H. In *A Free Song.* New York: G. Schirmer, 1943. Secular Cantata (no. 2): mixed chorus, 2 pf or orch, (pf red. by Paul Weissleder).

Look Down Fair Moon. *The Collected Writings of Walt Whitman* [Vol. 6] (1965).

5028 Crane, Joelle W. New York: Composers Facsimile Edn, 1976. Chorus: 4 S, 4 A, 2 T, 3 B, a cap.

5029 Hanna, James. In *War.* Hattiesburg, Miss.: Tritone Press, 1962. Song: low v, pf.

5030 Klein, John. Boston: Boston Music, 1949. Chorus: SATB, pf.

5031 Mollicone, Henry. MS, u.d., avail. ACA. Song: S, pf.

5032 Naginski, Charles. New York: G. Schirmer, 1942. Song: med. v, pf.

5033 Rorem, Ned. New York: Composers Editions, 1959; In *Five Poems of Walt Whitman.* New York: Boosey & Hawkes, 1970. Song: v, pf.

5034 Schuman, William. In *A Free Song*. New York: G. Schirmer, 1943. Secular cantata (no. 2): mixed chorus, 2 pf or orch (pf red by Paul Weissleder).

Mannahatta. *The Collected Writings of Walt Whitman* [Vol. 6] (1965).

5035 Lomon, Ruth. In *Phase 2*. u.p.: p.p., 1975. Song: S, vc and pf.

Memories. *The Collected Writings of Walt Whitman* [Vol. 6] (1965).

5036 Delius, Frederick. n.t. in *Songs of Farewell (Lieder des Abschieds)*. London: Winthrop Rogers, 1931. Chorus: SSAATTBB, pf or orch. Vocal score by Eric Fenby; words in Eng. and Ger., trans. by Jelka Delius. Recording: Angel, S 36285 (1966).

Mother and Babe. *The Collected Writings of Walt Whitman* [Vol. 6] (1965).

5037 Klein, John. In *Sentences from Whitman*. New York: Associated Music, 1946. Chorus: SSAA, opt pf.

5038 Schonthal, Ruth. In *By the Roadside: Six Songs to Poems by Walt Whitman*. New York: Oxford Univ. Press, 1979. Song: S, pf.

The Mystic Trumpeter. *The Collected Writings of Walt Whitman* [Vol. 6] (1965).

5039 Beckett, Wheeler. MS in C. Fischer rental, 1928. Setting for mixed chorus, T solo, orch; "Sing to My Soul." New York: C. Fischer, 1946. Setting for mixed chorus, T solo, pf. Words from sec. 8.

5040 Clutsam, George H. London: Hatzfeld, n.d. Setting for chorus, STBar soli, orch.

5041 Dello Joio, Norman. New York: G. Schirmer, 1945. Chorus: mixed voices, STBar soli, hn or pf.

5042 Farrar, Ernest. "O Glad, Culminating Song" in *Out of Doors* op. 14 no. 3. London: Stainer & Bell, 1923. Suite for chorus and orch. Words from sec. 8.

5043 Hanson, Howard. New York: C. Fischer, 1970. Chorus: SSAATTBB, narr., pf or orch (R).

5044 Harty, Hamilton. London: Novello, 1913. Setting for chorus, Bar solo, orch.

5045 Jacquet, H. Maurice. Boston: C.C. Birchard, 1927. Cantata: mixed voices, children's chorus, orch.

5046 Lees, Benjamin. In *Visions of Poets*. New York: Boosey & Hawkes, 1965. Dramatic Cantata: chorus, S and T soli, orch.

5047 Spencer, Williametta. Anaheim, Calif.: National Music, 1969. Chorus: SATB, pf.

5048 Zaninelli, Luigi. Delaware Water Gap, Pa.: Shawnee, 1972. Chorus: SATB, tpt, pf.

A Night Battle, over a Week Since. *The Collected Writings of Walt Whitman* [Vol. 7] (1965).

5049 Rorem, Ned. "A Night Battle" in *War Scenes*. New York: Boosey & Hawkes, 1971. Cycle: med.-low v, pf. Recording: Desto, DC 7101.

A Noiseless Patient Spider. *The Collected Writings of Walt Whitman* [Vol. 6] (1965).

5050 Kastle, Leonard. New York: G. Ricordi, 1956. Chorus: SATB, pf ad lib.

5051 Warfield, Gerald. MS, u.d., avail. ACA. Chorus: SATB or TTBB or SSAA (boys or women), a cap.

5052 Yanney, Yehuda. MS, u.d., avail ACA. Chorus: SSA, a cap.

Now Finale to the Shore. *The Collected Writings of Walt Whitman* [Vol. 6] (1965).

5053 Delius, Frederick. n.t. in *Songs of Farewell (Lieder des Abschieds)*. London: Winthrop Rogers, 1931. Chorus: SSAATTBB, pf or orch. Vocal score by Eric Fenby; words in Eng. and Ger., trans. by Jelka Delius. Recording: Angel, S 36285 (1966).

5054 Gustafson, Dwight. In *Three Songs of Parting*. u.p.: Shawnee, 1967. Chorus: SATB, pf.

O Captain! My Captain! *The Collected Writings of Walt Whitman* [Vol. 6] (1965).

5055 Anderson, Arthur O. Chicago: FitzSimmons, 1925. Setting for male chorus.

5056 Bergh, Arthur. "O Captain! My Captain!" op. 29. Chicago: Birchard, 1938. Chorus: SATB, pf.

5057 Bohannan, Jean. Boston: White-Smith, 1911. Chorus: TTBB, pf.

5058 Butcher, Frank C. "O Captain! My Captain!" op. 4. London: Novello, 1910. Song: v, pf.

5059 Damrosch, Walter. "An Abraham Lincoln Song." New York: M. Witmark, 1934. Setting for SSATTB chorus, Bar solo, pf or orch; Setting for chorus of liberated slaves, Bar solo, orch (1936).

5060 Earhart, Will. In coll. Ea. Unison voices, pf.

5061 Farwell, Arthur. Cincinnati: J. Church, 1918. Chorus: mixed voices, pf.

5062 Foster, Fay. In *Universal School Music Series.* Book 4. Ed. by Damrosch, Gartlan, and Gehrkens. New York: Hinds, Hayden & Eldredge, 1924. Setting for unison voices, pf.

5063 Gertz, Irving. Hollywood, Calif.: Middleroad Music, 1959 (Criterion). Chorus: SSATBarB, pf.

5064 Huss, Henry H. New York: G. Schirmer, 1910. Setting for male qrt, pf and org ad lib.

5065 Kelley, Edgar S. "O Captain! My Captain!" op. 19. In coll. TL. Chorus: SATB; Boston: C.C. Birchard, 1926. Chorus: SATB, pf.

5066 Lloyd, Charles H. London: Year Book Press, 1917. Unison song, pf.

5067 Lockwood, Normand. n.t. in *Elegy for a Hero.* Delaware Water Gap, Pa.: Shawnee, 1962. Cantata: SSAATTBarBarBB, a cap.

5068 Manney, Charles. Boston: O. Ditson, 1903. Song: B, pf.

5069 Mendelssohn, J. Arko. New York: Handy Bros., 1936. Chorus: TTBB, pf.

5070 Neidlinger, William H. In *Memories of President Lincoln.* Cincinnati: J. Church, 1920. Dramatic episode for Bar or T.

5071 Phippen, Joshua. Salem, Mass.: Essex Instit., 1909. Chorus: SSAATTBB, org ad lib.

5072 Remick, Bertha. Boston: C.C. Birchard, 1917. Unison song, pf. In coll ArJ.

5073 Rines, Robert H. "Captain! My Captain!" from the play, *A Whitman Portrait* by Paul Shyre. New York: Dramatists Play Service, 1966.

5074 Ringwald, Roy. n.t. in *The Song of America.* East Stroudsburg, Pa.: Shawnee, 1951. Cantata: SATB chorus, narr., pf 4 hands or orch.

5075 Rinker, Alton. In *American Poets' Suite.* Delaware Water Gap, Pa.: Shawnee, 1968. Chorus: SATB, pf. Arr. by Hawley Ades.

5076 Scott, Cyril. "My Captain!" op. 38. London: Elkin, 1904; Boston: A.P. Schmidt, 1904. Song: v, pf.

5077 Seymour, John L. "O Captain! My Captain!" op. 42. Sacramento: p.p., 1936. Choral ode for men's voices.

5078 Weill, Kurt. In *Three Walt Whitman Songs.* New York: Chappell, 1942. Song: v, pf.

5079 Wolpe, Stefan. In *Three Songs.* New York: Transcontinental Music, 1946. Song: med. v, pf.

5080 Wood, Charles. London: Boosey, 1899. Song: v, pf.

5081 Wyman, C.M., arr. from. In coll. LBR.

O Living Always, Always Dying. *The Collected Writings of Walt Whitman* [Vol. 6] (1965).

5082 Lomon, Ruth. In *Phase 2.* u.p.: p.p., 1975. Song: S, vc, pf.

O Sun of Real Peace. *The Collected Writings of Walt Whitman* [Vol. 6] (1965).

5083 Lees, Benjamin. In *Visions of Poets.* New York: Boosey & Hawkes, 1965. Dramatic Cantata: chorus, S and T soli, orch.

O Tan-Faced Prairie-Boy. *The Collected Writings of Walt Whitman* [Vol. 6] (1965).

5084 Elsmith, Leonard. In *Walt Whitman Songs.* New York: p.p., 1960. Song: med. v, pf.

O You Whom I Often and Silently Come. *The Collected Writings of Walt Whitman* [Vol. 6] (1965).

5085 Gassman, Remi. In *Three Love Lyrics from Whitman.* New York: Mercury, 1955. Song: S, cham orch.

5086 Harrison, Lou. "Fragment from Calamus." New York: Bomart, 1950. Song: Bar, pf.

5087 Reif, Paul. New York: Seesaw, 1971. Song: v, pf.

5088 Rorem, Ned. New York: Henmar, 1961. Song: v, pf. In coll. RFA.

Offerings. *The Collected Writings of Walt Whitman* [Vol. 6] (1965).

5089 Klein, John. In *Sentences from Whitman.* New York: Associated Music, 1946. Chorus: SSAA, opt pf.

Old Age's Lambent Peaks. *The Collected Writings of Walt Whitman* [Vol. 6] (1965).

5090 Lees, Benjamin. In *Visions of Poets.* New York: Boosey & Hawkes, 1965. Dramatic Cantata: chorus, S and T soli, orch.

An Old Man's Thought of School. *The Collected Writings of Walt Whitman* [Vol. 6] (1965).

5091 Hanson, Howard. "Song of Democracy" op. 44. New York: C. Fischer, 1957. Chorus: SATB, pf, or band or orch; Maurice E. Ford, arr. Chorus: TTBB, pf (1963).

Old War-Dreams. *The Collected Writings of Walt Whitman* [Vol. 6] (1965).

5092 Hall, Beatrice M. Paris: Senart, u.d. Song. Words in Eng. and Fr.

On the Beach at Night. *The Collected Writings of Walt Whitman* [Vol. 6] (1965).

5093 Bacon, Ernst. "The Lord Star." New York: Music Press, 1949. Chorus: 6-pt. mixed voices, Bar solo, pf or org, or orch (R); acc. originally for org, brass, and str.

5094 Bergsma, William. New York: C. Fischer, 1947. Chorus: SATB, a cap.

5095 Harrison, Julius. "Rhapsody." London: Boosey, 1932. Song: Bar, orch.

5096 Imbrie, Andrew. u.p.: Malcolm Music, 1961. Chorus: SATB, str orch.

5097 James, Philip. In *A Sea Symphony* [movement 4]. u.p.: Mills Music (R). Setting for B-Bar, pf or orch.

5098 Persichetti, Vincent. "The Pleiades" op. 107. Philadelphia: Elkan-Vogel, 1968. Chorus: SSSAAATTTBBB, tpt, str orch. A Note on the music says it may be performed by any size chorus with tpt and org, tpt and pf, or possibly with pf 3 hands.

On the Beach at Night Alone. *The Collected Writings of Walt Whitman* [Vol. 6] (1965).

5099 Crane, Joelle W. New York: Composers Facsimile Edn, 1977. Chorus: SSAATTBB, A solo, a cap.

5100 Strang, Gerald. n.t. in *Three Whitman Songs*. Los Angeles: Affiliated Musicians, 1953. Chorus: SATB, a cap.

5101 Vaughan Williams, Ralph. In *A Sea Symphony*. New York, London: Breitkopf & Härtel, 1909. Setting for chorus, S and Bar soli, orch.

Once I Pass'd through a Populous City. *The Collected Writings of Walt Whitman* [Vol. 6] (1965).

5102 Delius, Frederick. n.t. in *Idyll*. London: Hawkes, 1933. Setting for S and Bar soli, orch.

5103 Piket, Frederick. New York: Associated Music, 1955. Chorus: mixed voices, B solo, a cap; In *Six About Love*. New York: Associated Music, 1965. Chorus: SATB, B solo, a cap.

One Hour to Madness and Joy. *The Collected Writings of Walt Whitman* [Vol. 6] (1965).

5104 Delius, Frederick. n.t. in *Idyll*. London: Hawkes, 1933. Setting for S and Bar soli, orch.

One Thought Ever at the Fore. *The Collected Writings of Walt Whitman* [Vol. 6] (1965).

5105 Bacon, Ernst. In coll. BacSP. Song: v, pf; "The Divine Ship" in coll. BacQA, BacT.

5106 Stearns, Peter P. In *Whitman Cycle IV*. New York: Composers Facsimile Edn, 1959. Song: v, pf.

5107 Ward, Robert. "All Peoples of the Globe Together Sail" in *Fifth Symphony: Canticles of America*. New York: Highgate Press, 1979. Choral Symphony: mixed chorus, S and Bar soli, opt narr., orch.

One's-Self I Sing. *The Collected Writings of Walt Whitman* [Vol. 6] (1965).

5108 Harris, Roy. "Inscription" in *Symphony for Voices*. New York: G. Schirmer, 1939. Chorus: mixed voices, a cap.

5109 Norris, Homer A. In *The Flight of the Eagle*. Boston: Boston Music, 1903. Setting for STBar soli, pf.

Out of May's Shows Selected. *The Collected Writings of Walt Whitman* [Vol. 6] (1965).

5110 Delius, Frederick. u.t. in *Songs of Farewell (Lieder des Abschieds)*. London: Winthrop Rogers, 1931. Chorus: SSAATTBB, pf or orch. Vocal score by Eric Fenby; words in Eng. and Ger., trans. by Jelka Delius. Recording: Angel, S 36285 (1966).

5111 Jarrett, Jack. In *Choral Symphony on American Poems*. New York: C. Fischer, 1970. Chorus: SATB, pf; band or orch(R).

5112 Lockwood, Normand. "Apple Orchards" and "Apple Orchards II" in *4 Songs—A Cycle*. MS, u.d., avail. ACA. Song: S, pf (orig. for S, vn, org). 2 settings of this poem; "Apple Orchards." East Stroudsburg, Pa.: Shawnee, 1952. Chorus: mixed or treble voices, M or Bar solo, pf.

Out of the Cradle Endlessly Rocking. *The Collected Writings of Walt Whitman* [Vol. 6] (1965).

5113 Becker, John J. MS, u.d., avail. ACA. Setting for SATB chorus, S and T soli, narr., orch.

5114 Clarke, Henry L. "Shine! Shine! Shine! in *Four Elements*. MS, 1962, avail. ACA. Song: S, vc.

5115 Delius, Frederick. In *Sea Drift*. u.p.: Universal-Edition, 1918. Chorus: mixed voices, Bar solo, orch.

5116 Delius, Frederick. n.t. in *Idyll*. London: Hawkes, 1933. Setting for S and Bar soli, orch.

5117 Gassman, Remi. "Hither, My Love," "Shine! Shine!" in *Three Love Lyrics from Whitman*. New York: Mercury, 1955. Song: S, cham orch.

5118 Gilchrist, W.W. "A Summer's Morn." New York: O. Ditson, 1914. Setting for 3-pt. female voices.

5119 Gilchrist, W.W. "We Two Together" in coll. TL.

5120 Hartmann, Arthur. "Two Together." Chicago: Gamble-Hinged, 1911. Song: v, pf.

5121 Kernochan, Marshall R. "We Two Together." New York: Galaxy, 1911. Song: high and med. v edns, pf; In *Two Songs*. New York: Galaxy, 1933 (rev. edn).

5122 Lockwood, Normand. New York: G. Schirmer, 1939. Chorus: SATB, a cap.

5123 Manton, Robert W. "Love's Soliloquy." Boston: E.C. Schirmer, 1928.

5124 McKay, George F. In *Choral Rhapsody*. Boston: C.C. Birchard, 1942. Chorus: 6-pt. mixed voices, pf or orch.

5125 Raphling, Sam. "Shine! Great Sun!" New York: Beekman, 1963. Song: Bar, pf.

5126 Ryder, Arthur H. "Reminiscence" op. 6 no. 3. Boston: G. Schirmer, Jr., 1907. Song.

5127 Sanders, Robert. "Out of the Cradle." New York: Broude Bros., 1954. Chorus: SATB, S solo, a cap.

5128 Warner, Frank H. "We Two Together." Boston: White-Smith, 1941. Song: v, pf.

5129 Warren, Elinor R. "We Two." New York: G. Schirmer, 1947. Song: high, and med. or low, v edns, pf.

Out of the Rolling Ocean the Crowd. *The Collected Writings of Walt Whitman* [Vol. 6] (1965).

5130 Delius, Frederick. n.t. in *Idyll*. London: Hawkes, 1933. Setting for S and Bar soli, orch.

5131 Kernochan, Marshall R. "Out of the Rolling Ocean." Boston: C.W. Thompson, 1908. Song: med. v, pf; New York: Galaxy, 1932. Song: med. v, orch; New York: Galaxy, 1933 (rev edn).

5132 Vrionides, Christos and Rosina. New York: M. Baron, 1940. Chorus: SSAA.

Passage to India. *The Collected Writings of Walt Whitman* [Vol. 6] (1965).

5133 Delius, Frederick. "Passage to You" in *Songs of Farewell (Lieder des Abschieds)*. London: Winthrop Rogers, 1931. Chorus: SSAATTBB, pf or orch. Vocal score by Eric Fenby; words in Eng. and Ger., trans. by Jelka Delius. Recording: Angel, S 36285 (1966).

5134 Rogers, James H. "Sail Forth" in *In Memoriam*. New York: G. Schirmer, 1919. Cycle: med. v, pf. Words from sec. 9.

5135 Vaughan Williams, Ralph. "The Explorers" in *A Sea Symphony*. New York, London: Breitkopf & Härtel, 1909. Setting for chorus, S and Bar soli, orch. Words from secs. 5, 8, 9.

5136 Whitmer, Thomas C. u.t. [movement 1] in *Choral Rhapsody*. New York: H.W. Gray, 1928. Setting for chorus, solo qrt, pf or orch. Words from sec. 5 and 8.

Patrolling Barnegat. *The Collected Writings of Walt Whitman* [Vol. 6] (1965).

5137 Bonner, Eugene. "Patrolling Barnegat" op. 16. New York: G. Schirmer, 1927. Song: med. v, pf.

5138 Strang, Gerald. In *Three Whitman Excerpts*. Los Angeles: Affiliated Musicians, 1953. Chorus: SATB, a cap.

Perfections. *The Collected Writings of Walt Whitman* [Vol. 6] (1965).

5139 Klein, John. In *Four Whitman Sketches*. Boston: Boston Music, 1945. Chorus: SATB, a cap.

5140 Luening, Otto. "Only Themselves Understand Themselves." In *New Music* 8(4) (1935). Song: v, pf.

5141 Stout, Alan. "Only Themselves" in *Three Whitman Songs*. MS, 1971, avail. ACA. Song: Bar, pf.

Pioneers! O Pioneers! *The Collected Writings of Walt Whitman* [Vol. 6] (1965).

5142 Boughton, Rutland. "Pioneers." London: J. Curwen, 1925. Cantata: mixed chorus, T solo, pf or small orch.

5143 De Tar, Vernon. New York: Galaxy, 1936. Song: unison voices, pf.

5144 Grace, Harvey. "Pioneers." New York: C. Fischer, 1927. Marching Song: unison chorus, pf. In coll. CSB 5.

5145 Hoppin, Stuart B. "Pioneers." Boston: C.C. Birchard, 1938. Chorus: SATB, pf, orch, obl for 2 vn.

5146 James, Philip. "All the Past We Leave Behind" in coll. ChAH. Hymn. Text adapted.

5147 McDonald, Harl. "Pioneers, O Pioneers," "Have the Elder Races Halted?" "O You Daughters of the West," "All the Past We Leave Behind" in *Pioneers, O Pioneers*. Philadelphia: Elkan-Vogel, 1939. Cycle: mixed voices, a cap.

5148 McKay, George F. In *Choral Rhapsody*. Boston: C.C. Birchard, 1942. Choral Rhapsody: 6-pt. mixed voices, pf or orch.

5149 Ringwald, Roy. n.t. in *The Song of America*. East Stroudsburg, Pa.: Shawnee, 1951. Chorus: SATB, narr., pf 4 hands; "Pioneers! O Pioneers!" East Stroudsburg, Pa.: Shawnee, 1953. Chorus: TTBB. Recording: Decca, DAU 816.

5150 Schuman, William. "Pioneers!" London: J. & W. Chester, 1938. Chorus: SSAATTBB, a cap.

5151 Shaw, Martin. "Pioneers" in *Songs of Praise*. Ed. by Percy Dearmer, Ralph Vaughan Williams, and Martin Shaw. London: Oxford Univ. Press, 1931; In coll. SmNH, SmPS.

5152 Treharne, Bryceson. New York: R.L. Huntzinger, 1941. Chorus: TTBB or 4-pt. boys' voices, pf.

5153 Whitehead, Alfred. "Pioneers!" Boston: O. Ditson, 1933. Chorus: SATB, pf or org; also pubd for SAB school chorus, and unison choral song, pf or org.

5154 Whitmer, Thomas C. In *The Soul of America*. Boston: A.P. Schmidt, 1942. Chorus: mixed voices, pf or org or orch; augmented with an introduction for speech choir, 1948.

Poets to Come. *The Collected Writings of Walt Whitman* [Vol. 6] (1965).

5155 Sohal, Naresh. Sevenoaks, Kent: Novello, 1975. Part Song: SATB divisi, Bar solo, a cap.

Portals. *The Collected Writings of Walt Whitman* [Vol. 6] (1965).

5156 Dalmas, Philip. In *Four Songs from Whitman*. London: Novello, 1901. Song.

5157 Stout, Alan. In *Three Whitman Songs*. MS, 1971, avail. ACA. Song: Bar, pf.

Proud Music of the Storm. *The Collected Writings of Walt Whitman* [Vol. 6] (1965).

5158 Dello Joio, Norman. New York: E.B. Marks, 1967. Chorus: 7-pt. SATB, org or brass, 3 tpt, 3 hn, 2 t trb, 1 b trb, tuba (R). Words paraphrased.

5159 Whitmer, Thomas C. u.t. in *Choral Rhapsody*. New York: H.W. Gray, 1928. Setting for chorus, solo qrt, pf or orch.

Quicksand Years. *The Collected Writings of Walt Whitman* [Vol. 6] (1965).

5160 Adler, Samuel. In *Sixth String Quartet*. New York: C. Fischer, 1977. Song: med. v, str qrt.

Race of Veterans. *The Collected Writings of Walt Whitman* [Vol. 6] (1965).

5161 Bryson, Ernest. In *Drum Taps*. London: J. Curwen, 1919. Chorus: mixed voices, ad lib side drum, org, brass, str.

The Real War Will Never Get in the Books. *The Collected Writings of Walt Whitman* [Vol. 7] (1965).

5162 Rorem, Ned. In *War Scenes*. New York: Boosey & Hawkes, 1971. Cycle: med.-low v, pf. Recording: Desto, DC 7101.

Reconciliation. *The Collected Writings of Walt Whitman* [Vol. 6] (1965).

5163 Hopekirk, Helen. New York: G. Schirmer, 1915. Song: med. v, pf.

5164 Rorem, Ned. In *Five Poems of Walt Whitman*. New York: Boosey & Hawkes, 1970. Song: v, pf.

5165 Vaughan Williams, Ralph. n.t. in *Dona Nobis Pacem*. London: Oxford Univ. Press, 1936. Cantata: SATB chorus, S and Bar soli, orch (R) or pf and str orch (R).

Return of the Heroes. *The Collected Writings of Walt Whitman* [Vol. 6] (1965).

5166 Whitmer, Thomas C. In *The Soul of America*. Boston: A.P. Schmidt, 1942. Setting for mixed chorus, orch, or pf or org. Augmented with an intro. for speech choir, 1948. Uses 2 lines.

Roaming in Thought. *The Collected Writings of Walt Whitman* [Vol. 6] (1965).

5167 Klein, John. In *Four Whitman Sketches*. Boston: Boston Music, 1945. Chorus: SATB, a cap.

The Runner. *The Collected Writings of Walt Whitman* [Vol. 6] (1965).

5168 Klein, John. In *Sentences from Whitman*. New York: Associated Music, 1946. Chorus: SSAA, opt pf.

Salut au Monde. *The Collected Writings of Walt Whitman* [Vol. 6] (1965).

5169 Dello Joio, Norman. "Take Our Hand, Walt Whitman" in *Songs of Walt Whitman*. New York: E.B. Marks, 1966. Chorus: SATB, pf or orch (R). Words paraphrased.

5170 Whitmer, Thomas C. u.t. in *Choral Rhapsody*. New York: H.W. Gray, 1928. Setting for chorus, solo qrt, pf or orch.

The Ship Starting. *The Collected Writings of Walt Whitman* [Vol. 6] (1965).

5171 Booth, Guy. In *The Ship*. Boston: Boston Music, 1936. Chorus: mixed voices, a cap.

5172 Harris, George. In *Three Songs*. New York: G. Schirmer, 1925. Song: high v, pf.

5173 Lockwood, Normand. u.t. in *I Hear America Singing*. Delaware Water Gap, Pa.: Shawnee, 1954. Setting for mixed voices, pf.

5174 Naginski, Charles. New York: G. Schirmer, 1942. Song: med. v, pf.

5175 Sandby, Herman. New York: C. Fischer, 1914. Song: v, pf; "The

Ship Starting," "Skibet sejler," "Schiff segelt aus." Copenhagen: Skandinavisk og Borups Musikforlag, 1936. Song: v, pf. Words in Eng., Ger. (trans. by Max Hochdorf) and Dan. (trans. by Johannes V. Jensen).

A Sight in Camp in the Daybreak Gray and Dim. *The Collected Writings of Walt Whitman* [Vol. 6] (1965).

5176 Bryson, Ernest. "A Sight in Camp" in *Drum Taps*. London: J. Curwen, 1919. Chorus: mixed voices, ad lib side drum, org, brass, str.

5177 Cumming, Richard. "A Sight in Camp" in *We Happy Few*. New York: Boosey & Hawkes, 1969. Cycle: B-Bar, pf.

5178 Symons, Dom Thomas. "A Sight in Camp." London: J. Curwen, 1928. Song: med. v, pf. In coll. CAST.

The Sleepers. *The Collected Writings of Walt Whitman* [Vol. 6] (1965).

5179 Delius, Frederick. n.t. in *Idyll*. London: Hawkes, 1933. Setting for S and Bar soli, orch.

The Sobbing of the Bells. *The Collected Writings of Walt Whitman* [Vol. 6] (1965).

5180 Bacon, Ernst. In coll. BacSP. Song: v, pf.

5181 Hanna, James. Hattiesburg, Miss.: p.p., u.d. Setting for mixed chorus, pf.

Some Specimen Cases. *The Collected Writings of Walt Whitman* [Vol. 7] (1965).

5182 Rorem, Ned. "Specimen Case" in *War Scenes*. New York: Boosey & Hawkes, 1971. Cycle: med.-low v, pf. Recording: Desto, DC 7101.

Sometimes with One I Love. *The Collected Writings of Walt Whitman* [Vol. 6] (1965).

5183 Butterley, Nigel. Score with J. Albert & Son rental lib. Setting for S, Bar, male speaker, fl, cl, hn, 2 vn, pf.

5184 Rorem, Ned. New York: Composer's Editions Ltd., 1959; In *Five Poems of Walt Whitman*. New York: Boosey & Hawkes, 1970. Song: v, pf.

Song at Sunset. *The Collected Writings of Walt Whitman* [Vol. 6] (1965).

5185 Butt, James. "Sunset." London: Chappell, 1961. Song: v, pf.

5186 Holmboe, Virginia. "Song at Sunset" op. 138b. Copenhagen: W. Hansen, 1978. Setting for SATB.

5187 Whitmer, Thomas C. u.t. in *Choral Rhapsody*. New York: H.W. Gray, 1928. Setting for chorus, solo qrt, pf or orch.

Song for All Seas, All Ships. *The Collected Writings of Walt Whitman* [Vol. 6] (1965).

5188 Harris, Roy. In *Symphony for Voices*. New York: G. Schirmer, 1939. Chorus: mixed voices, a cap.

5189 Persichetti, Vincent. "Flaunt Out, O Sea" in *Celebrations* op. 103. Philadelphia: Elkan-Vogel, 1967. Cantata (no. 3): chorus, wind ens.

5190 Skolnik, Walter. Bryn Mawr, Pa.: Elkan-Vogel, u.d. Chorus: SATB, a cap.

5191 Vaughan Williams, Ralph. In *A Sea Symphony*. London: Breitkopf & Härtel, 1909. Setting for chorus, S and Bar soli, orch.

5192 Wagner, Joseph F. New York: Chappell, 1955. Cantata: SATB chorus, Bar solo, pf or orch (R).

A Song for Occupations. *The Collected Writings of Walt Whitman* [Vol. 6] (1965).

5193 Harris, Roy. New York: G. Schirmer, 1935. Chorus: SSAATTBB, a cap.

5194 Lockwood, Normand. u.t. in *I Hear America Singing*. Delaware Water Gap, Pa.: Shawnee, 1954. Setting for mixed voices, pf.

5195 Luening, Otto. "Lines from 'A Song for Occupations.' " New York: C.F. Peters, 1966. Chorus: SATB, a cap. Words from sec. 4.

5196 Williams, Ralph E. "Light and Shade." New York: Mills Music, 1955. Chorus: SATB, opt pf. Words from sec. 3.

5197 Wilson, Harry R. "All Music." New York: G. Schirmer, 1958. Chorus: SATB, incid. soli, a cap. Words from sec. 4.

A Song of Joys. *The Collected Writings of Walt Whitman* [Vol. 6] (1965).

5198 Creston, Paul. u.p.: F. Colombo, 1963. Song: high v, pf.

5199 Dello Joio, Norman. "A Jubilant Song." New York: G. Schirmer, 1946. Chorus: mixed voices, pf.

5200 Diemer, Emma L. "O to Make the Most Jubilant Song." New York: C. Fischer, 1972. Chorus: SATB, pf.

5200a Doherty, Anthony. Cincinnati: World Library, u.d. Chorus: SATB. Music not seen; text presumably from this poem.

Song of Myself. *The Collected Writings of Walt Whitman* [Vol. 6] (1965).

5201 Brunner, David L. "In Celebration." Delaware Water Gap, Pa.: Shawnee, 1978. Chorus: SSATB, a cap.

5202 Campbell-Tipton, Louis. "Rhapsodie" op. 32 no. 1. New York: G. Schirmer, 1913. Song: high and med.-low v edns, pf. Words in Eng. and Fr., trans. by Léon de Tinseau; words from sec. 21.

5203 Creston, Paul. "Whitman" in *The Celestial Vision* op. 60 no. 2. u.p.: Templeton Music, 1959. Chorus: TTBB, a cap.

5204 Gaul, Harvey B. "For the Numberless Unknown Heroes." Boston: O. Ditson, 1923. Paean: 8-pt. mixed voices. Words from sec. 18.

5205 Ives, Charles. "Walt Whitman." In coll. IOS, ITS. Song: v, pf. Words from sec. 20.

5206 Kagen, Sergius. "I Think I Could Turn." New York: Mercury, 1952. Song: B, pf. Words from sec. 32.

5207 Lees, Benjamin. "Song of Myself" (movements 5 and 9) in *Visions of Poets.* New York: Boosey & Hawkes, 1965. Dramatic Cantata: chorus, S and T soli, orch. Words from secs. 21, 22.

5208 Lister, Rodney. "The Second, Part III (A hum . . .)." MS, 1974, avail. ACA. Song: Bar, alto fl, e-hn, tbn, 2 perc, hp, vla, db. Words from sec. 5.

5209 Lockwood, Normand. u.t. in *I Hear America Singing.* Delaware Water Gap, Pa.: Shawnee, 1954. Setting for mixed voices, pf. Words from secs. 6, 8, 9.

5210 Norris, Homer A. "I Am the Poet of the Body," "I Am He that Walks" in *The Flight of the Eagle.* Boston: Boston Music, 1903. Setting for STBar soli, pf. Words from secs. 7, 20, 21, 45.

5211 Persichetti, Vincent. "I Celebrate Myself," "There Is That in Me" in *Celebrations.* op. 103. Philadelphia: Elkan-Vogel, 1967. Cantata (no. 3): chorus, wind ens. Words from secs. 1, 50.

5212 Pfautsch, Lloyd. n.t. in *I Hear America Singing.* Delaware Water Gap, Pa.: Shawnee, 1970. Chorus: SATB, a cap. Includes words from sec. 26.

5213 Whitmer, Thomas C. In *Choral Rhapsody.* New York: H.W. Gray, 1928. Setting for chorus, solo qrt, pf or orch. Words from secs. 46, 50.

5214 Williams, Ralph E. "The Good Earth." Park Ridge, Ill.: N.A. Kjos, 1967. Chorus: SATB, opt pf. Words from sec. 21.

Song of the Banner at Daybreak. *The Collected Writings of Walt Whitman* [Vol. 6] (1965).

5215 Schuman, William. "Song of the Banner" in *A Free Song.* New York: G. Schirmer, 1943. Secular cantata (no. 2): mixed chorus, orch or 2 pf (pf red. by Paul Weissleder). Words paraphrased.

Song of the Broad-Axe. *The Collected Writings of Walt Whitman* [Vol. 6] (1965).

   5216 "The Great City" in coll. CaCL. Setting for SATB

   5217 Lees, Benjamin. In *Visions of Poets*. New York: Boosey & Hawkes, 1965. Dramatic Cantata: chorus, S and T soli, orch. Words from sec. 1.

Song of the Exposition. *The Collected Writings of Walt Whitman* [Vol. 6] (1965).

   5218 Gertz, Irving. Hollywood, Calif.: Middleroad Music, 1959. Chorus: SSATBarB, pf. Words from sec. 9.

   5219 Lees, Benjamin. In *Visions of Poets*. New York: Boosey & Hawkes, 1965. Dramatic Cantata: chorus, S and T soli, orch. Words from secs. 1, 3.

   5220 Vaughan Williams, Ralph. "A Song for All Seas, All Ships" in *A Sea Symphony*. New York, London: Breitkopf & Härtel, 1909. Setting for chorus, S and Bar soli, orch. Words from sec. 8.

Song of the Open Road. *The Collected Writings of Walt Whitman* [Vol. 6] (1965).

   5221 Dello Joio, Norman. New York: C. Fischer, 1953. Chorus: SATB, tpt, pf. Words adapted.

   5222 Elsmith, Leonard. In *Walt Whitman Songs*. New York: p.p., 1960. Song: med. v, pf. Words from secs. 1, 4, 5.

   5223 Farrar, Ernest. In *Out of Doors* op. 14 no. 1. London: Stainer & Bell, 1923. Suite: chorus, orch. Words from sec. 1.

   5224 Malipiero, Riccardo. In *Sinfonia Cantata*. Milan: S. Zerboni, 1956. Setting for Bar, orch. Words from secs. 1, 9, 15.

   5225 Whitmer, Thomas C. In *Choral Rhapsody*. New York: H.W. Gray, 1928. Setting for chorus, solo qrt, pf or orch. Words from secs. 7, 8.

   5226 Wijdeveld, Wolfgang. In *Drei Liederen op tekst van Walt Whitman*. Amsterdam: Donemus, 1949. Song: med. v, vn, vc, cl. Words in Eng. from sec. 1.

Song of the Redwood-Tree. *The Collected Writings of Walt Whitman* [Vol. 6] (1965).

   5227 Hanna, James R. Northeaston, Mass.: Robert King, 1954. Setting for narr., 2 tpt, 2 hn, 2 trb, timp. Words adapted.

Song of the Universal. *The Collected Writings of Walt Whitman* [Vol. 6] (1965).

   5228 Norris, Homer A. "Come Said the Muse" in *The Flight of the Eagle*. Boston: Boston Music, 1903. Setting for STBar soli, pf. Words from secs. 1, 2, 3, 4.

5229 Persichetti, Vincent. "Sing Me the Universal" in *Celebrations* op. 103. Philadelphia: Elkan-Vogel, 1967. Cantata (no. 3): chorus, wind ens. Words from sec. 1.

5230 Riegger, Wallingford. "From Some Far Shore" op. 32b. New York: H. Flammer, 1948. Chorus: SATB, pf. Words from sec. 3.

5231 Valerio, Raphael. "And Thou America." Halesite, N.Y.: Camu Press, 1967. Chorus: mixed voices, pf. Words from sec. 4.

5232 Whitmer, Thomas C. In *Choral Rhapsody*. New York: H.W. Gray, 1928. Setting for chorus, solo qrt, pf or orch. Words from sec. 1.

Soon Shall the Winter's Foil Be Here. *The Collected Writings of Walt Whitman* [Vol. 6] (1965).

5233 Lees, Benjamin. In *Visions of Poets*. New York: Boosey & Hawkes, 1965. Dramatic Cantata: chorus, S and T soli, orch.

5234 Lockwood, Normand. "Winter's Foil" in *4 Songs—A Cycle*. MS, u.d., avail. ACA. Song: S, pf; orig. for S, vn, org.

Starting from Paumanok. *The Collected Writings of Walt Whitman* [Vol. 6] (1965).

5235 Amram, David. "Epilogue" in *A Year in Our Land*. New York: C.F. Peters, 1977. Cantata: SATB chorus, SATB soli, orch. Words from sec. 4.

5236 Kleinsinger, George. "And for the Past" in *I Hear America Singing*. New York: E.B. Marks, 1941. Cantata: SATB chorus, Bar solo, pf or orch (R). Words from sec. 16; with introductory narrative speech by soloist, "Sail, sail thy best, ship of Democracy."

5237 Kleinsinger, George. "For the Brood beyond Us" in *I Hear America Singing*. New York: E.B. Marks, 1941. Cantata: SATB chorus, Bar solo, pf or orch (R). Words from sec. 12; with introductory narrative speech by soloist, "Americanos! Conquerors!"

5238 Kleinsinger, George. "Interlink'd Food-Yielding Lands" in *I Hear America Singing*. New York: E.B. Marks, 1941. Cantata: SATB chorus, Bar solo, pf or orch (R). Words from sec. 14; with introductory narrative speech by soloist, "Then I saw new shapes arise."

5239 Kleinsinger, George. "See, Steamers Steaming" in *I Hear America Singing*. New York: E.B. Marks, 1941. Cantata: SATB chorus, Bar solo, pf or orch (R). Words from sec. 18; with introductory narrative speech by soloist, "But come my tan-faced children."

5240 Norris, Homer A. "O, Such Themes" in *The Flight of the Eagle*. Boston: Boston Music, 1903. Setting for STBar soli, pf. Text from secs. 3, 6, 7, 10, 12, 19.

5241 Whitmer, Thomas C. In *Choral Rhapsody*. New York: H.W. Gray, 1928. Setting for chorus, solo qrt, pf or orch. Text from sec. 6.

Sundown Lights. *The Collected Writings of Walt Whitman* [Vol. 7] (1965).

5242 Rorem, Ned. In *Sun*. New York: Boosey & Hawkes, 1969. Cycle: high v, pf or orch (R).

Supplement Hours. *The Collected Writings of Walt Whitman* [Vol. 6] (1965).

5243 Stearns, Peter P. "Sane, Random, Negligent Hours" in *Whitman Cycle IV*. New York: Composers Facsimile Edn, 1959. Cycle: v, pf.

Tears. *The Collected Writings of Walt Whitman* [Vol. 6] (1965).

5244 Crane, Joelle W. New York: Composers Facsimile Edn, 1976. Chorus: SSAATTBB, a cap.

5245 Dello Joio, Norman. In *Songs of Walt Whitman*. New York: E.B. Marks, 1966. Chorus: SATB, pf or orch (R).

5246 Hanna, James. In *Night*. Hattiesburg, Miss.: p.p., 1967. Cycle: v, vla, pf.

5247 Harris, Roy. In *Symphony for Voices*. New York: G. Schirmer, 1939. Chorus: mixed voices, a cap.

5248 Kaufer, Joseph. In *The Man with the Hoe and Other Songs*. Waukegan, Ill.: Lyric-Art, 1951. Song: high and med. v, pf.

5249 Stanford, Charles V. u.t. in *Songs of Faith by Walt Whitman* op. 97 no. 5. London: Boosey, 1908. Song: v, pf.

5250 Wijdeveld, Wolgang. In *Drei Liederen op tekst van Walt Whitman*. Amsterdam: Donemus, 1949. Song: med. v, vn, vc, cl. Text in Eng.

That Music Always Round Me. *The Collected Writings of Walt Whitman* [Vol. 6] (1965).

5251 Adler, Samuel. u.t. in *Sixth String Quartet*. New York: C. Fischer, 1977. Song: med. v, str qrt.

Then Shall Perceive. *The Collected Writings of Walt Whitman* [Vol. 6] (1965).

5252 Stearns, Peter P. "In Softness, Languor, Bloom, and Growth" in *Whitman Cycle IV*. New York: Composers Facsimile Edn, 1959. Song: v, pf.

These Carols. *The Collected Writings of Walt Whitman* [Vol. 6] (1965).

5253 Pfautsch, Lloyd. n.t. in *I Hear America Singing*. Delaware Water Gap, Pa.: Shawnee, 1970. Chorus: SATB, a cap.

This Day, O Soul. *The Collected Writings of Walt Whitman* [Vol. 6] (1965).

> 5254 Whitmer, Thomas C. In *Choral Rhapsody*. New York: H.W. Gray, 1928. Setting for chorus; solo qrt, pf or orch.

This Dust Was Once the Man. *The Collected Writings of Walt Whitman* [Vol. 6] (1965).

> 5255 Lockwood, Normand. n.t. in *Elegy for a Hero*. Delaware Water Gap, Pa.: Shawnee, 1962. Cantata: SSAATTBarBarBB, a cap.

This Moment Yearning and Thoughful. *The Collected Writings of Walt Whitman* [Vol. 6] (1965).

> 5256 Lockwood, Normand. Cincinnati: World Library Publications, u.d. Chorus: SATB, a cap.

> 5257 Strang, Gerald. n.t. in *Three Whitman Excerpts*. Los Angeles: Affiliated Musicians, 1953. Chorus: SATB, a cap.

Thought ["Of Equality—as if it harm'd me, giving others the same chances"]. *The Collected Writings of Walt Whitman* [Vol. 6] (1965).

> 5258 Klein, John. In *Sentences from Whitman*. New York: Associated Music, 1946. Chorus: SSAA, opt pf.

Thought ["Of Justice—as if Justice could be any thing but the ample same"]. *The Collected Writings of Walt Whitman* [Vol. 6] (1965).

> 5259 Klein, John. In *Four Whitman Sketches*. Boston: Boston Music, 1945. Chorus: SATB, a cap.

Thought ["Of obedience, faith, adhesivesness"]. *The Collected Writings of Walt Whitman* [Vol. 6] (1965).

> 5260 Schonthal, Ruth. In *By the Roadside: Six Songs to Poems by Walt Whitman*. New York: Oxford Univ. Press, 1979. Song: S, pf.

A Thought of Columbus. *The Collected Writings of Walt Whitman* [Vol. 6] (1965).

> 5261 Hamilton, John E. "To Columbus." u.p.: Presser, 1977. Setting for SATB, brass, perc.

Thou Mother with Thy Equal Brood. *The Collected Writings of Walt Whitman* [Vol. 6] (1965).

> 5262 Fitch, Theodore F. "Ship of Democracy." Boston: Boston Music, 1943. Chorus: SSAATTBB, a cap. Text from sec. 4.

5263 Hanson, Howard. "Song of Democracy." New York: C. Fischer, 1957. Chorus: mixed voices, orch, or band or pf. Text from sec. 4.

5264 Whitmer, Thomas C. In *The Soul of America*. Boston: A.P. Schmidt, 1942. Setting for mixed chorus, orch, or pf or org. Augmented with an introduction for speech choir, 1948; text from secs. 5, 6.

To a Certain Civilian. *The Collected Writings of Walt Whitman* [Vol. 6] (1965).

5265 Bryson, Ernest. In *Drum Taps*. London: J. Curwen, 1919. Chorus: mixed voices, ad lib side drum, org, brass, str.

To a Historian. *The Collected Writings of Walt Whitman* [Vol. 6] (1965).

5266 Persichetti, Vincent. "You Who Celebrate Bygones" in *Celebrations* op. 103. Philadelphia: Elkan-Vogel, 1967. Cantata (no. 3): chorus, wind ens.

To Old Age. *The Collected Writings of Walt Whitman* [Vol. 6] (1965).

5267 Klein, John. In *Sentences from Whitman*. New York: Associated Music, 1946. Chorus: SSAA, opt pf.

5268 Schonthal, Ruth. In *By A Roadside: Six Songs to Poems by Walt Whitman*. New York: Oxford Univ. Press, 1979. Song: S, pf.

To Soar in Freedom and in Fullness of Power. *The Collected Writings of Walt Whitman* [Vol. 6] (1965).

5269 Stearns, Peter P. "I Have Not So Much Emulated the Birds That Musically Sing" in *Whitman Cycle IV*. New York: Composers Facsimile Edn, 1959. Song: v, pf.

To the Soul. *The Collected Writings of Walt Whitman* [Vol. 6] (1965).

5270 Stanford, Charles V. u.t. in *Songs of Faith by Walt Whitman* op. 97 no. 4. London: Boosey, 1908. Song: v, pf.

To Thee Old Cause. *The Collected Writings of Walt Whitman* [Vol. 6] (1965).

5271 Hanson, Howard. In *Songs from "Drum Taps."* Glen Rock, N.J.: J. Fischer, 1935. Chorus: SSAATTBB, orch. Recording: Mercury, MG 50073 (1956).

5272 Harris, Roy. New York: Mills Music, 1941. Chorus: SATB, a cap.

To Think of Time. *The Collected Writings of Walt Whitman* [Vol. 6] (1965).

5273 Whitmer, Thomas C. In *Choral Rhapsody*. New York: H.W. Gray, 1928. Setting for chorus, solo qrt, pf or orch. Text from sec. 9.

To What You Said. *The Collected Writings of Walt Whitman* [Vol. 6] (1965).

> 5274 Bernstein, Leonard. In *Songfest*. New York: Boosey & Hawkes, 1977. Cycle: SAMTBarB, orch.

To You. *The Collected Writings of Walt Whitman* [Vol. 6] (1965).

> 5275 Persichetti, Vincent. "Stranger" in *Celebrations* op. 103. Philadelphia: Elkan-Vogel, 1967. Cantata (no. 3): chorus, wind ens.

> 5276 Rorem, Ned. Philadelphia: Elkan-Vogel, 1965. Song: v, pf; New York: Composers Edns, 1959.

> 5277 Shaw, Clifford. New York: Peer Intl., 1952. Song: med. v, pf.

Turn O Libertad. *The Collected Writings of Walt Whitman* [Vol. 6] (1965).

> 5278 Sessions, Roger. New York: E.B. Marks, 1952. Chorus: SATB, pf 4 hands, 2 pf, or orch (R).

Twilight. *The Collected Writings of Walt Whitman* [Vol. 6] (1965).

> 5279 Bacon, Ernst. In coll. BacSP; In *Ten Songs by Ernst Bacon*. San Francisco: Bacon, 1928.

> 5280 Dalmas, Philip. In *Four Songs from Whitman*. London: Novello, 1901. Song.

> 5281 Segerstam, Leif. In *Three Leaves of Grass*. London: Josef Weinberger, 1967. Song: high v, pf.

Vigil Strange I Kept on the Field One Night. *The Collected Writings of Walt Whitman* [Vol. 6] (1965).

> 5282 Dello Joio, Norman. "Vigil Strange." New York: Weaner-Levant, 1943. Chorus: SATB, pf 4 hands.

Visor'd. *The Collected Writings of Walt Whitman* [Vol. 6] (1965).

> 5283 Luening, Otto. New York: Composers Facsimile Edn, 1932; New York: Galaxy, 1976? Song: v, pf.

> 5284 Schonthal, Ruth. In *By the Roadside: Six Songs to Poems by Walt Whitman*. New York: Oxford Univ. Press, 1979. Song: S, pf.

Warble for Lilac-Time. *The Collected Writings of Walt Whitman* [Vol. 6] (1965).

> 5285 Carter, Elliott C. New York: Peer Intl., 1956. Song: v, pf; Song: v, orch (1977); New York: Peer International, 1978.

> 5286 Scott, Cyril. "Lilac-Time." London: Elkin, 1914. Song: v, pf.

Washington's Monument, February, 1885. *The Collected Writings of Walt Whitman* [Vol. 6] (1965).

5287 Lynn, George. "Washington's Monument." Golden, Colo.: Golden Music, 1965. Chorus: mixed voices, a cap.

5288 Vrionides, Christos and Rosina. "Washington's Monument." New York: M. Baron, 1940. Chorus: mixed voices, pf.

We Two, How Long We Were Fool'd. *The Collected Writings of Walt Whitman* [Vol. 6] (1965).

5289 Delius, Frederick. n.t. in *Idyll*. London: Hawkes, 1933. Setting for S and Bar soli, orch.

Weave in, My Hardy Life. *The Collected Writings of Walt Whitman* [Vol. 6] (1965).

5290 Van der Stucken, Frank. In coll. TFB, TFG, TFC 2, TL. Setting for SATB.

When I Heard the Learn'd Astronomer. *The Collected Writings of Walt Whitman* [Vol. 6] (1965).

5291 Bairstow, Edward C. London: Enoch, u.d. Song.

5292 Bedford, David. London: Universal Edition, 1975. Setting for T, wind ens.

5293 Farrar, Ernest. "The Astronomer" in *Out of Doors* op. 14 no. 2. London: Stainer & Bell, 1923. Suite: chorus, orch.

5294 Hanna, James. "Stars" in *Night*. Hattiesburg, Miss.: p.p., 1967. Cycle: v, vla, pf.

5295 Ivey, Jean E. "The Astronomer" in *Three Songs of Night*. New York: C. Fischer, 1973. Song: S, alto fl, cl, vla, vc, tape, pf.

5296 Spino, Pasquale J. In *Five Poetic Songs*. u.p.: J. Boonin, u.d. Chorus: SATB, a cap.

When I Peruse the Conquer'd Fame. *The Collected Writings of Walt Whitman* [Vol. 6] (1965).

5297 Diamond, David. "How It Was with Them" in *Three Songs*. New York: Leeds, 1950. Song: high v, pf.

When Lilacs Last in the Dooryard Bloom'd. *The Collected Writings of Walt Whitman* [Vol. 6] (1965).

5298 Abramson, Robert. "When Lilacs Last in the Dooryard Bloom'd," "Solitary Bird," "Come Lovely and Soothing Death" in *Three Elegies from Walt Whitman*. New York: Dow Music, 1957. Song: high and med. v edns, pf.

5299 Campbell-Tipton, Louis. "At the Tomb (Au pied d'une tombe)" in *Two Songs to Words by Walt Whitman* op. 33 no. 2. Boston: Boston Music, 1918. Song: high and low v edns, pf. Text in Eng. and Fr., trans. by Léon Tinseau.

5300 Campbell-Tipton, Louis. "Elegy (Elégie)" in *Two Songs to Words by Walt Whitman* op. 33 no. 1. Boston: Boston Music, 1918. Song: high and low v edns, pf. Text in Eng. and Fr., trans. by Léon Tinseau.

5301 Childs, Barney. MS, u.d., avail. ACA. Chorus: STB, cl, tpt, bsn, perc, concert band.

5302 Childs, Barney. "Quodlibet for Singers." MS, 1968, avail. ACA. Chorus: SATB, projections and tape. Uses a few adapted lines from sec. 16.

5303 Ching, James. "Ode to Death." London: Forsyth Bros., 1927. Cantata: chorus, T solo, orch.

5304 Davison, John. "Lo, This Land." New York: E.B. Marks, 1965. Chorus: SATB, pf or org; full orch or band (R).

5305 Foss, Lukas. n.t. in *American Cantata*. Paris and New York: Editions Salabert, 1976. Cantata: SATB chorus, T solo, male and female speakers, large or small orch. Words assembled by Foss and Ariel Sachs.

5306 Hawkins, John. n.t. in *Three Cavatinas*. Don Mills, Ont.: BMI Canada Ltd., 1969. Song: S, vn, vc, vib, cel, perc. Uses a few isolated words from sec. 16.

5307 Hindemith, Paul. "Sing on There in the Swamp" in *Nine English Songs*. New York: Associated Music, 1945. Song: S or M, pf.

5308 Hindemith, Paul. New York: Associated Music, 1948. Setting for chorus, M and Bar soli, orch. Recording: Columbia, ML 5973 (1964), MS 6573 (1964). Text in Eng. and Ger.

5309 Holst, Gustav. "Ode to Death" op. 38. London: Novello, 1922. Setting for mixed chorus, orch.

5310 Kleinsinger, George. "Come Lovely and Soothing Death." Boston: O. Ditson, 1954. Song: v, pf.

5311 Kleinsinger, George. "Farewell to a Hero." New York: Boosey & Hawkes, 1943. Cantata: chorus, narr. or B soli, pf or orch.

5312 Koepke, Paul. Chicago: Summy-Birchard, u.d. Setting for mixed chorus, pf.

5313 Lockwood, Normand. n.t. in *Elegy for a Hero*. Delaware Water Gap, Pa.: Shawnee, 1962. Cantata: SSAATTBarBarBB, a cap.

5314 Müller-Hermann, Johanna. "Lied der Erinnerung (In Memoriam)" op. 30. Vienna: Universal-Edition, 1930. Lyric Cantata: SATB chorus, SATB soli, org, orch. Pf/vocal score by Walter Hermann. Text in Eng. and Ger., trans. by Johannes Schlaf.

5315 Neidlinger, W.H. New York: G. Schirmer, 1897. Song: S, M, or Bar, pf; In *Memories of President Lincoln*. Cincinnati: J. Church, 1920. Dramatic episode for Bar or T.

5316 Raphling, Sam. In *I Hear America Singing*. New York: Beekman Music, 1960. Setting for chorus, med. v solo, orch. Text from sec. 16.

5317 Rogers, James H. "Dark Mother, Always Gliding Near" in *In Memoriam*. New York: G. Schirmer, 1919. Cycle: med. v, pf.

5318 Rogers, Winthrop. "When Lilacs Last," "The Thrush, the Hermit," "O Western Orb" in *Lilac and Star and Bird*. London: Winthrop Rogers, 1916. Song.

5319 Sanders, Robert. New York: Broude Bros., 1957. Chorus: SATB, a cap.

5320 Schuman, William. "To All, to Each" in *Carols of Death*. n.p.: Merion Music, 1959. Chorus: SATB, a cap.

5321 Sessions, Roger. Bryn Mawr, Pa.: Merion Music, 1974. Cantata: chorus, SCBar soli, orch.

5322 Shallenberg, Robert. "Lilacs." Cincinnati: Apogee Press, 1967. Chorus: SATB, a cap.

5323 Stanford, Charles V. "Elegiac Ode" op. 21. London: S. Lucas, Weber, 1884. Setting for chorus, soli, orch.

5324 Trubitt, Allen R. "The Carol of the Bird." Cincinnati: Westwood Press, 1967. Setting for mixed chorus, Bar solo, pf.

5325 Weill, Kurt. n.t. in *Street Scene*. New York: Chappell, 1948. Fragment of the poem used.

5326 Whitmer, Thomas C. In *Choral Rhapsody*. New York: H.W. Gray, 1928. Setting for chorus, solo qrt, pf or orch.

5327 Willingham, Lawrence. "Carol of the Thrush" op. 15. MS, 1977, avail. ACA. Song: S, fl, cl, vn, vla, vc.

5328 Wragg, Russell. "Lilacs." New York: R.L. Huntzinger, 1937. Song: v, pf. Text from sec. 1.

5329 Wright, Norman S. Los Angeles: Delkas Music, 1945. Song: v, pf.

Whispers of Heavenly Death. *The Collected Writings of Walt Whitman* [Vol. 6] (1965).

5330 Bacon, Ernst. In coll. BacSP. Song: v, pf; "On the Frontier" in coll. BacFS. Song: M, pf.

5331 Bonner, Eugene. In *Whispers of Heavenly Death*. London: J. & W. Chester, 1925. Song: v, pf or orch. Text in Eng. and Fr., trans. by Léon Bazalgette.

5332 Kastle, Leonard. New York: G. Ricordi, 1956. Chorus: SATB, pf ad lib.

5333 Luedeke, Raymond. MS, 1974, avail. ACA. Song: 2 S, pf.

5334 Vaughan Williams, Ralph. "Nocturne" in *Three Poems by Walt Whitman*. London: Oxford Univ. Press, 1925. Song: v, pf.

5335 Williams, David McK. New York: H.W. Gray, 1934. Anthem: mixed chorus, A solo, org or orch.

World Take Good Notice. *The Collected Writings of Walt Whitman* [Vol. 6] (1965).

5336 Bacon, Ernst. In *Six Songs*. *New Music* (Jan. 1942). Song: Bar or A, pf; "World Take Good Notice" in coll. BacT.

5337 Bryson, Ernest. "Race of Veterans" in *Drum Taps*. London: J. Curwen, 1918. Setting for mixed voices, side drum.

Year That Trembled and Reel'd Beneath Us. *The Collected Writings of Walt Whitman* [Vol. 6] (1965).

5338 Harris, Roy. "The Year That Trembled." u.p.: Mills Music, 1941. Chorus: SATB, a cap.

Years of the Modern. *The Collected Writings of Walt Whitman* [Vol. 6] (1965).

5339 Dello Joio, Norman. New York: Marks Music, 1968. Chorus: SATB, brass, perc. Text paraphrased.

Youth, Day, Old Age and Night. *The Collected Writings of Walt Whitman* [Vol. 6] (1965).

5340 Rorem, Ned. New York: Henmar, 1957. Song: high v, pf. In coll. RFA.

5341 Spalding, Eva R. "Jeunesse, jour, vieillese et nuit" in *Trois Melodies*. Paris: M. Senart, 1923. Song: v, pf. Text in Eng. and Fr., trans. by Léon Bazalgette.

5342 Wijdeveld, Wolfgang. In *Drei Liederen op tekst van Walt Whitman*. Amsterdam: Donemus, 1949. Song: med. v, vn, vc, cl. Text in Eng.

Miscellaneous

5343 Badings, Henk. "Cantata." New York: C.F. Peters, u.d. Setting for SATB, narr., winds (R).

5344 Bassett, Leslie. In *Celebration.* New York: C.F. Peters, u.d. Setting for SATB, narr., orch (R).

5345 Bliss, Arthur. "The City Arming" in *Morning Heroes.* London: Novello, 1930. Symphony: chorus, orator, orch. Text from movement 1.

5346 Bottje, Will G. "What Is a Man." MS, 1962, avail. ACA. Setting for SATB chorus, narr., 2 pf, band.

5347 Castérède, Jacques. "Hymn." New York: C.F. Peters, u.d. Setting for chorus, speaker, brass, perc, org.

5348 Crane, Joelle W. *Three Whitman Visions.* New York: Composers Facsimile Edn, 1977. Setting for 4 S, 4 A, 2 T, 2 B, A solo, a cap.

5348a Dello Joio, Norman. *As of a Dream.* New York: Associated Music Publishers, 1983. Masque: SATB chorus, soli, narr., orch, dancers (opt).

5349 Diemer, Emma L. "From This Hour, Freedom." New York: Lawson-Gould, 1978. Chorus: SATB, pf.

5350 Eastham, Clark. "Oh, to Sea." Chicago: Raymond A. Hoffman, 1940. Chorus.

5351 Felciano, Richard. "Cosmic Festival" in *Two Public Pieces.* Boston: E.C. Schirmer, u.d. Setting for unison voices, elec tape, with opt slides, film or dancers.

5352 Fine, Vivian. "Lines from Whitman" in *Five Songs.* New York: Composers Facsimile Edn, 1941. Song: med. or low v, pf.

5353 Hanna, James. "Turn, O Liberty" in *War.* Hattiesburg, Miss.: Tritone Press, 1962. Song: low v, pf.

5354 Hanson, Howard. *A Sea Symphony.* New York: C. Fischer, 1977. Chorus: SATB, pf or orch (R).

5355 Harris, George. "Leaves of Grass." London: A. & C. Black, 1922.

5356 James, Philip. "From 'Sea Drift' " in *A Sea Symphony* [movement 1]. u.p.: Mills Music (R). Setting for B-Bar, pf or orch.

5357 Kettering, Eunice L. "I Hear America Singing." Chicago: Somerset, 1970. Chorus: SATB, pf.

5358 Lovelock, William. "Vocalise" and "Death Carol." u.p.: Walton Music, 1975. Chorus.

5359 McKuen, Rod. "I Hear America Singing." Hollywood: Montcalm Productions, 1973. Suite: S, narr., orch.

5360 Moore, Mary C. "Consummation" in *Four Love Songs.* San Bruno, Calif.: W. Webster, 1933. Cycle: v, fl, pf, vn, vc; San Bruno, Calif.: W. Webster, 1939. Cycle: M or Bar, pf.

5361 Moss, Lawrence. "Unseen Leaves." New York: C. Fischer, 1976. Setting for S, ob, 2 tapes, slide proj., lights. Recording: Orion, ORS 78288 (1977).

5362 Norris, Homer A. "The Whole Earth" in *The Flight of the Eagle*. Boston: Boston Music, 1903. Setting for STBar.

5363 Riley, Dennis. "Cantata III." New York: C.F. Peters, u.d. Setting for SSAA, orch (R).

5364 Schickele, Peter. "I Saw the Vision of Armies" in *Baptism: A Journey through Our Time*. Recording: Vanguard, VSD 79275 (1968).

5365 Schuman, William. "Declaration Chorale." Bryn Mawr, Pa.: Merion Music, 1971. Chorus: SATB, a cap.

5366 Still, William G. In *Songs of Separation*. New York: Music Corp. of America, u.d. Song: med. v, pf.

5367 Tchesnokoff, A. "The Dead and the Living." Moscow, 1925.

5368 Vrionides, Christos. "What Is Grass" in *A Cycle of Whitman Poems*. New York: Composers Facsimile Edn, 1952. Setting for mixed chorus.

5369 Ward, Robert. "Behold, America" in *Fifth Symphony: Canticles of America*. New York: Highgate Press, 1979. Choral Symphony: mixed chorus, S and Bar soli, opt narr., orch. Text possibly from sec 8 of "Song of the Exposition."

JOHN GREENLEAF WHITTIER (1807–1892)

Currier, Thomas Franklin. *A Bibliography of John Greenleaf Whittier*. Cambridge, Mass.: Harvard Univ. Press, 1937 [CuBW].

Amy Wentworth. *In War-Time, and Other Poems* (1864).

5370 Hughes, Rupert. In *Five Homely Songs*. New York: G. Schirmer, 1920. Song: high or med. v, pf.

Andrew Rykman's Prayer. *In War Time, and Other Poems* (1864).

5371 Weber, C.M. von. "What Thou Wilt, O Father, Give" in coll. Par 4.

April. *The Chapel of the Hermits, and Other Poems* (1878).

5372 Grimm, C. Hugo. "April" [poem used as a basis of the Easter Cantata, "The Great Miracle"]. Cincinnati: J. Church, 1919.

At Last. *The Bay of Seven Islands, and Other Poems* (1878).

> 5373 Bishop, T. Brigham. Boston: O. Ditson, 1893. Sacred Song: med. v, pf.
>
> 5374 Flemming, Friedrich F. "When on My Day of Life the Night Is Falling" in coll. SmPS. Hymn.
>
> 5375 Foote, Arthur. Boston: A.P. Schmidt, 1916. Song: high v, pf.
>
> 5376 Goodell, Isaac. Haverhill, Mass.: Isaac Goodell, 1910. Quartet Hymn.
>
> 5377 Liddle, Samuel. London: Boosey, 1900. Sacred Song: 4 v edns, pf.
>
> 5378 Needham, Alicia Adelaide. London: Novello, 1901. Sacred Song: v, vn and org ad lib.

At Port Royal. *In War Time, and Other Poems* (1864).

> 5379 Battell, Robbins. "Song of the Negro Boatmen." New York: S.T. Gordon, 1862. Song: v, pf.
>
> 5380 Dadmun, J.W. "Song of the Negro Boatman." Boston: Russell & Patee, 1862. Arr. by Albert S. Allen.
>
> 5381 Emerson, L.O. "Negro Boatman's Song." Boston: O. Ditson, 1862. Song and Chorus.
>
> 5382 Goldbeck, Robert. "The Freedman's Song or the Song of the Negro Boatman." New York: Firth, Pond, 1862. Song: v, pf.
>
> 5383 Mayer, Ferdinand. "The 'Contraband' of Port Royal." Boston: Russell & Tolman, 1862.
>
> 5384 Merrill, H.T. "Song of the Negro Boatmen." Chicago: Root & Cady, 1862. Song: v, pf.
>
> 5385 Müller, Wenzel. "Song of the Negro Boatman" in coll. LBR. Song and Chorus, pf.
>
> 5386 Whiting, S.W. "Ole Massa on His Trabbels Gone." Boston: Ditson, 1862. Setting for SATB qrt.
>
> 5387 Wiebé, Edward. "Negro Boatman's Song." Boston: O. Ditson, 1862.

At School-Close. *The Vision of Echard, and Other Poems* (1878).

> 5388 Tschirch, R., adapted from. In coll. Ea.

Barbara Frietchie. *In War Time, and Other Poems* (1864).

> 5389 Jordan, Jules. Boston: O. Ditson, 1894. Patriotic Ballad: S solo, chorus, and orch; Boston: O. Ditson, 1913. Transposed from the original edn, and arranged for school use.
>
> 5390 Sloman, Elizabeth. New York: Wm. A. Pond, 1874. Song: med. or

low v, pf; New York: J.A. Parks, 1936. Setting for qrt or chorus of male voices, pf.

5391 Witt, Max S. New York: J.W. Stern, 1899. Song: v, pf. No mention of Whittier on the music. Text adapted.

5392 Zaninelli, Luigi. n.p.: Shawnee, 1960. Chorus: SATB, sn dr, b dr, pf 4 hands (opt brass and ww ens).

The Barefoot Boy. *The Panorama, and Other Poems* (1856).

5393 Johns, Clayton. In coll. TL, To.

The Brewing of Soma. *The Pennsylvania Pilgrim, and Other Poems* (1872).

5394 Bergh, Arthur. "Dear Lord and Father." New York: Chappell, 1955. Song: v, pf.

5395 Ender, Elizabeth. "Dear Lord and Father." Baltimore: G. Fred Kranz, 1941. Sacred Song: v, pf.

5396 Galbraith, J. Lamont. "Dear Lord and Father of Mankind." Bryn Mawr, Pa.: O. Ditson, 1912. Hymn-Anthem: SATB chorus, T solo, org.

5397 Gould, Nathaniel D. In coll. ChAH. Hymn.

5398 Ives, Charles. "Serenity" in *Seven Songs for Voice and Piano.* New York: Cos Cob, [NYPL ca. 1930]. Setting for unison chant, pf or solo v, pf.
> In coll. IOS, ISS.
> New York: Arrow Music, 1942. Setting for unison chant, pf or solo v, pf.

5399 Maker, F.C. "Dear Lord and Father of Mankind." In coll. Bo, GaL, Gord, LBW, SmPS, TFO.

5400 McKinney, Mathilde. "Dear Lord and Father of Mankind." New York: J. Fischer, 1950. Chorus: SA, pf.

5401 Steere, William C. "Dear Lord and Father." Bryn Mawr, Pa.: T. Presser, 1949. Song: med. v, pf.

5402 Stevens, Halsey. n.t. in *Three Hymns.* MS, 1955, avail. ACA. Hymn.

The Bridal of Pennacook. *Poems* (1849).

5403 Coleridge-Taylor, Samuel. "The Dark Eye Has Left Us" in *Six American Lyrics.* London: Novello, 1903. Song: C or Bar, pf.

5404 Dempster, William R. "The Dark Eye Has Left Us." Boston: O. Ditson, 1848. Song: v, pf.

5405 Fletcher, Percy E. "The Bridal of Weetamoo." Boston: O. Ditson, 1929. Choral Song: SSAA, pf.

5406 Jenkins, Cyril. "Song of Indian Women." London: Goodwin & Tabb, 1921. Song.

Centennial Hymn. *The Vision of Echard, and Other Poems* (1878).

5407 Carey, Henry. "Our Father's God, from out Whose Hand" in coll SmPS. Hymn.

5408 Paine, John Knowles. MS, 1876. Centennial Hymn Sung at the Opening of the Philadelphia Exhibition, 1876. Music may be found in the *Atlantic Monthly* (June 1876).
> Philadelphia: J.E. Ditson, 1876. Edns for mixed voices and men's voices.
> N. Clifford Page, arr. Boston: O. Ditson, 1930. Setting for 4-pt. chorus, pf.

5409 Smith, David S. Setting for SAB, T ad lib, pf. In coll. ArJ, TMT, To.

The Chapel of the Hermits. *The Chapel of the Hermits, and Other Poems* (1853).

5410 Darst, W. Glen. "God's Love and Blessing." New York: H.W. Gray, 1953. Anthem: SATB, keybd.

5411 Rossini, Gioacchino. "Faith." In coll. LAASR.

5412 Schumann, Robert, arr. from. n.t. in coll. SmPS. Hymn.

A Christmas Carmen. *Hazel-Blossoms* (1875).

5413 Batcheller, Daniel. "Sound over All Waters." Washington, D.C.: National Council for the Prevention of War, 1927. Setting in 4-pt. harmony.

5414 Besly, Maurice. "The Company of Heaven." London: Boosey, 1933. Song: med. v, pf.

5415 Browne, J. Lewis. "A Song of Great Joy." Cincinnati: W.H. Willis, 1901. Song: high, med., and low v edns, pf.

5416 Frackenpohl, Arthur. "Marches of Peace." Delaware Water Gap, Pa.: Shawnee, 1961. Chorus: SATB, pf or opt brass ens.

5417 Liddle, Samuel. "Hope of the Ages." New York and London: Boosey, 1900. Sacred Song: 4 v edns, org ad lib.

5418 Mueller, Carl F. "The Marches of Peace." New York: C. Fischer, 1957. Chorus: SATB, a cap. Also pubd for TTBB chorus, a cap, and SSA chorus, a cap.

5419 Pfautsch, Lloyd. "Canticle to Peace." Evanston: Summy-Birchard, 1958. Chorus: SATB, pf or band.

5420 Sudds, W.F. "Sound over the Waters." Boston: O. Ditson, 1896. Chorus.

5421 Treharne, Bryceson. "Rise, Hope of the Ages." u.p.: R.L. Huntz-inger, 1940. Chorus: SATB, pf; also pubd. for unison chorus.

5422 Weigl, Vally. "Peace Hymn." MS, 1958, avail. ACA. Chorus: SSA, pf.

The Dead Feast of the Kol-Folk. *The King's Missive, and Other Poems* (1881).

5423 Grimm, C. Hugo. "The Feast of the Kol-Folk." Reading: D.H. Vanderstucken, 1925. Exotic scene: SATB or SSA chorus, S solo, orch (R).

A Dream of Summer. *Poems* (1849).

5424 "A Dream of Summer." Arr. to a German Air in coll. LBR.

5425 Johns, Clayton. Boston: O. Ditson, 1907. Part Song: SATB, a cap.

The Drovers. *Songs of Labor, and Other Poems* (1850).

5426 Holst, Gustav. "Song of the Drovers." London: Novello, 1911. Trio: SSA, keybd.

"Ein Feste Burg ist Unser Gott." *In War Time, and Other Poems* (1864).

5427 Hutchinson, John W. "The Furnace Blast." New York: Firth, Pond, 1862. Chorus: SATB, pf.

5428 Perkins, W.O. "We Wait beneath the Surface Blast." Boston: O. Ditson, 1862. Song and qrt.

5429 Towne, T. Martin. "We Wait Beneath the Surface Blast." Chicago: H.M. Higgins, 1863. Setting for SATB qrt.

The Eternal Goodness. *The Tent on the Beach, and Other Poems* (1967).

5430 Bacon, Ernst. In *Five Hymns*. Boston: C.C. Birchard, 1952. Chorus: SATB, pf or org.

5431 Bond, Wm. H. Chicago: S. Brainard's, 1900. Setting for 4-pt. mixed chorus, org.

5432 Burnap, Uzziah C. n.t. in coll. SmPS. Hymn.

5433 Hawley, Charles B. Cincinnati: J. Church, 1907. Song: high and low v edns, pf.

5434 Homer, Sidney. "The Eternal Goodness" op. 21 no. 1. New York: G. Schirmer, 1909. Song: high and low v edns, pf.

5435 Irmer, W. "I Know Not What the Future Hath" in coll. LBR.

5436 Johnson, Herbert. Boston: Waldo Music, 1901. Song: high, med., and low v edns. Also pubd as a duet for high voices.

5437 Schulthes, W.A.F. "I Know Not What the Future Hath." In coll. LAS. SSI notes that the music is wrongly attributed to S. Webbe.

5438 Zaninelli, Luigi. "I Know Not What the Future Hath." Delaware Water Gap, Pa.: Shawnee, u.d. Chorus, mixed voices, pf.

Eva. *The Chapel of the Hermits, and Other Poems* (1853).

5439 Emilio, Manuel. "Little Eva: Uncle Tom's Guardian Angel." Boston: John P. Jewett, 1852. Song: A or Bar, pf. In coll. FSS 7.

The Eve of Election. *Home Ballads and Poems* (1860).

5440 Boyd, C.E. "Indian Summer" in coll. Gi 3, GiTh.

The Fishermen. *Songs of Labor, and Other Poems* (1850).

5441 Bissell, Alfred H. Boston: O. Ditson, 1884.

5442 Dethier, John V. Boston: C.C. Birchard, 1934. Chorus: SATB, pf or orch (R).

5443 Gilbert, H. In coll. JSE.

5444 Holst, Gustav. "Song of the Fishermen." London: Novello, 1911. Setting for SSA, pf; In *Songs of Land, Sea and Air*. Sevenoaks, Kent: Novello, 1979. Setting for SSA, pf.

5445 Kendall, Arthur S. Boston: Louis H. Ross, 1894. Song: v, pf.

5446 Neefe, Christian G. In coll. LBR.

For an Autumn Festival. *Home Ballads and Poems* (1860).

5447 André, Johann. In coll. LBR.

5448 Elliott, J.W. "Once More the Liberal Year Laughs Out." In coll. HC.

Garden [CuBW p. 250]. *The Bay of Seven Islands, and Other Poems* (1883).

5449 Foster, Myles B. "Thanksgiving." London: Novello, 1907.

Gone. *Poems* (1849).

5450 Stein, Theodor. In coll. LBR.

The Healer. *Hazel-Blossoms* (1875).

5451 Messer, M.J. Boston: C.W. Thompson, 1913. Sacred Song: M or Bar, pf.

The Henchman. *The Vision of Echard, and Other Poems* (1878).

5452 Neidlinger, W.H. "My Lady." New York: W. Maxwell, 1905. Song: 2 v edns, pf; In *Six Songs*. New York: W. Maxwell, 1907.

5453 Osgood, George L. "My Lady." Boston: O. Ditson, 1879. Song: v, pf.

"Her window opens to the bay." *The Tent on the Beach, and Other Poems* (1856).

5454 Stones, Alonzo. "The Sailor's Wife" op. 43 no. 2. New York: S.T. Gordon, 1877. Ballad.

The Huskers. *Song of Labor, and Other Poems* (1850).

5455 Burleigh, Cecil. "The Corn Song" op. 33 no. 3. New York: C Fischer, 1917. Song: v, pf.

5456 "The Corn Song." Arr. from a German Air. In coll. LBR.

5457 "The Corn Song." Adapted to a Scotch Air, tune of "Auld Land Syne." u.p.: Coe-Mortimer, n.d. Song: v, pf.

5458 Daniels, M.W. "The Corn Song" in coll. ArJ.

5459 Gaines, Samuel R. "The Corn Song." Boston: C.C. Birchard, 1935. Chorus: SATB, pf.

5460 Holst, Gustav. "Corn Song." London: Edward Arnold, 1918. Part Song: 2 voices, pf; H. Clough-Leiter, ed. "The Corn Song." Boston: E.C. Schirmer, 1929. Setting for unison and 2-pt. women's voices, pf; In *Songs of Land, Sea and Air*. Sevenoaks, Kent: Novello, 1979.

5461 Scott, B.M. "The Corn Song" in coll. DagR.

Hymn ["O Thou, whose presence went before"]. *Poems* (1837).

5462 Marshall, Leonard. n.t. in coll. ChAH. Hymn.

5463 "Song of the Free" in coll. LAASR.

Hymn for the Opening of Plymouth Church, St. Paul, Minnesota. *Hazel-Blossoms* (1875).

5464 "All Things Are Thine No Gift Have We." Arr. from *William Gardiner's Sacred Melodies*, 1815. In coll. SmPS. Hymn.

5465 MacMahon, Desmond. "All Things Are Thine." London: Novello, 1935. Unison song for voices, pf.

5466 Stevens, Halsey. n.t. in *Three Hymns*. MS, 1955, avail. ACA. Hymn.

Hymn of the Children. *The Vision of Echard, and Other Poems* (1878) [Originally titled, "Hymn. Sung at the Anniversary of the Children's Mission, Boston, 1878"].

5467 Rowley, Alec. "Thankfulness." London: Edward Arnold, 1936. Song for unison or massed singing, pf.

Hymn, Sung at Christmas by the Scholars of St. Helena's Island, S.C. *In War Time, and Other Poems* (1864).

　　5468 Methfessel, Albert G. "Hymn" in coll. LBR.

Hymns. From the French of Lamartine. 2 ["When the breath divine is flowing"]. *Poems* (1838).

　　5469 Loomis, Clarence. "Thou, O Father! Thou Alone." Chicago: C.F. Summy, 1920. Song: med. or low v, pf.

The Kansas Emigrants. *The Panorama, and Other Poems* (1856).

　　5470 Sullivan, M.D. "We Cross the Prairie As of Old." Boston: Wade, 1854. Song: v, pf.

Laus Deo! *National Lyrics* (1865).

　　5471 Battishill, J. In coll. LBR.

　　5472 Boott, Francis. Boston: O. Ditson, 1868. Song with SATB chorus ad lib, pf. In coll. BoS.

　　5473 Flagello, Nicolas. n.t. in *Te Deum for All Mankind*. New York: C. Fischer, 1969. Chorus: SATB, pf or orch (R).

　　5474 Ringwald, Roy. n.t. in *The Song of America*. East Stroudsburg, Pa.: Shawnee, 1951. Cantata: SATB chorus, narr., pf 4 hands or orch (R). Recording: Decca, DAU 816.

Lexington. *The Vision of Echard, and Other Poems* (1878).

　　5475 Earhart, W. In coll. Ea.

The Light That Is Felt. *Saint Gregory's Guest, and Recent Poems* (1886).

　　5476 Graham, F. Selwyn. London: C. Jefferys, n.d. Song.

　　5477 Ives, Charles E. New York: Mercury Music, 1950. Song: med. v, pf. In coll. TaCA.

　　5478 Methfessel, Albert G. In coll. LBR.

The Lumbermen. *Songs of Labor, and Other Poems* (1850).

　　5479 Baynon, Arthur. "The Song of the Lumbermen." London: Boosey, 1933. Chorus: SATB, pf.

　　5480 Calver, F. Leslie. Boston: A.P. Schmidt, 1927. Chorus: TTBB, keybd.

　　5481 Holst, Gustav. "Song of the Lumbermen." London: Edward Arnold, 1918. 2-pt. song; In *Songs of Land, Sea and Air*. Sevenoaks, Kent: Novello, 1979.

Mabel Martin. *Home Ballads and Poems* (1860).

> 5482 Birge, E.B. "The Husking" in coll. Par 4, ParO. Text from sec. 2 of the poem.

> 5483 MacKenzie, Alexander. "The Witch's Daughter" op. 66. London: Novello, 1904. Cantata: SATB chorus, S and Bar soli, pf or orch. Pf arr. by W.H. Bell. Words adapted.

> 5484 Skilton, Charles S. "The Witch's Daughter." New York: Fischer, 1918. Cantata: chorus, S and Bar soli, orch.

Maud Muller. *The Panorama, and Other Poems* (1856).

> 5485 Kountz, Richard. New York: H.W. Gray, 1924. Cantata: SATB chorus, soli, pf or org.

The Meeting. *Among the Hills, and Other Poems* (1869).

> 5486 Roberton, Hugh S. "Dedication." London: J. Curwen, 1935. Hymn: SATB, a cap.

Mountain Pictures. 1. *In War Time, and Other Poems* (1864).

> 5487 Burleigh, Cecil. "O Mountains of the North" op. 33 no. 4. New York: C. Fischer, 1917. Song: v, pf.

> 5488 Ross, Hugh, arr. "Our Native Hills." New York: Associated Music, 1932. Chorus: men's voices, unacc. Arr. from Sibelius' "Finlandia."

My Birthday. *The Pennsylvania Pilgrim, and Other Poems* (1872).

> 5489 Reichardt, Johann F. In coll. LBR.

My Playmate. *Home Ballads and Poems* (1860).

> 5490 Hodges, D.F. "Lingering Memories." Boston: G.D. Russell, 1874. Song: v, pf.

My Psalm. *Home Ballads and Poems* (1860).

> 5491 Hair, Frank N. Worcester, Mass.: C.L. Gorham, 1885; New York: Warner, Fitch, 1885. Song: S or T.

> 5492 Mozart, W.A. In coll. LBR.

> 5493 Silsby, Mae. "All As God Wills." Boston: O. Ditson, 1893. Sacred Song: A or Bar.

Our Country. *The Bay of Seven Islands, and Other Poems* (1883).

> 5494 Mendelssohn, Felix. In coll. LBR.

5495 Thompson, Van Denman. "A Prayer for Our Country." New York: H.W. Gray, 1948. Chorus: SATB, a cap.

Our Master. *The Tent on the Beach, and Other Poems* (1867).

5496 Allen, S. n.t. in coll. ChAH.

5497 Donizetti, G. "Immortal Love, Forever Full" in coll. LAS.

5498 Dykes, J.B. "We May Not Climb the Heav'nly Steeps." In coll. LAS.

5498a Hatch, Winnagene. "Immortal Love." Richmond, Va.: Richmond Music Press, 1983. Chorus: SATB, a cap.

5499 Henry, H.G. "Immortal Love."

5500 Hosmer, E.S. "We May Not Climb the Heavenly Steeps." Boston: O. Ditson, 1916. Hymn-Anthem: SATB chorus, A solo, org.

5501 Jewell, Lucina. "Immortal Love." New York: H.W. Gray, 1924. Anthem: SATB, org.

5502 Leo, Ernest A. "Immortal Love." New York: J.W. Stern, 1917. Sacred song.

5503 Mueller, Carl F. "Immortal Love, Forever Full." New York: H. Flammer, 1935. Anthem: SATB, org; Also pubd for 3-pt. female voices, org.

5504 Scott, Charles P. "Immortal Love." Boston: Boston Music, 1921. Hymn-Anthem: SATB chorus, STB soli,, org.

5505 Sleeper, H.D. "Our Lord and Master." Boston: Boston Music, 1926. Anthem: SATB, B or C soli, org.

5506 Stevens, Halsey. n.t. in *Three Hymns*. MS, 1955, avail. ACA. Hymn.

5507 Wallace, William V. n.t. in coll. SmPS, SmASH. Hymn. Arr. by Uzziah C. Burnap. In coll. Bo.

The Pipes at Lucknow. *Home Ballads and Poems* (1860).

5508 Wiebé, Edw. New York: S.N. Risley, 1858. Descriptive song.

The Poet and the Childern. *The Bay of Seven Islands, and Other Poems* (1883).

5509 Gumbert, Ferdinand. In coll. LBR.

The Poor Voter on Election Day. *The Chapel of the Hermits, and Other Poems* (1853).

5510 "The Poor Voter on Election Day." Arr. to a German air in coll. LBR.

The River-Path. *In War-Time, and Other Poems* (1864).

5511 Chadwick, G.W. In coll. Par 3, ParT 3.

A Sea Dream. *Hazel-Blossoms* (1875).

5512 Strelezki, Anton. "For Ever Dear." London: Phillips & Oliver, 1900; Boston: Boston Music, 1900. Song: 3 v edns.

Seed-Time and Harvest. *Songs of Labor, and Other Poems* (1850).

5513 Rowley, Alec. "Service." London: Novello, 1936. Unison song for massed voices, pf. In *The Musical Times*, vol. 77 no. 1117.

The Ship-Builders. *Songs of Labor, and Other Poems* (1850).

5514 Calver, F. Leslie. Boston: A.P. Schmidt, 1925. Chorus: TTBB, keybd.

5515 Holst, Gustav. "Song of the Ship-Builders." London: Novello, 1911. 2-pt. song, pf; In *Songs of Land, Sea and Air*. Sevenoaks, Kent: Novello, 1979. 2-pt. canon.

The Shoemakers. *Songs of Labor, and Other Poems* (1850).

5516 Holst, Gustav. "Song of the Shoemakers." London: Novello, 1911. Setting for SSA, pf; In *Songs of Land, Sea and Air*. Sevenoaks, Kent: Novello, 1979.

Skipper Ireson's Ride. *Home Ballads and Poems* (1860).

5517 Coerne, Louis A. "Skipper Ireson's Ride" op. 131. Boston: O. Ditson, 1920. Cantata: SATB chorus, Bar solo, orch (R).

5518 Rowley, Alec. "Old Floyd Ireson." London: Stainer & Bell, 1925. Part Song: SATB, a cap.

Sumner. *Hazel-Blossoms* (1875).

5519 Sharland, Joseph B. "There Is No End for Souls Like His." In coll. LBR.

The Three Bells. *The Pennsylvania Pilgrim, and Other Poems* (1872).

5520 Holden, Albert J. New York: Wm. Pond, 1882. Song: Bar.

The Two Angels. *The Vision of Echard, and Other Poems* (1878).

5521 Harling, W. Franke. Boston: Boston Music, 1914. Symphonic Ballad: male chorus, pf or orch.

5522 Mackenzie, A.C. London: J. Williams, 1895. Song.

The Vow of Washington. *At Sundown* (1890).

5523 Sloman, Elizabeth. New York: Wm. A. Pond, 1889. Song: v, pf.

We're Free [Poem not reprinted in a Whittier collection. For a publishing history, *see* CuBW pp. 381, 584–585].

5524 Cora, Karl. In *The Campaign: 2 Fremont Republican Songs*. Boston: N. Richardson, 1856. Song.

5525 Cora, Karl. "We See the Break of Day" in *The Campaign: 2 Lincoln Republican Songs*. Boston: Russell & Tolman, 1860. Song.

Worship. *Poems* (1849).

5526 Abt, Franz. "O Brother Man" in coll. SmPS. Hymn.

5527 Chase, Gilman. "O Brother Man." New York: Edwin H. Morris, 1950. Anthem: women's voices, org.

5528 Darke, Harold E. "O Brother Man" op. 41 no. 1. London: Oxford Univ. Press, 1935. Motet: SSATBB, a cap.

5529 Kirk, Theron. "O Brother Man." San Antonio: Southern Music, 1971. Chorus: SATB, pf or band.

5530 Ross, Hugh, arr. "O Brother Man." New York: G. Schirmer, 1945. Chorus: 3-pt. treble voices, Bar or M solo; pf or org, ob or e-hn ad lib. Cantiga of Montserrat Monastery, arr. after Felipe Pedrell by Hugh Ross.

5531 Shaw, Geoffrey. London: Novello, 1927. Anthem: SATB, org; In *The Musical Times* no. 967. Unison song for massed voices.

5532 Snow, Frances W. "Brotherhood." Boston: C.W. Homeyer, 1943. Motet: SATB, a cap.

5533 Thiman, Eric H. "O Brother Man." New York: H.W. Gray, 1956. Anthem: SATB, org.

5534 Ward-Casey, S. "O Brother Man." u.p.: York, Banks, 1937. Chorus: TTBB, a cap.

The Worship of Nature ["The harp at Nature's advent strung"]. *The Tent on the Beach, and Other Poems* (1867) [originally without title].

5535 "The Harp, at Nature's Advent Strung." Arr. to a German Air in coll. LBR.

5536 Wade, James C. n.t. in coll. SmPS. Hymn.

Miscellaneous

5537 Crotall, James H. "The Whistler." Philadelphia: M. D. Swisher, 1882. Song. There is no evidence the text is by John G. Whittier [CuBW p. 585].

5538 Edwards, Frank. "The First Green" in coll. ArF 2. Text: "Snows were melting down the vale...."

5539 Gilchrist, W.W. "Prayers of Love." Setting for SB, pf. In coll. TL.

5540 Jones, W.H. "Old Winter." In coll. NMS.

5541 Kay, Ulysses S. *Epigrams and Hymn.* New York: Pembroke Music, 1975. Chorus: mixed voices, org.

5542 King, Horatio C. "Absence." New York: Pond, 1878. Song: C, pf. Text from *The Tent on the Beach, and Other Poems.*

5543 Liszt, Franz. "Life's Closing Day (from Liebestraum)." York, Nebr.: J.A. Parks, 1937. Setting for male chorus or qrt, pf. Arr. by Marion Moore.

5544 Maker, F.C. Arr. by Gordon B. Nevin. "O Father, Haste the Promised Hour." New York: J. Fischer, 1933. Setting for 3-pt. mixed chorus, org.

5545 Entry cancelled.

5546 "Teacher's Hymn" in coll. Wig. Text: "Up to us sweet childhood looketh...."

5547 Thompson, Van Denman. "A Sweeter Song." New York: H.W. Gray, 1944. Anthem: SATB, a cap. Text: "A sweeter song will soon be heard...."

5548 Wallace, W.V. "Hymn of Adoration" in coll. MalS; "Serenity" in coll. Gi 3, GiTh.

5549 Whelpley, Benjamin. " 'Tis Spring-time on the Eastern Hills" op. 17 no. 3. Boston: Boston Music, 1913. Song: v, pf.

RICHARD WILBUR (B. 1921)

Beasts. *Things of This World* (1956).

5550 Cucinotta, Robert. New York: Lang Percussion, 1977. Song: B, perc.

The Beautiful Changes. *The Beautiful Changes and Other Poems* (1947).

5551 Binkerd, Gordon. New York: Boosey & Hawkes, u.d. Chorus: SSAA.

A Christmas Hymn. *Advice to a Prophet and Other Poems* (1961).

5552 Tollefson, Paulette. "A Stable Lamp Is Lighted" in *Contemporary Worship 1—Hymns*. Minneapolis: Augsburg, 1969. Hymn. In coll. LBW.

5553 Wyton, Alec. Minneapolis: Augsburg, 1982. Hymn: unison or 2-pt. voices, keybd.

Exeunt. *Things of This World* (1956).

5554 Wyner, Yehudi. In *Psalms and Early Songs*. New York: Associated Music, 1972. Song: med. v, pf.

Opposites (1973).

5555 Clarke, Henry L. "Of Nuts," "Of Standing Still," "Of Cheese," "Of Earth" in *Opposites*. MS, u.d., avail. ACA. Song: med. v, vla or vc.

Miscellaneous

5556 Bernstein, Leonard. *Candide*. New York: G. Schirmer, 1958. Comic Operetta based on Voltaire's satire. Book by Hellman; lyrics by Wilbur and others.

TENNESSEE WILLIAMS (1914–1983)

Cabin. *In the Winter of Cities* (1956).

5557 Bowles, Paul. In *Blue Mountain Ballads*. New York: G. Schirmer, 1946. Song: v, pf.

Covenant. *In the Winter of Cities* (1964).

5558 Benson, Warren. In *Shadow Wood*. New York: MCA Music, 1971. Cycle: S, large wind ens.

Heavenly Grass. *In the Winter of Cities* (1956).

5559 Bowles, Paul. In *Blue Mountain Ballads*. New York: G. Schirmer, 1946. Song: v, pf.

The Last Wine. *In the Winter of Cities* (1956).

5560 Benson, Warren. In *Shadow Wood*. New York: MCA Music, 1971. Cycle: S, large wind ens.

Lonesome Man. *In the Winter of Cities* (1956).

    5561 Bowles, Paul. In *Blue Mountain Ballads*. New York: G. Schirmer, 1946. Song: v, pf.

My Little One. *In the Winter of Cities* (1956).

    5562 Benson, Warren. In *Shadow Wood*. New York: MCA Music, 1971. Cycle: S, large wind ens.

Old Men Are Fond. *In the Winter of Cities* (1964).

    5563 Benson, Warren. In *Shadow Wood*. New York: MCA Music, 1971. Cycle: S, large wind ens.

Shadow Wood. *In the Winter of Cities* (1964).

    5564 Benson, Warren. In *Shadow Wood*. New York: MCA Music, 1971. Cycle: S, large wind ens.

Sugar in the Cane. *In the Winter of Cities* (1956).

    5565 Bowles, Paul. In *Blue Mountain Ballads*. New York: G. Schirmer, 1946. Song: v, pf.

Miscellaneous

    5566 Bowles, Paul. "Three." New York: Hargail Music, 1947. Song: v, pf. Text: "One I kept, two I lost. . . ."

    5567 Banfield, Raffaelo de. *Lord Byron's Love Letter*. New York: G. Ricordi, 1955. Opera, libretto by Williams.

WILLIAM CARLOS WILLIAMS (1883–1963)

Wallace, Emily M. *A Bibliography of William Carlos Williams*. Middletown, Conn.: Wesleyan Univ. Press, 1968, p. 258.

Approach of Winter. *Sour Grapes* (1921).

    5568 Holloway, Robin. In *This Is Just to Say*. London: Boosey & Hawkes, 1978. Cycle: T, pf.

The Bare Tree. *The Wedge* (1944).

5569 Holloway, Robin. In *This Is Just to Say*. London: Boosey & Hawkes, 1978. Cycle: T, pf.

Choral: The Pink Church. *Selected Poems* (1949).

5570 Thaew, Celia. In *Briarcliff Quarterly* 3(2) (Oct. 1946); music inserted between pages 192 and 193.

Conquest. *Al Que Quiere!* (1917).

5571 Holloway, Robin. "Conquest (Begun)" and "Conquest (Concluded)" in *This Is Just to Say*. London: Boosey & Hawkes, 1978. Cycle: T, pf.

The Counter. *The Collected Later Poems* [Rev. Edn] (1963).

5572 Holloway, Robin. "My Days Are Burning" in *This Is Just to Say*. London: Boosey & Hawkes, 1978. Cycle: T, pf.

The Dance. *The Wedge* (1944).

5573 Rorem, Ned. In *The Nantucket Songs*. New York: Boosey & Hawkes, 1981. Song: v, pf.

Danse Russe. *Al Que Quiere!* (1917).

5574 Heilner, Irwin. "Second Rhapsody." In *New Music* 8(4) (1935). Song: T, pf 4 hands.

The Descent. *The Desert Music and Other Poems* (1954).

5575 Fox, Fred. New York: Seesaw, 1972. Chorus: SSSAAATTTBBB, pf, perc.

El Hombre. *Al Que Quiere!* (1917).

5576 Spratlan, Lewis. "Morning Star" in *Images*. Northampton, Mass.: New Valley Music, 1977. Cycle: S, pf.

A Flowing River. *The Wedge* (1944).

5577 Holloway, Robin. In *This Is Just to Say*. London: Boosey & Hawkes, 1978. Cycle: T, pf.

The Fool's Song. *The Tempers* (1913).

5578 McGill, Josephine. New York: Boosey, 1915. Song: med. and low v edns, pf.

Iris. *Pictures from Brueghel* (1962).

5579 Spratlan, Lewis. In *Images*. Northampton, Mass.: New Valley Music, 1977. Cycle: S, pf.

Love Song. *Al Que Quiere!* (1917).

5580 Holloway, Robin. In *This Is Just to Say*. London: Boosey & Hawkes, 1978. Cycle: T, pf.

The Marriage of Souls. *The Collected Later Poems* [Rev. Edn] (1963).

5581 Holloway, Robin. In *This Is Just to Say*. London: Boosey & Hawkes, 1978. Cycle: T, pf.

Memory of April. *Sour Grapes* (1921).

5582 Holloway, Robin. In *This Is Just to Say*. London: Boosey & Hawkes, 1978. Cycle: T, pf.

Nantucket. *Collected Poems 1921–1931* (1934).

5583 Rorem, Ned. In *The Nantucket Songs*. New York: Boosey & Hawkes, 1981. Song: v, pf.

Paterson [Book II] (1948).

5584 Binkerd, Gordon W. "Nocturne." New York: Boosey & Hawkes, 1969. Chorus: SSAATTBB, pf red.

Perfection. *The Wedge* (1944).

5585 Holloway, Robin. In *This Is Just to Say*. London: Boosey & Hawkes, 1978. Cycle: T, pf.

Pictures from Brueghel. *Pictures from Brueghel* (1962).

5586 Luedeke, Raymond. In *Pictures from Brueghel*. MS, 1973, avail. ACA. Song: M and Bar, ww qnt. Setting of all 10 sections of the poem.

5587 Silsbee, Ann L. "Icarus." MS, 1977, avail. ACA. Chorus: SAAATTBB, 3 recorders, bongo drums.

Reverie and Invocation [Poem not reprinted elsewhere].

5588 Purdy, Stanley A. Rutherford, N.J.: Fairleigh Dickinson Univ. Press, 1964. Setting for chorus, pf or org.

Rogation Sunday. *The Collected Later Poems* [Rev. Edn] (1963).

5589 Canning, Thomas. "Rogation Hymn." MS, 1957, avail. ACA. Chorus: SATB, 2 tpt, 2 trb.

Spring Storm. *Sour Grapes* (1921).

> 5590 Holloway, Robin. In *This Is Just to Say*. London: Boosey & Hawkes, 1978. Cycle: T, pf.

This Is Just to Say. *Collected Poems 1921–1931* (1934).

> 5591 Holloway, Robin. In *This Is Just to Say*. London: Boosey & Hawkes, 1978. Cycle: T, pf.

The Widow's Lament in Springtime. *Sour Grapes* (1921).

> 5592 Babbitt, Milton. Hillsdale, N.Y.: Boelke-Bomart, 1959. Song: S, pf.

The Wildflower. *Spring and All* (1923).

> 5593 Holloway, Robin. In *This Is Just to Say*. London: Boosey & Hawkes, 1978. Cycle: T, pf.

Winter. *Collected Poems 1921–1931* (1934).

> 5594 Holloway, Robin. In *This Is Just to Say*. London: Boosey & Hawkes, 1978. Cycle: T, pf.

Miscellaneous

> 5595 Ordansky, Jerold A. In *Four Poems by William Carlos Williams*. MS, 1979, avail. ACA. Song: high v, pf.
>
> 5596 Robbins, Reginald C. "Phoenix" in *Songs by Reginald C. Robbins*. Hollywood: Golden West Music, 1941. Song: high v, pf.
>
> 5597 Williams, Joan F. "From Paterson." MS, u.d., avail. ACA. Song: v, tpt, vc, pf.

ELINOR WYLIE (1885–1928)

Beauty. *Nets to Catch the Wind* (1921).

> 5598 Woollen, Russell. In *3 Madrigals*. MS, 1961, avail. ACA. Chorus: SATB, a cap.

Bells in the Rain. *Nets to Catch the Wind* (1921).

> 5599 Duke, John. New York: C. Fischer, 1948. Song: high v, pf. In coll. TaCS.

5600 Woollen, Russell. In *Willow Brook Suite*. MS, 1964, avail. ACA. Song: med. and low v, pf.

The Bird. *Collected Poems* (1932).

5601 Duke, John. In *Two Songs*. New York: G. Schirmer, 1949. Song: S or T, pf.

5602 Hier, Ethel G. "The Bird in the Rain." New York: Composers Facsimile Edn, 1955. Song: v, pf. Music not seen; text presumably from this poem.

Fair Annet's Song. *Angels and Earthly Creatures: A Sequence of Sonnets* (1928).

5603 Bliss, Arthur. In *Seven American Poems*. London: Boosey, 1942. Song: low v, pf.

5604 Howe, Mary. In *English Songs, Part I*. New York: Galaxy Music, 1959. Song: v, pf.

5605 Nordoff, Paul. "Fair Annette's Song." New York: Associated Music, 1938. Song: S, pf.

Golden Bough. *Collected Poems* (1932).

5606 Robbins, Reginald C. Hollywood: Golden West Music, 1941. Song: high v, pf.

Let No Charitable Hope. *Black Armour: A Book of Poems* (1923).

5607 Rorem, Ned. In *Women's Voices*. New York: Boosey & Hawkes, 1979. Cycle: S, pf.

Little Elegy. *Angels and Earthly Creatures: A Sequence of Sonnets* (1929).

5608 Bliss, Arthur. In *Seven American Poems*. London: Boosey, 1942. Song: low v, pf.

5609 Duke, John. In *Two Songs*. New York: G. Schirmer, 1959. Song: S or T, pf.

5610 Howe, Mary. New York: G. Schirmer, 1939. Song: v, pf.

5611 Rorem, Ned. In *Two Songs*. New York: Hargail, 1952. Song: med. v, pf.

5612 Strilko, Anthony. New York: Beekman, 1962. Song: high v, pf.

Madman's Song. *Nets to Catch the Wind* (1921).

5613 Fetler, Paul. New York: Associated Music, 1957. Chorus: SATB, a cap.

5614 Woollen, Russell. In *Willow Brook Suite*. MS, 1964, avail. ACA. Song: med. and low v, pf.

Nebuchadnezzar. *Black Armour: A Book of Poems* (1923).

> 5615 Woollen, Russell. In *Willow Brook Suite*. MS, 1964, avail. ACA. Song: med. and low v, pf.

"Now shall the long homesickness have an end" [Sec. 1 pt. 1, "One Person"]. *Angels and Earthly Creatures: A Sequence of Sonnets* (1928).

> 5616 Levy, Marvin D. "One Person." New York: Boosey & Hawkes, 1967. Song: med. v, pf or orch (R). Words in Eng. and Ger.

On a Singing Girl. *Black Armour: A Book of Poems* (1923).

> 5617 Rorem, Ned. In *Two Songs*. New York: Hargail, 1952. Song: med. v, pf.

Ophelia. *Bookman* 54 (January 1922), p. 475.

> 5618 Strilko, Anthony. "Ophelia." New York: Beekman, 1958. Song: med. v, pf.

Peregrine. *Black Armour: A Book of Poems* (1923).

> 5619 Woollen, Russell. In *Willow Brook Suite*. MS, 1964, avail. ACA. Song: med. and low v, pf.

Pretty Words. *Collected Poems* (1932).

> 5620 Woollen, Russell. In *Willow Brook Suite*. MS, 1964, avail. ACA. Song: med. and low v, pf.

The Prinkin' Leddie. *Nets to Catch the Wind* (1921).

> 5621 Howe, Mary. New York: Galaxy, 1959. Song: T, pf; In *English Songs*. Part III. New York: Galaxy, 1959. Song: v, pf.

Shepherd's Holiday. *Collected Poems* (1932).

> 5622 Benjamin, Arthur. In *Three Songs*. London: Boosey, 1936. Song: v, pf.

Spring Pastoral. *Nets to Catch the Wind* (1921).

> 5623 Howe, Mary. New York: G. Schirmer, 1938. Chorus: SSA, pf. Recording: Composers Recordings, CRI SRD 145 (1961).

> 5624 Woollen, Russell. In *Willow Brook Suite*. MS, 1964, avail. ACA. Song: med. and low v, pf.

A Strange Story. *Trivial Breath* (1928).

5625 Howe, Mary. "When I Died in Berner's Street." New York: G. Schirmer, 1947. Song: v, pf.

Three Wishes. *Black Armour: A Book of Poems* (1923).

5626 Woollen, Russell. In *3 Madrigals*. MS, 1961, avail. ACA. Chorus: SATB, a cap.

To a Cough in the Street at Midnight. *Angels and Earthly Creatures: A Sequence of Sonnets* (1928).

5627 Woollen, Russell. In *Willow Brook Suite*. MS, 1964, avail. ACA. Song: med. and low v, pf.

Velvet Shoes. *Nets to Catch the Wind* (1921).

5628 Copley, Evan. Delaware Water Gap, Pa.: Shawnee, 1982. Chorus: SSA, pf.

5629 Duke, John. In *Two Lyrics by Elinor Wylie*. Boston: R.D. Row, 1950. Song: med.-high v, pf.

5630 Evans, Louise M. Chicago: R.A. Hoffman, 1943. Chorus: SSA, pf ad lib.

5631 Hageman, Richard. New York: Galaxy, 1954. Song: high v, pf.

5632 Howe, Mary. "Let Us Walk in the White Snow." New York: C. Fischer, 1948. Song: v, pf. In coll. TaCS.

5633 Robbins, Reginald C. Hollywood: Golden West Music, 1941. Song: high v, pf.

5634 Smith, Hale. In *The Valley Wind*. New York: E.B. Marks, 1974. Song: med. v, pf. In coll. PaAS.

5635 Thompson, Randall. Boston: E.C. Schirmer, 1938. Song: med. v, pf. In coll. UNSNV, WieF. Song: v, pf.

5636 Woollen, Russell. In *3 Madrigals*. MS, 1961, avail. ACA. Chorus: SATB, a cap.

Viennese Waltz. *Collected Poems* (1932).

5637 Duke, John. In *Two Lyrics by Elinor Wylie*. Boston: R.D. Row, 1950. Song: med.-high v, pf.

5638 Howe, Mary. New York: Galaxy, 1959. Song: v, pf; In *English Songs*. Part III. New York: Galaxy, 1959. Song: v, pf.

Miscellaneous

5639 Nordoff, Paul. "Elegy." New York: Associated Music, 1938. Song: med. v, pf.

5640 Woollen, Russell. "Song" in *Willow Brook Suite*. MS, 1964, avail.
ACA. Song: med. and low v, pf.

Index to Composers

Bornschein, Franz Carl (1879-1948)
Longfellow, 2911
J.R. Lowell, 3417
Robinson, 4204
Untermeyer, 4801a
Boros, David John (1944-1975)
Stevens, 4465
Borrow, W.
Longfellow, 2661
Bottje, Will Gay (b. 1925)
Dickinson, 1014
Lindsay, 2048
A. Lowell, 3317
Whitman, 5346
Boughton, Rutland (1878-1960)
Longfellow, 2930
Whitman, 4935, 5142
Boulez, Pierre (b. 1925)
Cummings, 474
Bowers, Clarence W.
Howells, 1628
Boweryem, George
J.R. Lowell, 3384
Bowles, Paul Frederic (b. 1910)
Stein, 4440, 4451
T. Williams, 5557, 5559, 5561, 5565,
5566
Boyd, Charles E.
Whittier, 5440
Boyd, Jack Arthur (b. 1932)
Bradstreet, 254
S. Crane, 366, 369, 374, 378
Whitman, 5004
Boyd, Wynn Leo (b. 1902)
Dunbar, 1049, 1052, 1062, 1063, 1089,
1097, 1098
Boyden, Georgie. *See* St. John, Georgie Boyden
Aldrich, 147
Boyle, George F. (1886-1948)
Dickinson, 732
Brabson, M.M.
Longfellow, 2628
Brackett, Frank Herbert
Aldrich, 139
Longfellow, 3142
B. Taylor, 4573, 4588
Bradley, Ruth Olive (b. ?1894)
Lindsay, 2032
Bradshaw, W.F.
Longfellow, 2472
Braine, Robert (1896-1940)
Freneau, 1282
Longfellow, 2983
Brandeis, Frederick (1932-1899)

Longfellow, 2234
Branscombe, Gena (1881-1977)
Longfellow, 2363
Braunschiedl, Johannes
Longfellow, 2364, 2871, 2938
Brazinski, Frank W. (b. 1932)
Hughes, 1659, 1689a, 1749, 1750, 1752,
1755
Breedlove, Leonard P.
MacLeish, 3475a
Brewer, Arthur Herbert, Sir (1865-1928)
Longfellow, 2281
Briccetti, Thomas (b. 1936)
Millay, 3578, 3611, 3644
Bricher, T.
Longfellow, 2681
Bricken, Carl Ernest (b. 1898)
Bynner, 338
Sandburg, 4257, 4375
Bridge, Frank (1879-1941)
Whitman, 5005
Briel, Marie
Lanier, 1951
Bright, [Robert] Houston (1916-1970)
Bryant, 291
Longfellow, 2905
Britten, Benjamin (1913-1976)
Eliot, 1138
R. Lowell, 3430
Britten, Emma, Mrs. *See* Harding, Emma
Broadhead, George Frederick (b. 1883)
Longfellow, 2364a
Brook, Harry
Bryant, 292
Brooks, Richard James (b. 1942)
Cummings, 574
Brown, A. Swan, Mrs.
Longfellow, 2958
Brown, Allyson
Dickinson, 749, 810, 900, 925
Brown, Obadiah Bruen (1829-1901)
Aldrich, 112
Holmes, 1477, 1597
Longfellow, 2150
Brown, William E.
Hillyer, 1427
Browne, John Lewis (1864-1933)
J.R. Lowell, 3393
Whittier, 5415
Bruen, C.
Holmes, 1566
Bruenner, Leopold (b. 1869)
Poe, 4010
Bruner, Jane W.

Poe, 3915a
Brunner, David L.
    Whitman, 5201
Brussels, Iris
    Millay, 3659
    Teasdale, 4633
Bryan, Robert
    Poe, 3916
Brydson, John Callis (b. 1900)
    Longfellow, 3068a, 3151a
Bryson, [Robert] Ernest (1867–1942)
    Whitman, 4834, 4859, 4869, 4913, 5161,
    5176, 5265, 5337
Bucalossi, Procida (b. 1859?)
    Longfellow, 2199, 3187
Bucci, Mark (b. 1924)
    Emerson, 1209
Buchanan, Annabel Morris (b. 1888)
    Millay, 3596
Buck, Dudley (1839–1909)
    Lanier, 1985, 1986
    Longfellow, 2480, 2654, 2714, 2851,
    2852, 3201
    Stedman, 4408, 4409, 4411, 4415, 4419,
    4422
    B. Taylor, 4548
Buck, Percy Carter, Sir (1871–1947)
    Bryant, 274
    Eliot, 1146
Bull, Clifton B.
    Teasdale, 4649
Bull, Harry G.
    Dunbar, 1086
Bullard, Frederick Field (1864–1904)
    Aldrich, 140
    Hovey, 1612, 1614, 1616, 1619, 1620,
    1621, 1622
    Longfellow, 2282
Bumstead, Gladys, Mrs (b. 1900)
    Lanier, 1987
Bunning, Herbert (1863–1937)
    Longfellow, 2959
Burck, Henry (1860?–1938)
    Longfellow, 2872
Burgstahler, Elton E. *See* Rau, Earl
Burleigh, Cecil (1885–1980)
    Bryant, 299
    Emerson, 1237
    Longfellow, 2365, 2552, 2618, 2624,
    2772, 2985
    J.R. Lowell, 3350, 3405, 3415, 3416
    Stedman, 4427
    Thoreau, 4778
    Whittier, 5455, 5487
Burleigh, Harry Thacker (1866–1949)

Dunbar, 1029
Hughes, 1743
Johnson, 1826, 1829, 1836, 1841, 1843,
    1844, 1845
Whitman, 4926
Burnap, Uzziah Christopher (1834–1900)
    Whittier, 5432
Burnes-Loughman, Mai
    Longfellow, 3152
Burr, Wilard (1852–1915)
    Longfellow, 3258
Burt, George James (b. 1929)
    Eliot, 1151
Burton, Frederick Russell (1861–1909)
    Holmes, 1482
    Longfellow, 2906, 2986, 2986a, 2986b
Burtt, Ben
    Millay, 3619
Busch, Carl (1862–1943)
    Bryant, 305
    Holmes, 1581
    Longfellow, 2302, 2398, 2494, 2641,
    2715, 2853, 2854, 2873, 2987, 2988,
    2989, 2990, 2991, 2992, 2993, 2994,
    2995, 2996, 2997, 2998, 3144
    J.R. Lowell, 3396
    Teasdale, 4709
Busch, Marie F.
    Dunbar, 1099
Butcher, Frank Charles (b. 1882)
    Whitman, 5058
Butler, Clarence
    Aldrich, 96
Butler, Eugene Sanders (b. 1935)
    Longfellow, 2356
Butt, James Basedon? (b. 1929)
    Whitman, 5185
Butterley, Nigel (b. 1935)
    Whitman, 5183
Butterworth, David Neil (b. 1934)
    Dickinson, 1014a
C.E.N.C.
    Longfellow, 2211
C.K.S.
    Longfellow, 2672
C.S.T.
    Longfellow, 2151
Cadman, Charles Wakefield (1881–1946)
    Dunbar, 1043
    Longfellow, 2212, 2723
    J.R. Lowell, 3418
    Miller, 3688
Cage, John (b. 1912)
    Cummings, 493, 523, 550, 634, 656,
    663, 669

Dickinson, Peter (b. 1934)
Cummings, 509a, 553a, 557a, 574a, 644a
Dickinson, 718, 866, 959

Dicks, Ernest Alfred
Longfellow, 3074

Dickson, Ellen (1819-1878); a.k.a. Dolores
Longfellow, 2202, 2501, 2684, 2700

Di Domenica, Robert (b. 1927)
Cullen, 433
Dunbar, 1035

Dieckmann, C.W.
Aldrich, 70

Diemer, Emma Lou (b. 1927)
Nash, 3729, 3731, 3738
Poe, 3952
Whitman, 5200, 5349

Diers, Ann MacDonald
Frost, 1327

Diggle, Roland (1885-1954)
Whitman, 4899, 5008

Dilworth, Don
Poe, 3918

Dinelli, Giuseppe
Longfellow, 2317

Dinerstein, Norman M. (b. 1937)
Dickinson, 698, 753, 765, 908

Distin, Theodore
Longfellow, 2318

Doellner, Robert
Poe, 3919

Doerinckel, Fred
Bryant, 297

Doherty, Anthony
Whitman, 5200a

Dolby, Charlotte Helen. *See* Sainton-Dolby,
Charlotte Helen

Dolliver, Sewall
B. Taylor, 4569

Dolores. *See* Dickson, Ellen

Donald, H.A.
Longfellow, 3010

Donato, Anthony (b. 1909)
Hughes, 1677
Van Doren, 4824

Done, Emily
Longfellow, 2663

Donizetti, Gaetano (1797-1848)
J.R. Lowell, 3351
Whittier, 5497

Donovan, Richard Frank (1891-1970)
Longfellow, 2554

Dormand, Frederic
Longfellow, 2502

Dorward, David Campbell (b. 1933)

Poe, 4013

Dougherty, Celius (b. 1902)
Cummings, 585, 617, 633, 643, 664
Dickinson, 709, 778
Frost, 1307
A. Lowell, 3310, 3312, 3314, 3321, 3331
Sandburg, 4376
Whitman, 4966

Dow, Howard M.
Longfellow, 2154

Downey, John W. (b. 1927)
Cummings, 649a

Downs, M.S.
B. Taylor, 4551, 4574

Dresel, Otto (1826-1890)
Holmes, 1449

Driver, J.M.
Longfellow, 2252

Dubensky, Arcady (1890-1966)
Poe, 4073

Dubois, Clement Francoise Theodore
Longfellow, 2368

Duffield, Brainerd
Melville, 3555

Duggan, Joseph Francis (1817-1900)
Poe, 3953

Dugmore, F.S.
Longfellow, 2740

Duke, John Woods (b. 1899)
Bynner, 341
Crapsey, 406
Cummings, 495, 504, 524, 653
Dickinson, 694, 713, 731, 734, 739, 790,
835, 855, 859, 936
Frost, 1286, 1303, 1328, 1339
Hillyer, 1407, 1419
MacLeish, 3438
Millay, 3671
Nathan, 3812, 3814
Prokosch, 4174
Robinson, 4185, 4202, 4205, 4209
Teasdale, 4624, 4646, 4651, 4715, 4738,
4742, 4760
Van Doren, 4817, 4818, 4819, 4823
Wylie, 5599, 5601, 5609, 5629, 5637

Duke, Vernon (b. 1903); pen name of
Vladimir Dukelsky
Nash, 3718, 3720, 3723, 3732, 3735,
3736, 3740, 3744, 3745, 3748, 3750,
3755, 3756, 3763, 3769, 3770, 3774,
3775, 3779, 3780, 3784, 3785, 3787,
3788, 3795, 3799, 3800

Dunham, Arthur
Markham, 3511

Dunham, Ervin
Markham, 3496, 3507, 3515

Dunhill, Thomas Frederick (1877–1946)
  Hovey, 1611
  Longfellow, 3075
Dunkley, Ferdinand Luis (1869–1956)
  Longfellow, 3259
  J.R. Lowell, 3398
Dunn, James Philip (1884–1936)
  Longfellow, 3283
  Poe, 4100
Dunne, John (1834–1883)
  Longfellow, 2532
Dunstan, Ralph (1857–1933)
  Longfellow, 2284
Dupont-Hansen, George
  Lanier, 1953
Durst, Sidney C.
  Bryant, 285a
Dyckman, H.W.
  Lanier, 1954
Dykes, John Bacchus, Rev. (1823–1876)
  Miller, 3682
  Whittier, 5498
Dyson, George, Sir (1883–1964)
  Longfellow, 2664
E.A.B.
  Longfellow, 2503, 3076
E.W.
  Longfellow, 2343
Earhart, Will (1871–1960)
  Hillyer, 1429, 1430
  Longfellow, 2285
  Whitman, 5060
  Whittier, 5475
Eastham, Clark
  Whitman, 4971, 5350
Edmunds, Christopher Montague (b. 1899)
  Longfellow, 2855
Edmunds, John (b. 1913)
  Poe, 4101
Edwards, Frank, pseud. *See* Loomis, Harvey Worthington
Edwards, Julian (1855–1910)
  Longfellow, 3047
Eisler, Paul (?1878–1951)
  Poe, 4055
Elgar, Edward [William], Sir (1857–1934)
  Harte, 1387
  Longfellow, 2187, 2847, 2856, 3077
Ella, R.J.
  Longfellow, 3175
Ellerton, John Lodge; pseud. of Lodge, John
  Longfellow, 2789
Elliot, Charles Samuel (1846–1910)
  Longfellow, 2119, 2155
Elliott, A.E.P.

  Longfellow, 2790
Elliott, James William (1833–1915)
  Whittier, 5448
Elmore, Robert Hall (b. 1913)
  Johnson, 1838
Elsmith, Leonard
  Whitman, 4946, 5084, 5222
Elvey, George [Job], Sir (1816–1893)
  Holmes, 1572
Elwell, Herbert (1898–1974)
  Aiken, 26
  Fletcher, 1268, 1270
  Frost, 1322, 1325
  Nathan, 3820
Ely, Thomas
  Longfellow, 3284
Eméleus, John
  Poe, 3954
Emerson, Luther Orlando (1820–1915)
  Bryant, 306
  Longfellow, 2741, 2791, 2818
  Whittier, 5381
Emilio, Manuel
  Whittier, 5439
Ender, Elizabeth
  Whittier, 5395
Enders, Harvey (1892–1947)
  Crapsey, 386
  Hughes, 1674
  Lindsay, 2043, 2065, 2077
Engel, A. Lehman (b. 1910)
  Cummings, 495a, 524a, 634a
Engel, Carl (1883–1944)
  Holmes, 1520
  A. Lowell, 3308, 3316, 3323, 3328, 3334
English, Granville (1895–1968)
  Dunbar, 1055
Epstein, Alvin (b. 1926)
  Nash, 3727
Epstein, David M. (b. 1930)
  Sandburg, 4265, 4278, 4331, 4370, 4374
Erickson, Elaine M. (b. 1941)
  Sandburg, 4289
Erickson, Frank (b. 1923)
  Emerson, 1220
Erlanger, Frédéric d', Baron (1868–1943)
  Longfellow, 2120
Erskine, Kennedy, Miss
  Longfellow, 3078
Escher, Rudolf (1912–1980)
  Dickinson, 1008, 740, 791, 943, 961, 982
Europe, James Reese (1881–1919)
  Johnson, 1866
Evans, Louise M.

Whittier, 5473

Flanagan, William (1923-1969)
Albee, 46, 47, 48
Melville, 3544, 3545, 3564, 3565, 3569, 3573, 3574
Moss, 3707, 3708, 3709, 3710, 3714
Stein, 4460
Whitman, 4958

Flemming, Friedrich Ferdinand (1778-1813)
Whittier, 5374

Fletcher, Percy E. (1879-1932)
Whittier, 5405

Flothius, Marius (b. 1914)
Teasdale, 4692

Floyd, Carlisle (b. 1926)
Melville, 3551

Foerster, Adolph Martin (1854-1927)
Longfellow, 3079
B. Taylor, 4590

Fontaine, Leon J.
Longfellow, 2659

Fontein-Tuinhout, F.R.
Longfellow, 2286, 2701, 2820

Foote, Arthur (1853-1937)
Aldrich, 100, 122, 129
Harte, 1388
Longfellow, 2122, 2931, 3011, 3036, 3153, 3261
Poe, 3957
B. Taylor, 4552
Whittier, 5375

Ford, Bertha
Aldrich, 130

Ford, John
Holmes, 1535

Forrester, James Cliffe (1860-1941)
Longfellow, 2504, 2878

Forster, Cuthbert
Longfellow, 2417

Forsyth, Cecil (1870-1941)
Poe, 4102

Fortescue, Marion T.
Miller, 3691d

Fortner, Jack
Cummings, 469, 490, 525, 578

Fortner, Wolfgang (b. 1907)
Eliot, 1147
Johnson, 1820

Foss, Lukas (b. 1922)
Sandburg, 4336
Stevens, 4523
Whitman, 5305

Fossier, J.
Stedman, 4420b

B. Taylor, 4597

Foster, Fay (1886-1960)
Aldrich, 101
Dunbar, 1076
Teasdale, 4638, 4662, 4693, 4707
Whitman, 5062

Foster, Myles Birket (1851-1922)
Whittier, 5449

Foulds, John Herbert (1880-1939)
Longfellow, 2098, 2843
Poe, 4093

Fox, Fred; pen name of Fox, Frederick Alfred (b. 1931)
Teasdale, 4694
W.C. Williams, 5575

Fox, George (1854-1902)
Poe, 3958

Fox, J. Bertram (1881-1946)
A. Lowell, 3309

Fox, Oscar J. (1879-1961)
Markham, 3519

Frackenpohl, Arthur (b. 1924)
Nash, 3717, 3722, 3733, 3758, 3759, 3765a, 3777, 3793, 3794, 3797
Whittier, 5416

Francis, G.T.
Longfellow, 2671, 3161

Frank, Marcel Gustave (b. 1906)
Whitman, 4937

Franke-Harling, William. *See* Harling, William Frank

Frederickson, Dolores
Teasdale, 4713

Freed, Arnold (b. 1926)
Frost, 1287

Freed, Isadore (1900-1960)
Dickinson, 780
Miller, 3685
Whitman, 4900

Freer, Eleanor Everest (1864-1942)
Aldrich, 50, 56
Lanier, 1993
Longfellow, 2542, 2645, 3048
B. Taylor, 4587

Frewin, Tom Harrison
Longfellow, 2879

Frith, Michael
Eliot, 1167

Frost, Charles Joseph (1848-1918)
Longfellow, 2702

Fryer, Herbert
Teasdale, 4670

Fuller, Jeanne Weaver (b. 1917)
Cummings, 559, 580

Fussell, Charles Clement (b. 1938)

Glazer, Frank
Frost, 1329

Glover, William Howard (1819–1875)
Longfellow, 2704

Glover, Stephen Ralph (1812–1870)
Longfellow, 2158, 2322, 2430, 2506, 2557, 2742, 2937, 3081

Glover, William L.
Aldrich, 144

Gluck, Christoph Willibald [Ritter von] (1714–1787)
B. Taylor, 4575, 4589

Godfrey, Percy
Longfellow, 2857

Goerdeler, R.
B. Taylor, 4576

Gold, Ernest (b. 1921)
Dickinson, 776, 848
Millay, 3661

Goldbeck, Robert (1839–1908)
Longfellow, 2431, 2792, 2881
Whittier, 5582

Golde, Walter H. (1887–1963)
Sandburg, 4264

Goldman, Maurice (b. 1910)
Lanier, 1956

Goldsborough, Arthur T.
Aldrich, 115

Goldstein, David
S.V. Benét, 220

Goldstein, William
Whitman, 4985

Golub, Peter
Dickinson, 1009
Pound, 4162

Goodall, Cecil
Longfellow, 2571

Goodell, Isaac
Whittier, 5376

Goodloe, Lucille E.
Hughes, 1669

Goodrich, A.J.
Holmes, 1530

Gordon, J. Hart
Longfellow, 2233

Gordon, Philip (b. 1894)
Frost, 1314
Longfellow, 2572, 2725, 2848

Gorst, Harold
Longfellow, 2793

Gould, John Edgar (1822–1875)
Longfellow, 2836

Gould, Monk
Longfellow, 2374

Gould, Nathaniel Duren (1781–1864)
Whittier, 5397

Gounod, Charles Francois (1818–1893)
Harte, 1382
Longfellow, 2123, 2159, 2573, 2583, 2882

Gow, George Coleman (1860–1938)
Lanier, 2022
Longfellow, 2323, 2607, 3012

Gower, Allis
Longfellow, 2324

Grace, Harvey (1874–1944)
Whitman, 5144

Graham, F. Selwyn
Whittier, 5476

Graham, Robert Virgil (b. ?1912)
Bynner, 309, 311, 340

Graham, Robert Z., pseud. *See* Loomis, Harvey Worthington

Graham, W.H.J.
Longfellow, 2507

Grahame, Murray
Longfellow, 2574

Granados [y campina], Enrique (1867–1916)
Johnson, 1867, 1868

Grant, Bartle
Longfellow, 3082

Grant-Schaefer, George Alfred (1872–1939)
Aldrich, 62
Holmes, 1455
Longfellow, 3013

Grantham, Donald, (b. 1947)
Dickinson, 688a, 726a, 866a, 885a, 940a, 968a, 1012a

Green, Ray (b. 1909)
Dickinson, 687, 906, 986, 990
Hughes, 1726, 1733
Sandburg, 4261, 4279, 4330, 4359

Gretchen, A.M.
Holmes, 1537

Griffes, Charles Tomlinson (1884–1920)
Lanier, 1994

Griffis, Elliot (1893–1967)
Poe, 4017, 4103, 4121

Grimm, Carl Hugo (1890–1978)
Whittier, 5372, 5423

Griswold, D.D.
Holmes, 1524

Griswold, Gertrude
Harte, 1371, 1397

Griswold, Ruth Redington
Lanier, 1957

Gross, A. Haller
B. Taylor, 4553

Hawley, Charles Beach (1858-1915)
Longfellow, 2124, 3085
B. Taylor, 4554
Whittier, 5433

Hawley, Stanley (1867-1916)
Longfellow, 2613
Poe, 3962, 4066, 4075

Hawtree, F.
Longfellow, 2092

Hay, Walter Cecil (b. 1828)
Longfellow, 2125

Haydn, Franz Joseph (1732-1809)
Holmes, 1507

Heap, Charles Swinnerton (1847-1900)
Poe, 3923

Heath, Fenno
Sandburg, 4300
Whitman, 4850

Heath, L.
Holmes, 1528

Hedge, Grace
Teasdale, 4653

Heider, Werner (b. 1930)
Pound, 4141

Heilner, Irwin (b. 1908)
Dickinson, 1006
Hughes, 1654, 1780
Levertov, 2030
Longfellow, 2241, 2598, 3162
W.C. Williams, 5574

Heinrich, Max (1853-1916)
Poe, 4076

Heins, Nicholas
Longfellow, 2433

Heise, Peter Arnold (1830-1879)
Holmes, 1546

Heiss, John C. (b. 1938)
Bryant, 293a, 304a
Dickinson, 749a, 807a
Longfellow, 3046a
Thoreau, 4777a

Heller, Hans Ewald (1894-1966)
Kreymborg, 1932

Heller, James (1892-1971)
Nathan, 3808, 3811, 3818, 3823, 3824, 3825

Helm, Everett (b. 1913)
Cummings, 515, 538
Nathan, 3807
Sandburg, 4338
Whitman, 4939

Helps, Robert (b. 1928)
Melville, 3546, 3547

Helyer, Marjorie
Lanier, 1959

Hemberger, Theodor (b. 1891)
Poe, 4077

Hempel, ?Charles Frederick (1811-1867)
Longfellow, 2821

Henderson
Poe, 4067, 4097

Henderson, Elizabeth
Whitman, 5011

Hennagin, Michael (b. 1936)
S. Crane, 358
Sandburg, 4256, 4275, 4309
Whitman, 4902, 4951, 4956, 4963

Hennings, R.E.
Holmes, 1538

Henriette
Harte, 1379

Henry, Bertram C.
Longfellow, 2884

Henry, Harold (1884-1956)
Harte, 1396

Henry, H.G.
Whittier, 5499

Henschel, [Isador] George, Sir (1850-1934)
Howells, 1634
Longfellow, 2126

Hensel, Richard (b. 1926)
Patchen, 3898, 3898a
Robinson, 4186, 4201, 4208

Herbert, Arthur
Longfellow, 2161

Herbert, Victor (1859-1924)
J.R. Lowell, 3382

Herman, Reinhold Ludwig (1849-1919)
Holmes, 1483

Herrmann, Bernard (1911-1975)
Anderson, 157

Herreshoff, Constance Mills
Millay, 3593, 3645

Hesser, Ernest George (b. 1883)
Longfellow, 2288

Heuberer, Charles F.
Longfellow, 2162, 2535, 3208, 3287

Heuser, Carl
Longfellow, 3086

Heward, Leslie Hays (1897-1943)
Holmes, 1497

Hewitt, Edward
Hillyer, 1432

Hewitt, George W.
Longfellow, 2744

Hews, George
Holmes, 1498

Heymann, Jacob
Longfellow, 2403, 2541

Lanier, 1969
  Patchen, 3889, 3892, 3894
Mills, Charles Henry (1873–1937)
  Longfellow, 3267
Minima
  Longfellow, 2709
Mirana; pseud. of Newton, William Edward, Mrs. (fl. 1870)
  Longfellow, 2275
Mirante, Thomas (b. 1931)
  Robinson, 4199
Mitchell, Ernest Edwin
  Longfellow, 3103
Mitchell, W.H.
  Longfellow, 2710
Mitchell, Walter
  Longfellow, 2917
Mocatta, Percy G.
  Longfellow, 2838
Moe, Daniel (b. 1926)
  Cummings, 511
Moir, Frank Lewis (b. 1852)
  Longfellow, 2514
Mollicone, Henry (b. 1946)
  Dickinson, 686, 719, 735, 757, 767
  Hillyer, 1415
  Patchen, 3879
  Sandburg, 4334
  Whitman, 5031
Molloy, James Lyman (1837–1909)
  Bryant, 262
  Longfellow, 2214
Monk, Edwin George (1819–1900)
  Longfellow, 2515
Montani, Nicola Aloysius (1880–1948)
  Poe, 3972
Montell, John B.
  Harte, 1389
Montgomery, William Henry (1811?–1886)
  Longfellow, 2537, 2691, 2751, 2827
Moody, D.B.
  Stedman, 4419a
Moore, Dorothy Rudd [Mrs. Kermit] (b. 1940)
  Cullen, 430, 434, 449
  Hughes, 1745, 1762, 1795
  Johnson, 1919
Moore, Douglas Stuart (1893–1969)
  S.V. Benét, 177, 187, 211, 227a
  Lindsay, 2037, 2072
  MacLeish, 3465
  Roethke, 4237
Moore, Mary Carr (1873–1957)
  Bryant, 281
  Holmes, 1575
  Whitman, 5360

Morgan, George Washbourne (1822–1892)
  Longfellow, 3178
Moritz, Edvard (1891–1974)
  Frost, 1298
Morrill, Dexter (b. 1938)
  Cummings, 586
  Millay, 3580
Morrill, Osma C.
  Longfellow, 2888
Morris, Haydn (1891–1965)
  Longfellow, 2551
Morrow, Katharine
  Longfellow, 2803
Morse, Constance
  B. Taylor, 4556
Morse, Richard W.
  Sandburg, 4267
Mortensen, Otto (b. 1907)
  Frost, 1333
  Hughes, 1683
  Johnson, 1840
  Nash, 3716
Morton, Marguerite W.
  Longfellow, 2193
Mosenthal, Joseph (1834–1896)
  Bryant, 294
  Longfellow, 2667a
  Stedman, 4407
Moss, Lawrence (b. 1927)
  Whitman, 5361
Moulton, Charles
  Longfellow, 2171
Mount, Julian; b. Hutchinson, William
  Poe, 3936, 4000
Mountfort, J.
  Longfellow, 2261
Mourant, Walter (b. 1910)
  Poe, 4108
Mozart, Wolfgang Amadeus (1756–1791)
  Aldrich, 82
  Hillyer, 1440
  Whittier, 5492
Muczynski, Robert (b. 1929)
  Dickinson, 782
Mueller, Carl Frank (b. 1892)
  Holmes, 1467
  Whittier, 5418, 5503
Mulder, Ernest Willem (1898–1959)
  Poe, 4128
Mulder, Herman (b. 1894)
  Poe, 3994
Müller-Hermann, Johanna (1878–1941)
  Whitman, 5314
Müller, Wenzel (1767–1835)
  Emerson, 1248

Roethke, 4217, 4225, 4228, 4229, 4233,
4236, 4239, 4242, 4246, 4248, 4249,
4251, 4253
Stein, 4438, 4459
Stevens, 4471, 4472, 4479, 4493, 4497,
4504, 4511
Whitman, 4838, 4953, 4957, 4965, 4986,
5033, 5049, 5088, 5162, 5164, 5182,
5184, 5242, 5276, 5340
W.C. Williams, 5573, 5583
Wylie, 5607, 5611, 5617
Rosewig, Albert Henry (1846–1929)
Longfellow, 2712
Rosibelli-Donimozarti, Maestro
J.R. Lowell, 3367a
Ross, Hugh (b. 1898)
Whittier, 5488, 5530
Ross, Orvis
Lanier, 1975
Ross, William
B. Taylor, 4582
Rossini, Gioacchino (1792–1868)
Holmes, 1547
Longfellow, 2177
Whittier, 5411
Rothwell, Walter Henry (1872–1927)
Untermeyer, 4790, 4801
Rotoli, Augusto (1847–1904)
Holmes, 1594
Rowley, Alec (1892–1958)
Whittier, 5467, 5513, 5518
Rowse, Albert
Poe, 4033
Roy, Klaus George (b. 1924)
Rich, 4178
Roy, William (1928–1958)
Dickinson, 860, 897
Teasdale, 4766
Royce, Edward (1886–1963)
Holmes, 1552
Poe, 4048, 4065, 4095
Royle, T. Popplewell
Poe, 4034
Rôze, Raymond (1875–1920); a.k.a.
Rôze-Perkins, J.H. Raymond
Poe, 4035
Rubel, Joseph
Hughes, 1737
Rudersdorff, ?Hermine (1822–1882)
Longfellow, 2808
Rummel, Walter Morse (1887–1953)
Pound, 4131, 4132, 4159, 4160
Russ, Elmo
Sandburg, 4270
Russell, [George] Alexander (1880–1953)

Lanier, 2000
Longfellow, 2441
Russell, John
Robinson, 4194
Rybner, Dagmar de Corval (b. 1890)
Teasdale, 4701, 4726, 4741
Ryder, Arthur Hilton (1875–1944)
Whitman, 5126
Rzewski, Frederic (b. 1938)
Hughes, 1673
S.D.S.
Holmes, 1542
J.R. Lowell, 3400
Saar, Louis Victor [Franz] (1868–1937)
Cooper, 350
Longfellow, 2921, 2952
Teasdale, 4730
Sacco, John Charles (b. 1905)
Crapsey, 403, 407, 411
Dickinson, 783
Teasdale, 4683
Sacco, P. Peter (b. 1928)
Emerson, 1236
Longfellow, 2390, 2907
J.R. Lowell, 3357
Saint-Saëns, Camille (1835–1921)
Nash, 3804
Sainton-Dolby, Charlotte Helen (1821–
1885); Dolby, Charlotte Helen; Sainton-
Dolby, Mme.
Aldrich, 150
Salter, Mary Elizabeth Turner (1856–1938);
Salter, Sumner, Mrs.
Dunbar, 1059
Saminsky, Lazare (1882–1959)
Lanier, 2009
Robinson, 4203
Thoreau, 4780
Sampson, Godfrey
Poe, 3980
Samuel, Gerhard (b. 1924)
Dickinson, 879
Samuels, Homer
Teasdale, 4642, 4727
Samuels, W.
Cullen, 450
Sandby, Herman (1881–1965)
Whitman, 5175
Sanders, Robert L. (1906–1924)
Whitman, 5127, 5319
Sandford, Lucy A.
Longfellow, 3113
Sargent, S.A.
Bryant, 284
Sargent, Paul (b. 1910)

Longfellow, 2230
Still, William Grant (1895-1978)
  Cullen, 437
  Dunbar, 1077, 1100
  Hughes, 1643, 1648a
  Whitman, 5366
Stilson, Harold W.
  Hughes, 1639
Stocker, M.A.
  Longfellow, 2760
Stoddard, L.E., Miss
  Longfellow, 2594
Stoepel, Robert August (1821-1887);
    Stöpel, Robert
  Longfellow, 2693, 3026
Stoessel, Albert (1894-1943)
  Whitman, 4854
Stoker, Richard (b. 1938)
  Emerson, 1211
Stone, David E. (b. 1922)
  Poe, 3982
Stone, Louise P.
  Sandburg, 4288
Stones, Alonzo
  Whittier, 5454
Storey-Smith, Warren. *See* Smith, Warren
    Storey
Stout, Alan (b. 1932)
  Whitman, 4841, 5141, 5157
Strachauer, Hermann
  Longfellow, 3044
Strang, Gerald (b. 1908)
  Whitman, 5100, 5138, 5257
Strassburg, Robert (b. 1915)
  Sandburg, 4315
Stravinsky, Igor [Fedorovich] (1882-1971)
  Eliot, 1143
Strelezki, Anton (1859-1907)
  Whittier, 5512
Strickland, William Bradley (b. 1914)
  Pound, 4156
Strilko, Anthony (b. 1931)
  Crapsey, 399, 416, 421
  Wylie, 5612, 5618
Strong, George Templeton (1856-1948)
  Poe, 3946
Sudds, William (1843-1920)
  Longfellow, 2179, 3120
  Whittier, 5420
Sullivan, Arthur Seymour, Sir (1842-1900)
  Longfellow, 2265, 2488, 2810
  Poe, 4119
Sullivan, Marion Dix, Mrs.
  Whittier, 5470

Sullivan, Thomas D.
  Longfellow, 2529
Sullivan, V.P. *See* Southey, Phimon L.
Sveinbjörnsson, Sveinbjörn (1847-1927)
  Longfellow, 2861
Swanson, Howard (1907-1978)
  Dunbar, 1042
  Eliot, 1162
  Hughes, 1686, 1688, 1716, 1720, 1724
  Lindsay, 2056
  Markham, 3516
  Sandburg, 4263, 4307, 4357
Swinstead, Felix Gerald (1880-1959)
  Longfellow, 2811
Sydeman, William J. (b. 1928)
  Dickinson, 747, 766, 793
Sydenham, Edwin Augustus (1847-1891)
  Poe, 4041
Sykes, Harold Hinchcliffe
  Poe, 3983
Symons, Dom Thomas (b. 1887)
  Whitman, 5178
Takacs, Jeno
  Longfellow, 2867a
Tarlow, Karen Anne (b. 1947)
  Cummings, 677
Tavener, John Kenneth (b. 1944)
  Eliot, 1132
Taylor, Clifford (b. 1923)
  Frost, 1299
  A. Lowell, 3313
Taylor, Cyril V. (b. 1907)
  Frost, 1321a
  Poe, 4114
Taylor, [Joseph] Deems (1885-1966)
  Holmes, 1468
  Millay, 3615
Taylor, Virgil Corydon (1817-1891)
  Holmes, 1579
Tchesnokoff, A.
  Whitman, 5367
Temple, Hope; pseud. of Davies, Dotie
    (1859-1938); a.k.a. Messager, Andre,
    Mrs.; Messager, André Charles Pros-
    per, Mrs.
  Longfellow, 2139
Tepé, Frank
  Longfellow, 2761
Tepper, Albert (b. 1921)
  Freneau, 1278
  Lindsay, 2049
Terry, Richard Runciman, Sir (1865-1938)
  Longfellow, 2180
Terschak, Adolf (1832-1901)
  Longfellow, 2530

Whittier, 5388

Tubb, Monte (b. 1933)
Cummings, 530

Tucker, Stephen
Harte, 1403

Tuckerman, Gustavius
Longfellow, 3252

Tuddenham, Horatio
Longfellow, 2473

Tullos, La Villa
Hughes, 1779, 1807

Turpin, Edmund Hart (1835–1907)
Longfellow, 2411

Tyson, Mildred Lund (b. ?1900); a.k.a.
Canfield, Harold, Mrs.
Teasdale, 4687

Ultan, Lloyd
Sandburg, 4268

Underhill, Charles Dudley
Aldrich, 110

Ung, Chinary (b. 1942)
Cummings, 456, 613

Urban, Francis
Lanier, 1981

Ursula
Poe, 4042a

Valerio, Raphael
Whitman, 5231

Van Antwerp, Yates
Holmes, 1472
Longfellow, 2396, 3150

Van Buskirk, Carl
Sandburg, 4316

Van Curt, W.E.
Longfellow, 2133

Van der Stucken, Frank [Valentin] (1858–
1929)
Whitman, 5290

Van der Water, Beardsley
Poe, 3947

Van Gelder, Martinus
Longfellow, 3124

Van Höveln-Carpé; b. Carpe, Myra Kinney
Poe, 3993, 3995, 4004, 4043, 4115

Van Vactor, David (b. 1906)
Longfellow, 2185

Vance, J.P.
Holmes, 1516

Vanderlip, Ruth W.
Millay, 3656

Vaughan Williams, Ralph (1872–1958)
Lanier, 1982
Longfellow, 3300
Whitman, 4831, 4855, 4884, 4907, 4908,

4920, 4996, 5101, 5135, 5165, 5191,
5220, 5334

Veazie, G.A., Jr.
Stedman, 4405a

Vercoe, Elizabeth
Plath, 3904, 3905
Rich, 4179, 4182
Sexton, 4396, 4397, 4398

Vernon, Mary Strawn
Longfellow, 2721

Verrall, John (b. 1908)
Freneau, 1285

Verrinder, Charles Garland
Longfellow, 2412

Vidal, Paul Antonin (1863–1931)
Markham, 3523

Vincent, Charles John (1852–1934)
Longfellow, 2899

Vogrich, Max [Wilhelm Karl] (1852–1916)
Poe, 3948

Volpé, A.D.
Longfellow, 2209, 2244

Vrionides, Christos (1894–1961)
Whitman, 4856, 5132, 5288, 5368

Wachtmesiter, Axel Raoul, Count (1865–
1947)
Markham, 3494, 3501, 3517

Wade, James Clifft (b. 1847)
Whitman, 5536

Wadsworth, W.
Longfellow, 2977

Wagenaar, Bernard (1894–1971)
Millay, 3600

Wagner, Carl
Longfellow, 3217

Wagner, Joseph Frederick (1900–1974)
Kreymborg, 1934, 1935, 1937, 1947
Whitman, 5192

Wainwright, John
Markham, 3524

Wakefield, Margaret, Miss
Longfellow, 2764

Walcott, Charles M.
Longfellow, 3301

Wald, George
Poe, 3984

Wald, Max R. (1889–1954)
Longfellow, 2105

Waldrop, Uda
Longfellow, 2405, 2978

Waley, Simon (1827–1875)
Longfellow, 2334

Walker, Ernest (1870–1949)
Longfellow, 3125

Wijdeveld, Wolfgang (b. 1910)
  Whitman, 5226, 5250, 5342
Wilder, Alec (1907–1980)
  Sandburg, 4294
Wilder, Burt Green (b. 1841)
  Holmes, 1554
Wilding-White, Raymond (b. 1922)
  Pound, 4139
Wiles, Cora Y.
  Harte, 1377
Wiley, Genevieve
  Untermeyer, 4795
Wilhelm, Carl Friedrich (1815–1873)
  Holmes, 1481
  B. Taylor, 4605
Wilkinson, Philip George (b. 1929)
  Poe, 3986
Willan, Healey (1880–1968)
  Whitman, 4885
Willeby, Charles (d. 1955)
  Dickinson, 1012
Willett, Chappie
  Hughes, 1809
Williams, Alice C.
  Whitman, 4886
Williams, Charles Lee (?1852–1935)
  Holmes, 1495
Williams, David H. (b. 1919)
  Lanier, 1983
  Teasdale, 4765
Williams, David McKinley (1887–1978)
  Whitman, 4910, 4959, 5335
Williams, Edgar W., Jr.
  Agee, 22
  Stevens, 4528
Williams, Egbert A.
  Johnson, 1920
Williams, Eliza
  Longfellow, 2353
Williams, Frances (d. 1978)
  Teasdale, 4647
Williams, Joan Franks (fl. 20th C.)
  W.C. Williams, 5597
Williams, Langton
  Longfellow, 2276
Williams, Ralph E.
  Whitman, 5196, 5214
Williams, Richard H.
  Aiken, 35
Williams, Vincent T.
  Masters, 3529
Williams, W.
  Longfellow, 3134
Willingham, Lawrence

Pound, 4160a
  Whitman, 5327
Willis, Richard M. (b. 1929)
  Patchen, 3886
Wills, Arthur (b. 1926)
  Eliot, 1172
Willis, H.B.
  Longfellow, 3135
Wills, Arthur
  Eliot, 1172
Wilson, H. Chilver
  Holmes, 1590
Wilson, Harry Robert (1901–1968)
  Lanier, 1984
  Poe, 3987
  Whitman, 5197
Wilson, Ira B. (1880–1950)
  Longfellow, 2232, 2307, 3030, 3031
Wilson, Mackenzie, Mrs.
  Longfellow, 2300
Wilson, R. Bruce
  Holmes, 1543
Wilson, R.H.
  Longfellow, 3273
Wilson, W.
  Longfellow, 3274
Wilson, William (fl. ca. 1830)
  Longfellow, 2301
Winslow, Richard Kenelm (b. 1918)
  E. Taylor, 4609
Wintle, Ogle
  Longfellow, 3247
Wirth, Carl Anton (b. 1912)
  Parker, 3843a
Wise, Jessie Moore (1883–1949)
  Markham, 3520
Wise, Michael
  Lindsay, 2062a
Withington, O.W.
  Longfellow, 3136
Witt, Max S.
  Whittier, 5391
Wolf-Ferrari, Ermanno (1876–1948)
  Longfellow, 3137
Wolfe, Jacques (1896–1973)
  Hughes, 1679
  Lindsay, 2041
  Longfellow, 3032
  Millay, 3606
  Sandburg, 4317, 4339
Wolpe, Stefan (1902–1972)
  Whitman, 5079
Wood, Albert H.
  Longfellow, 2769

Index to Titles of Literary Works

About the Compiler

Michael Hovland is completing his Ph.D. in English at the University of Iowa, where he teaches in the general education literature program. From 1982 to 1985 he was the advisor on literary figures for the *New Grove Dictionary of American Music*, to which he also contributed articles on seventeen American writers. He is currently compiling a bibliography of musical settings of American fiction and drama that will be a companion volume to *Musical Settings of American Poetry*.